CAMPBELL

essential
biology

Brief
Contents

CAMPBELL

essential
biology

1 Introduction: Biology Today

Why Biology Matters

If you've ever wondered what an unusual or especially beautiful animal is called, you're curious about taxonomy. ▶

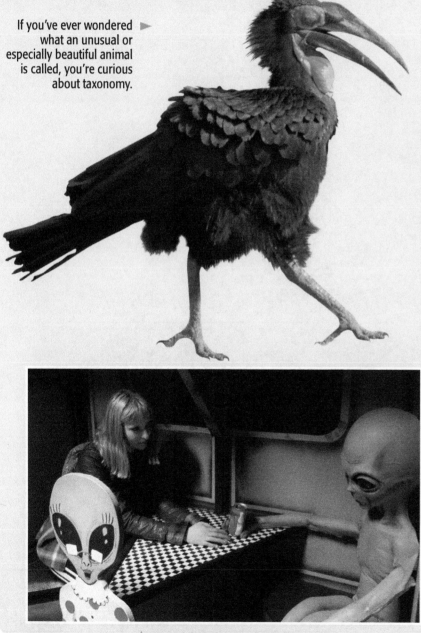

▲ One of the primary missions of the Mars rover is to search for signs of life.

Although you may not realize it, you use the scientific method every day. ▼

9 16

ISBN 10: 1-323-15269-5
ISBN 13: 978-1-323-15269-0

Eric J. Simon • Jean L. Dickey • Kelly A. Hogan • Jane B. Reece

Campbell Essential Biology

Second Custom Edition for the College of Southern Maryland
BIOLOGY 1020 Zoology

Taken from:
Campbell Essential Biology, Sixth Edition
by Eric J. Simon, Jean L. Dickey, Kelly A. Hogan, and Jane B. Reece

About the Authors

ERIC J. SIMON

is a professor in the Department of Biology and Health Science at New England College (Henniker, New Hampshire). He teaches introductory biology to science majors and nonscience majors, as well as upper-level courses in tropical marine biology and careers in science. Dr. Simon received a B.A. in biology and computer science and an M.A. in biology from Wesleyan University, and a Ph.D. in biochemistry from Harvard University. His research focuses on innovative ways to use technology to increase active learning in the science classroom, particularly for nonscience majors. Dr. Simon is also the author of the introductory biology textbook *Biology: The Core* and a coauthor of *Campbell Biology: Concepts & Connections*, 8th Edition.

To Muriel, my wonderful mother, who has always supported my efforts with love, compassion, great empathy, and an unwavering belief in me

JEAN L. DICKEY

is Professor Emerita of Biological Sciences at Clemson University (Clemson, South Carolina). After receiving her B.S. in biology from Kent State University, she went on to earn a Ph.D. in ecology and evolution from Purdue University. In 1984, Dr. Dickey joined the faculty at Clemson, where she devoted her career to teaching biology to nonscience majors in a variety of courses. In addition to creating content-based instructional materials, she developed many activities to engage lecture and laboratory students in discussion, critical thinking, and writing, and implemented an investigative laboratory curriculum in general biology. Dr. Dickey is the author of *Laboratory Investigations for Biology*, 2nd Edition, and is a coauthor of *Campbell Biology: Concepts & Connections*, 8th Edition.

To my mother, who taught me to love learning, and to my daughters, Katherine and Jessie, the twin delights of my life

KELLY A. HOGAN

is a faculty member in the Department of Biology and the Director of Instructional Innovation at the University of North Carolina at Chapel Hill, teaching introductory biology and introductory genetics to science majors. Dr. Hogan teaches hundreds of students at a time, using active-learning methods that incorporate technology such as cell phones as clickers, online homework, and peer evaluation tools. Dr. Hogan received her B.S. in biology at the College of New Jersey and her Ph.D. in pathology at the University of North Carolina, Chapel Hill. Her research interests relate to how large classes can be more inclusive through evidence-based teaching methods and technology. She provides faculty development to other instructors through peer coaching, workshops, and mentoring. Dr. Hogan is the author of *Stem Cells and Cloning*, 2nd Edition, and is lead moderator of the *Instructor Exchange*, a site within MasteringBiology® for instructors to exchange classroom materials and ideas. She is also a coauthor of *Campbell Biology: Concepts & Connections*, 8th Edition.

To the good-looking boy I met in my introductory biology course many moons ago—and to our two children, Jake and Lexi, who are everyday reminders of what matters most in life

JANE B. REECE

has worked in biology publishing since 1978, when she joined the editorial staff of Benjamin Cummings. Her education includes an A.B. in biology from Harvard University (where she was initially a philosophy major), an M.S. in microbiology from Rutgers University, and a Ph.D. in bacteriology from the University of California, Berkeley. At UC Berkeley, and later as a postdoctoral fellow in genetics at Stanford University, her research focused on genetic recombination in bacteria. Dr. Reece taught biology at Middlesex County College (New Jersey) and Queensborough Community College (New York). During her 12 years as an editor at Benjamin Cummings, she played a major role in a number of successful textbooks. She is the lead author of *Campbell Biology*, 10th Edition, and *Campbell Biology: Concepts & Connections*, 8th Edition.

To my wonderful coauthors, who have made working on our books a pleasure

NEIL A. CAMPBELL

(1946–2004) combined the inquiring nature of a research scientist with the soul of a caring teacher. Over his 30 years of teaching introductory biology to both science majors and nonscience majors, many thousands of students had the opportunity to learn from him and be stimulated by his enthusiasm for the study of life. While he is greatly missed by his many friends in the biology community, his coauthors remain inspired by his visionary dedication to education and are committed to searching for ever-better ways to engage students in the wonders of biology.

Detailed Contents

Appendices

Glossary

Index

Discover Why Biology *Matters*

Campbell Essential Biology highlights how the concepts that you learn in your biology class are relevant to your everyday life.

● **NEW! Why Biology Matters Photo Essays** use dynamic photographs and intriguing scientific observations to introduce each chapter. Each scientific tidbit is revisited in the chapter.

MasteringBiology®

NEW! Everyday Biology Videos briefly explore interesting and relevant biology topics that relate to concepts that students are learning in class. These 20 videos can be assigned in MasteringBiology with assessment questions.

15 The Evolution of Microbial Life

Why Microorganisms Matter

If your family took a vacation in which you traveled 1 mile for every million years in the history of life, you'd still be asking, "Are we there yet?" after driving from Miami to Seattle.

According to a recent study, infection by the parasite *Toxoplasma* makes mice lose their fear of cats.

▲ Seaweeds aren't just used for wrapping sushi—they're in your ice cream, too.

▲ You have microorganisms to thank for the clean water you drink every day.

292

● **UPDATED!** **Chapter Threads** weave a single compelling topic throughout the chapter. In Chapter 15, human microbiota are explored.

▼

 Human Microbiota BIOLOGY AND SOCIETY

Our Invisible Inhabitants

You probably know that your body contains trillions of individual cells, but did you know that they aren't all "you"? In fact, microorganisms residing in and on your body outnumber your own cells by 10 to 1. That means 100 trillion bacteria, archaea, and protists call your body home. Your skin, mouth, and nasal passages and your digestive and urogenital tracts are prime real estate for these microorganisms. Although each individual is so tiny that it would have to be magnified hundreds of times for you to see it, the weight of your microbial residents totals two to five pounds.

We acquire our microbial communities during the first two years of life, and they remain fairly stable thereafter. However, modern life is taking a toll on that stability. We alter the balance of these communities by taking antibiotics, purifying our water, sterilizing our food, attempting to germproof our surroundings, and scrubbing our skin and teeth. Scientists hypothesize that disrupting our microbial communities may increase our susceptibility to infectious diseases, predispose us to certain cancers, and contribute to conditions such as asthma and other allergies, irritable bowel syndrome, Crohn's disease, and autism. Researchers are even investigating whether having the wrong microbial community could make us fat. In addition, scientists are studying

Colorized scanning electron micrograph of bacteria on a human tongue (14,500×).

how our microbial communities have evolved over the course of human history. As you'll discover in the Evolution Connection section at the end of this chapter, for example, dietary changes invited decay-causing bacteria to make themselves at home on our teeth.

Throughout this chapter, you will learn about the benefits and drawbacks of human-microbe interactions. You will also sample a bit of the remarkable diversity of prokaryotes and protists. This chapter is the first of three that explore the magnificent diversity of life. And so it is fitting that we begin with the prokaryotes, Earth's first life-form, and the protists, the bridge between unicellular eukaryotes and multicellular plants, fungi, and animals.

293

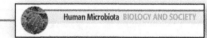 **Human Microbiota** BIOLOGY AND SOCIETY

Biology and Society essays relate biology to your life and interests. This example discusses the microorganisms that live in your own body.

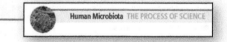 **Human Microbiota** THE PROCESS OF SCIENCE

Process of Science explorations give you real-world examples of how the scientific method is applied. Chapter 15 explores a recent investigation into the possible role of microbiota in obesity.

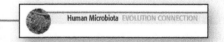 **Human Microbiota** EVOLUTION CONNECTION

Evolution Connection essays conclude each chapter by demonstrating how the theme of evolution runs throughout all of biology. The example in Chapter 15 discusses how changes in the typical human diet over generations is linked to bacteria that cause tooth decay.

● **Additional updated Chapter Threads and essays** include radioactivity in Chapter 2, muscle performance in Chapter 6, and theft of used cooking oil for biofuel recycling in Chapter 7.

Identify "Big Picture" Themes

Examples of major themes in biology are highlighted throughout the text to help you see how overarching biology concepts are interconnected.

● **NEW!** **Important Themes in Biology** are introduced in Chapter 1 to underscore unifying principles that run throughout biology.

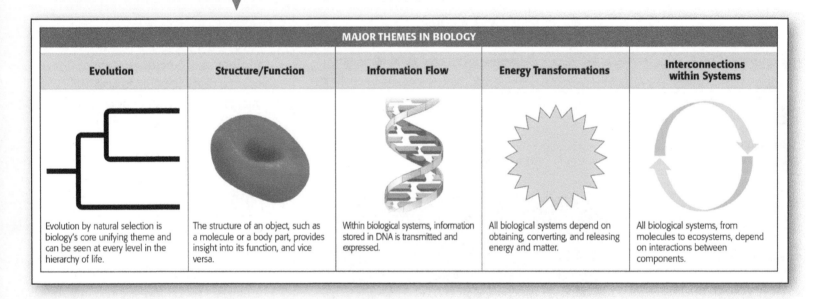

MAJOR THEMES IN BIOLOGY				
Evolution	**Structure/Function**	**Information Flow**	**Energy Transformations**	**Interconnections within Systems**
Evolution by natural selection is biology's core unifying theme and can be seen at every level in the hierarchy of life.	The structure of an object, such as a molecule or a body part, provides insight into its function, and vice versa.	Within biological systems, information stored in DNA is transmitted and expressed.	All biological systems depend on obtaining, converting, and releasing energy and matter.	All biological systems, from molecules to ecosystems, depend on interactions between components.

● These themes—Evolution, Structure/Function, Information Flow, Energy Transformations, and Interconnections within Systems—are **signaled with icons** throughout the text to help you notice the reoccurring examples of the major themes.

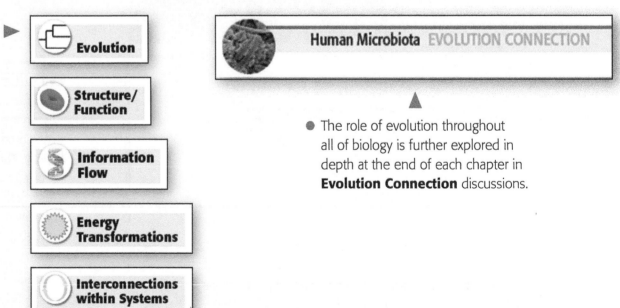

● The role of evolution throughout all of biology is further explored in depth at the end of each chapter in **Evolution Connection** discussions.

Recognize Analogies and Applications

Analogies and applications to everyday life make unfamiliar biology concepts easier to visualize and understand.

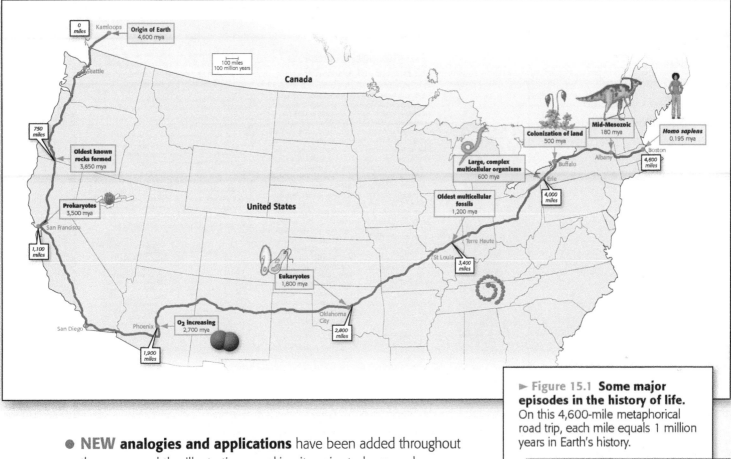

▶ Figure 15.1 **Some major episodes in the history of life.** On this 4,600-mile metaphorical road trip, each mile equals 1 million years in Earth's history.

If your family took a vacation in which you traveled 1 mile for every million years in the history of life, you'd still be asking, "Are we there yet?" after driving from Miami to Seattle.

● **NEW** **analogies and applications** have been added throughout the prose and the illustrations, making it easier to learn and remember key concepts for the first time. Examples include:

- comparing the significant differences between prokaryotic and eukaryotic cells to the differences between a bicycle and an SUV (Chapter 4)

- comparing the process of DNA winding into chromosomes with the act of winding yarn into a skein (Chapter 10)

- comparing a 4,600-mile road trip that describes the scale of biological evolution on Earth (Chapter 15)

- comparing signal transduction to email communication (Chapter 27*)

- comparing how dominoes relate to an action potential moving along an axon (Chapter 27*)

* Chapters 21–29 are included in the expanded version of the text that includes coverage of animal and plant anatomy and physiology.

Boost Your Scientific Literacy

A wide variety of exercises and assignments can help you move beyond memorization and think like a scientist.

● **UPDATED! Process of Science essays** appear in every chapter and walk through each step of the scientific method as it applies to a specific research question.

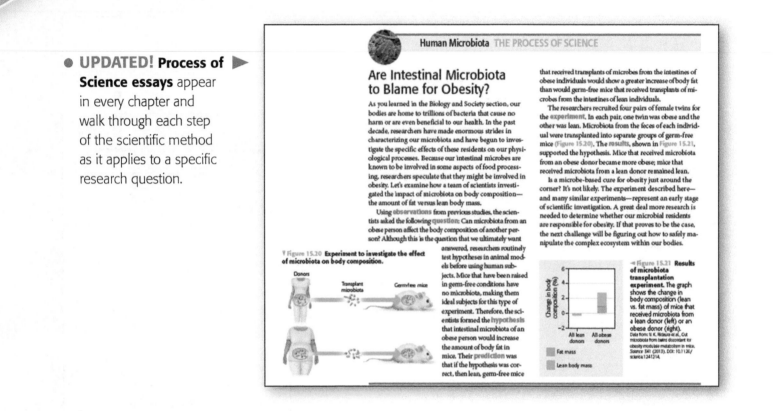

Human Microbiota THE PROCESS OF SCIENCE

Are Intestinal Microbiota to Blame for Obesity?

As you learned in the Biology and Society section, our bodies are home to trillions of bacteria that cause no harm or are even beneficial to our health. In the past decade, researchers have made enormous strides in characterizing our microbiota and have begun to investigate the specific effects of these residents on our physiological processes. Because our intestinal microbes are known to be involved in some aspects of food processing, researchers speculate that they might be involved in obesity. Let's examine how a team of scientists investigated the impact of microbiota on body composition—the amount of fat versus lean body mass.

Using observations from previous studies, the scientists asked the following question: Can microbiota from an obese person affect the body composition of another person? Although this is the question that we ultimately want answered, researchers routinely test hypotheses in animal models before using human subjects. Mice that have been raised in germ-free conditions have no microbiota, making them ideal subjects for this type of experiment. Therefore, the scientists formed the hypothesis that intestinal microbiota of an obese person would increase the amount of body fat in mice. Their prediction was that if the hypothesis was correct, then lean, germ-free mice

that received transplants of microbes from the intestines of obese individuals would show a greater increase of body fat than would germ-free mice that received transplants of microbes from the intestines of lean individuals.

The researchers recruited four pairs of female twins for the experiment. In each pair, one twin was obese and the other was lean. Microbiota from the feces of each individual were transplanted into separate groups of germ-free mice (Figure 15.20). The results, shown in Figure 15.21, supported the hypothesis. Mice that received microbiota from an obese donor became more obese; mice that received microbiota from a lean donor remained lean.

Is a microbe-based cure for obesity just around the corner? It's not likely. The experiment described here—and many similar experiments—represent an early stage of scientific investigation. A great deal more research is needed to determine whether our microbial residents are responsible for obesity. If that proves to be the case, the next challenge will be figuring out how to safely manipulate the complex ecosystem within our bodies.

▼ Figure 15.20 **Experiment to investigate the effect of microbiota on body composition.**

◄ Figure 15.21 **Results of microbiota transplantation experiment.** The graph shows the change in body composition (lean vs. fat mass) of mice that received microbiota from a lean donor (left) or an obese donor (right). Data from: V. K. Ridaura et al., Gut microbiota from twins discordant for obesity modulate metabolism in mice. *Science* 341 (2013), DOI: 10.1126/science.1241214.

MasteringBiology®

Part A · Designing a controlled experiment

In one experiment, scientists raised mice in germ-free conditions so the mice lacked intestinal microbes. The mice were fed a low-fat diet rich in the complex plant polysaccharides, such as cellulose, that are often called fiber.

When the mice were 12 weeks old, the scientists transplanted the microbial community from the intestine of a single "donor" mouse into all of the germ-free mice. Then they divided the mice randomly into two groups and fed each group a different diet.

- Group 1 (the control group) continued to eat a low-fat, high-fiber diet.
- Group 2 (the experimental group) ate a high-fat, high-sugar diet.

"Donor" mouse

Group 1: Control group — Low-fat, high-fiber diet

Germ-free mice

Group 2: Experimental group — High-fat, high-sugar diet

Mouse image: © Biochemistry Media Lab, University of Wisconsin · Madison. Used with permission.

◄ **NEW! Scientific Thinking Activities** are designed to help you develop an understanding of how scientific research is conducted.

NEW! Evaluating Science in the Media Activities challenge you to recognize validity, bias, purpose, and authority in everyday sources of information.

Learn to Interpret Data

Data interpretation is important for understanding biology and for making many important decisions in everyday life. Exercises in the text and online will help you develop this important skill.

● **NEW! Interpreting Data end-of-chapter questions** help you learn to use quantitative material by analyzing graphs and data. This example from Chapter 10 invites you to examine historical data of flu mortality. Other examples include:

- Chapter 13: Learn how markings on snail shells affect predation rates in an environment

- Chapter 15: Calculate how quickly bacteria can multiply on unrefrigerated food

14. **Interpreting Data** The graph below summarizes the number of children who died of all strains of flu from 2007 until 2013. Each bar represents the number of child deaths occurring in one week. Why does the graph have the shape it does, with a series of peaks and valleys? Looking over the Biology and Society section at the start of the chapter, why does the graph reach its highest points near the middle? Based on these data, when does flu season begin and end in a typical year?

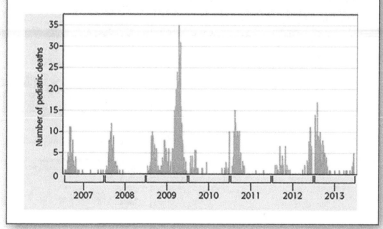

MasteringBiology®

Interpreting Data: Primary and Secondary Immune Responses

Use the graph at left to answer the questions.

© Pearson Education, Inc.

◀ **NEW! Interpreting Data Activities** help you build and practice data analysis skills.

Maximize Your Study Time

Campbell Essential Biology and the **MasteringBiology** homework, tutorial, and assessment program work hand-in-hand to help students succeed in introductory biology.

● **The Chapter Review** offers ▶ a built-in study guide that combines words with images to help you organize the key concepts. The unique figures in the Chapter Review synthesize information from the corresponding chapter, which helps you study more efficiently.

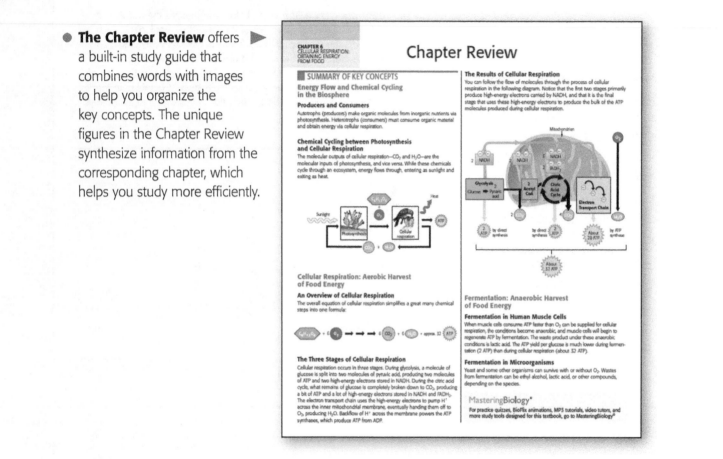

MasteringBiology®

MasteringBiology provides a wide range of activities and study tools to match your learning style, including BioFlix animations, MP3 audio tutorials, interactive practice quizzes, and more. Your instructor can assign activities for extra practice to monitor your progress in the course.

◀ **NEW!** **Essential Biology videos** introduce you to key concepts and vocabulary, and are narrated by authors Eric Simon and Kelly Hogan. Topics include the **Scientific Method, Molecules of Life, DNA Replication, Mechanisms of Evolution, Ecological Principles,** and more.

Learn Before, During, and After Class

MasteringBiology®

BEFORE CLASS

NEW! Dynamic Study Modules help you acquire, retain, and recall information faster and more efficiently than ever before. The convenient practice questions and detailed review explanations can be accessed on the go using a smartphone, tablet, or computer.

DURING CLASS

NEW! Learning Catalytics is a "bring your own device" assessment and classroom activity system that expands the possibilities for student engagement. Using Learning Catalytics, instructors can deliver a wide range of auto-gradable or open-ended questions that test content knowledge and build critical thinking skills using eighteen different answer types.

Mastering

Continuously Adaptive

Pre-lecture Assignments

Homework, Quizzing, and Testing

Learning Catalytics, Mastering Media

AFTER CLASS

- **Over 100 Coaching Activities** are created by the textbook author team and help you focus on learning key concepts and building your biology vocabulary.

- **NEW! Everyday Biology videos** briefly explore interesting and relevant biology topics that relate to concepts in the course.

Instructors: Extensive Resources for You

Extensive resources save valuable time both in course prep and during class.

- **The Instructor's Resource DVD for Campbell Essential Biology (with Physiology chapters)** organizes all instructor media resources by chapter into one convenient and easy-to-use package, including PowerPoint® slides, animations, lecture presentations, lecture questions to stimulate class discussions, quiz games, digital transparencies, and more (ISBN 0133950956 / 9780133950953).

- The **Test Bank** provides a variety of test questions, many art- or scenario-based, in both TestGen® and Microsoft® Word.

EXPANDED! Current Topic PowerPoint® presentations include new topics such as DNA Profiling, Stem Cells and Cloning, Diabetes, Biodiversity, and more. Each Powerpoint Presentation includes instructor teaching tips and active learning strategies to help you easily create a high-interest, active lecture.

MasteringBiology®

Selected materials from the Instructor Resources DVD can be accessed and downloaded from the Instructor Resources area of MasteringBiology.

The **Instructor Exchange** provides successful, class-tested active learning techniques and analogies from biology instructors around the nation, offering a springboard for quick ideas to create more compelling lectures. Co-author Kelly Hogan moderates contributions to the exchange.

Preface

This is a wonderful time to teach and learn biology. Opportunities to marvel at the natural world and the life within it abound. It's difficult to view a news website without finding stories that touch on biology and its intersection with society. In addition, the world of pop culture is rich with books, movies, TV shows, comic strips, and video games that feature biological wonders and challenge us to think about important biological concepts and their implications. Although some people *say* that they don't like biology (or, more often, science in general), nearly everyone will admit to an inborn biophilia. After all, most of us keep pets, tend a garden, enjoy zoos and aquariums, or appreciate time spent outdoors. Furthermore, nearly everyone realizes that the subject of biology has a significant impact on his or her own life through its connections to medicine, biotechnology, agriculture, environmental issues, forensics, and myriad other areas. But despite the inborn affinity that nearly everyone has for biology, it can be a struggle for nonscientists to delve into the subject. Our primary goal in writing *Campbell Essential Biology* is to help teachers motivate and educate the next generation of citizens by tapping into the inherent curiosity about life that we all share.

Goals of the Book

Although our world is rich with "teachable moments" and learning opportunities, the explosion of knowledge we have already witnessed in the 21st century threatens to bury a curious person under an avalanche of information. "So much biology, so little time" is the universal lament of biology educators. Neil Campbell conceived of *Campbell Essential Biology* as a tool to help teachers and students focus on the most important areas of biology. To that end, the book is organized into four core areas: cells, genes, evolution, and ecology. Dr. Campbell's vision, which we carry on and extend in this edition, has enabled us to keep *Campbell Essential Biology* manageable in size and thoughtful in the development of the concepts that are most fundamental to understanding life. We've aligned this new edition with today's "less is more" approach in biology education for nonscience majors—where the emphasis is on fewer topics and more focused explanations—and we never allow the content we do include to be diluted. Toward that end, in this new edition we removed some of the most technical details and terminology, which we hope will help nonscience major students to focus on the key topics in biology.

We formulated our approach after countless conversations with teachers and students in which we noticed some important trends in how biology is taught. In particular, many teachers identify three goals: (1) to engage students by relating the core content to their lives and the greater society; (2) to clarify the process of science by showing how it is applied in the real world and to give students practice in applying scientific and critical thinking skills themselves; and (3) to demonstrate how evolution serves as biology's unifying theme. To help achieve these goals, every chapter of this book includes three important features. First, a chapter-opening essay called Biology and Society highlights a connection between the chapter's core content and students' lives. Second, an essay called The Process of Science (found in the body of the chapter) describes how the scientific process has illuminated the topic at hand, using a classic or modern experiment as an example. Third, a chapter-closing Evolution Connection essay relates the chapter to biology's unifying theme of evolution. To maintain a cohesive narrative throughout each chapter, the content is tied together with a unifying chapter thread, a relevant high-interest topic that is woven throughout the three chapter essays and is touched on several additional times in the chapter. Thus, this unifying chapter thread ties together the three pedagogical goals of the course using a topic that is compelling and relevant to students.

New to This Edition

We hope that this latest edition of *Campbell Essential Biology* goes even further in helping students relate the material to their lives, understand the process of science, and appreciate how evolution is the unifying theme of biology. To this end, we've added significant new features and content to this edition:

- **Clarifying the importance of biology to students' lives.** Every student taking an introductory biology course should be made keenly aware of the myriad ways that biology affects his or her own life. To help put such issues front and center, and to "prime the learning pump" before diving into the content, we have included a new feature at the start of each chapter called Why It Matters. Every chapter begins with this new feature, which presents a series of attention-grabbing facts, in conjunction with compelling photographs that illustrate the importance of that chapter's topic to students' lives. These high-interest facts appear again in the chapter narrative, typeset in a design meant to capture students' attention and placed adjacent to the science discussion that explains the fact. Examples include: Why Macromolecules Matter ("A long-distance runner who carbo-loads the night before a race is banking glycogen to be used the next day") and Why Ecology Matters ("Producing the beef for a hamburger requires eight times as much land as producing the soybeans for a soyburger").
- **Major themes in biology incorporated throughout the book.** In 2009, the American Association for the Advancement of Science published a document that

served as a call to action in undergraduate biology education. The principles of this document, which is titled "Vision and Change," are becoming widely accepted throughout the biology education community. "Vision and Change" presents five core concepts that serve as the foundation of undergraduate biology. In this edition of *Campbell Essential Biology*, we repeatedly and explicitly link book content to each of the five themes. For example, the first theme, the relationship of structure to function, is illustrated in Chapter 2 in the discussion of how the unique chemistry of water accounts for its biological properties. The second theme, information flow, is explored in Chapter 10 in the discussion on how genes control traits. The third theme, interconnections within systems, is illustrated in Chapter 18 in the discussion on the global water cycle. The fourth theme, evolution, is called out in Chapter 17 in the discussion on the phylogeny of animals. The fifth theme, energy transformations, is explored in Chapter 6 in the discussion on the flow of energy through ecosystems. Readers will find at least one major theme called out in this way per chapter, which will help students see the connections between these major themes and the course content and instructors will have myriad easy-to-reference examples to help underscore these five themes. These specific examples are supplemented by many others throughout the text.

- **New unifying chapter threads.** As discussed earlier, every chapter in *Campbell Essential Biology* has a unique unifying chapter thread—a high-interest topic that helps to demonstrate the relevance of the chapter content. The chapter thread is incorporated into the three main essays of each chapter (Biology and Society, The Process of Science, and Evolution Connection) and appears throughout the chapter text. This sixth edition features many new chapter threads and essays, each of which highlights a current topic that applies biology to students' lives and to the greater society. For example, Chapter 2 presents a new thread on radioactivity, including discussions of its use in health care and as a tool to test evolutionary hypotheses. Chapter 15 features a new thread on human microbiota, including a recent investigation into the possible role of microbiota in obesity and an exploration of how the change from a hunter-gatherer lifestyle to a diet heavy in processed starch and sugar selected for oral bacteria that cause tooth decay.

- **Developing data literacy.** Many nonscience-major students express anxiety when faced with numerical data, yet the ability to interpret data can help with many important decisions we all face. To help foster critical thinking skills, we have incorporated a new feature called

Interpreting Data into the end-of-chapter assessments. These questions, one per chapter, offer students the opportunity to practice their science literacy skills. For example, in Chapter 10, students are asked to examine historical data of flu mortality, and in Chapter 15, students are tasked with calculating how quickly bacteria can multiply on unrefrigerated food. We hope that practice examining these simple yet relevant data sets will help students be more comfortable when they must confront numerical data in their own lives.

- **Updated content and figures.** As we do in every edition, we have made many significant updates to the content presented in the book. Examples of new or updated material include new discussions on epigenetics, metagenomics, and RNA interference; an examination of new genomic information on Neanderthals; updated climate change statistics; a discussion of advances in fetal genetic testing; and an updated discussion of new threats to biodiversity. We have also included nearly a dozen new examples of DNA profiling and a cutting-edge exploration of genetically modified foods. We also strive with each new edition to update our photos and illustrations. New figures include examples that show how a prion protein can cause brain damage (Figure 3.20) and how real data from DNA profiling can exonerate wrongly accused individuals (Figure 12.16).

- **New analogies.** As part of our continuing effort to help students visualize and relate to biology concepts, we have included numerous new analogies in this edition. For example, in Chapter 4, we compare the significant differences between prokaryotic and eukaryotic cells to the differences between a bicycle and an SUV. In Chapter 8, we compare the process of DNA winding into chromosomes with the act of winding yarn into a skein. Additional analogies, both narrative and visual, bring biological scale into focus, such as a 4,600-mile road trip that is used to help students imagine the scale of biological evolution on Earth (Figure 15.1).

- **MasteringBiology updates.** New whiteboard-style animated videos provide students with an introduction to key biological concepts so students can arrive to class better prepared to explore applications or dive into any topic more deeply. New Everyday Biology videos, produced by the BBC, promote connections between concepts and biology in everyday life, and Evaluating Science in the Media activities teach students how to be wise consumers of scientific information and coach them through critically evaluating the validity of scientific information on the Internet. New Scientific Thinking activities encourage students to develop scientific reasoning skills as they explore a current area of research and allows instructors to easily assess student mastery of these skills.

- **Teaching the Issues.** Because many instructors, including the authors, prefer to use current topics to demonstrate the relevance of biology to students' lives, we've expanded our series of Current Topic Instructor PowerPoints© with this edition. New topics include DNA Profiling, Stem Cells and Cloning, Diabetes, Biodiversity, and more. Each PowerPoint© Presentation includes instructor teaching tips and active learning strategies to easily create a high-interest, active lecture.

Attitudes about science and scientists are often shaped by a single required science class—*this* class. We hope to tap into the innate appreciation of nature we all share and nurture this affection into a genuine love of biology. In this spirit, we hope that this textbook and its supplements will encourage all readers to make biological perspectives a part of their personal worldviews. Please let us know how we are doing and how we can improve the next edition of *Campbell Essential Biology*.

ERIC SIMON
Department of Biology and
Health Science
New England College
Henniker, NH 03242
SimonBiology@gmail.com

JEAN DICKEY
Department of Biology
Clemson University
Clemson, SC 29634
dickeyj@clemson.edu

KELLY HOGAN
Department of Biology
University of North Carolina
Chapel Hill, NC 27599
leek@email.unc.edu

JANE REECE
C/O Pearson Education
1301 Sansome Street
San Francisco, CA 94111
JaneReece@cal.berkeley.edu

Acknowledgments

Throughout the process of planning and writing *Campbell Essential Biology*, the author team has had the great fortune of collaborating with an extremely talented group of publishing professionals and educators. Although the responsibility for any shortcomings lies solely with us, the merits of the book and its supplements reflect the contributions of a great many dedicated colleagues.

First and foremost, we must acknowledge our huge debt to Neil Campbell, the original author of this book and a source of ongoing inspiration for each of us. Although this edition has been carefully and thoroughly revised—to update its science, its connections to students' lives, its pedagogy, and its currency—it remains infused with Neil's founding vision and his commitment to share biology with introductory students.

This book could not have been completed without the efforts of the *Campbell Essential Biology* team at Pearson Education. Leading the team is acquisitions editor Alison Rodal, who is tireless in her pursuit of educational excellence and who inspires all of us to constantly seek better ways to help teachers and students. We also thank the Pearson Science executive team for their supportive leadership, in particular managing director of Arts, Science, Business and Engineering Paul Corey, vice president of science editorial Adam Jaworski, editor-in-chief Beth Wilbur, director of development Barbara Yien, executive editorial manager Ginnie Simione Jutson, and director of media development Lauren Fogel.

It is no exaggeration to say that the talents of the best editorial team in the industry are evident on every page of this book. The authors were continuously guided with great patience and skill by senior development editors Debbie Hardin, Julia Osborne, and Susan Teahan. We owe this editorial team—which include the wonderfully capable and friendly editorial assistant Alison Cagle—a deep debt of gratitude for their talents and hard work.

Once we formulated our words and images, the production and manufacturing teams transformed them into the final book. Project manager Lori Newman and program manager Leata Holloway oversaw the production process and kept everyone and everything on track. We also thank program manager team lead Mike Early and project manager team lead David Zielonka for their careful oversight. We hope you will agree that every edition of *Campbell Essential Biology* is distinguished by continuously updated and beautiful photography. For that we thank photo researcher Kristin Piljay, who constantly dazzles us with her keen ability to locate memorable images.

For the production and composition of the book, we thank senior project editor Norine Strang of S4Carlisle Publishing Services, whose professionalism and commitment to the quality of the finished product is visible throughout. The authors owe much to copyeditor Joanna Dinsmore and proofreader Pete Shanks for their keen eyes and attention to detail. We thank design manager Derek Bacchus (who is also responsible for the stunning cover design) and Gary Hespenheide of Hespenheide Design for the beautiful interior design, and we are grateful to Kristina Seymour and the artists at Precision Graphics for rendering clear and compelling illustrations. We also thank rights and permissions project manager Donna Kalal, manager of rights and permissions Rachel Youdelman, and text permissions project manager William Opaluch for keeping us within bounds. In the final stages of production, the talents of manufacturing buyer Stacy Weinberger shone.

Most instructors view the textbook as just one piece of the learning puzzle, with the book's supplements and media completing the picture. We are lucky to have a *Campbell Essential Biology* supplements team that is fully committed to the core goals of accuracy and readability. Project Manager Libby Reiser expertly coordinated the supplements, a difficult task given their number and variety. We also thank media project manager Eddie Lee for his work on the excellent Instructor Resources DVD that accompanies the text. We owe particular gratitude to the supplements authors, especially the indefatigable and eagle-eyed Ed Zalisko of Blackburn College, who wrote the Instructor Guide and the PowerPoint® Lectures; the highly skilled and multitalented Hilary Engebretson, of Whatcom Community College, who revised the Quiz Shows and Clicker questions; and Jean DeSaix (University of North Carolina at Chapel Hill), Justin Shaffer (University of California, Irvine), Kristen Miller (University of Georgia), and Suann Yang (Presbyterian College), our collaborative team of test bank authors for ensuring excellence in our assessment program. The authors also thank Justin Shaffer (University of California, Irvine), Suzanne Wakim (Butte Community College), and Eden Effert (Eastern Illinois University) for their fine work on the issues-based presentation Campbell Current Topics PowerPoint® Presentations. In addition, the authors thank Reading Quiz authors Amaya Garcia Costas, Montana State University, and Cindy Klevickis, James Madison University; Reading Quiz accuracy reviewer Veronica Menendez; Practice Test author Chris Romero, Front Range Community College; and Practice Test accuracy reviewer Justin Walgaurnery, University of Hawaii.

We wish to thank the talented group of publishing professionals who worked on the comprehensive media program that accompanies *Campbell Essential Biology with Physiology*. The team members dedicated to MasteringBiology™ are true "game changers" in the field of biology education. We thank content producer for media Daniel Ross for coordinating our multimedia plan. Vital contributions were also made by associate Mastering media producer Taylor Merck, senior content producer Lee Ann Doctor, and web developer Leslie Sumrall. We also thank Tania Mlawer and Sarah Jensen for their efforts to make our media products the best in the industry.

As educators and writers, we are very lucky to have a crack marketing team. Executive marketing manager Lauren Harp, director of marketing Christy Lesko, and field marketing manager

Amee Mosely seemed to be everywhere at once as they helped us achieve our authorial goals by keeping us constantly focused on the needs of students and instructors. For their amazing efforts with our marketing materials, we also thank copywriter supervisor Jane Campbell and designer Howie Severson.

We also thank the Pearson Science sales representatives, district and regional managers, and learning technology specialists for representing *Campbell Essential Biology with Physiology* on campuses. These representatives are our lifeline to the greater educational community, telling us what you like (and don't like) about this book and the accompanying supplements and media. Their enthusiasm for helping students makes them not only ideal ambassadors but also our partners in education. We urge all educators to take full advantage of the wonderful resource offered by the Pearson sales team.

Eric Simon would like to thank his colleagues at New England College for their support and for providing a model of excellence in education, in particular, Lori Bergeron, Deb Dunlop, Mark Mitch, Maria Colby, Sachie Howard, and Mark Watman. Eric would also like to acknowledge the contributions of Jim Newcomb for lending his keen eye for accuracy; Jay Withgott for sharing his expertise; Elyse Carter Vosen for providing much-needed social context; Jamey Barone for her sage sensitivity; and Amanda Marsh for her expert eye, sharp attention to detail, tireless commitment, constant support, compassion, and wisdom.

At the end of these acknowledgments, you'll find a list of the many instructors who provided valuable information about their courses, reviewed chapters, and/or conducted class tests of *Campbell Essential Biology with Physiology* with their students. All of our best ideas spring from the classroom, so we thank them for their efforts and support.

Most of all, we thank our families, friends, and colleagues, who continue to tolerate our obsession with doing our best for science education.

ERIC SIMON, JEAN DICKEY, KELLY HOGAN, JANE REECE

REVIEWERS OF THIS EDITION

Shazia Ahmed
Texas Woman's University

Tami Asplin
North Dakota State

TJ Boyle
Blinn College, Bryan Campus

Miriam Chavez
University of New Mexico, Valencia

Joe W. Conner
Pasadena City College

Michael Cullen
University of Evansville

Terry Derting
Murray State University

Danielle Dodenhoff
California State University, Bakersfield

Hilary Engebretson
Whatcom Community College

Holly Swain Ewald
University of Louisville

J. Yvette Gardner
Clayton State University

Sig Harden
Troy University

Jay Hodgson
Armstrong Atlantic State University

Sue Hum-Musser
Western Illinois University

Corey Johnson
University of North Carolina

Gregory Jones
Santa Fe College, Gainesville, Florida

Arnold J. Karpoff
University of Louisville

Tom Kennedy
Central New Mexico Community College

Erica Lannan
Prairie State College

Grace Lasker
Lake Washington Institute of Technology

Bill Mackay
Edinboro University

Mark Manteuffel
St. Louis Community College

Diane Melroy
University of North Carolina Wilmington

Kiran Misra
Edinboro University

Susan Mounce
Eastern Illinois University

Zia Nisani
Antelope Valley College

Michelle Rogers
Austin Peay State University

Bassam M. Salameh
Antelope Valley College

Carsten Sanders
Kuztown University

Justin Shaffer
University of California, Irvine

Jennifer Smith
Triton College

Ashley Spring
Eastern Florida State College

Michael Stevens
Utah Valley University

Chad Thompson
Westchester Community College

Melinda Verdone
Rock Valley College

Eileen Walsh
Westchester Community College

Kathy Watkins
Central Piedmont Community College

Wayne Whaley
Utah Valley University

Holly Woodruff (Kupfer)
Central Piedmont Community College

REVIEWERS OF PREVIOUS EDITIONS

Marilyn Abbott
Lindenwood College

Tammy Adair
Baylor University

Felix O. Akojie
Paducah Community College

Shireen Alemadi
Minnesota State University, Moorhead

William Sylvester Allred, Jr.
Northern Arizona University

Megan E. Anduri
California State University, Fullerton

Estrella Z. Ang
University of Pittsburgh

David Arieti
Oakton Community College

C. Warren Arnold
Allan Hancock Community College

Mohammad Ashraf
Olive-Harvey College

Heather Ashworth
Utah Valley University

Bert Atsma
Union County College

Yael Avissar
Rhode Island College

Barbara J. Backley
Elgin Community College

Gail F. Baker
LaGuardia Community College

Neil Baker
Ohio State University

Kristel K. Bakker
Dakota State University

Andrew Baldwin
Mesa Community College

Linda Barham
Meridian Community College

Charlotte Barker
Angelina College

Verona Barr
Heartland Community College

S. Rose Bast
Mount Mary College

Sam Beattie
California State University, Chico

Rudi Berkelhamer
University of California, Irvine

Penny Bernstein
Kent State University, Stark Campus

Suchi Bhardwaj
Winthrop University

Donna H. Bivans
East Carolina University

Andrea Bixler
Clarke College

Brian Black
Bay de Noc Community College

Allan Blake
Seton Hall University

Karyn Bledsoe
Western Oregon University

Judy Bluemer
Morton College

Sonal Blumenthal
University of Texas at Austin

Lisa Boggs
Southwestern Oklahoma State University

Dennis Bogyo
Valdosta State University

David Boose
Gonzaga University

Virginia M. Borden
University of Minnesota, Duluth

James Botsford
New Mexico State University

Cynthia Bottrell
Scott Community College

Richard Bounds
Mount Olive College

Cynthia Boyd
Hawkeye Community College

Robert Boyd
Auburn University

B. J. Boyer
Suffolk County Community College

Mimi Bres
Prince George's Community College

Patricia Brewer
University of Texas at San Antonio

Jerald S. Bricker
Cameron University

Carol A. Britson
University of Mississippi

George M. Brooks
Ohio University, Zanesville

Janie Sue Brooks
Brevard College

Steve Browder
Franklin College

Evert Brown
Casper College

Mary H. Brown
Lansing Community College

Richard D. Brown
Brunswick Community College

Steven Brumbaugh
Green River Community College

Joseph C. Bundy
University of North Carolina at Greensboro

Carol T. Burton
Bellevue Community College

Rebecca Burton
Alverno College

Warren R. Buss
University of Northern Colorado

Wilbert Butler
Tallahassee Community College

Miguel Cervantes-Cervantes
Lehman College, City University of New York

Maitreyee Chandra
Diablo Valley College

Bane Cheek
Polk Community College

Thomas F. Chubb
Villanova University

Reggie Cobb
Nash Community College

Pamela Cole
Shelton State Community College

William H. Coleman
University of Hartford

Jay L. Comeaux
McNeese State University

James Conkey
Truckee Meadows Community College

Karen A. Conzelman
Glendale Community College

Ann Coopersmith
Maui Community College

Erica Corbett
Southeastern Oklahoma State University

James T. Costa
Western Carolina University

Pat Cox
University of Tennessee, Knoxville

Laurie-Ann Crawford
Hawkeye Community College

Pradeep M. Dass
Appalachian State University

Paul Decelles
Johnson County Community College

Galen DeHay
Tri County Technical College

Cynthia L. Delaney
University of South Alabama

Jean DeSaix
University of North Carolina at Chapel Hill

Elizabeth Desy
Southwest State University

Edward Devine
Moraine Valley Community College

Dwight Dimaculangan
Winthrop University

Deborah Dodson
Vincennes Community College

Diane Doidge
Grand View College

Don Dorfman
Monmouth University

Richard Driskill
Delaware State University

Lianne Drysdale
Ozarks Technical Community College

Terese Dudek
Kishawaukee College

Shannon Dullea
North Dakota State College of Science

David A. Eakin
Eastern Kentucky University

Brian Earle
Cedar Valley College

Ade Ejire
Johnston Community College

Dennis G. Emery
Iowa State University

Renee L. Engle-Goodner
Merritt College

Virginia Erickson
Highline Community College

Carl Estrella
Merced College

Marirose T. Ethington
Genesee Community College

Paul R. Evans
Brigham Young University

Zenephia E. Evans
Purdue University

Jean Everett
College of Charleston

Dianne M. Fair
*Florida Community College
at Jacksonville*

Joseph Faryniarz
Naugatuck Valley Community College

Phillip Fawley
Westminster College

Lynn Fireston
Ricks College

Jennifer Floyd
Leeward Community College

Dennis M. Forsythe
The Citadel

Angela M. Foster
Wake Technical Community College

Brandon Lee Foster
Wake Technical Community College

Carl F. Friese
University of Dayton

Suzanne S. Frucht
Northwest Missouri State University

Edward G. Gabriel
Lycoming College

Anne M. Galbraith
University of Wisconsin, La Crosse

Kathleen Gallucci
Elon University

Gregory R. Garman
Centralia College

Wendy Jean Garrison
University of Mississippi

Gail Gasparich
Towson University

Kathy Gifford
Butler County Community College

Sharon L. Gilman
Coastal Carolina University

Mac Given
Neumann College

Patricia Glas
The Citadel

Ralph C. Goff
Mansfield University

Marian R. Goldsmith
University of Rhode Island

Andrew Goliszek
*North Carolina Agricultural and Technical
State University*

Tamar Liberman Goulet
University of Mississippi

Curt Gravis
Western State College of Colorado

Larry Gray
Utah Valley State College

Tom Green
West Valley College

Robert S. Greene
Niagara University

Ken Griffin
Tarrant County Junior College

Denise Guerin
Santa Fe Community College

Paul Gurn
Naugatuck Valley Community College

Peggy J. Guthrie
University of Central Oklahoma

Henry H. Hagedorn
University of Arizona

Blanche C. Haning
Vance-Granville Community College

Laszlo Hanzely
Northern Illinois University

Sherry Harrel
Eastern Kentucky University

Reba Harrell
Hinds Community College

Frankie Harris
Independence Community College

Lysa Marie Hartley
Methodist College

Janet Haynes
Long Island University

Michael Held
St. Peter's College

Consetta Helmick
University of Idaho

J. L. Henriksen
Bellevue University

Michael Henry
Contra Costa College

Linda Hensel
Mercer University

Jana Henson
Georgetown College

James Hewlett
Finger Lakes Community College

Richard Hilton
Towson University

Juliana Hinton
McNeese State University

Phyllis C. Hirsch
East Los Angeles College

W. Wyatt Hoback
University of Nebraska at Kearney

Elizabeth Hodgson
York College of Pennsylvania

A. Scott Holaday
Texas Tech University

Robert A. Holmes
Hutchinson Community College

R. Dwain Horrocks
Brigham Young University

Howard L. Hosick
Washington State University

Carl Huether
University of Cincinnati

Celene Jackson
Western Michigan University

John Jahoda
Bridgewater State College

Dianne Jennings
Virginia Commonwealth University

Richard J. Jensen
Saint Mary's College

Scott Johnson
Wake Technical Community College

Tari Johnson
Normandale Community College

Tia Johnson
Mitchell Community College

Greg Jones
Santa Fe Community College

John Jorstad
Kirkwood Community College

Tracy L. Kahn
University of California, Riverside

Robert Kalbach
Finger Lakes Community College

Mary K. Kananen
Pennsylvania State University, Altoona

Thomas C. Kane
University of Cincinnati

Arnold J. Karpoff
University of Louisville

John M. Kasmer
Northeastern Illinois University

Valentine Kefeli
Slippery Rock University

Dawn Keller
Hawkeye College

John Kelly
Northeastern University

Cheryl Kerfeld
University of California, Los Angeles

Henrik Kibak
*California State University,
Monterey Bay*

Kerry Kilburn
Old Dominion University

Joyce Kille-Marino
College of Charleston

Peter King
Francis Marion University

Peter Kish
*Oklahoma School of Science and
Mathematics*

Robert Kitchin
University of Wyoming

Cindy Klevickis
James Madison University

Richard Koblin
Oakland Community College

H. Roberta Koepfer
Queens College

Michael E. Kovach
Baldwin-Wallace College

Jocelyn E. Krebs
University of Alaska, Anchorage

Ruhul H. Kuddus
Utah Valley State College

Nuran Kumbaraci
Stevens Institute of Technology

Holly Kupfer
Central Piedmont Community College

Gary Kwiecinski
The University of Scranton

Roya Lahijani
Palomar College

James V. Landrum
Washburn University

Lynn Larsen
Portland Community College

Brenda Leady
University of Toledo

Siu-Lam Lee
University of Massachusetts, Lowell

Thomas P. Lehman
Morgan Community College

William Leonard
Central Alabama Community College

Shawn Lester
Montgomery College

Leslie Lichtenstein
Massasoit Community College

Barbara Liedl
Central College

Harvey Liftin
Broward Community College

David Loring
Johnson County Community College

Eric Lovely
Arkansas Tech University

Lewis M. Lutton
Mercyhurst College

Maria P. MacWilliams
Seton Hall University

Mark Manteuffel
St. Louis Community College

Lisa Maranto
Prince George's Community College

Michael Howard Marcovitz
Midland Lutheran College

Angela M. Mason
Beaufort County Community College

Roy B. Mason
Mt. San Jacinto College

John Mathwig
College of Lake County

Lance D. McBrayer
Georgia Southern University

Bonnie McCormick
University of the Incarnate Word

Katrina McCrae
Abraham Baldwin Agricultural College

Tonya McKinley
Concord College

Mary Anne McMurray
Henderson Community College

Maryanne Menvielle
California State University, Fullerton

Ed Mercurio
Hartnell College

Timothy D. Metz
Campbell University

Andrew Miller
Thomas University

David Mirman
Mt. San Antonio College

Nancy Garnett Morris
Volunteer State Community College

Angela C. Morrow
University of Northern Colorado

Patricia S. Muir
Oregon State University

James Newcomb
New England College

Jon R. Nickles
University of Alaska, Anchorage

Jane Noble-Harvey
University of Delaware

Michael Nosek
Fitchburg State College

Jeanette C. Oliver
Flathead Valley Community College

David O'Neill
Community College of Baltimore County

Sandra M. Pace
Rappahannock Community College

Lois H. Peck
University of the Sciences, Philadelphia

Kathleen E. Pelkki
Saginaw Valley State University

Jennifer Penrod
Lincoln University

Rhoda E. Perozzi
Virginia Commonwealth University

John S. Peters
College of Charleston

Pamela Petrequin
Mount Mary College

Paula A. Piehl
Potomac State College of West Virginia University

Bill Pietraface
State University of New York Oneonta

Gregory Podgorski
Utah State University

Rosamond V. Potter
University of Chicago

Karen Powell
Western Kentucky University

Martha Powell
University of Alabama

Elena Pravosudova
Sierra College

Hallie Ray
Rappahannock Community College

Jill Raymond
Rock Valley College

Dorothy Read
University of Massachusetts, Dartmouth

Nathan S. Reyna
Howard Payne University

Philip Ricker
South Plains College

Todd Rimkus
Marymount University

Lynn Rivers
Henry Ford Community College

Jennifer Roberts
Lewis University

Laurel Roberts
University of Pittsburgh

April Rottman
Rock Valley College

Maxine Losoff Rusche
Northern Arizona University

Michael L. Rutledge
Middle Tennessee State University

Mike Runyan
Lander University

Travis Ryan
Furman University

Tyson Sacco
Cornell University

Sarmad Saman
Quinsigamond Community College

Pamela Sandstrom
University of Nevada, Reno

Leba Sarkis
Aims Community College

Walter Saviuk
Daytona Beach Community College

Neil Schanker
College of the Siskiyous

Robert Schoch
Boston University

John Richard Schrock
Emporia State University

Julie Schroer
Bismarck State College

Karen Schuster
Florida Community College at Jacksonville

Brian W. Schwartz
Columbus State University

Michael Scott
Lincoln University

Eric Scully
Towson State University

Lois Sealy
Valencia Community College

Sandra S. Seidel
Elon University

Wayne Seifert
Brookhaven College

Susmita Sengupta
City College of San Francisco

Patty Shields
George Mason University

Cara Shillington
Eastern Michigan University

Brian Shmaefsky
Kingwood College

Rainy Inman Shorey
Ferris State University

Cahleen Shrier
Azusa Pacific University

Jed Shumsky
Drexel University

Greg Sievert
Emporia State University

Jeffrey Simmons
West Virginia Wesleyan College

Frederick D. Singer
Radford University

Anu Singh-Cundy
Western Washington University

Kerri Skinner
University of Nebraska at Kearney

Sandra Slivka
Miramar College

Margaret W. Smith
Butler University

Thomas Smith
Armstrong Atlantic State University

Deena K. Spielman
Rock Valley College

Minou D. Spradley
San Diego City College

Robert Stamatis
Daytona Beach Community College

Joyce Stamm
University of Evansville

Eric Stavney
Highline Community College

Bethany Stone
University of Missouri, Columbia

Mark T. Sugalski
New England College

Marshall D. Sundberg
Emporia State University

Adelaide Svoboda
Nazareth College

Sharon Thoma
Edgewood College

Kenneth Thomas
Hillsborough Community College

Sumesh Thomas
Baltimore City Community College

Betty Thompson
Baptist University

Paula Thompson
Florida Community College

Michael Anthony Thornton
Florida Agriculture and Mechanical University

Linda Tichenor
University of Arkansas, Fort Smith

John Tjepkema
University of Maine, Orono

Bruce L. Tomlinson
State University of New York, Fredonia

Leslie R. Towill
Arizona State University

Bert Tribbey
California State University, Fresno

Nathan Trueblood
California State University, Sacramento

Robert Turner
Western Oregon University

Michael Twaddle
University of Toledo

Virginia Vandergon
California State University, Northridge

William A. Velhagen, Jr.
Longwood College

Leonard Vincent
Fullerton College

Jonathan Visick
North Central College

Michael Vitale
Daytona Beach Community College

Lisa Volk
Fayetteville Technical Community College

Daryle Waechter-Brulla
University of Wisconsin, Whitewater

Stephen M. Wagener
Western Connecticut State University

Sean E. Walker
California State University, Fullerton

James A. Wallis
St. Petersburg Community College

Helen Walter
Diablo Valley College

Kristen Walton
Missouri Western State University

Jennifer Warner
University of North Carolina at Charlotte

Arthur C. Washington
Florida Agriculture and Mechanical University

Dave Webb
St. Clair County Community College

Harold Webster
Pennsylvania State University, DuBois

Ted Weinheimer
California State University, Bakersfield

Lisa A. Werner
Pima Community College

Joanne Westin
Case Western Reserve University

Wayne Whaley
Utah Valley State College

Joseph D. White
Baylor University

Quinton White
Jacksonville University

Leslie Y. Whiteman
Virginia Union University

Rick Wiedenmann
New Mexico State University at Carlsbad

Peter J. Wilkin
Purdue University North Central

Bethany Williams
California State University, Fullerton

Daniel Williams
Winston-Salem University

Judy A. Williams
Southeastern Oklahoma State University

Dwina Willis
Freed Hardeman University

David Wilson
University of Miami

Mala S. Wingerd
San Diego State University

E. William Wischusen
Louisiana State University

Darla J. Wise
Concord College

Michael Womack
Macon State College

Bonnie Wood
University of Maine at Presque Isle

Jo Wen Wu
Fullerton College

Mark L. Wygoda
McNeese State University

Calvin Young
Fullerton College

Shirley Zajdel
Housatonic Community College

Samuel J. Zeakes
Radford University

Uko Zylstra
Calvin College

Biology All Around Us BIOLOGY AND SOCIETY

An Innate Passion for Life

Do you like biology? Wait, let's put this question another way: Do you have a pet? Are you concerned with fitness or healthy eating? Have you ever visited a zoo or an aquarium for fun, taken a nature hike, or gathered shells on the beach? Do you like watching TV shows about sharks or dinosaurs? If you answered yes to any of these questions—well, then, it turns out that you do like biology!

Most of us have an inherent interest in life, an inborn curiosity about the natural world that leads us to study animals and plants and their habitats. We wrote *Essential Biology* to help you—a student with little or no college-level science experience—harness your innate enthusiasm for life. We'll use this passion to help you develop an understanding of the discipline of biology, one that you can apply to your own life and to the society in which you live. We believe that such a biological perspective is essential for any educated person, which is why we named our book *Essential Biology*. So, whatever your reasons for taking this course—even if only to fulfill your school's science requirement—you'll soon discover that exploring life is relevant and important to you, no matter your background or goals.

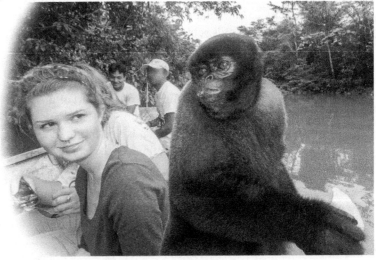

An inborn curiosity about nature. This student is interacting with a woolly monkey (*Lagothrix lagotricha*) during a school trip to the Amazon River in Peru.

To reinforce the fact that biology affects your everyday life in many ways, every chapter of *Essential Biology* opens with an essay—called Biology and Society—that will help you see the relevance of that chapter's material. Topics as varied as medical uses of radiation (Chapter 2), the importance of a flu shot (Chapter 10), and the community of microscopic organisms that live in and on your body (Chapter 15) help to illustrate biology's scope and show how the subject of biology is woven into the fabric of society. Throughout *Essential Biology*, we'll continuously emphasize these connections, pointing out many examples of how each topic can be applied to your life and the lives of those you care about.

The Scientific Study of Life

Now that we've established our goal—to examine how biology affects your life—a good place to start is with a basic definition: **Biology** is the scientific study of life. But have you ever looked up a word in the dictionary only to find that you need to look up some of the words within that definition to make sense of the original word? The definition of biology, although seemingly simple, raises more questions: What is a scientific study? And what does it mean to be alive? To help you get started with your investigation of biology, this first chapter of *Essential Biology* expands on important concepts within the definition of biology. First, we'll place the study of life in the broader context of science. Next, we'll investigate the nature of life by surveying the properties and scope of life. Finally, we'll introduce a series of broad themes you will encounter throughout your investigation of life, themes that serve as organizing principles for the information you will learn. Most important, throughout this chapter (and, indeed, throughout all of *Essential Biology*), we'll continue to provide examples of how biology affects *your* life, highlighting the relevance of this subject to society and everyone in it. ☑

The Process of Science

Recall the definition at the heart of this chapter: Biology is the scientific study of life. This leads to an obvious first question: What is a scientific study? Notice that biology is not defined as the "study of life" because there are many nonscientific ways that life can be studied. For example, extended meditation is a valid way of studying the nature of life—this approach might be well suited to a philosophy class, for example—but it does not qualify as biology because it is not a *scientific* means of studying life. How, then, do we tell the difference between science and other ways of trying to make sense of nature?

Science is an approach to understanding the natural world that is based on inquiry—a search for information, explanations, and answers to specific questions. This basic human drive to understand our natural world is manifest in two main scientific approaches: discovery science, which is mostly about *describing* nature, and hypothesis-driven science, which is mostly about *explaining* nature. Most scientists practice a combination of these two forms of inquiry.

Discovery Science

Scientists seek natural causes for natural phenomena. This limits the scope of science to the study of structures and processes that we can verifiably observe and measure, either directly or indirectly with the help of tools and technology, such as microscopes (Figure 1.1). Recorded observations are called **data**, and data are the items of information on which scientific inquiry is based. This dependence on verifiable data demystifies nature and distinguishes science from supernatural beliefs. Science can neither prove nor disprove that ghosts, deities, or spirits cause storms, eclipses, or illnesses,

▼ Figure 1.1 **The protist *Paramecium* viewed with three different types of microscopes.** Photographs taken with microscopes are called micrographs. Throughout this textbook, micrographs will have size notations along the side. For example, "LM 300×" indicates that the micrograph was taken with a light microscope and the objects are magnified to 300 times their original size.

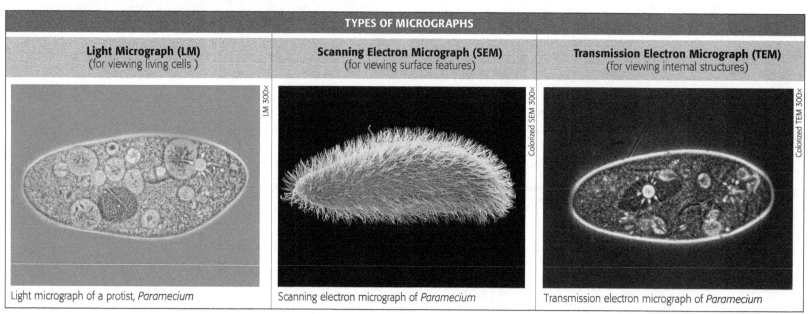

TYPES OF MICROGRAPHS

Light Micrograph (LM) (for viewing living cells)	**Scanning Electron Micrograph (SEM)** (for viewing surface features)	**Transmission Electron Micrograph (TEM)** (for viewing internal structures)
LM 300×	Colorized SEM 300×	Colorized TEM 300×
Light micrograph of a protist, *Paramecium*	Scanning electron micrograph of *Paramecium*	Transmission electron micrograph of *Paramecium*

◄ Figure 1.2 **Careful observation and measurement: the raw data for discovery science.** Dr. Jane Goodall spent decades recording her observations of chimpanzee behavior during field research in the jungles of Tanzania.

because such explanations are not measurable and are therefore outside the bounds of science.

Verifiable observations and measurements are the data of **discovery science**. In our quest to describe nature accurately, we discover its structure. Charles Darwin's careful description of the diverse plants and animals he observed in South America is an example of discovery science (as you'll learn in Chapter 13). More recently, Jane Goodall spent decades observing and recording the behavior of chimpanzees living in the jungles of Tanzania (Figure 1.2). And even more recently, molecular biologists have sequenced and analyzed huge amounts of DNA (an effort discussed in Chapter 12), gathering data that shed light on the genetic basis of life.

Hypothesis-Driven Science

The observations of discovery science motivate us to ask questions and seek explanations. Ideally, such investigations make use of the scientific method. As a formal process of inquiry, the **scientific method** consists of a series of steps (Figure 1.3). These steps provide a loose guideline for scientific investigations. There is no single formula for successfully discovering something new; instead, the scientific method suggests a broad outline for how discovery might proceed. The scientific method is a bit like an incomplete recipe: A basic outline of steps to be followed is presented, but the details of the dish are left to the cook. Similarly, working scientists do not typically follow the steps of the scientific method rigidly; different scientists proceed through the scientific method in different ways.

Most modern scientific investigations can be described as hypothesis-driven science. A **hypothesis** is a tentative answer to a question—a proposed explanation for a set of observations. A good hypothesis immediately leads to predictions that can be tested by experiments. Although

Observation	Question	Hypothesis	Prediction	Experiment
The TV remote doesn't work.	What's wrong with the remote?	The remote's batteries are dead.	If I replace the batteries, the remote will work.	I replace the batteries with new ones.

Experiment *does not support* hypothesis; revise hypothesis or pose new one.

Revise

Experiment *supports* hypothesis; make additional predictions and test them.

► Figure 1.3 **Applying the scientific method to a common problem.**

Although you may not realize it, you use the scientific method every day.

we don't think of it in those terms, we all use hypotheses in solving everyday problems. Imagine that you've completed your homework for the day and are going to reward yourself with some time in front of the TV. You press the power button on your TV remote, but the TV fails to turn on. That the TV does not turn on is an observation. The question that arises is obvious: Why didn't the remote turn on the TV? You could imagine a dozen possible explanations, but you can't possibly investigate them all simultaneously. Instead, you would focus on just one explanation (perhaps the most likely one based on past experience) and test it. That initial explanation is your hypothesis. For example, in this case, a reasonable hypothesis is that the batteries in the remote are dead.

Once a hypothesis is formed, an investigator can make predictions about what results are expected if that hypothesis is correct. We then test the hypothesis by performing an experiment to see whether or not the results are as predicted. This logical testing takes the form of "If . . . then" logic:

Observation: The TV remote doesn't work.

Question: What's wrong with the remote?

Hypothesis: The TV remote doesn't work because its batteries are dead.

Prediction: If I replace the batteries, then the remote will work.

Experiment: I replace the batteries with new ones.

Let's say that after you replace the batteries the remote still doesn't work. You would then formulate a second hypothesis and test it. Perhaps, for example, the TV is unplugged. Or you put in the new batteries incorrectly. You could continue to conduct additional experiments and formulate additional hypotheses until you reach a satisfactory conclusion to your initial question. As you do this, you are following the scientific method, and you are acting as a scientist.

Let's back up and examine what you would probably *not* do in this scenario: You most likely would not blame the malfunctioning remote on supernatural spirits, nor are you likely to meditate on the cause of the observed phenomenon. Your natural instinct is to formulate a hypothesis and then test it; the scientific method is probably your "go-to" method for solving problems. In fact, the scientific method is so deeply embedded in our society and in the way we think that most of us use it automatically (although we don't use the terminology presented here). The scientific method is therefore just a formalization of how you already think and act.

In every chapter of *Essential Biology*, we include examples of how the scientific method was used to learn about the material under discussion. In each of these sections (titled The Process of Science), we will, as a reminder, highlight the steps in the scientific method. The questions we will address include: Does lactose intolerance have a genetic basis (Chapter 3)? Why do dog coats come in so many varieties (Chapter 9)? Do the organisms living in your intestine affect your weight (Chapter 15)? As you become increasingly scientifically literate, you will arm yourself with the tools you need to evaluate claims that you hear. We are all bombarded by information every day—via commercials, websites, magazine articles, and so on—and it can be hard to filter out the bogus from the truly worthwhile. Having a firm grasp of science as a process of inquiry can therefore help you in many ways outside the classroom.

It is important to note that scientific investigations are not the only way of knowing nature. A comparative religion course would be a good way to learn about the diverse stories that focus on a supernatural creation of Earth and its life. Science and religion are two very different ways of trying to make sense of nature. Art is yet another way to make sense of the world around us. A broad education should include exposure to all these different ways of viewing the world. Each of us synthesizes our worldview by integrating our life experiences and multidisciplinary education. As a science textbook and part of that multidisciplinary education, *Essential Biology* showcases life in a purely scientific context. ☑

☑ CHECKPOINT

1. If you observe the squirrels on your campus and collect data on their dietary habits, what kind of science are you performing? If you come up with a tentative explanation for their dietary behavior and then test your idea, what kind of science are you performing?

2. Place these steps of the scientific method in their proper order: experiment, hypothesis, observation, prediction, results, question, revise/repeat.

Answers: 1. discovery science; hypothesis-driven science 2. observation, question, hypothesis, prediction, experiment, results, revise/repeat.

▼ Figure 1.4 **Some properties of life.** An object is considered alive if and only if it displays all of these properties simultaneously.

(a) **Order**

(b) **Regulation**

(c) **Growth and development**

(d) **Energy processing**

Theories in Science

Many people associate facts with science, but accumulating facts is not the primary goal of science. A telephone book is an impressive catalog of factual information, but it has little to do with science. It is true that facts, in the form of verifiable observations and repeatable experimental results, are the prerequisites of science. What really advances science, however, are new theories that tie together a number of observations that previously seemed unrelated. The cornerstones of science are the explanations that apply to the greatest variety of phenomena. People like Isaac Newton, Charles Darwin, and Albert Einstein stand out in the history of science not because they discovered a great many facts but because their theories had such broad explanatory power.

What is a scientific theory, and how is it different from a hypothesis? A scientific **theory** is much broader in scope than a hypothesis. A theory is a comprehensive explanation supported by abundant evidence, and it is general enough to spin off many new testable hypotheses. This is a hypothesis: "White fur is an adaptation that helps polar bears survive in an Arctic habitat." And this is another, seemingly unrelated hypothesis: "The unusual bone structure in a hummingbird's wings is an evolutionary adaptation that provides an advantage in gathering nectar from flowers." In contrast, the following theory ties together those seemingly unrelated hypotheses: "Adaptations to the local environment evolve by natural selection." This particular theory is one that we will describe later in this chapter.

Theories only become widely accepted by scientists if they are supported by an accumulation of extensive and varied evidence and if they have not been contradicted by any scientific data. The use of the term *theory* by scientists contrasts with our everyday usage, which implies untested speculation ("It's just a theory!"). In fact, we use the word "theory" in our everyday speech the way that a scientist uses the word "hypothesis." As you will soon learn, natural selection qualifies as a scientific theory because of its broad application and because it has been validated by a large number of observations and experiments. It is therefore not proper to say that natural selection is "just" a theory to imply that it is untested or lacking in evidence. In fact, any scientific theory is backed up by a wealth of supporting evidence, or else it wouldn't be referred to as a theory. ☑

☑ **CHECKPOINT**

You arrange to meet a friend for dinner at 6 P.M., but when the appointed hour comes, she is not there. You wonder why. Another friend says, "My theory is that she forgot." If your friend were speaking like a scientist, what would she have said?

Answer: "My hypothesis is that she forgot."

The Nature of Life

Recall once again our basic definition: Biology is the scientific study of life. Now that we have an understanding of what constitutes a scientific study, we can turn to the next question raised by this definition: What is life? Or, to put it another way, what distinguishes living things from nonliving things? The phenomenon of **life** seems to defy a simple, one-sentence definition. Yet even a small child instinctively knows that a dog or a bug or a plant is alive but a rock is not.

If I placed an object in front of you and asked you whether it was alive, what would you do? Would you poke it to see if it reacts? Would you watch it closely to see if it moves or breathes? Would you dissect it to look at its parts? Each of these ideas is closely related to how biologists actually define life: We recognize life mainly by what living things do. To start our investigation of biology, let's look at some properties that are shared by all living things.

The Properties of Life

Figure 1.4 highlights seven of the properties and processes associated with life. An object is generally considered to be alive if it displays all of these properties simultaneously. (a) *Order.* All living things exhibit

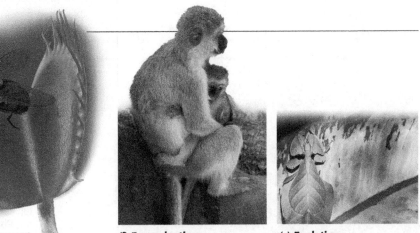

(e) Response to the environment

(f) Reproduction

(g) Evolution

complex but ordered organization, as seen in the structure of a pinecone. (b) *Regulation*. The environment outside an organism may change drastically, but the organism can adjust its internal environment, keeping it within appropriate limits. When it senses its body temperature dropping, a lizard can bask on a rock to absorb heat. (c) *Growth and development*. Information carried by DNA controls the pattern of growth and development in all organisms, including the crocodile. (d) *Energy processing*. Organisms take in energy and use it to perform all of life's activities; they emit energy as heat. A cheetah obtains energy by eating its kill, uses this energy to power running and other work, and continuously emits body heat into the environment. (e) *Response to the environment*. All organisms respond to environmental stimuli. A carnivorous Venus flytrap closes its leaves rapidly in response to the environmental stimulus of an insect touching the plant's sensory hairs. (f) *Reproduction*. Organisms reproduce their own kind. Thus, monkeys reproduce only monkeys—never lizards or cheetahs. (g) *Evolution*. Reproduction underlies the capacity of populations to change (evolve) over time. For example, the giant leaf insect (*Phyllium giganteum*) has evolved in a way that provides camouflage in its environment. Evolutionary change is a central, unifying phenomenon of all life.

Although we have no proof that life has ever existed anywhere other than Earth, biologists speculate that extraterrestrial life, if it exists, could be recognized by the same properties listed in Figure 1.4. The Mars rover *Curiosity* (**Figure 1.5**), which has

▲ Figure 1.5 **A view from the Mars rover *Curiosity* searching for signs of life.**

been exploring the surface of the red planet since 2012, contains several instruments designed to identify biosignatures, substances that provide evidence of past or present life. For example, *Curiosity* is using a suite of onboard instruments to detect chemicals that could provide evidence of energy processing by microscopic organisms. As of yet, no definitive signs of the properties of life have been detected, and the search continues. ☑

> One of the primary missions of the Mars rover is to search for signs of life.

✅ **CHECKPOINT**

Which properties of life apply to a car? Which do not?

Answer: A car demonstrates order, regulation, energy utilization, and response to the environment. But a car does not grow, reproduce, or evolve.

Life in Its Diverse Forms

The tarsier shown in **Figure 1.6** is just one of about 1.8 million identified species on Earth that displays all of the properties outlined in Figure 1.4. The diversity of known life—all the species that have been identified and named—includes at least 290,000 plants, 52,000 vertebrates (animals with backbones), and 1 million insects (more than half of all known forms of life). Biologists add thousands of newly identified species to the list each year. Estimates of the total number of species range from 10 million to more than 100 million. Whatever the actual number turns out to

◄ Figure 1.6 **A small sample of biological diversity.** A primate called a tarsier sits in a tree in a rainforest within the Philippines. The scientific name for this species is *Tarsius syrichta*.

Kingdom Plantae

Kingdom Fungi

Kingdom Animalia

Protists (multiple kingdoms)

▲ Figure 1.7 **The three domains of life.**

be, the enormous diversity of life presents organizational challenges to biologists who study it.

Grouping Species: The Basic Concept

To make sense of nature, people tend to group diverse items according to similarities. We may speak of "squirrels" and "butterflies," even though we recognize that each group actually includes many different species. A **species** is generally defined as a group of organisms that live in the same place and time and have the potential to interbreed with one another in nature to produce healthy offspring (more on this in Chapter 14). We may even sort groups into broader categories, such as rodents (which include squirrels) and insects (which include butterflies). **Taxonomy**, the branch of biology that names and classifies species, is the arrangement of species into a hierarchy of broader and broader groups. Have you ever seen a fish, or found a mushroom, or watched a bird and wondered what kind it was? If so, you were asking a question of taxonomy. Before we dive into biodiversity in greater detail in later chapters, let's summarize the broadest units of classification of life.

If you've ever wondered what an unusual or especially beautiful animal is called, you're curious about taxonomy.

The Three Domains of Life

On the broadest level, biologists divide the diversity of life into three domains: Bacteria, Archaea, and Eukarya (Figure 1.7). Every organism on Earth belongs to one of these three domains. The first two domains, Bacteria and Archaea, identify two very different groups of organisms that have prokaryotic cells—that is, relatively small and simple cells that lack a nucleus or other compartments bounded by internal membranes. All the eukaryotes (organisms with eukaryotic cells—that is, relatively large and complex cells that contain a nucleus and other membrane-enclosed compartments) are grouped into the domain Eukarya.

The domain Eukarya in turn includes three smaller divisions called kingdoms—Plantae, Fungi, and Animalia. Most members of the three kingdoms are multicellular. The kingdoms are distinguished partly by how the organisms obtain food. Plants produce their own sugars and other foods by photosynthesis. Fungi are mostly decomposers, obtaining food by digesting dead organisms and organic wastes. Animals—the kingdom to which we belong—obtain food by ingesting (eating) and digesting other organisms. Those eukaryotes that do not fit into any of the three kingdoms fall into a catch-all group called the protists. Most protists are single-celled; they include microscopic organisms such as amoebas. But protists also include certain multicellular forms, such as seaweeds. Scientists are in the process of organizing protists into multiple kingdoms, although they do not yet agree on exactly how to do this. ☑

☑ CHECKPOINT

1. Name the three domains of life. To which do you belong?
2. Name three kingdoms found within the domain Eukarya. Name a fourth group within this domain.

Major Themes in Biology

Biology is a big subject that, as new discoveries unfold every day, grows continuously in breadth and depth. Although we often focus on the details, it is important to recognize that there are broad themes running throughout the subject. These overarching principles unify all aspects of biology, from the microscopic world of cells to the global environment. Focusing on a few big picture ideas that cut across many topics within biology can help organize and make sense of all the information you will learn.

In this section, we'll describe five unifying themes that recur throughout our investigation of biology (Figure 1.8). You'll encounter these themes throughout subsequent chapters; we'll highlight each theme as it appears by using the icons from Figure 1.8 and repeating the section headings used below.

Evolution

Just as you have a family history, each species on Earth today represents one twig on a branching tree of life that extends back in time through ancestral species more and more remote. Species that are very similar, such as the brown bear and the polar bear, share a common ancestor at a relatively recent branch point on the tree of life (Figure 1.9). In addition, all bears can be traced back much farther in time to an ancestor common also to squirrels, humans, and all other mammals. All mammals have hair and milk-producing mammary glands, and such similarities are what we would expect if all mammals descended from a common ancestor, a first mammal. And mammals, reptiles, and all other vertebrates share a common ancestor

even more ancient than the common ancestor to mammals. Going farther back still, at the cellular level, all life displays striking similarities. For example, all living cells are surrounded by an outer plasma membrane of similar makeup and use structures called ribosomes to produce proteins.

The scientific explanation for the common characteristics found throughout such diverse species is evolution, the process that has transformed life on Earth from its earliest beginnings to the extensive variety we see today. Evolution is the fundamental principle of life and the core theme that unifies all of biology. The theory of evolution by natural selection, first described by Charles Darwin more than 150 years ago, is the one principle that makes sense of everything we know about living organisms. Any student of biology should begin by first understanding evolution. Evolution can help us investigate and understand every aspect of life, from the tiny organisms that occupy the most remote habitats, to the diversity of species in our local environment, to the stability of the global environment. In this section, we will present a basic introduction to this important topic. To emphasize evolution as the core theme of biology, we end each chapter of *Essential Biology* with an Evolution Connection section. You will learn, for example, how evolution can shed light on such topics as our quest to develop better biofuels (Chapter 7), how cancer cells grow and spread through the body (Chapter 10), and the development of antibiotic-resistant bacteria (Chapter 13).

The Darwinian View of Life

The evolutionary view of life came into focus in 1859 when English naturalist Charles Darwin published one

▼ Figure 1.8 **Five unifying themes that run throughout the discipline of biology.**

Evolution	Structure/Function	Information Flow	Energy Transformations	Interconnections within Systems
Evolution by natural selection is biology's core unifying theme and can be seen at every level in the hierarchy of life.	The structure of an object, such as a molecule or a body part, provides insight into its function, and vice versa.	Within biological systems, information stored in DNA is transmitted and expressed.	All biological systems depend on obtaining, converting, and releasing energy and matter.	All biological systems, from molecules to ecosystems, depend on interactions between components.

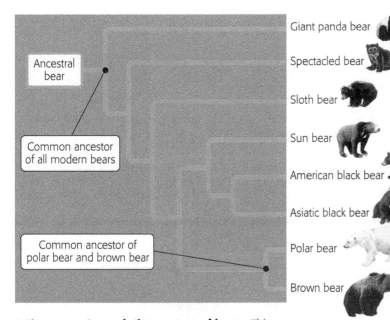

Giant panda bear

Spectacled bear

Sloth bear

Sun bear

American black bear

Asiatic black bear

Polar bear

Brown bear

Ancestral bear

Common ancestor of all modern bears

Common ancestor of polar bear and brown bear

▲ Figure 1.9 **An evolutionary tree of bears.** This tree represents a hypothesis (a tentative model) based on both the fossil record and a comparison of DNA sequences among modern bears. As new evidence about the evolutionary history of bears emerges, this tree will inevitably change.

reproductive success that Darwin called **natural selection** because the environment "selects" only certain heritable traits from those already existing. Natural selection does not promote or somehow encourage changes, but rather it serves to "edit" those changes that have already occurred. And the product of natural selection is adaptation, the accumulation of variations in a population over time. Returning to the example of bear evolution in Figure 1.9, one familiar adaptation in bears is fur color. Polar bears and brown (grizzly) bears each

▼ Figure 1.10 **Charles Darwin (1809–1882),** *The Origin of Species,* **and blue-footed boobies he observed on the Galápagos Islands.**

of the most important and influential books ever written: *On the Origin of Species by Means of Natural Selection* (Figure 1.10). First, Darwin presented a large amount of evidence in support of the evolutionary view that species living today descended from a succession of ancestral species. Darwin called this process "descent with modification." Darwin's phrase was an insightful one, because it captures the duality of life's unity (which is possible because of a shared descent) and diversity (which is possible because of gradual modification). In the Darwinian view, for example, the diversity of bears is based on different modifications of a common ancestor from which all bears descended.

Second, Darwin proposed a mechanism for descent with modification: the process of natural selection. In the struggle for existence, those individuals with heritable traits best suited to the local environment are more likely to survive and leave the greatest number of healthy offspring. Therefore, the traits that enhance survival and reproductive success will be represented in greater numbers in the next generation. It is this unequal

▲ Figure 1.11 **Finches of the Galápagos Islands.** Charles Darwin personally collected these finches during his time in the Galapagos.

display an evolutionary adaptation (white and brown fur, respectively) that resulted from natural selection operating in their respective environments. Presumably, natural selection tended to favor the fur color that provided each bear lineage with an appearance that provided an advantage in its home territory.

We now recognize many examples of natural selection in action. A classic example involves the finches (a kind of bird) of the Galápagos Islands (Figure 1.11). Over a span of two decades, researchers working on these isolated islands measured changes in beak size in a population of ground finch that prefers to eat small seeds. In dry years, when the preferred small seeds are in short supply, the birds instead have mostly large seeds to eat. Birds with larger, stronger beaks have a feeding advantage in such an environment, and greater reproductive success, and thus the average beak depth for the population increases during dry years. During wet years, small seeds become more abundant. Because smaller beaks are more efficient for eating the plentiful small seeds, the average beak depth decreases over generations. Such changes in structure are measurable evidence of natural selection in action.

The world is rich with examples of natural selection. Consider the development of antibiotic-resistant bacteria (Figure 1.12). Dairy and cattle farmers often add antibiotics to feed because doing so results in larger, more profitable animals. ❶ The members of the bacteria population will, through random chance, vary in their susceptibility to the antibiotic. ❷ Once the environment has been changed with the addition of antibiotics, some bacteria will succumb quickly and die, whereas others will survive. ❸ Those that do survive will have the potential to multiply, producing offspring that will likely inherit the traits that enhance survival. ❹ Over many generations, bacteria that are resistant to antibiotics will thrive in greater and greater numbers. Thus, feeding antibiotics to cows may promote the evolution of antibiotic-resistant bacterial populations that are not susceptible to standard drug treatments.

Observing Artificial Selection

Darwin found convincing evidence of the power of natural selection in examples of *artificial* selection, the purposeful breeding of domesticated plants and animals by humans. People have been modifying other species

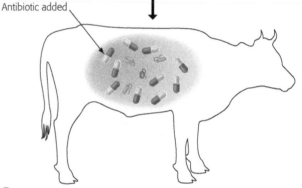

❶ **Population with varied inherited traits.** Initially, the population of bacteria varies in its ability to resist the antibiotic. By random chance, a few bacteria are somewhat resistant.

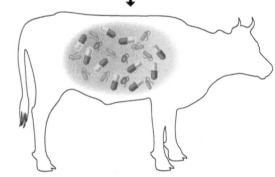

❷ **Elimination of individuals with certain traits.** The majority of bacteria are susceptible to the effects of the antibiotic and so will die off. The few resistant bacteria will tend to survive.

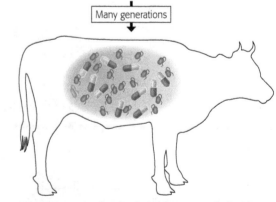

❸ **Reproduction of survivors.** The selective pressure of the antibiotic favors survival and reproductive success of the few resistant bacteria. Thus, genes for anitbiotic resistance are passed along to the next generation in greater frequency.

Many generations

❹ **Increasing frequency of traits that enhance survival and reproductive success.** Generation after generation, the bacteria population adapts to its environment through natural selection.

▲ Figure 1.12 **Natural selection in action.**

for millennia by selecting breeding stock with certain traits. For example, the plants we grow for food today bear little resemblance to their wild ancestors. Have you ever had wild blueberries or wild strawberries? They are much different (and, in many ways, much less desirable) than their modern kin. This is because we have customized crop plants through many generations of artificial selection by selecting different parts of the plant to accentuate. All the vegetables shown in Figure 1.13 (and more) have a common ancestor in one species of wild mustard (shown in the center of the figure). The power of selective breeding is also apparent in our pets, which

have been bred for looks and for useful characteristics. For example, all domesticated dogs are descended from wolves, but people in different cultures have customized hundreds of dog breeds as different as basset hounds and Saint Bernards (Figure 1.14). The tremendous variety of modern dogs reflects thousands of years of artificial selection. You may not realize it, but you are exposed to the products of artificial selection every day!

Darwin's publication of *On the Origin of Species* fueled an explosion in biological research that continues today. Over the past century and a half, a tremendous amount of evidence has accumulated in support of Darwin's theory

▶ Figure 1.13 **The artificial selection of food crops.**

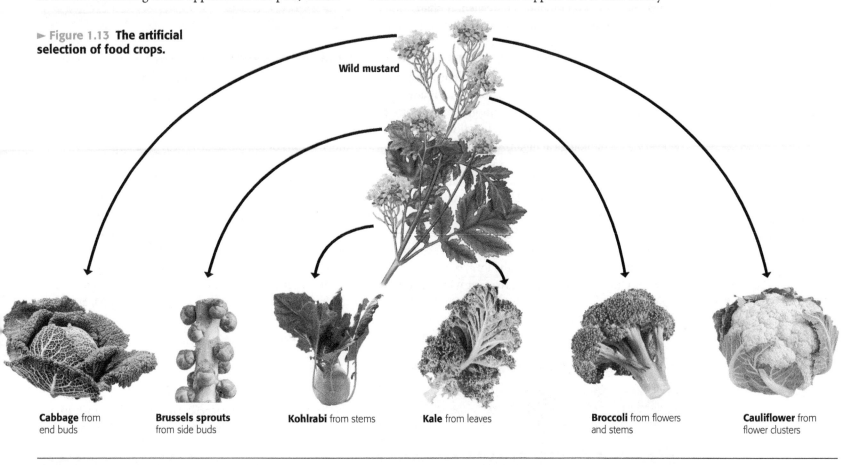

Wild mustard

Cabbage from end buds

Brussels sprouts from side buds

Kohlrabi from stems

Kale from leaves

Broccoli from flowers and stems

Cauliflower from flower clusters

▼ Figure 1.14 **The artificial selection of pets.**

Artificial selection

Gray wolves

Domesticated dogs

of evolution by natural selection, making it one of biology's best-demonstrated, most comprehensive, and longest-held theories. Throughout *Essential Biology*, you will learn more about how natural selection works and see other examples of how natural selection affects your life. ☑

Structure/Function — The Relationship of Structure to Function

When considering useful objects in your home, you may realize that form and function are related. A chair, for example, cannot have just any shape; it must have a stable base to stand on and a flat area for holding your weight. The function of the chair constrains the possible shapes it may have. Similarly, within biological systems, structure (the shape of something) and function (what it does) are often related, with each providing insight into the other.

The correlation of structure and function can be seen at every level of biological organization. Consider your lungs, which function to exchange gases with the environment: Your lungs bring in oxygen (O_2) and take out carbon dioxide (CO_2). The structure of your lungs correlates with this function (Figure 1.15). Increasingly smaller branches of your lungs end in millions of tiny sacs in which the gases cross from the air to your blood, and vice versa. This branched structure (the form of the lungs) provides a tremendous surface area over which a very high volume of air may pass (the function of the lungs). Cells, too, display a correlation of structure and function. As oxygen enters the blood in the lungs, for example,

▲ Figure 1.15 **Structure/function: human lungs.** The structure of your lungs correlates with their function.

▼ Figure 1.16 **Structure/function: red blood cells.** As oxygen enters the blood in the lungs, it diffuses into red blood cells.

Colorized SEM 5,400x

it diffuses into red blood cells (Figure 1.16). The concave indentations of red blood cells provide a large surface area through which oxygen can diffuse.

Throughout the textbook, we will see the structure/function principle apply to all levels of biological organization, from the structure of cells and their components, to DNA replication, to the internal organization of plants and animals. Some specific examples of the correlation of structure and function that you will encounter include explaining why ice floats (Chapter 2), the importance of a protein's shape (Chapter 3), and structural adaptations within the bodies of plants (Chapter 16). ☑

Information Flow — Information Flow

For life's functions to proceed in an orderly manner, information must be received, transmitted, and used. Such information flow is apparent at all levels of biological organization. At the microscopic scale, every cell contains information in the form of **genes**, hereditary units of information consisting of specific sequences of DNA passed on from the previous generation. At the organismal level, as every multicellular organism develops from an embryo, information exchanged among cells enables the overall body plan to take shape in an organized fashion (as you'll see in Chapter 8). Once the organism is mature, information about the internal conditions of its body is used to keep those conditions within a range that allows for life.

Although bacteria and humans inherit different genes, that information is encoded in an identical chemical language common to all organisms. In fact, the language of life has an alphabet of just four letters. The chemical names of DNA's four molecular building blocks are abbreviated as A, G, C, and T (Figure 1.17). A typical gene is hundreds to thousands of chemical "letters" in length. A gene's meaning to a cell is encoded in its specific sequence of these letters, just as the message of this sentence is encoded in its arrangement of the 26 letters of the English alphabet.

The entire set of genetic information that an organism inherits is called its **genome**. The nucleus of each human cell contains a genome that is about 3 billion chemical letters long. In recent years, scientists have tabulated virtually the entire sequence of the genome from humans and hundreds of other organisms. As this work progresses, biologists will continue to learn the functions of the genes and how their activities are coordinated in the development and functioning of an organism. The emerging field of genomics—a branch of biology that studies whole genomes—is a striking example of how the flow of information can inform our study of life at its many levels.

How is all this information used within your body? At any given moment, your genes are producing thousands of different proteins that control your body's processes. (You'll learn the details of how proteins are

▲ Figure 1.18 **Biotechnology.** Since the 1970s, applications of biology have revolutionized medicine.

▶ Figure 1.17 **The language of DNA.** Every molecule of DNA is constructed from four kinds of chemical building blocks that are chained together, shown here as simple shapes and letters.

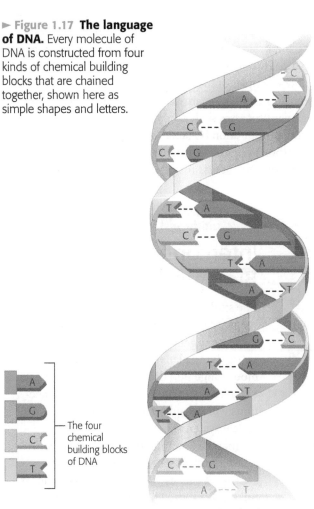

The four chemical building blocks of DNA

A DNA molecule

produced from DNA in Chapter 10.) Food is broken down, new body tissues are built, cells divide, signals are sent—all under the control of proteins, all of which are built from information stored in your DNA. For example, structures within your body assess the amount of glucose in your blood and, in response, secrete varying amounts of hormones that keep blood glucose levels within acceptable values. The information in one of your genes translates to "Make insulin." Insulin, produced by cells within the pancreas, is a chemical that helps regulate your body's use of glucose as a fuel.

People with type 1 diabetes often have a mutation (error) in a different gene that causes the body's immune cells to attack and destroy the insulin-producing pancreas cells. The breakdown of the normal flow of information within the body leads to disease. Some people with diabetes regulate their sugar levels by injecting themselves with insulin produced by genetically engineered bacteria. These bacteria can make insulin because the human gene has been transplanted into them. This example of genetic engineering was one of the earliest successes of biotechnology, a field that has transformed the pharmaceutical industry and extended millions of lives (Figure 1.18). And biotechnology is only possible because biological information, written in the universal chemical language of DNA, is used in a similar manner by all life on Earth. ☑

Energy Transformations **Pathways that Transform Energy and Matter**

Movement, growth, reproduction, and the various cellular activities of life are work, and work requires energy. The input of energy, primarily from the sun, and the

☑ **CHECKPOINT**

Which is bigger: gene or genome?

Answer: genome (because your genome consists of all your genes)

transformation of energy from one form to another make life possible (Figure 1.19). At their source, most ecosystems are solar powered. The energy that enters an ecosystem as sunlight is captured by plants and other photosynthetic organisms (producers) that absorb the sun's energy and convert it, storing it as chemical bonds within sugars and other complex molecules. These molecules then become food for a series of consumers, such as animals, that feed on producers. Consumers can use the food as a source of energy by breaking chemical bonds or as building blocks for making molecules needed by the organism. In other words, the molecules consumed can be used as both a source of energy and a source of matter. In the process of these energy conversions between and within organisms, some energy is converted to heat, which is then lost from the ecosystem. Thus, energy flows through an ecosystem, entering as light and exiting as heat. This is represented by wavy lines in Figure 1.19.

Every object in the universe, both living and nonliving, is composed of matter. In contrast to energy flowing through an ecosystem, matter is recycled within an ecosystem. This is represented by the blue circle in Figure 1.19. For example, minerals that plants absorb from the soil can eventually be recycled back into to the soil when plants are decomposed by microorganisms. Decomposers, such as fungi and many bacteria, break down waste products and the remains of dead organisms, changing complex molecules into simple nutrients. The action of decomposers ensures that nutrients are

available to be taken up from the soil by plants again, thereby completing the cycle.

Within all living cells, a vast network of interconnected chemical reactions (collectively referred to as metabolism) continually converts energy from one form to another as matter is recycled. For example, as food molecules are broken down into simpler molecules, energy stored in the chemical bonds is released. This energy can be captured and used by the body (to power muscle contractions, for example). The atoms that made up the food can then be recycled (to build new muscle tissue, for example). Within all living organisms—there is a never-ending "chemical square dance" in which molecules swap chemical partners as they receive, convert, and release matter and energy. The importance of energy and matter transformations is made clear by examining what happens when they are disrupted. Cyanide is one of the deadliest known poisons. Ingesting just 200 milligrams (about half the size of a tablet of aspirin) causes death in humans. Cyanide is so toxic because it blocks an essential step within the metabolic pathway that harvests energy from glucose. When even a single protein within this pathway becomes inhibited, cells lose the ability to extract the energy stored in the chemical bonds of glucose. The rapid death that follows is a macabre illustration of the importance of energy and matter transformations to life. Throughout your study of biology, you will see more examples of the how living organisms regulate the transformation of energy and matter, from microscopic cellular processes such as photosynthesis (Chapter 7) and cellular respiration (Chapter 8), to ecosystem-wide cycles of carbon and other nutrients (Chapter 20), to global cycles of water across the planet (Chapter 18). ☑

☑ CHECKPOINT

What is the key difference between how energy and matter move in ecosystems?

Answer: Energy moves through an ecosystem (entering and exiting), whereas matter is recycled within an ecosystem.

▼ Figure 1.19 **Nutrient and energy flow in an ecosystem.** Nutrients are recycled within an ecosystem, whereas energy flows into and then out of an ecosystem.

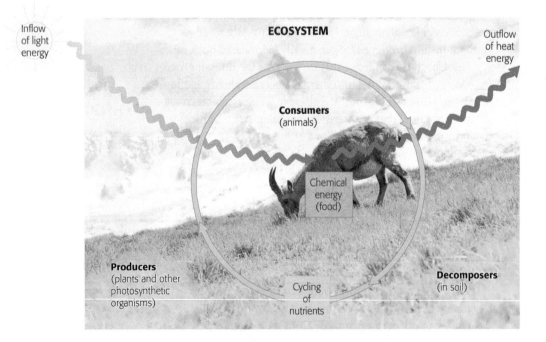

Inflow of light energy

ECOSYSTEM

Outflow of heat energy

Consumers (animals)

Chemical energy (food)

Producers (plants and other photosynthetic organisms)

Cycling of nutrients

Decomposers (in soil)

⬭ **Interconnections within Systems**

Interconnections within Biological Systems

The study of life extends from the microscopic scale of the molecules and cells that make up organisms to the global scale of the entire living planet. We can divide this enormous range into different levels of biological organization. There are many interconnections within and between these levels of biological systems.

Imagine zooming in from space to take a closer and closer look at life on Earth. Figure 1.20 takes you on a tour that spans the full scope of life. The top of the figure shows the global scale of the entire **biosphere**, which

▼ Figure 1.20 **Zooming in on life.**

② Ecosystems
An ecosystem consists of all living organisms in a particular area and all the nonliving components of the environment with which life interacts, such as soil, water, and light.

③ Communities
All organisms in an ecosystem (such as the iguanas, crabs, seaweed, and even bacteria in this ecosystem) are collectively called a community.

① Biosphere
Earth's biosphere includes all life and all the places where life exists.

④ Populations
Within communities are various populations, groups of interacting individuals of one species, such as a group of iguanas.

⑤ Organisms
An organism is an individual living thing, like this iguana.

⑥ Organ Systems and Organs
An organism's body consists of several organ systems, each of which contains two or more organs. For example, the iguana's circulatory system includes its heart and blood vessels.

⑩ Molecules and Atoms
Finally, we reach molecules, the chemical level in the hierarchy. Molecules are clusters of even smaller chemical units called atoms. Each cell consists of an enormous number of chemicals that function together to give the cell the properties we recognize as life. DNA, the molecule of inheritance and the substance of genes, is shown here as a computer graphic. Each sphere in the DNA model represents a single atom.

← Atom

⑨ Organelles
Organelles are functional components of cells, such as the nucleus that houses the DNA.

Nucleus

⑧ Cells
The cell is the smallest unit that can display all the characteristics of life.

⑦ Tissues
Each organ is made up of several different tissues, such as the heart muscle tissue shown here. A tissue consists of a group of similar cells performing a specific function.

Colorized LM 60x

consists of all the environments on Earth that support life—including soil; oceans, lakes, and other bodies of water; and the lower atmosphere. At the other extreme of biological size and complexity are microscopic molecules such as DNA, the chemical responsible for inheritance. Zooming outward from bottom to top in the figure, you can see that it takes many molecules to build a cell, many cells to make a tissue, multiple tissues to make an organ, and so on. At each new level, novel properties emerge that are absent from the preceding one. These emergent properties are due to the specific arrangement and interactions of parts in an increasingly complex system. Such properties are called emergent because they emerge as complexity increases. For example, life emerges at the level of the cell; a test tube full of molecules is not alive. The saying "the whole is greater than the sum of its parts" captures this idea. Emergent properties are not unique to life. A box of camera parts won't do anything, but if the parts are arranged and interact in a certain way, you can capture photographs. Add structures from a phone, and your camera and phone can interact to gain the ability to send photos to friends instantly. New properties emerge as the complexity increases. Compared to such nonliving examples, however, the unrivaled complexity of biological systems makes the emergent properties of life especially fascinating to study.

Consider another example of interconnectedness within biological systems, one that operates on a much larger scale: global climate. As the composition of the atmosphere changes, patterns of temperature are changing across the planet. This affects the makeup of ecosystems by changing patterns of weather and availability of

water. In turn, biological communities and populations are altered. For example, because of changing weather patterns and water levels, the range of several species of disease-causing mosquitoes has drifted north, bringing illnesses (such as malaria) to areas not previously affected by them. When someone is bit by a malaria-carrying mosquito, his or her body will be affected by an illness that occurs at a cellular level. Throughout our study of life, we will see countless interconnections that operate within and between every level of the biological hierarchy shown in Figure 1.20.

From the interactions within the biosphere to the molecular machinery within cells, biologists are investigating life at its many levels. Zooming in at ever-finer resolution illustrates the principle of reductionism—the approach of reducing complex systems to simpler components that are more manageable to study. Reductionism is a powerful strategy in biology. For example, by studying the molecular structure of DNA that had been extracted from cells, James Watson and Francis Crick inferred the chemical basis of biological inheritance. In this reductionist spirit, we will begin our investigation of biology by studying the chemistry of life (Chapter 2). ☑

☑ CHECKPOINT

What is the smallest level of biological organization that can display all the characteristics of life?

Answer: a cell

Chapter Review

SUMMARY OF KEY CONCEPTS

The Scientific Study of Life

Biology is the scientific study of life. It is important to distinguish scientific investigations from other ways of thinking, and to distinguish living objects from nonliving ones.

The Process of Science

Only scientific means of investigating life qualify as biology.

Discovery Science

Describing the natural world with verifiable data is the hallmark of discovery science.

Hypothesis-Driven Science

A scientist formulates a hypothesis (tentative explanation) to account for observations of the natural world. The hypothesis may then be tested via the steps of the scientific method:

Revise and repeat

Observation → Question → Hypothesis → Prediction → Experiment

Theories in Science

A theory is a broad and comprehensive statement about the world that is supported by the accumulation of a great deal of verifiable evidence.

The Nature of Life

The Properties of Life

All life displays a common set of characteristics:

Order   Regulation   Growth and development   Energy processing

Response to the environment   Reproduction   Evolution

Life in Its Diverse Forms

Biologists organize living organisms into three domains. The domain Eukarya is further divided into three kingdoms (distinguished partly by their means of obtaining food) and one catch-all group:

Life		
Prokaryotes	**Eukaryotes**	
	Plantae Fungi Animalia	Protists (all other eukaryotes)
	Three kingdoms	
Domain Bacteria	**Domain Archaea**	**Domain Eukarya**

Major Themes in Biology

Throughout your study of biology, you will frequently come upon examples of five unifying themes: evolution, the relationship of structure to function, the flow of information through biological systems, energy transformations, and interconnections with biological systems.

MAJOR THEMES IN BIOLOGY				
Evolution	**Structure/ Function**	**Information Flow**	**Energy Transformations**	**Interconnections within Systems**

Evolution

Charles Darwin established the ideas of evolution ("descent with modification") via natural selection (unequal reproductive success) in his 1859 publication *The Origin of Species*. Natural selection leads to adaptations to the environment, which—when passed from generation to generation—is the mechanism of evolution.

The Relationship of Structure to Function

At all levels of biology, structure and function are related. Changing structure often results in an altered function, and learning about a component's function will often give insight into its structure.

Information Flow

Throughout living systems, information is stored, transmitted, and used. Within your body, genes provide instructions for building proteins, which perform many of life's tasks.

Pathways That Transform Energy and Matter

Within ecosystems, nutrients are recycled, but energy flows through.

Interconnections within Biological Systems

Life can be studied on many scales, from molecules to the entire biosphere. As complexity increases, novel properties emerge. For example, the cell is the smallest unit that can possibly display all of the characteristics of life.

MasteringBiology®

For practice quizzes, BioFlix animations, MP3 tutorials, video tutors, and more study tools designed for this textbook, go to MasteringBiology®

SELF-QUIZ

1. Which of the following is *not* a characteristic of all living organisms?
   a. capable of self-reproduction
   b. composed of multiple cells
   c. complex yet organized
   d. uses energy

2. Place the following levels of biological organization in order from smallest to largest: atom, biosphere, cell, ecosystem, molecule, organ, organism, population, tissue. Which is the smallest level capable of demonstrating all of the characteristics of life?

3. Plants use the process of photosynthesis to convert the energy in sunlight to chemical energy in the form of sugar. While doing so, they consume carbon dioxide and water and release oxygen. Explain how this process functions in both the cycling of chemical nutrients and the flow of energy through an ecosystem.

4. For each of the following organisms, match its description to its most likely domain and/or kingdom:
   a. A foot-tall organism capable of producing its own food from sunlight
   b. A microscopic, simple, nucleus-free organism found living in a riverbed
   c. An inch-tall organism growing on the forest floor that consumes material from dead leaves
   d. A thimble-sized organism that feeds on algae growing in a pond

   1. Bacteria
   2. Eukarya/Animalia
   3. Eukarya/Fungi
   4. Eukarya/Plantae

5. How does natural selection cause a population to become adapted to its environment over time?

6. Which of the following statements best describes the logic of the scientific method?
   a. If I generate a testable hypothesis, tests and observations will support it.
   b. If my prediction is correct, it will lead to a testable hypothesis.
   c. If my observations are accurate, they will support my hypothesis.
   d. If my hypothesis is correct, I can expect certain test results.

7. Which of the following statements best distinguishes hypotheses from theories in science?
   a. Theories are hypotheses that have been proved.
   b. Hypotheses are tentative guesses; theories are correct answers to questions about nature.
   c. Hypotheses usually are narrow in scope; theories have broad explanatory power.
   d. Hypotheses and theories mean essentially the same thing in science.

8. _____ is the core idea that unifies all areas of biology.

9. Match each of the following terms to the phrase that best describes it.
   a. Natural selection   1. A testable idea
   b. Evolution   2. Descent with modification
   c. Hypothesis   3. Unequal reproductive success
   d. Biosphere   4. All life-supporting environments on Earth

Answers to these questions can be found in Appendix: Self-Quiz Answers.

THE PROCESS OF SCIENCE

10. The fruits of wild species of tomato are tiny compared with the giant beefsteak tomatoes available today. This difference in fruit size is almost entirely due to the larger number of cells in the domesticated fruits. Plant biologists have recently discovered genes that are responsible for controlling cell division in tomatoes. Why would such a discovery be important to producers of other kinds of fruits and vegetables? To the study of human development and disease? To our basic understanding of biology?

11. **Interpreting Data** Trans fats are a form of dietary fat that can have significant health consequences. The graph below represents data from a 2004 study that compared the amount of trans fats found in adipose tissue (body fat) of 79 heart attack patients and 167 people who did not have a heart attack. Write a one-sentence summary of the results presented in the graph.

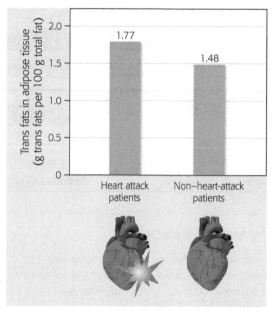

Data from: P. M. Clifton et al., *Trans* fatty acids in adipose tissue and the food supply are associated with myocardial infarction. *Journal of Nutrition* 134: 874–879 (2004).

BIOLOGY AND SOCIETY

12. The news media and popular magazines frequently report stories that are connected to biology. In the next 24 hours, record all such stories you hear or read about from three different sources and briefly describe the biological connections you perceive in each story.

13. If you pay attention, you will find yourself conducting many hypothesis-driven experiments each day. Over the next day, try to think of a good example where you performed a simple experiment to test a hypothesis about some observation. Write the experience out as a story, and then rewrite it using the steps of the scientific method (observation, question, hypothesis, prediction, and so on).

Unit 1
Cells

2 Essential Chemistry for Biology

Chapter Thread: **Radioactivity**

3 The Molecules of Life

Chapter Thread: **Lactose Intolerance**

4 A Tour of the Cell

Chapter Thread: **Humans Versus Bacteria**

5 The Working Cell

Chapter Thread: **Nanotechnology**

6 Cellular Respiration: Obtaining Energy from Food

Chapter Thread: **Exercise Science**

7 Photosynthesis: Using Light to Make Food

Chapter Thread: **Biofuels**

2 Essential Chemistry for Biology

Too little of the essential element copper in your diet causes anemia, but too much causes kidney and liver damage. ▶

Sodium is an explosive solid and chlorine is a poisonous gas, but when combined they form a common ingredient in your diet: table salt. ▶

▲ Lemon juice has roughly the same acidity as the food-digesting chemicals in your stomach.

Radioactivity BIOLOGY AND SOCIETY

Radiation and Health

The word "radioactive" probably sets off alarm bells in your mind: "Danger! Hazardous!" It is true that radiation, high-energy particles emitted by radioactive substances, can penetrate living tissues and kill cells by damaging DNA. But you probably know that radiation can also be medically beneficial by, for example, helping to treat cancer. So what determines whether radiation is harmful or helpful to an organism's health?

Radiation is most dangerous when exposure is uncontrolled and covers most or all of the body, as happens when a person is exposed to radioactive fallout from a nuclear detonation or accident. In contrast, controlled medical radiation therapy exposes only a small part of the body to a precise dosage of radiation. For example, when treating cancer, carefully calibrated radiation beams are aimed from several angles, intersecting only at the tumor. This provides a deadly dose to cancerous cells but mostly spares surrounding healthy tissues. Radiation therapy is also used to treat Graves' disease, a condition in which an overactive thyroid gland (located in the neck) causes a variety of physical symptoms, including shaking, swelling behind the eyeballs, and heart irregularities. Individuals with Graves' disease may be treated with a "cocktail" containing radioactive iodine. Because the thyroid produces a variety of hormones that use iodine, the radioactive iodine accumulates in this gland, where it then provides a steady low dose of radiation that can, over time, destroy enough thyroid tissue to reduce symptoms.

Pros and cons of radiation. Radiation can be harmful if it is released into the environment, but physicians use controlled doses of radiation to diagnose and treat several diseases.

What makes something radioactive? To understand this question, we have to look to the most basic level of all living things: the atoms that make up all matter. Many questions about life—for example, why is radiation harmful to cells?—can be reduced to questions about chemicals and their interactions—for example, how does radiation affect the atoms in living issues? Knowledge of chemistry is therefore essential to understanding biology. In this chapter, we'll review some basic chemistry that you can apply throughout your study of life. We'll start with an examination of molecules, atoms, and their components. Next, we'll discuss water, one of life's most important molecules, and its crucial role in sustaining life on Earth.

Some Basic Chemistry

Why would a biology textbook include a chapter on chemistry? Well, take any biological system apart and you eventually end up at the chemical level. In fact, you can think of your body as a big watery container of chemicals undergoing a continuous series of chemical reactions. Viewed this way, your metabolism—the sum total of all the chemical reactions that occur in your body—is like a giant square dance, with chemical partners constantly swapping atoms as they move to and fro. Beginning at this basic biological level, let's explore the chemistry of life.

Matter: Elements and Compounds

You and everything that surrounds you is made of matter, the physical "stuff" of the universe. Matter is found on Earth in three physical states: solid, liquid, and gas. Defined more formally, **matter** is anything that occupies space and has mass. **Mass** is a measure of the amount of material in an object. All matter is composed of chemical elements. An **element** is a substance that cannot be broken down into other substances by chemical reactions. Think of it this way: When you burn wood, you are left with ash. But when you burn ash, you only get more ash. That is because wood is a complex mixture of elements, while ash is a pure element (carbon) that cannot be further broken down. There are 92 naturally occurring elements; examples are carbon, oxygen, and gold. Each element has a symbol derived from its English, Latin, or German name. For instance, the symbol for gold, Au, is from the Latin word *aurum*. All the elements—the 92 that occur naturally and

> Too little of the essential element copper in your diet causes anemia, but too much causes kidney and liver damage.

Mercury (Hg)

Copper (Cu)

Lead (Pb)

► **Figure 2.1 Abbreviated periodic table of the elements.** In the full periodic table (see Appendix B), each entry contains the element symbol in the center, with the atomic number above and the atomic mass below. The element highlighted here is carbon (C).

Carbon (C): 18.5%

Oxygen (O): 65.0%

Calcium (Ca): 1.5%
Phosphorus (P): 1.0%
Potassium (K): 0.4%
Sulfur (S): 0.3%
Sodium (Na): 0.2%
Chlorine (Cl): 0.2%
Magnesium (Mg): 0.1%

Hydrogen (H): 9.5%

Nitrogen (N): 3.3%

Trace elements: less than 0.01%

Boron (B)	Manganese (Mn)
Chromium (Cr)	Molybdenum (Mo)
Cobalt (Co)	Selenium (Se)
Copper (Cu)	Silicon (Si)
Fluorine (F)	Tin (Sn)
Iodine (I)	Vanadium (V)
Iron (Fe)	Zinc (Zn)

▲ Figure 2.2 **Chemical composition of the human body.** Notice that just 4 elements make up 96% of your weight.

several dozen that are human-made—are listed in the **periodic table of the elements**, a familiar fixture in any chemistry or biology lab (**Figure 2.1**; see Appendix B for a full version).

Of the naturally occurring elements, 25 are essential to people. (Other organisms need fewer; plants, for example, typically need 17.) Four of these elements—oxygen (O), carbon (C), hydrogen (H), and nitrogen (N)—make up about 96% of the weight of the body (**Figure 2.2**). Much of the remaining 4% is accounted for by 7 elements, most of which are probably familiar to you, such as calcium (Ca). Calcium, important for building strong bones and teeth, is found abundantly in milk and dairy products as well as sardines and green, leafy vegetables (kale and broccoli, for example).

Less than 0.01% of your weight is made up of 14 trace elements. **Trace elements** are required in only very small amounts, but you cannot live without them. The average person, for example, needs only a tiny speck of iodine each day. Iodine is an essential ingredient of hormones produced by the thyroid gland, located in the neck. An iodine deficiency causes the thyroid gland to enlarge, a condition called goiter. Therefore, consuming foods that are naturally rich in iodine—such as green vegetables, eggs, kelp, and dairy products—prevents goiter. The addition of iodine to table salt ("iodized salt") has nearly eliminated goiter in industrialized nations, but many thousands of people in developing countries are still affected (**Figure 2.3**). Another trace element is fluorine,

Atomic number
(number of protons)

6

Element symbol

C

Atomic mass
(mass of average atom of that element)

12.01

H																	He
Li	Be											B	C	N	O	F	Ne
Na	Mg											Al	Si	P	S	Cl	Ar
K	Ca	Sc	Ti	V	Cr	Mn	Fe	Co	Ni	Cu	Zn	Ga	Ge	As	Se	Br	Kr
Rb	Sr	Y	Zr	Nb	Mo	Tc	Ru	Rh	Pd	Ag	Cd	In	Sn	Sb	Te	I	Xe
Cs	Ba	La	Hf	Ta	W	Re	Os	Ir	Pt	Au	Hg	Tl	Pb	Bi	Po	At	Rn
Fr	Ra	Ac	Rf	Db	Sg	Bh	Hs	Mt	Ds	Rg	Cn						

Ce	Pr	Nd	Pm	Sm	Eu	Gd	Tb	Dy	Ho	Er	Tm	Yb	Lu
Th	Pa	U	Np	Pu	Am	Cm	Bk	Cf	Es	Fm	Md	No	Lr

▼ Figure 2.3 Diet and goiter.

Goiter, an enlargement of the thyroid gland, shown here in a Malaysian woman, can occur when a person's diet does not include enough iodine, a trace element.

Eating iodine-rich foods can prevent goiter.

which (in the form of fluoride) is added to dental products and drinking water and helps maintain healthy bones and teeth. Many prepared foods are fortified with trace mineral elements. Look at the side of a cereal box and you'll probably see iron listed; you can actually see the iron yourself if you crush the cereal and stir a magnet through it. Be grateful for this additive: It helps prevent anemia due to iron deficiency, one of the most common nutritional deficiencies among Americans.

Elements can combine to form **compounds**, substances that contain two or more elements in a fixed ratio. In everyday life, compounds are much more common than pure elements. Familiar examples of compounds include table salt and water. Table salt is sodium chloride, NaCl, consisting of equal parts of the elements sodium (Na) and chlorine (Cl). A molecule of water, H_2O, has two atoms of hydrogen and one atom of oxygen. Most of the compounds in living organisms contain several different elements. DNA, for example, contains carbon, nitrogen, oxygen, hydrogen, and phosphorus. ☑

Atoms

Each element is made up of one kind of atom, and the atoms in an element are different from the atoms of other elements. An **atom** is the smallest unit of matter that still retains the properties of an element. In other words, the smallest amount of the element carbon is one carbon atom. Just how small is this "piece" of carbon? It would

take about a million carbon atoms to stretch across the period at the end of this sentence.

The Structure of Atoms

Atoms are composed of subatomic particles, of which the three most important are protons, electrons, and neutrons. A **proton** is a subatomic particle with a single unit of positive electrical charge (+). An **electron** is a subatomic particle with a single negative charge (−). A **neutron** is electrically neutral (has no charge).

Figure 2.4 shows a simplified model of an atom of the element helium (He), the lighter-than-air gas used to inflate party balloons. Each atom of helium has 2 neutrons (◯) and 2 protons (⊕) tightly packed into the **nucleus**, the atom's central core. Two electrons (⊖) move around the nucleus in a spherical cloud at nearly the speed of light. The electron cloud is much bigger than the nucleus. If the atom were the size of a baseball stadium, the nucleus would be the size of a pea on the pitcher's mound and the electrons would be two gnats buzzing around the bleachers. When an atom has an equal number of protons and electrons, its net electrical charge is zero and so the atom is neutral.

All atoms of a particular element have the same unique number of protons. This number is the element's **atomic number**. Thus, an atom of helium, with 2 protons, has an atomic number of 2, and no other element has 2 protons. The periodic table of elements (Appendix B) lists elements in order of atomic number. Note that in these atoms, the atomic number is also the number of electrons. A standard atom of any element has an equal number of protons and electrons, and thus its net electrical charge is 0 (zero). An atom's **mass number** is the sum of the number of protons and neutrons. For helium, the mass number is 4. The mass of a proton and the mass of a neutron are almost identical and are expressed in a unit of measurement called the dalton. Protons and neutrons each have masses close to 1 dalton. An electron has only about 1/2,000 the mass of a proton, so its mass is approximated as zero. An atom's **atomic mass**, which is listed in the periodic table as the bottom number (under the element symbol), is close to its mass number—the sum of its protons and neutrons—but may differ slightly because it represents an average of all the naturally occurring forms of that element.

Isotopes

Some elements can exist in different forms called **isotopes**, which have the same numbers of protons and electrons as a standard atom of that element but different numbers

Sodium is an explosive solid and chlorine is a poisonous gas, but when combined they form a common ingredient in your diet: table salt.

▼ Figure 2.4 A simplified model of a helium atom. This model shows the subatomic particles in an atom of helium. The electrons move very fast, creating a spherical cloud of negative charge surrounding the positively charged nucleus.

2 ⊕ Protons
2 ◯ Neutrons — Nucleus
2 ⊖ Electrons

Nucleus

Electron cloud containing two electrons

☑ CHECKPOINT

How many of the naturally occurring elements are used by your body? Which four are the most abundant in living cells?

Answer: 25; oxygen, carbon, hydrogen, and nitrogen

of neutrons. In other words, isotopes are forms of an element that differ in mass. As shown in Table 2.1, the isotope carbon-12 (named for its mass number), which has 6 neutrons and 6 protons, makes up about 99% of all naturally occurring carbon. Most of the other 1% of carbon on Earth is the isotope carbon-13, which has 7 neutrons and 6 protons. A third isotope, carbon-14, which has 8 neutrons and 6 protons, occurs in minute quantities. All three isotopes have 6 protons—otherwise, they would not be carbon. Both carbon-12 and carbon-13 are stable isotopes, meaning that their nuclei remain intact more or less forever. The isotope carbon-14, on the other hand, is radioactive. A **radioactive isotope** is one in which the nucleus decays spontaneously, shedding particles and energy.

Radiation from decaying isotopes can damage cellular molecules and thus can pose serious health risks. In 1986,

Table 2.1	Isotopes of Carbon		
	Carbon-12	**Carbon-13**	**Carbon-14**
Protons	6 ⎤ mass	6 ⎤ mass	6 ⎤ mass
	⎦ number	⎦ number	⎦ number
Neutrons	6 ⎦ 12	7 ⎦ 13	8 ⎦ 14
Electrons	6	6	6

☑ CHECKPOINT

By definition, all atoms of carbon have exactly 6 _____, but the number of _____ varies from one isotope to another.

Answer: protons; neutrons

the explosion of a nuclear reactor at Chernobyl, Ukraine, released large amounts of radioactive isotopes, killing 30 people within a few weeks. Millions of people in the surrounding areas were exposed, causing an estimated 6,000 cases of thyroid cancer. The 2011 post-tsunami Fukushima nuclear disaster in Japan, did not result in any immediate deaths due to radiation exposure, but scientists are carefully monitoring the people who live in the area to watch for any long-term health consequences.

Natural sources of radiation can also pose a threat. Radon, a radioactive gas, can cause lung cancer. Radon may contaminate buildings where underlying rocks naturally contain the radioactive element uranium. Homeowners can install a radon detector or test their home to ensure that radon levels are safe.

Although radioactive isotopes can cause harm when uncontrolled, they have many uses in biological research and medicine. In the Biology and Society section, we discussed how radioactivity can be used to treat diseases such as cancer and Graves' disease. Let's take a look at another beneficial use of radioactivity: the diagnosis of disease. ☑

 Radioactivity THE PROCESS OF SCIENCE

Can Radioactive Tracers Identify Brain Diseases?

Cells use radioactive isotopes the same way they use nonradioactive isotopes of the same element. Once the cell takes up a radioactive isotope, the location and concentration of the isotope can be detected because of the radiation it emits. This makes radioactive isotopes useful as tracers—biological spies, in effect—for monitoring living organisms. For example, a medical diagnostic tool called a PET scan works by detecting small amounts of radiation emitted by radioactive materials that were purposefully introduced into the body (Figure 2.5).

In 2012, researchers published a study that used PET scans to investigate Alzheimer's disease. In Alzheimer's disease, a patient gradually loses his or her memory and can become confused, forgetful, and unable to perform normal daily tasks. The disease inevitably leads to a loss of bodily functions

▲ Figure 2.5 **A PET scan.** This monitor shows the images produced by a PET scanner. PET scans can be used to diagnose several diseases, including epilepsy, cancer, and Alzheimer's disease.

and death. A definitive diagnosis of Alzheimer's is difficult because it is hard to distinguish from other age-related disorders. Early detection and treatment of Alzheimer's could benefit many patients and their families.

The **observation** that the brains of people with Alzheimer's are often filled with clumps of a protein called amyloid led the researchers to **question** whether these clumps could be detected by a PET scan. The researchers formed the **hypothesis** that a molecule called florbetapir, which contains the radioactive isotope fluorine-18, could be detected by PET scans after it binds to amyloid deposits in living patients. The researchers' **prediction** was that using florbetapir during PET scans could help with diagnosis.

Their **experiment** involved 229 patients who had been diagnosed with mental decline. Of these, 113 patients showed amyloid deposits in their PET scans. This information led doctors to change the diagnosis in 55% of the patients, sometimes changing the diagnosis to Alzheimer's and sometimes changing it to a different disease. Furthermore, the PET scan data led to changes in treatment (such as different drugs) in 87% of cases. These **results** indicate that radioisotope scans can indeed alter diagnoses and affect treatment. Researchers hope that this will lead to improved outcomes for patients suffering from this debilitating condition.

Chemical Bonding and Molecules

Of the three subatomic particles we've discussed—protons, neutrons, and electrons—only electrons are directly involved in chemical reactions. The number of electrons in an atom determines the chemical properties of that atom. Chemical reactions enable atoms to transfer or share electrons. These interactions usually result in atoms staying close together, held by attractions called **chemical bonds**. In this section, we will discuss three types of chemical bonds: ionic, covalent, and hydrogen bonds.

Ionic Bonds

Table salt is an example of how the transfer of electrons can bond atoms together. As discussed earlier, the two ingredients of table salt are the elements sodium (Na) and chlorine (Cl). When in close proximity to each other, a chlorine atom strips an electron from a sodium atom (Figure 2.6). Before this electron transfer, both the sodium and chlorine atoms are electrically neutral. Because electrons are negatively charged, the electron transfer moves one unit of negative charge from sodium to chlorine. This action makes both atoms **ions**, atoms or molecules that are electrically charged as a result of gaining or losing electrons. In this case, the loss of an electron results in the sodium ion having a charge of $+1$, whereas chlorine's gain of an electron results in it having a charge of -1. The sodium ion (Na^+) and chloride ion (Cl^-) are then held together by an **ionic bond**, the attraction between oppositely charged ions. Compounds, such as table salt, that are held together by ionic bonds are called ionic compounds. (Note that negatively charged ions often have names ending in "-ide," like "chloride" or "fluoride.") ✓

Covalent Bonds

In contrast to the complete *transfer* of electrons in ionic bonds, a **covalent bond** forms when two atoms *share* one or more pairs of electrons. Of the bonds we've discussed, covalent bonds are the strongest; these are the bonds that hold atoms together in a **molecule**. For example, in Figure 2.7, you can see that each of the two hydrogen atoms in a molecule of formaldehyde (CH_2O, a common disinfectant and preservative) shares one pair of electrons with the carbon atom. The oxygen atom shares two pairs of electrons with the carbon, forming a double bond. Notice that each atom of hydrogen (H) can form one covalent bond, oxygen (O) can form two, and carbon (C) can form four.

▼ Figure 2.6 **Electron transfer and ionic bonding.** When a sodium atom and a chlorine atom meet, the electron transfer between the two atoms results in two ions with opposite charges.

An electron is stripped from sodium and added to chlorine.

Na
Sodium atom

Cl
Chlorine atom

Na⁺
Sodium ion

Cl⁻
Chloride ion

The attraction between the ions—an ionic bond—holds the ions together.

Sodium chloride (NaCl)

☑ **CHECKPOINT**

When a lithium ion (Li^+) joins a bromide ion (Br^-) to form lithium bromide, the resulting bond is a(n) _____ bond.

Answer: ionic

▼ Figure 2.7 **Alternative ways to represent a molecule.** A molecular formula, such as CH_2O, tells you the number of each kind of atom in a molecule but not how they are attached together. This figure shows four common ways of representing the arrangement of atoms in molecules.

Name (molecular formula)	Electron configuration	Structural formula	Space-filling model	Ball-and-stick model
	Shows how each atom completes its outer shell by sharing electrons	Represents each covalent bond (a pair of shared electrons) with a line	Shows the shape of a molecule by symbolizing atoms with color-coded balls	Represents atoms with "balls" and bonds with "sticks"
Formaldehyde (CH_2O)				

Double bond (two pairs of shared electrons)

Single bond (a pair of shared electrons)

Hydrogen Bonds

A molecule of water (H_2O) consists of two hydrogen atoms joined to one oxygen atom by single covalent bonds. (The covalent bonds between the atoms are represented as the "sticks" here in a ball-and-stick illustration, and the atoms are shown as the "balls"):

However, the electrons are not shared equally between the oxygen and hydrogen atoms. The two yellow arrows shown in the space-filling model here indicate the stronger pull on the shared electrons that oxygen has compared with its hydrogen partners:

The unequal sharing of negatively charged electrons, combined with its V shape, makes a water molecule polar. A **polar molecule** is one with an uneven distribution of charge that creates two poles, one positive pole and one negative pole. In the case of water, the oxygen end of the molecule has a slight negative charge, and the region around the two hydrogen atoms is slightly positive.

The polarity of water results in weak electrical attractions between neighboring water molecules. Because opposite charges attract, water molecules tend to orient such that a hydrogen atom from one water molecule is near the oxygen atom of an adjacent water molecule. These weak attractions are called **hydrogen bonds** (Figure 2.8). As you will see later in this chapter, the ability of water to form hydrogen bonds has many crucial implications for life on Earth.

Chemical Reactions

The chemistry of life is dynamic. Your cells are constantly rearranging molecules by breaking existing chemical

bonds and forming new ones in a "chemical square dance." Such changes in the chemical composition of matter are called **chemical reactions**. An example of a chemical reaction is the breakdown of hydrogen peroxide (a common disinfectant that you may have poured on a cut):

Let's translate the chemical shorthand: Two molecules of hydrogen peroxide ($2\ H_2O_2$) react to form two molecules of water ($2\ H_2O$) and one molecule of oxygen (O_2, which is responsible for the fizzing that happens when hydrogen peroxide interacts with blood). The arrow in this equation indicates the conversion of the starting materials, the **reactants** ($2\ H_2O_2$), to the **products** ($2\ H_2O$ and O_2).

Notice that the same total numbers of hydrogen and oxygen atoms are present in reactants (to the left of the arrow) and products (to the right), although they are grouped differently. Chemical reactions cannot create or destroy matter; they can only rearrange it. These rearrangements usually involve the breaking of chemical bonds in reactants and the forming of new bonds in products.

This discussion of water molecules as the product of a chemical reaction is a good conclusion to this section on basic chemistry. Water is a substance so important in biology that we'll take a closer look at its life-supporting properties in the next section. ✓

Hydrogen bond ─⊏ ┊

(−)

(+)

H
|
O — H

Slightly positive charge

Slightly negative charge

(+) ┈ (−)

(−)

(+)

(+) ┈ (−)

◄ Figure 2.8 **Hydrogen bonding in water.** The charged regions of the polar water molecules are attracted to oppositely charged areas of neighboring molecules. Each molecule can hydrogen-bond to a maximum of four partners.

☑ **CHECKPOINT**

Predict the formula for the compound that results when a molecule of sulfur trioxide (SO_3) combines with a molecule of water to produce a single molecule of product. (*Hint*: In chemical reactions, no atoms are gained or lost.)

Answer: H_2SO_4 (sulfuric acid, which is a component of acid rain)

Water and Life

Life on Earth began in water and evolved there for 3 billion years before spreading onto land. Modern life, even land-dwelling life, is still tied to water. You've had personal experience with this dependence on water every time you seek liquids to quench your thirst. Inside your body, your cells are surrounded by a fluid that's composed mostly of water, and your cells themselves range from 70% to 95% in water content.

The abundance of water is a major reason that Earth is habitable. Water is so common that it is easy to overlook the fact that it is an exceptional substance with many extraordinary properties (Figure 2.9). We can trace water's unique life-supporting properties to the structure and interactions of its molecules.

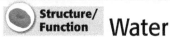

Structure/Function Water

The unique properties of water on which all life on Earth depends are a prime example of one of biology's overarching themes: the relationship of structure and function. The structure of water molecules—the polarity and the hydrogen bonding that results (see Figure 2.8)—explains most of water's life-supporting functions. We'll explore four of those properties here: the cohesive nature of water, the ability of water to moderate temperature, the biological significance of ice floating, and the versatility of water as a solvent.

The Cohesion of Water

Water molecules stick together as a result of hydrogen bonding. In a drop of water, any particular set of hydrogen bonds lasts for only a few trillionths of a second, yet at any instant, huge numbers of hydrogen bonds exist between molecules of liquid water. This tendency of molecules of the same kind to stick together, called **cohesion**, is much stronger for water than for most other liquids. The cohesion of water is important in the living world. Trees, for example, depend on cohesion to help transport water from their roots to their leaves (Figure 2.10).

Related to cohesion is surface tension, a measure of how difficult it is to stretch or break the surface of a liquid. Hydrogen bonds give water unusually high surface tension, making it behave as though it were coated with an invisible film (Figure 2.11). Other

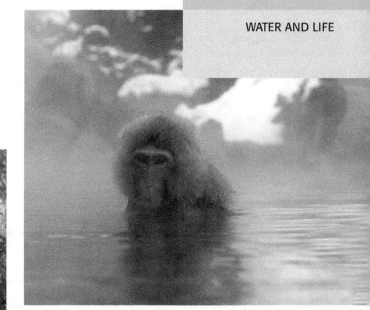

▲ **Figure 2.9 A watery world.** In this photograph, you can see water as liquid (which covers three-quarters of Earth's surface), ice (in the form of snow), and vapor (as steam).

Microscopic water-conducting tubes

Cohesion due to hydrogen bonds between water molecules

Colorized SEM 150×

▲ **Figure 2.10 Cohesion and water transport in plants.** The evaporation of water from leaves pulls water upward from the roots through microscopic tubes in the trunk of the tree. Because of cohesion, the pulling force is relayed through the tubes all the way down to the roots. As a result, water rises against the force of gravity.

▼ **Figure 2.11 A raft spider walking on water.** The cumulative strength of hydrogen bonds among water molecules allows this spider to walk on pond water without breaking the surface.

liquids have much weaker surface tension; an insect, for example, could not walk on the surface of a cup of gasoline (which is why gardeners sometimes use gas to drown bugs removed from flower bushes).

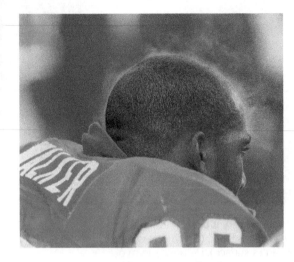

▲ Figure 2.12 **Sweating as a mechanism of evaporative cooling.**

How Water Moderates Temperature

If you've ever burned your finger on a metal pot while waiting for the water in it to boil, you know that water heats up much more slowly than metal. In fact, because of hydrogen bonding, water has a stronger resistance to temperature change than most other substances.

When water is heated, the heat energy first disrupts hydrogen bonds and then makes water molecules jostle around faster. The temperature of the water doesn't go up until the water molecules start to speed up. Because heat is first used to break hydrogen bonds rather than raise the temperature, water absorbs and stores a large amount of heat while warming up only a few degrees. Conversely, when water cools, hydrogen bonds form, a process that releases heat. Thus, water can release a relatively large amount of heat to the surroundings while the water temperature drops only slightly.

Earth's giant water supply—the oceans, seas, lakes, and rivers—enables temperatures on the planet to stay within limits that permit life by storing a huge amount of heat from the sun during warm periods and giving off heat that warms the air during cold periods. That's why coastal areas generally have milder climates than inland regions. Water's resistance to temperature change also stabilizes ocean temperatures, creating a favorable environment for marine life. You may have noticed that the water temperature at the beach fluctuates much less than the air temperature.

Another way that water moderates temperature is by **evaporative cooling**. When a substance evaporates (changes from a liquid to a gas), the surface of the liquid that remains cools down. This occurs because the molecules with the greatest energy (the "hottest" ones) tend to vaporize first. Think of it like this: If the five fastest runners on your track team quit school, it would lower the average speed of the remaining team. Evaporative cooling helps prevent some land-dwelling creatures from overheating; it's why sweating helps you dissipate excess body heat (Figure 2.12). And the expression "It's not the heat, it's the humidity" has its basis in the difficulty of sweating when the air is already saturated with water vapor.

The Biological Significance of Ice Floating

When most liquids get cold, their molecules move closer together. If the temperature is cold enough, the liquid freezes and becomes a solid. Water, however, behaves differently. When water molecules get cold enough, they move apart, with each molecule staying at "arm's length" from its neighbors, forming ice. A chunk of ice floats because it is less dense than the liquid water in which it is floating. Floating ice is a consequence of hydrogen bonding. In contrast to the short-lived and constantly changing hydrogen bonds in liquid water, those in solid ice last longer, with each molecule bonded to four neighbors. As a result, ice is a spacious crystal (Figure 2.13).

► Figure 2.13 **Why ice floats.** Compare the tightly packed molecules in liquid water with the spaciously arranged molecules in the ice crystal. The less dense ice floats atop the denser water.

Liquid water
Hydrogen bonds constantly break and re-form.

Hydrogen bond

Ice
Stable hydrogen bonds hold molecules apart, making ice less dense than water.

How does floating ice help support life on Earth? When a deep body of water cools and a layer of ice forms on top, the floating ice acts as an insulating "blanket" over the liquid water, allowing life to persist under the frozen surface. But imagine what would happen if ice were denser than water: Ice would sink during winter. All ponds, lakes, and even the oceans would eventually freeze solid without the insulating protection of the top layer of ice. Then, during summer, only the upper few inches of the oceans would thaw. It's hard to imagine life persisting under such conditions.

Water as the Solvent of Life

If you've ever stirred sugar into coffee or added salt to soup, you know that you can dissolve sugar or salt in water. This results in a mixture known as a **solution**, a liquid consisting of a homogeneous mixture of two or more substances. The dissolving agent is called the **solvent**, and any substance that is dissolved is called a **solute**. When water is the solvent, the resulting solution is called an **aqueous solution**. The fluids of organisms are aqueous solutions. For example, tree sap is an aqueous solution consisting of sugar and minerals dissolved in water.

Water can dissolve an enormous variety of solutes necessary for life, providing a medium for chemical reactions. For example, water can dissolve salt ions, as shown in Figure 2.14. Each ion becomes surrounded by oppositely charged regions of water molecules. Solutes that are polar molecules, such as sugars, dissolve by orienting locally charged regions of their molecules toward water molecules in a similar way.

We have discussed four special properties of water, each a consequence of water's unique chemical structure. Next, we'll look at aqueous solutions in more detail. ☑

Acids, Bases, and pH

In aqueous solutions, most of the water molecules are intact. However, some of the water molecules break apart into hydrogen ions (H^+) and hydroxide ions (OH^-). A balance of these two highly reactive ions is critical for the proper functioning of chemical processes within organisms.

A chemical compound that releases H^+ to a solution is called an **acid**. One example of a strong acid is hydrochloric acid (HCl), the acid in your stomach that aids in digestion of food. In solution, HCl breaks apart into the ions H^+ and Cl^-. A **base** (or alkali) is a compound that accepts H^+ and removes them from solution. Some bases, such as sodium hydroxide (NaOH), do this by releasing OH^-, which combines with H^+ to form H_2O.

To describe the acidity of a solution, chemists use the **pH scale**, a measure of the hydrogen ion (H^+) concentration in a solution. The scale ranges from 0 (most acidic) to 14 (most basic).

Lemon juice has roughly the same acidity as the food-digesting chemicals in your stomach.

▲ Figure 2.14 **A crystal of table salt (NaCl) dissolving in water.** As a result of electrical charge attractions, H_2O molecules surround the sodium and chloride ions, dissolving the crystal in the process.

Chloride ion in solution

Sodium ion in solution

Cl⁻   Na⁺

Cl⁻   Na⁺

Salt crystal

Each pH unit represents a tenfold change in the concentration of H^+ (**Figure 2.15**). For example, lemon juice at pH 2 has 100 times more H^+ than an equal amount of tomato juice at pH 4. Aqueous solutions that are neither acidic nor basic (such as pure water) are said to be neutral; they have a pH of 7. They do contain some H^+

and OH^-, but the concentrations of the two ions are equal. The pH of the solution inside most living cells is close to 7.

Even a slight change in pH can be harmful to an organism because the molecules in cells are extremely sensitive to H^+ and OH^- concentrations. Biological fluids contain **buffers**, substances that minimize changes in pH by accepting H^+ when that ion is in excess and donating H^+ when it is depleted. For example, buffer in contact lens solution helps protect the surface of the eye from potentially painful changes in pH. This buffering process, however, is not foolproof, and changes in environmental pH can profoundly affect ecosystems. For example, about 25% of the carbon dioxide (CO_2) generated by people (primarily by burning fossil fuels) is absorbed by the oceans. When CO_2 dissolves in seawater, it reacts with water to form carbonic acid (**Figure 2.16**), which lowers ocean pH. The resulting ocean acidification can greatly change marine environments. Oceanographers have calculated that the pH of the ocean is lower now than at any time in the past 420,000 years, and it is continuing to drop.

The effects of ocean acidification—including coral bleaching and changes in metabolism among a wide variety of sea creatures—are daunting reminders that the chemistry of life is linked to the chemistry of the environment. It reminds us, too, that chemistry happens on a global scale, because industrial processes in one region of the world often cause ecosystem changes in another part of the world. ☑

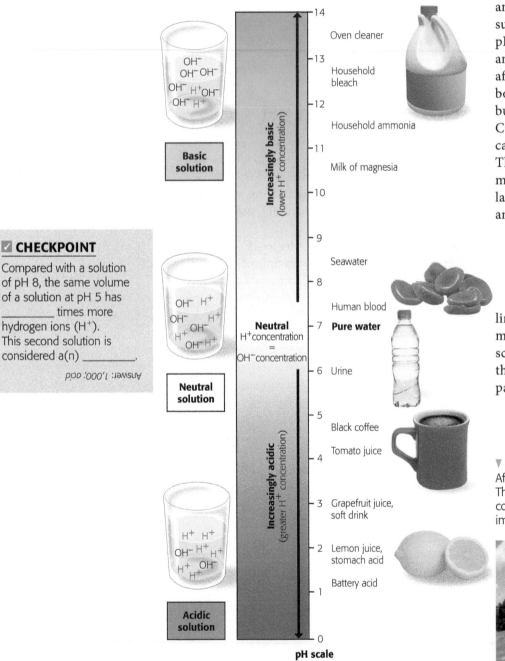

▲ **Figure 2.15 The pH scale.** A solution having a pH of 7 is neutral, meaning that its H^+ and OH^- concentrations are equal. The lower the pH below 7, the more acidic the solution, or the greater its excess of H^+ compared with OH^-. The higher the pH above 7, the more basic the solution, or the greater the deficiency of H^+ relative to OH^-.

▼ **Figure 2.16 Ocean acidification by atmospheric CO_2.** After dissolving in seawater, CO_2 reacts to form carbonic acid. This acid then undergoes further chemical reactions that disrupt coral growth. Such acidification can cause drastic changes in important marine ecosystems.

Radioactivity as an Evolutionary Clock

Throughout this chapter, we have highlighted ways—both helpful and harmful—that radioactivity can affect the health of living organisms. In addition to detecting and treating diseases, another helpful application of radioactivity involves the natural process of radioactive decay, which can be used to obtain important data about the evolutionary history of life on Earth.

Fossils—both preserved imprints and remains of dead organisms—are reliable chronological records of life because we can determine their ages through radiometric dating (Figure 2.17), which is based on the decay of radioactive isotopes. For example, carbon-14 is a radioactive isotope with a half-life of 5,700 years. It is present in trace amounts in the environment. **①** A living organism assimilates the different isotopes of an element in proportions that reflect their relative abundances in the environment. In this example, carbon-14 is taken up in trace quantities, along with much larger quantities of the more common carbon-12. **②** At the time of death, the organism ceases to take in carbon from the environment. From this moment forward, the amount of carbon-14 relative to carbon-12 in the fossil declines: The carbon-14 in the body decays into carbon-12, but no new carbon-14 is added. Because the half-life of carbon-12 is known, the ratio of the two isotopes (carbon-14 to carbon-12) is a reliable indicator of the age of the fossil. In this case, it takes 5,700 years for half of the radioactive carbon-14 to decay; half of the remainder is present after another 5,700 years; and so on. **③** A fossil's age can be estimated by measuring the ratio of the two isotopes to learn how many half-life reductions have occurred since it died. For example, if the ratio of carbon-14 to carbon-12 in this fossil was found to be $\frac{1}{8}$th that of the environment, this fossil would be about 17,100 (5,700 × 3 half-lives) years old.

Using such techniques, scientists can estimate the ages of fossils from around the world and place them in an ordered sequence called the fossil record. The fossil record is one of the most important and convincing sets of evidence that led Charles Darwin to formulate the theory of natural selection (as you'll see later, in Chapter 14). Every time a new fossil is dated, it can be placed within the vast history of life on Earth.

▼ Figure 2.17 **Radiometric dating.** Living organisms incorporate the carbon-14 isotope (represented here with blue dots). But no new carbon-14 is introduced once an organism dies, and the carbon-14 that remains slowly decays into carbon-12. By measuring the amount of carbon-14 in a fossil, scientists can estimate its age.

Chapter Review

■ SUMMARY OF KEY CONCEPTS

Some Basic Chemistry

Matter: Elements and Compounds

Matter consists of elements and compounds, which are combinations of two or more elements. Of the 25 elements essential for life, oxygen, carbon, hydrogen, and nitrogen are the most abundant in living matter.

Atoms

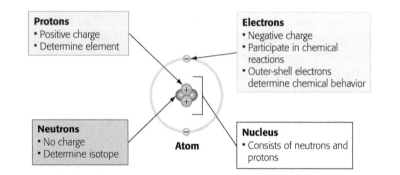

Protons
- Positive charge
- Determine element

Electrons
- Negative charge
- Participate in chemical reactions
- Outer-shell electrons determine chemical behavior

Neutrons
- No charge
- Determine isotope

Atom

Nucleus
- Consists of neutrons and protons

Chemical Bonding and Molecules

Transfer of one or more electrons produces attractions between oppositely charged ions:

Attraction between oppositely charged ions holds the ions in an ionic bond.

Lithium ion   Fluoride ion

Lithium fluoride (ionic compound)

A molecule consists of two or more atoms connected by covalent bonds, which are formed by electron sharing:

Electron sharing

Atoms joined into a molecule via covalent bonds

Water is a polar molecule; the slightly positively charged H atoms in one water molecule may be attracted to the partial negative charge of O atoms in neighboring water molecules, forming weak but important hydrogen bonds:

Hydrogen bond

Chemical Reactions

By breaking bonds in reactants and forming new bonds in products, chemical reactions rearrange matter.

Water and Life

Structure/Function: Water

The cohesion (sticking together) of water molecules is essential to life. Water moderates temperature by absorbing heat in warm environments and releasing heat in cold environments. Evaporative cooling also helps stabilize the temperatures of oceans and organisms. Ice floats because it is less dense than liquid water, and the insulating properties of floating ice prevent the oceans from freezing solid. Water is a very good solvent, dissolving a great variety of solutes to produce aqueous solutions.

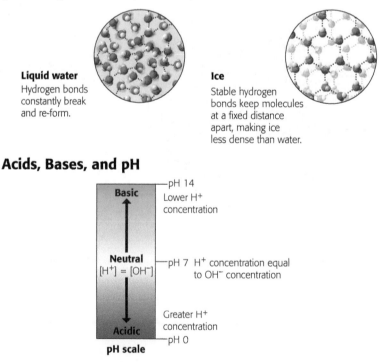

Liquid water
Hydrogen bonds constantly break and re-form.

Ice
Stable hydrogen bonds keep molecules at a fixed distance apart, making ice less dense than water.

Acids, Bases, and pH

Basic — pH 14 Lower H^+ concentration

Neutral
$[H^+] = [OH^-]$ — pH 7 H^+ concentration equal to OH^- concentration

Acidic — Greater H^+ concentration — pH 0

pH scale

MasteringBiology®

For practice quizzes, BioFlix animations, MP3 tutorials, video tutors, and more study tools designed for this textbook, go to MasteringBiology®

SELF-QUIZ

1. An atom can be changed into an ion by adding or removing _____. An atom can be changed into a different isotope by adding or removing _____.

2. If you change the number of _____, the atom becomes a different element.

3. A nitrogen atom has 7 protons, and the most common isotope of nitrogen has 7 neutrons. A radioactive isotope of nitrogen has 9 neutrons. What are the atomic numbers and mass numbers of the stable and radioactive forms of nitrogen?

4. Why are radioactive isotopes useful as tracers in research on the chemistry of life?

5. What is chemically nonsensical about this structure?
H—C≡C—H

6. Why is it unlikely that two neighboring water molecules would be arranged like this?

7. Which of the following is not a chemical reaction?
   a. Sugar ($C_6H_{12}O_6$) and oxygen gas (O_2) combine to form carbon dioxide (CO_2) and water (H_2O).
   b. Sodium metal and chlorine gas unite to form sodium chloride.
   c. Hydrogen gas combines with oxygen gas to form water.
   d. Ice melts to form liquid water.

8. Some people in your study group say they don't understand what a polar molecule is. You explain that a polar molecule
   a. is slightly negative at one end and slightly positive at the other end.
   b. has an extra electron, giving it a positive charge.
   c. has an extra electron, giving it a negative charge.
   d. has covalent bonds.

9. Explain how the unique properties of water result from the fact that water is a polar molecule.

10. Explain why it is unlikely that life could exist on a planet where the main liquid is methane, a nonpolar molecule that does not form hydrogen bonds.

11. A can of cola consists mostly of sugar dissolved in water, with some carbon dioxide gas that makes it fizzy and makes the pH less than 7. Describe the cola using the following terms: solute, solvent, acidic, aqueous solution.

Answers to these questions can be found in Appendix: Self-Quiz Answers.

THE PROCESS OF SCIENCE

12. Animals obtain energy through a series of chemical reactions in which sugar ($C_6H_{12}O_6$) and oxygen gas (O_2) are reactants. This process produces water (H_2O) and carbon dioxide (CO_2) as waste products. How might you use a radioactive isotope to find out whether the oxygen in CO_2 comes from sugar or from oxygen gas?

13. This diagram shows the arrangement of electrons around the nucleus of a fluorine atom (left) and a potassium atom (right). Predict what kind of bond forms when a fluorine atom comes into contact with a potassium atom.

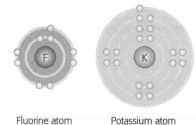

Fluorine atom   Potassium atom

14. **Interpreting Data** As discussed in the text and shown in Figure 2.17, radiometric dating can be used to determine the age of biological materials. The calculation of age depends on the half-life of the radioisotope under consideration. For example, carbon-14 makes up about 1 part per trillion of naturally occurring carbon. When an organism dies, its body contains 1 carbon-14 atom per trillion total carbon atoms. After 5,700 years (the half-life of carbon-14), its body contains one-half as much carbon-14; the other half has decayed and is no longer present. French scientists used carbon-14 dating to determine the age of prehistoric wall paintings in the Niaux caves. They determined that the paintings were made using natural dyes approximately 13,000 years ago. Using your knowledge of radiometric dating, how much carbon-14 must the scientists have found in the cave paintings to support this result? Express your answer in both percentage of carbon-14 remaining and in parts of carbon-14 per trillion.

BIOLOGY AND SOCIETY

15. Critically evaluate this statement: "It's paranoid to worry about contaminating the environment with chemical wastes; this stuff is just made of the same atoms that were already present in our environment."

16. A major source of the CO_2 that causes ocean acidification is emissions from coal-burning power plants. One way to reduce these emissions is to use nuclear power to produce electricity. The proponents of nuclear power contend that it is the only way that the United States can increase its energy production while reducing air pollution, because nuclear power plants emit little or no acid-precipitation-causing pollutants. What are some of the benefits of nuclear power? What are the possible costs and dangers? Do you think we ought to increase our use of nuclear power to generate electricity? If a new power plant were to be built near your home, would you prefer it to be a coal-burning plant or a nuclear plant?

3 The Molecules of Life

Why Macromolecules Matter

If you drink coffee, odds are good that you spooned beets into your cup today—in the form of table sugar.

A long-distance runner who carbo-loads the night before a race is banking glycogen to be used the next day.

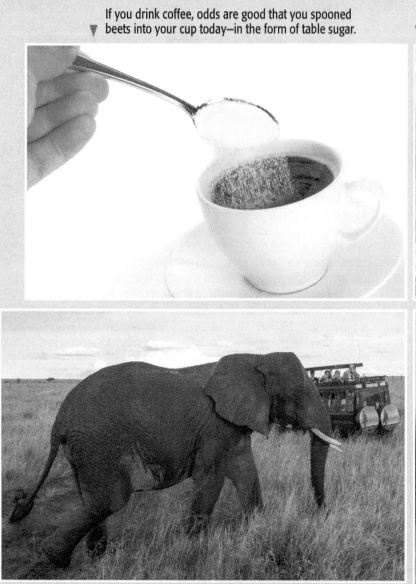

▲ The structure of your DNA is nearly indistinguishable from the DNA of a mosquito or an elephant: The differences in animal species result from the way nucleotides are arranged.

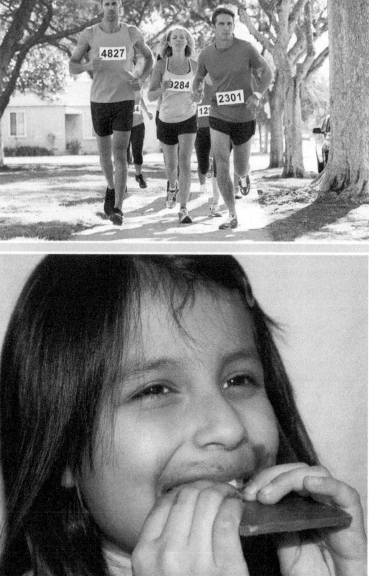

▲ Chocolate melts in your mouth (and in your hands) because of the structure of cocoa butter, which is high in saturated fats.

Lactose Intolerance BIOLOGY AND SOCIETY

Got Lactose?

You've probably seen ads that associate a milk mustache with good health. Indeed, milk is a very healthy food: It's rich in protein, minerals, and vitamins, and can be low in fat. But for the majority of adults in the world, a glass of milk delivers a heavy dose of digestive discomfort that can include bloating, gas, and abdominal pain. These are symptoms of lactose intolerance, the inability to digest lactose, the main sugar found in milk.

For people with lactose intolerance, the problem starts when lactose enters the small intestine. To absorb this sugar, digestive cells in the small intestine must produce a molecule called lactase. Lactase is an enzyme, a protein that helps drive chemical reactions—in this case, the breakdown of lactose into smaller sugars. Most people are born with the ability to digest lactose. But after about age 2, lactase levels in most people decline significantly. Lactose that is not broken down in the small intestine passes into the large intestine, where bacteria feed on it and belch out gaseous by-products. An accumulation of gas produces uncomfortable symptoms. Sufficient lactase can thus mean the difference between delight and discomfort when someone drinks a tall glass of chocolate milk.

There is no treatment for the underlying cause of lactose intolerance: the decreased production of lactase. So what are the options for people who do not produce enough of this enzyme? The first option is

Lactose-rich chocolate milk. Lactose digestion results from interactions between several classes of the body's molecules.

avoiding lactose-containing foods; abstinence is always the best form of protection! Alternatively, substitutes are available, such as milk made from soy or almonds, or cow's milk that has been pretreated with lactase. If you are lactose intolerant and pizza is your staple food, you can buy lactose-free cheese (made from soy) or you can make your own mozzarella from lactose-free milk. Also, lactase in pill form can be taken along with food to ease digestion by artificially providing the enzyme that the body naturally lacks.

Lactose intolerance illustrates one way the interplay of biological molecules can affect your health. Such molecular interactions, repeated in countless variations, drive all biological processes. In this chapter, we'll explore the structure and function of large molecules that are essential to life. We'll start with an overview of carbon and then examine four classes of molecules: carbohydrates, lipids, proteins, and nucleic acids. Along the way, we'll look at where these molecules occur in your diet and the important roles they play in your body.

Organic Compounds

A cell is mostly made up of water, but the rest is mainly carbon-based molecules. When it comes to the chemistry of life, carbon plays the leading role. This is because carbon is unparalleled in its ability to form the skeletons of large, complex, diverse molecules that are necessary for life's functions. The study of carbon-based molecules, which are called **organic compounds**, lies at the heart of any study of life.

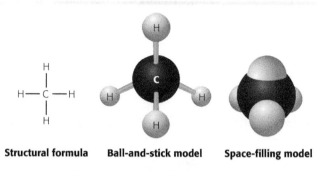

Structural formula   Ball-and-stick model   Space-filling model

▲ Figure 3.2 **Methane, a simple organic compound.**

Carbon Chemistry

Carbon is a versatile molecule ingredient because an atom of carbon can share electrons with other atoms in four covalent bonds that can branch off in four directions. Because carbon can use one or more of its bonds to attach to other carbon atoms, it is possible to construct an endless diversity of carbon skeletons varying in size and branching pattern (Figure 3.1). Thus, molecules with multiple carbon "intersections" can form very elaborate shapes. The carbon atoms of organic compounds can also bond with other elements, most commonly hydrogen, oxygen, and nitrogen.

One of the simplest organic compounds is methane, CH_4, with a single carbon atom bonded to four hydrogen atoms (Figure 3.2). Methane is abundant in natural gas and is also produced by prokaryotes that live in swamps (in the form of swamp gas) and in the digestive

tracts of grazing animals, such as cows. Larger organic compounds (such as octane, with eight carbons) are the main molecules in the gasoline we burn in cars and other machines. Organic compounds are also important fuels in your body; the energy-rich parts of fat molecules have a structure similar to gasoline (Figure 3.3).

The unique properties of an organic compound depend not only on its carbon skeleton but also on the atoms attached to the skeleton. In an organic compound, the groups of atoms directly involved in chemical reactions are called **functional groups**. Each functional group plays a particular role during chemical reactions. Two examples of functional groups are the hydroxyl group (—OH, found in alcohols such as isopropyl rubbing alcohol) and the carboxyl group (—COOH, found in all proteins). Many biological molecules have two or more functional groups. Keeping in mind this basic scheme—carbon skeletons with attached functional groups—we are now ready to explore how our cells make large molecules out of smaller ones.

▼ Figure 3.1 **Variations in carbon skeletons.** All of these examples are organic compounds that consist only of carbon and hydrogen. Notice that each carbon atom forms four bonds and each hydrogen atom forms one bond. One line represents a single bond (sharing of one pair of electrons) and two lines represent a double bond (sharing of two pairs of electrons).

Carbon skeletons vary in length

Carbon skeletons may have double bonds, which can vary in location

Double bond

Carbon skeletons may be unbranched or branched

Carbon skeletons may be arranged in rings

▼ Figure 3.3 **Hydrocarbons as fuel.** Energy-rich organic compounds in gasoline provide fuel for machines, and energy-rich molecules in fats provide fuel for cells.

Octane

Dietary fat

Giant Molecules from Smaller Building Blocks

On a molecular scale, the members of three categories of biological molecules—carbohydrates (such as those found in starchy foods like French fries and bagels), proteins (such as enzymes and the components of your hair), and nucleic acids (such as DNA)—are gigantic; in fact, biologists call them **macromolecules** (*macro* means "big"). Despite the size of macromolecules, their structures can be easily understood because they are **polymers**, large molecules made by stringing together many smaller molecules called **monomers**. A polymer is like a necklace made by joining together many monomer "beads" or a train made from a chain of box cars. Although, at first, the structure of a long train may seem very complex, it can be easily understood by asking two questions: What kind of cars make up the train? How are they joined together? Similarly, even large and complex biological macromolecules can be understood by considering which monomers make them up and how those monomers are attached together.

Cells link monomers together to form a polymer through a **dehydration reaction**. As the name implies, this chemical reaction involves removing a molecule of water (Figure 3.4a). For each monomer added to a chain, a water molecule (H_2O) is formed by the release of two hydrogen atoms and one oxygen atom from the reactants. This same type of dehydration reaction occurs regardless of the specific monomers involved and the type of polymer the cell is producing. Therefore, you'll see this type of reaction repeated many times throughout this chapter.

Organisms not only make macromolecules but also break them down. For example, you must digest macromolecules in food to make their monomers available to your cells, which can then rebuild the monomers into the macromolecules that make up your body. Converting macromolecules is like taking apart a car (food) made of interlocking toy blocks and then using these blocks to assemble a new car of your own design (your own body's molecules). The breakdown of polymers occurs by a process called **hydrolysis** (Figure 3.4b). Hydrolysis means to break (*lyse*) with water (*hydro*). Cells break bonds between monomers by adding water to them, a process that is essentially the reverse of a dehydration reaction. Imagine disassembling a long train by throwing water at the junctions between cars. Each time you add water, one more car or set of cars is broken free. You learned in the Biology and Society section about one real-world example of a hydrolysis reaction: the breakdown of lactose into its monomers by the enzyme lactase. ☑

☑ CHECKPOINT

1. Chemical reactions that build polymers from _____ are called _____ reactions because they release a molecule of water.
2. The reverse type of reaction, one that breaks larger molecules down into smaller molecules, is called _____.

Answers: 1. monomers; dehydration 2. hydrolysis

▼ Figure 3.4 **Synthesis and breakdown of polymers.** For simplicity, the only atoms shown in these diagrams are hydrogens and hydroxyl groups (—OH) in strategic locations.

(a) Building a polymer chain. A polymer grows in length when an incoming monomer and the monomer at the end of the polymer each contribute atoms to form a water molecule. The monomers replace the lost covalent bonds with a bond between each other.

(b) Breaking a polymer chain. Hydrolysis reverses the process by adding a water molecule, which breaks the bond between two monomers, creating two smaller molecules from one bigger one.

Large Biological Molecules

There are four categories of large, important biological molecules found in all living creatures: carbohydrates, lipids, proteins, and nucleic acids. For each category, we'll explore the structure and function of these large molecules by first learning about the smaller molecules used to build them.

Carbohydrates

Carbohydrates, or "carbs," are a class of molecules that includes sugars and polymers of sugars. Some examples are the small sugar molecules dissolved in soft drinks and the long starch molecules in spaghetti and bread. In animals, carbohydrates are a primary source of dietary energy and raw material for manufacturing other kinds of organic compounds; in plants, they serve as a building material for much of the plant body.

Monosaccharides

Simple sugars, or **monosaccharides** (from the Greek *mono*, single, and *sacchar*, sugar), are the monomers of carbohydrates; they cannot be broken down into smaller sugars. Common examples are glucose, found in soft drinks, and fructose, found in fruit. Both of these simple sugars are also in honey (Figure 3.5). The molecular formula for glucose is $C_6H_{12}O_6$. Fructose has the same formula, but its atoms are arranged differently. Glucose and fructose are examples of **isomers**, molecules that have the same molecular formula but different structures. Isomers are like anagrams—words that contain the same letters in a different order, such as *heart* and *earth*. Because molecular shape is so important, seemingly minor differences in the arrangement of atoms give isomers different properties, such as how they react with other molecules. In this case, the rearrangement of functional groups makes fructose taste much sweeter than glucose.

It is convenient to draw sugars as if their carbon skeletons were linear. When dissolved in water, however, many monosaccharides form rings when one end of the molecule forms a bond with another part of the molecule (Figure 3.6). You'll notice this ring shape in the depiction of the structure of many carbohydrates in this chapter.

Monosaccharides, particularly glucose, are the main fuel molecules for cellular work. Like an automobile engine consuming gasoline, your cells break down glucose molecules and extract their stored energy, giving off carbon dioxide as "exhaust." The rapid conversion of glucose to cellular energy is why a solution of glucose dissolved in water (often called dextrose) is given as an IV to sick or injured patients; the glucose provides an immediate energy source to tissues in need of repair. ✓

► Figure 3.5
Monosaccharides (simple sugars). Glucose and fructose, both of which are found in honey, are isomers, molecules with the same atoms arranged differently.

Glucose
$C_6H_{12}O_6$

Fructose
$C_6H_{12}O_6$

Isomers
(same formula, different arrangements)

▼ Figure 3.6 **The ring structure of glucose.**

(a) Linear and ring structures. The carbon atoms are numbered so you can relate the linear and ring versions of the molecule. As the double arrows indicate, ring formation is a reversible process, but at any instant in an aqueous solution, most glucose molecules are rings.

(b) Abbreviated ring structure. In this book, we'll use this abbreviated ring symbol for glucose. Each unmarked corner represents a carbon and its attached atoms.

Disaccharides

A **disaccharide**, or double sugar, is constructed from two monosaccharides by a dehydration reaction. The disaccharide lactose, sometimes called "milk sugar," is made from the monosaccharides glucose and galactose (Figure 3.7). Another common disaccharide is maltose, naturally found in germinating seeds. It is used in making beer, malt whiskey and liquor, malted milk shakes, and malted milk ball candy. A molecule of maltose consists of two glucose monomers joined together.

The most common disaccharide is sucrose (table sugar), which consists of a glucose monomer linked to a fructose monomer. Sucrose is the main carbohydrate in plant sap, and it nourishes all the parts of the plant. Sugar manufacturers extract sucrose from the stems of sugarcane or (much more often in the United States) the roots of sugar beets. Another common sweetener is high-fructose corn syrup (HFCS), made through a commercial process that uses an enzyme to convert natural glucose in corn syrup to the much sweeter fructose. HFCS is a clear, goopy liquid containing about 55% fructose; it is much cheaper than sucrose and easier to mix into drinks and processed foods. If you read the label on a soft drink, you're likely to find that high-fructose corn syrup is one of the first ingredients listed (Figure 3.8).

The average American consumes about 45 kilograms (kg)—a whopping 100 pounds—of sweeteners per year, mainly in the form of sucrose and HFCS. This national "sweet tooth" persists in spite of our growing awareness about how sugar can negatively affect our health. Sugar is a major cause of tooth decay, and overconsumption increases the risk of developing diabetes and heart disease. Moreover, high sugar consumption tends to replace eating more varied and nutritious foods. The description of sugars as "empty calories" is accurate in the sense that most sweeteners contain only negligible

If you drink coffee, odds are good that you spooned beets into your cup today—in the form of table sugar.

▼ Figure 3.7 **Disaccharide (double sugar) formation.** To form a disaccharide, two simple sugars are joined by a dehydration reaction, in this case forming a bond between monomers of glucose and galactose to make the double sugar lactose.

Glucose   Galactose

Lactose

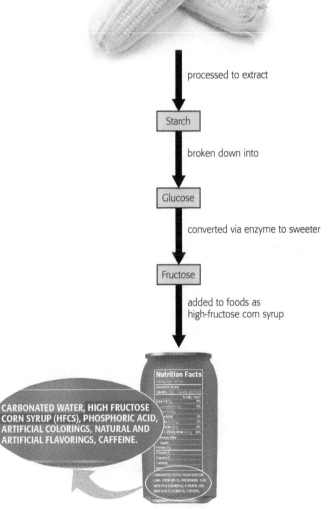

◄ Figure 3.8 **High-fructose corn syrup.** Many processed foods include high-fructose corn syrup, an artificial sweetener made by chemically treating sugars extracted from corn.

processed to extract

Starch

broken down into

Glucose

converted via enzyme to sweeter

Fructose

added to foods as high-fructose corn syrup

CARBONATED WATER, HIGH FRUCTOSE CORN SYRUP (HFCS), PHOSPHORIC ACID, ARTIFICIAL COLORINGS, NATURAL AND ARTIFICIAL FLAVORINGS, CAFFEINE.

amounts of nutrients other than carbohydrates. For good health, we also require proteins, fats, vitamins, and minerals. And we need to include substantial amounts of complex carbohydrates—that is, polysaccharides—in our diet. Let's examine these macromolecules next. ☑

Polysaccharides

Complex carbohydrates, or **polysaccharides**, are long chains of sugars—polymers of monosaccharides. One familiar example is starch, a storage polysaccharide found in plants. **Starch** consists of long strings of glucose monomers (Figure 3.9a). Plant cells store starch, providing a sugar stockpile that can be tapped when needed. Potatoes and grains, such as wheat, corn, and rice, are the major sources of starch in our diet. Animals can digest starch because enzymes within their digestive systems break the bonds between glucose monomers through hydrolysis reactions.

Animals store excess glucose in the form of a polysaccharide called **glycogen**. Like starch, glycogen is a polymer of glucose monomers, but glycogen is more extensively branched (Figure 3.9b). Most of your glycogen is stored in liver and muscle cells, which break down the glycogen to release glucose when you need energy. This is why some athletes "carbo-load," consuming large amounts of starchy foods the night before an athletic event. The

A long-distance runner who carbo-loads the night before a race is banking glycogen to be used the next day.

starch is converted to glycogen, which is then available for rapid use during physical activity the next day.

Cellulose, the most abundant organic compound on Earth, forms cable-like fibrils in the tough walls that enclose plant cells and is a major component of wood and other structural components of plants (Figure 3.9c). We take advantage of that structural strength when we use lumber as a building material. Cellulose is also a polymer of glucose, but its glucose monomers are linked together in a unique way. Unlike the glucose linkages in starch and glycogen, those in cellulose cannot be broken by any enzyme produced by animals. Grazing animals and wood-eating insects such as termites are able to derive nutrition from cellulose because microorganisms inhabiting their digestive tracts break it down. The cellulose in plant foods that you eat, commonly known as dietary fiber (your grandma might call it "roughage") passes through your digestive tract unchanged. Because it remains undigested, fiber does not provide nutrients, but it does help keep your digestive system healthy. The passage of cellulose stimulates cells lining the digestive tract to secrete mucus, which allows food to pass smoothly. The health benefits of dietary fiber include lowering the risk of heart disease, diabetes, and gastrointestinal disease. However, most Americans do not get the recommended levels of fiber in their diet. Foods rich in fiber include fruits and vegetables, whole grains, bran, and beans.

▼ Figure 3.9 **Three common polysaccharides.**

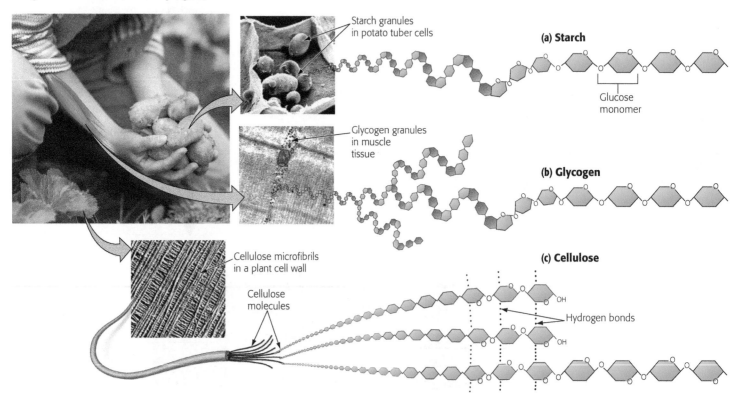

Starch granules in potato tuber cells

(a) Starch

Glucose monomer

Glycogen granules in muscle tissue

(b) Glycogen

Cellulose microfibrils in a plant cell wall

Cellulose molecules

(c) Cellulose

Hydrogen bonds

Lipids

Almost all carbohydrates are **hydrophilic** ("water-loving") molecules that dissolve readily in water. In contrast, **lipids** are **hydrophobic** ("water-fearing"); they do not mix with water. You've probably seen this chemical behavior when you combine oil and vinegar: The oil, which is a type of lipid, separates from the vinegar, which is mostly water (**Figure 3.10**). If you shake vigorously, you can force a temporary mixture long enough to douse your salad, but what remains in the bottle will quickly separate. Lipids also differ from carbohydrates, proteins, and nucleic acids in that they are neither huge macromolecules nor are they necessarily polymers built from repeating monomers. Lipids are a diverse group of molecules made from different molecular building blocks. In this section, we'll look at two types of lipids: fats and steroids.

Fats

A typical **fat** consists of a glycerol molecule joined with three fatty acid molecules by dehydration reactions (**Figure 3.11a**). The resulting fat molecule is called a **triglyceride** (**Figure 3.11b**), a term you may hear in the results of a blood test. A fatty acid is a long molecule that stores a lot of energy. A pound of fat packs more than twice as much energy as a pound of carbohydrate. The downside to this energy efficiency in fats is that it is very difficult for a person trying to lose weight to "burn off" excess fat. We stock these long-term food stores in specialized reservoirs called adipose cells, which swell and shrink when we deposit and withdraw fat from them. This adipose tissue, or body fat, not only stores energy but also cushions vital organs and insulates us, helping maintain a constant, warm body temperature.

Notice in Figure 3.11b that the bottom fatty acid bends where there is a double bond in the carbon skeleton. That fatty acid is **unsaturated** because it has fewer than the maximum number of hydrogens at the double bond. The other two fatty acids in the fat molecule lack double bonds in their tails. Those fatty acids are **saturated**, meaning that they contain the maximum number of hydrogen atoms, giving them a straight shape. A saturated fat is one with all three of its fatty acid tails saturated. If one or more of the fatty acids is unsaturated, then it's an unsaturated fat, like the one in Figure 3.11b. A polyunsaturated fat has several double bonds within its fatty acids.

Most animal fats, such as lard and butter, have a relatively high proportion of saturated fatty acids. The linear shape of saturated fatty acids allows these molecules to stack easily (like bricks in a wall), so saturated

◄ Figure 3.10 **The separation of hydrophobic (oil) and hydrophilic (vinegar) components in salad dressing.**

Oil (hydrophobic)

Vinegar (hydrophilic)

▼ Figure 3.11 **The synthesis and structure of a triglyceride molecule.**

Fatty acid

Glycerol

(a) A dehydration reaction linking a fatty acid to glycerol

(b) A fat molecule with a glycerol "head" and three energy-rich hydrocarbon fatty acid "tails"

43

fats tend to be solid at room temperature (Figure 3.12). Diets rich in saturated fats may contribute to cardiovascular disease by promoting atherosclerosis. In this condition, lipid-containing deposits called plaque build up along the inside walls of blood vessels, reducing blood flow and increasing risk of heart attacks and strokes.

Plant and fish fats are relatively high in unsaturated fatty acids. The bent shape of unsaturated fatty acids makes them less likely to form solids (imagine trying to build a wall using bent bricks!). Most unsaturated fats are liquid at room temperature. Fats that are primarily unsaturated include vegetable oils (such as corn and canola oil) and fish oils (such as cod liver oil).

Although plant oils tend to be low in saturated fat, tropical plant fats are an exception. Cocoa butter, a main ingredient in chocolate, contains a mix of saturated and unsaturated fat that gives chocolate a melting point near body temperature. Thus, chocolate stays solid at room temperature but melts in your mouth, creating a pleasing "mouth feel" that is one of the reasons chocolate is so appealing.

Sometimes a food manufacturer wants to use a vegetable oil but needs the food product to be solid, as with margarine or peanut butter. To achieve the desired texture, the manufacturer can convert unsaturated fats to saturated fats by adding hydrogen, a process called **hydrogenation**. Unfortunately, hydrogenation can also create **trans fats**, a type of unsaturated fat that is particularly bad for your health. Since 2006, the U.S. Food and Drug Administration has required that trans fats be listed on nutrition labels. But even if a label on a hydrogenated product says 0 grams (g) of trans fats per serving, the product might actually have up to 0.5 g per serving (which legally can be rounded down to 0). Furthermore, trans fats are often found in fast foods, such as French fries and battered-and-fried foods, that may not have labels. Due to the increased awareness of their unhealthy nature, trans fats are becoming less common as food manufacturers substitute other forms of fat. Indeed, trans fats may soon be a dietary thing of the past. New York City banned restaurants from serving trans fats in 2006, and California followed suit in 2010. The countries of Iceland, Switzerland, and Denmark have effectively removed trans fats from the food supply. In the United States, the Food and Drug Administration has ruled that trans fats are not "generally regarded as safe," a designation that will likely result in a phasing out of trans fats from the American food supply.

Although trans fats should generally be avoided and saturated fats limited, it is not true that *all* fats are unhealthy. In fact, some fats perform important functions within the body and are beneficial and even essential to a healthy diet. For example, fats containing omega-3 fatty acids have been shown to reduce the risk of heart disease and relieve the symptoms of arthritis and inflammatory bowel disease. Some sources of these beneficial fats are nuts and oily fish such as salmon. ✓

> Chocolate melts in your mouth (and in your hands) because of the structure of cocoa butter, which is high in saturated fats.

✓ **CHECKPOINT**

What are unsaturated fats? What kinds of unsaturated fat are particularly unhealthy? What kinds of unsaturated fat are most healthful?

Answer: fats with less than the maximum number of hydrogens because of double bonds between some carbons; trans fats; fats containing omega-3 fatty acids

▼ Figure 3.12 **Types of fats.**

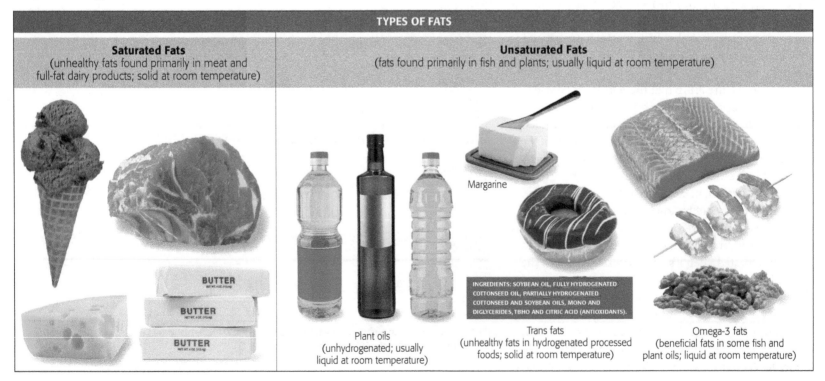

TYPES OF FATS	
Saturated Fats (unhealthy fats found primarily in meat and full-fat dairy products; solid at room temperature)	**Unsaturated Fats** (fats found primarily in fish and plants; usually liquid at room temperature)

INGREDIENTS: SOYBEAN OIL, FULLY HYDROGENATED COTTONSEED OIL, PARTIALLY HYDROGENATED COTTONSEED AND SOYBEAN OILS, MONO AND DIGLYCERIDES, TBHO AND CITRIC ACID (ANTIOXIDANTS).

Margarine

Plant oils (unhydrogenated; usually liquid at room temperature)

Trans fats (unhealthy fats in hydrogenated processed foods; solid at room temperature)

Omega-3 fats (beneficial fats in some fish and plant oils; liquid at room temperature)

Steroids

Steroids are lipids that are very different from fats in structure and function. All steroids have a carbon skeleton with four fused rings. Different steroids vary in the functional groups attached to this set of rings, and these chemical variations affect their function. One common steroid is cholesterol, which has a bad reputation because of its association with cardiovascular disease. However, cholesterol is a key component of the membranes that surround your cells. It is also the "base steroid" from which your body produces other steroids, such as the hormones estrogen and testosterone (Figure 3.13), which are responsible for the development of female and male sex characteristics, respectively.

Anabolic steroids are synthetic variants of testosterone. In human males, testosterone causes buildup of muscle and bone mass during puberty and maintains masculine traits throughout life. Because anabolic steroids resemble testosterone, they mimic some of its effects. Anabolic steroids are prescribed to treat diseases that cause muscle wasting, such as cancer and AIDS. However, individuals sometimes abuse anabolic steroids to build up their muscles quickly. In recent years, many famous athletes have admitted using chemically modified ("designer") performance-enhancing anabolic steroids (Figure 3.14). Such revelations have raised questions about the validity of home run records and other athletic accomplishments.

Using anabolic steroids is indeed a fast way to increase body size beyond what hard work can produce. But at what cost? Steroid abuse may cause violent mood swings ("roid rage"), depression, liver damage, high cholesterol, shrunken testicles, reduced sex drive, and infertility. Symptoms related to sexuality occur because artificial anabolic steroids often cause the body to reduce its output of natural sex hormones. Most athletic organizations ban the use of anabolic steroids because of their many potential health hazards coupled with the unfairness of an artificial advantage. ☑

Cholesterol

can be converted by the body to

Testosterone

A type of estrogen

▲ Figure 3.13 **Examples of steroids.** The molecular structures of the steroids shown here are abbreviated by omitting all the atoms that make up the rings. The subtle difference between testosterone and estrogen influences the development of the anatomical and physiological differences between male and female mammals, including lions and humans. This example illustrates the importance of molecular structure to function.

Alex Rodriguez

Mark McGwire

Floyd Landis

Ben Johnson

► Figure 3.14 **Steroids and the modern athlete.** Each of the athletes shown here—baseball players Alex Rodriguez and Mark McGwire, Tour de France cyclist Floyd Landis, and Olympic sprinter Ben Johnson—has admitted to steroid use.

☑ **CHECKPOINT**

What steroid acts as the molecular building block of the human steroid hormones?

Answer: cholesterol

Proteins

A **protein** is a polymer of amino acid monomers. Proteins account for more than 50% of the dry weight of most cells, and they are instrumental in almost everything cells do (Figure 3.15). Proteins are the "worker bees" of your body: Chances are, if something is getting done, there is a protein doing it. Your body has tens of thousands of different kinds of proteins, each with a unique three-dimensional shape corresponding to a specific function. In fact, proteins are the most structurally sophisticated molecules in your body.

The Monomers of Proteins: Amino Acids

All proteins are made by stringing together a common set of 20 kinds of amino acids. Every **amino acid** consists of a central carbon atom bonded to four covalent partners. Three of those attachments are common to all 20 amino acids: a carboxyl group (—COOH), an amino group (—NH₂), and a hydrogen atom. The variable component of amino acids is called the side chain (or R group, for radical group); it is attached to the fourth bond of the central carbon (Figure 3.16a). Each type of amino acid has a unique side chain which gives that amino acid its special chemical properties (Figure 3.16b). Some amino acids have very simple side chains; the amino acid glycine, for example, has a single hydrogen as its side chain. Other amino acids have more complex side chains, some with branches or rings within them. ☑

☑ **CHECKPOINT**

1. Which of the following is *not* made of protein: hair, muscle, cellulose, or enzymes?
2. What are the monomers of all proteins? What is the one part of an amino acid that varies?

Answers: 1. Cellulose is a carbohydrate. 2. amino acids; the side chain

▼ Figure 3.16 **Amino acids.** All amino acids share common functional groups but vary in their side chains.

(a) The general structure of an amino acid.

Hydrophobic side chain

Hydrophilic side chain

Leucine   **Serine**

(b) Examples of amino acids with hydrophobic and hydrophilic side chains. The side chain of the amino acid leucine is hydrophobic. In contrast, the side chain of the amino acid serine has a hydroxyl group (–OH), which is hydrophilic.

▼ Figure 3.15 **Some of the varied roles played by proteins.**

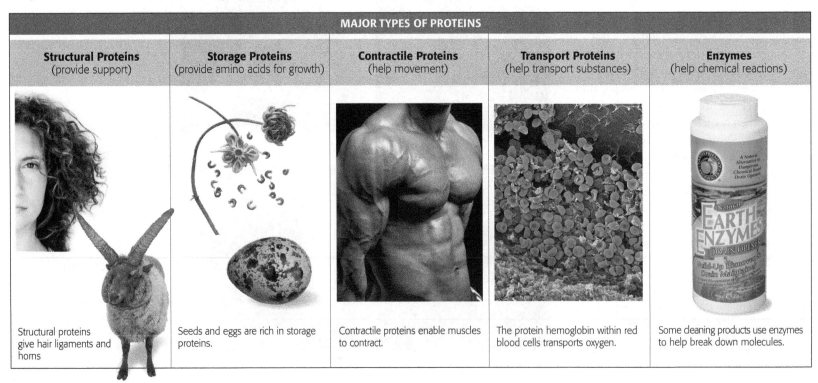

MAJOR TYPES OF PROTEINS				
Structural Proteins (provide support)	**Storage Proteins** (provide amino acids for growth)	**Contractile Proteins** (help movement)	**Transport Proteins** (help transport substances)	**Enzymes** (help chemical reactions)
Structural proteins give hair ligaments and horns	Seeds and eggs are rich in storage proteins.	Contractile proteins enable muscles to contract.	The protein hemoglobin within red blood cells transports oxygen.	Some cleaning products use enzymes to help break down molecules.

Structure/Function   Protein Shape

Cells link amino acid monomers together by—can you guess?—dehydration reactions. The bond that joins adjacent amino acids is called a **peptide bond** (Figure 3.17). The resulting long chain of amino acids is called a **polypeptide**. A functional protein is one or more polypeptide chains precisely twisted, folded, and coiled into a molecule of unique shape. The difference between a polypeptide and a protein can be likened to the relationship between a long strand of yarn and a sweater. To be functional, the long fiber (the yarn) must be precisely knit into a specific shape (the sweater).

How is it possible to make the huge variety of proteins found in your body from just 20 kinds of amino acids? The answer is arrangement. You know that you can make many different English words by varying the sequence of just 26 letters. Though the protein alphabet is slightly smaller (just 20 "letters"), the "words" are much longer, with a typical polypeptide being hundreds or thousands of amino acids in length. Just as each word is constructed from a unique succession of letters, each protein has a unique linear sequence of amino acids.

The amino acid sequence of each polypeptide determines the three-dimensional structure of the protein. And it is a protein's three-dimensional structure that enables the molecule to carry out its specific function. Nearly all proteins work by recognizing and binding to some other molecule. For example, the specific shape of lactase enables it to recognize and attach to lactose, its molecular target. For all proteins, structure and function are interrelated: What a protein does is a consequence of its shape. The twists and turns of the protein in Figure 3.18 may appear haphazard, but they represent this protein's specific three-dimensional shape, and without that exact shape, the protein could not do its job.

▼ Figure 3.18 **The structure of a protein.** The chain below, drawn in serpentine fashion so that it fits on the page, shows the amino acid sequence of a polypeptide found in lysozyme, an enzyme in your tears and sweat that helps prevent bacterial infections. The names of the amino acids are given as their three-letter abbreviations; for example, the amino acid alanine is abbreviated "ala." This amino acid sequence folds into a protein of specific shape, shown at bottom in two computer-generated representations. Without this specific shape, the protein could not perform its function.

One amino acid (alanine)

The amino acid sequence of lysozyme

Here you can see how the polypeptide folds into a compact shape.

Carboxyl group + Amino group

Side chain   Amino acid   Side chain   Amino acid

Dehydration reaction H_2O

Peptide bond

▲ Figure 3.17 **Joining amino acids.** A dehydration reaction links adjacent amino acids by a peptide bond.

This model allows you to see the details of the protein's structure.

Changing a single letter can drastically affect the meaning of a word—"tasty" versus "nasty," for instance. Similarly, even a slight change in the amino acid sequence can affect a protein's ability to function. For example, the substitution of one amino acid for another at a particular position in hemoglobin, the blood protein that carries oxygen, causes sickle-cell disease, an inherited blood disorder (Figure 3.19). Even though 145 out of the 146 amino acids in hemoglobin are correct, that one change is enough to cause the protein to fold into a different shape, which alters its function, which in turn causes disease. Misfolded proteins are associated with

several severe brain disorders. For example, the diseases shown in Figure 3.20 are all caused by prions, misfolded versions of normal brain proteins. Prions can infiltrate the brain, converting normally folded proteins into the abnormal shape. Clustering of the misfolded proteins eventually disrupts brain function.

In addition to dependence on the amino acid sequence, a protein's shape is sensitive to the environment. An unfavorable change in temperature, pH, or some other factor can cause a protein to unravel. If you cook an egg, the transformation of the egg white from clear to opaque is caused by proteins in the egg white coming apart. One of the reasons why extremely high fevers are so dangerous is that some proteins in the body lose their shape above 104°F.

What determines a protein's amino acid sequence? The amino acid sequence of each polypeptide chain is specified by a gene. And this relationship between genes and proteins brings us to this chapter's last category of large biological molecules: nucleic acids. ☑

☑ CHECKPOINT

How can changing an amino acid alter the function of a protein?

Answer: Changing an amino acid may alter the shape of the protein, which changes its function.

Amino acid sequence of normal hemoglobin

Normal hemoglobin peptide

Normal red blood cell

SEM 500×

(a) Normal hemoglobin. Red blood cells of humans are normally disk-shaped. Each cell contains millions of molecules of the protein hemoglobin, which transports oxygen from the lungs to other organs of the body.

Amino acid sequence of sickle-cell hemoglobin

Sickle-cell hemoglobin polypeptide

Sickled red blood cell

SEM 500×

(b) Sickle-cell hemoglobin. A slight change in the amino acid sequence of hemoglobin causes sickle-cell disease. The inherited substitution of one amino acid—valine in place of the amino acid glutamic acid—occurs at the 6th position of the polymer. Such abnormal hemoglobin molecules tend to crystallize, deforming some of the cells into a sickle shape. Someone with the disease suffers from dangerous episodes when the angular cells clog tiny blood vessels, impeding blood flow.

► Figure 3.19 **A single amino acid substitution in a protein causes sickle-cell disease.**

► Figure 3.20 **How an improperly folded protein can lead to brain disease.** Here, you can see how prion proteins bring about the destruction of brain tissue, as well as several examples (right) of the resulting disease.

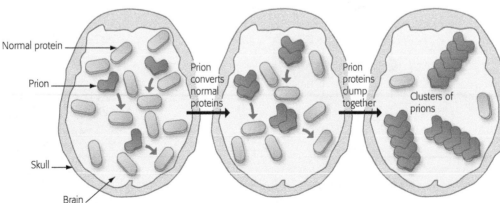

Normal protein

Prion

Prion converts normal proteins

Prion proteins clump together

Clusters of prions

Skull

Brain

Prions in cattle cause mad cow disease, formally called bovine spongiform encephalopathy (BSE).

First described among one tribe in Papua New Guinea in the 1950s, kuru is a human brain disease transmitted by cannibalistic ingestion of an infected person's brain, which transfers the prion to a new host.

Prions cause fatal weight loss in several animals, including deer, elk, and moose.

Nucleic Acids

Nucleic acids are macromolecules that store information and provide the instructions for building proteins. The name *nucleic* comes from the fact that DNA is found in the nuclei of eukaryotic cells. There are actually two types of nucleic acids: **DNA** (which stands for deoxyribonucleic acid) and **RNA** (for ribonucleic acid). The genetic material that humans and all other organisms inherit from their parents consists of giant molecules of DNA. The DNA resides in the cell as one or more very long fibers called chromosomes. A **gene** is a unit of inheritance encoded in a specific stretch of DNA that programs the amino acid sequence of a polypeptide. Those programmed instructions, however, are written in a chemical code that must be translated from "nucleic acid language" to "protein language" (Figure 3.21). A cell's RNA molecules help make this translation (see Chapter 10).

Nucleic acids are polymers made from monomers called **nucleotides** (Figure 3.22). Each nucleotide contains three parts. At the center of each nucleotide is a five-carbon sugar (blue in the figure), deoxyribose in DNA and ribose in RNA. Attached to the sugar is a negatively charged phosphate group (yellow) containing a phosphorus atom bonded to oxygen atoms (PO_4^-). Also attached to the sugar is a nitrogen-containing base (green) made of one or two rings. The sugar and phosphate are the same in all nucleotides; only the base varies. Each DNA nucleotide has one of four possible nitrogenous bases: adenine (abbreviated A), guanine (G), cytosine (C), or thymine (T) (Figure 3.23). Thus, all genetic information is written in a four-letter alphabet.

▼ Figure 3.22 **A DNA nucleotide.** A DNA nucleotide monomer consists of three parts: a sugar (deoxyribose), a phosphate, and a nitrogenous (nitrogen-containing) base.

(a) Atomic structure

(b) Symbol used in this book

▼ Figure 3.23 **The nitrogenous bases of DNA.** Notice that adenine and guanine have double-ring structures. Thymine and cytosine have single-ring structures.

Adenine (A)

Guanine (G)

Thymine (T)

Cytosine (C)

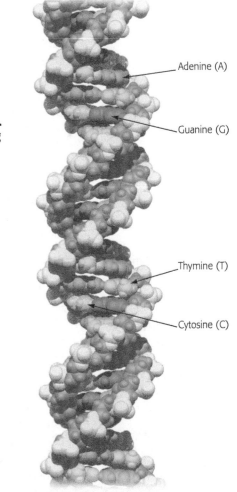

Space-filling model of DNA (showing the four bases in four different colors)

▼ Figure 3.21 **Building a protein.** Within the cell, a gene (a segment of DNA) provides the directions to build a molecule of RNA, which can then be translated into a protein.

Dehydration reactions link nucleotide monomers into long chains called polynucleotides (Figure 3.24a). In a polynucleotide, nucleotides are joined by covalent bonds between the sugar of one nucleotide and the phosphate of the next. This bonding results in a **sugar-phosphate backbone**, a repeating pattern of sugar-phosphate-sugar-phosphate, with the bases (A, T, C, or G) hanging off the backbone like appendages. With different combinations of the four bases, the number of possible polynucleotide sequences is vast. One long polynucleotide may contain many genes, each a specific series of hundreds or thousands of nucleotides. This sequence is a code that provides instructions for building a specific polypeptide from amino acids.

> The structure of your DNA is nearly indistinguishable from the DNA of a mosquito or an elephant: The differences in animal species result from the way nucleotides are arranged.

A molecule of cellular DNA is double-stranded, with two polynucleotide strands coiled around each other to form a **double helix** (Figure 3.24b). Think of a candy cane or a barber pole that has two intertwined spirals, one red and one white. In the central core of the helix (corresponding to the interior of the candy cane), the bases along one DNA strand hydrogen-bond to bases along the other strand. The bonds are individually weak, but collectively they zip the two strands together into a very stable double helix formation. To understand how DNA strands are bonded, think of Velcro, in which two strips are held together by hook-and-loop bonds, each of which is weak but which collectively form a tight grip. Because of the way the functional groups hang off the bases, the base pairing in a DNA double helix is specific: The base A can pair only with T, and G can pair only with C. Thus, if you know the sequence of bases along one DNA strand, you also know the sequence along the complementary strand in the double helix. This unique base pairing is the basis of DNA's ability to act as the molecule of inheritance (as discussed in Chapter 10).

There are many similarities between DNA and RNA. Both are polymers of nucleotides, for example, and both are made of nucleotides consisting of a sugar, a phosphate, and a base. But there are three important differences. (1) As its name *ribonucleic acid* denotes, its sugar is ribose rather than deoxyribose. (2) Instead of the base thymine, RNA has a similar but distinct base called uracil (U) (Figure 3.25). Except for the presence of ribose and uracil, an RNA polynucleotide chain is identical to a DNA polynucleotide chain. (3) RNA is usually found in living cells in single-stranded form, whereas DNA usually exists as a double helix.

Now that we've examined the structure of nucleic acids, we'll look at how a change in nucleotide sequence can affect protein production. To illustrate this point, we'll return to a familiar condition. ☑

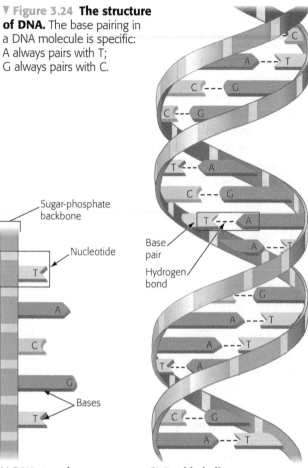

▼ Figure 3.24 **The structure of DNA.** The base pairing in a DNA molecule is specific: A always pairs with T; G always pairs with C.

Sugar-phosphate backbone

Nucleotide

Bases

Base pair

Hydrogen bond

(a) DNA strand
(polynucleotide)

(b) Double helix
(two polynucleotide strands)

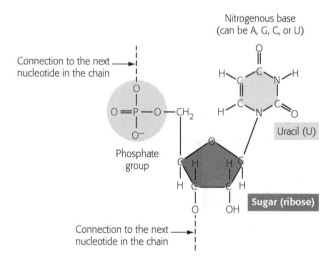

▼ Figure 3.25 **An RNA nucleotide.** Notice that this RNA nucleotide differs from the DNA nucleotide in Figure 3.22 in two ways: The RNA sugar is ribose rather than deoxyribose, and the base is uracil (U) instead of thymine (T). The other three kinds of RNA nucleotides have the bases A, C, and G, as in DNA.

Nitrogenous base (can be A, G, C, or U)

Connection to the next nucleotide in the chain

Phosphate group

Uracil (U)

Sugar (ribose)

Connection to the next nucleotide in the chain

Does Lactose Intolerance Have a Genetic Basis?

The enzyme lactase, like all proteins, is encoded by a DNA gene. A reasonable hypothesis is that lactose-intolerant people have a defect in their lactase gene. However, this hypothesis is not supported by **observation**. Even though lactose intolerance runs in families, most lactose-intolerant people have a normal version of the lactase gene. This raises the following **question**: What is the genetic basis for lactose intolerance?

A group of Finnish and American scientists proposed the **hypothesis** that lactose intolerance can be correlated with a single nucleotide at a particular site within one chromosome. They made the **prediction** that this site would be near, though not within, the lactase gene. In their **experiment**, they examined the genes of 196 lactose-intolerant people from nine Finnish families. Their **results** showed a 100% correlation between lactose intolerance and a nucleotide at a site approximately

Human cell (DNA in 46 chromosomes)
Chromosome 2 (one DNA molecule)
Section of chromosome 2
DNA
Lactase gene
14,000 nucleotides
C at this site causes lactose intolerance
T at this site causes lactose tolerance

◄ **Figure 3.26 A genetic cause of lactose intolerance.** A research study showed a correlation between lactose intolerance and a nucleotide at a specific location on one chromosome.

14,000 nucleotides away from the lactase gene—a relatively short distance in terms of the whole chromosome (Figure 3.26). Other experiments showed that depending on the nucleotide sequence within this region of the DNA molecule, the action of the lactase gene is ramped up or down (in a way that likely involves producing a regulatory protein that interacts with the nucleotides near the lactase gene). This study shows how a small change in a DNA nucleotide sequence can have a major effect on the production of a protein and the well-being of an organism.

The Evolution of Lactose Intolerance in Humans

As you'll recall from the Biology and Society section, most people in the world are lactose intolerant as adults and thus do not easily digest the milk sugar lactose. In fact, lactose intolerance is found in 80% of African Americans and Native Americans and 90% of Asian Americans but only in about 10% of Americans of northern European descent. And as discussed in the Process of Science section, lactose intolerance appears to have a genetic basis.

From an evolutionary perspective, it is reasonable to infer that lactose intolerance is rare among northern Europeans because the ability to tolerate lactose offered a survival advantage to their ancestors. In northern Europe's relatively cold climate, only one crop harvest a year is possible. Therefore, herd animals were a main source of food for early humans in that region. Cattle were first domesticated in northern Europe about 9,000 years ago (Figure 3.27). With milk and other dairy products at hand year-round, natural selection would have favored

anyone with a mutation that kept the lactase gene switched on beyond infanthood. In cultures where dairy products were not a staple in the diet, natural selection would not favor such a mutation.

Researchers wondered whether the genetic basis for lactose tolerance in northern Europeans might be present in other cultures that kept dairy herds. To find out, they compared the genetic makeup and lactose tolerance of 43 ethnic groups in East Africa. The researchers identified three other genetic changes that keep the lactase gene permanently active. These mutations appear to have occurred beginning around 7,000 years ago, about the time that archaeological evidence shows domestication of cattle in these African regions.

Genetic changes that confer a selective advantage, such as surviving cold winters or withstanding drought by drinking milk, spread rapidly in these early peoples. Whether or not you can digest milk is therefore an evolutionary record of the cultural history of your ancestors.

▲ **Figure 3.27 A prehistoric cave painting in Lascaux, France, of wild cattle.** The cow-like animal on the right is an auroch, the first species of domesticated cattle in Europe. Aurochs migrated from Asia about 250,000 years ago but became extinct in 1627.

Chapter Review

SUMMARY OF KEY CONCEPTS

Organic Compounds

Carbon Chemistry

Carbon atoms can form large, complex, diverse molecules by bonding to four potential partners, including other carbon atoms. In addition to variations in the size and shape of carbon skeletons, organic compounds vary in the presence and locations of different functional groups.

Giant Molecules from Smaller Building Blocks

Large Biological Molecules

Large Biological Molecules	Functions	Components	Examples
Carbohydrates	Dietary energy; storage; plant structure	Monosaccharide	Monosaccharides: glucose, fructose; disaccharides: lactose, sucrose; polysaccharides: starch, cellulose
Lipids	Long-term energy storage (fats); hormones (steroids)	Components of a triglyceride	Fats (triglycerides); steroids (testosterone, estrogen)
Proteins	Enzymes, structure, storage, contraction, transport, etc.	Amino acid	Lactase (an enzyme); hemoglobin (a transport protein)
Nucleic acids	Information storage	Nucleotide	DNA, RNA

Carbohydrates

Simple sugars (monosaccharides) provide cells with energy and building materials. Double sugars (disaccharides), such as sucrose, consist of two monosaccharides joined by a dehydration reaction. Polysaccharides are long polymers of sugar monomers. Starch in plants and glycogen in animals are storage polysaccharides. The cellulose of plant cell walls, which is indigestible by animals, is an example of a structural polysaccharide.

Lipids

Lipids are hydrophobic. Fats, a type of lipid, are the major form of long-term energy storage in animals. A molecule of fat, or triglyceride, consists of three fatty acids joined by dehydration reactions to a molecule of glycerol. Most animal fats are saturated, meaning that their fatty acids have the maximum number of hydrogens. Plant oils contain mostly unsaturated fats, having fewer hydrogens in the fatty acids because of double bonding in the carbon skeletons. Steroids, including cholesterol and the sex hormones, are also lipids.

Proteins

There are 20 types of amino acids, the monomers of proteins. They are linked by dehydration reactions to form polymers called polypeptides. A protein consists of one or more polypeptides folded into a specific three-dimensional shape. The shape of a protein determines its function. Changing the amino acid sequence of a polypeptide may alter the shape and therefore the function of the protein. Shape is sensitive to environment, and if a protein loses its shape because of an unfavorable environment, its function may also be lost.

Nucleic Acids

Nucleic acids include RNA and DNA. DNA takes the form of a double helix, two DNA strands (polymers of nucleotides) held together by hydrogen bonds between nucleotide components called bases. There are four kinds of DNA bases: adenine (A), guanine (G), thymine (T), and cytosine (C). A always pairs with T, and G always pairs with C. These base-pairing rules enable DNA to act as the molecule of inheritance. RNA has U (uracil) instead of T.

DNA double helix   **DNA strand**   **DNA nucleotide**

MasteringBiology®

For practice quizzes, BioFlix animations, MP3 tutorials, video tutors, and more study tools designed for this textbook, go to MasteringBiology®

SELF-QUIZ

1. One isomer of methamphetamine is the addictive illegal drug known as "crank." Another isomer is a medicine for sinus congestion. How can you explain the differing effects of the two isomers?

2. Monomers are joined together to form larger polymers through _____. Such a reaction releases a molecule of _____.

3. Polymers are broken down into the monomers that make them up through the chemical reaction called _____.

4. Which of the following terms includes all the others in the list?
   a. polysaccharide
   b. carbohydrate
   c. monosaccharide
   d. disaccharide

5. When two molecules of glucose ($C_6H_{12}O_6$) are joined together by a dehydration reaction, what are the formulas of the two products? (*Hint*: No atoms are gained or lost.)

6. One molecule of dietary fat is made by joining three molecules of _____ to one molecule of _____. What is the formal name of the resulting molecule?

7. Which of the following statements about saturated fats is true?
   a. Saturated fats contain one or more double bonds along the tails.
   b. Saturated fats contain the maximum number of hydrogens along the tails.
   c. Saturated fats make up the majority of most plant oils.
   d. Saturated fats are typically healthier for you than unsaturated fats.

8. Humans and other animals cannot digest wood because they
   a. cannot digest any carbohydrates.
   b. cannot chew it fine enough.
   c. lack the enzyme needed to break down cellulose.
   d. get no nutrients from it.

9. Explain how it could be possible to change an amino acid within a protein but not affect that protein's function.

10. Most proteins can easily dissolve in water. Knowing that, where within the overall three-dimensional shape of a protein would you most likely find hydrophobic amino acids?

11. A shortage of phosphorus in the soil would make it especially difficult for a plant to manufacture
    a. DNA.
    b. proteins.
    c. cellulose.
    d. fatty acids.

12. A glucose molecule is to _____ as a nucleotide is to a _____.

13. Name three similarities between DNA and RNA. Name three differences.

14. What is the structure of a gene? What is the function of a gene?

Answers to these questions can be found in Appendix: Self-Quiz Answers.

THE PROCESS OF SCIENCE

15. A food manufacturer is advertising a new cake mix as fat-free. Scientists at the Food and Drug Administration (FDA) are testing the product to see if it truly lacks fat. Hydrolysis of the cake mix yields glucose, fructose, glycerol, a number of amino acids, and several kinds of molecules with long chains. Further analysis shows that most of the chains have a carboxyl group at one end. What would you tell the food manufacturer if you were a spokesperson for the FDA?

16. Imagine that you have produced several versions of lactase, each of which differs from normal lactase by a single amino acid. Describe a test that could indirectly determine which of the versions significantly alters the three-dimensional shape of the protein.

17. **Interpreting Data** Below is a typical food label for one cookie. One gram of fat packs 9 Calories, and 1 gram of carbohydrates or protein packs 4 Calories. The top of the label shows that each cookie contains 140 Calories in total. What percentage of the Calories in this cookie are from fat, carbohydrates, and protein?

Nutrition Facts

Serving Size 1 Cookie (28 g /1 oz)
Servings Per Container 8

Amount Per Serving

Calories 140   Calories from Fat 60

	% Daily Value*
Total Fat 7g	11%
Saturated Fat 3g	15%
Trans Fat 0g	
Cholesterol 10mg	3%
Sodium 80mg	3%
Total Carbohydrate 18g	6%
Dietary Fiber 1g	4%
Sugars 10g	
Protein 2g	

BIOLOGY AND SOCIETY

18. Some amateur and professional athletes take anabolic steroids to help them build strength ("bulk up"). The health risks of this practice are extensively documented. Apart from these health issues, what is your opinion about the ethics of athletes using chemicals to enhance performance? Is this a form of cheating, or is it just part of the preparation required to stay competitive in a sport where anabolic steroids are commonly used? Defend your opinion.

19. Heart disease is the leading cause of death among people in the United States and other industrialized nations. Fast food is a major source of unhealthy fats that contribute significantly to heart disease. Imagine you're a juror sitting on a trial where a fast-food manufacturer is being sued for producing a harmful product. To what extent do you think manufacturers of unhealthy foods should be held responsible for the health consequences of their products? As a jury member, how would you vote?

20. Each year, industrial chemists develop and test thousands of new organic compounds for use as insecticides, fungicides, and weed killers. In what ways are these chemicals useful and important to us? In what ways can they be harmful? Is your general opinion of such chemicals positive or negative? What influences have shaped your feelings about these chemicals?

4 A Tour of the Cell

Mushrooms, ▶
amoebas, and you
are all made up of the
same kind of cells.

The caffeine that gives your cup
of tea a kick also protects tea plants
▼ from herbivores.

▲ Without the cytoskeleton, your cells would collapse in on themselves,
much like a house collapses when the infrastructure fails.

Humans Versus Bacteria BIOLOGY AND SOCIETY

Antibiotics: Drugs That Target Bacterial Cells

Antibiotics—drugs that disable or kill infectious bacteria—are a marvel of modern medicine. The first antibiotic to be discovered was penicillin in 1920. A revolution in human health rapidly followed. Fatality rates of many diseases (such as bacterial pneumonia and surgical infections) plummeted, saving millions of lives. In fact, human health care improved so quickly and so profoundly that some doctors in the early 1900s predicted the end of infectious diseases altogether. Alas, this did not come to pass (see the Evolution Connection section in Chapter 13 for a discussion of why infectious diseases were not so easily defeated).

The goal of antibiotic treatment is to knock out invading bacteria while doing no damage to the human host. So how does an antibiotic zero in on its target among trillions of human cells? Most antibiotics are so precise because they bind to structures found only in bacterial cells. For example, the common antibiotics erythromycin and streptomycin bind to the bacterial ribosome, a vital cellular structure responsible for the production of proteins. The ribosomes of humans are different enough from those of bacteria that the antibiotics bind only to bacterial ribosomes, leaving human ribosomes unaffected. Ciprofloxacin (commonly referred to as Cipro) is the antibiotic of choice to combat anthrax-causing bacteria. This drug targets an enzyme that bacteria need to maintain their chromosome structure. Your cells can survive just fine in the presence of Cipro because human chromosomes have a sufficiently different makeup than bacterial chromosomes. Other drugs, such as penicillin, ampicillin, and bacitracin, disrupt the synthesis of cell walls, a structure found in most bacteria that is absent from the cells of humans and other animals.

This discussion of how various antibiotics target bacteria underscores the main point of this chapter: To understand how life works—whether in bacteria or in your own body—you first need to learn about cells. On the scale of biological organization, cells occupy a special place: They are the simplest objects that can be alive. Nothing smaller than a cell is capable of displaying all of life's properties. In this chapter, we'll explore the microscopic structure and function of cells. Along the way, we'll further consider how the ongoing battle between humans and infectious bacteria is affected by the cellular structures present on both sides.

Colorized TEM 3,200×

Two kinds of cells. In this micrograph, *Helicobacter pylori* bacteria (green) can be seen mingling with cells within the human stomach. This species of bacteria causes stomach ulcers.

The Microscopic World of Cells

Each cell in your body is a miniature marvel. If the world's most sophisticated jumbo jet was reduced to microscopic size, its intricacy would pale next to a living cell.

Organisms are either single-celled, such as most prokaryotes and protists, or multicelled, such as plants, animals, and most fungi. Your own body is a cooperative society of trillions of cells of many specialized types. As you read this page, muscle cells allow you to scan your eye across the words, while sensory cells in your eye gather information and send it to brain cells, which interpret the words. Everything you do—every action and every thought—is possible because of processes that occur at the cellular level.

Figure 4.1 shows the size range of cells compared with objects both larger and smaller. Notice that the scale along the left side of the figure increases by powers of 10 to accommodate the range of sizes shown. Starting at the top with 10 meters (m), each subsequent mark represents a tenfold decrease in length. Most cells are between 1 and 100 μm in diameter (yellow region of the figure) and are therefore visible only with a microscope. There are some interesting exceptions: an ostrich egg is a single cell about 6 inches across and weighing about 3 pounds; nerve cells in your body can stretch several feet long; and nerve cells in giant squid can be more than 30 feet long!

How do new living cells arise? First formulated in the 1800s, the **cell theory** states that all living things are composed of cells and that all cells come from earlier cells. So every cell in your body (and in every other living organism on Earth) was formed by division of a previously living cell. (That raises an obvious question: how did the first cell evolve? This fascinating topic will be addressed in Chapter 15.) With that introduction, let's begin to explore the variety of cells found among life on Earth.

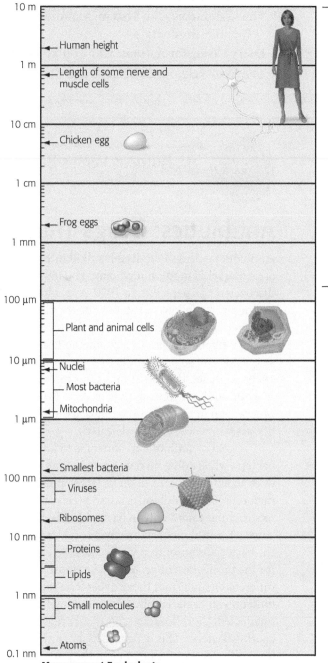

Measurement Equivalents

1 meter (m) = 100 cm = 1,000 mm = about 39.4 inches

1 centimeter (cm) = 10^{-2} $\left(\frac{1}{100}\right)$ m = about 0.4 inch

1 millimeter (mm) = 10^{-3} $\left(\frac{1}{1,000}\right)$ m = $\frac{1}{10}$ cm

1 micrometer (μm) = 10^{-6} m = 10^{-3} mm

1 nanometer (nm) = 10^{-9} m = 10^{-3} μm

▲ Figure 4.1 **The size range of cells.** Starting at the top of this scale with 10 m (10 meters) and going down, each measurement along the left side marks a tenfold decrease in size.

Table 4.1 — Comparing Prokaryotic and Eukaryotic Cells

Prokaryotic cells	Eukaryotic cells
Plasma membrane of identical structure	
Cytoplasm occupies entire interior of cell	Cytoplasm occupies the region between the nucleus and the plasma membrane
Single circular chromosome in nucleoid region	One or more linear chromosomes in nucleus
Both have ribosomes, but structure differs slightly	
First evolved approximately 3.5 billion years ago	First evolved approximately 2.1 billion years ago
Smaller, simpler	Larger, more complex
No membrane-bound organelles	Membrane-bound organelles (for example, nucleus, ER)
Most are surrounded by cell walls; some have capsules, pili, and/or flagella	Plant cells surrounded by cell walls; animal cells surrounded by extracellular matrix

The Two Major Categories of Cells

The countless cells that exist on Earth can be placed into two basic categories: prokaryotic cells and eukaryotic cells (Table 4.1). **Prokaryotic cells** are found in organisms of the domains Bacteria and Archaea, known as prokaryotes (see Figure 1.7). Organisms of the domain Eukarya—including protists, plants, fungi, and animals—are composed of **eukaryotic cells** and are called eukaryotes.

All cells, whether prokaryotic or eukaryotic, have several features in common. They are all bounded by a barrier called a **plasma membrane**, which regulates the traffic of molecules between the cell and its surroundings. Inside all cells is a thick, jellylike fluid called the **cytosol**, in which cellular components are suspended. All cells have one or more **chromosomes** carrying genes made of DNA. And all cells have **ribosomes** that build proteins according to instructions from the genes. Because of structural differences between bacteria and eukaryotes, as mentioned in the Biology and Society section at the beginning of the chapter, some antibiotics—such as streptomycin—target prokaryotic ribosomes, crippling protein synthesis in the bacterial invaders but not in the eukaryotic host (you).

Mushrooms, amoebas, and you are all made up of the same kind of cells.

Although they have many similarities, prokaryotic and eukaryotic cells differ in several important ways. Fossil evidence shows that prokaryotes were the first life on Earth, appearing more than

☑ **CHECKPOINT**

1. Name four structures found in both prokaryotic and eukaryotic cells.

2. How is the nucleoid region of a prokaryotic cell different from the nucleus of a eukaryotic cell?

Answers: 1. plasma membrane, chromosomes, cytosol, and ribosomes. 2. There is no membrane enclosing the prokaryotic nucleoid region.

3.5 billion years ago. In contrast, the first eukaryotes did not appear until around 2.1 billion years ago. Prokaryotic cells are usually much smaller—about one-tenth the length of a typical eukaryotic cell—and are simpler in structure. Think of a prokaryotic cell as being like a bicycle, whereas a eukaryotic cell is like a sports utility vehicle. Both a bike and an SUV get you from place to place, but one is much smaller and contains many fewer parts than the other. Similarly, prokaryotic cells and eukaryotic cells perform similar functions, but prokaryotes cells are much smaller and less complex. The most significant structural difference between the two types of cells is that eukaryotic cells have **organelles** ("little organs"), membrane-enclosed structures that perform specific functions, and prokaryotic cells do not. The most important organelle is the **nucleus**, which houses most of a eukaryotic cell's DNA. The nucleus is surrounded by a double membrane. A prokaryotic cell lacks a nucleus; its DNA is coiled into a "nucleus-like" region called the **nucleoid**, which is not partitioned from the rest of the cell by membranes.

Consider this analogy: A eukaryotic cell is like an office building that is separated into cubicles. Within each cubicle, a specific function is performed, thus dividing the labor among many internal compartments. One cubicle may hold the accounting department, for example, while another is home to the sales force. The "cubicle walls" within eukaryotic cells are made from membranes that help maintain a unique chemical environment inside each cubicle. In contrast, the interior of a prokaryotic cell is like an open warehouse. The spaces for specific tasks within a "prokaryotic warehouse" are distinct but they are not separated by physical barriers.

Figure 4.2 depicts an idealized prokaryotic cell and a micrograph of an actual bacterium. Surrounding the plasma membrane of most prokaryotic cells is a rigid cell wall, which protects the cell and helps maintain its shape. Recall from the Biology and Society section at the beginning of the chapter that bacterial cell walls are the targets of some antibiotics. In some prokaryotes, a sticky outer coat called a capsule surrounds the cell wall. Capsules provide protection and help prokaryotes stick to surfaces and to other cells in a colony. For example, capsules help bacteria in your mouth stick together to form harmful dental plaque. Prokaryotes can have short projections called pili, which can also attach to surfaces. Many prokaryotic cells have flagella, long projections that propel them through their liquid environment. ☑

An Overview of Eukaryotic Cells

All eukaryotic cells—whether from animals, plants, protists, or fungi—are fundamentally similar to one another and quite different from prokaryotic cells. **Figure 4.3** provides overviews of an idealized animal cell and plant cell. No real cell looks quite like these because living cells have many more copies of most of the structures shown; each of your cells have hundreds of mitochondria and millions of ribosomes, for example. To keep from getting lost on our tour of the cell, throughout this chapter we'll use miniature versions of the diagrams in Figure 4.3 as road maps, highlighting the structure we're

▼ **Figure 4.2 A prokaryotic cell.** A drawing of an idealized prokaryotic cell (right) is shown alongside a micrograph of *Helicobacter pylori* (left), a bacterium that causes stomach ulcers.

Colorized TEM 18,700×

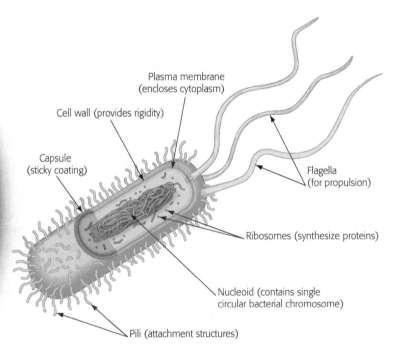

Plasma membrane (encloses cytoplasm)

Cell wall (provides rigidity)

Capsule (sticky coating)

Flagella (for propulsion)

Ribosomes (synthesize proteins)

Nucleoid (contains single circular bacterial chromosome)

Pili (attachment structures)

discussing. Notice that the structures are color-coded; we'll use this color scheme throughout this book.

The region of the cell outside the nucleus and within the plasma membrane is called the **cytoplasm**. (This term is also used to refer to the interior of a prokaryotic cell.) The cytoplasm of a eukaryotic cell consists of various organelles suspended in the liquid cytosol. As you can see in Figure 4.3, most organelles are found in both animal and plant cells. But you'll notice some important differences—for example, only plant cells have chloroplasts (where photosynthesis occurs) and a cell wall (which provides stiffness to plant structures), and only animal cells have lysosomes (bubbles of digestive enzymes surrounded by membranes). In the rest of this section, we'll take a closer look at the architecture of eukaryotic cells, beginning with the plasma membrane. ☑

▼ Figure 4.3 **An idealized animal cell and plant cell.** For now, the labels on the drawings are just words, but these organelles will come to life as we take a closer look at how each part of the cell functions.

Idealized animal cell

Idealized plant cell

Membrane Structure

Before we enter the cell to explore the organelles, let's make a quick stop at the surface of this microscopic world: the plasma membrane. To help you understand the structure and function of the cell membrane, imagine you want to create a new homestead in the wilderness. You will probably want to start by fencing your property to protect it from the outside world. Similarly, the plasma membrane is the boundary that separates the living cell from its nonliving surroundings. The plasma membrane is a remarkable film, so thin that you would have to stack 8,000 of these membranes to equal the thickness of one piece of paper. Yet the plasma membrane can regulate the traffic of chemicals into and out of the cell. As with all things biological, the structure of the plasma membrane correlates with its function.

✅ **CHECKPOINT**

What function does the organization of phospholipids into a bilayer in water serve?

Answer: The bilayer structure shields the hydrophobic tails of the phospholipids from water while exposing the hydrophilic heads to water.

Structure/ Function **The Plasma Membrane**

The plasma membrane and other membranes of the cell are composed mostly of **phospholipids**. The structure of phospholipid molecules is well suited to their function as a major constituent of biological membranes. Each phospholipid is composed of two distinct regions—a "head" with a negatively charged phosphate group and two nonpolar fatty acid "tails." Phospholipids group together to form a two-layer sheet called a **phospholipid bilayer**. As you can see in Figure 4.4a, the phospholipids' hydrophilic ("water-loving") heads are arranged to face outward, exposed to the aqueous solutions on both sides of a membrane. Their hydrophobic ("water-fearing") tails are arranged inward, mingling with each other and shielded from water. Suspended in the phospholipid bilayer of most membranes are proteins that help regulate traffic across the membrane; these proteins also perform other functions (Figure 4.4b). (You'll learn more about membrane proteins in Chapter 5.)

Membranes are not static sheets of molecules locked rigidly in place, however. In fact, the texture of a cellular membrane is similar to salad oil. The phospholipids and most of the proteins can therefore drift about within the membrane. Thus, a membrane is a **fluid mosaic**—fluid because the molecules can move freely past one another and mosaic because of the diversity of proteins that float like icebergs in the phospholipid sea. Next, we'll see how some bacteria can cause illness by piercing the plasma membrane. ✅

▼ Figure 4.4 **The plasma membrane structure.**

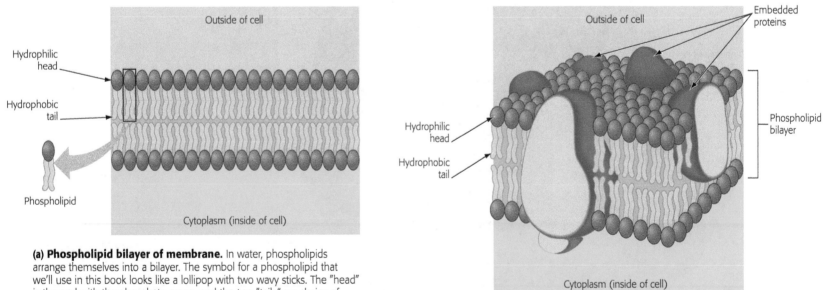

(a) Phospholipid bilayer of membrane. In water, phospholipids arrange themselves into a bilayer. The symbol for a phospholipid that we'll use in this book looks like a lollipop with two wavy sticks. The "head" is the end with the phosphate group, and the two "tails" are chains of carbon and hydrogen. The bilayer arrangement keeps the heads exposed to water while keeping the tails in the oily interior of the membrane.

(b) Fluid mosaic model of membrane. Membrane proteins, like the phospholipids, have both hydrophilic and hydrophobic regions.

Humans Versus Bacteria THE PROCESS OF SCIENCE

What Makes a Superbug?

Some bacteria cause disease by rupturing the plasma membrane of human immune cells. One example is a common bacteria called *Staphylococcus aureus* (commonly referred to as "staph" or SA). These bacteria, found on your skin, are usually harmless but may multiply and spread, causing a "staph infection." Staph infections typically occur in hospitals and can cause serious, even life-threatening conditions, such as pneumonia or necrotizing fasciitis ("flesh-eating disease").

Most staph infections can be treated with antibiotics. But particularly dangerous strains of *S. aureus*—known as MRSA (for multidrug-resistant SA)—are unaffected by all of the commonly used antibiotics. In recent years, MRSA infections have become more common in hospitals, gyms, and schools. In one study, scientists from the National Institutes of Health (NIH) studied a particular deadly MRSA strain. They began with the **observation** that other bacteria use a protein called PSM to disable human immune cells by forming holes that rip apart the plasma membrane. This observation led them to **question** whether PSM plays a role in MRSA infection (Figure 4.5). Their **hypothesis** was that MRSA bacteria lacking the ability to produce PSM would be less deadly than normal MRSA strains that produced PSM.

In their **experiment**, scientists infected seven mice with a normal MRSA strain and eight mice with a MRSA strain genetically engineered to not produce PSM. The **results** were striking: All seven mice infected with the normal MRSA strain died, while five of the eight mice infected with the strain that did not produce PSM survived. Immune cells from all of the dead mice had holes within the plasma membrane. The researchers concluded that normal MRSA strains use the

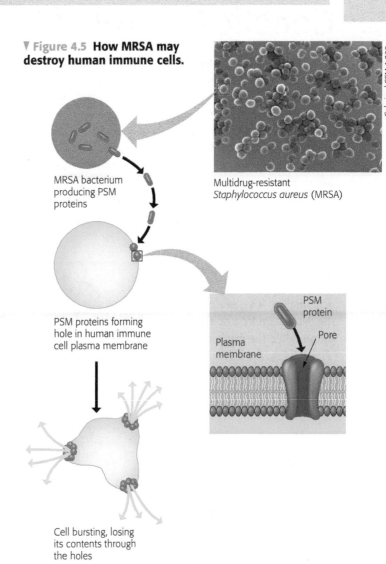

▼ Figure 4.5 **How MRSA may destroy human immune cells.**

Colorized SEM 1,300×

MRSA bacterium producing PSM proteins

Multidrug-resistant *Staphylococcus aureus* (MRSA)

PSM proteins forming hole in human immune cell plasma membrane

PSM protein

Pore

Plasma membrane

Cell bursting, losing its contents through the holes

membrane-destroying PSM protein, but other factors must come into play because three mice died even in the absence of PSM. The deadly effects of MRSA are therefore a reminder of the critical role played by the plasma membrane and another example of the ongoing battle between humans and disease-causing bacteria.

Cell Surfaces

Surrounding their plasma membranes, plant cells have a cell wall made from cellulose fibers, which are long chains of polysaccharide (see Figure 3.9c). The walls protect the cells, maintain cell shape, and keep cells from absorbing so much water that they burst. Plant cells are connected to each other via channels that pass through the cell walls, joining the cytoplasm of each cell to that of its neighbors. These channels allow water and other small molecules to move between cells, integrating the activities of a tissue.

Animal cells lack a cell wall, but most animal cells secrete a sticky coat called the **extracellular matrix**. Fibers made of the protein collagen (also found in your skin, cartilage, bones, and tendons) hold cells together in tissues and can also have protective and supportive functions. In addition, the surfaces of most animal cells contain cell junctions, structures that connect cells together into tissues, allowing the cells to function in a coordinated way. ☑

☑ **CHECKPOINT**

What polysaccharide is the primary component of plant cell walls?

Answer: cellulose

The Nucleus and Ribosomes: Genetic Control of the Cell

If you think of the cell as a factory, then the nucleus is its control center. Here, the master plans are stored, orders are given, changes are made in response to external factors, and the process of making new factories is initiated. The factory supervisors are the genes, the inherited DNA molecules that direct almost all the business of the cell. Each gene is a stretch of DNA that stores the information necessary to produce a particular protein. Proteins can be likened to workers on the factory floor because they do most of the actual work of the cell.

nuclear envelope is similar in structure to the plasma membrane: a phospholipid bilayer with associated proteins. Pores in the envelope allow certain materials to pass between the nucleus and the surrounding cytoplasm. (As you'll soon see, among the most important materials that passes between the nucleus and cytoplasm through the nuclear pores are molecules of RNA that carry instructions for building proteins.) Within the nucleus, long DNA molecules and associated proteins form fibers called **chromatin**. Each long chromatin fiber constitutes one chromosome (**Figure 4.7**). The number of chromosomes in a cell depends on the species; for example, each human body cell has 46 chromosomes, whereas rice cells have 24 and dog cells have 78 (see Figure 8.2 for more examples). The **nucleolus** (shown in Figure 4.6), a prominent structure within the nucleus, is the site where the components of ribosomes are made. We'll examine ribosomes next. ☑

☑ CHECKPOINT

What is the relationship between chromosomes, chromatin, and DNA?

Answer: Chromosomes are made of chromatin, which is a combination of DNA and proteins.

The Nucleus

The nucleus is separated from the cytoplasm by a double membrane called the **nuclear envelope** (**Figure 4.6**). Each membrane of the

▼ Figure 4.6 **The nucleus.**

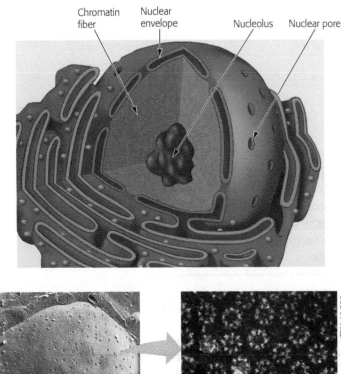

Chromatin fiber
Nuclear envelope
Nucleolus
Nuclear pore

TEM 8,800×

TEM 12,500×

Surface of nuclear envelope

Nuclear pores

▼ Figure 4.7 **The relationship between DNA, chromatin, and a chromosome.**

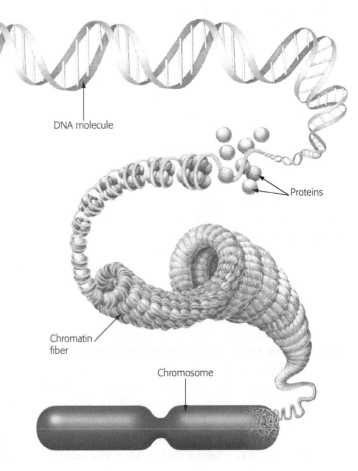

DNA molecule

Proteins

Chromatin fiber

Chromosome

Ribosomes

The small blue dots in the cells in Figure 4.3 and outside the nucleus in Figure 4.6 represent the ribosomes. Ribosomes are responsible for protein synthesis (Figure 4.8). In eukaryotic cells, the components of ribosomes are made in the nucleus and then transported through the pores of the nuclear envelope into the cytoplasm. It is in the cytoplasm that the ribosomes begin their work. Some ribosomes are suspended in the cytosol, making proteins that remain within the fluid of the cell. Other ribosomes are attached to the outside of the nucleus or an organelle called the endoplasmic reticulum (Figure 4.9), making proteins that are incorporated into membranes or secreted by the cell. Free and bound ribosomes are structurally identical, and ribosomes can switch locations, moving between the endoplasmic reticulum and the cytosol. Cells that make a lot of proteins have a large number of ribosomes. For example, each cell in your pancreas that produces digestive enzymes may contain a few million ribosomes.

How DNA Directs Protein Production

Like a company executive, the DNA doesn't actually do any of the work of the cell. Instead, the DNA "executive" issues orders that result in work being done by the protein "workers." Figure 4.10 shows the sequence of events during protein production in a eukaryotic cell (with the DNA and other structures being shown disproportionately large in relation to the nucleus). ❶ DNA transfers its coded information to a molecule called messenger RNA (mRNA). Like a middle manager, the mRNA molecule carries the order to "build this type of protein." ❷ The mRNA exits the nucleus through pores in the nuclear envelope and travels to the cytoplasm, where it binds to a ribosome. ❸ The ribosome moves along the mRNA, translating the genetic message into a protein with a specific amino acid sequence. (You'll learn how the message is translated in Chapter 10.) In this way, information carried by the DNA can direct the work of the entire cell without the DNA ever leaving the protective confines of the nucleus. ☑

☑ CHECKPOINT

1. What is the function of ribosomes?
2. What is the role of mRNA in making a protein?

Answers: 1. protein synthesis 2. A molecule of mRNA carries the genetic message from a gene (DNA) to ribosomes that translate it into protein.

▶ **Figure 4.8 A computer model of a ribosome in the process of synthesizing a protein.**

Ribosome

mRNA

Protein

▼ **Figure 4.9 ER-bound ribosomes.**

TEM 50,000×

Ribosomes attached to endoplasmic reticulum visible as tiny dark blue dots

◀ **Figure 4.10**
DNA → RNA → protein. Inherited genes in the nucleus control protein production and hence the activities of the cell.

DNA

❶ Synthesis of mRNA in the nucleus

mRNA

Nucleus

Cytoplasm

❷ Movement of mRNA into cytoplasm via nuclear pore

mRNA

Ribosome

❸ Synthesis of protein in the cytoplasm

Protein

The Endomembrane System: Manufacturing and Distributing Cellular Products

Like an office partitioned into cubicles, the cytoplasm of a eukaryotic cell is partitioned by organelle membranes (see Figure 4.3). Some of the membranes are physically connected, and others are linked by **vesicles** (sacs made of membrane) that transfer membrane segments between organelles. Together, these organelles form the **endomembrane system**. This system includes the nuclear envelope, the endoplasmic reticulum, the Golgi apparatus, lysosomes, and vacuoles.

The Endoplasmic Reticulum

The **endoplasmic reticulum (ER)** is one of the main manufacturing facilities within a cell. It produces an enormous variety of molecules. Connected to the nuclear envelope, the ER forms an extensive labyrinth of tubes and sacs running throughout the cytoplasm (Figure 4.11). A membrane separates the internal ER compartment from the cytosol. There are two components that make up the ER: rough ER and smooth ER. These two types of ER are physically connected but differ in structure and function.

Rough ER

The "rough" in **rough ER** refers to ribosomes that stud the outside of its membrane. One of the functions of rough ER is to make more membrane. Phospholipids made by enzymes of the rough ER are inserted into the ER membrane. In this way, the ER membrane grows, and portions of it can bubble off and be transferred to other parts of the cell. The ribosomes attached to the rough ER produce proteins that will be inserted into the growing ER membrane, transported to other organelles, and eventually exported. Cells that secrete a lot of protein—such as the cells of your salivary glands, which secrete enzymes into your mouth—are especially rich in rough ER. As shown in Figure 4.12, **①** some products manufactured by rough ER are **②** chemically modified and then **③** packaged into **transport vesicles**, sacs made of membrane that bud off from the rough ER. The transport vesicles may then be **④** dispatched to other locations in the cell.

▼ Figure 4.11 **The endoplasmic reticulum (ER).** In this drawing, the flattened sacs of rough ER and the tubes of smooth ER are connected. Notice that the ER is also connected to the nuclear envelope (the nucleus has been omitted from the illustration for clarity).

▼ Figure 4.12 **How rough ER manufactures and packages secretory proteins.**

③ Proteins to be secreted depart in transport vesicles.

④ Vesicles bud off from the ER. Proteins are secreted from the cell when vesicles fuse with the plasma membrane.

② Proteins are often modified in the ER.

① A ribosome links amino acids into a polypeptide, which threads through the membrane into the interior of the ER.

Ribosome

Protein

Transport vesicle

Rough ER

Polypeptide

Nuclear envelope

Ribosomes

Rough ER

Smooth ER

Smooth ER

The "smooth" in **smooth ER** refers to the fact that this organelle lacks the ribosomes that populate the surface of rough ER (see Figure 4.11). A diversity of enzymes built into the smooth ER membrane enables this organelle to perform many functions. One is the synthesis of lipids, including steroids (see Figure 3.13). For example, the cells in ovaries or testes that produce the steroid sex hormones are enriched with smooth ER. In liver cells, enzymes of the smooth ER detoxify circulating drugs such as barbiturates, amphetamines, and some antibiotics (which is why antibiotics don't persist in the bloodstream after combating an infection). As liver cells are exposed to a drug, the amounts of smooth ER and its detoxifying enzymes increase. This can strengthen the body's tolerance of the drug, meaning that higher doses will be required in the future to achieve the desired effect. The growth of smooth ER in response to one drug can also increase tolerance of other drugs. For example, barbiturate use, such as frequently taking sleeping pills, may make certain antibiotics less effective by accelerating their breakdown in the liver.

The Golgi Apparatus

Working in close partnership with the ER, the **Golgi apparatus**, an organelle named for its discoverer (Italian scientist Camillo Golgi), who first described this structure in 1898, receives, refines, stores, and distributes chemical products of the cell (Figure 4.13). You can think of the Golgi apparatus as a detailing facility that receives shipments of newly manufactured cars (proteins), puts on the finishing touches, stores the completed cars, and then ships them out when needed.

Products made in the ER reach the Golgi apparatus in transport vesicles. The Golgi apparatus consists of a stack of membrane plates, looking much like a pile of pita bread. ❶ One side of a Golgi stack serves as a receiving dock for vesicles from the ER. ❷ Proteins within a vesicle are usually modified by enzymes during their transit from the receiving to the shipping side of the Golgi apparatus. For example, molecular identification tags may be added that serve to mark and sort protein molecules into different batches for different destinations. ❸ The shipping side of a Golgi stack is a depot from which finished products can be carried in transport vesicles to other organelles or to the plasma membrane. Vesicles that bind with the plasma membrane transfer proteins to it or secrete finished products to the outside of the cell. ☑

☑ **CHECKPOINT**

1. What makes rough ER rough?
2. What is the relationship between the Golgi apparatus and the ER in a protein-secreting cell?

Answers: **1.** *ribosomes attached to the membrane* **2.** *The Golgi apparatus receives proteins from the ER via vesicles, processes the proteins, and then dispatches them in vesicles.*

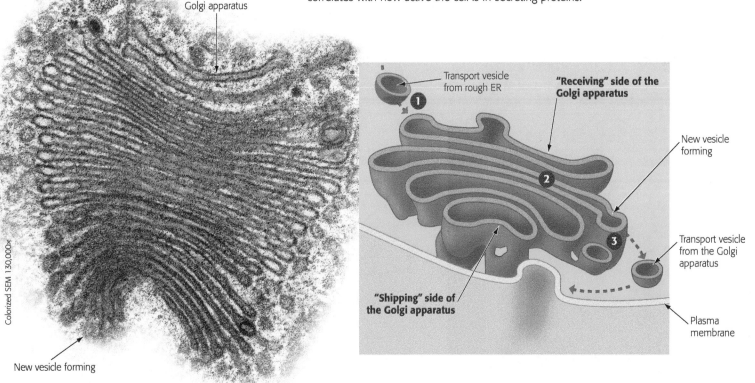

▼ **Figure 4.13 The Golgi apparatus.** The Golgi consists of flattened sacs arranged something like a stack of pita bread. The number of stacks in a cell (from a few to hundreds) correlates with how active the cell is in secreting proteins.

"Receiving" side of the Golgi apparatus

New vesicle forming

Colorized SEM 130,000×

Transport vesicle from rough ER

"Receiving" side of the Golgi apparatus

New vesicle forming

Transport vesicle from the Golgi apparatus

"Shipping" side of the Golgi apparatus

Plasma membrane

65

Lysosomes

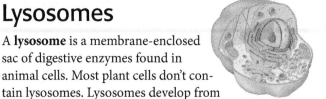

A **lysosome** is a membrane-enclosed sac of digestive enzymes found in animal cells. Most plant cells don't contain lysosomes. Lysosomes develop from vesicles that bud off from the Golgi apparatus. Enzymes within a lysosome can break down large molecules such as proteins, polysaccharides, fats, and nucleic acids. The lysosome provides a compartment where the cell can digest these molecules safely, without unleashing the digestive enzymes on the cell itself.

Lysosomes have several types of digestive functions. Many single-celled protists engulf nutrients into tiny cytoplasmic sacs called food vacuoles. Lysosomes fuse with the food vacuoles, exposing the food to digestive enzymes **(Figure 4.14a)**. Small molecules that result from this digestion, such as amino acids, leave the lysosome and nourish the cell. Lysosomes also help destroy harmful bacteria. For example, your white blood cells ingest bacteria into vacuoles, and lysosomal enzymes that are emptied into these vacuoles rupture the bacterial cell walls. In addition, without harming the cell, a lysosome can engulf and digest parts of another organelle, essentially recycling it by making its molecules available for the construction of new organelles **(Figure 4.14b)**. With the help of lysosomes, a cell can thereby continually renew itself. Lysosomes also have sculpting functions in embryonic development. In an early human embryo, lysosomes release enzymes that digest webbing between fingers of the developing hand.

The importance of lysosomes to cell function and human health is made clear by hereditary disorders called lysosomal storage diseases. A person with such a disease is missing one or more of the digestive enzymes normally found within lysosomes. The abnormal lysosomes become engorged with indigestible substances, and this eventually interferes with other cellular functions. Most of these diseases are fatal in early childhood. In Tay-Sachs disease, for example, lysosomes lack a lipid-digesting enzyme. As a result, nerve cells die as they accumulate excess lipids, ravaging the nervous system. Fortunately, lysosomal storage diseases are rare. ☑

▼ Figure 4.14 **Two functions of lysosomes.**

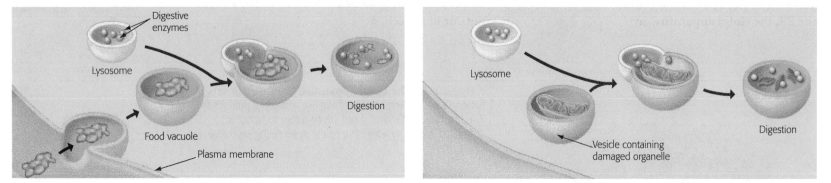

(a) **A lysosome digesting food**

Digestive enzymes

Lysosome

Food vacuole

Plasma membrane

Digestion

(b) **A lysosome breaking down the molecules of damaged organelles**

Lysosome

Vesicle containing damaged organelle

Digestion

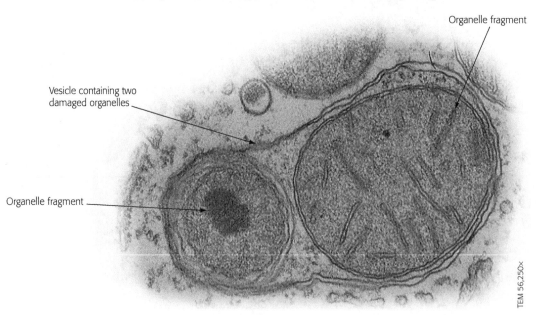

Organelle fragment

Vesicle containing two damaged organelles

Organelle fragment

TEM 56,250x

Vacuoles

Vacuoles are large sacs made of membrane that bud off from the ER or Golgi apparatus. Vacuoles have a variety of functions. For example, Figure 4.14a shows a food vacuole budding from the plasma membrane. Certain freshwater protists have contractile vacuoles that pump out excess water that flows into the cell (Figure 4.15a).

Another type of vacuole is a **central vacuole**, a versatile compartment that can account for more than half the volume of a mature plant cell (Figure 4.15b). A central vacuole stores organic nutrients, such as proteins stockpiled in the vacuoles of seed cells. It also contributes to plant growth by absorbing water and causing cells to expand. In the cells of flower petals, central

The caffeine that gives your cup of tea a kick also protects tea plants from herbivores.

vacuoles may contain pigments that attract pollinating insects. Central vacuoles may also contain poisons that protect against plant-eating animals. Some important crop plants produce and store large amounts of toxic chemicals—harmful to animals that might graze on the plant but useful to us—such as tobacco plants (which store nicotine) and coffee and tea plants (which store caffeine).

Figure 4.16 will help you review how organelles of the endomembrane system are related. Note that a product made in one part of the endomembrane system may exit the cell or become part of another organelle without crossing a membrane. Also note that membrane made by the ER can become part of the plasma membrane through the fusion of a transport vesicle. In this way, even the plasma membrane is related to the endomembrane system. ☑

☑ **CHECKPOINT**

Place the following cellular structures in the order they would be used in the production and secretion of a protein: Golgi apparatus, nucleus, plasma membrane, ribosome, transport vesicle.

Answer: nucleus, ribosome, transport vesicle, Golgi apparatus, plasma membrane

▼ Figure 4.15 **Two types of vacuoles.**

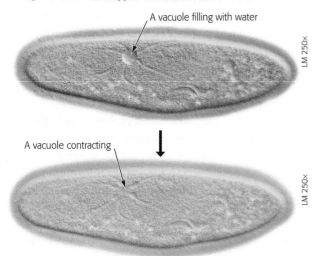

A vacuole filling with water

A vacuole contracting

LM 250×

LM 250×

(a) Contractile vacuole in *Paramecium*. A contractile vacuole fills with water and then contracts to pump the water out of the cell.

Central vacuole

Colorized TEM 1,700×

(b) Central vacuole in a plant cell. The central vacuole (colorized blue in this micrograph) is often the largest organelle in a mature plant cell.

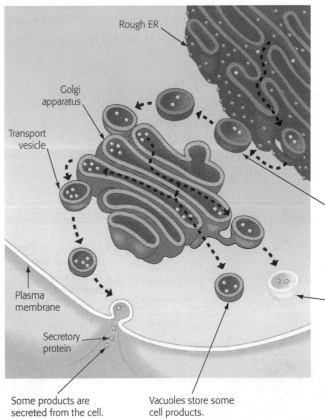

Rough ER

Golgi apparatus

Transport vesicle

Plasma membrane

Secretory protein

Transport vesicles carry enzymes and other proteins from the rough ER to the Golgi for processing.

Lysosomes carrying digestive enzymes can fuse with other vesicles.

Some products are secreted from the cell.

Vacuoles store some cell products.

▲ Figure 4.16 **Review of the endomembrane system.** The dashed arrows show some of the pathways of cell product distribution and membrane migration via transport vesicles.

Energy Transformations

Chloroplasts and Mitochondria

One of the central themes of biology is the transformation of energy: how it enters living systems, is converted from one form to another, and is eventually given off as heat. To follow the energy through living systems, we must consider the two organelles that act as cellular power stations: chloroplasts and mitochondria.

Chloroplasts

Most of the living world runs on the energy provided by photosynthesis, the conversion of light energy from the sun to the chemical energy of sugar and other organic molecules. **Chloroplasts**, which are unique to the photosynthetic cells of plants and algae, are the organelles that perform photosynthesis.

A chloroplast is partitioned into compartments by two membranes, one inside the other (Figure 4.17). The stroma is a thick fluid found inside the innermost membrane. Suspended in that fluid, the interior of a network of membrane-enclosed disks and tubes forms another compartment. Notice in Figure 4.17 that the disks occur in interconnected stacks called grana (singular, *granum*) that resemble stacks of poker chips. The grana are a chloroplast's solar power packs, the structures that trap light energy and convert it to chemical energy (as detailed in Chapter 7).

Mitochondria

In contrast to chloroplasts (found only in plant cells), mitochondria are found in almost all eukaryotic cells, including those of plants and animals. **Mitochondria** (singular, *mitochondrion*) are the organelles

in which cellular respiration takes place; during cellular respiration, energy is harvested from sugars and transformed into another form of chemical energy called ATP (adenosine triphosphate). Cells use molecules of ATP as a direct energy source.

An envelope of two membranes encloses the mitochondrion, and the inner membrane encloses a thick fluid called the mitochondrial matrix (Figure 4.18). The inner membrane of the envelope has numerous infoldings called cristae. The cristae create a large surface area in which many of the enzymes and other molecules that function in cellular respiration are embedded, thereby maximizing ATP output. (You'll learn more about how mitochondria convert food energy to ATP energy in Chapter 6.)

Besides their ability to provide cellular energy, mitochondria and chloroplasts share another feature: They contain their own DNA that encodes some of their own proteins made by their own ribosomes. Each chloroplast and mitochondrion contains a single circular DNA chromosome that resembles a prokaryotic chromosome. In fact, mitochondria and chloroplasts can grow and pinch in two, reproducing themselves. This is evidence that mitochondria and chloroplasts evolved from ancient free-living prokaryotes that established residence within other, larger host prokaryotes. This phenomenon, where one species lives inside a host species, is a special type of symbiosis (see Chapter 16 for further information). Over time, mitochondria and chloroplasts likely became increasingly interdependent with the host prokaryote, eventually evolving into a single organism with inseparable parts. The DNA found within mitochondria and chloroplasts is therefore likely remnants of this ancient evolutionary event. ☑

☑ CHECKPOINT

1. What does photosynthesis accomplish?
2. What is cellular respiration?

Answers: 1. the conversion of light energy to chemical energy stored in food molecules 2. a process that converts the chemical energy of sugars and other food molecules to chemical energy in the form of ATP

▼ Figure 4.17 **The chloroplast: site of photosynthesis.**

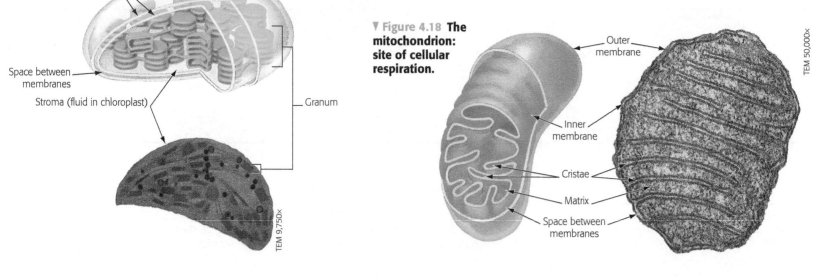

Inner and outer membranes

Space between membranes

Stroma (fluid in chloroplast)

Granum

TEM 9,750x

▼ Figure 4.18 **The mitochondrion: site of cellular respiration.**

Outer membrane

Inner membrane

Cristae

Matrix

Space between membranes

TEM 50,000x

The Cytoskeleton: Cell Shape and Movement

If someone asked you to describe a house, you would most likely mention the various rooms and their locations. You probably would not think to mention the foundation and beams that support the house. Yet these structures perform an extremely important function. Similarly, cells have an infrastructure called the **cytoskeleton**, a network of protein fibers extending throughout the cytoplasm. The cytoskeleton serves as both skeleton and "muscles" for the cell, functioning in support and movement.

> Without the cytoskeleton, your cells would collapse in on themselves, much like a house collapses when the infrastructure fails.

Maintaining Cell Shape

One function of the cytoskeleton is to give mechanical support to the cell and maintain its shape. This is especially important for animal cells, which lack rigid cell walls. The cytoskeleton contains several types of fibers made from different types of protein. One important type of fiber forms **microtubules**, hollow tubes of protein **(Figure 4.19a)**. The other kinds of cytoskeletal fibers, called intermediate filaments and microfilaments, are thinner and solid.

Just as the bony skeleton of your body helps fix the positions of your organs, the cytoskeleton provides anchorage and reinforcement for many organelles in a cell. For instance, the nucleus is held in place by a "cage" of cytoskeletal filaments. Other organelles use the cytoskeleton for movement. For example, a lysosome might reach a food vacuole by gliding along a microtubule track. Microtubules also guide the movement of chromosomes when cells divide (via the mitotic spindle— see Chapter 8).

A cell's cytoskeleton is dynamic: It can be quickly dismantled in one part of the cell by removing protein subunits and re-formed in a new location by reattaching the subunits. Such rearrangement can provide rigidity in a new location, change the shape of the cell, or even cause the whole cell or some of its parts to move. This process contributes to the amoeboid (crawling) movements of the protist *Amoeba* (Figure 4.19b) and movement of some of our white blood cells. ☑

▼ Figure 4.19 **The cytoskeleton.**

LM 2,500x

(a) Microtubules in the cytoskeleton. In this micrograph of animal cells, the cytoskeleton microtubules are labeled with a fluorescent yellow dye.

(b) Microtubules and movement. The crawling movement of an *Amoeba* is due to the rapid degradation and rebuilding of microtubules.

LM 250x

Cilia and Flagella

In some eukaryotic cells, microtubules are arranged into structures called flagella and cilia, extensions from a cell that aid in movement. Eukaryotic **flagella** (singular, *flagellum*) propel cells with an undulating, whiplike motion. They often occur singly, such as in human sperm cells (**Figure 4.20a**), but may also appear in groups on the outer surface of protists. **Cilia** (singular, *cilium*) are generally shorter and more numerous than flagella and move in a coordinated back-and-forth motion, like the rhythmic oars of a crew team. Both cilia and flagella propel various protists through water (**Figure 4.20b**). Though different in length, number per cell, and beating pattern, cilia and flagella have the same basic architecture. Not all animals have cilia or flagella—many do not—and they are almost never found on plant cells.

Some cilia extend from nonmoving cells that are part of a tissue layer. There, they move fluid over the tissue's surface. For example, cilia lining your windpipe clean your respiratory system by sweeping mucus with trapped debris out of your lungs (**Figure 4.20c**). Tobacco smoke can inhibit or destroy these cilia, interfering with the normal cleansing mechanisms and allowing more toxin-laden smoke particles to reach the lungs. Frequent coughing—common in heavy smokers—then becomes the body's attempt to cleanse the respiratory system.

Because human sperm rely on flagella for movement, it's easy to understand why problems with flagella can lead to male infertility. Interestingly, some men with a type of hereditary sterility also suffer from respiratory problems. Because of a defect in the structure of their flagella and cilia, the sperm of men afflicted with this disorder cannot swim normally within the female reproductive tract to fertilize an egg (causing sterility), and their cilia do not sweep mucus out of their lungs (causing recurrent respiratory infections). ☑

☑ CHECKPOINT

Compare and contrast cilia and flagella.

Answer: Cilia and flagella have the same basic structure, are made from microtubules, and help move cells or move fluid over cells. Cilia are short and numerous and move back and forth. Flagella are longer, often occurring singly, and they undulate.

▼ Figure 4.20 **Examples of flagella and cilia.**

Colorized SEM 2,500×

(a) Flagellum of a human sperm cell. A eukaryotic flagellum undulates in a whiplike motion, driving a cell such as this sperm cell through its fluid environment.

Colorized SEM 500×

(b) Cilia on a protist. Cilia are shorter and more numerous than flagella and move with a back-and-forth motion. As shown here, a layer of beating cilia covers *Paramecium*, a freshwater protist that can dart rapidly through its watery environment.

Colorized SEM 3,000×

(c) Cilia lining the respiratory tract. The cilia lining your respiratory tract sweep mucus with trapped debris out of your lungs. This helps keep your airway clear and prevents infections.

The Evolution of Bacterial Resistance in Humans

Individuals with variations that make them better suited for the local environment will survive and reproduce more often (on average) than those who lack such variations. When the advantageous variations have a genetic basis, the offspring of individuals with the variations will more often also have the favorable adaptions, giving them a survival and reproductive advantage. In this way, repeated over many generations, natural selection promotes evolution of the population.

Within a human population, the persistent presence of a disease can provide a new basis for measuring those individuals who are best suited for survival in the local environment. For example, a recent evolutionary study examined people living in Bangladesh. This population has been exposed to the disease cholera—caused by an infectious bacterium—for millennia (Figure 4.21). After cholera bacteria enter a victim's digestive tract (usually through contaminated drinking water), the bacteria produce a toxin that binds to intestinal cells.

There, the toxin alters proteins in the plasma membrane, causing the cells to excrete fluid. The resulting diarrhea, which spreads the bacteria by shedding it back into the environment, can cause severe dehydration and death if untreated.

Because Bangladeshis have lived for so long in an environment that teems with cholera bacteria, one might expect that natural selection would favor those individuals who have some resistance to the bacteria. Indeed, recent studies of people from Bangladesh revealed mutations in several genes that appear to confer an increased resistance to cholera. Researchers discovered one mutation in a gene that encodes for the plasma membrane proteins that are the targets of the cholera bacteria. Although the mechanism is not yet understood, these genes appear to offer a survival advantage by making the proteins somewhat more resistant to attack by the cholera toxin. Because such genes offer a survival advantage within this population, they have slowly spread through the Bangladeshi population over the past 30,000 years. In other words, the Bangladeshi population is evolving increased resistance to cholera.

In addition to providing insight into the recent evolutionary past, data from this study reveal potential ways that humans might thwart the cholera bacterium. Perhaps pharmaceutical companies can exploit the proteins produced by the identified mutations to create a new generation of antibiotics. If so, this will represent another way that biologists have applied lessons learned from our understanding of evolution to improve human health. It also reminds us that we humans, like all life on Earth, are shaped by evolution due to changes in our environment, including the presence of infectious microorganisms that live around us.

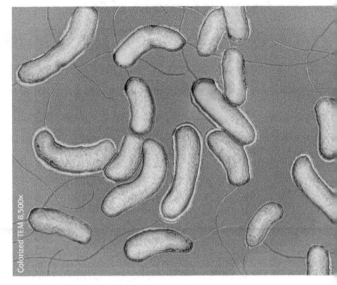

▼ Figure 4.21 People living in Bangladesh appear to have evolved resistance to *Vibrio cholerae*, the bacterium that causes the deadly disease cholera.

Chapter Review

■ SUMMARY OF KEY CONCEPTS

The Microscopic World of Cells

The Two Major Categories of Cells

CATEGORIES OF CELLS	
Prokaryotic Cells	**Eukaryotic Cells**
• Smaller • Simpler • Lack membrane-bound organelles • Found in bacteria and archaea	• Larger • More complex • Have membrane-bound organelles • Found in protists, plants, fungi, animals

An Overview of Eukaryotic Cells

Membranes partition eukaryotic cells into a number of functional compartments. The largest organelle is usually the nucleus. Other organelles are located in the cytoplasm, the region outside the nucleus and within the plasma membrane.

Membrane Structure

The Plasma Membrane

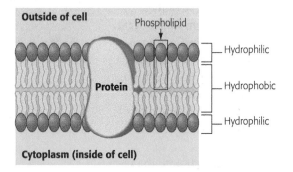

Cell Surfaces

The walls that encase plant cells support plants against the pull of gravity and also prevent cells from absorbing too much water. Animal cells are coated by a sticky extracellular matrix.

The Nucleus and Ribosomes: Genetic Control of the Cell

The Nucleus

An envelope consisting of two membranes encloses the nucleus. Within the nucleus, DNA and proteins make up chromatin fibers; each very long fiber is a single chromosome. The nucleus also contains the nucleolus, which produces components of ribosomes.

Ribosomes

Ribosomes produce proteins in the cytoplasm using messages produced by the DNA.

How DNA Directs Protein Production

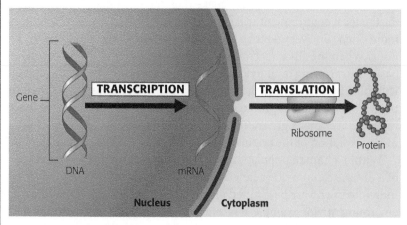

The Endomembrane System: Manufacturing and Distributing Cellular Products

The Endoplasmic Reticulum

The ER consists of membrane-enclosed tubes and sacs within the cytoplasm. Rough ER, named because of the ribosomes attached to its surface, makes membrane and secretory proteins. The functions of smooth ER include lipid synthesis and detoxification.

The Golgi Apparatus

The Golgi apparatus refines certain ER products and packages them in transport vesicles targeted for other organelles or export from the cell.

Lysosomes

Lysosomes, sacs containing digestive enzymes, aid digestion and recycling within the cell.

Vacuoles

Vacuoles include the contractile vacuoles that expel water from certain freshwater protists and the large, multifunctional central vacuoles of plant cells.

Energy Transformations: Chloroplasts and Mitochondria

Chloroplasts and Mitochondria

The Cytoskeleton: Cell Shape and Movement

Maintaining Cell Shape

Microtubules are an important component of the cytoskeleton, an organelle that gives support to, and maintains the shape of, cells.

Cilia and Flagella

Cilia and eukaryotic flagella are appendages that aid in movement, and they are made primarily of microtubules. Cilia are short and numerous and move the cell via coordinated beating. Flagella are long, often occur singly, and propel a cell with whiplike movements.

MasteringBiology®

For practice quizzes, BioFlix animations, MP3 tutorials, video tutors, and more study tools designed for this textbook, go to MasteringBiology®

SELF-QUIZ

1. You look into a microscope and view an unknown cell. What might you see that would tell you whether the cell is prokaryotic or eukaryotic?
   a. a rigid cell wall
   b. a nucleus
   c. a plasma membrane
   d. ribosomes

2. Explain how each word in the term *fluid mosaic* describes the structure of a membrane.

3. Identify which of the following structures includes all the others in the list: rough ER, smooth ER, endomembrane system, the Golgi apparatus.

4. The ER has two distinct regions that differ in structure and function. Lipids are synthesized within the _____, and proteins are synthesized within the _____.

5. A type of cell called a lymphocyte makes proteins that are exported from the cell. You can track the path of these proteins within the cell from production through export by labeling them with radioactive isotopes. Identify which of the following structures would be radioactively labeled in your experiment, listing them in the order in which they would be labeled: chloroplasts, Golgi apparatus, plasma membrane, smooth ER, rough ER, nucleus, mitochondria.

6. Name two similarities in the structure or function of chloroplasts and mitochondria. Name two differences.

7. Match the following organelles with their functions:
   a. ribosomes   1. movement
   b. microtubules   2. photosynthesis
   c. mitochondria   3. protein synthesis
   d. chloroplasts   4. digestion
   e. lysosomes   5. cellular respiration

8. DNA controls the cell by transmitting genetic messages that result in protein production. Place the following organelles in the order that represents the flow of genetic information from the DNA through the cell: nuclear pores, ribosomes, nucleus, rough ER, Golgi apparatus.

9. Compare and contrast cilia and flagella.

Answers to these questions can be found in Appendix: Self-Quiz Answers.

THE PROCESS OF SCIENCE

10. The cells of plant seeds store oils in the form of droplets enclosed by membranes. Unlike the membranes you learned about in this chapter, the oil droplet membrane consists of a single layer of phospholipids rather than a bilayer. Draw a model for a membrane around an oil droplet. Explain why this arrangement is more stable than a bilayer.

11. Imagine that you are a pediatrician and one of your patients is a newborn who may have a lysosomal storage disease. You remove some cells from the patient and examine them under the microscope. What would you expect to see? Design a series of tests that could reveal whether the patient is indeed suffering from a lysosomal storage disease.

12. **Interpreting Data** A population of bacteria may evolve resistance to a drug over time. Draw a graph that represents such a change. Label the *x*-axis as "time" and the *y*-axis as "population size." Draw a line on the graph that represents how the size of the population might change over time after the introduction of a new antibiotic. Label the point on your line where the new drug was introduced, and then indicate how the population size might change over time after that introduction.

BIOLOGY AND SOCIETY

13. Doctors at a university medical center removed John Moore's spleen, which is a standard treatment for his type of leukemia. The disease did not recur. Researchers kept the spleen cells alive in a nutrient medium. They found that some cells produced a blood protein that showed promise as a treatment for cancer and AIDS. The researchers patented the cells. Moore sued, claiming a share in profits from any products derived from his cells. The U.S. Supreme Court ruled against Moore, stating that his lawsuit "threatens to destroy the economic incentive to conduct important medical research." Moore argued that the ruling left patients "vulnerable to exploitation at the hands of the state." Do you think Moore was treated fairly? What else would you like to know about this case that might help you decide?

14. Scientists are learning to manipulate living cells in various ways, changing their genetic composition and the way they function. Some biotechnology companies have sought to patent their unique engineered cell lines. Do you think it is in society's best interest to allow cells to be patented? Why or why not? Do you think the same patent rules should apply whether the cells originate from a human or from a bacterium?

The Working Cell

Why Cellular Functions Matter

Both nerve gas and
insecticides work by
crippling a vital enzyme. ▶

For thousands of years, people have used osmosis
▼ to preserve food through salt and sugar curing.

▲ You'd have to walk more than 2 hours to burn
the calories in half a pepperoni pizza.

Nanotechnology BIOLOGY AND SOCIETY

Harnessing Cellular Structures

Imagine a tiny movable "car" with balls of carbon atoms for wheels, or a three-dimensional relief map of the world carved onto an object 1,000 times smaller than a grain of sand. These are real-world examples of nanotechnology, the manipulation of materials at the molecular scale. When designing devices of such small size, researchers often turn to living cells for inspiration. After all, you can think of a cell as a machine that continuously and efficiently performs a variety of functions, such as movement, energy processing, and production of various products. Let's consider one example of cell-based nanotechnology and see how it relates to working cells.

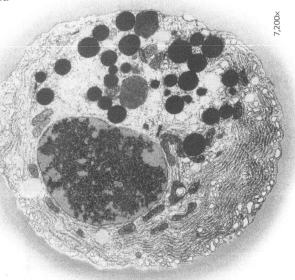

Researchers at Cornell University are attempting to harvest the energy-producing capability of human sperm cells. Like other cells, a sperm cell generates energy by breaking down sugars and other molecules that pass through its plasma membrane. Enzymes within the cell carry out a process called glycolysis. During glycolysis, the energy released from the breakdown of glucose is used to produce molecules of ATP. Within a living sperm, the ATP produced during glycolysis and other processes provides the energy that propels the sperm through the female reproductive tract. In an attempt to harness this energy-producing system, the Cornell researchers attached three glycolysis enzymes to a computer chip. The enzymes continued to function in this artificial system, producing energy from sugar. The hope is that a larger set of enzymes can eventually be used to power microscopic robots. Such nanorobots could use glucose from the bloodstream to power the delivery of drugs to body tissues, among many other possible tasks. This example is only a glimpse into the incredible potential of new technologies inspired by working cells.

Cellular structures. Even the smallest cell, such as this one from a human pancreas, is a miniature machine of startling complexity.

In this chapter, we'll explore three processes common to all living cells: energy metabolism, the use of enzymes to speed chemical reactions, and transport regulation by the plasma membrane. Along the way, we'll further consider nanotechnologies that mimic the natural activities of living cells.

Some Basic Energy Concepts

Energy makes the world go round—both on a planetary scale and on a cellular scale. But what exactly is energy? Our first step in understanding the working cell is to learn a few basic concepts about energy.

Conservation of Energy

Energy is defined as the capacity to cause change. Some forms of energy are used to perform work, such as moving an object against an opposing force—for example, lifting a barbell against the force of gravity. Imagine a diver climbing to the top of a platform and then diving off (Figure 5.1). To get to the top of the platform, the diver must perform work to overcome the opposing force of gravity. Specifically, chemical energy from food is converted to **kinetic energy**, the energy of motion. In this case, the kinetic energy takes the form of muscle movement propelling the diver to the top of the platform.

What happens to the kinetic energy when the diver reaches the top of the platform? Does it disappear at that point? In fact, it does not. A physical principle known as **conservation of energy** explains that it is not possible to destroy or create energy. Energy can only be converted from one form to another. A power plant, for example, does not make energy; it merely converts it from one form (such as energy stored in coal) to a more convenient form (such as electricity). That's what happens in the diver's climb up the steps. The kinetic energy of muscle movement is stored as **potential energy**, the energy an object has because of its location or structure. The energy contained by water behind a dam or by a compressed spring are examples of potential energy. In our example, the diver at the top of the platform has potential energy because of his elevated location. Then the act of diving off the platform into the water converts the potential energy back to kinetic energy. Life depends on countless similar conversions of energy from one form to another. ☑

► Figure 5.1 **Energy conversions during a dive.**

On the platform, the diver has more potential energy.

Climbing the steps converts kinetic energy of muscle movement to potential energy.

Diving converts potential energy to kinetic energy.

In the water, the diver has less potential energy.

Heat

If energy cannot be destroyed, where has the energy gone in our example when the diver hits the water? The energy has been converted to **heat**, a type of kinetic energy contained in the random motion of atoms and molecules. The friction between the body and its surroundings generated heat in the air and then in the water.

All energy conversions generate some heat. Although releasing heat does not destroy energy, it does make it more difficult to harness for useful work. Heat is energy in its most disordered, chaotic form, the energy of aimless molecular movement.

Entropy is a measure of the amount of disorder, or randomness, in a system. Consider an analogy from your own room. It's easy to increase the chaos—in fact, it seems to happen spontaneously! But it requires the expenditure of significant energy to restore order once again.

Every time energy is converted from one form to another, entropy increases. The energy conversions during the climb up the ladder and the dive from the platform increased entropy as the diver emitted heat to the surroundings. To climb up the steps again for another dive, the diver must use additional stored food energy. This conversion will also create heat and therefore increase entropy. ✓

Chemical Energy

How can molecules derived from the food we eat provide energy for our working cells? The molecules of food, gasoline, and other fuels have a form of potential energy called **chemical energy**, which arises from the arrangement of atoms and can be released by a chemical reaction. Carbohydrates, fats, and gasoline have structures that make them especially rich in chemical energy.

Living cells and automobile engines use the same basic process to make the chemical energy stored in their fuels available for work (Figure 5.2). In both cases, this process breaks organic fuel into smaller waste molecules that have much less chemical energy than the fuel molecules did, thereby releasing energy that can be used to perform work.

For example, the engine of an automobile mixes oxygen with gasoline (which is why all cars require an air intake system) in an explosive chemical reaction that breaks down the fuel molecules and pushes the pistons that eventually move the wheels. The waste products emitted from the car's exhaust pipe are mostly carbon dioxide and water. Only about 25% of the energy that an automobile engine extracts from its fuel is converted to the kinetic energy of the car's movement. Most of

☑ CHECKPOINT

Which form of energy is most randomized and difficult to put to work?

Answer: heat

◄ Figure 5.2 **Energy conversions in a car and a cell.** In both a car and a cell, the chemical energy of organic fuel molecules is harvested using oxygen. This chemical breakdown releases energy stored in the fuel molecules and produces carbon dioxide and water. The released energy can be used to perform work.

Fuel rich in chemical energy	Energy conversion	Waste products poor in chemical energy

Octane (from gasoline) + Oxygen

Heat energy

Combustion Kinetic energy of movement

Carbon dioxide + Water

Energy conversion in a car

Glucose (from food) + Oxygen

Heat energy

Cellular respiration ATP Energy for cellular work

Carbon dioxide + Water

Energy conversion in a cell

the rest is converted to heat—so much that the engine would melt if the car's radiator did not disperse heat into the atmosphere. That is why high-end performance cars need sophisticated air flow systems to avoid overheating.

Cells also use oxygen in reactions that release energy from fuel molecules. As in a car engine, the "exhaust" from such reactions in cells is mostly carbon dioxide and water. The combustion of fuel in cells is called cellular respiration, which is a more gradual and efficient "burning" of fuel compared with the explosive combustion in an automobile engine. Cellular respiration is the energy-releasing chemical breakdown of fuel molecules and the storage of that energy in a form the cell can use to perform work. (We will discuss the details of cellular respiration in Chapter 6.) You convert about 34% of your food energy to useful work, such as movement of your muscles. The rest of the energy released by the breakdown of fuel molecules generates body heat. Humans and many other animals can use this heat to keep the body at an almost constant temperature (37°C, or 98.6°F, in the case of humans), even when the surrounding air is much colder. You've probably noticed how quickly a crowded room warms up—it's all that released metabolic heat energy! The liberation of heat energy also explains why you feel hot after exercise. Sweating and other cooling mechanisms enable your body to lose the excess heat, much as a car's radiator keeps the engine from overheating.

Food Calories

Read any packaged food label and you'll find the number of calories in each serving of that food. Calories are units of energy. A **calorie** (cal) is the amount of energy that can raise the temperature of 1 gram (g) of water by 1°C. You could actually measure the caloric content of a peanut by burning it under a container of water to convert all of the stored chemical energy to heat and then measuring the temperature increase of the water.

Calories are tiny units of energy, so using them to describe the fuel content of foods is not practical. Instead, it's conventional to use kilocalories (kcal), units of 1,000 calories. In fact, the Calories (capital C) on a food package are actually kilocalories. For example, one peanut has about 5 Calories. That's a lot of energy, enough to increase the temperature of 1 kg (a little more than a quart) of water by 5°C. And just a handful of peanuts contains enough Calories, if converted to heat, to boil 1 kg of water. In living organisms, of course, food isn't used to boil water but instead used to fuel the activities of life. Figure 5.3 shows the number of Calories in several foods and how many Calories are burned by some typical activities. ✓

You'd have to walk more than 2 hours to burn the calories in half a pepperoni pizza.

✓ CHECKPOINT

According to Figure 5.3, how long would you have to ride your bicycle to burn off the energy in a cheeseburger?

Answer: a little more than a half hour (1 cheeseburger = 295 Calories; 1 hour of cycling consumes 490 Calories, so 295/490 = 0.6 hours, or about 36 minutes)

▼ Figure 5.3 **Some caloric accounting.**

Food	Food Calories
Cheeseburger	295
Spaghetti with sauce (1 cup)	241
Baked potato (plain, with skin)	220
Fried chicken (drumstick)	193
Bean burrito	189
Pizza with pepperoni (1 slice)	181
Peanuts (1 ounce)	166
Apple	81
Garden salad (2 cups)	56
Popcorn (plain, 1 cup)	31
Broccoli (1 cup)	25

(a) Food Calories (kilocalories) in various foods

Activity	Food Calories consumed per hour by a 150-pound person*
Running (7 min/mi)	979
Dancing (fast)	510
Bicycling (10 mph)	490
Swimming (2 mph)	408
Walking (3 mph)	245
Dancing (slow)	204
Playing the piano	73
Driving a car	61
Sitting (writing)	28

*Not including energy necessary for basic functions, such as breathing and heartbeat

(b) Food Calories (kilocalories) we burn in various activities

ATP and Cellular Work

The carbohydrates, fats, and other fuel molecules we obtain from food cannot be used directly as fuel for our cells. Instead, the chemical energy released by the breakdown of organic molecules during cellular respiration is used to generate molecules of ATP. These molecules of ATP then power cellular work. ATP acts like an energy shuttle, storing energy obtained from food and then releasing it as needed at a later time. Such energy transformations are essential for all life on Earth.

The Structure of ATP

The abbreviation ATP stands for adenosine triphosphate. **ATP** consists of an organic molecule called adenosine plus a tail of three phosphate groups (Figure 5.4). The triphosphate tail is the "business" end of ATP, the part that provides energy for cellular work. Each phosphate group is negatively charged. Negative charges repel each other. The crowding of negative charges in the triphosphate tail contributes to the potential energy of ATP. It's analogous to storing energy by compressing a spring; if you release the spring, it will relax, and you can use that springiness to do some useful work. For ATP power, it is release of the phosphate at the tip of the triphosphate tail that makes energy available to working cells. What remains is **ADP**, adenosine diphosphate (two phosphate groups instead of three, shown on the right side of Figure 5.4).

Phosphate Transfer

When ATP drives work in cells by being converted to ADP, the released phosphate groups don't just fly off into space. ATP energizes other molecules in cells by transferring phosphate groups to those molecules. When a target molecule accepts the third phosphate group, it becomes energized and can then perform work in the cell. Imagine a bicyclist pedaling up a hill. In the muscle cells of the rider's legs, ATP transfers phosphate groups to motor proteins. The proteins then change shape, causing the muscle cells to contract (Figure 5.5a). This contraction provides the mechanical energy needed to propel the rider. ATP also enables the transport of ions and other dissolved substances across the membranes of the rider's nerve cells (Figure 5.5b), helping them send signals to her legs. And ATP drives the production of a cell's large molecules from smaller molecular building blocks (Figure 5.5c).

▼ Figure 5.4 **ATP power.** Each (P) in the triphosphate tail of ATP represents a phosphate group, a phosphorus atom bonded to oxygen atoms. The transfer of a phosphate from the triphosphate tail to other molecules provides energy for cellular work.

▼ Figure 5.5 **How ATP drives cellular work.** Each type of work shown here is powered when an enzyme transfers phosphate from ATP to a recipient molecule.

(a) Motor protein performing mechanical work (moving a muscle fiber)

(b) Transport protein performing transport work (importing a solute)

(c) Chemical reactants performing chemical work (promoting a chemical reaction)

☑ **CHECKPOINT**

1. Explain how ATP powers cellular work.
2. What is the source of energy for regenerating ATP from ADP?

Answers: 1. ATP transfers a phosphate to another molecule, increasing that molecule's energy. 2. chemical energy harvested from sugars and other organic fuels via cellular respiration

The ATP Cycle

Your cells spend ATP continuously. Fortunately, it is a renewable resource. ATP can be restored by adding a phosphate group back to ADP. That takes energy, like recompressing a spring. And that's where food enters the picture. The chemical energy that cellular respiration harvests from sugars and other organic fuels is put to work regenerating a cell's supply of ATP. Cellular work spends ATP, which is recycled when ADP and phosphate are combined using energy released by cellular respiration (Figure 5.6). Thus, energy from processes that yield energy, such as the breakdown of organic fuels, is transferred to processes that consume energy, such as muscle

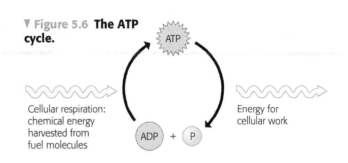

▼ Figure 5.6 **The ATP cycle.**

Cellular respiration: chemical energy harvested from fuel molecules

Energy for cellular work

contraction and other cellular work. The ATP cycle can run at an astonishing pace: Up to 10 million ATPs are consumed and recycled each second in a working muscle cell. ☑

Enzymes

A living organism contains a vast collection of chemicals, and countless chemical reactions constantly change the organism's molecular makeup. In a sense, a living organism is a complex "chemical square dance," with the molecular "dancers" continually changing partners via chemical reactions. The total of all the chemical reactions in an organism is called **metabolism**. But almost no metabolic reactions occur without help. Most require the assistance of **enzymes**, proteins that speed up chemical reactions without being consumed by those reactions. All living cells contain thousands of different enzymes, each promoting a different chemical reaction.

☑ **CHECKPOINT**

How does an enzyme affect the activation energy of a chemical reaction?

Answer: An enzyme lowers the activation energy.

Activation Energy

For a chemical reaction to begin, chemical bonds in the reactant molecules must be broken. (The first step in swapping partners during a square dance is to let go of your current partner's hand.) This process requires that the molecules absorb energy from their surroundings. In other words, for most chemical reactions, a cell has to spend a little energy to make more. You can easily relate this concept to your own life: it takes effort to clean your room, but this will save you more energy in the long run because you won't have to hunt for your belongings. The energy that must be invested to start a reaction is called **activation energy** because it activates the reactants and triggers the chemical reaction.

Enzymes enable metabolism to occur by reducing the amount of activation energy required to break the bonds of reactant molecules. If you think of the activation energy as a barrier to a chemical reaction, an enzyme's function is to lower that barrier (Figure 5.7). It does so by binding to reactant molecules and putting them under physical or chemical stress, making it easier to break their bonds and start a reaction. In our analogy of cleaning your room, this is like a friend offering to help you. You start and end in the same place whether solo or assisted, but your friend's help lowers your activation energy, making it more likely that you'll proceed. Next, we'll return to our theme of nanotechnology to see how enzymes can be engineered to be even more efficient. ☑

▼ Figure 5.7 **Enzymes and activation energy.**

(a) Without enzyme. A reactant molecule must overcome the activation energy barrier before a chemical reaction can break the molecule into products.

(b) With enzyme. An enzyme speeds the chemical reaction by lowering the activation energy barrier.

Nanotechnology THE PROCESS OF SCIENCE

Can Enzymes Be Engineered?

Like all other proteins, enzymes are encoded by genes. **Observations** of genetic sequences suggest that many of our genes were formed through a type of molecular evolution: One ancestral gene duplicated, and the two copies diverged over time via random genetic changes, eventually becoming distinct genes for enzymes with different functions.

The natural evolution of enzymes raises a **question**: Can laboratory methods mimic this process through artificial selection? A group of researchers at two California biotechnology companies formed the **hypothesis** that an artificial process could be used to modify the gene that codes for the enzyme lactase (which breaks down the sugar lactose) into a new gene coding for a new enzyme with a new function. Their **experiment** used a procedure called directed evolution. In this process, many copies of the gene for the starting lactase enzyme were mutated at random (**Figure 5.8**). The researchers tested the enzymes resulting from these mutated genes to determine which enzymes best displayed a new activity (in this case, breaking down a different sugar). The genes for the enzymes that did show the new activity were then subjected to several more rounds of duplication, mutation, and screening.

After seven rounds, the **results** indicated that directed evolution had produced a new enzyme with a novel function. Researchers have used similar methods to produce many artificial enzymes with desired properties, such as one that produces an antibiotic with tenfold greater efficiency, ones that remain stable and productive under high-heat industrial conditions, and one that greatly improves the production of cholesterol-lowering drugs. These results show that directed evolution is another example of how scientists can mimic the natural processes of cells for their own purposes.

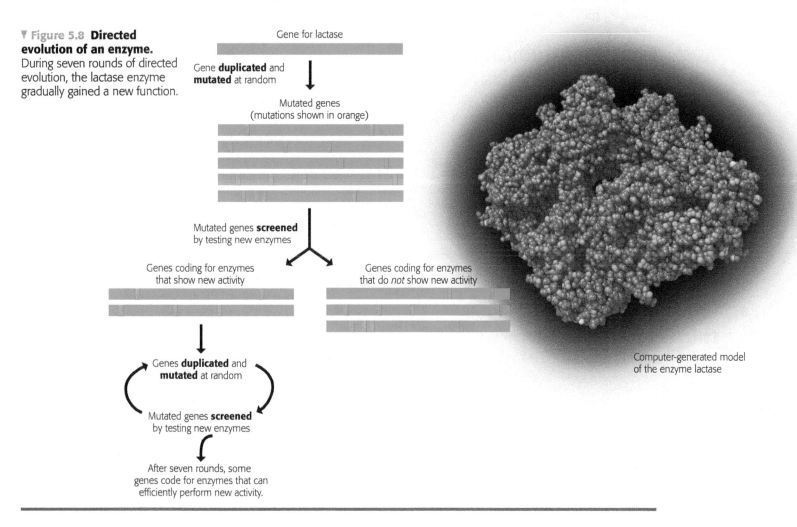

▼ Figure 5.8 **Directed evolution of an enzyme.** During seven rounds of directed evolution, the lactase enzyme gradually gained a new function.

Gene for lactase

Gene **duplicated** and **mutated** at random

Mutated genes (mutations shown in orange)

Mutated genes **screened** by testing new enzymes

Genes coding for enzymes that show new activity

Genes coding for enzymes that do *not* show new activity

Genes **duplicated** and **mutated** at random

Mutated genes **screened** by testing new enzymes

After seven rounds, some genes code for enzymes that can efficiently perform new activity.

Computer-generated model of the enzyme lactase

Structure/ Function ## Enzyme Activity

An enzyme is very selective in the reaction it catalyzes. This selectivity is based on the enzyme's ability to recognize a certain reactant molecule, which is called the enzyme's **substrate**. A region of the enzyme called the **active site** has a shape and chemistry that fits the substrate molecule. The active site is typically a pocket or groove on the surface of the enzyme. When a substrate slips into this docking station, the active site changes shape slightly to embrace the substrate and catalyze the reaction. This interaction is called **induced fit** because the entry of the substrate induces the enzyme to change shape slightly, making the fit between substrate and active site snugger. Think of a handshake: As your hand makes contact with another hand, it changes shape slightly to make a better fit.

After the products are released from the active site, the enzyme can accept another molecule of substrate. In fact, the ability to function repeatedly is a key characteristic of enzymes. **Figure 5.9** follows the action of the enzyme lactase, which breaks down the disaccharide lactose (the substrate). This enzyme is underproduced or defective in lactose-intolerant people. Like lactase, many enzymes are named for their substrates, with an *-ase* ending. ✓

Enzyme Inhibitors

Certain molecules can inhibit a metabolic reaction by binding to an enzyme and disrupting its function (**Figure 5.10**). Some of these **enzyme inhibitors** are substrate imposters that plug up the active site. (You can't shake a person's hand if someone else puts a banana in it first!) Other inhibitors bind to the enzyme at a site remote from the active site, but the binding changes the enzyme's shape. (Imagine trying to shake hands when someone is tickling your ribs, causing you to clench your hand.) In each case, an inhibitor disrupts the enzyme by altering its shape—a clear example of the link between structure and function.

In some cases, the binding of an inhibitor is reversible. For example, if a cell is producing more of a certain product than it needs, that product may reversibly inhibit an enzyme required for its production. This feedback regulation keeps the cell from wasting resources that could be put to better use.

Many beneficial drugs work by inhibiting enzymes. Penicillin blocks the active site of an enzyme that bacteria use in making cell walls. Ibuprofen inhibits an enzyme involved in sending pain signals. Many cancer drugs inhibit enzymes that promote cell division. Many toxins and poisons also work as inhibitors. Nerve gases (a form of chemical warfare) irreversibly bind to the active site of an enzyme vital to transmitting nerve impulses, leading to rapid paralysis and death. Many pesticides are toxic to insects because they inhibit this same enzyme.

Both nerve gas and insecticides work by crippling a vital enzyme.

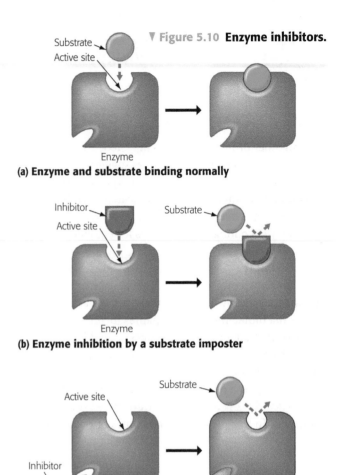

▼ Figure 5.10 **Enzyme inhibitors.**

Substrate
Active site
Enzyme

(a) Enzyme and substrate binding normally

Inhibitor
Active site
Substrate
Enzyme

(b) Enzyme inhibition by a substrate imposter

Active site
Substrate
Inhibitor
Enzyme

(c) Inhibition of an enzyme by a molecule that causes the active site to change shape

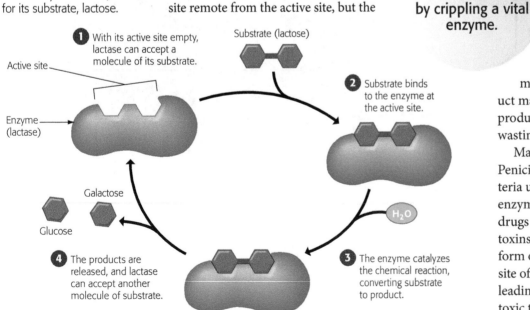

▼ Figure 5.9 **How an enzyme works.** Our example is the enzyme lactase, named for its substrate, lactose.

Active site

Enzyme (lactase)

Galactose

Glucose

1 With its active site empty, lactase can accept a molecule of its substrate.

Substrate (lactose)

2 Substrate binds to the enzyme at the active site.

H_2O

3 The enzyme catalyzes the chemical reaction, converting substrate to product.

4 The products are released, and lactase can accept another molecule of substrate.

Membrane Function

So far, we have discussed how cells control the flow of energy and how enzymes affect the pace of chemical reactions. In addition to these vital processes, cells must also regulate the flow of materials to and from the environment. The plasma membrane consists of a double layer of fat (a phospholipid bilayer) with embedded proteins (see Figure 4.4). **Figure 5.11** describes the major functions of these membrane proteins. Of all the functions shown in the figure, one of the most important is the regulation of transport in and out of the cell. A steady traffic of small molecules moves across a cell's plasma membrane in both directions. But this traffic flow is never willy-nilly. Instead, all biological membranes are selectively permeable—that is, they only allow certain molecules to pass. Let's explore this in more detail.

Passive Transport: Diffusion across Membranes

Molecules are restless. They constantly vibrate and wander randomly. One result of this motion is **diffusion**, the movement of molecules spreading out evenly into the available space. Each molecule moves randomly, but the overall diffusion of a population of molecules is usually directional, from a region where the molecules are more concentrated to a region where they are less concentrated. For example, imagine many molecules of perfume inside a bottle. If you remove the bottle top, every molecule of perfume will move randomly about, but the overall movement will be out of the bottle, and the room will eventually smell of the perfume. You could, with great effort, return the perfume molecules to its bottle, but the molecules would never all return spontaneously.

▼ **Figure 5.11 Primary functions of membrane proteins.** An actual cell may have just a few of the types of proteins shown here, and many copies of each particular protein may be present.

Enzymatic activity. This protein and the one next to it are enzymes, having an active site that fits a substrate. Enzymes may form an assembly line that carries out steps of a pathway.

Cytoplasm

Fibers of extracellular matrix

Cell signaling. A binding site fits the shape of a chemical messenger. The messenger may cause a change in the protein that relays the message to the inside of the cell.

Attachment to the cytoskeleton and extracellular matrix. Such proteins help maintain cell shape and coordinate changes.

Cytoskeleton

Cytoplasm

Transport. A protein may provide a channel that a chemical substance can pass through.

Intercellular joining. Proteins may link adjacent cells.

Cell-cell recognition. Some proteins with chains of sugars serve as identification tags recognized by other cells.

For an example closer to a living cell, imagine a membrane separating pure water from a mixture of dye dissolved in water (Figure 5.12). Assume that this membrane has tiny holes that allow dye molecules to pass. Although each dye molecule moves randomly, there will be a net migration across the membrane to the side that began as pure water. Movement of the dye will continue until both solutions have equal concentrations. After that, there will be a dynamic equilibrium: Molecules will still be moving, but at that point as many dye molecules move in one direction as in the other.

Diffusion of dye across a membrane is an example of **passive transport**—*passive* because the cell does not expend any energy for the diffusion to happen. But remember that the cell membrane is selectively permeable. For example, small molecules such as oxygen (O_2) generally pass through more readily than larger molecules such as amino acids. But the membrane is relatively impermeable to even some very small substances, such as most ions, which are too hydrophilic to pass through the phospholipid bilayer. In passive transport, a substance diffuses down its **concentration gradient**, from where the substance is more concentrated to where it is less concentrated.

In our lungs, for example, there is more oxygen gas (O_2) in the air than in the blood. Therefore, oxygen moves by passive transport from the air into the bloodstream.

Substances that do not cross membranes spontaneously—or otherwise cross very slowly—can be transported via proteins that act as corridors for specific molecules (see Figure 5.11). This assisted transport is called **facilitated diffusion**. For example, water molecules can move through the plasma membrane of some cells via transport proteins—each of which can help 3 billion water molecules per second pass through! People with a rare mutation in the gene that encodes these water-transport proteins have defective kidneys that cannot reabsorb water; such people must drink 20 liters of water every day to prevent dehydration. On the flip side, a common complication of pregnancy is fluid retention, the culprit responsible for swollen ankles and feet, often caused by increased synthesis of water channel proteins. Other specific transport proteins move glucose across cell membranes 50,000 times faster than diffusion. Even at this rate, facilitated diffusion is a type of passive transport because it does not require the cell to expend energy. As in all passive transport, the driving force is the concentration gradient. ☑

▼ Figure 5.12 **Passive transport: diffusion across a membrane.**
A substance will diffuse from where it is more concentrated to where it is less concentrated. Put another way, a substance tends to diffuse down its concentration gradient.

(a) Passive transport of one type of molecule. The membrane is permeable to these dye molecules, which diffuse down the concentration gradient. At equilibrium, the molecules are still restless, but the rate of transport is equal in both directions.

(b) Passive transport of two types of molecules. If solutions have two or more solutes, each will diffuse down its own concentration gradient.

Osmosis and Water Balance

The diffusion of water across a selectively permeable membrane is called **osmosis** (Figure 5.13). A **solute** is a substance that is dissolved in a liquid solvent, and the resulting mixture is called a **solution**. For example, a solution of salt water contains salt (the solute) dissolved in water (the solvent). Imagine a membrane separating two solutions with different concentrations of a solute. The solution with a higher concentration of solute is

▼ Figure 5.13 **Osmosis.** A membrane separates two solutions with different sugar concentrations. Water molecules can pass through the membrane, but sugar molecules cannot.

said to be **hypertonic** to the other solution. The solution with the lower solute concentration is said to be **hypotonic** to the other. Note that the hypotonic solution, by having the lower solute concentration, has the higher water concentration (less solute = more water). Therefore, water will diffuse across the membrane along its concentration gradient from an area of higher water concentration (hypotonic solution) to one of lower water concentration (hypertonic solution). This reduces the difference in solute concentrations and changes the volumes of the two solutions.

People can take advantage of osmosis to preserve foods. Salt is often applied to meats—like pork and cod—to cure them; the salt causes water to move out of food-spoiling bacteria and fungi. Food can also be preserved in honey because a high sugar concentration draws water out of food.

When the solute concentrations are the same on both sides of a membrane, water molecules will move at the same rate in both directions, so there will be no net change in solute concentration. Solutions of equal solute concentration are said to be **isotonic**. For example, many marine animals, such as sea stars and crabs, are isotonic to seawater, so that overall they neither gain nor lose water from the environment. In hospitals, intravenous (IV) fluids administered to patients must be isotonic to blood cells to avoid harm.

Water Balance in Animal Cells

The survival of a cell depends on its ability to balance water uptake and loss. When an animal cell is immersed in an isotonic solution, the cell's volume remains constant because the cell gains water at the same rate that it loses water (Figure 5.14a, top). But what happens if an animal cell is in contact with a hypotonic solution, which has a lower solute concentration than the cell? Due to osmosis, the cell would gain water, swell, and possibly burst (lyse) like an overfilled water balloon (Figure 5.14b, top). A hypertonic environment is also harsh on an animal cell; the cell shrivels from water loss (Figure 5.14c, top).

For an animal to survive a hypotonic or hypertonic environment, the animal must have a way to balance the uptake and loss of water. The control of water balance is called **osmoregulation**. For example, a freshwater fish has kidneys and gills that work constantly to prevent an excessive buildup of water in the body. Humans can suffer consequences of osmoregulation failure. Dehydration (consumption of too little water) can cause fatigue and even death. Drinking too much water—called hyponatremia or "water intoxication"—can also cause death by overdiluting necessary ions.

Animal cell

Normal

Lysing

Shriveled

Plant cell

H_2O

Plasma membrane

Flaccid (wilts)

Turgid (normal)

Shriveled

(a) Isotonic solution

(b) Hypotonic solution

(c) Hypertonic solution

◄ **Figure 5.14 Osmotic environments.** Animal cells (such as a red blood cell) and plant cells behave differently in different osmotic environments.

Water Balance in Plant Cells

Problems of water balance are somewhat different for cells that have rigid cell walls, such as those from plants, fungi, many prokaryotes, and some protists. A plant cell immersed in an isotonic solution is flaccid (floppy), and the plant wilts (Figure 5.14a, bottom). In contrast, a plant cell is turgid (very firm) and healthiest in a hypotonic environment, with a net inflow of water (Figure 5.14b, bottom). Although the elastic cell wall expands a bit, the back pressure it exerts prevents the cell from taking in too much water and bursting. Turgor is necessary for plants to retain their upright posture and the extended state of their leaves (Figure 5.15). However, in a hypertonic environment, a plant cell is no better off than an animal cell. As a plant cell loses water, it shrivels, and its plasma membrane pulls away from the cell wall (Figure 5.14c, bottom). This usually kills the cell. Thus, plant cells thrive in a hypotonic environment, whereas animal cells thrive in an isotonic one. ☑

> For thousands of years, people have used osmosis to preserve food through salt and sugar curing.

▼ **Figure 5.15 Plant turgor.** Watering a wilted plant will make it regain its turgor.

☑ CHECKPOINT

1. An animal cell shrivels when it is _____ compared with its environment.
2. The cells of a wilted plant are _____ compared with their environment.

Answers: 1. hypertonic 2. isotonic

Active Transport: The Pumping of Molecules across Membranes

In contrast to passive transport, **active transport** requires that a cell expend energy to move molecules across a membrane. Cellular energy (usually provided by ATP) is used to drive a transport protein that pumps a solute *against* the concentration gradient—that is, in the direction that is opposite the way it would naturally flow (Figure 5.16). Movement against a force, like rolling a boulder uphill against gravity, requires a considerable expenditure of energy.

Active transport allows cells to maintain internal concentrations of small solutes that differ from environmental concentrations. For example, compared with its surroundings, an animal nerve cell has a much higher concentration of potassium ions and a much lower concentration of sodium ions. The plasma membrane helps maintain these differences by pumping sodium out of the cell and potassium into the cell. This particular case of active transport (called the sodium-potassium pump) is vital to the nervous system of most animals. ☑

▲ Figure 5.16 **Active transport.** Transport proteins are specific in their recognition of atoms or molecules. This transport protein (purple) has a binding site that accepts only a certain solute. Using energy from ATP, the protein pumps the solute against its concentration gradient.

Exocytosis and Endocytosis: Traffic of Large Molecules

So far, we've focused on how water and small solutes enter and leave cells by moving through the plasma membrane. The story is different for large molecules such as proteins, which are much too big to fit through the membrane. Their traffic into and out of the cell depends on the ability of the cell to package large molecules inside sacs called vesicles. You have already seen an example of this: During protein production by the cell, secretory proteins exit the cell from transport vesicles that fuse with the plasma membrane, spilling the contents outside the cell (see Figures 4.12 and 4.16). That process is called **exocytosis** (Figure 5.17). When you cry, for example, cells in your tear glands use exocytosis to export the salty tears. In your brain, the exocytosis of neurotransmitter chemicals such as dopamine helps neurons communicate.

In **endocytosis**, a cell takes material in via vesicles that bud inward (Figure 5.18). For example, in a process called **phagocytosis** ("cellular eating"), a cell engulfs a particle and packages it within a food vacuole. Other times, a cell "gulps" droplets of fluid into vesicles. Endocytosis can also be triggered by the binding of certain external molecules to specific receptor proteins built into the plasma membrane. This binding causes the local region of the membrane to form a vesicle that transports the specific substance into the cell. In human liver cells, this process is used to take up cholesterol from the blood. An inherited defect in the receptors on liver cells can lead to an inability to process cholesterol, which can lead to heart attacks at ages as young as 5. Cells of your immune system use endocytosis to engulf and destroy invading bacteria and viruses.

Because all cells have a plasma membrane, it is logical to infer that membranes first formed early in the evolution of life on Earth. In the final section of this chapter, we'll consider the evolution of membranes.

▼ Figure 5.17 **Exocytosis.**

▼ Figure 5.18 **Endocytosis.**

Nanotechnology EVOLUTION CONNECTION

The Origin of Membranes

By simulating conditions found on the early Earth, scientists have been able to demonstrate that many of the molecules important to life can form spontaneously. (See Figure 15.3 and the accompanying text for a description of one such experiment.) Such results suggest that phospholipids, the key ingredients in all membranes, were probably among the first organic compounds that formed from chemical reactions on the early Earth. Once formed, they could self-assemble into simple membranes. When a mixture of phospholipids and water is shaken, for example, the phospholipids organize into bilayers, forming water-filled bubbles of membrane (Figure 5.19). This assembly requires neither genes nor other information beyond the properties of the phospholipids themselves.

The tendency of lipids in water to spontaneously form membranes has led biomedical engineers to produce liposomes (a type of artificial vesicle) that can encase particular chemicals. In the future, these engineered liposomes may be used to deliver nutrients or medications to specific sites within the body. In fact, as of 2012, 12 drugs have been approved for delivery via liposomes, including ones that target fungal infections, influenza, and hepatitis. Thus, membranes—like the other cellular components discussed in the Biology and Society and the Process of Science sections—have inspired novel nanotechnologies.

The formation of membrane-enclosed collections of molecules would have been a critical step in the evolution of the first cells. A membrane can enclose a solution that is different in composition from its surroundings. A plasma membrane that allows cells to regulate their chemical exchanges with the environment is a basic requirement for life. Indeed, all cells are enclosed by a plasma membrane that is similar in structure and function—illustrating the evolutionary unity of life.

▼ Figure 5.19 **The spontaneous formation of membranes: a key step in the origin of life.**

Water-filled bubble made of phospholipids

Colorized LM 75x

Chapter Review

■ SUMMARY OF KEY CONCEPTS

Some Basic Energy Concepts

Conservation of Energy

Machines and organisms can transform kinetic energy (energy of motion) to potential energy (stored energy) and vice versa. In all such energy transformations, total energy is conserved. Energy cannot be created or destroyed.

Heat

Every energy conversion releases some randomized energy in the form of heat. Entropy is a measure of disorder, or randomness.

Chemical Energy

Molecules store varying amounts of potential energy in the arrangement of their atoms. Organic compounds are relatively rich in such chemical energy. The combustion of gasoline within a car's engine and the breakdown of glucose via cellular respiration within living cells are both examples of how the chemical energy stored in molecules can be converted to useful work.

Food Calories

Food Calories, actually kilocalories, are units used to measure the amount of energy in our foods and the amount of energy we expend in various activities.

ATP and Cellular Work

Your cells recycle ATP: as ATP is broken down to ADP to drive cellular work, new molecules of ATP are built from ADP using energy obtained from food.

Enzymes

Activation Energy

Enzymes are biological catalysts that speed up metabolic reactions by lowering the activation energy required to break the bonds of reactant molecules.

Enzyme Activity

The entry of a substrate into the active site of an enzyme causes the enzyme to change shape slightly, allowing for a better fit and thereby promoting the interaction of enzyme with substrate.

Enzyme Inhibitors

Enzyme inhibitors are molecules that can disrupt metabolic reactions by binding to enzymes, either at the active site or elsewhere.

Membrane Function

Proteins embedded in the plasma membrane perform a wide variety of functions, including regulating transport, anchoring to other cells or substances, promoting enzymatic reactions, and recognizing other cells.

Passive Transport, Osmosis, and Active Transport

Most animal cells require an isotonic environment, with equal concentrations of water within and outside the cell. Plant cells need a hypotonic environment, which causes water to flow inward, keeping walled cells turgid.

Exocytosis and Endocytosis: Traffic of Large Molecules

Exocytosis is the secretion of large molecules within vesicles. Endocytosis is the import of large substances via vesicles into the cell.

MasteringBiology®

For practice quizzes, BioFlix animations, MP3 tutorials, video tutors, and more study tools designed for this textbook, go to MasteringBiology®

SELF-QUIZ

1. Describe the energy transformations that occur when you climb to the top of a stairway.

2. _____ is the capacity to perform work, while _____ is a measure of randomness.

3. The label on a candy bar says that it contains 150 Calories. If you could convert all of that energy to heat, you could raise the temperature of how much water by 15°C?

4. Why does removing a phosphate group from the triphosphate tail in a molecule of ATP release energy?

5. Your digestive system uses a variety of enzymes to break down large food molecules into smaller ones that your cells can assimilate. A generic name for a digestive enzyme is hydrolase. What is the chemical basis for that name? (*Hint*: Review Figure 3.4.)

6. Explain how an inhibitor can disrupt an enzyme's action without binding to the active site.

7. If someone at the other end of a room smokes a cigarette, you may breathe in some smoke. The movement of smoke is similar to what type of transport?
   a. osmosis
   b. diffusion
   c. facilitated diffusion
   d. active transport

8. Explain why it is not enough just to say that a solution is "hypertonic."

9. What is the primary difference between passive and active transport in terms of concentration gradients?

10. Which of these types of cellular transport require(s) energy?
    a. facilitated diffusion
    b. active transport
    c. osmosis
    d. a and b

Answers to these questions can be found in Appendix: Self-Quiz Answers.

THE PROCESS OF SCIENCE

11. HIV, the virus that causes AIDS, depends on an enzyme called reverse transcriptase to multiply. Reverse transcriptase reads a molecule of RNA and creates a molecule of DNA from it. A molecule of AZT, the first drug approved to treat AIDS, has a shape very similar to (but a bit different than) that of the DNA base thymine. Propose a model for how AZT inhibits HIV.

12. Gaining and losing weight are matters of caloric accounting: Calories in the food you eat minus Calories that you spend in activity. One pound of human body fat contains approximately 3,500 Calories. Using Figure 5.3, compare ways you could burn off those Calories. How far would you have to run, swim, or walk to burn the equivalent of 1 pound

of fat, and how long would it take? Which method of burning Calories appeals the most to you? The least? How much of each food would you have to consume in order to gain a single pound? How does one pound's worth of food compare with one pound's worth of exercise? Does it seem like an even trade-off?

13. **Interpreting Data** The graph below illustrates the course of a chemical reaction with and without an enzyme. Which curve represents the reaction in the presence of the enzyme? What energy changes are represented by the lines labeled a, b, and c?

BIOLOGY AND SOCIETY

14. Obesity is a serious health problem for many Americans. Several popular diet plans advocate low-carbohydrate diets. Most low-carb dieters compensate by eating more protein and fat. What are the advantages and disadvantages of such a diet? Should the government regulate the claims of diet books? How should the claims be tested? Should diet proponents be required to obtain and publish data before making claims?

15. As discussed in the Biology and Society section, the creation and manufacture of nanotechnology devices have the potential to significantly improve human health. But do such devices also have the potential to do harm or to be abused? In what ways might they be? Can you imagine rules or regulations that would allow for beneficial uses of nanorobots without allowing for harm?

16. Lead acts as an enzyme inhibitor, and it can interfere with the development of the nervous system. One manufacturer of lead-acid batteries instituted a "fetal protection policy" that banned female employees of childbearing age from working in areas where they might be exposed to high levels of lead. These women were transferred to lower-paying jobs in lower-risk areas. Some employees challenged the policy in court, claiming that it deprived women of job opportunities available to men. The U.S. Supreme Court ruled the policy illegal. But many people are uncomfortable about the "right" to work in an unsafe environment. What rights and responsibilities of employers, employees, and government agencies are in conflict? What criteria should be used to decide who can work in a particular environment?

6 Cellular Respiration: Obtaining Energy from Food

Why Cellular Respiration Matters

About 20% of the energy produced by your body each day is used to sustain your brain.

You have something in common with a sports car: You both require an air intake system to burn fuel efficiently.

550

▲ Similar metabolic processes produce alcohol, pepperoni, soy sauce, rising bread, and acid in your muscles after a hard workout.

Exercise Science BIOLOGY AND SOCIETY

Getting the Most Out of Your Muscles

Serious athletes train extensively to reach the peak of their physical potential. A key aspect of athletic conditioning involves increasing aerobic capacity, the ability of the heart and lungs to deliver oxygen to body cells. For many endurance athletes, such as long-distance runners or cyclists, the rate at which oxygen is provided to working muscles is the limiting factor in their performance.

Why is oxygen so important? Whether you are exercising or just going about your daily tasks, your muscles need a continuous supply of energy to perform work. Muscle cells obtain this energy from the sugar glucose through a series of chemical reactions that depend upon a constant input of oxygen (O_2). Therefore, to keep moving, your body needs a steady supply of O_2.

When there is enough oxygen reaching your cells to support their energy needs, metabolism is said to be aerobic. As your muscles work harder, you breathe faster and deeper to inhale more O_2. If you continue to pick up the pace, you will approach your aerobic capacity, the maximum rate at which O_2 can be taken in and used by your muscle cells and therefore the most strenuous exercise that your body can maintain aerobically. Exercise physiologists (scientists who study how the body works during physical activity) therefore use oxygen-monitoring equipment to precisely determine the maximum possible aerobic output for any given person. Such data allow a well-trained athlete to stay within aerobic limits, ensuring the maximum possible output—in other words, his or her best effort.

If you work even harder and exceed your aerobic capacity, the demand for oxygen in your muscles will outstrip your

The science of exercise. Exercise physiologists can help athletes perform their best by carefully monitoring the consumption of oxygen and the production of carbon dioxide.

body's ability to deliver it; metabolism then becomes anaerobic. With insufficient O_2, your muscle cells switch to an "emergency mode" in which they break down glucose very inefficiently and produce lactic acid as a by-product. As lactic acid and other by-products accumulate, muscle activity is impaired. Your muscles can work under these conditions for only a few minutes before they give out.

Every living organism depends on processes that provide energy. In fact, we need energy to walk, talk, and think—in short, to stay alive. The human body has trillions of cells, all hard at work, all demanding fuel continuously. In this chapter, you'll learn how cells harvest food energy and put it to work with the help of oxygen. Along the way, we'll consider the implications of how the body responds to exercise.

Energy Flow and Chemical Cycling in the Biosphere

All life requires energy. In almost all ecosystems on Earth, this energy originates with the sun. During **photosynthesis**, plants convert the energy of sunlight to the chemical energy of sugars and other organic molecules (as we'll discuss in Chapter 7). Humans and other animals depend on this conversion for our food and more. You're probably wearing clothing made of a product of photosynthesis—cotton. Most of our homes are framed with lumber, which is wood produced by photosynthetic trees. Even textbooks are printed on a material (paper) that can be traced to photosynthesis in plants. But from an animal's point of view, photosynthesis is primarily about providing food.

Producers and Consumers

Plants and other **autotrophs** ("self-feeders") are organisms that make all their own organic matter—including carbohydrates, lipids, proteins, and nucleic acids—from nutrients that are entirely inorganic: carbon dioxide from the air and water and minerals from the soil. In other words, autotrophs make their own food; they don't need to eat to gain energy to power their cellular processes. In contrast, humans and other animals are **heterotrophs** ("other-feeders"), organisms that cannot make organic molecules from inorganic ones. Therefore, we must eat organic material to get our nutrients and provide energy for life's processes.

Most ecosystems depend entirely on photosynthesis for food. For this reason, biologists refer to plants and other autotrophs as **producers**. Heterotrophs, in contrast, are **consumers**, because they obtain their food by eating plants or by eating animals that have eaten plants (Figure 6.1). We animals and other heterotrophs depend on autotrophs for organic fuel and for the raw organic materials we need to build our cells and tissues. ☑

Chemical Cycling between Photosynthesis and Cellular Respiration

The chemical ingredients for photosynthesis are carbon dioxide (CO_2), a gas that passes from the air into a plant via tiny pores, and water (H_2O), which is absorbed from the soil by the plant's roots. Inside leaf cells, organelles called chloroplasts use light energy to rearrange the atoms of these ingredients to produce sugars—most

► Figure 6.1 **Producer and consumer.** A giraffe (consumer) eating leaves produced by a photosynthetic plant (producer).

importantly glucose ($C_6H_{12}O_6$)—and other organic molecules (Figure 6.2). You can think of chloroplasts as tiny solar-powered sugar factories. A by-product of photosynthesis is oxygen gas (O_2) that is released through pores into the atmosphere.

Both animals and plants use the organic products of photosynthesis as sources of energy. A chemical process called cellular respiration uses O_2 to convert the energy stored in the chemical bonds of sugars to another source of chemical energy called ATP. Cells expend ATP for almost all their work. In both plants and animals, the production of ATP during cellular respiration occurs mainly in the organelles called mitochondria (see Figure 4.18).

You might notice in Figure 6.2 that energy takes a one-way trip through an ecosystem, entering as sunlight and exiting as heat. Chemicals, in contrast, are recycled. Notice also in Figure 6.2 that the waste products of cellular respiration are CO_2 and H_2O—the very same ingredients used as inputs for photosynthesis. Plants store chemical energy via photosynthesis and then harvest this energy via cellular respiration. (Note that plants perform *both* photosynthesis to produce fuel molecules *and* cellular respiration to burn them, while animals perform *only* cellular respiration.) Plants usually make more organic molecules than they need for fuel. This photosynthetic surplus provides material for the plant to grow or can be stored (as starch in potatoes, for example). Thus, when you consume a carrot, potato, or turnip, you are eating the energy reservoir that plants (if unharvested) would have used to grow the following spring.

People have always taken advantage of plants' photosynthetic abilities by eating them. More recently, engineers have managed to tap into this energy reserve to produce liquid biofuels, primarily ethanol (see Chapter 7 for a discussion of biofuels). But no matter the end product, you can trace the energy and raw materials for growth back to solar-powered photosynthesis. ☑

☑ CHECKPOINT

What is misleading about the following statement? "Plants have chloroplasts that perform photosynthesis, whereas animals have mitochondria that perform cellular respiration."

Answer: It implies that cellular respiration does not also occur in plants. It does.

◀ Figure 6.2 **Energy flow and chemical cycling in ecosystems.** Energy flows through an ecosystem, entering as sunlight and exiting as heat. In contrast, chemical elements are recycled within an ecosystem.

Sunlight energy enters ecosystem

Photosynthesis
(in chloroplasts)
converts light energy
to chemical energy

$C_6H_{12}O_6$
Glucose
+
O_2
Oxygen

CO_2
Carbon dioxide
+
H_2O
Water

Cellular respiration
(in mitochondria)
harvests food energy
to produce ATP

ATP drives cellular work

Heat energy exits ecosystem

Cellular Respiration:
Aerobic Harvest of Food Energy

We usually use the word *respiration* to mean breathing. Although respiration on the organismal level should not be confused with cellular respiration, the two processes are closely related (Figure 6.3). Cellular respiration requires a cell to exchange two gases with its surroundings. The cell takes in oxygen in the form of the gas O_2. It gets rid of waste in the form of the gas carbon dioxide, or CO_2. Respiration, or breathing, results in the exchange of these same gases between your blood and the

You have something in common with a sports car: You both require an air intake system to burn fuel efficiently.

outside air. Oxygen present in the air you inhale diffuses across the lining of your lungs and into your bloodstream. And the CO_2 in your bloodstream diffuses into your lungs and exits your body when you exhale. Every molecule of CO_2 that you exhale was originally formed in one of the mitochondria of your body's cells.

Internal combustion engines, like the ones found in cars, use O_2 (via the air intakes) to break down gasoline. A cell also requires O_2 to break down its fuel (see Figure 5.2). Cellular respiration—a biological version of internal combustion—is the main way that chemical energy is harvested from food and converted to ATP energy (see Figure 5.6). Cellular respiration is an **aerobic** process, which is just another way of saying that it requires oxygen. Putting all this together, we can now define **cellular respiration** as the aerobic harvesting of chemical energy from organic fuel molecules. ☑

▼ Figure 6.3 **How breathing is related to cellular respiration.** When you inhale, you breathe in O_2. The O_2 is delivered to your cells, where it is used in cellular respiration. Carbon dioxide, a waste product of cellular respiration, diffuses from your cells to your blood and travels to your lungs, where it is exhaled.

Energy Transformations — An Overview of Cellular Respiration

One of biology's overarching themes is that all living organisms depends on transformations of energy and matter. We see examples of such transformations throughout the study of life, but few are as important as the conversion of energy in fuel (food molecules) to a form that cells can use directly. Most often, the fuel molecule used by cells is glucose, a simple sugar (monosaccharide) with the formula $C_6H_{12}O_6$ (see Figure 3.6). (Less often, other organic molecules are used to gain energy.) This equation summarizes the transformation of glucose during cellular respiration:

The series of arrows in this formula represents the fact that cellular respiration consists of many chemical steps. A specific enzyme catalyzes each reaction—more than two dozen reactions in all—in the pathway. In fact, these reactions constitute one of the most important metabolic pathways for nearly every eukaryotic cell—those found in plants, fungi, protists, and animals. This pathway provides the energy these cells need to maintain the functions of life.

The many chemical reactions that make up cellular respiration can be grouped into three main stages: glycolysis, the citric acid cycle, and electron transport. **Figure 6.4** is a road map that will help you follow the three stages of respiration and see where each stage occurs in your cells. During **glycolysis**, a molecule of glucose is split into two molecules of a compound called pyruvic acid. The enzymes for glycolysis are located in the cytoplasm. The **citric acid cycle** (also called the Krebs cycle) completes the breakdown of glucose all the way to CO_2, which is then released as a waste product. The enzymes for the citric acid cycle are dissolved in the fluid within mitochondria. Glycolysis and the citric acid cycle generate a small amount of ATP directly. They generate much more ATP indirectly, via reactions that transfer electrons from fuel molecules to a molecule called NAD^+ (<u>n</u>icotinamide <u>a</u>denine <u>d</u>inucleotide) that cells make from niacin, a B vitamin. The electron transfer forms a molecule called **NADH** (the H represents the transfer of hydrogen along with the electrons) that acts as a shuttle carrying high-energy electrons from one area of the cell to another. The third stage of cellular respiration is **electron transport**. Electrons captured from food by the NADH formed in the first two stages are stripped of their energy, a little bit at a time, until they are finally combined with oxygen to form water. The proteins and other molecules that make up electron transport chains are embedded within the inner membrane of the mitochondria. The transport of electrons from NADH to oxygen releases the energy your cells use to make most of their ATP.

The overall equation for cellular respiration shows that the atoms of the reactant molecules glucose and oxygen are rearranged to form the products carbon dioxide and water. But don't lose track of why this process occurs: The main function of cellular respiration is to generate ATP for cellular work. In fact, the process can produce around 32 ATP molecules for each glucose molecule consumed. ☑

☑ **CHECKPOINT**

Which stages of cellular respiration take place in the mitochondria? Which stage takes place outside the mitochondria?

Answer: the citric acid cycle and electron transport; glycolysis

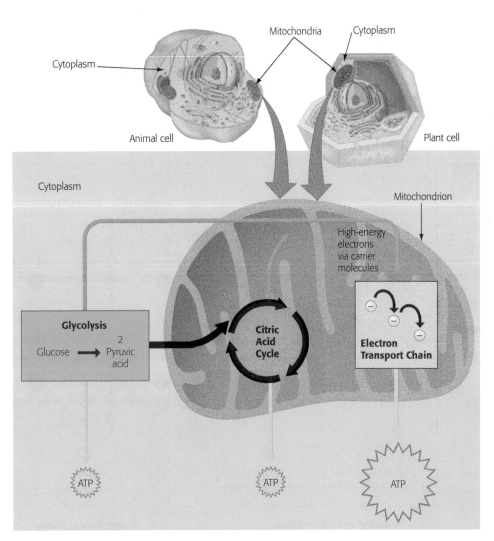

► Figure 6.4 **A road map for cellular respiration.**

The Three Stages of Cellular Respiration

Now that you have a big-picture view of cellular respiration, let's examine the process in more detail. A small version of Figure 6.4 will help you keep the overall process of cellular respiration in plain view as we take a closer look at its three stages.

Stage 1: Glycolysis

The word *glycolysis* means "splitting of sugar" (Figure 6.5), and that's just what happens. ❶ During glycolysis, a six-carbon glucose molecule is broken in half, forming two three-carbon molecules. Notice in Figure 6.5 that the initial split requires an energy investment of two ATP molecules per glucose. ❷ The three-carbon molecules then donate high-energy electrons to NAD$^+$, forming NADH. ❸ In addition to NADH, glycolysis also makes four ATP molecules directly when enzymes transfer phosphate groups

from fuel molecules to ADP (Figure 6.6). Glycolysis thus produces a net of two molecules of ATP per molecule of glucose. (This fact will become important during our later discussion of fermentation.) What remains of the fractured glucose at the end of glycolysis are two molecules of pyruvic acid. The pyruvic acid still holds most of the energy of glucose, and that energy is harvested in the second stage of cellular respiration, the citric acid cycle.

▼ Figure 6.6 **ATP synthesis by direct phosphate transfer.** Glycolysis generates ATP when enzymes transfer phosphate groups directly from fuel molecules to ADP.

▼ Figure 6.5 **Glycolysis.** In glycolysis, a team of enzymes splits glucose, eventually forming two molecules of pyruvic acid. After investing 2 ATP at the start, glycolysis generates 4 ATP directly. More energy will be harvested later from high-energy electrons used to form NADH and from the two molecules of pyruvic acid.

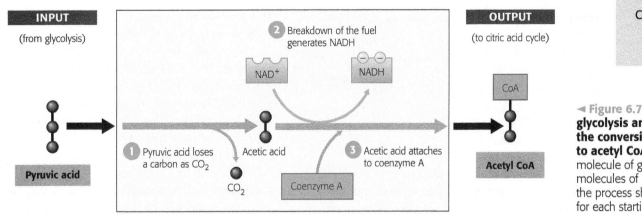

INPUT (from glycolysis)

OUTPUT (to citric acid cycle)

2 Breakdown of the fuel generates NADH

NAD⁺

NADH

CoA

1 Pyruvic acid loses a carbon as CO_2

Acetic acid

3 Acetic acid attaches to coenzyme A

Coenzyme A

CO_2

Pyruvic acid

Acetyl CoA

◄ **Figure 6.7 The link between glycolysis and the citric acid cycle: the conversion of pyruvic acid to acetyl CoA.** Remember that one molecule of glucose is split into two molecules of pyruvic acid. Therefore, the process shown here occurs twice for each starting glucose molecule.

Stage 2: The Citric Acid Cycle

The two molecules of pyruvic acid, the fuel that remains after glycolysis, are not quite ready for the citric acid cycle. The pyruvic acid must be "groomed"—converted to a form the citric acid cycle can use **(Figure 6.7)**. ❶ First, each pyruvic acid loses a carbon as CO_2. This is the first of this waste product we've seen so far in the breakdown of glucose. The remaining fuel molecules, each with only two carbons left, are called acetic acid (the acid that's in vinegar). ❷ Electrons are stripped from these molecules and transferred to another molecule of NAD⁺, forming more NADH. ❸ Finally, each acetic acid is attached to a molecule called coenzyme A (CoA), an enzyme derived from the B vitamin pantothenic acid, to form acetyl CoA. The CoA escorts the acetic acid into

the first reaction of the citric acid cycle. The CoA is then stripped and recycled.

The citric acid cycle finishes extracting the energy of sugar by dismantling the acetic acid molecules all the way down to CO_2 **(Figure 6.8)**. ❶ Acetic acid joins a four-carbon acceptor molecule to form a six-carbon product called citric acid (for which the cycle is named). For every acetic acid molecule that enters the cycle as fuel, ❷ two CO_2 molecules eventually exit as a waste product. Along the way, the citric acid cycle harvests energy from the fuel. ❸ Some of the energy is used to produce ATP directly. However, the cycle captures much more energy in the form of ❹ NADH and ❺ a second, closely related electron carrier called $FADH_2$. ❻ All the carbon atoms that entered the cycle as fuel are accounted for as CO_2 exhaust, and the four-carbon acceptor molecule is recycled. We have tracked only one acetic acid molecule through the citric acid cycle here. But because glycolysis splits glucose in two, the citric acid cycle occurs twice for each glucose molecule that fuels a cell. ☑

☑ CHECKPOINT

Two molecules of what compound are produced by glycolysis? Does this molecule enter the citric acid cycle?

Answer: Pyruvic acid. No; it is first converted to acetic acid.

► **Figure 6.8 The citric acid cycle.**

INPUT

OUTPUT

Citric acid

❶ Acetic acid

ADP + P

3 NAD⁺

FAD

Citric Acid Cycle

❻ Acceptor molecule

2 CO_2 ❷

ATP ❸

3 NADH ❹

$FADH_2$ ❺

Stage 3: Electron Transport

Let's take a closer look at the path that electrons take on their way from glucose to oxygen (Figure 6.9). During cellular respiration, the electrons gathered from food molecules "fall" in a stepwise cascade, losing energy at each step. In this way, cellular respiration unlocks chemical energy in small amounts, bit by bit, that cells can put to productive use. The first stop in the path down the cascade is NAD^+. The transfer of electrons from organic fuel (food) to NAD^+ converts it to NADH. The electrons have now taken one baby step down in their trip from glucose to oxygen. The rest of the cascade consists of an **electron transport chain**.

Each link in an electron transport chain is actually a molecule, usually a protein (shown as purple circles in Figure 6.9). In a series of reactions, each member of the chain transfers electrons. With each transfer, the electrons give up a small amount of energy that can then be used indirectly to generate ATP. The first molecule of the chain accepts electrons from NADH. Thus, NADH carries electrons from glucose and other fuel molecules and deposits them at the top of an electron transport chain. The electrons cascade down the chain, from molecule to molecule, like an electron bucket brigade. The molecule at the bottom of the chain finally "drops"

the electrons to oxygen. At the same time, oxygen picks up hydrogen, forming water.

The overall effect of all this transfer of electrons during cellular respiration is a "downward" trip for electrons from glucose to NADH to an electron transport chain to oxygen. During the stepwise release of chemical energy in the electron transport chain, our cells make most of their ATP.

It is actually oxygen, the "electron grabber," at the end, that makes it all possible. By pulling electrons down the transport chain from fuel molecules, oxygen functions somewhat like gravity pulling objects downhill. This role as a final electron acceptor is how the oxygen we breathe functions in our cells and why we cannot survive more than a few minutes without it. Viewed this way, drowning is deadly because it deprives cells of the final "electron grabbers" (oxygen) needed to drive cellular respiration.

The molecules of electron transport chains are built into the inner membranes of mitochondria (see

▼ Figure 6.9 **The role of oxygen in harvesting food energy.** In cellular respiration, electrons "fall" in small steps from food to oxygen, producing water. NADH transfers electrons from food to an electron transport chain. The attraction of oxygen to electrons "pulls" the electrons down the chain.

Figure 4.18). Because these membranes are highly folded, their large surface area can accommodate thousands of copies of the electron transport chain—another good example of how biological structure fits function. Each chain acts as a chemical pump that uses the energy released by the "fall" of electrons to move hydrogen ions (H^+) across the inner mitochondrial membrane. This pumping causes ions to become more concentrated on one side of the membrane than on the other. Such a difference in concentration stores potential energy, similar to the way water can be stored behind a dam. There

is a tendency for hydrogen ions to gush back to where they are less concentrated, just as there is a tendency for water to flow downhill. The inner membrane temporarily "dams" hydrogen ions.

The energy of dammed water can be harnessed to perform work. Gates in a dam allow the water to rush downhill, turning giant turbines, and this work can be used to generate electricity. Your mitochondria have structures that act like turbines. Each of these miniature machines, called an **ATP synthase**, is constructed from proteins built into the inner mitochondrial membrane, adjacent to the proteins of the electron transport chains. **Figure 6.10** shows a simplified view of how the energy previously stored in NADH and $FADH_2$ can now be used to generate ATP. **1** NADH and **2** $FADH_2$ transfer electrons to an electron transport chain. **3** The electron transport chain uses this energy supply to pump H^+ across the inner mitochondrial membrane. **4** Oxygen pulls electrons down the transport chain. **5** The H^+ concentrated on one side of the membrane rushes back "downhill" through an ATP synthase. This action spins a component of the ATP synthase, just as water turns the turbines in a dam. **6** The rotation activates parts of the synthase molecule that attach phosphate groups to ADP molecules to generate ATP.

The poison cyanide produces its deadly effect by binding to one of the protein complexes in the electron transport chain (marked with a skull-and-crossbones symbol in Figure 6.10). When bound there, cyanide blocks the passage of electrons to oxygen. This blockage is like clogging a dam. As a result, no H^+ gradient is generated, and no ATP is made. Cells stop working, and the organism dies. ☑

☑ **CHECKPOINT**

What is the potential energy source that drives ATP production by ATP synthase?

Answer: a concentration gradient of H^+ across the inner membrane of a mitochondrion

▼ Figure 6.10 **How electron transport drives ATP synthase machines.**

The Results of Cellular Respiration

When taking cellular respiration apart to see how all the molecular nuts and bolts of its metabolic machinery work, it's easy to lose sight of its overall function: to generate about 32 molecules of ATP per molecule of glucose (the actual number can vary by a few, depending on the organism and molecules involved). **Figure 6.11** will help you keep track of the ATP molecules generated. As we discussed, glycolysis and the citric acid cycle each contribute 2 ATP by directly making it. The rest of the ATP molecules are produced by ATP synthase, powered by the "fall" of electrons from food to oxygen. The electrons are carried from the organic fuel to electron transport chains by NADH and FADH$_2$. Each electron pair "dropped" down a transport chain from NADH or FADH$_2$ can power the synthesis of a few ATP. You can visualize the process like this: Energy flows from glucose to carrier molecules and ultimately to ATP.

We have seen that glucose can provide the energy to make the ATP our cells use for all their work. All of the energy-consuming activities of your body—moving your muscles, maintaining your heartbeat and temperature, and even the thinking that goes on within your brain—can be traced back to ATP and, before that, the glucose that was used to make it. The importance of glucose is underscored by the severity of diseases in which glucose balance is disturbed. Diabetes, which affects more than 20 million Americans, is caused by an inability to properly regulate glucose levels in the blood due to problems with the hormone insulin. If left untreated, a glucose imbalance can lead to a variety of problems, including cardiovascular disease, coma, and even death.

> About 20% of the energy produced by your body each day is used to sustain your brain.

But even though we have concentrated on glucose as the fuel that is broken down during cellular respiration, respiration is a versatile metabolic furnace that can "burn" many other kinds of food molecules. **Figure 6.12** diagrams some metabolic routes for the use of carbohydrates, fats, and proteins as fuel for cellular respiration. Taken together, all of these food molecules make up your calorie-burning metabolism. ✓

▼ Figure 6.12 **Energy from food.** The monomers from carbohydrates (polysaccharides and sugars), fats, and proteins can all serve as fuel for cellular respiration.

► Figure 6.11 **A summary of ATP yield during cellular respiration.**

Fermentation: Anaerobic Harvest of Food Energy

Although you must breathe to stay alive, some of your cells can work for short periods without oxygen. This **anaerobic** ("without oxygen") harvest of food energy is called fermentation.

Fermentation in Human Muscle Cells

You know by now that as your muscles work, they require a constant supply of ATP, which is generated by cellular respiration. As long as your blood provides your muscle cells with enough O_2 to keep electrons "falling" down transport chains in mitochondria, your muscles will work aerobically.

But under strenuous conditions, your muscles can spend ATP faster than your bloodstream can deliver O_2; when this happens, your muscle cells begin to work anaerobically. After functioning anaerobically for about 15 seconds, muscle cells will begin to generate ATP by the process of fermentation. **Fermentation** relies on glycolysis, the first stage of cellular respiration. Glycolysis does not require O_2 but does produce two ATP molecules for each glucose molecule broken down to pyruvic acid. That isn't very efficient compared with the 32 or so ATP molecules each glucose molecule generates during cellular respiration, but it can energize muscles for a short burst of activity. However, in such situations your cells will have to consume more glucose fuel per second because so much less ATP per glucose molecule is generated under anaerobic conditions.

To harvest food energy during glycolysis, NAD^+ must be present to receive electrons (see Figure 6.9). This is no problem under aerobic conditions, because the cell regenerates NAD^+ when NADH drops its electron cargo down electron transport chains to O_2. However, this recycling of NAD^+ cannot occur under anaerobic conditions because there is no O_2 to accept the electrons. Instead, NADH disposes of electrons by adding them to the pyruvic acid produced by glycolysis **(Figure 6.13)**. This restores NAD^+ and keeps glycolysis working.

The addition of electrons to pyruvic acid produces a waste product called lactic acid. The lactic acid by-product is eventually transported to the liver, where liver cells convert it back to pyruvic acid. Exercise physiologists have long speculated about the role that lactic acid plays in muscle fatigue, as you'll see next. ☑

☑ **CHECKPOINT**

How many molecules of ATP can be produced from one molecule of glucose during fermentation?

Answer: two

▼ Figure 6.13 **Fermentation: producing lactic acid.** Glycolysis produces ATP even in the absence of O_2. This process requires a continuous supply of NAD^+ to accept electrons from glucose. The NAD^+ is regenerated when NADH transfers the electrons it removed from food to pyruvic acid, thereby producing lactic acid (or other waste products, depending on the species of organism).

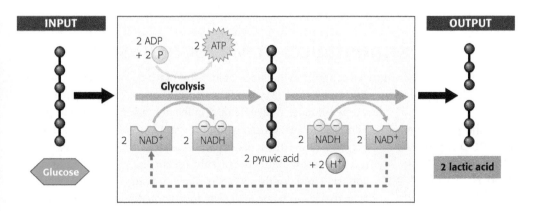

INPUT

2 ADP + 2 P → 2 ATP

Glycolysis

2 NAD⁺   2 NADH   2 NADH   2 NAD⁺

2 pyruvic acid + 2 H⁺

Glucose

OUTPUT

2 lactic acid

Exercise Science THE PROCESS OF SCIENCE

What Causes Muscle Burn?

You may have heard that the burn you experience after hard exercise ("Feel the burn!") is due to the buildup of lactic acid in your muscles. This idea originated with the work of a British biologist named A.V. Hill. Considered one of the founders of the field of exercise physiology, Hill won a 1922 Nobel Prize for his investigations of muscle contraction.

In 1929, Hill performed a classic experiment that began with the **observation** that muscles produce lactic acid under anaerobic conditions. Hill asked the **question**, Does the buildup of lactic acid cause muscle fatigue? To find out, Hill developed a technique for electrically stimulating dissected frog muscles in a laboratory solution. He formed the **hypothesis** that a buildup of lactic acid would cause muscle activity to stop.

Hill's **experiment** tested frog muscles under two different sets of conditions (Figure 6.14). First, he showed that muscle performance declined when lactic acid could not diffuse away from the muscle tissue. Next, he showed that when lactic acid was allowed to diffuse away, performance improved significantly. These **results** led Hill to the conclusion that the buildup of lactic acid is the primary cause of muscle failure under anaerobic conditions.

Given his scientific stature (he was considered the world's leading authority on muscle activity), Hill's conclusion went unchallenged for many decades. Gradually, however, evidence that contradicted Hill's results began to accumulate. For example, the effect that Hill demonstrated did not appear to occur at human body temperature. And certain individuals who are unable to accumulate lactic acid have muscles that fatigue

more rapidly, which is the opposite of what you would expect. Recent experiments have directly refuted Hill's conclusions. Research indicates that increased levels of other ions may be to blame, and the role of lactic acid in muscle fatigue remains a hotly debated topic.

The changing view of lactic acid's role in muscle fatigue illustrates an important point about the process of science: It is dynamic and subject to constant adjustment as new evidence is uncovered. This would not have surprised Hill, who himself observed that all scientific hypotheses may become obsolete, and that changing conclusions in light of new evidence is necessary for the advancement of science.

▼ Figure 6.14 **A. V. Hill's 1929 apparatus for measuring muscle fatigue.**

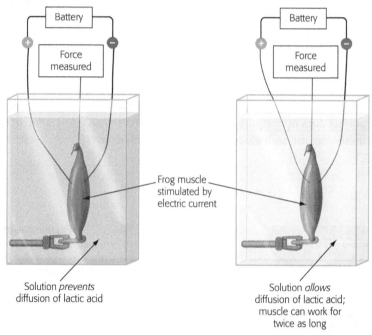

Solution *prevents* diffusion of lactic acid

Frog muscle stimulated by electric current

Solution *allows* diffusion of lactic acid; muscle can work for twice as long

Fermentation in Microorganisms

Our muscles cannot rely on lactic acid fermentation for very long. However, the two ATP molecules produced per glucose molecule during fermentation is enough to sustain many microorganisms. We have domesticated such microbes to transform milk into cheese, sour cream, and yogurt. These foods owe their sharp or sour flavor mainly to lactic acid. The food industry

Similar metabolic processes produce alcohol, pepperoni, soy sauce, rising bread, and acid in your muscles after a hard workout.

also uses fermentation to produce soy sauce from soybeans, to pickle cucumbers, olives, and cabbage, and to produce meat products like sausage, pepperoni, and salami.

Yeast, a microscopic fungus, is capable of both cellular respiration and fermentation. When kept in an anaerobic environment, yeast cells ferment sugars and other foods to stay alive. As they do, the yeast produce ethyl alcohol as a waste product instead of lactic acid (Figure 6.15). This alcoholic fermentation also releases CO_2. For thousands of years, people have put yeast to work producing alcoholic beverages such as beer and wine. And as every baker knows, the CO_2 bubbles from fermenting yeast also cause bread dough to rise. (The alcohol produced in fermenting bread is burned off during baking.) ☑

☑ **CHECKPOINT**

What kind of acid builds up in human muscle during strenuous activity?

Answer: lactic acid

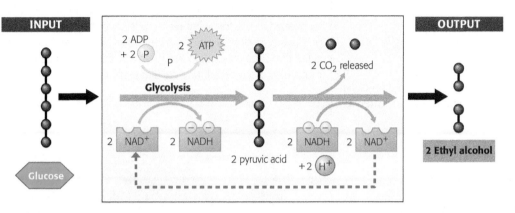

▲ Figure 6.15 **Fermentation: producing ethyl alcohol.** The alcohol produced by yeast as bread rises is burned off during baking.

Exercise Science EVOLUTION CONNECTION

The Importance of Oxygen

In the Biology and Society and the Process of Science sections, we have been reminded of the important role that oxygen plays during aerobic exercise. But in the last section on fermentation, we learned that exercise can continue on a limited basis even under anaerobic (oxygen-free) conditions. Both aerobic and anaerobic respiration start with glycolysis, the splitting of glucose to form pyruvic acid. Glycolysis is thus the universal energy-harvesting process of life.

The role of glycolysis in both respiration and fermentation has an evolutionary basis. Ancient prokaryotes probably used glycolysis to make ATP long before oxygen was present in Earth's atmosphere. The oldest known fossils of bacteria date back more than 3.5 billion years, but significant levels of O_2 did not accumulate in the atmosphere until about 2.7 billion years ago (Figure 6.16). For almost one billion years, prokaryotes must have generated ATP exclusively from glycolysis.

The fact that glycolysis occurs in almost all organisms suggests that it evolved very early in ancestors common to all the domains of life. The location of glycolysis within the cell also implies great antiquity; the pathway does not require any of the membrane-enclosed organelles of the eukaryotic cell, which evolved more than a billion years after the prokaryotic cell. Glycolysis is a metabolic heirloom from early cells that continues to function in fermentation and as the first stage in the breakdown of organic molecules by cellular respiration. The ability of our muscles to function anaerobically can therefore be viewed as a vestige of our ancient ancestors who relied exclusively on this metabolic pathway.

▼ Figure 6.16 **A time line of oxygen and life on Earth.**

O_2 present in Earth's atmosphere

Billions of years ago

0

2.1 — First eukaryotic organisms

2.2 — Atmospheric oxygen reaches 10% of modern levels

2.7 — Atmospheric oxygen first appears

3.5 — Oldest prokaryotic fossils

4.5 — Origin of Earth

Chapter Review

▉ SUMMARY OF KEY CONCEPTS

Energy Flow and Chemical Cycling in the Biosphere

Producers and Consumers

Autotrophs (producers) make organic molecules from inorganic nutrients via photosynthesis. Heterotrophs (consumers) must consume organic material and obtain energy via cellular respiration.

Chemical Cycling between Photosynthesis and Cellular Respiration

The molecular outputs of cellular respiration—CO_2 and H_2O—are the molecular inputs of photosynthesis, and vice versa. While these chemicals cycle through an ecosystem, energy flows through, entering as sunlight and exiting as heat.

Cellular Respiration: Aerobic Harvest of Food Energy

An Overview of Cellular Respiration

The overall equation of cellular respiration simplifies a great many chemical steps into one formula:

The Three Stages of Cellular Respiration

Cellular respiration occurs in three stages. During glycolysis, a molecule of glucose is split into two molecules of pyruvic acid, producing two molecules of ATP and two high-energy electrons stored in NADH. During the citric acid cycle, what remains of glucose is completely broken down to CO_2, producing a bit of ATP and a lot of high-energy electrons stored in NADH and $FADH_2$. The electron transport chain uses the high-energy electrons to pump H^+ across the inner mitochondrial membrane, eventually handing them off to O_2, producing H_2O. Backflow of H^+ across the membrane powers the ATP synthases, which produce ATP from ADP.

The Results of Cellular Respiration

You can follow the flow of molecules through the process of cellular respiration in the following diagram. Notice that the first two stages primarily produce high-energy electrons carried by NADH, and that it is the final stage that uses these high-energy electrons to produce the bulk of the ATP molecules produced during cellular respiration.

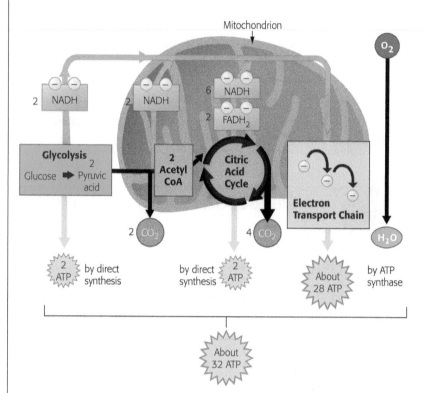

Fermentation: Anaerobic Harvest of Food Energy

Fermentation in Human Muscle Cells

When muscle cells consume ATP faster than O_2 can be supplied for cellular respiration, the conditions become anaerobic, and muscle cells will begin to regenerate ATP by fermentation. The waste product under these anaerobic conditions is lactic acid. The ATP yield per glucose is much lower during fermentation (2 ATP) than during cellular respiration (about 32 ATP).

Fermentation in Microorganisms

Yeast and some other organisms can survive with or without O_2. Wastes from fermentation can be ethyl alcohol, lactic acid, or other compounds, depending on the species.

MasteringBiology®

For practice quizzes, BioFlix animations, MP3 tutorials, video tutors, and more study tools designed for this textbook, go to MasteringBiology®

SELF-QUIZ

1. Which of the following statements is a correct distinction between autotrophs and heterotrophs?
   a. Only heterotrophs require chemical compounds from the environment.
   b. Cellular respiration is unique to heterotrophs.
   c. Only heterotrophs have mitochondria.
   d. Only autotrophs can live on nutrients that are entirely inorganic.

2. Why are plants called producers? Why are animals called consumers?

3. How is your breathing related to your cellular respiration?

4. Of the three stages of cellular respiration, which produces the most ATP molecules per glucose?

5. The final electron acceptor of electron transport chains in mitochondria is _____.

6. The poison cyanide acts by blocking a key step in the electron transport chain. Knowing this, explain why cyanide kills so quickly.

7. Cells can harvest the most chemical energy from which of the following?
   a. an NADH molecule
   b. a glucose molecule
   c. six CO_2 molecules
   d. two pyruvic acid molecules

8. _____ is a metabolic pathway common to both fermentation and cellular respiration.

9. Sports physiologists at an Olympic training center want to monitor athletes to determine at what point their muscles are functioning anaerobically. They can do this by checking for a buildup of
   a. ADP.
   b. lactic acid.
   c. carbon dioxide.
   d. oxygen.

10. A glucose-fed yeast cell is moved from an aerobic environment to an anaerobic one. For the cell to continue to generate ATP at the same rate, approximately how much glucose must it consume in the anaerobic environment compared with the aerobic environment?

Answers to these questions can be found in Appendix: Self-Quiz Answers.

THE PROCESS OF SCIENCE

11. Your body makes NAD^+ from two B vitamins, niacin and riboflavin. You need only tiny amounts of these vitamins. The U.S. Food and Drug Administration's recommended dietary allowances are 20 mg daily for niacin and 1.7 mg daily for riboflavin. These amounts are thousands of times less than the amount of glucose your body needs each day to fuel its energy requirements. How many NAD^+ molecules are needed for the breakdown of each glucose molecule? Why do you think your daily requirement for these substances is so small?

12. **Interpreting Data** The basal metabolic rate (BMR) is the amount of energy that must be consumed by a person at rest to maintain his or her body weight. BMR depends on several factors, including sex, age, height, and weight. The following graph shows the BMR for a 6'0" 45-year-old male. For this person, how does BMR correlate with weight? How many more calories must a 250-pound man consume to maintain his weight than a 200 pound man? Why would BMR depend on weight?

BMR by weight

BIOLOGY AND SOCIETY

13. As discussed in the Biology and Society section, the delivery of oxygen to muscles is the limiting factor for many athletes. Some athletes seek to improve their athletic performance through blood doping, which can artificially increase athletic capacity. Other athletes achieve the same result by training at high altitude (which promotes the formation of more red blood cells by the bone marrow). If two athletes achieve exactly the same result—one due to injecting her own blood and one due to training at altitude—why do you think the former is considered cheating but the latter is not? What would you do to enforce antidoping rules in sports at all levels (high school, college, Olympic, professional)?

14. Nearly all human societies use fermentation to produce alcoholic drinks. The technology dates back to the earliest civilizations. Suggest a hypothesis for how people first discovered fermentation.

15. The consumption of alcohol by a pregnant woman can cause a series of birth defects called fetal alcohol syndrome (FAS). Symptoms of FAS include head and facial irregularities, heart defects, mental retardation, and behavioral problems. The U.S. Surgeon General's Office recommends that pregnant women abstain from drinking alcohol, and the government has mandated that a warning label be placed on liquor bottles. Imagine you are a server in a restaurant. An obviously pregnant woman orders a strawberry daiquiri. How would you respond? Is it the woman's right to make those decisions about her unborn child's health? Do you bear any responsibility in the matter? Is a restaurant responsible for monitoring the dietary habits of its customers?

7 Photosynthesis: Using Light to Make Food

If you want to reduce the rate of global climate change, plant a tree.

Nearly all life on Earth—including you—can trace its source of energy back to the sun.

Protecting yourself from short wavelengths of light can be lifesaving.

Biofuels BIOLOGY AND SOCIETY

A Greasy Crime Wave

In September 2013, police in Ocala, Florida, arrested two men and charged them with organized fraud and grand theft. Their crime? The men were caught red-handed with more than 700 gallons of stolen used cooking oil pilfered from a variety of local eateries. Why would anyone steal that nasty stuff? The reason is simple: Remnants of restaurant deep fryers, sometimes called "liquid gold," fetch about $2 per pound when sold to recyclers. That makes the burglars' haul worth more than $5,000. Why is grease so valuable?

As fossil fuel supplies dwindle and prices rise, the need for reliable, renewable sources of energy increases. In response, scientists are researching better ways to harness biofuels, energy obtained from living material. Some researchers focus on burning plant matter directly (wood pellet boilers, for example), and others focus on using plant material to produce biofuels that can be burned.

There are several types of biofuels. Bioethanol is a type of alcohol (the same kind found in alcoholic drinks) that is made from wheat, corn, sugar beets, and other food crops. Starch made naturally by plants is converted to glucose and then fermented to ethanol by microorganisms such as single-celled algae. Bioethanol can be used directly as a fuel source in specially designed vehicles, but it is more commonly used as a gasoline additive that can increase fuel efficiency while decreasing vehicle emissions. You may have noticed a sticker on a gas pump that declares the percentage of ethanol in that gasoline; most cars today run on a blend of 85% gasoline and 15% ethanol. Many car manufacturers are producing "flexible-fuel" vehicles that can run on any combination of gasoline and bioethanol. Although bioethanol does reduce carbon emissions and is a renewable resource, its production raises the prices of food crops (which become more expensive as acreage is diverted to biofuel production).

Cellulosic ethanol is a form of bioethanol made from cellulose found in nonedible plant material such as wood, grass, or scraps from crops. Biodiesel, the most common biofuel in Europe, is made from plant oils such as recycled frying oil. Like bioethanol, it can be used on its own or as an emissions-reducing additive to standard diesel. In a strange twist, rising values for diesel have sparked a greasy crime wave as thieves tap into this new and largely unguarded source of raw material. Today, only about 2.7% of the world's fuel used for driving is provided by biofuels, but the International Energy Agency has set a goal of 25% by 2050.

Using biofuels. Biofuels are added to most gasoline in the United States.

When we derive energy from biofuels, we are actually tapping into the energy of the sun, which drives photosynthesis in plants. Photosynthesis is the process by which plants use light to make sugars from carbon dioxide—sugars that are food for the plant and the starting point for most of our own food. In this chapter, we'll first examine some basic concepts of photosynthesis; then we'll look at the specific mechanisms involved in this process.

The Basics of Photosynthesis

The process of photosynthesis is the ultimate source of energy for nearly every ecosystem on Earth. **Photosynthesis** is a process whereby plants, algae (which are protists), and certain bacteria transform light energy into chemical energy, using carbon dioxide and water as starting materials and releasing oxygen gas as a by-product. The chemical energy produced via photosynthesis is stored in the bonds of sugar molecules.

Nearly all life on Earth—including you—can trace its source of energy back to the sun.

Organisms that generate their own organic matter from inorganic ingredients are called autotrophs (see Chapter 6). Plants and other organisms that do this by photosynthesis—photoautotrophs—are the producers for most ecosystems (Figure 7.1). Not only do photoautotrophs feed us, they also clothe us (as the source of cotton fibers), house us (wood), and provide energy for warmth, light, and transportation (biofuels).

Chloroplasts: Sites of Photosynthesis

Photosynthesis in plants and algae occurs within light-absorbing organelles called **chloroplasts** (see Chapter 4, especially Figure 4.17). All green parts of a plant have chloroplasts and thus can carry out photosynthesis. In most plants, however, the leaves have the most chloroplasts (about 500,000 per square millimeter of leaf surface—that's equivalent to about 300 million chloroplasts in a leaf the size of a standard postage stamp). Their green color is from **chlorophyll**, a pigment (light-absorbing molecule) in the chloroplasts that plays a central role in converting solar energy to chemical energy.

Chloroplasts are concentrated in the interior cells of leaves (Figure 7.2), with a typical cell containing 30–40 chloroplasts. Carbon dioxide (CO_2) enters a leaf, and oxygen (O_2) exits, by way of tiny pores called **stomata** (singular, *stoma*, meaning "mouth"). The carbon dioxide that enters the leaf is the source of carbon for much of the body of the plant, including the sugars and starches that we eat. So the bulk of the body of a plant derives from the air, not the soil. As proof of this idea, consider hydroponics, a means of growing plants using only air and water; no soil whatsoever is involved. In addition to carbon dioxide, photosynthesis requires water, which is absorbed by the plant's roots and transported to the leaves, where veins carry it to the photosynthetic cells.

Membranes within the chloroplast form the framework where many of the reactions of photosynthesis occur. Like a mitochondrion, a chloroplast has a double-membrane envelope. The chloroplast's inner membrane encloses a compartment filled with **stroma**, a thick fluid. (It's easy to confuse two terms associated with photosynthesis: *stomata* are pores through which

▼ Figure 7.1 **A diversity of photoautotrophs.**

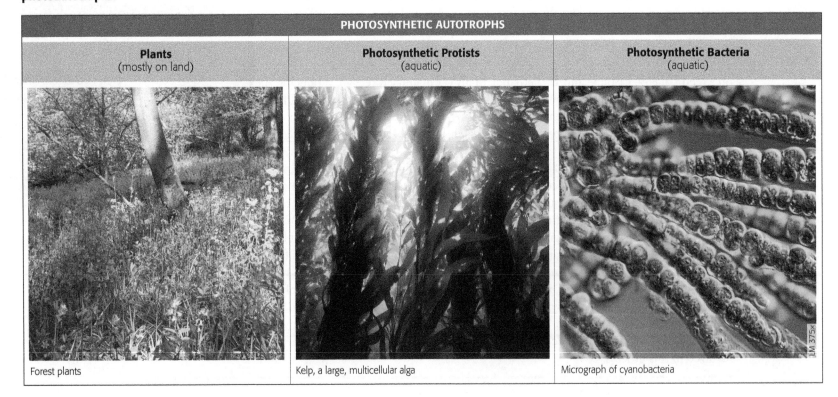

PHOTOSYNTHETIC AUTOTROPHS

| **Plants** (mostly on land) | **Photosynthetic Protists** (aquatic) | **Photosynthetic Bacteria** (aquatic) |

Forest plants

Kelp, a large, multicellular alga

Micrograph of cyanobacteria

LM 375×

gases are exchanged, and *stroma* is the fluid within the chloroplast.) Suspended in the stroma are interconnected membranous sacs called **thylakoids**. The thylakoids are concentrated in stacks called **grana** (singular, *granum*). The chlorophyll molecules that capture light energy are built into the thylakoid membranes. The structure of a chloroplast—with its stacks of disks—aids its function by providing a large surface area for the reactions of photosynthesis. ☑

Interior cell

Inner and outer membranes

Stroma   Thylakoid

Thylakoid space

Granum

LM 2,000×

Chloroplast

Photosynthetic cells   Vein (transports water and nutrients)

CO₂   O₂   Stomata

Colorized TEM 1,000×

Leaf cross section

► Figure 7.2 **Journey into a leaf.** This series of blowups takes you into a leaf's interior, then into a plant cell, and finally into a chloroplast, the site of photosynthesis.

☑ **CHECKPOINT**

Photosynthesis takes place within organelles called _____ using gases that are exchanged via pores called _____.

Answer: chloroplasts; stomata

Energy Transformations

An Overview of Photosynthesis

The following chemical equation, simplified to highlight the relationship between photosynthesis and cellular respiration, provides a summary of the reactants and products of photosynthesis:

Light energy

$$6\ CO_2 + 6\ H_2O \longrightarrow C_6H_{12}O_6 + 6\ O_2$$

Notice that the reactants of photosynthesis—carbon dioxide (CO_2) and water (H_2O)—are the same as the waste products of cellular respiration (see Figure 6.2). Also notice that photosynthesis produces what respiration uses—glucose ($C_6H_{12}O_6$) and oxygen (O_2). In other words, photosynthesis recycles the "exhaust" of cellular respiration and rearranges its atoms to produce food and oxygen. Photosynthesis is a chemical transformation that requires a lot of energy, and sunlight absorbed by chlorophyll provides that energy.

Recall that cellular respiration is a process of electron transfer (see Chapter 6). A "fall" of electrons from food molecules to oxygen to form water releases the energy that mitochondria can use to make ATP (see Figure 6.9). The opposite occurs in photosynthesis: Electrons are boosted "uphill" and added to carbon dioxide to produce

sugar. Hydrogen is moved along with the electrons being transferred from water to carbon dioxide. This transfer of hydrogen requires the chloroplast to split water molecules into hydrogen and oxygen. The hydrogen is transferred along with electrons to carbon dioxide to form sugar. The oxygen escapes through stomata in leaves into the atmosphere as O_2, a waste product of photosynthesis.

The overall equation for photosynthesis is a simple summary of a complex process. Like many energy-producing processes within cells, photosynthesis is a multistep chemical pathway, with each step in the path producing products that are used as reactants in the next step. This is a clear example of one of biology's major themes: the use of metabolic pathways to obtain, process, and store energy. To help get a better overview, let's take a look at the two stages of photosynthesis: the light reactions and the Calvin cycle (**Figure 7.3**).

▼ Figure 7.3 **A road map for photosynthesis.** We'll use a smaller version of this road map for orientation as we take a closer look at the light reactions and the Calvin cycle.

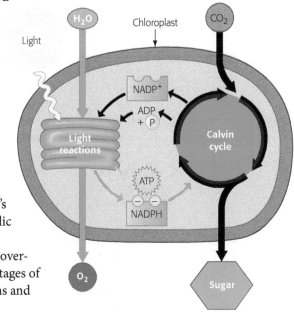

H_2O Chloroplast CO_2

Light

$NADP^+$

$ADP + P$

Light reactions

Calvin cycle

ATP

NADPH

O_2 Sugar

In the **light reactions**, chlorophyll in the thylakoid membranes absorbs solar energy (the "photo" part of photosynthesis), which is then converted to the chemical energy of ATP (the molecule that drives most cellular work) and **NADPH** (an electron carrier). During the light reactions, water is split, providing a source of electrons and giving off O_2 gas as a by-product.

The **Calvin cycle** uses the products of the light reactions to power the production of sugar from carbon dioxide (the "synthesis" part of photosynthesis). The enzymes that drive the Calvin cycle are dissolved in the stroma. ATP generated by the light reactions provides the energy for sugar synthesis. And the NADPH produced by the light reactions provides the high-energy electrons that drive the synthesis of glucose from carbon dioxide. Thus, the Calvin cycle indirectly depends on light to produce sugar because it requires the supply of ATP and NADPH produced by the light reactions.

The initial incorporation of carbon from CO_2 into organic compounds is called **carbon fixation**. This process has important implications for global climate, because the removal of carbon from the air and its incorporation into plant material can help reduce the concentration of carbon dioxide in the atmosphere. Deforestation, which removes a lot of photosynthetic plant life, thereby reduces the ability of the biosphere to absorb carbon. Planting new forests can have the opposite effect of fixing carbon from the atmosphere, potentially reducing the effect of the gases that contribute to global climate change. ☑

> If you want to reduce the rate of global climate change, plant a tree.

The Light Reactions: Converting Solar Energy to Chemical Energy

Chloroplasts are solar-powered sugar factories. Let's look at how they convert sunlight to chemical energy.

The Nature of Sunlight

Sunlight is a type of energy called radiation or electromagnetic energy. Electromagnetic energy travels through space as rhythmic waves, like the ripples made by a pebble dropped into a pond. The distance between the crests of two adjacent waves is called a **wavelength**. The full range of radiation, from the very short wavelengths of gamma rays to the very long wavelengths of radio signals, is called the **electromagnetic spectrum** (Figure 7.4). Visible light is the fraction of the spectrum that our eyes see as different colors.

When sunlight shines on a pigmented material, certain wavelengths (colors) of the visible light are absorbed and disappear from the light that is reflected by the material. For example, we see a pair of jeans as blue because pigments in the fabric absorb the other colors, leaving only light in the blue part of the spectrum to be reflected from the fabric to our eyes. In the 1800s,

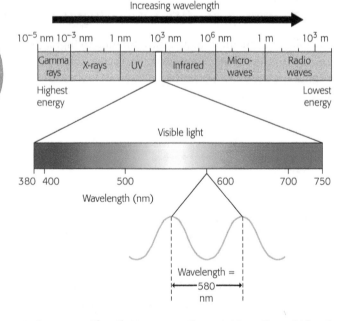

▲ Figure 7.4 **The electromagnetic spectrum.** The middle of the figure expands the thin slice of the spectrum that is visible to us as different colors of light, from about 380 nanometers (nm) to about 750 nm in wavelength. The bottom of the figure shows electromagnetic waves of one particular wavelength of visible light.

botanists (biologists who study plants) discovered that only certain wavelengths of light are used by plants, as we'll see next.

What Colors of Light Drive Photosynthesis?

In 1883, German biologist Theodor Engelmann made the **observation** that certain bacteria living in water tend to cluster in areas with higher oxygen concentrations. He already knew that light passed through a prism would separate into the different wavelengths (colors). Engelmann soon began to **question** whether he could use this information to determine which wavelengths of light work best for photosynthesis.

Engelmann's **hypothesis** was that oxygen-seeking bacteria would congregate near regions of algae performing the most photosynthesis (and hence producing the most oxygen). Engelmann began his **experiment** by laying a string of freshwater algal cells within a drop of water on a microscope slide. He then added oxygen-sensitive bacteria to the drop. Next, using a prism, he created a spectrum of light and shined it on the slide. His **results**, summarized in **Figure 7.5**, showed that most bacteria congregated around algae exposed to red-orange and blue-violet light, with very few bacteria moving to the area of green light. Other experiments have since verified that chloroplasts absorb light mainly in the blue-violet and red-orange part of the spectrum and that those wavelengths of light are the ones mainly responsible for photosynthesis.

Variations of this classic experiment are still performed today. For example, biofuel researchers test different species of algae to determine which wavelengths of light result in optimal fuel production. Biofuel facilities of the future may use a variety of species that take advantage of the full spectrum of light that shines down on them.

◄ **Figure 7.5 Investigating how light wavelength affects photosynthesis.** When algal cells are placed on a microscope slide, oxygen-seeking bacteria migrate toward algae exposed to certain colors of light. These results suggest that blue-violet and orange-red wavelengths best drive photosynthesis, while green wavelengths do so only a little bit.

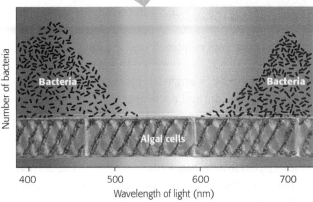

Chloroplast Pigments

The selective absorption of light by leaves explains why they appear green to us; light of that color is poorly absorbed by chloroplasts and is thus reflected or transmitted toward the observer (Figure 7.6). Energy cannot be destroyed, so the absorbed energy must be converted to other forms. Chloroplasts contain several different pigments that absorb light of different wavelengths.

► **Figure 7.6 Why are leaves green?** Chlorophyll and other pigments in chloroplasts reflect or transmit green light while absorbing other colors.

Chlorophyll *a*, the pigment that participates directly in the light reactions, absorbs mainly blue-violet and red light. A very similar molecule, chlorophyll *b*, absorbs mainly blue and orange light. Chlorophyll *b* does not participate directly in the light reactions, but it conveys absorbed energy to chlorophyll *a*, which then puts the energy to work in the light reactions.

Chloroplasts also contain a family of yellow-orange pigments called carotenoids, which absorb mainly blue-green light. Some carotenoids have a protective function: They dissipate excess light energy that would otherwise damage chlorophyll. Some carotenoids are human nutrients: beta-carotene (a bright orange/red pigment found in pumpkins, sweet potatoes, and carrots) is converted to vitamin A in the body, and lycopene (a bright red pigment found in tomatoes, watermelon, and red peppers) is an antioxidant that is being studied for potential anti-cancer properties. Additionally, the spectacular colors of fall foliage in some parts of the world are due partly to the yellow-orange light reflected from carotenoids (Figure 7.7). The decreasing temperatures in autumn cause a decrease in the levels of chlorophyll, allowing the colors of the longer-lasting carotenoids to be seen in all their fall glory.

All of these chloroplast pigments are built into the thylakoid membranes (see Figure 7.2). There the pigments are organized into light-harvesting complexes called photosystems, our next topic. ☑

▲ Figure 7.7 **Photosynthetic pigments.** Falling autumn temperatures cause a decrease in the levels of green chlorophyll within the foliage of leaf-bearing trees. This decrease allows the colors of the carotenoids to be seen.

☑ **CHECKPOINT**

What is the specific name of the pigment that absorbs energy during the light reactions?

Answer: chlorophyll a

How Photosystems Harvest Light Energy

Thinking about light as waves explains most of light's properties. However, light also behaves as discrete packets of energy called photons. A **photon** is a fixed quantity of light energy. The shorter the wavelength of light, the greater the energy of a photon. A photon of violet light, for example, packs nearly twice as much energy as a photon of red light. This is why short-wavelength light—such as ultraviolet light and X-rays—can be damaging; photons at these wavelengths carry enough energy to damage proteins and DNA, potentially leading to cancerous mutations.

Protecting yourself from short wavelengths of light can be lifesaving.

When a pigment molecule absorbs a photon, one of the pigment's electrons gains energy. This electron is now said to be "excited"; that is, the electron has been raised from its starting state (called the ground state) to an excited state. The excited state is highly unstable, so an excited electron usually loses its excess energy and falls back to its ground state almost immediately (Figure 7.8a). Most pigments release heat energy as their light-excited electrons fall back to their ground state. (That's why a surface with a lot of pigment, such as a black driveway, gets so hot on a sunny day.) But some pigments emit light as well as heat after absorbing

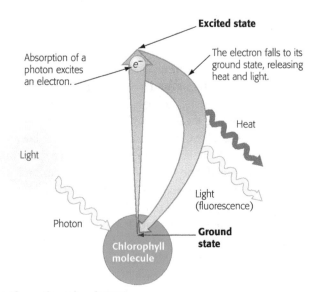

(a) **Absorption of a photon**

(b) **Fluorescence of a glow stick.** Breaking a vial within a glow stick starts a chemical reaction that excites electrons within a fluorescent dye. As the electrons fall from their excited state to the ground state, the excess energy is emitted as light.

▲ Figure 7.8 **Excited electrons in pigments.**

Chloroplast

Cluster of pigment molecules associated with membrane proteins

Photon

Primary electron acceptor

Electron transfer

Reaction-center chlorophyll *a*

Reaction center

Pigment molecules

Thylakoid membrane

Transfer of energy

Photosystem

▲ Figure 7.9 **A photosystem: light-gathering molecules that focus light energy onto a reaction center.**

photons. The fluorescent light emitted by a glow stick is caused by a chemical reaction that excites electrons of a fluorescent dye (Figure 7.8b). The excited electrons quickly fall back down to their ground state, releasing energy in the form of fluorescent light.

In the thylakoid membrane, chlorophyll molecules are organized with other molecules into photosystems. Each **photosystem** has a cluster of a few hundred pigment molecules, including chlorophylls *a* and *b* and some carotenoids (Figure 7.9). This cluster of pigment

molecules functions as a light-gathering antenna. When a photon strikes one of the pigment molecules, the energy jumps from molecule to molecule until it arrives at the reaction center of the photosystem. The reaction center consists of chlorophyll *a* molecules that sit next to another molecule called a primary electron acceptor. This primary electron acceptor traps the light-excited electron (e^-) from the chlorophyll *a* in the reaction center. Another team of molecules built into the thylakoid membrane then uses that trapped energy to make ATP and NADPH. ☑

How the Light Reactions Generate ATP and NADPH

Two photosystems cooperate in the light reactions (Figure 7.10). ❶ Photons excite electrons in the chlorophyll of the first photosystem. These photons are then trapped by the primary electron acceptor. This photosystem then replaces the lost electrons by extracting new ones from water. This is the step that releases O_2 during photosynthesis. ❷ Energized electrons from the first photosystem pass down an electron transport chain to the second photosystem. The chloroplast uses the energy released by this electron "fall" to make ATP. ❸ The second photosystem transfers its light-excited electrons to $NADP^+$, reducing it to NADPH.

► Figure 7.10 **The light reactions of photosynthesis.** The orange arrows trace a light-driven flow of electrons from H_2O to NADPH. These electrons also produce ATP.

NADP⁺

Primary electron acceptor

$2e^-$

Energy to make ATP

❷

Primary electron acceptor

$2e^-$

$2e^-$

❸

NADPH

Electron transport chain

Light

Light

$2e^-$

❶

Reaction-center chlorophyll

Second photosystem

Reaction-center chlorophyll

First photosystem

H_2O

$2e^-$

$2 H^+ + \frac{1}{2} O_2$

☑ **CHECKPOINT**

1. Why is water required as a reactant in photosynthesis? (*Hint*: Review Figures 7.10 and 7.11.)
2. In addition to conveying electrons between photosystems, the electron transport chains of chloroplasts provide the energy for the synthesis of _____.

Answers: 1. The splitting of water provides electrons for converting NAD$^+$ to NADPH. 2. ATP

Figure 7.11 shows the location of the light reactions in the thylakoid membrane. The two photosystems and the electron transport chain that connects them transfer electrons from H_2O to NADP$^+$, producing NADPH. Notice that the mechanism of ATP production during the light reactions is very similar to the mechanism we saw in cellular respiration (see Figure 6.10). In both cases, an electron transport chain pumps hydrogen ions (H$^+$) across a membrane—the inner mitochondrial membrane in the case of respiration and the thylakoid membrane in photosynthesis. And in both cases, ATP synthases use the energy stored by the H$^+$ gradient to make ATP. The main difference is that food provides the high-energy electrons in cellular respiration, whereas light-excited electrons flow down the transport chain during photosynthesis. The traffic of electrons shown in Figures 7.10 and 7.11 is analogous to the cartoon in **Figure 7.12**.

We have seen how the light reactions absorb solar energy and convert it to the chemical energy of ATP and NADPH. Notice again, however, that the light reactions did not produce any sugar. That's the job of the Calvin cycle, as we'll see next. ☑

▼ Figure 7.12 **The light reactions illustrated using a hard-hat analogy.**

▼ Figure 7.11 **How the thylakoid membrane converts light energy to the chemical energy of NADPH and ATP.**

The Calvin Cycle: Making Sugar from Carbon Dioxide

If chloroplasts are solar-powered sugar factories, then the Calvin cycle is the actual sugar-manufacturing machinery. This process is called a cycle because its starting material is regenerated. With each turn of the cycle, there are chemical inputs and outputs. The inputs are CO_2 from the air as well as ATP and NADPH produced by the light reactions. Using carbon from CO_2, energy from ATP, and high-energy electrons from NADPH, the Calvin cycle constructs an energy-rich sugar molecule called glyceraldehyde 3-phosphate (G3P). The plant cell can then use G3P as the raw material to make the glucose and other organic compounds (such as cellulose and starch) that it needs. Figure 7.13 presents the basics of the Calvin cycle, emphasizing inputs and outputs. Each ● symbol represents a carbon atom, and each ⓟ symbol represents a phosphate group. ☑

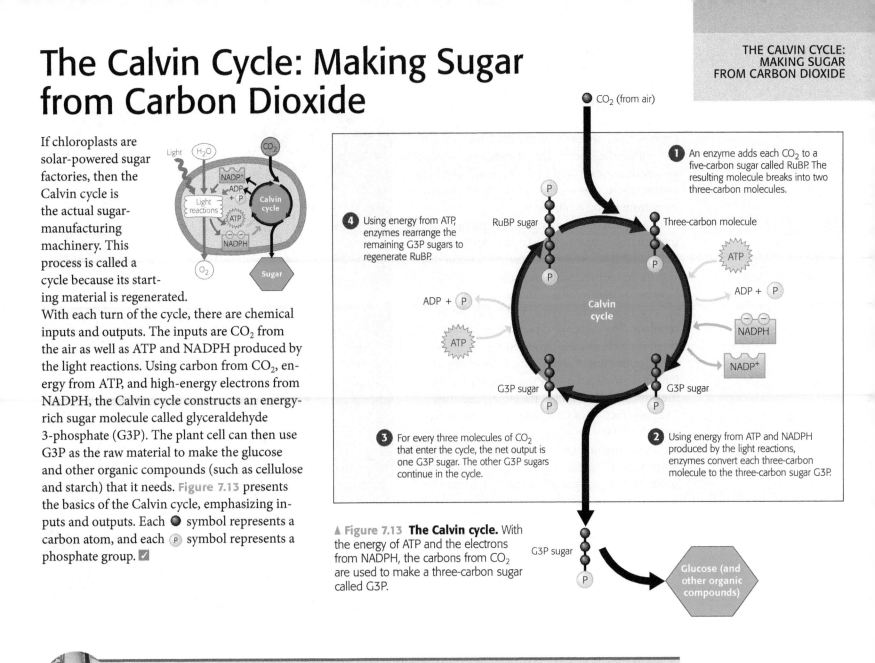

1 An enzyme adds each CO_2 to a five-carbon sugar called RuBP. The resulting molecule breaks into two three-carbon molecules.

4 Using energy from ATP, enzymes rearrange the remaining G3P sugars to regenerate RuBP.

3 For every three molecules of CO_2 that enter the cycle, the net output is one G3P sugar. The other G3P sugars continue in the cycle.

2 Using energy from ATP and NADPH produced by the light reactions, enzymes convert each three-carbon molecule to the three-carbon sugar G3P.

▲ Figure 7.13 **The Calvin cycle.** With the energy of ATP and the electrons from NADPH, the carbons from CO_2 are used to make a three-carbon sugar called G3P.

Biofuels EVOLUTION CONNECTION

Creating a Better Biofuel Factory

Throughout this chapter, we've studied how plants convert solar energy to chemical energy via photosynthesis. Such transformations are vital to our welfare and to Earth's ecosystems. As discussed in the Biology and Society section, scientists are attempting to tap into the "green energy" of photosynthesis to produce biofuels. But the production of biofuels is highly inefficient. In fact, it is usually far more costly to produce biofuels than to extract the equivalent amount of fossil fuels.

Biomechanical engineers are working to solve this dilemma by turning to an obvious example: evolution by natural selection. In nature, organisms with genes that make them better suited to their local environment will, on average, more often survive and pass those genes on to the next generation. Repeated over many generations, genes that enhance survival within that environment will become more common, and the species evolves.

When trying to solve an engineering problem, scientists can impose their own desired outcomes using a process called directed evolution (see the Process of Science section in Chapter 5 for another example).

☑ CHECKPOINT

What is the function of NADPH in the Calvin cycle?

Answer: It provides the high-energy electrons that are added to CO_2 to form G3P (a sugar).

115

During this process, scientists in the laboratory (instead of the natural environment) determine which organisms are the fittest. Directed evolution of biofuel production often involves microscopic algae (Figure 7.14) rather than plants because algae are easier to manipulate and maintain within the laboratory. Furthermore, some algae produce nearly half their own body weight in hydrocarbons that are only a few chemical steps away from useful biofuels.

In a typical directed evolution experiment, the researcher starts with a large collection of individual alga—sometimes naturally occurring species and sometimes transgenic algae that have been engineered to carry useful genes, such as fungal genes for enzymes that break down cellulose. The algae are exposed to mutation-promoting chemicals. This produces a highly varied collection of algae that can be screened for the desired outcome: the ability to produce the most useful biofuel in the largest quantity. The tiny fraction of total algae that can best perform this task is grown and subjected to another round of mutation and selection. After many repetitions, the algae may slowly improve their ability to efficiently produce biofuels. Many research laboratories—some within major petroleum companies—are using such methods and may someday produce an alga that can provide the ultimate source of green energy, an achievement that would highlight how lessons from natural evolution can be applied to improve our lives.

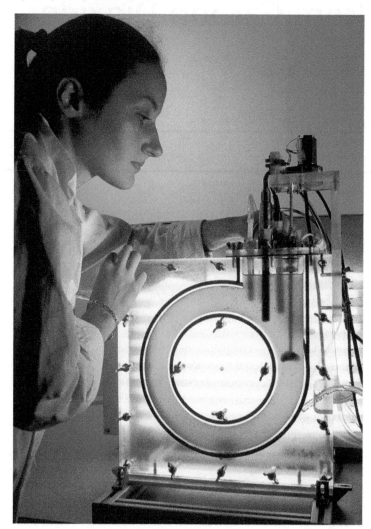

▼ Figure 7.14 **Microscopic biofuel factories.** This researcher is monitoring a reaction chamber in which microscopic algae are using light to produce biofuels.

Chapter Review

SUMMARY OF KEY CONCEPTS

The Basics of Photosynthesis

Photosynthesis is a process whereby light energy is transformed into chemical energy stored as bonds in sugars made from carbon dioxide and water.

Chloroplasts: Sites of Photosynthesis

Chloroplasts contain a thick fluid called stroma surrounding a network of membranes called thylakoids.

Energy Transformation: An Overview of Photosynthesis

The overall process of photosynthesis can be divided into two stages connected by energy- and electron-carrying molecules:

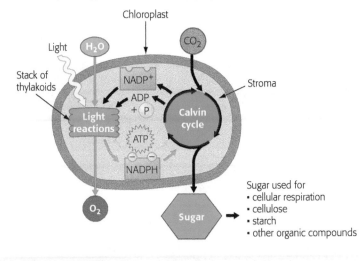

The Light Reactions: Converting Solar Energy to Chemical Energy

The Nature of Sunlight

Visible light is part of the spectrum of electromagnetic energy. It travels through space as waves. Different wavelengths of light appear as different colors; shorter wavelengths carry more energy.

Chloroplast Pigments

Pigment molecules absorb light energy of certain wavelengths and reflect other wavelengths. We see the reflected wavelengths as the color of the pigment. Several chloroplast pigments absorb light of various wavelengths and convey it to other pigments, but it is the green pigment chlorophyll *a* that participates directly in the light reactions.

How Photosystems Harvest Light Energy and How the Light Reactions Generate ATP and NADPH

The Calvin Cycle: Making Sugar from Carbon Dioxide

Within the stroma (fluid) of the chloroplast, carbon dioxide from the air and ATP and NADPH produced during the light reactions are used to produce G3P, an energy-rich sugar molecule that can be used to make glucose and other organic molecules.

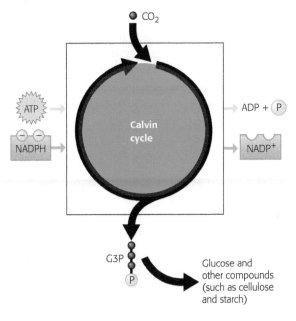

MasteringBiology®

For practice quizzes, BioFlix animations, MP3 tutorials, video tutors, and more study tools designed for this textbook, go to MasteringBiology®

SELF-QUIZ

1. The light reactions take place in the structures of the chloroplast called the _____, while the Calvin cycle takes place in the _____.

2. In terms of the spatial organization of photosynthesis within the chloroplast, what is the advantage of the light reactions producing NADPH and ATP on the stroma side of the thylakoid membrane?

3. Which of the following are inputs to photosynthesis? Choose all that apply. Which are outputs? Choose all that apply.
   a. CO_2
   b. O_2
   c. sugar
   d. H_2O
   e. light

4. Explain how the name "photosynthesis" describes what this process accomplishes.

5. What color of light is the least effective in driving photosynthesis? Why?

6. When light strikes chlorophyll molecules, they lose electrons, which are ultimately replaced by splitting molecules of _____.

7. Which of the following are produced by reactions that take place in the thylakoids and are consumed by reactions in the stroma?

   a. CO_2 and H_2O
   b. $NADP^+$ and ADP
   c. ATP and NADPH
   d. glucose and O_2

8. The reactions of the Calvin cycle are not directly dependent on light, and yet they usually do not occur at night. Why?

9. Of the following metabolic processes, which one is common to photosynthesis and cellular respiration?

   a. reactions that convert light energy to chemical energy
   b. reactions that split H_2O molecules and release O_2
   c. reactions that store energy by pumping H^+ across membranes
   d. reactions that convert CO_2 to sugar

Answers to these questions can be found in Appendix: Self-Quiz Answers.

THE PROCESS OF SCIENCE

10. Tropical rain forests cover only about 3% of Earth's surface, but they are estimated to be responsible for more than 20% of global photosynthesis. For this reason, rain forests are often referred to as the "lungs" of the planet, providing O_2 for life all over Earth. However, most experts believe that rain forests make little or no net contribution to global O_2 production. From your knowledge of photosynthesis and cellular respiration, can you explain why they might think this? (*Hint:* What happens to the energy stored as sugars in the body of a plant when that plant dies or parts of it are eaten by animals?)

11. Suppose you wanted to discover whether the oxygen atoms in the glucose produced by photosynthesis come from H_2O or CO_2. Explain how you could use a radioactive isotope to find out.

12. **Interpreting Data** The graph above right is called an absorption spectrum. Each line on the graph is made by shining light of varying wavelengths through a sample. For each wavelength, the amount of that light absorbed by the sample is recorded. This graph combines three such measurements, one each for the pigments chlorophyll *a*, chlorophyll *b*, and the carotenoids. Notice that the graphs for the chlorophyll pigments match the data presented in Figure 7.5. Imagine a plant that lacks chlorophyll and relies only on carotenoids for photosynthesis. What colors of light would work best for this plant? How would this plant appear to your eye?

BIOLOGY AND SOCIETY

13. There is strong evidence that Earth is getting warmer because of an intensified greenhouse effect resulting from increased CO_2 emissions from industry, vehicles, and the burning of forests. Global climate change could influence agriculture, melt polar ice, and flood coastal regions. In response to these threats, 192 parties have accepted the Kyoto Protocol, which calls for mandatory reductions of greenhouse gas emissions in 30 industrialized nations by 2012. The United States has signed but not ratified (put into effect) the agreement, instead proposing a more modest set of voluntary goals allowing businesses to decide whether they wish to participate and providing tax incentives to encourage them to do so. The reasons given for rejecting the agreement are that it might hurt the American economy and that some less industrialized countries (such as India) are exempted from it, even though they produce a lot of pollution. Do you agree with this decision? In what ways might efforts to reduce greenhouse gases hurt the economy? How can those costs be weighed against the costs of global climate change? Should poorer nations carry an equal burden to reduce their emissions?

14. Burning biomass to produce electricity avoids many of the problems associated with gathering, refining, transporting, and burning fossil fuels. Yet the use of biomass as fuel is not without its own set of problems. What challenges might arise from a large-scale conversion to biomass energy? How do these challenges compare with those encountered with fossil fuels? Which set of challenges do you think is more likely to be overcome? Does one energy source have more benefits and fewer costs than the others? Explain.

Unit 2
Genetics

8 Cellular Reproduction: Cells from Cells

Chapter Thread: **Life with and without Sex**

9 Patterns of Inheritance

Chapter Thread: **Dog Breeding**

10 The Structure and Function of DNA

Chapter Thread: **The Deadliest Virus**

11 How Genes Are Controlled

Chapter Thread: **Cancer**

12 DNA Technology

Chapter Thread: **DNA Profiling**

8 Cellular Reproduction: Cells from Cells

▲ In certain species of sea star, a severed arm may be able to regrow a whole new body.

◄ Having too few or too many chromosomes is almost always fatal.

If stretched out, the DNA ► in any one of your cells would be taller than you.

▲ Every tumor is the result of a malfunction in cell division.

Life with and without Sex BIOLOGY AND SOCIETY

Virgin Birth of a Dragon

Zookeepers at the Chester Zoo in England were startled to discover that Flora, a female Komodo dragon—*Varanus komodoensis*, the largest living species of lizard, capable of growing up to 10 feet long—had laid a clutch of 25 eggs. It wasn't surprising that a captive Komodo dragon would breed. In fact, Flora was at the

The Komodo dragon. The Komodo is the world's largest lizard and is found in the wild only on three islands in Indonesia.

zoo for that very reason: She was one of two female Komodo dragons that were part of a captive breeding program intended to help repopulate the species. What made Flora's clutch of eggs so remarkable is that she had not yet been in the company of a male, let alone mated with one. As far as anyone knew, Komodo dragons, like the vast majority of animal species, create offspring only through sexual reproduction involving the union of a male's sperm and a female's egg. But despite Flora's virginity, eight of her eggs developed normally and hatched into live, healthy Komodo dragons.

DNA analysis confirmed that Flora's offspring derived their genes solely from her. The new dragons must have resulted from parthenogenesis, the production of offspring by a female without involvement of a male. Parthenogenesis is one form of asexual reproduction, the creation of a new generation without participation of sperm and egg. Parthenogenesis is rare among vertebrates (animals with backbones), although it has been documented in species as diverse as sharks (including the hammerhead), domesticated birds, and now Komodo dragons. Soon, zoologists identified a second Komodo at a different zoo who had also borne young by parthenogenesis. This same Komodo dragon later had additional offspring via sexual reproduction—indicating that this species is capable of switching between two reproductive modes. Biologists are investigating the evolutionary basis of this phenomenon and considering what implications it may have on efforts to repopulate this rare species.

The ability of organisms to procreate is the one characteristic that best distinguishes living things from nonliving matter. All organisms—from bacteria to lizards to you—are the result of repeated cell divisions. The perpetuation of life therefore depends on cell division, the production of new cells. In this chapter, we'll look at how individual cells are copied and then see how cell reproduction underlies the process of sexual reproduction. Throughout our discussion, we'll consider examples of asexual and sexual reproduction among both plants and animals.

What Cell Reproduction Accomplishes

When you hear the word *reproduction*, you probably think of the birth of new organisms. But reproduction actually occurs much more often at the cellular level. Consider the skin on your arm. Skin cells are constantly reproducing themselves and moving outward toward the surface, replacing dead cells that have rubbed off. This renewal of your skin goes on throughout your life. And when your skin is injured, additional cell reproduction helps heal the wound.

When a cell undergoes reproduction, or **cell division**, the two "daughter" cells that result are genetically identical to each other and to the original "parent" cell. (Biologists traditionally use the word *daughter* in this context to refer to offspring cells, but of course cells lack gender.) Before the parent cell splits into two, it duplicates its **chromosomes**, the structures that contain most of the cell's DNA. Then, during cell division, each daughter cell receives one identical set of chromosomes from the original parent cell.

As summarized in **Figure 8.1**, cell division plays several important roles in the lives of organisms. For example, within your body, millions of cells must divide every second to replace damaged or lost cells. Another function of cell division is growth. All of the trillions of cells in your body are the result of repeated cell divisions that began in your mother's body with a single fertilized egg cell.

Another vital function of cell division is reproduction. Many single-celled organisms, such as amoebas,

In certain species of sea star, a severed arm may be able to regrow a whole new body.

reproduce by dividing in half, and the offspring are genetic replicas of the parent. Because it does not involve fertilization of an egg by a sperm, this type of reproduction is called **asexual reproduction**.

Offspring produced by asexual reproduction inherit all of their chromosomes from a single parent and are thus genetic duplicates.

Many multicellular organisms can reproduce asexually as well. For example, some sea star species have the ability to grow new individuals from fragmented pieces. And if you've ever grown a houseplant from a clipping, you've observed asexual reproduction in plants. In asexual reproduction, there is one simple principle of inheritance: The lone parent and each of its offspring have identical genes. The type of cell division responsible for asexual reproduction and for the growth and maintenance of multicellular organisms is called mitosis.

Sexual reproduction is different; it requires fertilization of an egg by a sperm. The production of **gametes**—egg and sperm—involves a special type of cell division called meiosis, which occurs only in reproductive organs. As we'll discuss later, a gamete has only half as many chromosomes as the parent cell that gave rise to it.

In summary, two kinds of cell division are involved in the lives of sexually reproducing organisms: mitosis for growth and maintenance and meiosis for reproduction. The remainder of the chapter is divided into two main sections, one devoted to each type of cell division. ☑

► Figure 8.1 **Three functions of cell division by mitosis.**

FUNCTIONS OF CELL DIVISION BY MITOSIS

Cell Replacement	Growth via Cell Division

Division of a human kidney cell into two

LM 590×

The cells of an early human embryo

Colorized SEM 810×

The Cell Cycle and Mitosis

Almost all of the genes of a eukaryotic cell—around 21,000 in humans—are located on chromosomes in the cell nucleus. (The main exceptions are genes on small DNA molecules found in mitochondria and chloroplasts.) Because chromosomes are the lead players in cell division, we'll focus on them before turning our attention to the cell as a whole.

If stretched out, the DNA in any one of your cells would be taller than you.

Most of the time, the chromosomes exist as thin fibers that are much longer than the nucleus they are stored in. In fact, if fully extended, the DNA in just one of your cells would be more than 6 feet long! Chromatin in this state is too thin to be seen using a light microscope. As a cell

Eukaryotic Chromosomes

Each eukaryotic chromosome contains one very long DNA molecule, typically bearing thousands of genes. The number of chromosomes in a eukaryotic cell depends on the species (Figure 8.2). For example, human body cells have 46 chromosomes, while the body cells of a dog have 78 and those of a koala bear have 16. Chromosomes are made up of a material called **chromatin**, fibers composed of roughly equal amounts of DNA and protein molecules. The protein molecules help organize the chromatin and help control the activity of its genes.

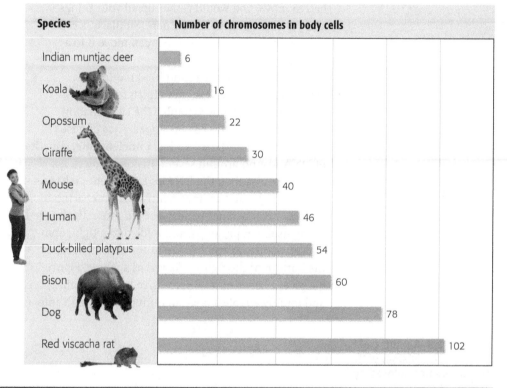

Species	Number of chromosomes in body cells
Indian muntjac deer	6
Koala	16
Opossum	22
Giraffe	30
Mouse	40
Human	46
Duck-billed platypus	54
Bison	60
Dog	78
Red viscacha rat	102

▶ Figure 8.2 **The number of chromosomes in the cells of selected mammals.** Notice that humans have 46 chromosomes and that the number of chromosomes does not correspond to the size or complexity of an organism.

Asexual Reproduction

LM 250x

Reproduction of an amoeba

Fragmentation and regeneration of a sea star. The sea star on the right lost and replaced an arm. The severed arm grew into the new sea star on the left.

Reproduction of an African violet from a clipping (large leaf)

prepares to divide, its chromatin fibers coil up, forming compact chromosomes that become visible under a light microscope (Figure 8.3).

Such long molecules of DNA can fit into the tiny nucleus because within each chromosome the DNA is packed into an elaborate, multilevel system of coiling and folding. A crucial aspect of DNA packing is the association of the DNA with small proteins called **histones**. Why is it necessary for a cell's chromosomes to be compacted in this way? Imagine that your belongings are spread out around your room. If you had to move, you would gather up all your things and put them in small containers. Similarly, a cell must compact its DNA before it can move it to a new cell.

Figure 8.4 presents a simplified model of DNA packing. First, histones attach to the DNA. In electron micrographs, the combination of DNA and histones has the appearance of beads on a string. Each "bead," called a **nucleosome**, consists of DNA wound around several histone molecules. When not dividing, the DNA of active genes takes on this lightly packed arrangement. When preparing to divide, chromosomes condense even more: the beaded string itself wraps, loops, and folds into a tight, compact structure, as you can see in the chromosome at the bottom of the figure. Viewed as a whole, Figure 8.4 gives a sense of how successive levels of coiling and folding enable a huge amount of DNA to fit into a

cell's tiny nucleus. Think of a DNA as a length of yarn; a chromosome is then like a skein of yarn, one very long piece that is folded into a tight package for easier handling.

▼ Figure 8.4 **DNA packing in a eukaryotic chromosome.** Successive levels of coiling of DNA and associated proteins ultimately result in highly compacted chromosomes. The fuzzy appearance of the final chromosome at the bottom arises from the intricate twists and folds of the chromatin fibers.

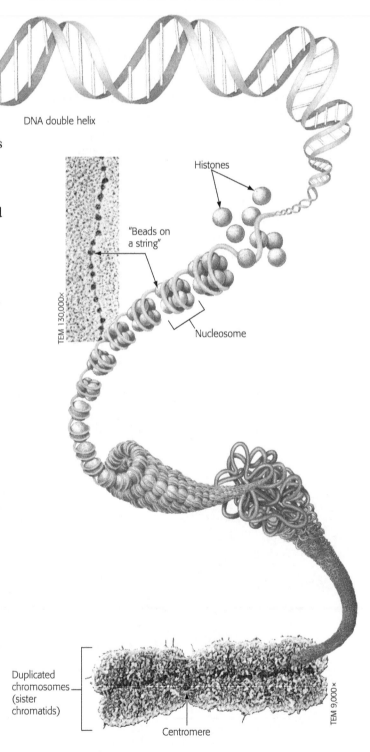

DNA double helix

Histones

"Beads on a string"

Nucleosome

TEM 130,000×

Duplicated chromosomes (sister chromatids)

Centromere

TEM 9,000×

▼ Figure 8.3 **A plant cell just before division, with chromosomes colored by stains.**

LM 1,400×

Chromosomes

Information Flow Duplicating Chromosomes

Think of the chromosomes as being like a detailed instruction manual on how to run a cell; during division, the original cell must pass on a copy of the manual to the new cell while also retaining a copy for itself. Before a cell begins the division process, it must therefore duplicate all of its chromosomes. The DNA molecule of each chromosome is copied through the process of DNA replication (discussed in detail in Chapter 10), and new histone protein molecules attach as needed. The result is that—at this point—each chromosome consists of two copies called **sister chromatids**, which contain identical genes. At the bottom of Figure 8.4, the two sister chromatids are joined together most tightly at a narrow "waist" called the **centromere**.

▲ **Figure 8.5 Duplication and distribution of a single chromosome.** During cell reproduction, the cell duplicates each chromosome and distributes the two copies to the daughter cells.

When the cell divides, the sister chromatids of a duplicated chromosome separate from each other (Figure 8.5). Once separated from its sister, each chromatid is considered a full-fledged chromosome, and it is identical to the original chromosome. One of the new chromosomes goes to one daughter cell, and the other goes to the other daughter cell. In this way, each daughter cell receives a complete and identical set of chromosomes. A dividing human skin cell, for example, has 46 duplicated chromosomes, and each of the two daughter cells that result from it has 46 single chromosomes.

The Cell Cycle

The rate at which a cell divides depends on its role within the organism's body. Some cells divide once a day, others less often, and some highly specialized cells, such as mature muscle cells, do not divide at all.

The **cell cycle** is the ordered sequence of events that extends from the time a cell is first formed from a dividing parent cell until its own division into two cells. Think of the cell cycle as the "lifetime" of a cell, from its "birth" to its own reproduction. As Figure 8.6 shows, most of the cell cycle is spent in **interphase**. Interphase is a time when a cell goes about its usual business, performing its normal functions within the organism. For example, during interphase a cell in your stomach lining might make and release enzyme molecules that aid in digestion. While in interphase, a cell roughly doubles everything in its cytoplasm. It increases its supply of proteins, increases the number of many of its organelles (such as mitochondria and ribosomes), and grows in size. Typically, interphase lasts for at least 90% of the cell cycle.

From the standpoint of cell reproduction, the most important event of interphase is chromosome duplication, when the DNA in the nucleus is precisely doubled. The period when this occurs is called the S phase (for DNA *synthesis*). The interphase periods before and after the S phase are called the G_1 and G_2 phases, respectively (G stands for *gap*). During G_1, each chromosome is single, and the cell performs its normal functions. During G_2 (after DNA duplication during the S phase), each chromosome in the cell consists of two identical sister chromatids, and the cell prepares to divide.

The part of the cell cycle when the cell is actually dividing is called the **mitotic (M) phase**. It includes two overlapping stages, mitosis and cytokinesis. In **mitosis**, the nucleus and its contents, most importantly the duplicated chromosomes, divide and are evenly distributed, forming two daughter nuclei. During **cytokinesis**, the cytoplasm (along with all the organelles) is divided in two. The combination of mitosis and cytokinesis produces two genetically identical daughter cells, each fully equipped with a nucleus, cytoplasm, organelles, and plasma membrane. ✓

☑ CHECKPOINT

1. A duplicated chromosome consists of two sister _____ joined together at the _____.
2. What are the two broadest divisions of the cell cycle? What two processes are involved in the actual duplication of the cell?

Answers: 1. chromatids; centromere 2. interphase and the mitotic phase; mitosis and cytokinesis

▼ **Figure 8.6 The eukaryotic cell cycle.** The cell cycle extends from the "birth" of a cell (just after the point indicated by the dark blue arrow at the bottom of the cycle), resulting from cell reproduction, to the time the cell itself divides in two. (During interphase, the chromosomes are diffuse masses of thin fibers; they do not actually appear in the rodlike form you see here.)

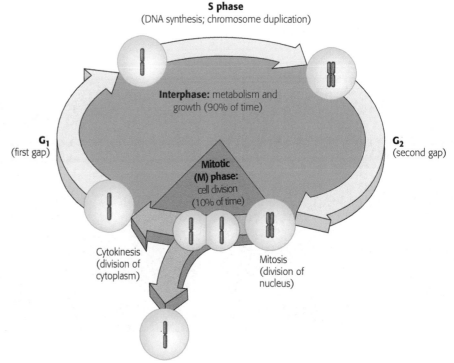

S phase
(DNA synthesis; chromosome duplication)

Interphase: metabolism and growth (90% of time)

G_1 (first gap)

G_2 (second gap)

Mitotic (M) phase: cell division (10% of time)

Cytokinesis (division of cytoplasm)

Mitosis (division of nucleus)

Mitosis and Cytokinesis

Figure 8.7 illustrates the cell cycle for an animal cell using drawings, descriptions, and photomicrographs. The micrographs running along the bottom row of the page show dividing cells from a salamander, with chromosomes depicted in blue. The drawings in the top row include details that are not visible in the micrographs. In these cells, we illustrate just four chromosomes to keep the process a bit simpler to follow; remember that one of your cells actually contains 46 chromosomes. The text within the figure describes

▼ Figure 8.7 **Cell reproduction: A dance of the chromosomes.** After the chromosomes duplicate during interphase, the elaborately choreographed stages of mitosis—prophase, metaphase, anaphase, and telophase—distribute the duplicate sets of chromosomes to two separate nuclei. Cytokinesis then divides the cytoplasm, yielding two genetically identical daughter cells.

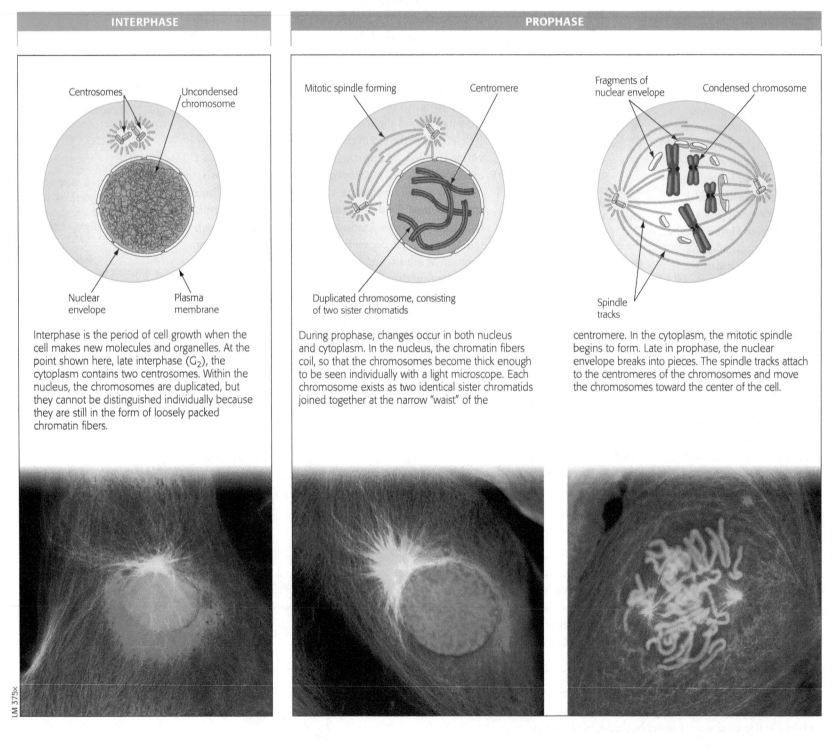

INTERPHASE

Centrosomes
Uncondensed chromosome

Nuclear envelope
Plasma membrane

Interphase is the period of cell growth when the cell makes new molecules and organelles. At the point shown here, late interphase (G_2), the cytoplasm contains two centrosomes. Within the nucleus, the chromosomes are duplicated, but they cannot be distinguished individually because they are still in the form of loosely packed chromatin fibers.

PROPHASE

Mitotic spindle forming
Centromere

Fragments of nuclear envelope
Condensed chromosome

Duplicated chromosome, consisting of two sister chromatids

Spindle tracks

During prophase, changes occur in both nucleus and cytoplasm. In the nucleus, the chromatin fibers coil, so that the chromosomes become thick enough to be seen individually with a light microscope. Each chromosome exists as two identical sister chromatids joined together at the narrow "waist" of the

centromere. In the cytoplasm, the mitotic spindle begins to form. Late in prophase, the nuclear envelope breaks into pieces. The spindle tracks attach to the centromeres of the chromosomes and move the chromosomes toward the center of the cell.

LM 375x

the events occurring at each stage. Study this figure carefully (it has a lot of information and it's important!) and notice the striking changes in the nucleus and other cellular structures.

Biologists distinguish four main stages of mitosis: **prophase**, **metaphase**, **anaphase**, and **telophase**. The timing of these stages is not precise, and they overlap a bit. Think of stages in your own life—infancy, childhood, adulthood, old age—and you'll realize that the stages run into each other and vary from individual to individual; so it is with the stages of mitosis.

The chromosomes are the stars of the mitotic drama, and their movements depend on the **mitotic spindle**, a football-shaped structure of microtubule tracks (colored green in the figure) that guides the separation of the two sets of daughter chromosomes. The tracks of spindle microtubules grow from structures within the cytoplasm called centrosomes.

METAPHASE

Condensed chromosomes align

The mitotic spindle is now fully formed. The centromeres of all the chromosomes line up between the two poles of the spindle. For each chromosome, the tracks of the mitotic spindle attached to the two sister chromatids pull toward opposite poles. This tug of war keeps the chromosomes in the middle of the cell.

ANAPHASE

Separated chromosomes

Anaphase begins suddenly when the sister chromatids of each chromosome separate. Each is now considered a full-fledged (daughter) chromosome. The chromosomes move toward opposite poles of the cell as the spindle tracks shorten. Simultaneously, the tracks not attached to chromosomes lengthen, pushing the poles farther apart and elongating the cell.

TELOPHASE

Nuclear envelope forming   Cleavage furrow

Telophase begins when the two groups of chromosomes have reached opposite ends of the cell. Telophase is the reverse of prophase: Nuclear envelopes form, the chromosomes uncoil, and the spindle disappears. Mitosis, the division of one nucleus into two genetically identical daughter nuclei, is now finished. Cytokinesis, the division of the cytoplasm, usually occurs with telophase. In animals, a cleavage furrow pinches the cell in two, producing two daughter cells.

▼ Figure 8.8 **Cytokinesis in animal and plant cells.**

SEM 100x

Cleavage
furrow

Wall of
parent cell

Cell plate
forming

Daughter
nucleus

LM 640x

Cleavage furrow

Contracting ring of
microfilaments

Daughter cells

(a) Animal cell cytokinesis

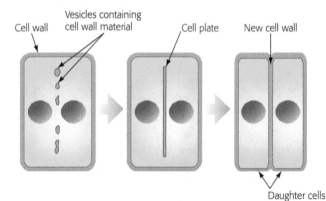

Cell wall

Vesicles containing
cell wall material

Cell plate

New cell wall

Daughter cells

(b) Plant cell cytokinesis

☑ **CHECKPOINT**

An organism called a
plasmodial slime mold is
one huge cytoplasmic mass
with many nuclei. Explain
how a variation in the cell
cycle could cause this
"monster cell" to arise.

*Answer: Mitosis occurs repeatedly
without cytokinesis.*

Cytokinesis, the division of the cytoplasm into two cells, usually begins during telophase, overlapping the end of mitosis. In animal cells, the cytokinesis process is known as **cleavage**. The first sign of cleavage is the appearance of a cleavage furrow, an indentation at the equator of the cell. A ring of microfilaments in the cytoplasm just under the plasma membrane contracts, like the pulling of a drawstring on a hooded sweatshirt, deepening the furrow and pinching the parent cell in two **(Figure 8.8a)**.

Cytokinesis in a plant cell occurs differently. Vesicles containing cell wall material collect at the middle of the cell. The vesicles fuse, forming a membranous disk called the **cell plate**. The cell plate grows outward, accumulating more cell wall material as more vesicles join it. Eventually, the membrane of the cell plate fuses with the plasma membrane, and the cell plate's contents join the parental cell wall. The result is two daughter cells **(Figure 8.8b)**. ☑

Cancer Cells: Dividing Out of Control

For a plant or animal to grow and maintain its tissues normally, it must be able to control the timing of cell division—speeding up, slowing down, or turning the process off/on as needed. The sequential events of the cell cycle are directed by a **cell cycle control system** that consists of specialized proteins within the cell. These proteins integrate information from the environment and from other body cells and send "stop" and "go-ahead" signals at certain key points during the cell cycle. For example, the cell cycle normally halts within the G_1 phase of interphase unless the cell receives a go-ahead signal via certain control proteins. If that signal never arrives,

> Every tumor is the result of a malfunction in cell division.

the cell will switch into a permanently nondividing state. Some of your nerve and muscle cells, for example, are arrested this way. If the go-ahead signal is received and the G_1 checkpoint is passed, the cell will usually complete the rest of the cycle.

What Is Cancer?

Cancer, which currently claims the lives of one out of every five people in the United States and other industrialized nations, is a disease of the cell cycle. Cancer cells do not respond normally to the cell cycle control system; they divide excessively and may invade other tissues of the body. If unchecked, cancer cells may continue to divide until they kill the host. Cancer cells are thus referred to as "immortal" since, unlike other human cells, they will never cease dividing. In fact, thousands of laboratories around the world today use HeLa cells, a laboratory strain of human cells that were originally obtained from a woman named Henrietta Lacks, who died of cervical cancer in 1951.

The abnormal behavior of cancer cells begins when a single cell undergoes genetic changes (mutations) in one or more genes that encode for proteins in the cell cycle control system. These changes cause the cell to grow abnormally. The immune system generally recognizes and destroys such cells. However, if the cell evades destruction, it may proliferate to form a **tumor**, an abnormally growing mass of body cells. If the abnormal cells remain at the original site, the lump is called a **benign tumor**. Benign tumors can cause problems if they grow large and disrupt certain organs, such as the brain, but often they can be completely removed by surgery and are rarely deadly.

In contrast, a **malignant tumor** is one that has the potential to spread into neighboring tissues and other parts of the body, forming new tumors **(Figure 8.9)**. A malignant tumor may or may not have actually begun to spread, but once it does, it will soon displace normal tissue and interrupt organ function. An individual with a malignant tumor is said to have **cancer**. The spread of cancer cells beyond their original site is called **metastasis**. Cancers are named according to where they originate. Liver cancer, for example, always begins in liver tissue and may spread from there.

Cancer Treatment

Once a tumor starts growing in the body, how can it be treated? There are three main types of cancer treatment. Surgery to remove a tumor is usually the first step. For many benign tumors, surgery may be sufficient. If it is not, doctors turn to treatments that attempt to stop cancer cells from dividing. In **radiation therapy**, parts of the body that have cancerous tumors are exposed to concentrated beams of high-energy radiation, which often harm cancer cells more than normal cells. Radiation therapy is often effective against malignant tumors that have not yet spread. However, there is sometimes enough damage to normal body cells to produce side effects, such as nausea and hair loss.

Chemotherapy, the use of drugs to disrupt cell division, is used to treat widespread or metastatic tumors. Chemotherapy drugs work in a variety of ways. Some prevent cell division by interfering with the mitotic spindle. For example, paclitaxel (trade name Taxol) freezes the spindle after it forms, keeping it from functioning. Paclitaxel is made from a chemical discovered in the bark of the Pacific yew, a tree found mainly in the northwestern United States. It has fewer side effects than many other anticancer drugs and seems to be effective against some hard-to-treat cancers of the ovary and breast. Another drug, vinblastine, prevents the mitotic spindle from forming in the first place. Vinblastine was first obtained from the periwinkle plant, which is native to the tropical rain forests of Madagascar. Given these examples, preserving biodiversity may be the key to discovering the next generation of lifesaving anticancer drugs.

Cancer Prevention and Survival

Although cancer can strike anyone, there are certain lifestyle changes you can make to reduce your chances of developing cancer or increase your chances of surviving it. Not smoking, exercising adequately (usually defined as at least 150 minutes of moderate exercise each week), avoiding overexposure to the sun, and eating a high-fiber, low-fat diet can all help reduce the likelihood of getting cancer. Seven types of cancer can be easily detected: skin and oral (via physical exam), breast (via self-exams or mammograms for higher-risk women and women 50 and older), prostate (via rectal exam), cervical (via Pap smear), testicular (via self-exam), and colon (via colonoscopy). Regular visits to the doctor can help identify tumors early, which is the best way to increase the chance of successful treatment. ☑

☑ **CHECKPOINT**

What differentiates a benign tumor from a malignant tumor?

Answer: A benign tumor remains at its point of origin, whereas a malignant tumor can spread.

▼ Figure 8.9 **Growth and metastasis of a malignant tumor of the breast.**

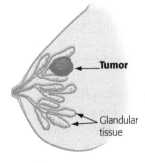

A tumor grows from a single cancer cell.

Cancer cells invade neighboring tissue.

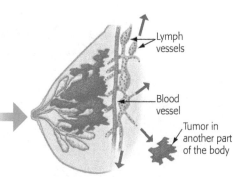

Metastasis: Cancer cells spread through lymph and blood vessels to other parts of the body.

Meiosis, the Basis of Sexual Reproduction

Only maple trees produce more maple trees, only goldfish make more goldfish, and only people make more people. These simple facts of life have been recognized for thousands of years and are reflected in the age-old saying, "Like begets like." But in a strict sense, "Like begets like" applies only to asexual reproduction, where offspring inherit all their DNA from a single parent. Asexual offspring are exact genetic replicas of that one parent and of each other, and their appearances are very similar.

The family photo in Figure 8.10 makes the point that in a sexually reproducing species, like does not exactly beget like. You probably resemble your biological parents more closely than you resemble strangers, but you do not look exactly like your parents or your siblings—unless you are an identical twin. Each offspring of sexual reproduction inherits a unique combination of genes from its two parents, and this combined set of genes programs a unique combination of traits. As a result, sexual reproduction can produce tremendous variety among offspring.

▲ **Figure 8.10 The varied products of sexual reproduction.** Every child inherits a unique combination of genes from his or her parents and displays a unique combination of traits.

Sexual reproduction depends on the cellular processes of meiosis and fertilization. But before discussing these processes, we need to return to chromosomes and the role they play in the life cycle of sexually reproducing organisms.

Homologous Chromosomes

If we examine cells from different individuals of a single species—sticking to one sex, for now—we find that they have the same number and types of chromosomes. Viewed with a microscope, your chromosomes would look exactly like those of Angelina Jolie (if you're a woman) or Brad Pitt (if you're a man).

A typical body cell, called a **somatic cell**, has 46 chromosomes in humans. A technician can break open a human cell in metaphase of mitosis, stain the chromosomes with dyes, take a picture with the aid of a microscope, and arrange the chromosomes in matching pairs by size. The resulting display is called a **karyotype** (Figure 8.11). Notice in the figure that each chromosome is duplicated, with two sister chromatids joined along their length; within the white box, for example, the left "stick" is actually a pair of sister chromatids stuck together (as shown in the drawing to the left). Notice also that almost every chromosome has a twin that resembles it in length and centromere position; in the figure, the white box surrounds one set of twin chromosomes. The two chromosomes of such a matching pair, called **homologous chromosomes**, carry genes controlling the same inherited characteristics. For example, if a gene influencing freckles is located at a particular place on one chromosome—within the yellow band in the drawing in Figure 8.11, for instance—then the homologous chromosome has that same gene in the same location. However, the two homologous chromosomes may have different versions of the same gene. Let's restate this concept because it often confuses students: A pair of homologous chromosomes has two nearly identical chromosomes, each of which consists of two identical sister chromatids after chromosome duplication.

In human females, the 46 chromosomes fall neatly into 23 homologous pairs. For a male, however, the chromosomes in one pair do not look alike. This nonmatching pair, only partly homologous, is the male's sex chromosomes. **Sex chromosomes** determine a person's sex (male versus female). In mammals, males have one X chromosome and one Y chromosome. Females have

▼ Figure 8.11 **Pairs of homologous chromosomes in a human male karyotype.** This karyotype shows 22 completely homologous pairs (autosomes) and a 23rd pair that consists of an X chromosome and a Y chromosome (sex chromosomes). With the exception of X and Y, the homologous chromosomes of each pair match in size, centromere position, and staining pattern.

Pair of homologous chromosomes

Centromere

One duplicated chromosome

Sister chromatids

LM 3,600×

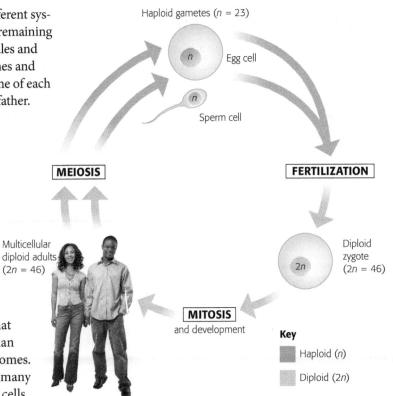

two X chromosomes. (Other organisms have different systems; in this chapter, we focus on humans.) The remaining chromosomes (44 in humans), found in both males and females, are called **autosomes**. For both autosomes and sex chromosomes, you inherited one chromosome of each pair from your mother and the other from your father.

Gametes and the Life Cycle of a Sexual Organism

The **life cycle** of a multicellular organism is the sequence of stages leading from the adults of one generation to the adults of the next. Having two sets of chromosomes, one inherited from each parent, is a key factor in the life cycle of humans and all other species that reproduce sexually. **Figure 8.12** shows the human life cycle, emphasizing the number of chromosomes.

Humans (as well as most other animals and many plants) are **diploid** organisms because all body cells contain pairs of homologous chromosomes. In other words, all your chromosomes come in matching sets. This is similar to shoes in your closet: You may have 46 shoes, but they are organized as 23 pairs, with the members of each pair being nearly identical to each other. The total number of chromosomes, 46 in humans, is the diploid number (abbreviated $2n$). The gametes, egg and sperm cells, are not diploid. Made by meiosis in an ovary or testis, each gamete has a single set of chromosomes: 22 autosomes plus a sex chromosome, either X or Y. A cell with a single chromosome set is called a **haploid** cell; it has only one member of each pair of homologous chromosomes. To visualize the haploid state, imagine your closet containing only one shoe from each pair. For humans, the haploid number, n, is 23.

In the human life cycle, a haploid sperm fuses with a haploid egg in a process called **fertilization**. The resulting fertilized egg, called a **zygote**, is diploid. It has two sets of chromosomes, one set from each parent. The life cycle is completed as a sexually mature adult develops from the zygote. Mitotic cell division ensures that all somatic cells of the human body receive a copy of all of the zygote's 46 chromosomes. Thus, every one of the trillions of cells in your body can trace its ancestry back through mitotic divisions to the single zygote produced when your father's sperm and your mother's egg fused about nine months before you were born (although you probably don't want to dwell on those details!).

◀ **Figure 8.12 The human life cycle.** In each generation, the doubling of chromosome number that results from fertilization is offset by the halving of chromosome number during meiosis.

Producing haploid gametes by meiosis keeps the chromosome number from doubling in every generation. To illustrate, **Figure 8.13** tracks one pair of homologous chromosomes. ❶ Each of the chromosomes is duplicated during interphase (before mitosis). ❷ The first division, meiosis I, segregates the two chromosomes of the homologous pair, packaging them in separate (haploid) daughter cells. But each chromosome is still doubled. ❸ Meiosis II separates the sister chromatids. Each of the four daughter cells is haploid and contains only a single chromosome from the pair of homologous chromosomes.

▼ Figure 8.13 **How meiosis halves chromosome number.**

131

The Process of Meiosis

Meiosis, the process of cell division that produces haploid gametes in diploid organisms, resembles mitosis, but with two important differences. The first difference is that, during meiosis, the number of chromosomes is cut in half. In meiosis, a cell that has duplicated its chromosomes undergoes two consecutive divisions, called meiosis I and meiosis II. Because one duplication of the chromosomes is followed by two divisions, each of the four daughter cells resulting from meiosis has a haploid set of chromosomes—half as many chromosomes as the starting cell.

The second difference of meiosis compared with mitosis is an exchange of genetic material—pieces of chromosomes—between homologous chromosomes. This exchange, called crossing over, occurs during the first prophase of meiosis. We'll look more closely at crossing over later. For now, study Figure 8.14, including the text below it, which describes the stages of meiosis in detail for a hypothetical animal cell containing four chromosomes.

As you go through Figure 8.14, keep in mind the difference between homologous chromosomes and sister chromatids: The two chromosomes of a homologous pair are individual chromosomes that were inherited

▼ Figure 8.14 **The stages of meiosis.**

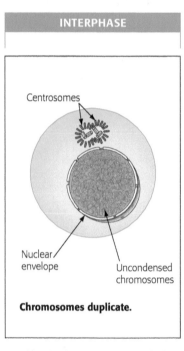

INTERPHASE

Centrosomes

Nuclear envelope

Uncondensed chromosomes

Chromosomes duplicate.

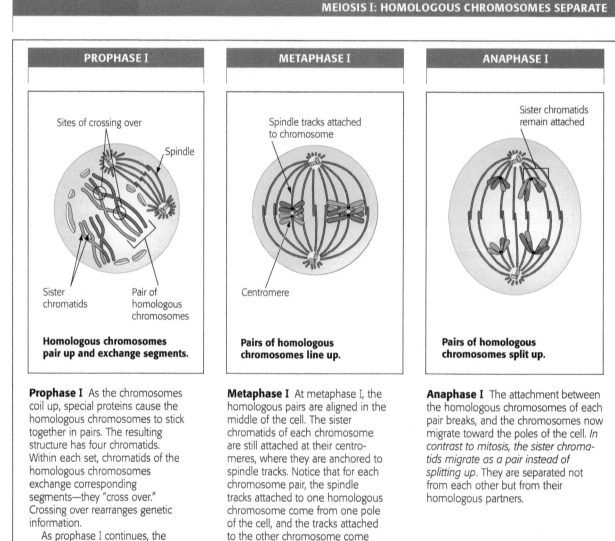

MEIOSIS I: HOMOLOGOUS CHROMOSOMES SEPARATE

PROPHASE I

Sites of crossing over

Spindle

Sister chromatids

Pair of homologous chromosomes

Homologous chromosomes pair up and exchange segments.

METAPHASE I

Spindle tracks attached to chromosome

Centromere

Pairs of homologous chromosomes line up.

ANAPHASE I

Sister chromatids remain attached

Pairs of homologous chromosomes split up.

As with mitosis, meiosis is preceded by an interphase during which the chromosomes duplicate. Each chromosome then consists of two identical sister chromatids. The chromosomes consist of uncondensed chromatin fibers.

Prophase I As the chromosomes coil up, special proteins cause the homologous chromosomes to stick together in pairs. The resulting structure has four chromatids. Within each set, chromatids of the homologous chromosomes exchange corresponding segments—they "cross over." Crossing over rearranges genetic information.

As prophase I continues, the chromosomes coil up further, a spindle forms, and the homologous pairs are moved toward the center of the cell.

Metaphase I At metaphase I, the homologous pairs are aligned in the middle of the cell. The sister chromatids of each chromosome are still attached at their centromeres, where they are anchored to spindle tracks. Notice that for each chromosome pair, the spindle tracks attached to one homologous chromosome come from one pole of the cell, and the tracks attached to the other chromosome come from the opposite pole. With this arrangement, the homologous chromosomes are poised to move toward opposite poles of the cell.

Anaphase I The attachment between the homologous chromosomes of each pair breaks, and the chromosomes now migrate toward the poles of the cell. *In contrast to mitosis, the sister chromatids migrate as a pair instead of splitting up.* They are separated not from each other but from their homologous partners.

from different parents, one from the mother and one from the father. The members of a pair of homologous chromosomes in Figure 8.14 (and later figures) are identical in size and shape but colored in the illustrations differently (red versus blue) to remind you that they differ in this way. In the interphase just before meiosis, each chromosome duplicates to form sister chromatids that remain together until anaphase of meiosis II. Before crossing over occurs, sister chromatids are identical and carry the same versions of all their genes. ✓

LM 900x

Meiosis II in a lily cell

✓ **CHECKPOINT**

If a single diploid somatic cell with 18 chromosomes undergoes meiosis and produces sperm, the result will be _____ sperm, each with _____ chromosomes. (Provide two numbers.)

Answer: four, nine

MEIOSIS II: SISTER CHROMATIDS SEPARATE

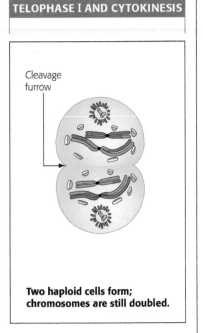

TELOPHASE I AND CYTOKINESIS

Cleavage furrow

Two haploid cells form; chromosomes are still doubled.

PROPHASE II

METAPHASE II

ANAPHASE II

Sister chromatids separate

TELOPHASE II AND CYTOKINESIS

Haploid daughter cells forming

During another round of cell division, the sister chromatids finally separate; four haploid daughter cells result, containing single chromosomes.

Telophase I and Cytokinesis In telophase I, the chromosomes arrive at the poles of the cell. When they finish their journey, each pole has a haploid chromosome set, although each chromosome is still in duplicate form. Usually, cytokinesis occurs along with telophase I, and two haploid daughter cells are formed.

The Process of Meiosis II Meiosis II is essentially the same as mitosis. The important difference is that meiosis II starts with a haploid cell that has *not* undergone chromosome duplication during the preceding interphase.

During prophase II, a spindle forms and moves the chromosomes toward the middle of the cell. During metaphase II, the chromosomes are aligned as they are in mitosis, with the tracks attached to the sister chromatids of each chromosome coming from opposite poles.

In anaphase II, the centromeres of sister chromatids separate, and the sister chromatids of each pair move toward opposite poles of the cell. In telophase II, nuclei form at the cell poles, and cytokinesis occurs at the same time. There are now four haploid daughter cells, each with single chromosomes.

133

Review: Comparing Mitosis and Meiosis

You have now learned the two ways that cells of eukaryotic organisms divide (Figure 8.15). Mitosis—which provides for growth, tissue repair, and asexual reproduction—produces daughter cells that are genetically identical to the parent cell. Meiosis, needed for sexual reproduction, yields genetically unique haploid daughter cells—cells with only one member of each homologous chromosome pair.

For both mitosis and meiosis, the chromosomes duplicate only once, in the preceding interphase. Mitosis involves one division of the nucleus and cytoplasm (duplication, then division in half), producing two

► Figure 8.15 **Comparing mitosis and meiosis.** The events unique to meiosis occur during meiosis I: In prophase I, duplicated homologous chromosomes pair along their lengths, and crossing over occurs between homologous (nonsister) chromatids. In metaphase I, pairs of homologous chromosomes (rather than individual chromosomes) are aligned at the center of the cell. During anaphase I, sister chromatids of each chromosome stay together and go to the same pole of the cell as homologous chromosomes separate. At the end of meiosis I, there are two haploid cells, but each chromosome still has two sister chromatids.

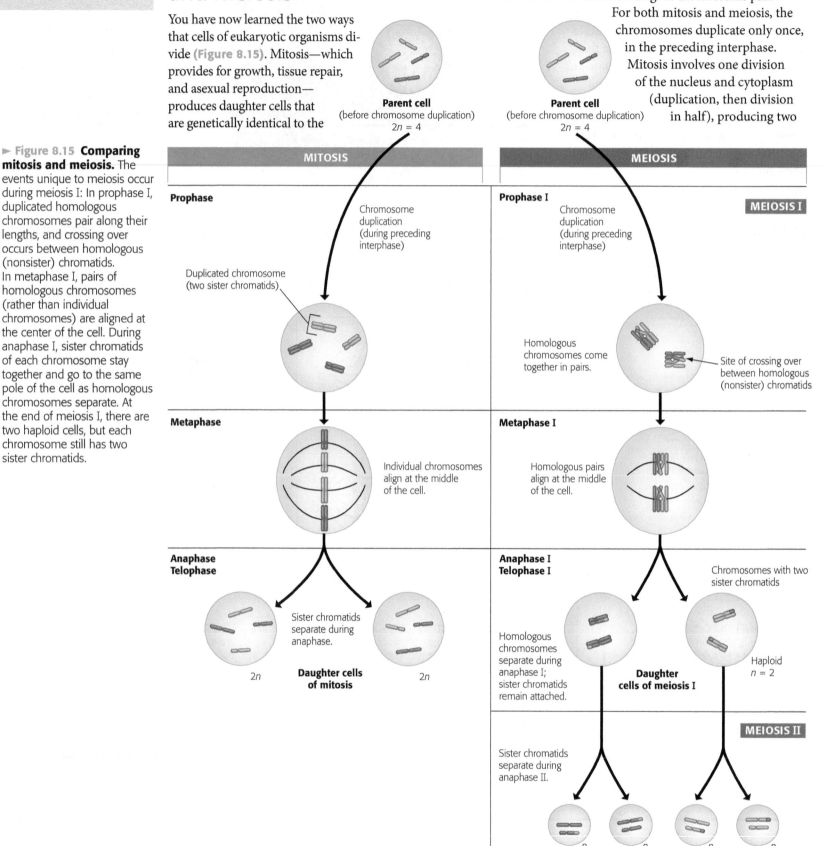

diploid cells. Meiosis entails two nuclear and cytoplasmic divisions (duplication, division in half, then division in half again), yielding four haploid cells.

Figure 8.15 compares mitosis and meiosis, tracing these two processes for a diploid parent cell with four chromosomes. As before, homologous chromosomes are those matching in size. (Imagine that the red chromosomes were inherited from the mother and the blue chromosomes from the father.) Notice that all the events unique to meiosis occur during meiosis I. Meiosis II is virtually identical to mitosis in that it separates sister chromatids. But unlike mitosis, meiosis II yields daughter cells with a haploid set of chromosomes. ☑

The Origins of Genetic Variation

As we discussed earlier, offspring that result from sexual reproduction are genetically different from their parents and from one another. How does meiosis produce such genetic variation?

Independent Assortment of Chromosomes

Figure 8.16 illustrates one way in which meiosis contributes to genetic variety. The figure shows how the arrangement of homologous chromosomes at metaphase of meiosis I affects the resulting gametes. Once again, our example is from a hypothetical diploid organism with four chromosomes (two pairs of homologous chromosomes), with colors used to differentiate homologous chromosomes (red for chromosomes inherited from the mother and blue for chromosomes from the father).

When aligned during metaphase I, the side-by-side orientation of each homologous pair of chromosomes is a matter of chance—either the red or blue chromosome may be on the left or right. Thus, in this example, there are two possible ways that the chromosome pairs can align during metaphase I. In possibility 1, the chromosome pairs are oriented with both red chromosomes on the same side (blue/red and blue/red). In this case, each of the gametes produced at the end of meiosis II has only red or only blue chromosomes (combinations a and b). In possibility 2, the chromosome pairs are oriented differently (blue/red and red/blue). This arrangement produces gametes with one red and one blue chromosome (combinations c and d). Thus, with the two possible arrangements shown in this example, the organism will produce gametes with four different combinations of chromosomes. For a species with more than two pairs of chromosomes, such as humans, every chromosome pair orients independently of all the others at metaphase I. (Chromosomes X and Y behave as a homologous pair in meiosis.)

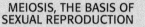

☑ CHECKPOINT

True or false: Both mitosis and meiosis are preceded by chromosome duplication.

Answer: true

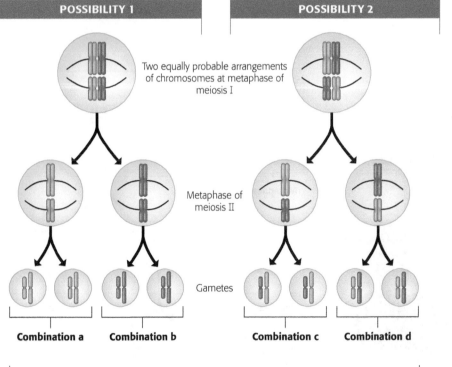

| POSSIBILITY 1 | POSSIBILITY 2 |

Two equally probable arrangements of chromosomes at metaphase of meiosis I

Metaphase of meiosis II

Gametes

Combination a **Combination b** **Combination c** **Combination d**

Because possibilities 1 and 2 are equally likely, the four possible types of gametes will be made in approximately equal numbers.

◄ Figure 8.16 **Results of alternative arrangements of chromosomes at metaphase of meiosis I.** The arrangement of chromosomes at metaphase I determines which chromosomes will be packaged together in the haploid gametes.

For any species, the total number of chromosome combinations that can appear in gametes is 2^n, where n represents the haploid number. For the hypothetical organism in Figure 8.16, $n = 2$, so the number of chromosome combinations is 2^2, or 4. For a human ($n = 23$), there are 2^{23}, or about 8 million, possible chromosome combinations! This means that every gamete a person produces contains one of about 8 million possible combinations of maternal and paternal chromosomes. When you consider that a human egg cell with about 8 million possibilities is fertilized at random by a human sperm cell with about 8 million possibilities (Figure 8.17), you can see that a single man and a single woman can produce zygotes with 64 trillion combinations of chromosomes!

Crossing Over

So far, we have focused on genetic variety in gametes and zygotes at the whole-chromosome level. We'll now take a closer look at **crossing over**, the exchange of corresponding segments between nonsister chromatids of homologous chromosomes, which occurs during prophase I of meiosis. Figure 8.18 shows crossing over between two homologous chromosomes and the resulting gametes. At the time that crossing over begins very early in prophase I, homologous chromosomes

are closely paired all along their lengths, with a precise gene-by-gene alignment.

The exchange of segments between nonsister chromatids—one maternal chromatid and one paternal chromatid of a homologous pair—adds to the genetic variety resulting from sexual reproduction. In Figure 8.18, if there were no crossing over, meiosis could produce only two types of gametes: the ones ending up with chromosomes that exactly match the parents' chromosomes, either all blue or all red (as in Figure 8.16). With crossing over, gametes arise

▼ **Figure 8.17 The process of fertilization: a close-up view.** Here you see many human sperm contacting an egg. Only one sperm can add its chromosomes to produce a zygote.

Colorized LM 1320×

▼ Figure 8.18 **The results of crossing over during meiosis for a single pair of homologous chromosomes.** A real cell has multiple pairs of homologous chromosomes that produce a huge variety of recombinant chromosomes in the gametes.

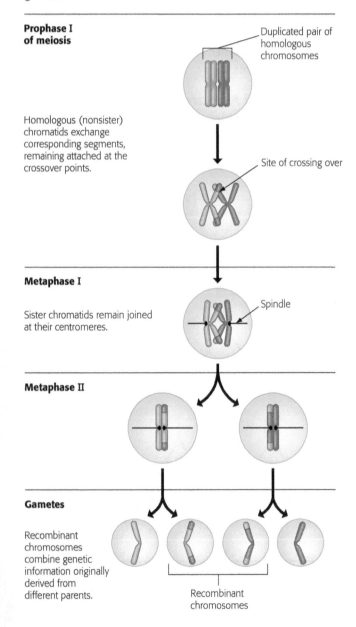

Prophase I of meiosis

Duplicated pair of homologous chromosomes

Homologous (nonsister) chromatids exchange corresponding segments, remaining attached at the crossover points.

Site of crossing over

Metaphase I

Sister chromatids remain joined at their centromeres.

Spindle

Metaphase II

Gametes

Recombinant chromosomes combine genetic information originally derived from different parents.

Recombinant chromosomes

with chromosomes that are partly from the mother and partly from the father. These chromosomes are called "recombinant" because they result from genetic recombination, the production of gene combinations different from those carried by the parental chromosomes.

Because most chromosomes contain thousands of genes, a single crossover event can affect many genes. When we also consider that multiple crossovers can occur in each pair of homologous chromosomes, it's not surprising that gametes and the offspring that result from them are so incredibly varied. ✓

☑ **CHECKPOINT**

Name two events during meiosis that contribute to genetic variety among gametes. During what stages of meiosis does each occur?

Answer: crossing over between homologous chromosomes during prophase I and independent orientation/assortment of the pairs of homologous chromosomes at metaphase I

Life with and without Sex THE PROCESS OF SCIENCE

Do All Animals Have Sex?

As discussed in the Biology and Society section, some species such as Komodo dragons can reproduce via both sexual and asexual routes. Although some animal species can reproduce asexually, very few animals reproduce *only* asexually. In fact, evolutionary biologists have traditionally considered asexual reproduction an evolutionary dead end (for reasons we'll discuss in the Evolution Connection section at the end of the chapter).

To investigate a case in which asexual reproduction seemed to be the norm, researchers from Harvard University studied a group of animals called bdelloid rotifers (Figure 8.19). This class of nearly microscopic freshwater invertebrates includes more than 300 known species. Despite hundreds of years of **observations**, no one had ever found bdelloid rotifer males or evidence of sexual reproduction. But the possibility remained that bdelloids had sex very infrequently or that the males were impossible to recognize by appearance. Thus, the Harvard research team posed the following **question**: Does this entire class of animals reproduce solely by asexual means?

The researchers formed the **hypothesis** that bdelloid rotifers have indeed thrived for millions of years without sexually reproducing. But how could this hypothesis be tested? In most species, the two versions of a gene in a pair of homologous chromosomes are very similar due to the constant trading of genes during sexual reproduction. If a species has survived without sex for millions of years, the researchers reasoned, then changes in the DNA sequences of homologous genes should accumulate independently, and the two versions of the genes should have significantly diverged from each other over time. This led to the **prediction** that bdelloid rotifers would display much more variation in their pairs of homologous genes than most organisms.

In a simple but elegant **experiment**, the researchers compared the sequences of a particular gene in bdelloid and non-bdelloid rotifers. Their **results** were striking. Among non-bdelloid rotifers that reproduce sexually, the two homologous versions of the gene were nearly identical, differing by only 0.5% on average. In contrast, the two versions of the same gene in bdelloid rotifers differed by 3.5–54%. These data provided strong evidence that bdelloid rotifers have evolved for millions of years without any sexual reproduction.

▶ Figure 8.19
A bdelloid rotifer.

LM 300x

When Meiosis Goes Awry

So far, our discussion of meiosis has focused on the process as it normally and correctly occurs. But what happens when there is an error in the process? Such a mistake can result in genetic abnormalities that range from mild to severe to fatal.

How Accidents during Meiosis Can Alter Chromosome Number

Within the human body, meiosis occurs repeatedly as the testes or ovaries produce gametes. Almost always, chromosomes are distributed to daughter cells without any errors. But occasionally there is a mishap, called a **nondisjunction**, in which the members of a chromosome pair fail to separate at anaphase. Nondisjunction can occur during meiosis I or II (Figure 8.20). In either case, gametes with abnormal numbers of chromosomes are the result.

Figure 8.21 shows what can happen when an abnormal gamete produced by nondisjunction unites with a normal gamete during fertilization. When a normal sperm fertilizes an egg cell with an extra chromosome,

the result is a zygote with a total of $2n + 1$ chromosomes. Because mitosis duplicates the chromosomes as they are, the abnormality will be passed to all embryonic cells. If the organism survives, it will have an abnormal karyotype and probably a medical disorder caused by the abnormal number of genes. ☑

☑ **CHECKPOINT**

Explain how nondisjunction in meiosis could result in a diploid gamete.

Answer: A diploid gamete would result if there were nondisjunction of all the chromosomes during meiosis I or II.

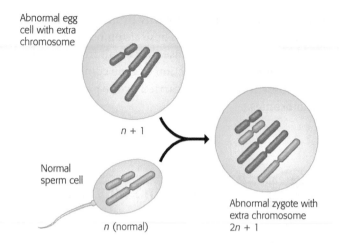

▲ Figure 8.21 **Fertilization after nondisjunction in the mother.**

▼ Figure 8.20 **Two types of nondisjunction.** In both examples in the figure, the cell at the top is diploid ($2n$), with two pairs of homologous chromosomes.

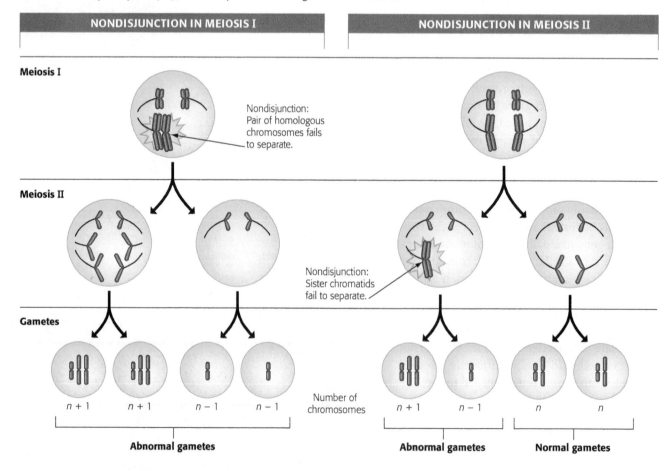

Down Syndrome: An Extra Chromosome 21

Figure 8.11 showed a normal human complement of 23 pairs of chromosomes. Compare it with the karyotype in **Figure 8.22**; besides having two X chromosomes (because it's from a female), the karyotype in Figure 8.22 has three number 21 chromosomes. Because this person is triploid for chromosome 21 (instead of the usual diploid condition),

Having too few or too many chromosomes is almost always fatal.

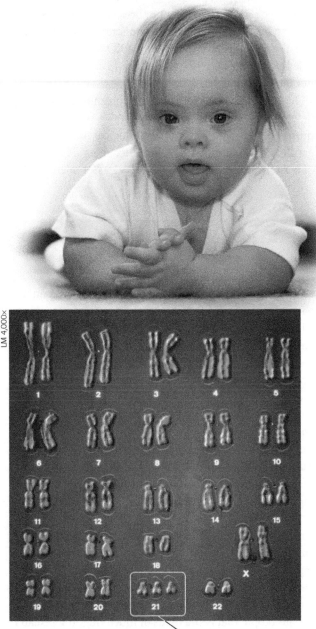

▼ Figure 8.22 **Trisomy 21 and Down syndrome.** This child displays the characteristic facial features of Down syndrome. The karyotype (bottom) shows trisomy 21; notice the three copies of chromosome 21.

LM 4,000×

Trisomy 21

they have 47 chromosomes in total. This condition is called **trisomy 21**.

In most cases, a human embryo with an atypical number of chromosomes is spontaneously aborted (miscarried) long before birth, often before the woman is even aware that she is pregnant. In fact, some doctors speculate that miscarriages due to genetic defects occur in nearly one-quarter of all pregnancies, although this number is difficult to verify. However, some aberrations in chromosome number seem to upset the genetic balance less drastically, and individuals with such abnormalities can survive. These people usually have a characteristic set of symptoms, called a syndrome. A person with trisomy 21 has a condition called **Down syndrome** (named after John Langdon Down, an English physician who first described this condition in 1866).

Affecting about 1 out of every 700 children, trisomy 21 is the most common chromosome number abnormality and the most common serious birth defect in the United States. Down syndrome includes characteristic facial features—frequently a fold of skin at the inner corner of the eye, a round face, and a flattened nose—as well as short stature, heart defects, and susceptibility to leukemia and Alzheimer's disease. People with Down syndrome usually have a life span shorter than normal. They also exhibit varying degrees of developmental delays. However, some individuals with the syndrome may live to middle age or beyond, and many are socially adept and can function well within society. Although no one is sure why, the risk of Down syndrome increases with the age of the mother, climbing to about 1% risk for mothers at age 40. The fetuses of pregnant women age 35 and older are therefore candidates for chromosomal prenatal screenings (see Chapter 9). ☑

Abnormal Numbers of Sex Chromosomes

Trisomy 21 is an autosomal nondisjunction. Nondisjunction in meiosis can also lead to abnormal numbers of sex chromosomes, X and Y. Unusual numbers of sex chromosomes seem to upset the genetic balance less than unusual numbers of autosomes. This may be because the Y chromosome is very small and carries relatively few genes. Furthermore, mammalian cells normally operate with only one functioning X chromosome because other copies of the chromosome become inactivated in each cell (see Chapter 11).

☑ **CHECKPOINT**

What does it mean to refer to a disease as a "syndrome," as with AIDS?

Answer: A syndrome displays a set of multiple symptoms rather than just a single symptom.

Table 8.1	Abnormalities of Sex Chromosome Number in Humans		
Sex Chromosomes	**Syndrome**	**Origins of Nondisjunction**	**Frequency in Population**
XXY	Klinefelter syndrome (male)	Meiosis in egg or sperm formation	$\frac{1}{2,000}$
XYY	None (normal male)	Meiosis in sperm formation	$\frac{1}{2,000}$
XXX	None (normal female)	Meiosis in egg or sperm formation	$\frac{1}{1,000}$
XO	Turner syndrome (female)	Meiosis in egg or sperm formation	$\frac{1}{5,000}$

Table 8.1 lists the most common human sex chromosome abnormalities. An extra X chromosome in a male, making him XXY, produces a condition called Klinefelter syndrome. If untreated, men with this disorder have male sex organs, but the testes are abnormally small, the individual is sterile, and he often has breast enlargement and other feminine body contours. These symptoms can be reduced through administration of the sex hormone testosterone. Klinefelter syndrome is also found in individuals with more than three sex chromosomes, such as XXYY, XXXY, or XXXXY. These abnormal numbers of sex chromosomes result from multiple nondisjunctions.

Human males with a single extra Y chromosome (XYY) do not have any well-defined syndrome, although they tend to be taller than average. Females with an extra X chromosome (XXX) cannot be distinguished from XX females except by karyotype.

Females who are lacking an X chromosome are designated XO; the O indicates the absence of a second sex chromosome. These women have Turner syndrome. They have a characteristic appearance, including short stature and often a web of skin extending between the neck and shoulders. Women with Turner syndrome are of normal intelligence, but are sterile. If left untreated, they have poor development of breasts and other secondary sex characteristics. Administration of estrogen can alleviate those symptoms. The XO condition is the sole known case where having only 45 chromosomes is not fatal in humans.

Notice the crucial role of the Y chromosome in determining a person's sex. In general, a single Y chromosome is enough to produce biological maleness, regardless of the number of X chromosomes. The absence of a Y chromosome results in biological femaleness. ☑

CHECKPOINT

Why is an individual more likely to survive with an abnormal number of sex chromosomes than an abnormal number of autosomes?

Answer: because the Y chromosome is very small and extra X chromosomes are inactivated

Life with and without Sex EVOLUTION CONNECTION

▼ Figure 8.23 **Sexual and asexual reproduction.** Many plants, such as this strawberry, have the ability to reproduce both sexually (via flowers that produce fruit) and asexually (via runners).

The Advantages of Sex

Throughout this chapter, we've examined cell division within the context of reproduction. Like the Komodo dragon discussed in the Biology and Society section, many species (including a few dozen animal species, but many more among the plant kingdom) can reproduce both sexually and asexually (Figure 8.23). An important advantage of asexual reproduction is that there is no need for a partner. Asexual reproduction may thus confer an evolutionary advantage when organisms are sparsely distributed (on an isolated island, for example) and unlikely to meet a mate. Furthermore, if an organism is superbly suited to a stable environment, asexual reproduction has the advantage of passing on its entire genetic legacy intact. Asexual reproduction also eliminates the need to expend energy forming gametes and copulating with a partner.

In contrast to plants, the vast majority of animals reproduce by sexual means. There are exceptions, such as the few species that can reproduce via parthenogenesis and the bdelloid rotifers discussed in the Process of Science section. But most animals reproduce only through sex. Therefore, sex must enhance evolutionary fitness. But how? The answer remains elusive. Most hypotheses focus on the unique combinations of genes formed during meiosis and fertilization. By producing offspring of varied genetic makeup, sexual reproduction may enhance survival by speeding adaptation to a changing environment. Another idea is that shuffling genes during sexual reproduction might reduce the incidence of harmful genes more rapidly. But for now, one of biology's most basic questions—Why have sex?—remains a hotly debated topic that is the focus of much ongoing research.

Runner

Chapter Review

■ SUMMARY OF KEY CONCEPTS

What Cell Reproduction Accomplishes

Cell reproduction, also called cell division, produces genetically identical daughter cells:

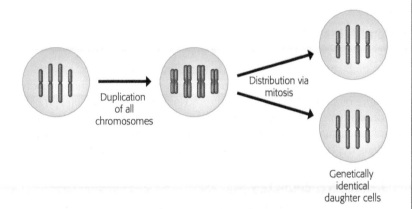

Duplication of all chromosomes

Distribution via mitosis

Genetically identical daughter cells

Some organisms use mitosis (ordinary cell division) to reproduce. This is called asexual reproduction, and it results in offspring that are genetically identical to the lone parent and to each other. Mitosis also enables multicellular organisms to grow and develop and to replace damaged or lost cells. Organisms that reproduce sexually, by the union of a sperm with an egg cell, carry out meiosis, a type of cell division that yields gametes with only half as many chromosomes as body (somatic) cells.

The Cell Cycle and Mitosis

Eukaryotic Chromosomes

The genes of a eukaryotic genome are grouped into multiple chromosomes in the nucleus. Each chromosome contains one very long DNA molecule, with many genes, that is wrapped around histone proteins. Individual chromosomes are coiled up and therefore visible with a light microscope only when the cell is in the process of dividing; otherwise, they are in the form of thin, loosely packed chromatin fibers.

Information Flow: Duplicating Chromosomes

Because chromosomes contain the information needed to control cellular processes, they must be copied and distributed to daughter cells. Before a cell starts dividing, the chromosomes duplicate, producing sister chromatids (containing identical DNA) joined together at the centromere.

Chromosome (one long piece of DNA)

Centromere

Sister chromatids

Duplicated chromosome

The Cell Cycle

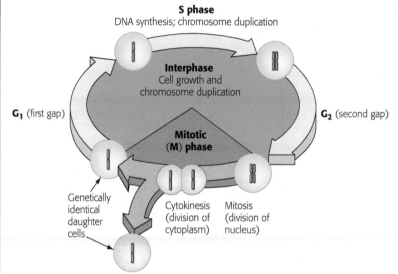

S phase
DNA synthesis; chromosome duplication

Interphase
Cell growth and chromosome duplication

G_1 (first gap)

G_2 (second gap)

Mitotic (M) phase

Genetically identical daughter cells

Cytokinesis (division of cytoplasm)

Mitosis (division of nucleus)

Mitosis and Cytokinesis

Mitosis is divided into four phases: prophase, metaphase, anaphase, and telophase. At the start of mitosis, the chromosomes coil up and the nuclear envelope breaks down (prophase). Next, a mitotic spindle made of microtubule tracks moves the chromosomes to the middle of the cell (metaphase). The sister chromatids then separate and are moved to opposite poles of the cell (anaphase), where two new nuclei form (telophase). Cytokinesis overlaps the end of mitosis. In animals, cytokinesis occurs by cleavage, which pinches the cell in two. In plants, a membranous cell plate divides the cell in two. Mitosis and cytokinesis produce genetically identical cells.

Cancer Cells: Dividing Out of Control

When the cell cycle control system malfunctions, a cell may divide excessively and form a tumor. Cancer cells may grow to form malignant tumors, invade other tissues (metastasize), and even kill the host. Surgery can remove tumors, and radiation and chemotherapy are effective as treatments because they interfere with cell division. You can increase the likelihood of surviving some forms of cancer through lifestyle changes and regular screenings.

Meiosis, the Basis of Sexual Reproduction

Homologous Chromosomes

The somatic cells (body cells) of each species contain a specific number of chromosomes; human cells have 46, made up of 23 pairs of homologous chromosomes. The chromosomes of a homologous pair carry genes for the same characteristics at the same places. Mammalian males have X and Y sex chromosomes (only partly homologous), and females have two X chromosomes.

Gametes and the Life Cycle of a Sexual Organism

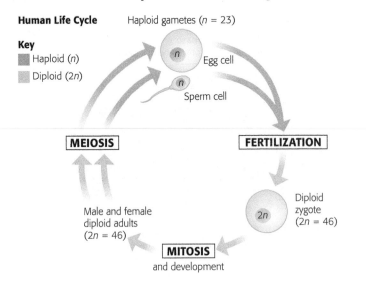

Human Life Cycle

Haploid gametes ($n = 23$)

Key
- Haploid (n)
- Diploid ($2n$)

Egg cell

Sperm cell

MEIOSIS

FERTILIZATION

Male and female diploid adults ($2n = 46$)

Diploid zygote ($2n = 46$)

MITOSIS
and development

The Process of Meiosis

Meiosis, like mitosis, is preceded by chromosome duplication. But in meiosis, the cell divides twice to form four daughter cells. The first division, meiosis I, starts with the pairing of homologous chromosomes. In crossing over, homologous chromosomes exchange corresponding segments. Meiosis I separates the members of the homologous pairs and produces two daughter cells, each with one set of (duplicated) chromosomes. Meiosis II is essentially the same as mitosis; in each of the cells, the sister chromatids of each chromosome separate.

Review: Comparing Mitosis and Meiosis

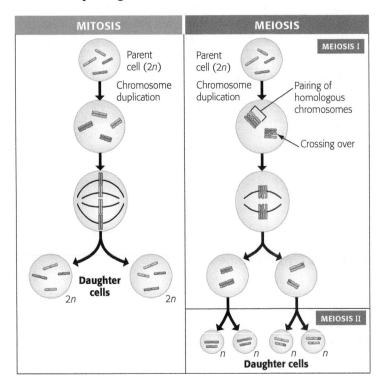

MITOSIS	MEIOSIS

Parent cell ($2n$)

Chromosome duplication

MEIOSIS I

Parent cell ($2n$)

Chromosome duplication

Pairing of homologous chromosomes

Crossing over

Daughter cells

$2n$ $2n$

MEIOSIS II

n n n n

Daughter cells

The Origins of Genetic Variation

Because the chromosomes of a homologous pair come from different parents, they carry different versions of many of their genes. The large number of possible arrangements of chromosome pairs at metaphase of meiosis I leads to many different combinations of chromosomes in eggs and sperm. Random fertilization of eggs by sperm greatly increases the variation. Crossing over during prophase of meiosis I increases variation still further.

When Meiosis Goes Awry

Sometimes a person has an abnormal number of chromosomes, which causes problems. Down syndrome is caused by an extra copy of chromosome 21. The abnormal chromosome count is a product of nondisjunction, the failure of a pair of homologous chromosomes to separate during meiosis I or of sister chromatids to separate during meiosis II. Nondisjunction can also produce gametes with extra or missing sex chromosomes, which lead to varying degrees of malfunction but do not usually affect survival.

MasteringBiology®

For practice quizzes, BioFlix animations, MP3 tutorials, video tutors, and more study tools designed for this textbook, go to MasteringBiology®

SELF-QUIZ

1. Which of the following is not a function of mitosis in humans?
   a. repair of wounds
   b. growth
   c. production of gametes from diploid cells
   d. replacement of lost or damaged cells

2. In what sense are the two daughter cells produced by mitosis identical?

3. Why is it difficult to observe individual chromosomes during interphase?

4. A biochemist measures the amount of DNA in cells growing in the laboratory. The quantity of DNA in a cell would be found to double
   a. between prophase and anaphase of mitosis.
   b. between the G_1 and G_2 phases of the cell cycle.
   c. during the M phase of the cell cycle.
   d. between prophase I and prophase II of meiosis.

5. Which two phases of mitosis are essentially opposites in terms of changes in the nucleus?

6. Complete the following table to compare mitosis and meiosis:

	Mitosis	Meiosis
a. Number of chromosomal duplications		
b. Number of cell divisions		
c. Number of daughter cells produced		
d. Number of chromosomes in daughter cells		
e. How chromosomes line up during metaphase		
f. Genetic relationship of daughter cells to parent cells		
g. Functions performed in the human body		

7. If an intestinal cell in a dog contains 78 chromosomes, a dog sperm cell would contain _____ chromosomes.

8. A micrograph of a dividing cell from a mouse shows 19 chromosomes, each consisting of two sister chromatids. During which stage of meiosis could this micrograph have been taken? (Explain your answer.)

9. Tumors that remain at their site of origin are called _____, and tumors that have cells that can migrate to other body tissues are called _____.

10. A diploid body (somatic) cell from a fruit fly contains eight chromosomes. This means that _____ different combinations of chromosomes are possible in its gametes.

11. Although nondisjunction is a random event, there are many more individuals with an extra chromosome 21, which causes Down syndrome, than individuals with an extra chromosome 3 or chromosome 16. Propose an explanation for this.

Answers to these questions can be found in Appendix: Self-Quiz Answers.

THE PROCESS OF SCIENCE

12. A mule is the offspring of a horse and a donkey. A donkey sperm contains 31 chromosomes and a horse egg has 32 chromosomes, so the zygote contains a total of 63 chromosomes. The zygote develops normally. The combined set of chromosomes is not a problem in mitosis, and the mule combines some of the best characteristics of horses and donkeys. However, a mule is sterile; meiosis cannot occur normally in its testes or ovaries. Explain why mitosis is normal in cells containing both horse and donkey chromosomes but the mixed set of chromosomes interferes with meiosis.

13. You prepare a slide with a thin slice of an onion root tip. You see the following view in a light microscope. Identify the stage of mitosis for each of the outlined cells, a–d.

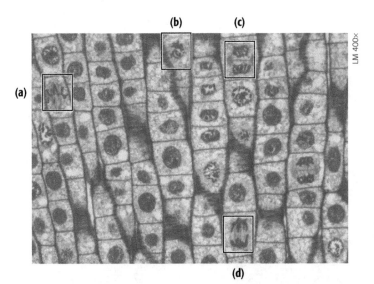

14. Interpreting Data The graph in the right hand column shows the incidence of Down syndrome in the offspring of normal parents as the age of the mother increases. For women under the age of 30, how many infants with Down syndrome are born per 1,000 births? How many for women at age 40? At age 50? How many times more likely is a 50-year-old woman to give birth to a baby with Down syndrome than a 30-year-old woman?

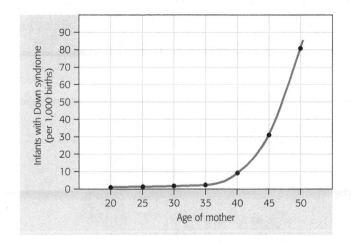

BIOLOGY AND SOCIETY

15. As described in the Biology and Society section, some species (including some endangered species) have been shown to be capable of reproduction via parthenogenesis, without participation of a mate. What implications might this have on efforts to repopulate endangered species? What drawbacks might a parthenogenesis program have on the well-being of the species it targets?

16. Every year, about a million Americans are diagnosed with cancer. This means that about 75 million Americans now living will eventually have cancer, and one in five will die of the disease. There are many kinds of cancers and many causes of the disease. For example, smoking causes most lung cancers. Overexposure to ultraviolet rays in sunlight causes most skin cancers. There is evidence that a high-fat, low-fiber diet is a factor in breast, colon, and prostate cancers. And agents in the workplace, such as asbestos and vinyl chloride, are also implicated as causes of cancer. Hundreds of millions of dollars are spent each year in the search for effective treatments for cancer, yet far less money is spent on preventing cancer. Why might this be true? What kinds of lifestyle changes can you make to help reduce your risk of cancer? What kinds of prevention programs could be initiated or strengthened to encourage these changes? What factors might impede such changes and programs? Should we devote more of our resources to treating cancer or to preventing it? Defend your position.

17. The practice of buying and selling gametes, particularly eggs from fertile women, is becoming increasingly common in the United States and some other industrialized countries. Do you have any objections to this type of transaction? Would you be willing to sell your gametes? At any price? Whether you are willing to do so or not, do you think that other people should be restricted from doing so?

9 Patterns of Inheritance

Why Genetics Matters

Hemophilia is more prevalent among European royalty than commoners because of past intermarriage.

▲ Your mother's genes had no role in determining your sex.

Because the environment helps shape your appearance, identical twins aren't identical in every way. ▶

Dog Breeding BIOLOGY AND SOCIETY

Our Longest-Running Genetic Experiment

The adorable canine in the photo to the right is a purebred Cavalier King Charles Spaniel. If you were to mate two purebred "Cavs," you'd expect the offspring to display the traits that distinguish this breed, such as a silky coat, long elegant ears, and gentle eyes. This is a reasonable expectation because each purebred dog has a well-documented pedigree that includes several generations of ancestors with similar genetic makeup and appearance. But similarities among purebred Cavaliers extend beyond mere appearance; Cavs are generally energetic, obedient, sweet, and gentle—traits that make these dogs particularly well suited to act as companion or therapy dogs. Such behavioral similarities suggest that dog breeders can select for personality as well as physical traits. Cavaliers have four standard coat types—Blenheim (chestnut brown on white, seen at right, named after Blenheim Palace in England, where such dogs were first bred), black and tan, ruby, and tricolor (black, white, and tan)—reminding us that even within a purebred line, there remains significant variation of certain traits.

Breeding a best friend. Dogs, such as this Cavalier King Charles Spaniel, are one of humankind's longest running genetic experiments.

Purebred pooches are living proof that dogs are more than man's best friend: They are also one of our longest-running genetic experiments. Evidence (which we'll explore at the end of this chapter) suggests that people have selected and mated dogs with preferred traits for more than 15,000 years. Nearly every modern Cavalier, for example, can trace its ancestry back to a single pair that were brought to America by a breeder in 1952. These original dogs were chosen due to their desired shape and temperament. Similar choices were made for every modern dog breed. Over thousands of years, such genetic tinkering has led to the incredible variety of body types and behaviors we have today, from huge, docile Great Danes to tiny, spunky Chihuahuas.

Although people have been applying genetics for thousands of years—by breeding food crops (such as wheat, rice, and corn) as well as domesticated animals (such as cows, sheep, and goats)—the biological principles underlying genetics have only recently been understood. In this chapter, you will learn the basic rules of how genetic traits are passed from generation to generation and how the behavior of chromosomes (the topic of Chapter 8) accounts for these rules. In the process, you will learn how to predict the ratios of offspring with particular traits. At several points in the chapter, we'll return to the subject of dog breeding to help illustrate genetic principles.

Genetics and Heredity

Heredity is the transmission of traits from one generation to the next. **Genetics**, the scientific study of heredity, began in the 1860s, when an Augustinian monk named Gregor Mendel (Figure 9.1) deduced its fundamental principles by breeding garden peas. Mendel lived and worked in an abbey in Brunn, Austria (now Brno, in the Czech Republic). Strongly influenced by his study of physics, mathematics, and chemistry at the University of Vienna, his research was both experimentally and mathematically rigorous, and these qualities were largely responsible for his success.

▲ Figure 9.1
Gregor Mendel.

In a paper published in 1866, Mendel correctly argued that parents pass on to their offspring discrete genes (which he termed "heritable factors") that are responsible for inherited traits, such as purple flowers or round seeds in pea plants. (It is interesting to note that Mendel's publication came just seven years after Darwin's 1859 publication of *On the Origin of Species*, making the 1860s a banner decade in the advent of modern biology.) In his paper, Mendel stressed that genes retain their individual identities generation after generation, no matter how they are mixed up or temporarily masked.

reach the carpel. When he wanted to fertilize one plant with pollen from a different plant, he pollinated the plants by hand, as shown in Figure 9.3. Thus, Mendel was always sure of the parentage of his new plants.

Each of the characters Mendel chose to study, such as flower color, occurred in two distinct traits. Mendel worked with his plants until he was sure he had purebred varieties—that is, varieties for which self-fertilization produced offspring all identical to the parent. For instance, he identified a purple-flowered variety that, when self-fertilized, always produced offspring plants that had all purple flowers.

Next Mendel was ready to ask what would happen when he crossed different purebred varieties with each other. For example, what offspring would result if plants with purple flowers and plants with white flowers were

▼ Figure 9.3 **Mendel's technique for cross-fertilizing pea plants.**

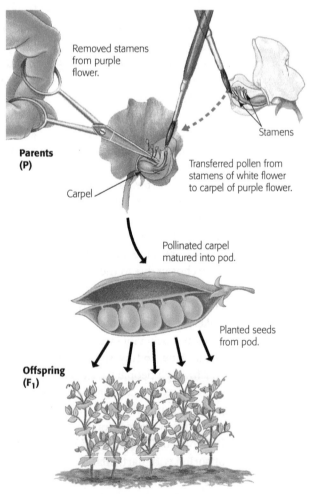

Removed stamens from purple flower.

Stamens

Parents (P)

Transferred pollen from stamens of white flower to carpel of purple flower.

Carpel

Pollinated carpel matured into pod.

Planted seeds from pod.

Offspring (F₁)

In an Abbey Garden

Mendel probably chose to study garden peas because they were easy to grow and they came in many readily distinguishable varieties. For example, one variety has purple flowers and another variety has white flowers. A heritable feature that varies among individuals, such as flower color, is called a **character**. Each variant of a character, such as purple or white flowers, is called a **trait**.

Perhaps the most important advantage of pea plants as an experimental model was that Mendel could strictly control their reproduction. The petals of a pea flower (Figure 9.2) almost completely enclose the egg-producing organ (the carpel) and the sperm-producing organs (the stamens). Consequently, in nature, pea plants usually self-fertilize because sperm-carrying pollen grains released from the stamens land on the tip of the egg-containing carpel of the same flower. Mendel could ensure self-fertilization by covering a flower with a small bag so that no pollen from another plant could

▼ Figure 9.2 **The structure of a pea flower.** To reveal the reproductive organs—the stamens and carpel—one of the petals has been removed in this drawing.

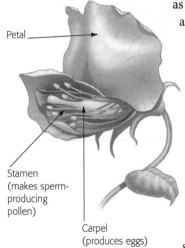

Petal

Stamen (makes sperm-producing pollen)

Carpel (produces eggs)

cross-fertilized as shown in Figure 9.3? The offspring of two different purebred varieties are called **hybrids**, and the cross-fertilization itself is referred to as a genetic **cross**. The parental plants are called the **P generation**, and their hybrid offspring are the **F₁ generation** (F for *filial*, from the Latin for "son" or "daughter"). When F₁ plants self-fertilize or fertilize each other, their offspring are the **F₂ generation**. ✓

Mendel's Law of Segregation

Mendel performed many experiments in which he tracked the inheritance of characters, such as flower color, that occur as two alternative traits (Figure 9.4). The results led him to formulate several hypotheses about inheritance. Let's look at some of his experiments and follow the reasoning that led to his hypotheses.

▼ **Figure 9.4 The seven characters of pea plants studied by Mendel.** Each character comes in the two alternative traits shown here.

	Dominant	Recessive
Flower color	Purple	White
Flower position	Axial	Terminal
Seed color	Yellow	Green
Seed shape	Round	Wrinkled
Pod shape	Inflated	Constricted
Pod color	Green	Yellow
Stem length	Tall	Dwarf

✓ **CHECKPOINT**

Why was the development of purebred pea plant varieties critical to Mendel's work?

Answer: Purebred varieties allowed Mendel to predict the outcome of specific crosses and therefore to run controlled experiments.

Monohybrid Crosses

Figure 9.5 shows a cross between a purebred pea plant with purple flowers and a purebred pea plant with white flowers. This is called a **monohybrid cross** because only one character is being studied—flower color in this case. Mendel saw that the F₁ plants all had purple flowers. Was the factor responsible for inheritance of white flowers now lost as a result of the cross? By mating the F₁ plants with each other, Mendel found the answer to this question to be no. Of the 929 F₂ plants he bred, about three-fourths (705) had purple flowers and one-fourth (224) had white flowers; that is, there were about three purple F₂ plants for every white plant, or a 3:1 ratio of purple to white. Mendel figured out that the gene for white flowers did not disappear in the F₁ plants but was somehow hidden or masked when the purple-flower factor was present. He also deduced that the F₁ plants must have carried two factors for the flower-color character, one for purple and one for white. From these results and others, Mendel developed four hypotheses:

1. *There are alternative versions of genes that account for variations in inherited characters.* For example, the gene for flower color in pea plants exists in one form for purple and another for white. The alternative versions of a gene are called **alleles**.

2. *For each inherited character, an organism inherits two alleles, one from each parent.* These alleles may be the same or different. An organism that has two identical alleles for a gene is said to be **homozygous** for that gene (and is called a homozygote). An organism that has two different alleles for a gene is said to be **heterozygous** for that gene (and is called a heterozygote).

3. *If the two alleles of an inherited pair differ, then one determines the organism's appearance and is called the **dominant allele**; the other has no noticeable effect on the organism's appearance and is called the **recessive allele**.* Geneticists use uppercase italic letters (such as P) to represent dominant alleles and lowercase italic letters (such as p) to represent recessive alleles.

4. *A sperm or egg carries only one allele for each inherited character because the two alleles for a character segregate (separate) from each other during the production of gametes.* This statement is called the **law of segregation**. When sperm and egg unite at fertilization, each contributes its alleles, restoring the paired condition in the offspring.

Figure 9.6 illustrates Mendel's law of segregation, which explains the inheritance pattern shown in Figure 9.5. Mendel's hypotheses predict that when alleles segregate during gamete formation in the F₁ plants, half the gametes will receive a purple-flower allele (P) and the other half a white-flower allele (p). During pollination among the F₁ plants, the gametes unite randomly. An egg with a purple-flower allele has an equal chance of being fertilized by a sperm with a purple-flower allele or one with a white-flower allele (that is, a P egg may fuse with a P sperm or a p sperm). Because the same is true for an egg with a white-flower allele (a p egg with a P sperm or p sperm), there are a total of four equally likely combinations of sperm and egg.

The diagram at the bottom of Figure 9.6, called a **Punnett square**, repeats the cross shown in Figure 9.5 in a way that highlights the four possible combinations of gametes and the resulting four possible offspring in the F₂ generation. Each square represents an equally probable product of fertilization. For example, the box in the upper right corner of the Punnett square shows the genetic combination resulting from a p sperm fertilizing a P egg.

According to the Punnett square, what will be the physical appearance of these F₂ offspring? One-fourth of the plants have two alleles specifying purple flowers (PP); clearly, these plants will have purple flowers. One-half (two-fourths) of the F₂ offspring have inherited one

▼ **Figure 9.5 Mendel's cross tracking one character (flower color).** Note the 3:1 ratio of purple flowers to white flowers in the F₂ generation.

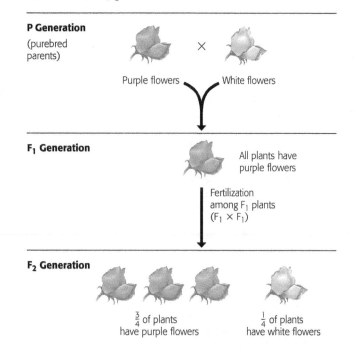

P Generation
(purebred parents)

×

Purple flowers   White flowers

F₁ Generation

All plants have purple flowers

Fertilization among F₁ plants
(F₁ × F₁)

F₂ Generation

¾ of plants have purple flowers   ¼ of plants have white flowers

▼ Figure 9.6 **The law of segregation.**

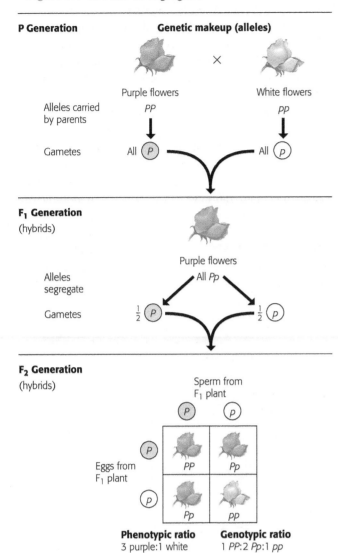

P Generation

Genetic makeup (alleles)

Purple flowers × White flowers

PP Alleles carried by parents *pp*

Gametes All $\textcircled{P}$ All $\textcircled{p}$

F₁ Generation (hybrids)

Purple flowers
All *Pp*

Alleles segregate

Gametes $\frac{1}{2}$ $\textcircled{P}$ $\frac{1}{2}$ $\textcircled{p}$

F₂ Generation (hybrids)

Sperm from F₁ plant

$\textcircled{P}$ $\textcircled{p}$

Eggs from F₁ plant $\textcircled{P}$ *PP* *Pp*

$\textcircled{p}$ *Pp* *pp*

Phenotypic ratio
3 purple:1 white

Genotypic ratio
1 *PP*:2 *Pp*:1 *pp*

Mendel found that each of the seven characters he studied had the same inheritance pattern: A parental trait disappeared in the F₁ generation, only to reappear in one-fourth of the F₂ offspring. The underlying mechanism is explained by Mendel's law of segregation: Pairs of alleles segregate (separate) during gamete formation; the fusion of gametes at fertilization creates allele pairs again. Research since Mendel's day has established that the law of segregation applies to all sexually reproducing organisms, including people.

Genetic Alleles and Homologous Chromosomes

Before continuing with Mendel's experiments, let's consider how an understanding of chromosomes (see Chapter 8) fits with what we've said about genetics so far. The diagram in **Figure 9.7** shows a pair of homologous chromosomes—chromosomes that carry alleles of the same genes. Recall that every diploid cell, whether from a pea plant or a person, has pairs of homologous chromosomes. One member of each pair comes from the organism's female parent and the other member of each pair comes from the male parent. Each labeled band on the chromosomes in the figure represents a gene **locus** (plural, *loci*), a specific location of a gene along the chromosome. You can see the connection between Mendel's law of segregation and homologous chromosomes: Alleles (alternative versions) of a gene reside at the same locus on homologous chromosomes. However, the two chromosomes may bear either identical alleles or different ones at any one locus. In other words, the organisms may be homozygous or heterozygous for the gene at that locus. We will return to the chromosomal basis of Mendel's law later in the chapter. ☑

---

allele for purple flowers and one allele for white flowers (*Pp*); like the F₁ plants, these plants will also have purple flowers, the dominant trait. (Note that *Pp* and *pP* are equivalent and usually written as *Pp*.) Finally, one-fourth of the F₂ plants have inherited two alleles specifying white flowers (*pp*) and will express this recessive trait. Thus, Mendel's model accounts for the 3:1 ratio that he observed in the F₂ generation.

Geneticists distinguish between an organism's physical appearance, called its **phenotype** (such as purple or white flowers), and its genetic makeup, called its **genotype** (such as *PP*, *Pp*, or *pp*). Now we can see that Figure 9.5 shows only the phenotypes and Figure 9.6 both the genotypes and phenotypes in our sample cross. For the F₂ plants, the ratio of plants with purple flowers to those with white flowers (3:1) is called the phenotypic ratio. The genotypic ratio is 1(*PP*):2(*Pp*):1(*pp*).

▼ Figure 9.7 **The relationship between alleles and homologous chromosomes.** The matching colors of corresponding loci highlight the fact that homologous chromosomes carry alleles for the same genes at the same positions along their lengths.

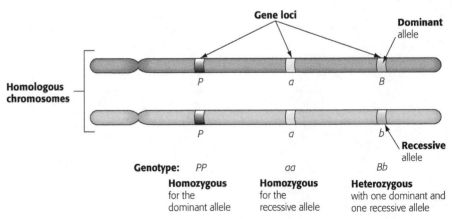

Gene loci

Dominant allele

Homologous chromosomes

P *a* *B*

P *a* *b*

Recessive allele

Genotype: *PP* *aa* *Bb*

Homozygous for the dominant allele

Homozygous for the recessive allele

Heterozygous with one dominant and one recessive allele

Mendel's Law of Independent Assortment

In addition to flower color, Mendel studied two other pea plant characters: seed shape (round versus wrinkled) and seed color (yellow versus green). From tracking these characters one at a time in monohybrid crosses, Mendel knew that the allele for round shape (designated R) was dominant to the allele for wrinkled shape (r) and that the allele for yellow seed color (Y) was dominant to the allele for green seed color (y). What would result from a **dihybrid cross**, the mating of parental varieties differing in two characters? Mendel crossed homozygous plants having round-yellow seeds (genotype $RRYY$) with plants having wrinkled-green seeds ($rryy$). As shown in Figure 9.8, the union of RY and ry gametes from the P generation yielded

hybrids heterozygous for both characters ($RrYy$)—that is, dihybrids. As we would expect, all of these offspring, the F_1 generation, had round-yellow seeds (the two dominant traits). But were the two characters transmitted from parents to offspring as a package, or was each character inherited independently of the other?

The question was answered when Mendel crossed the F_1 plants with each other. If the genes for the two characters were inherited together (Figure 9.8a), then the F_1 hybrids would produce only the same two kinds of gametes that they received from their parents. In that case, the F_2 generation would show a 3:1 phenotypic ratio (three plants with round-yellow seeds for every one with wrinkled-green seeds), as in the Punnett square in Figure 9.8a. If, however, the two seed characters sorted independently, then the F_1 generation would produce four gamete genotypes—RY, rY, Ry, and ry—in equal

▼ **Figure 9.8 Testing alternative hypotheses for gene assortment in a dihybrid cross.** Only hypothesis B was supported by Mendel's data.

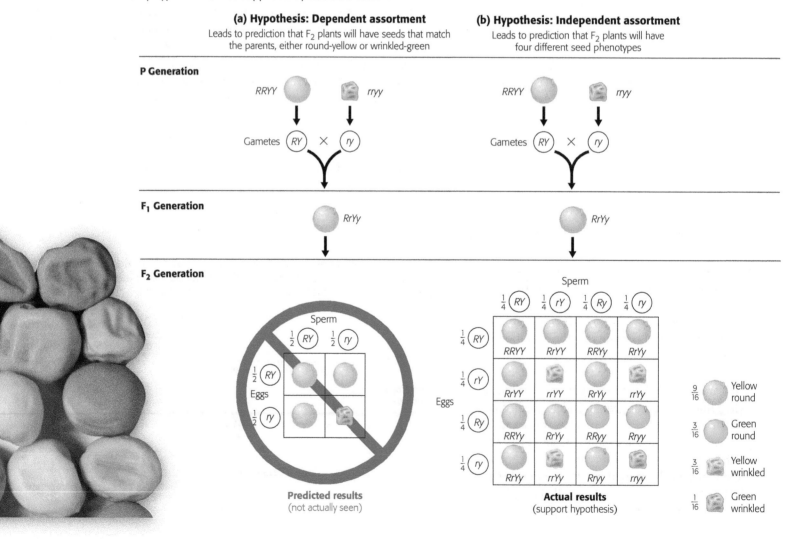

quantities. The Punnett square in Figure 9.8b shows all possible combinations of alleles that can result in the F_2 generation from the union of four kinds of sperm with four kinds of eggs. If you study the Punnett square, you'll see that it predicts nine different genotypes in the F_2 generation. These nine genotypes will produce four different phenotypes in a ratio of 9:3:3:1.

The Punnett square in Figure 9.8b also reveals that a dihybrid cross is equivalent to two monohybrid crosses occurring simultaneously. From the 9:3:3:1 ratio, we can see that there are 12 plants in the F_2 generation with round seeds compared to 4 with wrinkled seeds, and 12 yellow-seeded plants compared to four green-seeded ones. These 12:4 ratios each reduce to 3:1, which is the F_2 ratio for a monohybrid cross. Mendel tried his seven pea characters in various dihybrid combinations and always observed a 9:3:3:1 ratio (or two simultaneous 3:1 ratios) of phenotypes in the F_2 generation. These results supported the hypothesis that *each pair of alleles segregates independently of the other pairs of alleles during gamete formation*. In other words, the inheritance of one character has no effect on the inheritance of another. This is called Mendel's **law of independent assortment**.

For another application of the law of independent assortment, examine the dog breeding experiment described in Figure 9.9. The inheritance of two characters in Labrador retrievers is controlled by separate genes: black versus chocolate coat color, and normal vision versus the eye disorder progressive retinal atrophy (PRA). Black Labs have at least one copy of an allele called *B*. The *B* allele is dominant to *b*, so only the coats of dogs with genotype *bb* are chocolate in color. The allele that causes PRA, called *n*, is recessive to allele *N*, which is necessary for normal vision. Thus, only dogs of genotype *nn* become blind from PRA. If you mate two doubly heterozygous (*BbNn*) Labs (bottom of Figure 9.9), the phenotypic ratio of the offspring (F_2) is 9:3:3:1. These results resemble the F_2 results in Figure 9.8, demonstrating that the coat color and PRA genes are inherited independently. ✓

☑ **CHECKPOINT**

Looking at Figure 9.9, what is the ratio of black coat to chocolate coat in Labs? Of normal vision to blindness?

Answer: 3:1; 3:1

▼ Figure 9.9 **Independent assortment of genes in Labrador retrievers.**
Blanks in the genotypes indicate alleles that can be either dominant or recessive.

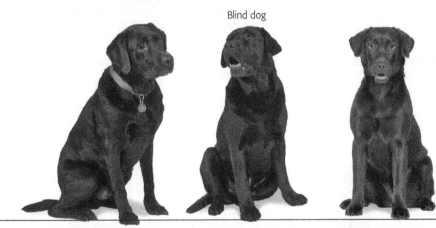

Phenotypes	Black coat, normal vision	Black coat, blind (PRA)	Chocolate coat, normal vision	Chocolate coat, blind (PRA)
Genotypes	B_N_	B_nn	bbN_	bbnn

(a) Possible phenotypes of Labrador retrievers

Mating of double heterozygotes
(black coat, normal vision)
BbNn ━ ✕ ━ BbNn

Phenotypic ratio of offspring	9 black coat, normal vision	3 black coat, blind (PRA)	3 chocolate coat, normal vision	1 chocolate coat, blind (PRA)

(b) A Labrador dihybrid cross

Using a Testcross to Determine an Unknown Genotype

Suppose you have a Labrador retriever with a chocolate coat. Consulting Figure 9.9, you can tell that its genotype must be *bb*, the only combination of alleles that produces the chocolate-coat phenotype. But what if you have a black Lab? It could have one of two possible genotypes—*BB* or *Bb*—and there is no way to tell which genotype is the correct one by looking at the dog. To determine your dog's genotype, you could perform a **testcross**, a mating between an individual of dominant phenotype but unknown genotype (your black Lab) and a homozygous recessive individual—in this case, a *bb* chocolate Lab.

Figure 9.10 shows the offspring that could result from such a mating. If, as shown on the left, the black Lab parent's genotype is *BB*, we would expect all the offspring to be black, because a cross between genotypes *BB* and *bb* can produce only *Bb* offspring. On the other hand, if the black Lab parent is *Bb*, we would expect both black (*Bb*) and chocolate (*bb*) offspring. Thus, the appearance of the offspring may reveal the original black dog's genotype. ☑

▼ **Figure 9.10** **A Labrador retriever testcross.** To determine the genotype of a black Lab, it can be crossed with a chocolate Lab (homozygous recessive, *bb*). If all the offspring are black, the black parent most likely had genotype *BB*. If any of the offspring are chocolate, the black parent must be heterozygous (*Bb*).

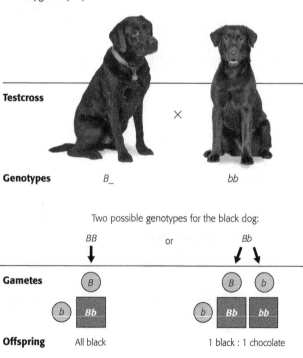

The Rules of Probability

Mendel's strong background in mathematics served him well in his studies of inheritance. For instance, he understood that genetic crosses obey the rules of probability—the same rules that apply when tossing coins, rolling dice, or drawing cards. An important lesson we can learn from tossing coins is that for each and every toss, the probability of heads is $\frac{1}{2}$. Even if heads has landed five times in a row, the probability of the next toss coming up heads is still $\frac{1}{2}$. In other words, the outcome of any particular toss is unaffected by what has happened on previous attempts. Each toss is an independent event.

If two coins are tossed simultaneously, the outcome for each coin is an independent event, unaffected by the other coin. What is the chance that both coins will land heads-up? The probability of such a dual event is the product of the separate probabilities of the independent events—for the coins, $\frac{1}{2} \times \frac{1}{2} = \frac{1}{4}$. This is called the **rule of multiplication**, and it holds true for independent events that occur in genetics as well as coin tosses, as shown in Figure 9.11. In our dihybrid cross of Labradors (see Figure 9.9), the genotype of the F₁ dogs

▼ **Figure 9.11** **Segregation of alleles and fertilization as chance events.** When heterozygotes (*Bb*) form gametes, segregation of alleles during sperm and egg formation is like two separately tossed coins (that is, two independent events).

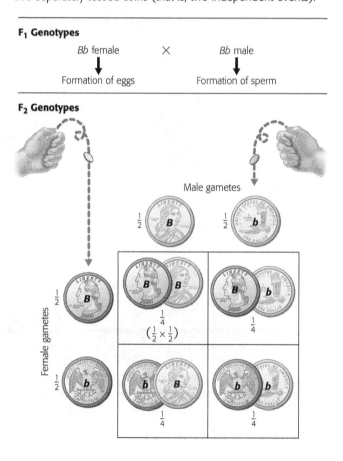

for coat color was *Bb*. What is the probability that a particular F$_2$ dog will have the *bb* genotype? To produce a *bb* offspring, both egg and sperm must carry the *b* allele. The probability that an egg from a *Bb* dog will have the *b* allele is $\frac{1}{2}$, and the probability that a sperm will have the *b* allele is also $\frac{1}{2}$. By the rule of multiplication, the probability that two *b* alleles will come together at fertilization is $\frac{1}{2} \times \frac{1}{2} = \frac{1}{4}$. This is exactly the answer given by the Punnett square in Figure 9.11. If we know the genotypes of the parents, we can predict the probability for any genotype among the offspring. By applying the rules of probability to segregation and independent assortment, we can solve some rather complex genetics problems. ☑

Family Pedigrees

Mendel's laws apply to the inheritance of many human traits. **Figure 9.12** illustrates alternative forms of three human characters that are each thought to be determined by simple dominant-recessive inheritance of one gene. (The genetic basis of many other human characters—such as eye and hair color—is much more complex and poorly understood.) If we call the dominant allele of any such gene *A*, the dominant phenotype results from either the homozygous genotype *AA* or the heterozygous genotype *Aa*. Recessive phenotypes result only from the homozygous genotype *aa*. In genetics, the word *dominant* does not imply that a phenotype is either normal or more common than a recessive phenotype; **wild-type traits** (those seen most often in nature) are not necessarily specified by dominant alleles. In genetics, dominance means that a heterozygote (*Aa*), carrying only a single copy of a dominant allele, displays the dominant phenotype. By contrast, the phenotype of the corresponding recessive allele is seen only in a homozygote (*aa*). Recessive traits may in fact be more common in the population than dominant ones. For example, the absence of freckles (*ff*) is more common than their presence (*FF* or *Ff*).

How can human genetics be studied? Researchers working with pea plants or Labrador retrievers can perform testcrosses. But geneticists who study people obviously cannot control the mating of their research participants. Instead, they must analyze the results of matings that have already occurred. First, the geneticist collects as much information as possible about a family's history for a trait. Then the researcher assembles this information into a family tree, called a **pedigree**. (You may associate pedigrees with purebred animals such as racehorses and champion dogs, but they can be used to represent human matings just as well.) To analyze a pedigree, the geneticist applies logic and Mendel's laws.

Freckles

Widow's peak

Free earlobe

No freckles

Straight hairline

Attached earlobe

DOMINANT TRAITS

RECESSIVE TRAITS

◄ Figure 9.12 **Examples of inherited human traits thought to be controlled by a single gene.**

Let's apply this approach to the example in **Figure 9.13**, a pedigree tracing the incidence of free versus attached earlobes. The letter *F* stands for the dominant allele for free earlobes, and *f* symbolizes the recessive allele for attached earlobes. In the pedigree, ☐ represents a male, ○ represents a female, colored symbols (▨ and ⬤) indicate that the person has the trait being investigated (in this case, attached earlobes), and an unshaded symbol represents a person who does not have the trait (that person has free earlobes). The earliest (oldest) generation is at the top of the pedigree, and the most recent generation is at the bottom.

By applying Mendel's laws, we can deduce that the attached allele is recessive because that is the only way that Kevin can have attached earlobes when neither of his parents (Hal and Ina) do. We can therefore label all the individuals with attached earlobes in the pedigree (that is, all those with colored circles or squares) as homozygous recessive (*ff*).

Mendel's laws enable us to deduce the genotypes for most of the people in the pedigree. For example, Hal and Ina must have carried the *f* allele (which they passed on to Kevin) along with the *F* allele that gave them free earlobes. The same must be true of Aaron and Betty because they both have free earlobes but Fred and Gabe have attached earlobes. For each of these cases, Mendel's laws and simple logic allow us to definitively assign a genotype.

Notice that we cannot deduce the genotype of every member of the pedigree. For example, Lisa must have at least one *F* allele, but she could be *FF* or *Ff*. We cannot distinguish between these two possibilities using the available data. Perhaps future generations will provide the data that solve this mystery. ☑

Human Disorders Controlled by a Single Gene

The human genetic disorders listed in **Table 9.1** are known to be inherited as dominant or recessive traits controlled by a single gene. These disorders therefore show simple inheritance patterns like the ones Mendel studied in pea plants. The genes involved are all located on autosomes, chromosomes other than the sex chromosomes X and Y.

Recessive Disorders

Most human genetic disorders are recessive. They range in severity from harmless to life-threatening. Most people who have recessive disorders are born to normal parents who are both heterozygotes—that is, parents who are **carriers** of the recessive allele for the disorder but appear normal themselves.

Using Mendel's laws, we can predict the fraction of affected offspring that is likely to result from a marriage between two carriers. Consider a form of inherited deafness caused by a recessive allele. Suppose two heterozygous carriers (*Dd*) have a child. What is the probability that the child will be deaf? As the Punnett square

▼ **Figure 9.13 A family pedigree showing inheritance of free versus attached earlobes.**

First generation
(grandparents)

Aaron *Ff* Betty *Ff*   Cletus *ff* Debbie *Ff*

Second generation
(parents, aunts, and uncles)

Evelyn *FF or Ff* Fred *ff* Gabe *ff* Hal *Ff* Ina *Ff* Julia *ff*

Third generation
(brother and sister)

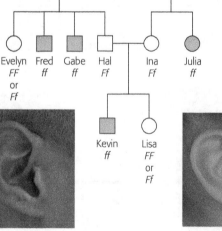

Kevin *ff* Lisa *FF or Ff*

Female **Male**

⬤ ▨ Attached

○ ☐ Free

Table 9.1	Some Autosomal Disorders in People
Disorder	**Major Symptoms**
Recessive Disorders	
Albinism	Lack of pigment in skin, hair, and eyes
Cystic fibrosis	Excess mucus in lungs, digestive tract, liver; increased susceptibility to infections; death in early childhood unless treated
Phenylketonuria (PKU)	Accumulation of phenylalanine in blood; lack of normal skin pigment; mental retardation unless treated
Sickle-cell disease	Sickled red blood cells; damage to many tissues
Tay-Sachs disease	Lipid accumulation in brain cells; mental deficiency; blindness; death in childhood
Dominant Disorders	
Achondroplasia	Dwarfism
Alzheimer's disease (one type)	Mental deterioration; usually strikes late in life
Huntington's disease	Mental deterioration and uncontrollable movements; strikes in middle age
Hypercholesterolemia	Excess cholesterol in blood; heart disease

in **Figure 9.14** shows, each child of two carriers has a $\frac{1}{4}$ chance of inheriting two recessive alleles. Thus, we can say that about one-fourth of the children of this couple are likely to be deaf. We can also say that a hearing child from such a family has a $\frac{2}{3}$ chance of being a carrier (that is, on average, two out of three of the offspring with the hearing phenotype will be *Dd*). We can apply this same method of pedigree analysis and prediction to any genetic trait controlled by a single gene.

The most common lethal genetic disease in the United States is **cystic fibrosis (CF)**. Affecting about 30,000 Americans, the recessive CF allele is carried by about 1 in 31 Americans. A person with two copies of this allele has cystic fibrosis, which is characterized by an excessive secretion of very thick mucus from the lungs, pancreas, and other organs. This mucus can interfere with breathing, digestion, and liver function and makes the person vulnerable to recurrent bacterial infections. Although there is no cure for this fatal disease, a special diet, antibiotics to prevent infection, frequent pounding of the chest and back to clear the lungs, and other treatments can greatly extend life. Once invariably fatal in childhood, advances in CF treatment have raised the median survival age of Americans with CF to 37. ☑

Dominant Disorders

A number of human disorders are caused by dominant alleles. Some are harmless, such as extra fingers and toes or digits that are webbed. A serious but nonlethal disorder caused by a dominant allele is achondroplasia, a form of dwarfism in which the head and torso develop

▼ Figure 9.14 **Predicted offspring when both parents are carriers for a recessive disorder.**

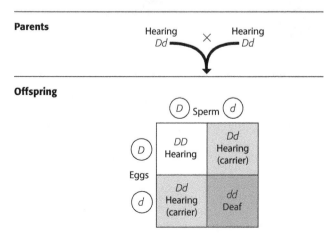

Parents

Hearing *Dd* ✕ Hearing *Dd*

Offspring

	Sperm D	Sperm d
Eggs D	DD Hearing	Dd Hearing (carrier)
Eggs d	Dd Hearing (carrier)	dd Deaf

☑ **CHECKPOINT**

A man and a woman who are both carriers of cystic fibrosis have had three children without cystic fibrosis. If the couple has a fourth child, what is the probability that the child will have the disorder?

Answers: $\frac{1}{4}$ (The genotypes and phenotypes of their other children are irrelevant.)

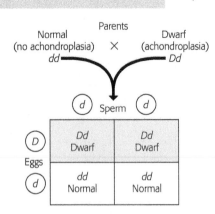

▲ Figure 9.15 A Punnett square illustrating a family with and without achondroplasia.

normally but the arms and legs are short. The homozygous dominant genotype (*AA*) causes death of the embryo, and therefore only heterozygotes (*Aa*), individuals with a single copy of the defective allele, have this disorder. This also means that a person with achondroplasia has a 50% chance of passing the condition on to any children (Figure 9.15). Therefore, all those who do not have achondroplasia, more than 99.99% of the population, are homozygous for the recessive allele (*aa*). This example makes it clear that a dominant allele is not necessarily more common in a population than the corresponding recessive allele.

Dominant alleles that cause lethal disorders are much less common than lethal recessive alleles. One example is the allele that causes Huntington's disease, a degeneration of the nervous system that usually does not begin until middle age. Once the deterioration of the nervous system begins, it is irreversible and inevitably fatal. Because the allele for Huntington's disease is dominant, any child born to a parent with the allele has a 50% chance of inheriting the allele and the disorder. This example makes it clear that a dominant allele is not necessarily "better" than the corresponding recessive allele.

One way that geneticists study human traits is to find similar genes in animals, which can then be studied in greater detail through controlled matings and other experiments. Let's return to the chapter thread—dog breeding—to investigate the furry coats of man's best friend.

Dog Breeding THE PROCESS OF SCIENCE

What Is the Genetic Basis of Coat Variation in Dogs?

You've probably made the **observation** that compared with most mammals, dogs come in a wide variety of physical types. For instance, dog coats can be short or long, straight or curly or wire-haired (having a "moustache" and "eyebrows"). Sometimes a single breed, such as the fox terrier, may display two or more of these variations (Figure 9.16).

In 2005, the complete genome of a dog—the sequence of all the DNA of a female boxer named Tasha—was published. Since that time, canine geneticists have added a wealth of data from other breeds. In 2009, an international group of researchers set out to investigate the **question** of the genetic basis for canine coats. They proposed the **hypothesis** that a comparison of genes from a wide variety of dogs with different coats would identify the genes responsible. They made the **prediction** that mutations in just a few genes could account for the coat appearance. Their **experiment** compared DNA sequences in 622 dogs from dozens of breeds. Their **results** identified three genes that in different combinations produced seven different coat appearances, from very short hair to full, thick, wired hair. The difference between the two dogs in the photo, for example, is due to a change in a single gene that regulates keratin, a protein that is one of the primary structural components of hair.

This experiment shows how the extreme range of phenotypes in dogs combined with the availability of genome sequences can be used to provide insight into interesting genetic questions. Indeed, similar research has uncovered the genetic basis of other dog traits, such as body size, hairlessness, and coat color.

▼ Figure 9.16 Smooth versus wired fox terrier. The fox terrier, like several other breeds, comes in smooth (left) and wired (right) coats.

Genetic Testing

Until relatively recently, the onset of symptoms was the only way to know if a person had inherited an allele that might lead to disease. Today, there are many tests that can detect the presence of disease-causing alleles in an individual's genome.

Most genetic tests are performed during pregnancy if the prospective parents are aware that they have an increased risk of having a baby with a genetic disease. Genetic testing before birth usually requires the collection of fetal cells. In amniocentesis, a physician uses a needle to extract about 2 teaspoons of the fluid that bathes the developing fetus (Figure 9.17). In chorionic villus sampling, a physician inserts a narrow, flexible tube through the mother's vagina and into her uterus, removing some placental tissue. Once cells are obtained, they can be screened for genetic diseases.

Because amniocentesis and chorionic villus sampling have risks of complications, these techniques are usually reserved for situations in which the possibility of a genetic disease is high. Alternatively, blood tests on the mother at 15 to 20 weeks of pregnancy can help identify fetuses at risk for certain birth defects. The most widely used blood test measures levels of a protein called AFP in the mother's blood; abnormally high levels may indicate developmental defects in the fetus, while abnormally low levels may indicate Down syndrome. For a more complete risk profile, a woman's doctor may order a "triple screen test," which measures AFP as well as two other hormones produced by the placenta. Abnormal levels of these substances in the maternal blood may also point to a risk of Down syndrome. Newer genetic screening procedures involve isolating tiny amounts of fetal cells or DNA released into the mother's bloodstream. Because they are more accurate and can be performed earlier and more safely than other tests, these newer technologies are gradually replacing more invasive screening methods.

As genetic testing becomes more routine, geneticists are working to make sure that the tests do not cause more problems than they solve. Geneticists stress that patients seeking genetic testing should receive counseling both before and after to explain the test and to help them cope with the results. Identifying a genetic disease early can give families time to prepare—emotionally, medically, and financially. Advances in biotechnology offer possibilities for reducing human suffering, but not before key ethical issues are resolved. The dilemmas posed by human genetics reinforce one of this book's themes: the immense social implications of biology. ☑

☑ **CHECKPOINT**

Peter is a 28-year-old man whose father died of Huntington's disease. Peter's mother shows no signs of the disease. What is the probability that Peter has inherited Huntington's disease?

Answers: ½

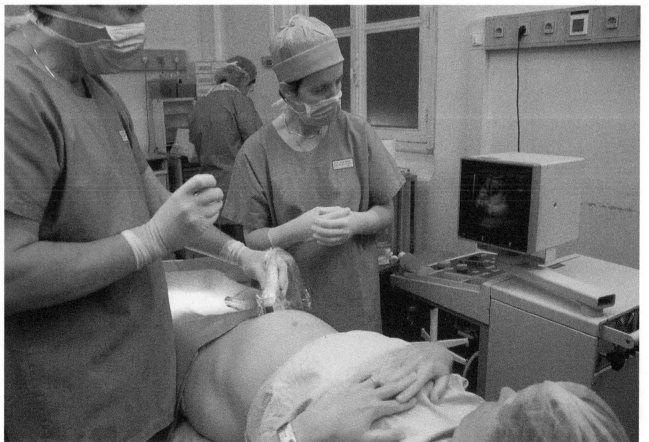

◄ Figure 9.17
Amniocentesis. A doctor uses a sonogram to help guide the removal of fetal cells for genetic testing.

Variations on Mendel's Laws

Mendel's two laws explain inheritance in terms of genes that are passed along from generation to generation according to simple rules of probability. These laws are valid for all sexually reproducing organisms, including garden peas, Labrador retrievers, and people. But just as the basic rules of musical harmony cannot account for all the rich sounds of a symphony, Mendel's laws stop short of explaining some patterns of genetic inheritance. In fact, for most sexually reproducing organisms, cases in which Mendel's rules can strictly account for the patterns of inheritance are relatively rare. More often, the observed inheritance patterns are more complex. Next, we'll look at several extensions to Mendel's laws that help account for this complexity.

Incomplete Dominance in Plants and People

The F$_1$ offspring of Mendel's pea crosses always looked like one of the two parent plants. In such situations, the dominant allele has the same effect on the phenotype whether present in one or two copies. But for some characters, the appearance of F$_1$ hybrids falls between the phenotypes of the two parents, an effect called **incomplete dominance**. For instance, when red snapdragons are crossed with white snapdragons, all the F$_1$ hybrids have pink flowers (Figure 9.18). And in the F$_2$ generation, the genotypic ratio and the phenotypic ratio are the same: 1:2:1.

We also see examples of incomplete dominance in people. One case involves a recessive allele (*h*) that causes hypercholesterolemia, dangerously high levels of cholesterol in the blood. Normal individuals are homozygous dominant, *HH*. Heterozygotes (*Hh*) have blood cholesterol levels about twice what is normal. Such heterozygotes are very prone to cholesterol buildup in artery walls and may have heart attacks from blocked heart arteries by their mid-30s. Hypercholesterolemia is even more serious in homozygous individuals (*hh*). Homozygotes have about five times the normal amount of blood cholesterol and may have heart attacks as early as age 2. If we look at the molecular basis for hypercholesterolemia, we can understand the intermediate phenotype of heterozygotes (Figure 9.19). The *H* allele specifies a cell-surface receptor protein that liver cells use to mop up excess low-density lipoprotein (LDL, or "bad cholesterol") from the blood. With only half as many receptors as *HH* individuals, heterozygotes can remove much less excess cholesterol.

▼ Figure 9.18 **Incomplete dominance in snapdragons.**
Compare this diagram with Figure 9.6, where one of the alleles displays complete dominance.

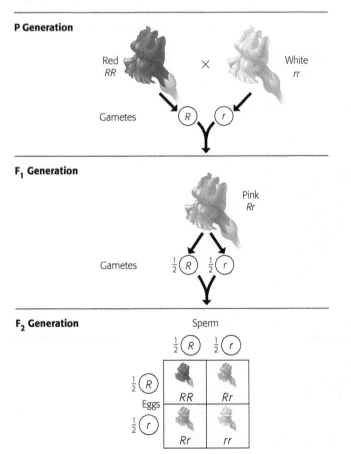

▼ Figure 9.19 **Incomplete dominance in human hypercholesterolemia.**
LDL receptors on liver cells promote the breakdown of cholesterol carried in the bloodstream by LDL (low-density lipoprotein). This process helps prevent the accumulation of cholesterol in the arteries. Having too few receptors allows dangerous levels of LDL to build up in the blood.

ABO Blood Groups: An Example of Multiple Alleles and Codominance

So far, we have discussed inheritance patterns involving only two alleles per gene (*H* versus *h*, for example). But most genes can be found in populations in more than two forms, known as multiple alleles. Although each individual carries, at most, two different alleles for a particular gene, in cases of multiple alleles, more than two possible alleles exist in the population.

The **ABO blood groups** in humans involve three alleles of a single gene. Various combinations of these three alleles produce four phenotypes: A person's blood type may be A, B, AB, or O. These letters refer to two carbohydrates, designated A and B, that may be found on the surface of red blood cells (**Figure 9.20**). A person's red blood cells may be coated with carbohydrate A (giving them type A blood), carbohydrate B (type B), both (type AB), or neither (type O). (In case you are wondering, the "positive" and "negative" notations associated with blood types—referred to as the Rh blood group system—are due to inheritance of a separate, unrelated gene.)

Matching compatible blood groups is critical for safe blood transfusions. If a donor's blood cells have a carbohydrate (A or B) that is foreign to the recipient, then the recipient's immune system produces blood proteins called antibodies that bind to the foreign carbohydrates and cause the donor blood cells to clump together, potentially killing the recipient.

The four blood groups result from various combinations of the three different alleles: I^A (for the ability to make substance A), I^B (for B), and i (for neither A nor B). Each person inherits one of these alleles from each parent. Because there are three alleles, there are six possible genotypes, as listed in Figure 9.21. Both the I^A and I^B alleles are dominant to the i allele. Thus, $I^A I^A$ and $I^A i$ people have type A blood, and $I^B I^B$ and $I^B i$ people have type B. Recessive homozygotes (ii) have type O blood with neither carbohydrate. Finally, people of genotype $I^A I^B$ make *both* carbohydrates. In other words, the I^A and I^B alleles are **codominant**, meaning that both alleles are expressed in heterozygous individuals ($I^A I^B$) who have type AB blood. Notice that type O blood reacts with no others, making such a person a universal donor. A person with type AB blood is a universal receiver. Be careful to distinguish codominance (the expression of both alleles) from incomplete dominance (the expression of one intermediate trait). ☑

☑ CHECKPOINT

1. Why is a testcross unnecessary to determine whether a snapdragon with red flowers is homozygous or heterozygous?
2. Maria has type O blood, and her sister has type AB blood. What are the genotypes of the girls' parents?

Answers: 1. Only plants homozygous for the dominant allele have red flowers; heterozygotes have pink flowers. 2. One parent is $I^A i$, and the other parent is $I^B i$.

▼ **Figure 9.20** **Multiple alleles for the ABO blood groups.** The three versions of the gene responsible for blood type may produce carbohydrate A (allele I^A), carbohydrate B (allele I^B), or neither carbohydrate (allele i). Because each person carries two alleles, six genotypes are possible that result in four different phenotypes. The clumping reaction that occurs between antibodies and foreign blood cells is the basis of blood-typing (shown in the photograph at right) and of the adverse reaction that occurs when someone receives a transfusion of incompatible blood.

Blood Group (Phenotype)	Genotypes	Red Blood Cells	Antibodies Present in Blood	Reactions When Blood from Groups Below Is Mixed with Antibodies from Groups at Left			
				O	A	B	AB
A	$I^A I^A$ or $I^A i$	Carbohydrate A	Anti-B				
B	$I^B I^B$ or $I^B i$	Carbohydrate B	Anti-A				
AB	$I^A I^B$		—				
O	ii		Anti-A Anti-B				

▼ Figure 9.21 **Sickle-cell disease: multiple effects of a single human gene.**

Individual homozygous for sickle-cell allele

Sickle-cell (abnormal) hemoglobin

Abnormal hemoglobin crystallizes into long, flexible chains, causing red blood cells to become sickle-shaped.

Colorized SEM 4,000×

Sickled cells can lead to a cascade of symptoms, such as weakness, pain, organ damage, and paralysis.

Structure/Function Pleiotropy and Sickle-Cell Disease

Our genetic examples to this point have been cases in which each gene specifies only one hereditary character. But in many cases, one gene influences several characters, a property called **pleiotropy**.

An example of pleiotropy in humans is sickle-cell disease (sometimes called sickle-cell anemia), a disorder characterized by a diverse set of symptoms. The direct effect of the sickle-cell allele is to make red blood cells produce abnormal hemoglobin proteins (see Figure 3.19). These abnormal molecules tend to link together and crystallize, especially when the oxygen content of the blood is lower than usual because of high altitude, overexertion, or respiratory ailments. As the hemoglobin crystallizes, the normally disk-shaped red blood cells deform to a sickle shape with jagged edges (**Figure 9.21**). As is so often the case in biology, altering structure affects function. Because of their shape, sickled cells do not flow smoothly in the blood and tend to accumulate and clog tiny blood vessels. Blood flow to body parts is reduced, resulting in periodic fever, severe pain, and damage to the heart, brain, and kidneys. The abnormal sickled cells are destroyed by the body, causing anemia and general weakness. Blood transfusions and drugs may relieve some of the symptoms, but there is no cure, and sickle-cell disease kills about 100,000 people in the world annually. ☑

Polygenic Inheritance

Mendel studied genetic characters that could be classified on an either-or basis, such as purple or white flower color. However, many characters, such as human skin color and height, vary along a continuum in a population. Many such features result from **polygenic inheritance**, the additive effects of two or more genes on a single phenotypic character. (This is the logical opposite of pleiotropy, in which one gene affects several characters.)

There is evidence that height in people is controlled by several genes that are inherited separately. (In actuality, human height is probably affected by a great number of genes, but we'll simplify here.) Let's consider three genes, with a tall allele for each (A, B, and C) contributing one "unit" of tallness to the phenotype and being incompletely dominant to the other alleles (a, b, and c).

☑ **CHECKPOINT**

How does sickle-cell disease exemplify the concept of pleiotropy?

Answer: Homozygotes for the sickle-cell allele have abnormal hemoglobin, and its effect on the shape of red blood cells leads to a cascade of traits affecting many organs of the body.

A person who is AABBCC would be very tall, while an aabbcc individual would be very short. An AaBbCc person would be of intermediate height. Because the alleles have an additive effect, the genotype AaBbCc would produce the same height as any other genotype with just three tallness alleles, such as AABbcc. The Punnett square in **Figure 9.22** shows all possible genotypes from

▲ Figure 9.22 **A model for polygenic inheritance of height.**

a mating of two triple heterozygotes (*AaBbCd*). The row of figures below the Punnett square shows the seven height phenotypes that would theoretically result. This hypothetical example shows how inheritance of three genes could lead to seven different versions of a trait at the frequencies indicated by the bars in the graph at the bottom of the figure.

Epigenetics and the Role of Environment

If we examine a real human population for height, we would see more height phenotypes than just seven. The true range might be similar to the entire distribution of height under the bell-shaped curve in Figure 9.22. In fact, no matter how carefully we characterize the genes for height, a purely genetic description will always be incomplete. This is because height is also influenced by environmental factors, such as nutrition and exercise.

Many phenotypic characters result from a combination of heredity and environment. For example, the leaves of a tree all have the same genotype, but they vary in size, shape, and color, depending on exposure to wind and sun and the tree's nutritional state. For people, exercise alters build; experience improves performance on intelligence tests; and social and cultural factors can greatly affect appearance. As geneticists learn more and more about our genes, it's becoming clear that many human characters—such as risk of heart disease, cancer, alcoholism, and schizophrenia—are influenced by both genes *and* environment.

Whether human characters are more influenced by genes or by the environment—nature or nurture—is a very old and hotly contested issue. For some characters, such as the ABO blood group, a given genotype mandates an exact phenotype, and the environment plays no role whatsoever. In contrast, the number of blood cells in a drop of your blood varies quite a bit, depending on such factors as the altitude, your physical activity, and whether or not you have a cold.

Spending time with identical twins will convince anyone that environment, and not just genes, affects a person's traits (Figure 9.23). In general, only genetic

> Because the environment helps shape your appearance, identical twins aren't identical in every way.

influences are inherited, and any effects of the environment are not usually passed to the next generation. In recent years, however, biologists have begun to recognize the importance of **epigenetic inheritance**, the transmission of traits by mechanisms not directly involving DNA sequence. For example, DNA and/or protein components of chromosomes can be chemically modified by adding or removing chemical groups. Over a lifetime, the environment plays a role in these changes, which may explain how one identical twin can suffer from a genetically based disease whereas the other twin does not, despite their identical genomes. Recent research has shown that young identical twins are essentially indistinguishable in terms of their epigenetic markers, but epigenetic differences accumulate as they age, resulting in substantial differences in gene expression between older twins. Epigenetic modifications—and the changes in gene activity that result—may even be carried on to the next generation. For example, some research suggests that epigenetic changes may underlie certain instincts in animals, allowing behaviors learned by one generation (such as avoiding certain stimuli) to be passed on to the next generation via chromosomal modifications.

Unlike alterations to the DNA sequence, chemical changes to the chromosomes can be reversed (by processes that are not yet fully understood). Research into the importance of epigenetic inheritance is a very active area of biology, and new discoveries that alter our understanding of genetics are sure to follow. ☑

☑ CHECKPOINT

If you produced cloned mice, how would you predict the number of epigenetic differences among the clones to change as they age?

Answer: You would expect the number of epigenetic differences to be low at first and then gradually increase as the clones age.

▶ Figure 9.23 **As a result of environmental influences, even identical twins can look different.**

The Chromosomal Basis of Inheritance

It was not until many years after Mendel's death that biologists understood the significance of his work. Cell biologists worked out the processes of mitosis and meiosis in the late 1800s (see Chapter 8). Then, around 1900, researchers began to notice parallels between the behavior of chromosomes and the behavior of genes. One of biology's most important concepts began to emerge.

The **chromosome theory of inheritance** states that genes are located at specific positions (loci) on chromosomes and that the behavior of chromosomes during meiosis and fertilization accounts for inheritance patterns. Indeed, it is chromosomes that undergo segregation and independent assortment during meiosis and thus account for Mendel's laws. Figure 9.24 correlates the results of the dihybrid cross in Figure 9.8b with the movement of chromosomes through meiosis. Starting with two purebred parental plants, the diagram follows two genes on different chromosomes—one for seed shape (alleles *R* and *r*) and one for seed color (alleles *Y* and *y*)—through the F_1 and F_2 generations. ☑

Linked Genes

Realizing that genes are on chromosomes when they segregate leads to some important conclusions about the ways genes can be inherited. The number of genes in a cell is far

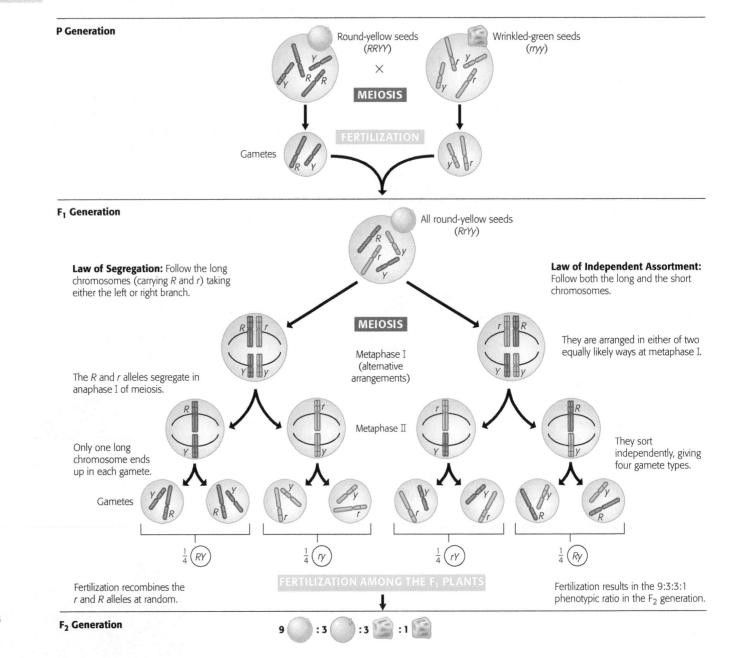

P Generation

Round-yellow seeds (*RRYY*)   ×   Wrinkled-green seeds (*rryy*)

MEIOSIS

FERTILIZATION

Gametes

F_1 Generation

All round-yellow seeds (*RrYy*)

Law of Segregation: Follow the long chromosomes (carrying *R* and *r*) taking either the left or right branch.

Law of Independent Assortment: Follow both the long and the short chromosomes.

MEIOSIS

Metaphase I (alternative arrangements)

They are arranged in either of two equally likely ways at metaphase I.

The *R* and *r* alleles segregate in anaphase I of meiosis.

Metaphase II

Only one long chromosome ends up in each gamete.

They sort independently, giving four gamete types.

Gametes

$\frac{1}{4}$ (*RY*) $\frac{1}{4}$ (*ry*) $\frac{1}{4}$ (*rY*) $\frac{1}{4}$ (*Ry*)

Fertilization recombines the *r* and *R* alleles at random.

FERTILIZATION AMONG THE F_1 PLANTS

Fertilization results in the 9:3:3:1 phenotypic ratio in the F_2 generation.

F_2 Generation

9 : 3 : 3 : 1

▶ Figure 9.24 **The chromosomal basis of Mendel's laws.**

greater than the number of chromosomes; each chromosome therefore carries hundreds or thousands of genes. Genes located near each other on the same chromosome, called **linked genes**, tend to travel together during meiosis and fertilization. Such genes are often inherited as a set and therefore often do not follow Mendel's law of independent assortment. For closely linked genes, the inheritance of one does in fact correlate with the inheritance of the other, producing results that do not follow the standard ratios predicted by Punnett squares. In contrast, genes located far apart on the same chromosome usually do sort independently because of crossing over (see Figure 8.18).

The patterns of genetic inheritance we've discussed so far have always involved genes located on autosomes, not on the sex chromosomes. We're now ready to look at the role of sex chromosomes and the inheritance patterns exhibited by the characters they control. As you'll see, genes located on sex chromosomes produce some unusual patterns of inheritance. ☑

Sex Determination in Humans

Many animals, including all mammals, have a pair of sex chromosomes—designated X and Y—that determine an individual's sex (Figure 9.25). Individuals with one X chromosome and one Y chromosome are males; XX individuals are females. Human males and females both have 44 autosomes (chromosomes other than sex chromosomes). As a result of chromosome segregation during

> Your mother's genes had no role in determining your sex.

meiosis, each gamete contains one sex chromosome and a haploid set of autosomes (22 in humans). All eggs contain a single X chromosome. Of the sperm cells, half contain an X chromosome and half contain a Y chromosome. An offspring's sex depends on whether the sperm cell that fertilizes the egg bears an X or a Y.

Sex-Linked Genes

Besides bearing genes that determine sex, the sex chromosomes also contain genes for characters unrelated to maleness or femaleness. A gene located on a sex chromosome is called a **sex-linked gene**. The human X chromosome contains approximately 1,100 genes, whereas the Y chromosome contains genes that encode for only about 25 proteins (most of which affect only the testes); therefore, most sex-linked genes are found on the X chromosome.

A number of human conditions, including redgreen colorblindness, hemophilia, and a type of muscular dystrophy, result from sex-linked recessive alleles. Red-green colorblindness is a common sex-linked disorder that is caused by a malfunction of light-sensitive cells in the eyes. (Colorblindness is actually a large class of disorders involving several sex-linked genes, but we will focus on just one specific type of colorblindness here.) A person with normal color vision can see more than 150 colors. In contrast, someone with redgreen colorblindness can see fewer than 25. Figure 9.26 shows a simple test for red-green

☑ **CHECKPOINT**

What are linked genes? Why do they often disobey Mendel's law of independent assortment?

Answer: Genes located near each other on the same chromosome. Because they often travel together during meiosis and fertilization, linked genes tend to be inherited together rather than independently.

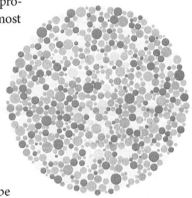

▲ Figure 9.26 **A test for red-green colorblindness.** Can you see a green numeral 7 against the reddish background? If not, you probably have some form of red-green colorblindness, a sex-linked trait.

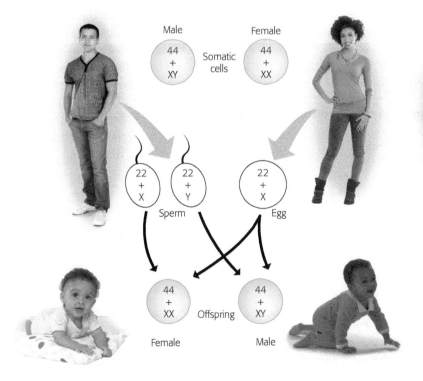

Male — Somatic cells

44 + XY

Female

44 + XX

Sperm: 22 + X, 22 + Y

Egg: 22 + X

Offspring: 44 + XX (Female), 44 + XY (Male)

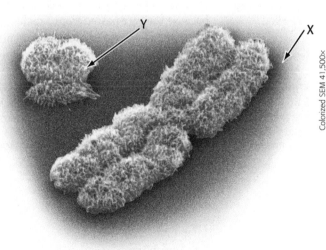

Colorized SEM 41,500×

Y   X

▲ Figure 9.25 **The chromosomal basis of sex determination in humans.** The micrograph above shows human X and Y chromosomes in a duplicated state.

163

colorblindness. Mostly males are affected, but heterozygous females have some defects, too.

Because they are located on the sex chromosomes, sex-linked genes exhibit unusual inheritance patterns. **Figure 9.27a** (below) illustrates what happens when a colorblind male has offspring with a homozygous female with normal color vision. All the children have normal color vision, suggesting that the allele for wild-type (normal) color vision is dominant. If a female carrier mates with a male who has normal color vision, the classic 3:1 phenotypic ratio of normal color vision to colorblindness appears among the children **(Figure 9.27b)**. However, there is a surprising twist: The colorblind trait shows up only in males. All the females have normal vision, while half the males are colorblind and half are normal. This is because the gene involved in this inheritance pattern is located exclusively on the X chromosome; there is no corresponding locus on the Y. Thus, females (XX) carry two copies of the gene for this character, and males (XY) carry only one. Because the colorblindness allele is recessive, a female will be colorblind only if she receives that allele on both X chromosomes **(Figure 9.27c)**. For a male, however, a single copy of the recessive allele confers colorblindness. For this reason, recessive sex-linked traits are expressed much more frequently in men than in women. For example, colorblindness is about 20-fold more common among males than among females. This inheritance pattern is why people often say that certain genes "skip a generation"—because they are passed from a male (in generation 1) to a female carrier (who does not express it in generation 2) back to a male (in generation 3).

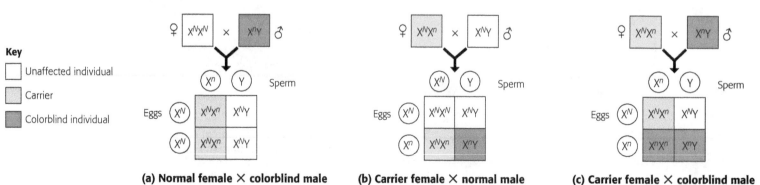

▲ Figure 9.28 **Hemophilia in the royal family of Russia.** The photograph shows Queen Victoria's granddaughter Alexandra, her husband Nicholas, who was the last czar of Russia, their son Alexis, and their daughters. In the pedigree, half-colored symbols represent heterozygous carriers of the hemophilia allele and fully colored symbols represent a person with hemophilia.

Hemophilia is a sex-linked recessive trait with a long, well-documented history. Hemophiliacs bleed excessively when injured because they have inherited an abnormal allele for a factor involved in blood clotting. The most seriously affected individuals may bleed to death after relatively minor bruises or cuts. A high incidence of hemophilia plagued the royal families of Europe. Queen Victoria (1819–1901) of England was a carrier of the hemophilia allele. She passed it on to one of her sons and two of her daughters. Through marriage, her daughters then introduced the disease into the royal families of Prussia, Russia, and Spain. In this way, the former practice of strengthening international alliances by marriage effectively spread hemophilia through the royal families of several nations **(Figure 9.28)**. ✓

> Hemophilia is more prevalent among European royalty than commoners because of past intermarriage.

▼ Figure 9.27 **Inheritance of colorblindness, a sex-linked recessive trait.** We use an uppercase *N* for the dominant, normal color-vision allele and *n* for the recessive, colorblind allele. To indicate that these alleles are on the X chromosome, we show them as superscripts to the letter X. The Y chromosome does not have a gene locus for vision; therefore, the male's phenotype results entirely from the sex-linked gene on his single X chromosome.

Key
- ☐ Unaffected individual
- ◻ Carrier
- ◼ Colorblind individual

(a) **Normal female × colorblind male**

(b) **Carrier female × normal male**

(c) **Carrier female × colorblind male**

Barking Up the Evolutionary Tree

As we've seen throughout this chapter, dogs are more than man's best friend: They are also one of our longest-running genetic experiments. About 15,000 years ago, in East Asia, people began to cohabit with ancestral canines that were predecessors of both modern wolves and dogs. As people moved into permanent, geographically isolated settlements, populations of canines were separated from one another and eventually became inbred.

Different groups of people chose dogs with different traits. A 2010 study indicated that small dogs were first bred within early agricultural settlements of the Middle East around 12,000 years ago. Elsewhere, herders selected dogs for controlling flocks while hunters chose dogs for retrieving prey. Continued over millennia, such genetic tinkering has resulted in a diverse array of dog body types and behaviors. In each breed, a distinct genetic makeup results in a distinct set of physical and behavioral traits.

As discussed in the Process of Science section, our understanding of canine evolution took a big leap forward

when researchers sequenced the complete genome of a dog. Using the genome sequence and other data, canine geneticists produced an evolutionary tree based on a genetic analysis of 85 breeds (Figure 9.29). The analysis shows that the canine family tree includes a series of well-defined branch points. Each fork represents a purposeful selection by people that produced a genetically distinct subpopulation with specific desired traits.

The genetic tree shows that the most ancient breeds, those most closely related to the wolf, are Asian species such as the shar-pei and Akita. Subsequent genetic splits created distinct breeds in Africa (basenji), the Arctic (Alaskan malamute and Siberian husky), and the Middle East (Afghan hound and saluki). The remaining breeds, primarily of European ancestry, were developed most recently and can be grouped by genetic makeup into those bred for guarding (for example, the rottweiler), herding (such as sheepdogs), and hunting (including the Labrador retriever and beagle). The formulation of an evolutionary tree for the domestic dog shows that new technologies can provide important insights into genetic and evolutionary questions about life on Earth.

► Figure 9.29 **An evolutionary tree of dog breeds.** Genetic analysis has revealed the ancestral history of various dog breeds.

Chapter Review

SUMMARY OF KEY CONCEPTS

Genetics and Heredity

Gregor Mendel, the first to study the science of heredity by analyzing patterns of inheritance, emphasized that genes retain permanent identities.

In an Abbey Garden

Mendel started with purebred varieties of pea plants representing two alternative variants of a hereditary character. He then crossed the different varieties and traced the inheritance of traits from generation to generation.

Mendel's Law of Segregation

Pairs of alleles separate during gamete formation; fertilization restores the pairs.

If an individual's genotype (genetic makeup) has two different alleles for a gene and only one influences the organism's phenotype (appearance), that allele is said to be dominant and the other allele recessive. Alleles of a gene reside at the same locus, or position, on homologous chromosomes. When the allele pair matches, the organism is homozygous; when the alleles are different, the organism is heterozygous.

Mendel's Law of Independent Assortment

By following two characters at once, Mendel found that the alleles of a pair segregate independently of other allele pairs during gamete formation.

Using a Testcross to Determine an Unknown Genotype

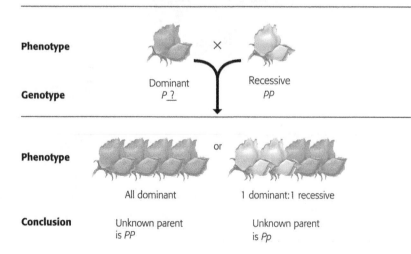

The Rules of Probability

Inheritance follows the rules of probability. The chance of inheriting a recessive allele from a heterozygous parent is $\frac{1}{2}$. The chance of inheriting it from both of two heterozygous parents is $\frac{1}{2} \times \frac{1}{2} = \frac{1}{4}$, illustrating the rule of multiplication for calculating the probability of two independent events.

Family Pedigrees

The inheritance of many human traits, from freckles to genetic diseases, follows Mendel's laws and the rules of probability. Geneticists can use family pedigrees to determine patterns of inheritance and individual genotypes.

Human Disorders Controlled by a Single Gene

For traits that vary within a population, the one most commonly found in nature is called the wild type. Many inherited disorders in humans are controlled by a single gene with two alleles. Most of these disorders, such as cystic fibrosis, are caused by autosomal recessive alleles. A few, such as Huntington's disease, are caused by dominant alleles.

Variations on Mendel's Laws

Incomplete Dominance in Plants and People

ABO Blood Groups: An Example of Multiple Alleles and Codominance

Within a population, there are often multiple kinds of alleles for a character, such as the three alleles for the ABO blood groups. The alleles determining blood groups are codominant; that is, both are expressed in a heterozygote.

Structure/Function: Pleiotropy and Sickle-Cell Disease

In pleiotropy, one gene (such as the sickle-cell disease gene) can affect many characters (such as the multiple symptoms of the disease).

Polygenic Inheritance

Epigenetics and the Role of Environment

Many phenotypic characters result from a combination of genetic and environmental effects, but only genetic influences are biologically heritable. Epigenetic inheritance, the transmission of traits from one generation to the next by means of chemical modifications to DNA and proteins, may explain how environmental factors can affect genetic traits.

The Chromosomal Basis of Inheritance

Genes are located on chromosomes. The behavior of chromosomes during meiosis and fertilization accounts for inheritance patterns.

Linked Genes

Certain genes are linked: They tend to be inherited as a set because they lie close together on the same chromosome.

Sex Determination in Humans

In humans, sex is determined by whether a Y chromosome is present. A person who inherits two X chromosomes develops as a female. A person who inherits one X and one Y chromosome develops as a male.

Sex-Linked Genes

Their inheritance of genes on the X chromosome reflects the fact that females have two homologous X chromosomes, but males have only one. Most sex-linked human disorders, such as red-green colorblindness and hemophilia, are due to recessive alleles and are seen mostly in males. A male receiving a single sex-linked recessive allele from his mother will have the disorder; a female has to receive the allele from both parents to be affected.

Sex-Linked Traits			
Female: Two alleles	Genotype	$X^N X^N$	$X^N X^n$	$X^n X^n$
	Phenotype	Normal female	Carrier female	Affected female (rare)

Male: One allele	Genotype	$X^N Y$	$X^n Y$
	Phenotype	Normal male	Affected male

MasteringBiology®

For practice quizzes, BioFlix animations, MP3 tutorials, video tutors, and more study tools designed for this textbook, go to MasteringBiology®

1. The genetic makeup of an organism is called its _____, and the physical traits of an organism are called its _____.

2. Which of Mendel's laws is represented by each statement?
   a. Alleles of each pair of homologous chromosomes separate independently during gamete formation.
   b. Alleles segregate during gamete formation; fertilization creates pairs of alleles once again.

3. Edward was found to be heterozygous (*Ss*) for the sickle-cell trait. The alleles represented by the letters *S* and *s* are
   a. on the X and Y chromosomes.
   b. linked.
   c. on homologous chromosomes.
   d. both present in each of Edward's sperm cells.

4. Whether an allele is dominant or recessive depends on
   a. how common the allele is, relative to other alleles.
   b. whether it is inherited from the mother or the father.
   c. whether it or another allele determines the phenotype when both are present.
   d. whether or not it is linked to other genes.

5. Two fruit flies with eyes of the usual red color are crossed, and their offspring are as follows: 77 red-eyed males, 71 ruby-eyed males, 152 red-eyed females. The gene that controls whether eyes are red or ruby is _____, and the allele for ruby eyes is _____.
   a. autosomal (carried on an autosome); dominant
   b. autosomal; recessive
   c. sex-linked; dominant
   d. sex-linked; recessive

6. All the offspring of a white hen and a black rooster are gray. The simplest explanation for this pattern of inheritance is
   a. pleiotropy.
   b. sex linkage.
   c. codominance.
   d. incomplete dominance.

7. A man who has type B blood and a woman who has type A blood could have children of which of the following phenotypes? (*Hint*: Review Figure 9.20.)
   a. A, B, or O
   b. AB only
   c. AB or O
   d. A, B, AB, or O

8. Duchenne muscular dystrophy is a sex-linked recessive disorder characterized by a progressive loss of muscle tissue. Neither Rudy nor Carla has Duchenne muscular dystrophy, but their first son does have it. If the couple has a second child, what is the probability that he or she will also have the disease?

9. Adult height in people is at least partially hereditary; tall parents tend to have tall children. But people come in a range of sizes, not just tall or short. What extension of Mendel's model could produce this variation in height?

10. A purebred brown mouse is repeatedly mated with a purebred white mouse, and all their offspring are brown. If two of these brown offspring are mated, what fraction of the F_2 mice will be brown?

11. How could you determine the genotype of one of the brown F_2 mice in problem 10? How would you know whether a brown mouse is homozygous? Heterozygous?

12. Tim and Jan both have freckles (a dominant trait), but their son Michael does not. Show with a Punnett square how this is possible. If Tim and Jan have two more children, what is the probability that *both* of them will have freckles?

13. Incomplete dominance is seen in the inheritance of hypercholesterolemia. Mack and Toni are both heterozygous for this character, and both have elevated levels of cholesterol. Their daughter Katerina has a cholesterol level six times normal; she is apparently homozygous, *hh*. What fraction of Mack and Toni's children are likely to have elevated but not extreme levels of cholesterol, like their parents? If Mack and Toni have one more child, what is the probability that the child will suffer from the more serious form of hypercholesterolemia seen in Katerina?

14. Why was Henry VIII wrong to blame his wives for always producing daughters?

15. Both parents of a boy are phenotypically normal, but their son suffers from hemophilia, a sex-linked recessive disorder. Draw a pedigree that shows the genotypes of the three individuals. What fraction of the couple's children are likely to suffer from hemophilia? What fraction are likely to be carriers?

16. Heather was surprised to discover that she suffered from red-green colorblindness. She told her biology professor, who said, "Your father is colorblind, too, right?" How did her professor know this? Why did her professor not say the same thing to the colorblind males in the class?

17. In rabbits, black hair depends on a dominant allele, *B*, and brown hair on a recessive allele, *b*. Short hair is due to a dominant allele, *S*, and long hair to a recessive allele, *s*. If a true-breeding black short-haired male is mated with a brown long-haired female, describe their offspring. What will be the genotypes of the offspring? If two of these F_1 rabbits are mated, what phenotypes would you expect among their offspring? In what proportions?

Answers to these questions can be found in Appendix: Self-Quiz Answers.

THE PROCESS OF SCIENCE

18. In 1981, a stray cat with unusual curled-back ears was adopted by a family in Lakewood, California. Hundreds of descendants of this cat have since been born, and cat fanciers hope to develop the "curl" cat into a show breed. The curl allele is apparently dominant and carried on an autosome. Suppose you owned the first curl cat and wanted to develop a purebred variety. Describe tests that would determine whether the curl gene is dominant or recessive and whether it is autosomal or sex-linked.

19. Interpreting Data As shown in the Punnett square below, one variety of deafness is caused by an autosomal recessive allele. Two parents who do not show any signs of the disease but are carriers could therefore have a child who is deaf, because that child could inherit one recessive deafness-causing gene from each parent. Imagine that a deaf male mates with a hearing female. We know the deaf male must have the genotype *dd*, but the female could be either *Dd* or *DD*. Such a mating is essentially a testcross, like the one shown in Figure 9.10. If the parents' first child has hearing, can you say with certainty what the mother's genotype must be? What if the couple has four children (none twins), all with hearing—can you say with certainty the mother's genotype? What would it take for a definitive genotype to be assigned?

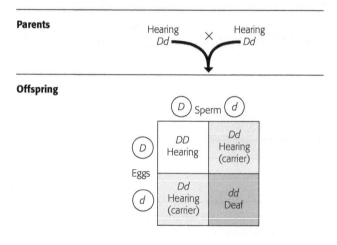

BIOLOGY AND SOCIETY

20. There are now nearly 200 recognized breeds of dog, from the Affenpinscher to the Yorkshire Terrier. But several of these suffer from medical problems due to the inbreeding required to establish the breed. For example, nearly every Cavalier King Charles (discussed in the Biology and Society essay) suffers from heart murmurs caused

by a genetically defective heart valve. Such problems are likely to remain as long as the organizations that oversee dog breeding maintain strict pedigree requirements. Some people are suggesting that every breed be allowed to mix with others to help introduce new gene lines free of the congenital defects. Why do you think the governing societies are resistant to such cross-breed mixing? What would you do if you were in charge of addressing the genetic defects that currently plague some breeds?

21. Gregor Mendel never saw a gene, yet he concluded that some inherited factors were responsible for the patterns of inheritance he observed in peas. Similarly, maps of *Drosophila* chromosomes (and the very idea that genes are carried on chromosomes) were conceived by observing the patterns of inheritance of linked genes, not by observing the genes directly. Is it legitimate for biologists to claim the existence of objects and processes they cannot actually see? How do scientists know whether an explanation is correct?

22. Many infertile couples turn to in vitro fertilization to try to have a baby. In this technique, sperm and ova are collected and used to create eight-cell embryos for implantation into a woman's uterus. At the eight-cell stage, one of the fetal cells can be removed without causing harm to the developing fetus. Once removed, the cell can be genetically tested. Some couples may know that a particular genetic disease runs in their family. They might wish to avoid implanting any embryos with the disease-causing genes. Do you think this is an acceptable use of genetic testing? What if a couple wanted to use genetic testing to select embryos for traits unrelated to disease, such as freckles? Do you think that couples undergoing in vitro fertilization should be allowed to perform whatever genetic tests they wish? Or do you think that there should be limits on what tests can be performed? How do you draw the line between genetic tests that are acceptable and those that are not?

10 The Structure and Function of DNA

A single molecular "typo" in DNA can result in a life-threatening disease.

Because all life on Earth shares a universal genetic code, your DNA could be used to genetically modify a monkey.

Mad cow disease is caused by an abnormal molecule of protein.

Enzymes help maintain the integrity of your DNA to greater than 99.999% accuracy.

The Deadliest Virus BIOLOGY AND SOCIETY

The First 21st-Century Pandemic

In 2009, a cluster of unusual flu cases was reported in and around Mexico City. Despite a near total shutdown of the city, the new flu virus, called 2009 H1N1, quickly spread to California and Texas. This strain was originally misnamed the "swine flu"; in fact, pigs had little impact on the spread of this virus, which, like most flu viruses, is passed from person to person through respiratory fluids. Nonetheless, the new strain received heavy media attention and caused considerable worry among the general public. In June 2009, the World Health Organization (WHO) declared H1N1 to be the first influenza pandemic (global epidemic) of the 21st century; the last flu pandemic was in 1968. In response, the WHO unveiled a comprehensive effort to contain H1N1, including increased surveillance, development of rapid testing procedures, the issuance of travel warnings, recommendations for increased sanitation (hand washing, etc.), and the production, stockpiling, and distribution of antiviral drugs. By 2010, cases of H1N1 had been confirmed in 214 countries.

Scientists soon determined that H1N1 was a hybrid flu strain, created when a previously known flu virus (which itself originated through a combination of viruses from birds, swine, and people) mixed with an Asian swine flu virus. This novel combination of genes produced some unusual features in the H1N1 strain. Most significantly, it infected

The H1N1 influenza virus. Citizens of Russia try to protect themselves from H1N1 infection in late fall 2009.

young, healthy people, whereas the flu usually affects the elderly or people who are already sick. Many countries participated in the WHO-coordinated response, including widespread distribution of a new vaccine. As a result, the virus was contained, and WHO declared the pandemic over in August 2010. The WHO confirmed that this virus killed about 18,000 people, and estimates of the total number of unreported deaths topped 250,000.

You may wonder, What's the big deal about the flu? The flu is not merely a seasonal inconvenience. In fact, the influenza virus may be the deadliest pathogen known to science. In a typical year in the United States, more than 20,000 people die from influenza infection. And that is considered a good year. Once every few decades, a new flu strain explodes on the scene, causing pandemics and widespread death. H1N1 pales in comparison to the deadliest outbreak: the pandemic of 1918–1919, which in just 18 months killed 40 million people worldwide—that's more people than have died of AIDS since it was discovered more than 30 years ago. Given the nature of the threat, it's no surprise that health workers remain vigilant, always aware that a new and deadly flu virus may appear at any time.

The flu virus, like all viruses, consists of a relatively simple structure of nucleic acid (RNA in this case) and protein. Combating any virus requires a detailed understanding of life at the molecular level. In this chapter, we will explore the structure of DNA, how it replicates and mutates, and how it controls the cell by directing the synthesis of RNA and protein.

DNA: Structure and Replication

DNA was known to be a chemical component of cells by the late 1800s, but Gregor Mendel and other early geneticists did their work without any knowledge of DNA's role in heredity. By the late 1930s, experimental studies had convinced most biologists that one specific kind of molecule, rather than a complex chemical mixture, is the basis of inheritance. Attention focused on chromosomes, which were already known to carry genes. By the 1940s, scientists knew that chromosomes consist of two types of chemicals: DNA and protein. And by the early 1950s, a series of discoveries had convinced the scientific world that DNA was the molecule that acts as the hereditary material. This breakthrough ushered in the field of **molecular biology**, the study of heredity at the molecular level.

What came next was one of the most celebrated quests in the history of science: the effort to figure out the structure of DNA. A good deal was already known about DNA. Scientists had identified all its atoms and knew how they were bonded to one another. What was not understood was the specific three-dimensional arrangement of atoms that gives DNA its unique properties—the capacity to store genetic information, copy it, and pass it from generation to generation. The race was on to discover the link between the structure and function of this important molecule. We will describe that momentous discovery shortly. First, let's review the underlying chemical structure of DNA and its chemical cousin RNA.

DNA and RNA Structure

Both DNA and RNA are nucleic acids, which consist of long chains (polymers) of chemical units (monomers) called **nucleotides**. (For an in-depth refresher, see Figures 3.21–3.25.) A diagram of a nucleotide polymer, or **polynucleotide**, is shown in Figure 10.1. Polynucleotides can be very long and may have any sequence of the four different types of nucleotides (abbreviated A, C, T, and G), so a tremendous variety of polynucleotide chains is possible.

Nucleotides are joined together by covalent bonds between the sugar of one nucleotide and the phosphate of the next. This results in a repeating pattern of sugar-phosphate-sugar-phosphate, which is known as a **sugar-phosphate backbone**. The nitrogenous bases are arranged like ribs that project from this backbone. You can think of a polynucleotide as a long ladder split in

DNA double helix

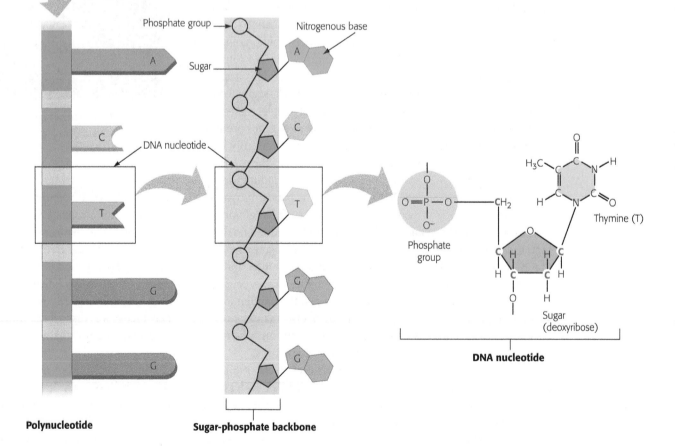

► Figure 10.1 **The chemical structure of a DNA polynucleotide.** A molecule of DNA contains two polynucleotides, each a chain of nucleotides. Each nucleotide consists of a nitrogenous base, a sugar (blue), and a phosphate group (gold).

Polynucleotide

Sugar-phosphate backbone

half longwise, with rungs that come in four colors. The sugars and phosphates make up the side of the ladder, with the sugars acting as the half-rungs.

Moving from left to right across Figure 10.1, we can zoom in to see that each nucleotide consists of three components: a nitrogenous base, a sugar (blue), and a phosphate group (gold). Examining a single nucleotide even more closely, we see the chemical structure of its three components. The phosphate group, with a phosphorus atom (P) at its center, is the source of the *acid* in nucleic acid. Each phosphate has a negative charge on one of its oxygen atoms. The sugar has five carbon atoms (shown in red): four in its ring and one extending above the ring. The ring also includes an oxygen atom. The sugar is called *deoxyribose* because, compared with the sugar ribose, it is missing an oxygen atom. The full name for **DNA** is *deoxyribonucleic acid*, with *nucleic* referring to DNA's location in the nuclei of eukaryotic cells. The nitrogenous base (thymine, in our example) has a ring of nitrogen and carbon atoms with various chemical groups attached. Nitrogenous bases are basic (having a high pH, the opposite of acidic), hence their name.

The four nucleotides found in DNA differ only in their nitrogenous bases (see Figure 3.23 for a review).

The bases can be divided into two types. **Thymine (T)** and **cytosine (C)** are single-ring structures. **Adenine (A)** and **guanine (G)** are larger, double-ring structures. Instead of thymine, RNA has a similar base called **uracil (U).** And RNA contains a slightly different sugar than DNA (ribose instead of deoxyribose, accounting for the names RNA vs. DNA). Other than that, RNA and DNA polynucleotides have the same chemical structure. **Figure 10.2** is a computer graphic of a piece of RNA polynucleotide about 20 nucleotides long. ☑

▶ **Figure 10.2** **An RNA polynucleotide.** The yellow used for the phosphorus atoms and the blue of the sugar atoms make it easy to spot the sugar-phosphate backbone.

☑ **CHECKPOINT**

Compare and contrast the chemical components of DNA and RNA.

Answer: Both are polymers of nucleotides (a sugar + a nitrogenous base + a phosphate group). In RNA, the sugar is ribose; in DNA, it is deoxyribose. Both RNA and DNA have the bases A, G, and C, but DNA has T and RNA has U.

Watson and Crick's Discovery of the Double Helix

The celebrated partnership that solved the puzzle of DNA structure began soon after a 23-year-old newly minted American Ph.D. named James D. Watson journeyed to Cambridge University in England. There, a more senior scientist, Francis Crick, was studying protein structure with a technique called X-ray crystallography. While visiting the laboratory of Maurice Wilkins at King's College in London, Watson saw an X-ray image of DNA produced by Wilkins's colleague Rosalind Franklin. The data produced by Franklin turned out to be the key to the puzzle. A careful study of the image enabled Watson to figure out that the basic shape of DNA is a helix (spiral) with a uniform diameter. The thickness of the helix suggested that it was made up of two polynucleotide strands—in other words, a **double helix**. But how were the nucleotides arranged in the double helix?

Using wire models, Watson and Crick began trying to construct a double helix that conformed to all known data about DNA **(Figure 10.3)**. Watson placed the backbones on the outside of the model, forcing the nitrogenous bases to swivel to the interior of the molecule. As he did this, it occurred to him that the four kinds of bases must pair in a specific way. This idea of specific base pairing was a flash of inspiration that enabled Watson and Crick to solve the DNA puzzle.

▼ **Figure 10.3** **Discoverers of the double helix.**

James Watson (left) and **Francis Crick.** The discoverers of the structure of DNA are shown in 1953 with their model of the double helix.

Rosalind Franklin Using X-rays, Franklin generated some of the key data that provided insight into the structure of DNA.

At first, Watson imagined that the bases paired like with like—for example, A with A, C with C. But that kind of pairing did not fit with the fact that the DNA molecule has a uniform diameter. An AA pair (made of two double-ringed bases) would be almost twice as wide as a CC pair (made of two single-ringed bases), resulting in an uneven molecule. It soon became apparent that a double-ringed base on one strand must always be paired with a single-ringed base on the opposite strand. Moreover, Watson and Crick realized that the chemical structure of each kind of base dictated the pairings even more specifically.

Each base has protruding chemical groups that can best form hydrogen bonds with just one appropriate partner. This would be like having four colors of snap-together puzzle pieces and realizing that only certain colors can snap together (e.g., red can only snap together with blue). Similarly, adenine can best form hydrogen bonds with thymine, and guanine with cytosine. In the biologist's shorthand: A pairs with T, and G pairs with C. A is also said to be "complementary" to T, and G to C.

If you imagine a polynucleotide strand as a half ladder, then you can picture the model of the DNA double helix proposed by Watson and Crick as a full ladder twisted into a spiral (Figure 10.4). Figure 10.5 shows three more detailed representations of the double helix. The ribbonlike diagram in Figure 10.5a symbolizes the bases with shapes that emphasize their complementarity. Figure 10.5b is a more chemically precise version showing only four base pairs, with the helix untwisted and the individual hydrogen bonds specified by dashed lines. Figure 10.5c is a computer model showing part of a double helix in detail.

Although the base-pairing rules dictate the side-by-side combinations of bases that form the rungs of the double helix, they place no restrictions on the sequence of nucleotides along the length of a DNA strand. In fact, the sequence of bases can vary in countless ways.

In 1953, Watson and Crick rocked the scientific world with a succinct paper proposing their molecular model for

▶ Figure 10.4 **A rope-ladder model of a double helix.** The ropes at the sides represent the sugar-phosphate backbones. Each rung stands for a pair of bases connected by hydrogen bonds.

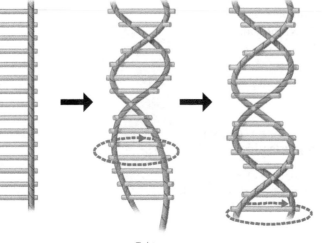

Twist

▼ Figure 10.5 **Three representations of DNA.**

Hydrogen bond

(a) Ribbon model. The sugar-phosphate backbones are blue ribbons, and the bases are complementary shapes in shades of green and orange.

(b) Atomic model. In this more chemically detailed structure, you can see the individual hydrogen bonds (dashed lines). You can also see that the strands run in opposite directions: Notice that the sugars on the two strands are upside down with respect to each other.

(c) Computer model. Each atom is shown as a sphere, creating a space-filling model.

DNA. Few milestones in the history of biology have had as broad an impact as their double helix, with its A-T and C-G base pairing. In 1962, Watson, Crick, and Wilkins received the Nobel Prize for their work. (Franklin deserved a share of the prize, but she had died from cancer in 1958, and Nobel prizes are never granted posthumously.)

In their 1953 paper, Watson and Crick wrote that the structure they proposed "immediately suggests a possible copying mechanism for the genetic material." In other words, the structure of DNA points toward a molecular explanation for life's unique properties of reproduction and inheritance. Understanding how the arrangement of parts within DNA affects it actions within a cell is an excellent example of biology's important theme of the relationship of structure to function, as we see next.

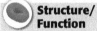 **Structure/ Function**

DNA Replication

Every cell contains a DNA "cookbook" that provides complete information on how to make and maintain that cell. When a cell reproduces, it must duplicate this information, providing one copy to the new offspring cell while keeping one copy for itself. Thus, each cell must have a means of copying the DNA instructions. In a clear demonstration of how the structure of a biological system can provide insight into its function, Watson and Crick's model of DNA suggests that each DNA strand serves as a mold, or template, to guide reproduction of the other strand. If you know the sequence of bases in one strand of the double helix, you can very easily determine the sequence of bases in the other strand by applying the base-pairing rules: A pairs with T (and T with A), and G pairs with C (and C with G). For example, if one polynucleotide has the sequence AGTC, then the complementary polynucleotide in that DNA molecule must have the sequence TCAG.

Figure 10.6 shows how this model can account for the direct copying of a piece of DNA. The two strands of parental DNA separate, and each becomes a template for the assembly of a complementary strand from a supply of free nucleotides. The nucleotides are lined up one at a time along the template strand in accordance with the base-pairing rules. Enzymes link the nucleotides to form new DNA strands. The completed new molecules, identical to the parental molecule, are known as daughter DNA molecules (no gender should be inferred from this name).

The process of DNA replication requires the co-operation of more than a dozen enzymes and other proteins. The enzymes that make the covalent bonds between the nucleotides of a new DNA strand are called **DNA polymerases**. As an incoming nucleotide

Enzymes help maintain the integrity of your DNA to greater than 99.999% accuracy.

base-pairs with its complement on the template strand, a DNA polymerase adds it to the end of the growing daughter strand. The process is both fast (a rate of 50 nucleotides per second is typical) and amazingly accurate, with fewer than one in a billion bases incorrectly paired. In addition to their roles in DNA replication, DNA polymerases and some of the associated proteins can repair DNA that has been damaged by toxic chemicals or high-energy radiation, such as X-rays and ultraviolet light.

DNA replication begins on a double helix at specific sites, called origins of replication. Replication then proceeds in both directions, creating what are called replication "bubbles" (Figure 10.7). The parental DNA strands open up as daughter strands elongate on both sides of each bubble. The DNA molecule of a typical eukaryotic chromosome has many origins where replication can start simultaneously, shortening the total time needed for the process. Eventually, all the bubbles merge, yielding two completed double-stranded daughter DNA molecules.

DNA replication ensures that all the body cells in a multicellular organism carry the same genetic information. It is also the means by which genetic information is passed along to offspring. ☑

Parental (old) DNA molecule

Daughter (new) strand

Parental (old) strand

Daughter DNA molecules (double helices)

▲ Figure 10.6 **DNA replication.** Replication results in two daughter DNA molecules, each consisting of one old strand and one new strand. The parental DNA untwists as its strands separate, and the daughter DNA rewinds as it forms.

▼ Figure 10.7 **Multiple "bubbles" in replicating DNA.**

Origin of replication
Origin of replication
Parental strands

Origin of replication
Parental strand
Daughter strand

Bubble

Two daughter DNA molecules

☑ CHECKPOINT

1. How does complementary base pairing make DNA replication possible?
2. What enzymes connect nucleotides together during DNA replication?

Answers: 1. When the two strands of the double helix separate, each serves as a template on which nucleotides can be arranged by specific base pairing into new complementary strands. 2. DNA polymerases

Information Flow

From DNA to RNA to Protein

Now that we've seen how the structure of DNA allows it to be copied, let's explore how DNA provides instructions to a cell and to an organism as a whole.

How an Organism's Genotype Determines Its Phenotype

We can now define genotype and phenotype (terms first introduced in Chapter 9) with regard to the structure and function of DNA. An organism's *genotype*, its genetic makeup, is the heritable information contained in the sequence of nucleotide bases in its DNA. The *phenotype*, the organism's physical traits, arises from the actions of a wide variety of proteins. For example, structural proteins help make up the body of an organism, and enzymes catalyze the chemical reactions that are necessary for life.

DNA specifies the synthesis of proteins. However, a gene does not build a protein directly. Instead, DNA dispatches instructions in the form of RNA, which in turn programs protein synthesis. This fundamental concept in biology is summarized in Figure 10.8. The molecular "chain of command" is from DNA in the nucleus (purple area in the figure) to RNA to protein synthesis in the cytoplasm (blue area). The two stages are **transcription**, the transfer of genetic information from DNA into an RNA molecule, and **translation**, the transfer of the information from RNA into a polypeptide (protein strand). The relationship between genes and proteins is thus one of information flow: The function of a DNA gene is to dictate the production of a polypeptide. ✅

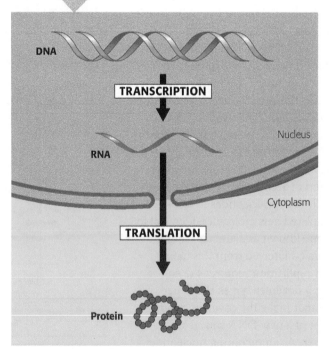

▼ Figure 10.8 **The flow of genetic information in a eukaryotic cell.** A sequence of nucleotides in the DNA is transcribed into a molecule of RNA in the cell's nucleus. The RNA travels to the cytoplasm, where it is translated into the specific amino acid sequence of a protein.

DNA

TRANSCRIPTION

RNA

Nucleus

Cytoplasm

TRANSLATION

Protein

From Nucleotides to Amino Acids: An Overview

Genetic information in DNA is transcribed into RNA and then translated into polypeptides, which then fold into proteins. But how do these processes occur? Transcription and translation are linguistic terms, and it is useful to think of nucleic acids and proteins as having languages. To understand how genetic information passes from genotype to phenotype, we need to see how the chemical language of DNA is translated into the different chemical language of proteins.

What exactly is the language of nucleic acids? Both DNA and RNA are polymers made of nucleotide monomers strung together in specific sequences that convey information, much as specific sequences of letters convey information in English. In DNA, the monomers are the four types of nucleotides, which differ in their nitrogenous bases (A, T, C, and G). The same is true for RNA, although it has the base U instead of T.

The language of DNA is written as a linear sequence of nucleotide bases, such as the blue sequence you see on the enlarged DNA strand in Figure 10.9. Every gene is made up of a specific sequence of bases, with special sequences marking the beginning and the end. A typical gene is a few thousand nucleotides in length.

When a segment of DNA is transcribed, the result is an RNA molecule. The process is called transcription because the nucleic acid language of DNA has simply been rewritten (transcribed) as a sequence of bases of RNA; the language is still that of nucleic acids. The nucleotide bases of the RNA molecule are complementary to those on the DNA strand. As you will soon see, this is because the RNA was synthesized using the DNA as a template.

Translation is the conversion of the nucleic acid language to the polypeptide language. Like nucleic acids, polypeptides are straight polymers, but the monomers that make them up—the letters of the polypeptide alphabet—are the 20 amino acids common to all organisms (represented as purple shapes in Figure 10.9). The sequence of nucleotides of the RNA molecule dictates the sequence of amino acids of the polypeptide. But remember, RNA is only a messenger; the genetic information that dictates the amino acid sequence originates in DNA.

What are the rules for translating the RNA message into a polypeptide? In other words, what is the correspondence between the nucleotides of an RNA molecule and the amino acids of a polypeptide? Keep in mind that there are only four different kinds of nucleotides in DNA (A, G, C, T) and RNA (A, G, C, U). During translation, these four must somehow specify 20 amino acids. If each nucleotide base coded for one amino acid, only 4 of the 20 amino acids could be accounted for. In fact, triplets of bases are the smallest "words" of uniform length that can specify all the amino acids. There can be 64 (that is, 4^3) possible code words of this type—more than enough to specify the 20 amino acids. Indeed, there are enough triplets to allow more than one coding for each amino acid. For example, the base triplets AAA and AAG both code for the same amino acid.

Experiments have verified that the flow of information from gene to protein is based on a triplet code. The genetic instructions for the amino acid sequence of a polypeptide chain are written in DNA and RNA as a series of three-base words called **codons**. Three-base codons in the DNA are transcribed into complementary three-base codons in the RNA, and then the RNA codons are translated into amino acids that form a polypeptide. As summarized in Figure 10.9, one DNA codon (three nucleotides) → one RNA codon (three nucleotides) → one amino acid. Next we turn to the codons themselves. ☑

☑ **CHECKPOINT**

How many nucleotides are necessary to code for a polypeptide that is 100 amino acids long?

Answer: 300

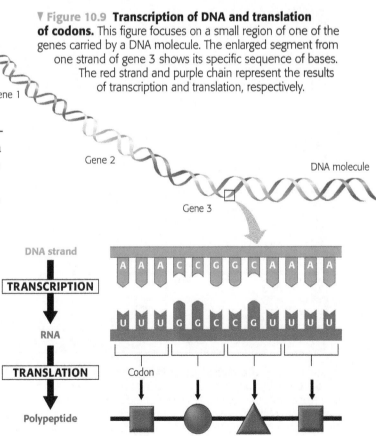

▼ Figure 10.9 **Transcription of DNA and translation of codons.** This figure focuses on a small region of one of the genes carried by a DNA molecule. The enlarged segment from one strand of gene 3 shows its specific sequence of bases. The red strand and purple chain represent the results of transcription and translation, respectively.

Gene 1

Gene 2

Gene 3

DNA molecule

DNA strand

TRANSCRIPTION

RNA

TRANSLATION

Polypeptide

A A A C C G G C A A A A

U U U G G C C G U U U U

Codon

Amino acid

The Genetic Code

The **genetic code** is the set of rules that convert a nucleotide sequence in RNA to an amino acid sequence. As Figure 10.10 shows, 61 of the 64 triplets code for amino acids. The triplet AUG has a dual function: It codes for the amino acid methionine (abbreviated Met) and can also provide a signal for the start of a polypeptide chain. Three codons (UAA, UAG, and UGA) do not designate amino acids. They are the stop codons that instruct the ribosomes to end the polypeptide.

Notice in Figure 10.10 that a given RNA triplet always specifies a given amino acid. For example, although codons UUU and UUC both specify phenylalanine (Phe), neither of them ever represents any other amino acid. The codons in the figure are the triplets found in RNA. They have a straightforward, complementary relationship to the codons in DNA. The nucleotides making up the codons occur in a linear order along the DNA and RNA, with no gaps separating the codons.

The genetic code is nearly universal, shared by organisms from the simplest bacteria to the most complex plants and animals. The universality of the genetic vocabulary suggests that it arose very early in evolution and was passed on over the eons to all the organisms living on Earth today. In fact, such universality is the key to modern DNA technologies. Because diverse organisms share a common genetic code, it is possible to program one species to produce a protein from another species by transplanting DNA (Figure 10.11). This allows scientists to mix and match genes from various species—a procedure with many useful genetic engineering applications in agriculture, medicine, and research (see Chapter 12 for further discussion of genetic engineering). Besides having practical purposes, a shared genetic vocabulary also reminds us of the evolutionary kinship that connects all life on Earth. ☑

> Because all life on Earth shares a universal genetic code, your DNA could be used to genetically modify a monkey.

▼ Figure 10.11 **A pig expressing a foreign gene.** The glowing porker in the middle was created when researchers incorporated a jelly (jellyfish) gene for a protein called green fluorescent protein (GFP) into the DNA of a standard pig.

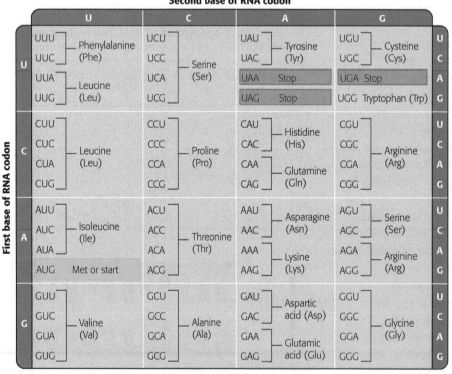

Second base of RNA codon

	U	C	A	G	
U	UUU ⎫ Phenylalanine (Phe) UUC ⎭ UUA ⎫ Leucine (Leu) UUG ⎭	UCU ⎫ UCC ⎪ Serine (Ser) UCA ⎪ UCG ⎭	UAU ⎫ Tyrosine (Tyr) UAC ⎭ UAA Stop UAG Stop	UGU ⎫ Cysteine (Cys) UGC ⎭ UGA Stop UGG Tryptophan (Trp)	U C A G
C	CUU ⎫ CUC ⎪ Leucine (Leu) CUA ⎪ CUG ⎭	CCU ⎫ CCC ⎪ Proline (Pro) CCA ⎪ CCG ⎭	CAU ⎫ Histidine (His) CAC ⎭ CAA ⎫ Glutamine (Gln) CAG ⎭	CGU ⎫ CGC ⎪ Arginine (Arg) CGA ⎪ CGG ⎭	U C A G
A	AUU ⎫ AUC ⎪ Isoleucine (Ile) AUA ⎭ AUG Met or start	ACU ⎫ ACC ⎪ Threonine (Thr) ACA ⎪ ACG ⎭	AAU ⎫ Asparagine (Asn) AAC ⎭ AAA ⎫ Lysine (Lys) AAG ⎭	AGU ⎫ Serine (Ser) AGC ⎭ AGA ⎫ Arginine (Arg) AGG ⎭	U C A G
G	GUU ⎫ GUC ⎪ Valine (Val) GUA ⎪ GUG ⎭	GCU ⎫ GCC ⎪ Alanine (Ala) GCA ⎪ GCG ⎭	GAU ⎫ Aspartic acid (Asp) GAC ⎭ GAA ⎫ Glutamic acid (Glu) GAG ⎭	GGU ⎫ GGC ⎪ Glycine (Gly) GGA ⎪ GGG ⎭	U C A G

First base of RNA codon / Third base of RNA codon

▲ Figure 10.10 **The dictionary of the genetic code, listed by RNA codons.** Practice using this dictionary by finding the codon UGG. (It is the only codon for the amino acid tryptophan, Trp.) Notice that the codon AUG (highlighted in green) not only stands for the amino acid methionine (Met), but also functions as a signal to "start" translating the RNA at that place. Three of the 64 codons (highlighted in red) function as "stop" signals that mark the end of a genetic message, but do not encode any amino acids.

Transcription: From DNA to RNA

Let's look more closely at transcription, the transfer of genetic information from DNA to RNA. If you think of your DNA as a cookbook, then transcription is the process of copying one recipe onto an index card (a molecule of RNA) for immediate use. Figure 10.12a is a close-up view of this process. As with DNA replication, the two DNA strands must first separate at the place where the process will start. In transcription, however, only one of the DNA strands serves as a template for the newly forming RNA molecule; the other strand is unused. The nucleotides that make up the new RNA molecule take their place one at a time along the DNA template strand by forming hydrogen bonds with the nucleotide bases there. Notice that the RNA nucleotides follow the usual base-pairing rules, except that U, rather than T, pairs with A. The RNA nucleotides are linked by the transcription enzyme **RNA polymerase**.

Figure 10.12b is an overview of the transcription of an entire gene. Special sequences of DNA nucleotides tell the RNA polymerase where to start and where to stop the transcribing process.

❶ Initiation of Transcription

The "start transcribing" signal is a nucleotide sequence called a **promoter**, which is located in the DNA at the beginning of the gene. A promoter is a specific place where RNA polymerase attaches. The first phase of transcription, called initiation, is the attachment of RNA polymerase to the promoter and the start of RNA synthesis. For any gene, the promoter dictates which of the two DNA strands is to be transcribed (the particular strand varies from gene to gene).

❷ RNA Elongation

During the second phase of transcription, elongation, the RNA grows longer. As RNA synthesis continues, the RNA strand peels away from its DNA template, allowing the two separated DNA strands to come back together in the region already transcribed.

❸ Termination of Transcription

In the third phase, termination, the RNA polymerase reaches a special sequence of bases in the DNA template called a **terminator**. This sequence signals the end of the gene. At this point, the polymerase molecule detaches from the RNA molecule and the gene, and the DNA strands rejoin.

In addition to producing RNA that encodes amino acid sequences, transcription makes two other kinds of RNA that are involved in building polypeptides. We discuss these kinds of RNA a little later. ☑

☑ CHECKPOINT

How does RNA polymerase "know" where to start transcribing a gene?

Answer: It recognizes the gene's promoter, a specific nucleotide sequence.

▼ Figure 10.12 **Transcription.**

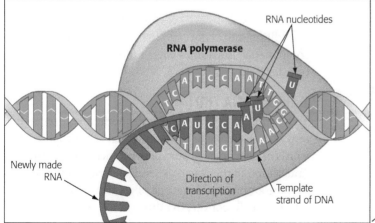

(a) A close-up view of transcription. As RNA nucleotides base-pair one by one with DNA bases on one DNA strand (called the template strand), the enzyme RNA polymerase (orange) links the RNA nucleotides into an RNA chain.

(b) Transcription of a gene. The transcription of an entire gene occurs in three phases: initiation, elongation, and termination of the RNA. The section of DNA where the RNA polymerase starts is called the promoter; the place where it stops is called the terminator.

The Processing of Eukaryotic RNA

In the cells of prokaryotes, which lack nuclei, the RNA transcribed from a gene immediately functions as **messenger RNA (mRNA)**, the molecule that is translated into protein. But this is not the case in eukaryotic cells. The eukaryotic cell not only localizes transcription in the nucleus but also modifies, or processes, the RNA transcripts there before they move to the cytoplasm for translation by the ribosomes.

One kind of RNA processing is the addition of extra nucleotides to the ends of the RNA transcript. These additions, called the **cap** and **tail**, protect the RNA from attack by cellular enzymes and help ribosomes recognize the RNA as mRNA.

Another type of RNA processing is made necessary in eukaryotes by noncoding stretches of nucleotides that interrupt the nucleotides that actually code for amino acids. It is as if nonsense words were randomly interspersed within a recipe that you copied. Most genes of plants and animals, it turns out, include such internal noncoding regions, which are called **introns**. The coding regions—the parts of a gene that are expressed—are called **exons**. As Figure 10.13 illustrates, both exons and introns are transcribed from DNA into RNA. However, before the RNA leaves the nucleus, the introns are removed, and the exons are joined to produce an mRNA molecule with a continuous coding sequence. This process is called **RNA splicing**. RNA splicing is believed to play a significant role in humans in allowing our approximately 21,000 genes to produce many thousands more

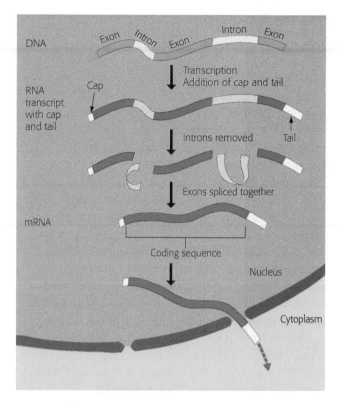

▲ Figure 10.13 **The production of messenger RNA (mRNA) in a eukaryotic cell.** Note that the molecule of mRNA that leaves the nucleus is substantially different from the molecule of RNA that was first transcribed from the gene. In the cytoplasm, the coding sequence of the final mRNA will be translated.

polypeptides. This is accomplished by varying the exons that are included in the final mRNA.

With capping, tailing, and splicing completed, the "final draft" of eukaryotic mRNA is ready for translation. ☑

☑ **CHECKPOINT**
Why is a final mRNA often shorter than the DNA gene that coded for it?

Answer: because introns are removed from the RNA

Translation: The Players

As we have already discussed, translation is a conversion between different languages—from the nucleic acid language to the protein language—and it involves more elaborate machinery than transcription.

Messenger RNA (mRNA)
The first important ingredient required for translation is the mRNA produced by transcription. Once it is present, the machinery used to translate mRNA requires enzymes and sources of chemical energy, such as ATP. In addition, translation requires two other important components: ribosomes and a kind of RNA called transfer RNA.

Transfer RNA (tRNA)
Translation of any language into another requires an interpreter, someone or something that can recognize the words of one language and convert them to the other. Translation of the genetic message carried in mRNA into the amino acid language of proteins also requires an interpreter. To convert the three-letter words (codons) of nucleic acids to the amino acid words of proteins, a cell uses a molecular interpreter, a type of RNA called **transfer RNA (tRNA)**, depicted in Figure 10.14.

▼ Figure 10.14 **The structure of tRNA.** At one end of the tRNA is the site where an amino acid will attach (purple), and at the other end is the three-nucleotide anticodon where the mRNA will attach (light green).

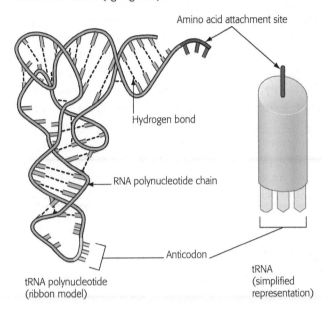

Amino acid attachment site

Hydrogen bond

RNA polynucleotide chain

Anticodon

tRNA polynucleotide
(ribbon model)

tRNA
(simplified
representation)

Ribosomes

Ribosomes are the organelles in the cytoplasm that coordinate the functioning of mRNA and tRNA and actually make polypeptides. As you can see in **Figure 10.15a**, a ribosome consists of two subunits. Each subunit is made up of proteins and a considerable amount of yet another kind of RNA, **ribosomal RNA (rRNA)**. A fully assembled ribosome has a binding site for mRNA on its small subunit and binding sites for tRNA on its large subunit. **Figure 10.15b** shows how two tRNA molecules get together with an mRNA molecule on a ribosome. One of the tRNA binding sites, the P site, holds the tRNA carrying the growing polypeptide chain, while another, the A site, holds a tRNA carrying the next amino acid to be added to the chain. The anticodon on each tRNA base-pairs with a codon on the mRNA. The subunits of the ribosome act like a vise, holding the tRNA and mRNA molecules close together. The ribosome can then connect the amino acid from the tRNA in the A site to the growing polypeptide. ☑

☑ **CHECKPOINT**

What is an anticodon?

Answer: An anticodon is the base triplet of a tRNA molecule that couples the tRNA to a complementary codon in the mRNA. The base pairing of anticodon to codon is a key step in translating mRNA to a polypeptide.

A cell that is producing proteins has in its cytoplasm a supply of amino acids. But amino acids themselves cannot recognize the codons arranged in sequence along messenger RNA. It is up to the cell's molecular interpreters, tRNA molecules, to match amino acids to the appropriate codons to form the new polypeptide. To perform this task, tRNA molecules must carry out two distinct functions: (1) pick up the appropriate amino acids and (2) recognize the appropriate codons in the mRNA. The unique structure of tRNA molecules enables them to perform both tasks.

As shown on the left in Figure 10.14, a tRNA molecule is made of a single strand of RNA—one polynucleotide chain—consisting of about 80 nucleotides. The chain twists and folds upon itself, forming several double-stranded regions in which short stretches of RNA base-pair with other stretches. At one end of the folded molecule is a special triplet of bases called an **anticodon**. The anticodon triplet is complementary to a codon triplet on mRNA. During translation, the anticodon on the tRNA recognizes a particular codon on the mRNA by using base-pairing rules. At the other end of the tRNA molecule is a site where one specific kind of amino acid attaches. Although all tRNA molecules are similar, there are slightly different versions of tRNA for each amino acid.

▼ Figure 10.15 **The ribosome.**

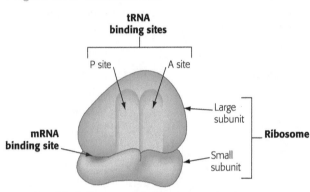

tRNA
binding sites

P site   A site

mRNA
binding site

Large
subunit

Small
subunit

Ribosome

(a) A simplified diagram of a ribosome. Notice the two subunits and sites where mRNA and tRNA molecules bind.

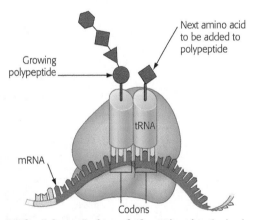

Growing
polypeptide

Next amino acid
to be added to
polypeptide

mRNA

tRNA

Codons

(b) The "players" of translation. When functioning in polypeptide synthesis, a ribosome holds one molecule of mRNA and two molecules of tRNA. The growing polypeptide is attached to one of the tRNAs.

181

▼ Figure 10.16 **A molecule of mRNA.**

Cap

Start of genetic message

End

Tail

Translation: The Process

Translation is divided into the same three phases as transcription: initiation, elongation, and termination.

Initiation

This first phase brings together the mRNA, the first amino acid with its attached tRNA, and the two subunits of a ribosome. An mRNA molecule, even after splicing, is longer than the genetic message it carries (Figure 10.16). Nucleotide sequences at either end of the molecule (pink) are not part of the message, but along with the cap and tail in eukaryotes, they help the mRNA bind to the ribosome. The initiation process determines exactly where translation will begin so that the mRNA codons will be translated into the correct sequence of amino acids. Initiation occurs in two steps, as shown in Figure 10.17 ❶. An mRNA molecule binds to a small ribosomal subunit. A special initiator tRNA then binds to the **start codon**, where translation is to begin on the mRNA. The initiator tRNA carries the amino acid methionine (Met); its anticodon, UAC, binds to the start codon, AUG ❷. A large ribosomal subunit binds to the small one, creating a functional ribosome. The initiator tRNA fits into the P site on the ribosome.

Elongation

Once initiation is complete, amino acids are added one by one to the first amino acid. Each addition occurs in the three-step elongation process shown in Figure 10.18. ❶ The anticodon of an incoming tRNA molecule, carrying its amino acid, pairs with the mRNA codon in the A site of the ribosome. ❷ The polypeptide leaves the tRNA in the P site and attaches to the amino acid on the tRNA in the A site. The ribosome creates a new peptide bond. Now the chain has one more amino acid. ❸ The P site tRNA now leaves the ribosome, and the ribosome moves the remaining tRNA, carrying the growing polypeptide, to the P site. The mRNA and tRNA move as a unit. This movement brings into the A site the next mRNA codon to be translated, and the process can start again with step 1.

Termination

Elongation continues until a **stop codon** reaches the ribosome's A site. Stop codons—UAA, UAG, and UGA—do not code for amino acids but instead tell translation to stop. The completed polypeptide, typically several hundred amino acids long, is freed, and the ribosome splits back into its subunits. ☑

▼ Figure 10.17 **The initiation of translation.**

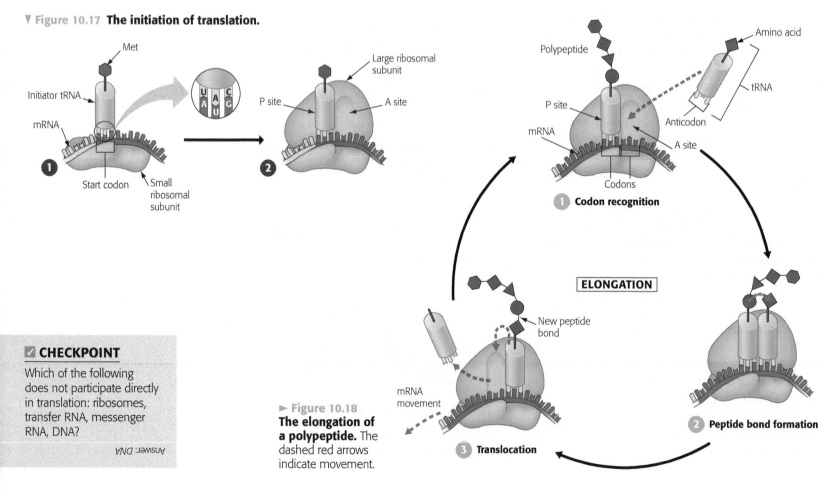

Met

Initiator tRNA

mRNA

❶

Start codon

Small ribosomal subunit

P site

A site

Large ribosomal subunit

❷

Polypeptide

Amino acid

tRNA

Anticodon

P site

mRNA

A site

Codons

❶ **Codon recognition**

ELONGATION

New peptide bond

mRNA movement

❸ **Translocation**

❷ **Peptide bond formation**

► Figure 10.18 **The elongation of a polypeptide.** The dashed red arrows indicate movement.

Review: DNA → RNA → Protein

Figure 10.19 reviews the flow of genetic information in the cell, from DNA to RNA to protein. In eukaryotic cells, transcription (DNA → RNA) occurs in the nucleus, and the RNA is processed before it enters the cytoplasm. Translation (RNA → protein) is rapid; a single ribosome can make an average-sized polypeptide in less than a minute. As it is made, a polypeptide coils and folds, assuming its final three-dimensional shape.

What is the overall significance of transcription and translation? These are the processes whereby genes control the structures and activities of cells—or, more broadly, the way the genotype produces the phenotype. The flow of information originates with the specific sequence of nucleotides in a DNA gene. The gene dictates the transcription of a complementary sequence of nucleotides in mRNA. In turn, the information within the mRNA specifies the sequence of amino acids in a polypeptide. Finally, the proteins that form from the polypeptides determine the appearance and capabilities of the cell and organism.

For decades, the DNA → RNA → protein pathway was believed to be the sole means by which genetic information controls traits. In recent years, however, this notion has been challenged by discoveries that point to more complex roles for RNA. (We will explore some of these special properties of RNA in Chapter 11.) ☑

☑ **CHECKPOINT**

1. Transcription is the synthesis of _____, using _____ as a template.
2. Translation is the synthesis of _____, with one _____ determining each amino acid in the sequence.
3. Which organelle coordinates translation?

Answers: 1. mRNA; DNA 2. protein (polypeptides); codon 3. ribosomes

▼ Figure 10.19 **A summary of transcription and translation.** This figure summarizes the main stages in the flow of genetic information from DNA to protein in a eukaryotic cell.

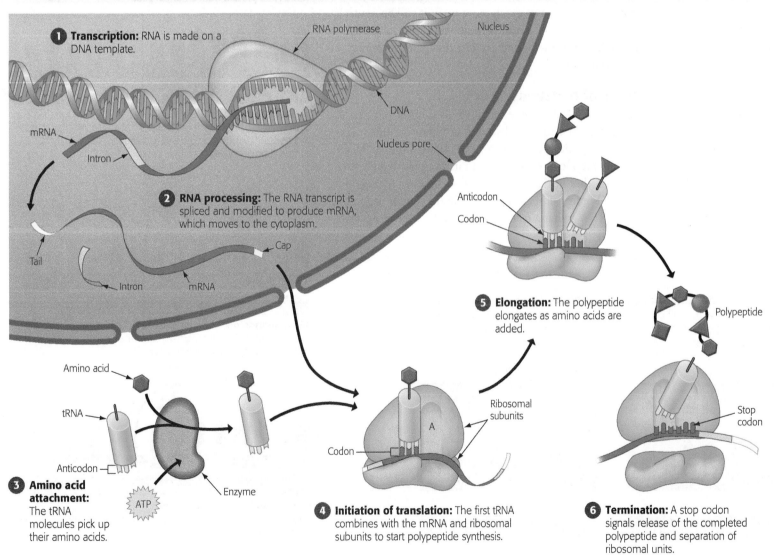

1 **Transcription:** RNA is made on a DNA template.

RNA polymerase

Nucleus

DNA

mRNA

Intron

Nucleus pore

2 **RNA processing:** The RNA transcript is spliced and modified to produce mRNA, which moves to the cytoplasm.

Anticodon

Codon

Tail

Cap

Intron

mRNA

5 **Elongation:** The polypeptide elongates as amino acids are added.

Polypeptide

Amino acid

tRNA

Ribosomal subunits

Stop codon

Anticodon

Codon

A

Codon

Enzyme

ATP

3 **Amino acid attachment:** The tRNA molecules pick up their amino acids.

4 **Initiation of translation:** The first tRNA combines with the mRNA and ribosomal subunits to start polypeptide synthesis.

6 **Termination:** A stop codon signals release of the completed polypeptide and separation of ribosomal units.

Mutations

Since discovering how genes are translated into proteins, scientists have been able to describe many heritable differences in molecular terms. For instance, sickle-cell disease can be traced to a change in a single amino acid in one of the polypeptides in the hemoglobin protein (see Figure 3.19). This difference is caused by a single nucleotide difference in the DNA coding for that polypeptide (Figure 10.20).

A single molecular "typo" in DNA can result in a life-threatening disease.

Any change in the nucleotide sequence of a cell's DNA is called a **mutation**. Mutations can involve large regions of a chromosome or just a single nucleotide pair, as in sickle-cell disease. Occasionally, a base substitution leads to an improved protein or one with new capabilities that enhance the success of the mutant organism and its descendants. Much more often, though, mutations are harmful. Think of a mutation as a typo in a recipe; occasionally, such a typo might lead to an improved recipe, but much more often it will be neutral, mildly bad, or disastrous. Let's consider how mutations involving only one or a few nucleotide pairs can affect gene translation.

Types of Mutations

Mutations within a gene can be divided into two general categories: nucleotide substitutions and nucleotide insertions or deletions (Figure 10.21). A substitution is the replacement of one nucleotide and its base-pairing partner with another nucleotide pair. For example, in the second row in Figure 10.21, A replaces G in the fourth codon of the mRNA. What effect can a substitution have? Because the genetic code is redundant, some substitution mutations have no effect at all. For example, if a mutation causes an mRNA codon to change from GAA to GAG, no change in the protein product would result because GAA and GAG both code for the same amino acid (Glu). Such a change is called a silent mutation. In our recipe example, changing "1¼ cup sugar" to "1¼ cup sugor"

▼ Figure 10.21 **Three types of mutations and their effects.** Mutations are changes in DNA, but they are shown here in mRNA and the polypeptide product.

mRNA and protein from a normal gene

(a) Base substitution. Here, an A replaces a G in the fourth codon of the mRNA. The result in the polypeptide is a serine (Ser) instead of a glycine (Gly). This amino acid substitution may or may not affect the protein's function.

(b) Nucleotide deletion. When a nucleotide is deleted, all the codons from that point on are misread. The resulting polypeptide is likely to be completely nonfunctional.

(c) Nucleotide insertion. As with a deletion, inserting one nucleotide disrupts all codons that follow, most likely producing a nonfunctional polypeptide.

▼ Figure 10.20 **The molecular basis of sickle-cell disease.** The sickle-cell allele differs from its normal counterpart, a gene for hemoglobin, by only one nucleotide (orange). This difference changes the mRNA codon from one that codes for the amino acid glutamic acid (Glu) to one that codes for valine (Val).

would probably be translated the same way, just like the translation of a silent mutation does not change the meaning of the message.

Other substitutions involving a single nucleotide do change the amino acid coding. Such mutations are called missense mutations. For example, if a mutation causes an mRNA codon to change from GGC to AGC, the resulting protein will have a serine (Ser) instead of a glycine (Gly) at this position. Some missense mutations have little or no effect on the shape or function of the resulting protein; imagine changing a recipe from "1¼ cups sugar" to "1⅓ cups sugar"—this will probably have a negligible effect on your final product. However, other substitutions, as we saw in the sickle-cell case, cause changes in the protein that prevent it from performing normally. This would be like changing "1¼ cups sugar" to "6¼ cups sugar"—this one change is enough to ruin the recipe.

Some substitutions, called nonsense mutations, change an amino acid codon into a stop codon. For example, if an AGA (Arg) codon is mutated to a UGA (stop) codon, the result will be a prematurely terminated protein, which probably will not function properly. In our recipe analogy, this would be like stopping food preparation before the end of the recipe, which is almost certainly going to ruin the dish.

Mutations involving the deletion or insertion of one or more nucleotides in a gene, called frameshift mutations, often have disastrous effects (see Figure 10.21b and c). Because mRNA is read as a series of nucleotide triplets during translation, adding or subtracting nucleotides may alter the triplet grouping of the genetic message. All the nucleotides after the insertion or deletion will be regrouped into different codons. Consider this recipe example: Add one cup egg nog. Deleting the second letter produces an entirely nonsensical message— ado nec upe ggn og—which will not produce a useful product. Similarly, a frameshift mutation most often produces a nonfunctioning polypeptide.

Mutagens

Mutations can occur in a number of ways. Spontaneous mutations result from random errors during DNA replication or recombination. Other sources of mutation are physical and chemical agents called **mutagens**. The most common physical mutagen is high-energy radiation, such as X-rays and ultraviolet (UV) light. Chemical mutagens are of various types. One type, for example, consists of chemicals that are similar to normal DNA bases but that base-pair incorrectly when incorporated into DNA.

Because many mutagens can act as carcinogens, agents that cause cancer, you would do well to avoid them as much as possible. What can you do to avoid exposure to mutagens? Several lifestyle practices can help, including not smoking and wearing protective clothing and sunscreen to minimize direct exposure to the sun's UV rays. But such precautions are not foolproof, and it is not possible to avoid mutagens (such as UV radiation and secondhand smoke) entirely.

Although mutations are often harmful, they can also be beneficial, both in nature and in the laboratory. Mutations are one source of the rich diversity of genes in the living world, a diversity that makes evolution by natural selection possible **(Figure 10.22)**. Mutations are also essential tools for geneticists. Whether naturally occurring or created in the laboratory, mutations are responsible for the different alleles needed for genetic research. ☑

☑ **CHECKPOINT**

1. What would happen if a mutation changed a start codon to some other codon?
2. What happens when one nucleotide is lost from the middle of a gene?

Answers: **1.** mRNA transcribed from the mutated gene would be nonfunctional because ribosomes would not initiate translation. **2.** In the mRNA, the reading of the triplets downstream from the deletion is shifted, leading to a long string of incorrect amino acids in the polypeptide.

▼ **Figure 10.22 Mutations and diversity.** Mutations are one source of the diversity of life visible in this scene from the Isle of Staffa, in the North Atlantic.

185

Viruses and Other Noncellular Infectious Agents

Viruses share some of the characteristics of living organisms, such as having genetic material in the form of nucleic acid packaged within a highly organized structure. A virus is generally not considered alive, however, because it is not cellular and cannot reproduce on its own. (See Figure 1.4 to review the properties of life.) A **virus** is an infectious particle consisting of little more than "genes in a box": a bit of nucleic acid wrapped in a protein coat and, in some cases, an envelope of membrane (Figure 10.23). A virus cannot reproduce on its own, and thus it can multiply only by infecting a living cell and directing the cell's molecular machinery to make more viruses. In this section, we'll look at viruses that infect different types of host organisms, starting with bacteria.

Bacteriophages

Viruses that attack bacteria are called **bacteriophages** ("bacteria-eaters"), or **phages** for short. Figure 10.24 shows a micrograph of a bacteriophage called T4 infecting an *Escherichia coli* bacterium. The phage consists of a molecule of DNA enclosed within an elaborate structure made of proteins. The "legs" of the phage bend when they touch the cell surface. The tail is a hollow rod enclosed in a springlike sheath. As the legs bend, the spring compresses, the bottom of the rod punctures the cell membrane, and the viral DNA passes from inside the head of the virus into the cell.

Once they infect a bacterium, most phages enter a reproductive cycle called the **lytic cycle**. The lytic cycle gets its name from the fact that after many copies of the phage are produced within the bacterial cell, the bacterium lyses (breaks open). Some viruses can also reproduce by an alternative route—the **lysogenic cycle**. During a lysogenic cycle, viral DNA replication occurs without phage production or the death of the cell.

Protein coat   DNA

▼ Figure 10.24 **Bacteriophages (viruses) infecting a bacterial cell.**

Head

Bacteriophage
(200 nm tall)

Tail

Bacterial cell

DNA
of virus

Colorized TEM 225,000×

▲ Figure 10.23 **Adenovirus.** A virus that infects the human respiratory system, an adenovirus consists of DNA enclosed in a protein coat shaped like a 20-sided polyhedron, shown here in a computer-generated model that is magnified approximately 500,000 times the actual size. At each corner of the polyhedron is a protein spike, which helps the virus attach to a susceptible cell.

Figure 10.25 illustrates the two kinds of cycles for a phage named lambda that can infect *E. coli* bacteria. At the start of infection, **1** lambda binds to the outside of a bacterium and injects its DNA inside. **2** The injected lambda DNA forms a circle. In the lytic cycle, this DNA immediately turns the cell into a virus-producing factory. **3** The cell's own machinery for DNA replication, transcription, and translation is hijacked by the virus and used to produce copies of the virus. **4** The cell lyses, releasing the new phages.

In the lysogenic cycle, **5** the viral DNA is inserted into the bacterial chromosome. Once there, the phage DNA is referred to as a **prophage**, and most of its genes are inactive. Survival of the prophage depends on the reproduction of the cell where it resides. **6** The host cell replicates the prophage DNA along with its cellular DNA and then, upon dividing, passes on both the prophage and the cellular DNA to its two daughter cells. A single infected bacterium can quickly give rise to a large population of bacteria that all carry prophages. The prophages may remain in the bacterial cells indefinitely. **7** Occasionally, however, a prophage leaves its chromosome; this event may be triggered by environmental conditions such as exposure to a mutagen. Once separate, the lambda DNA usually switches to the lytic cycle, which results in the production of many copies of the virus and lysing of the host cell.

Sometimes the few prophage genes active in a lysogenic bacterial cell can cause medical problems. For example, the bacteria that cause diphtheria, botulism, and scarlet fever would be harmless to people if it were not for the prophage genes they carry. Certain of these genes direct the bacteria to produce toxins that make people ill. ☑

☑ **CHECKPOINT**

Describe one way some viruses can perpetuate their genes without immediately destroying the cells they infect.

Answer: Some viruses can insert their DNA into the DNA of the cell they infect (the lysogenic cycle). The viral DNA is replicated along with the cell's DNA every time the cell divides.

▼ Figure 10.25 **Alternative phage reproductive cycles.** Certain phages can undergo alternative reproductive cycles. After entering the bacterial cell, the phage DNA can either integrate into the bacterial chromosome (lysogenic cycle) or immediately start the production of progeny phages (lytic cycle), destroying the cell. Once it enters a lysogenic cycle, the phage's DNA may be carried in the host cell's chromosome for many generations.

Phage lambda

E. coli

Phage

Newly released phage may infect another cell

1 Phage attaches to cell.

Phage DNA

Bacterial chromosome (DNA)

Phage injects DNA

4 Cell lyses, releasing phages.

LYTIC CYCLE

Phages assemble

2 Phage DNA circularizes.

LYSOGENIC CYCLE

7 Occasionally a prophage may leave the bacterial chromosome.

Many cell divisions

6 Lysogenic bacterium reproduces normally, replicating the prophage at each cell division.

Prophage

3 New phage DNA and proteins are synthesized.

OR

5 Phage DNA is inserted into the bacterial chromosome.

Plant Viruses

Viruses that infect plant cells can stunt plant growth and diminish crop yields. Most known plant viruses have RNA rather than DNA as their genetic material. Many of them, like the tobacco mosaic virus (TMV) shown in Figure 10.26, are rod-shaped with a spiral arrangement of proteins surrounding the nucleic acid. TMV, which infects tobacco and related plants, causing discolored spots on the leaves, was the first virus ever discovered (in 1930).

To infect a plant, a virus must first get past the plant's epidermis, an outer protective layer of cells. For this reason, a plant damaged by wind, chilling, injury, or insects is more susceptible to infection than a healthy plant. Some insects carry and transmit plant viruses, and farmers and gardeners may unwittingly spread plant viruses through the use of pruning shears and other tools.

There is no cure for most viral plant diseases, and agricultural scientists focus on preventing infection and on breeding or genetically engineering varieties of crop plants that resist viral infection. In Hawaii, for example, the spread of papaya ringspot potyvirus (PRSV) by aphids wiped out the native papaya (Hawaii's second largest crop) in certain island regions. But since 1998, farmers have been able to plant a genetically engineered PRSV-resistant strain of papaya, and papayas have been reintroduced into their old habitats. ☑

▼ Figure 10.26 **Tobacco mosaic virus.** The photo shows the mottling of leaves in tobacco mosaic disease. The rod-shaped virus causing the disease has RNA as its genetic material.

RNA

Protein

Tobacco mosaic virus

Animal Viruses

Viruses that infect animal cells are common causes of disease. As discussed in the Biology and Society section, no virus is a greater human health threat than the influenza (flu) virus (Figure 10.27). Like many animal viruses, this one has an outer envelope made of phospholipid membrane, with projecting spikes of protein. The envelope enables the virus to enter and leave a host cell. Many viruses, including those that cause the flu, common cold, measles, mumps, AIDS, and polio, have RNA as their genetic material. Diseases caused by DNA viruses include hepatitis, chicken pox, and herpes infections.

Membranous envelope

Protein spike

RNA

Protein coat

► Figure 10.27 **An influenza virus.** The genetic material of this virus consists of eight separate molecules of RNA, each wrapped in a protein coat.

Figure 10.28 shows the reproductive cycle of the mumps virus, a typical RNA virus. Once a common childhood disease characterized by fever and swelling of the salivary glands, mumps has become quite rare in industrialized nations due to widespread vaccination. When the virus contacts a susceptible cell, protein spikes on its outer surface attach to receptor proteins on the cell's plasma membrane. **①** The viral envelope fuses with the cell's membrane, allowing the protein-coated RNA to enter the cytoplasm. **②** Enzymes then remove the protein coat. **③** An enzyme that entered the cell as part of the virus uses the virus's RNA genome as a template for making complementary strands of RNA. The new strands have two functions: **④** They serve as mRNA for the synthesis of new viral proteins, and **⑤** they serve as templates for synthesizing new viral genome RNA. **⑥** The new coat proteins assemble around the new viral RNA. **⑦** Finally, the viruses leave the cell by cloaking themselves in plasma membrane. In other words, the virus obtains its envelope from the cell, budding off the cell without necessarily rupturing it.

Not all animal viruses reproduce in the cytoplasm. For example, herpesviruses—which cause chicken pox, shingles, cold sores, and genital herpes—are enveloped DNA viruses that reproduce in a host cell's nucleus, and they get their envelopes from the cell's nuclear membrane. Copies of the herpesvirus DNA usually remain behind in the nuclei of certain nerve cells. There they remain dormant until some sort of stress, such as a cold, sunburn, or emotional stress, triggers virus production, resulting in unpleasant symptoms. Once acquired, herpes infections may flare up repeatedly throughout a person's life. More than 75% of American adults carry herpes simplex 1 (which causes cold sores), and more than 20% carry herpes simplex 2 (which causes genital herpes).

The amount of damage a virus causes the body depends partly on how quickly the immune system responds to fight the infection and partly on the ability of the infected tissue to repair itself. We usually recover completely from colds because our respiratory tract tissue can efficiently replace damaged cells. In contrast, the poliovirus attacks nerve cells, which are not usually replaceable. The damage to such cells by polio is permanent. In such cases, the only medical option is to prevent the disease with vaccines.

How effective are vaccines? We'll examine this question next using the example of the flu vaccine. ☑

☑ CHECKPOINT

Why is infection by herpesvirus permanent?

Answer: because herpesvirus leaves viral DNA in the nuclei of nerve cells

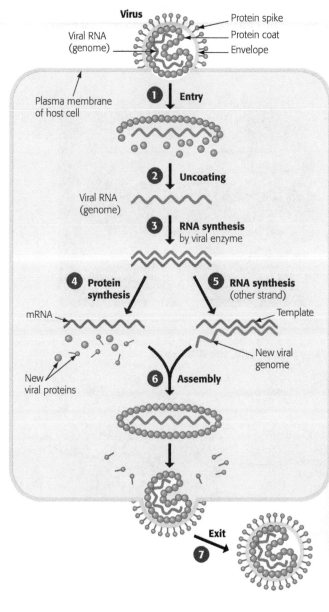

▼ Figure 10.28 **The reproductive cycle of an enveloped virus.** This virus is the one that causes mumps. Like the flu virus, it has a membranous envelope with protein spikes, but its genome is a single molecule of RNA.

Virus
Protein spike
Protein coat
Envelope
Viral RNA (genome)
Plasma membrane of host cell
① Entry
② Uncoating
Viral RNA (genome)
③ RNA synthesis by viral enzyme
④ Protein synthesis
⑤ RNA synthesis (other strand)
mRNA
Template
New viral proteins
New viral genome
⑥ Assembly
Exit
⑦

Mumps virus
Protein spike
Envelope
Colorized TEM 294,000×

Do Flu Vaccines Protect the Elderly?

Yearly flu vaccinations are recommended for nearly all people over the age of six months. But how can we be sure they are effective? Because elderly people often have weaker immune systems than younger people and because the elderly account for a significant slice of total health-care spending, they are an important population for vaccination efforts. Epidemiologists (scientists who study the distribution, causes, and control of diseases in populations) have made the **observation** that vaccination rates among the elderly rose from 15% in 1980 to 65% in 1996. This observation has led them to ask an important and basic **question:** Do flu vaccines decrease the mortality rate as a result of the flu among those elderly people who receive them? To find out, researchers investigated data from the general population. Their **hypothesis** was that elderly people who were immunized would have fewer hospital stays and deaths during the winter after vaccination. Their **experiment** followed tens of thousands of people over the age of 65 during the ten flu seasons of the 1990s. The **results** are summarized in **Figure 10.29**. People who were vaccinated had a 27% less chance of being hospitalized during the next flu season and a 48% less chance of dying. But could some factor other than flu shots be at play? For example, maybe people who choose to be vaccinated are healthier for other reasons. As a control, the researchers examined health data for the summer (when flu is not a factor). During these months, there was no difference in the hospitalization rates and only 16% fewer deaths for the immunized, suggesting that flu vaccines provide a significant health benefit among the elderly during the flu season.

► Figure 10.29 **The effect of flu vaccines on the elderly.** Receiving a flu vaccine greatly reduced the risk of hospitalization and death in the flu season following the shot. The reduction was much smaller or nonexistent in later summer months.

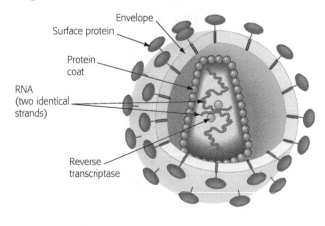

HIV, the AIDS Virus

The devastating disease **AIDS** (acquired immunodeficiency syndrome) is caused by **HIV** (human immunodeficiency virus), an RNA virus with some nasty twists. In outward appearance, HIV (**Figure 10.30**) resembles the mumps virus. Its envelope enables HIV to enter and leave a cell much the way the mumps virus does. But HIV has a different mode of reproduction. It is a **retrovirus**, an RNA virus that reproduces by means of a DNA molecule, the reverse of the usual DNA → RNA flow of genetic information. These viruses carry molecules of an enzyme called **reverse transcriptase**, which catalyzes reverse transcription: the synthesis of DNA on an RNA template.

▼ Figure 10.30 **HIV, the AIDS virus.**

Figure 10.31 illustrates what happens after HIV RNA is uncoated in the cytoplasm of a cell. The reverse transcriptase (green) **1** uses the RNA as a template to make a DNA strand and then **2** adds a second, complementary DNA strand. **3** The resulting double-stranded viral DNA then enters the cell nucleus and inserts itself into the chromosomal DNA, becoming a **provirus**. Occasionally, the provirus is **4** transcribed into RNA **5** and translated into viral proteins. **6** New viruses assembled from these components eventually leave the cell and can then infect other cells. This is the standard reproductive cycle for retroviruses.

HIV infects and eventually kills several kinds of white blood cells that are important in the body's immune system. The loss of such cells causes the body to become susceptible to other infections that it would normally be able to fight off. Such secondary infections cause the syndrome (a collection of symptoms) that eventually

kills AIDS patients. Since it was first recognized in 1981, HIV has infected tens of millions of people worldwide, resulting in millions of deaths.

Although there is as yet no cure for AIDS, its progression can be slowed by two categories of anti-HIV drugs. Both types of medicine interfere with the reproduction of the virus. The first type inhibits the action of enzymes called proteases, which help produce the final versions of HIV proteins. The second type, which includes the drug AZT, inhibits the action of the HIV enzyme reverse transcriptase. The key to AZT's effectiveness is its shape. The shape of a molecule of AZT is very similar to the shape of part of the T (thymine) nucleotide **(Figure 10.32)**. In fact, AZT's shape is so similar to the T nucleotide that AZT can bind to reverse transcriptase, essentially taking the place of T. But unlike thymine, AZT cannot be incorporated into a growing DNA chain. Thus, AZT "gums up the works," interfering with the synthesis of HIV DNA. Because this synthesis is an essential step in the reproductive cycle of HIV, AZT may block the spread of the virus within the body.

Many HIV-infected people in the United States and other industrialized countries take a "drug cocktail" that contains both reverse transcriptase inhibitors and protease inhibitors, and the combination seems to be much more effective than the individual drugs in keeping the virus at bay and extending patients' lives. In fact, the death rate from HIV infection can be lowered by 80% with proper treatment. However, even in combination, the drugs do not completely rid the body of the virus. Typically, HIV reproduction and the symptoms of AIDS return if a patient discontinues the medications. Because AIDS has no cure yet, prevention (namely, avoiding unprotected sex, and staying away from needle sharing) is the only healthy option. ☑

☑ **CHECKPOINT**

Why is HIV called a retrovirus?

Answer: Because it synthesizes DNA from its RNA genome. This is the reverse ("retro") of the usual DNA → RNA information flow.

▼ **Figure 10.31 The behavior of HIV nucleic acid in an infected cell.**

HIV (red dots) infecting a white blood cell

SEM 5,500x

▼ **Figure 10.32 AZT and the T nucleotide.** The anti-HIV drug AZT (right) has a chemical shape very similar to part of the T (thymine) nucleotide of DNA.

Part of a T nucleotide   AZT

Viroids and Prions

Viruses may be small and simple, but they are giants compared to two other classes of pathogens: viroids and prions. Viroids are small, circular RNA molecules that infect plants. Viroids do not encode proteins but can nonetheless replicate in host plant cells using cellular enzymes. These small RNA molecules may cause disease by interfering with the regulatory systems that control plant growth.

Even stranger are infectious proteins called **prions**. Prions cause a number of brain diseases in various animal species, including scrapie in sheep and goats, chronic wasting disease in deer and elk, and mad cow disease (formally called bovine spongiform encephalopathy, or BSE), which infected more than

> Mad cow disease is caused by an abnormal molecule of protein.

2 million cattle in the United Kingdom in the 1980s. In humans, prions cause Creutzfeldt-Jakob disease, an extremely rare, incurable, and inevitably fatal deterioration of the brain.

How can a protein cause disease? A prion is thought to be a misfolded form of a protein normally present in brain cells. When a prion enters a cell containing the normal form of protein, the prion somehow converts the normal protein molecules to the misfolded prion version. The abnormal proteins clump together, which may lead to loss of brain tissue (although how this occurs is the subject of much debate and ongoing research). To date, there is no known cure for prion diseases, so hope rests on understanding and preventing the process of infection. ☑

The Deadliest Virus EVOLUTION CONNECTION

Emerging Viruses

Viruses that suddenly come to the attention of medical scientists are called **emerging viruses**. H1N1 (discussed in the Biology and Society section) is one example; another is West Nile virus, which appeared in North America in 1999 and has since spread to all 48 contiguous U.S. states. West Nile virus is spread primarily by mosquitoes, which carry the virus in blood sucked from one victim and can transfer it to another victim. West Nile virus cases surged in 2012, especially in Texas, claiming nearly 300 lives (Figure 10.33).

How do such viruses burst on the human scene, giving rise to new diseases? One way is by the mutation of existing viruses. RNA viruses tend to have unusually high rates of mutation because errors in replicating their RNA genomes are not subject to proofreading mechanisms that help reduce errors during DNA replication. Some mutations enable existing viruses to evolve into new strains that can cause disease in individuals who have developed resistance to the ancestral virus. This is why we need yearly flu vaccines: Mutations create new influenza virus strains to which people have no immunity.

New viral diseases also arise from the spread of existing viruses from one host species to another. Scientists estimate that about three-quarters of new human diseases originated in other animals. The spread of a viral disease from a small, isolated population can also lead to widespread epidemics. For instance, AIDS went unnamed and virtually unnoticed for decades before it began to spread around the world. In this case, technological and social factors, including affordable international travel, blood transfusions, sexual activity, and the abuse of intravenous drugs, allowed a previously rare human disease to become a global scourge.

Acknowledging the persistent threat that viruses pose to human health, Nobel Prize winner Joshua Lederberg once warned: "We live in evolutionary competition with microbes. There is no guarantee that we will be the survivors." If we someday manage to control HIV, influenza, and other emerging viruses, this success will likely arise from our understanding of molecular biology.

▶ Figure 10.33 **Mapping the West Nile virus outbreak of 2012.**

Incidence per 100,000

☐ 0.00	☐ 0.50–0.99
☐ 0.01–0.024	☐ ≥1.00
☐ 0.25–0.49	

Chapter Review

SUMMARY OF KEY CONCEPTS

DNA: Structure and Replication

DNA and RNA Structure

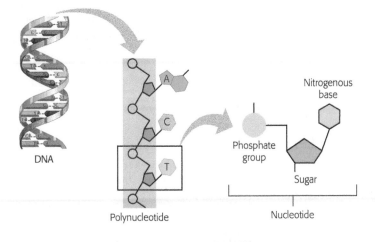

DNA

Polynucleotide

Phosphate group

Sugar

Nitrogenous base

Nucleotide

	DNA	RNA
Nitrogenous base	C G A T	C G A U
Sugar	Deoxy-ribose	Ribose
Number of strands	2	1

Structure/Function: Watson and Crick's Discovery of the Double Helix

Watson and Crick worked out the three-dimensional structure of DNA: two polynucleotide strands wrapped around each other in a double helix. Hydrogen bonds between bases hold the strands together. Each base pairs with a complementary partner: A with T, and G with C.

DNA Replication

The structure of DNA, with its complementary base pairing, allows it to function as the molecule of heredity through DNA replication.

New daughter strand

Parental DNA molecule

Identical daughter DNA molecules

Information Flow: From DNA to RNA to Protein

How an Organism's Genotype Determines Its Phenotype

The information constituting an organism's genotype is carried in the sequence of its DNA bases. The genotype controls phenotype through the expression of proteins.

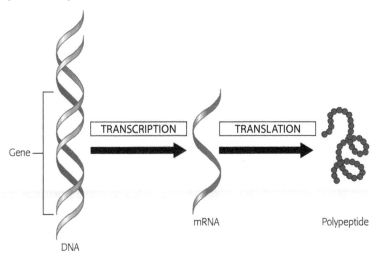

Gene

TRANSCRIPTION

TRANSLATION

DNA

mRNA

Polypeptide

From Nucleotides to Amino Acids: An Overview

The DNA of a gene is transcribed into RNA using the usual base-pairing rules, except that an A in DNA pairs with U in RNA. In the translation of a genetic message, each triplet of nucleotide bases in the RNA, called a codon, specifies one amino acid in the polypeptide.

The Genetic Code

In addition to codons that specify amino acids, the genetic code has one codon that is a start signal and three that are stop signals for translation. The genetic code is redundant: There is more than one codon for most amino acids.

Transcription: From DNA to RNA

In transcription, RNA polymerase binds to the promoter of a gene, opens the DNA double helix there, and catalyzes the synthesis of an RNA molecule using one DNA strand as a template. As the single-stranded RNA transcript peels away from the gene, the DNA strands rejoin.

The Processing of Eukaryotic RNA

The RNA transcribed from a eukaryotic gene is processed before leaving the nucleus to serve as messenger RNA (mRNA). Introns are spliced out, and a cap and tail are added.

Translation: The Players

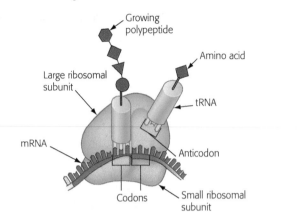

Translation: The Process

In initiation, a ribosome assembles with the mRNA and the initiator tRNA bearing the first amino acid. Beginning at the start codon, the codons of the mRNA are recognized one by one by tRNAs bearing succeeding amino acids. The ribosome bonds the amino acids together. With each addition, the mRNA moves by one codon through the ribosome. When a stop codon is reached, the completed polypeptide is released.

Review: DNA → RNA → Protein

The sequence of codons in DNA, via the sequence of codons in mRNA, spells out the primary structure of a polypeptide.

Mutations

Mutations are changes in the DNA base sequence, caused by errors in DNA replication or recombination or by mutagens. Substituting, deleting, or inserting nucleotides in a gene has varying effects on the polypeptide and organism.

Type of Mutation	Effect
Substitution of one DNA base for another	**Silent** mutations result in no change to amino acids.
	Missense mutations swap one amino acid for another.
	Nonsense mutations change an amino acid codon to a stop codon.
Insertions or **deletions** of DNA nucleotides	Frameshift mutations can alter the triplet grouping of codons and greatly change the amino acid sequence.

Viruses and Other Noncellular Infectious Agents

Viruses are infectious particles consisting of genes packaged in protein.

Bacteriophages

When phage DNA enters a lytic cycle inside a bacterium, it is replicated, transcribed, and translated. The new viral DNA and protein molecules then assemble into new phages, which burst from the cell. In the lysogenic cycle, phage DNA inserts into the cell's chromosome and is passed on to generations of daughter cells. Much later, it may initiate phage production.

Plant Viruses

Viruses that infect plants can be a serious agricultural problem. Most have RNA genomes. Viruses enter plants via breaks in the plant's outer layers.

Animal Viruses

Many animal viruses, such as flu viruses, have RNA genomes; others, such as hepatitis viruses, have DNA. Some animal viruses "steal" a bit of cell membrane as a protective envelope. Some, such as the herpesvirus, can remain latent inside cells for long periods.

HIV, the AIDS Virus

HIV is a retrovirus. Inside a cell it uses its RNA as a template for making DNA, which is then inserted into a chromosome.

Viroids and Prions

Even smaller than viruses, viroids are small molecules of RNA that can infect plants. Prions are infectious proteins that cause a number of degenerative brain diseases in humans and other animals.

MasteringBiology®

For practice quizzes, BioFlix animations, MP3 tutorials, video tutors, and more study tools designed for this textbook, go to MasteringBiology®

SELF-QUIZ

1. A molecule of DNA contains two polymer strands called _____, made by bonding together many monomers called _____.
2. Name the three parts of every nucleotide.
3. Which of the following correctly ranks nucleic acid structures in order of size, from largest to smallest?
   a. gene, chromosome, nucleotide, codon
   b. chromosome, gene, codon, nucleotide
   c. nucleotide, chromosome, gene, codon
   d. chromosome, nucleotide, gene, codon
4. A scientist inserts a radioactively labeled DNA molecule into a bacterium. The bacterium replicates this DNA molecule and distributes one daughter molecule (double helix) to each of two daughter cells. How much radioactivity will the DNA in each of the two daughter cells contain? Why?
5. The nucleotide sequence of a DNA codon is GTA. What would be the nucleotide sequence of an mRNA molecule transcribed from this DNA? In the process of protein synthesis, a tRNA pairs with the mRNA codon. What is the nucleotide sequence of the tRNA anticodon that corresponds to this mRNA codon? What amino acid is attached to the tRNA (see Figure 10.10)?
6. Describe the process by which the information in a gene is transcribed and translated into a protein. Correctly use these terms in your description: tRNA, amino acid, start codon, transcription, mRNA, gene, codon, RNA polymerase, ribosome, translation, anticodon, peptide bond, stop codon.

7. Match the following molecules with the cellular process or processes in which they are primarily involved.

a. ribosomes
b. tRNA
c. DNA polymerases
d. RNA polymerase
e. mRNA

1. DNA replication
2. transcription
3. translation

8. A geneticist finds that a particular mutation has no effect on the polypeptide encoded by the gene. This mutation probably involves

a. deletion of one nucleotide.
b. alteration of the start codon.
c. insertion of one nucleotide.
d. substitution of one nucleotide.

9. Scientists have discovered how to put together a bacteriophage with the protein coat of phage A and the DNA of phage B. If this composite phage were allowed to infect a bacterium, the phages produced in the cell would have

a. the protein of A and the DNA of B.
b. the protein of B and the DNA of A.
c. the protein and DNA of A.
d. the protein and DNA of B.

10. How do some viruses reproduce without ever having DNA?

11. HIV requires an enzyme called _____ to convert its RNA genome to a DNA version. Why is this enzyme a particularly good target for anti-AIDS drugs? (*Hint*: Would you expect such a drug to harm the human host?)

Answers to these questions can be found in Appendix: Self-Quiz Answers.

THE PROCESS OF SCIENCE

12. A cell containing a single chromosome is placed in a medium containing radioactive phosphate, making any new DNA strands formed by DNA replication radioactive. The cell replicates its DNA and divides. Then the daughter cells (still in the radioactive medium) replicate their DNA and divide, resulting in a total of four cells. Sketch the DNA molecules in all four cells, showing a normal (nonradioactive) DNA strand as a solid line and a radioactive DNA strand as a dashed line.

13. In a classic 1952 experiment, biologists Alfred Hershey and Martha Chase labeled two batches of bacteriophages, one with radioactive sulfur (which only tags protein) and the other with radioactive phosphorus (which only tags DNA). In separate test tubes, they allowed each batch of phages to bind to nonradioactive bacteria and inject its DNA. After a few minutes, they separated the bacterial cells from the viral parts that remained outside the bacterial cells and measured the radioactivity of both portions. What results do you think they obtained? How would these results help them to determine which viral component—DNA or protein—was the infectious portion?

14. **Interpreting Data** The graph below summarizes the number of children who died of all strains of flu from 2007 until 2013. Each bar represents the number of child deaths occurring in one week. Why does the graph have the shape it does, with a series of peaks and valleys? Looking over the Biology and Society section at the start of the chapter, why does the graph reach its highest points near the middle? Based on these data, when does flu season begin and end in a typical year?

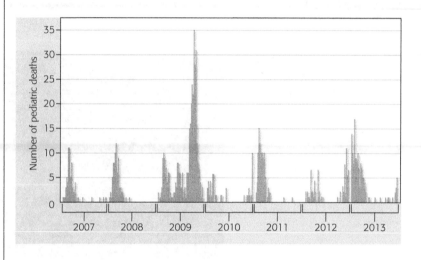

BIOLOGY AND SOCIETY

15. Scientists at the National Institutes of Health (NIH) have worked out thousands of sequences of genes and the proteins they encode, and similar analyses are being carried out at universities and private companies. Knowledge of the nucleotide sequences of genes might be used to treat genetic defects or produce lifesaving medicines. NIH and some U.S. biotechnology companies have applied for patents on their discoveries. In Britain, the courts have ruled that a naturally occurring gene cannot be patented. Do you think individuals and companies should be able to patent genes and gene products? Before answering, consider the following: What are the purposes of a patent? How might the discoverer of a gene benefit from a patent? How might the public benefit? What negative effects might result from patenting genes?

16. Your college roommate seeks to improve her appearance by visiting a tanning salon. How would you explain the dangers of this to her?

17. Flu vaccines have been shown to be safe, are very reliable at reducing the risk of hospitalization or death from influenza, and are inexpensive. Should children be required to obtain a flu vaccine before going to school? What about hospital workers before reporting to work? Defend your answers to these questions.

Why Gene Regulation Matters

Someday a DNA chip might report on the activities of all your genes. ▶

▼ Cloning may help save the giant panda from extinction.

▲ Lifestyle choices you make can dramatically affect your risk of cancer.

Cancer BIOLOGY AND SOCIETY

Tobacco's Smoking Gun

When European explorers returned from their first voyages to the Americas, they brought back tobacco, a common trade item among Native Americans. The novelty of smoking tobacco quickly spread through Europe. To keep up with demand, the southern United States soon became a major tobacco producer. Over time, smoking increased in popularity around the world, and by the 1950s, about half of all Americans smoked more than a pack of cigarettes each day. In these early days, little attention was paid to purported health risks; in fact, cigarette advertising often touted the "health benefits" of tobacco, claiming that use of the product had a soothing effect on the throat and helped the smoker remain calm and lose weight.

By the 1960s, however, doctors began to notice a disturbing trend: The rate of lung cancer had increased dramatically. Although the disease was rare in 1930, by 1955 it had become the deadliest form of cancer among American men. In fact, by 1990, lung cancer was killing more than twice as many men each year as any other type of cancer. But a few vocal skeptics, mostly tied to groups with an economic interest in the tobacco industry, doubted the link between smoking and cancer. They pointed out that the evidence was purely statistical or based on animal studies; no direct proof, they said, had been found that tobacco smoke causes cancer in humans.

Colorized SEM 450×

Human cancer cells. These tumor cells have lost the ability to control their growth.

The "smoking gun" of proof was found in 1996 when researchers added one component of tobacco smoke, called BPDE, to human lung cells growing in the lab. The researchers showed that BPDE binds to a gene within these cells called *p53*. That gene codes for a protein that helps suppress the formation of tumors. The researchers showed that BPDE causes mutations in the *p53* gene that deactivate the protein; with this important tumor-suppressor protein deactivated, tumors grow. This work directly linked a chemical in tobacco smoke to the formation of human lung tumors. Since that time, a mountain of experimental data and statistical studies has removed any scientific doubt of the link between smoking and cancer.

How can a mutation in a gene lead to cancer? It turns out that many cancer-associated genes encode proteins that turn other genes on or off. When these proteins malfunction, the cell may become cancerous. In fact, the ability to properly control which genes are active at any given time is crucial to normal cell function. How genes are controlled and how the regulation of genes affects cells and organisms—including ways this topic affects your own life—are the subjects of this chapter.

How and Why Genes Are Regulated

Every cell in your body—and, indeed, all the cells in the body of every sexually reproducing organism—was produced through successive rounds of mitosis starting from the zygote, the original cell that formed after fusion of sperm and egg. Mitosis exactly duplicates the chromosomes. Therefore, every cell in your body has the same DNA as the zygote. To put it another way: Every somatic (body) cell contains every gene. However, the cells in your body are specialized in structure and function; a neuron, for example, looks and acts nothing like a red blood cell. But if every cell contains identical genetic instructions, how do cells develop differently from one another? To help you understand this idea, imagine that every restaurant in your hometown uses the same cookbook. If that were the case, how could each restaurant develop a unique menu? The answer is obvious: Even though each restaurant has the same cookbook, different restaurants pick and choose different recipes from this book to prepare. Similarly, cells with the same genetic information can develop into different types of cells through **gene regulation**, mechanisms that turn on certain genes while other genes remain turned off. Regulating gene activity allows for specialization of cells within the body, just as regulating which recipes are used allows for varying menus in multiple restaurants.

As an example of gene regulation, consider the development of a unicellular zygote into a multicellular organism. During embryonic growth, groups of cells follow different paths, and each group becomes a particular kind of tissue. In the mature organism, each cell type—neuron or red blood cell, for instance—has a different pattern of turned-on genes.

What does it mean to say that genes are turned on or off? Genes determine the nucleotide sequence of specific mRNA molecules, and mRNA in turn determines the sequence of amino acids in proteins (in summary: DNA → RNA → protein; see Chapter 10). A gene that is turned on is being transcribed into mRNA, and that message is being translated into specific proteins. The overall process by which genetic information flows from genes to proteins is called **gene expression**.

As an illustration of this principle, Figure 11.1 shows the patterns of gene expression for four genes in three different specialized cells of an adult human. Note that the genes for "housekeeping" enzymes, such as those that provide energy via glycolysis, are "on" in all the cells. In contrast, the genes for some proteins, such as insulin and hemoglobin, are expressed only by particular kinds of cells. One protein, hemoglobin, is not expressed in any of the cell types shown in the figure. ☑

Gene Regulation in Bacteria

To understand how a cell can regulate gene expression, consider the relatively simple case of bacteria. In the course of their lives, bacteria must regulate their genes in response to environmental changes. For example,

☑ CHECKPOINT

If your blood cells and skin cells have the same genes, how can they be so different?

Answer: Each cell type expresses different genes than the other cell type.

► Figure 11.1 **Patterns of gene expression in three types of human cells.** Different types of cells express different combinations of genes. The specialized proteins whose genes are represented here are an enzyme involved in glucose digestion; an antibody, which aids in fighting infection; insulin, a hormone made in the pancreas; and the oxygen transport protein hemoglobin, which is expressed only in red blood cells.

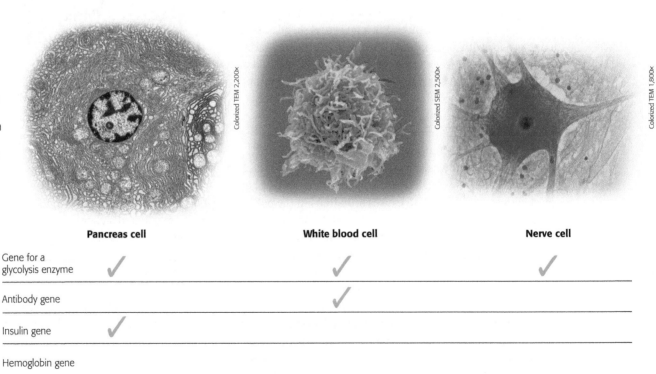

	Pancreas cell	White blood cell	Nerve cell
Gene for a glycolysis enzyme	✓	✓	✓
Antibody gene		✓	
Insulin gene	✓		
Hemoglobin gene			

Key

✓ = Active gene

when a nutrient is plentiful, bacteria do not squander valuable resources to make the nutrient from scratch. Bacterial cells that can conserve resources and energy have a survival advantage over cells that are unable to do so. Thus, natural selection has favored bacteria that express only the genes whose products are needed by the cell.

Imagine an *Escherichia coli* bacterium living in your intestines. It will be bathed in various nutrients, depending on what you eat. If you drink a milk shake, for example, there will be a sudden rush of the sugar lactose. In response, *E. coli* will express three genes for enzymes that enable the bacterium to absorb and digest this sugar. After the lactose is gone, these genes are turned off; the bacterium does not waste its energy continuing to produce these enzymes when they are not needed. Thus, a bacterium can adjust its gene expression to changes in the environment.

How does a bacterium "know" if lactose is present or not? In other words, how does the presence or absence of lactose influence the activity of the genes that code for the lactose enzymes? The key is the way the three lactose-digesting genes are organized: They are adjacent in the DNA and turned on and off as a single unit. This regulation is achieved through short stretches of DNA that help turn all three genes on and off at once, coordinating their expression. Such a cluster of related genes and sequences that control them is called an **operon** (Figure 11.2). The operon considered here, the *lac* (short for lactose) operon, illustrates principles of gene regulation that apply to a wide variety of prokaryotic genes.

How do DNA control sequences turn genes on or off? One control sequence, called a **promoter** (green in the figure), is the site where the enzyme RNA polymerase attaches and initiates transcription—in our example, transcription of the genes for lactose-digesting enzymes. Between the promoter and the enzyme genes, a DNA segment called an **operator** (yellow) acts as a switch that is turned on or off, depending on whether a specific protein is bound there. The operator and protein together determine whether RNA polymerase can attach to the promoter and start transcribing the genes (light blue). In the *lac* operon, when the operator switch is turned on, all the enzymes needed to metabolize lactose are made at once.

The top half of Figure 11.2 shows the *lac* operon in "off" mode, its status when there is no lactose available. Transcription is turned off because ❶ a protein called a **repressor** ( ) binds to the operator ( ) and ❷ physically blocks the attachment of RNA polymerase ( ) to the promoter ( ).

The bottom half of Figure 11.2 shows the operon in "on" mode, when lactose is present. The lactose ( )

interferes with attachment of the *lac* repressor to the operator by ❶ binding to the repressor and ❷ changing the repressor's shape. In its new shape ( ), the repressor cannot bind to the operator, and the operator switch remains on. ❸ RNA polymerase is no longer blocked, so it can now bind to the promoter and from there ❹ transcribe the genes for the lactose enzymes into mRNA. ❺ Translation produces all three lactose enzymes (purple).

Many operons have been identified in bacteria. Some are quite similar to the *lac* operon, whereas others have somewhat different mechanisms of control. For example, operons that control amino acid synthesis cause bacteria to stop making these molecules when they are already present in the environment, saving materials and energy for the cells. In these cases, the amino acid *activates* the repressor. Armed with a variety of operons, *E. coli* and other prokaryotes can thrive in frequently changing environments. ☑

▼ Figure 11.2 **The *lac* operon of *E. coli*.**

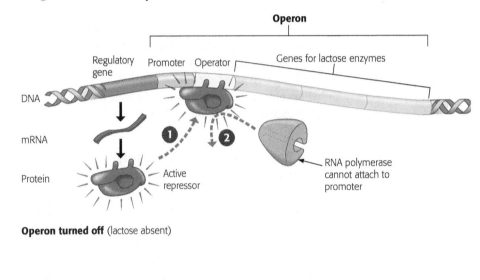

Operon turned off (lactose absent)

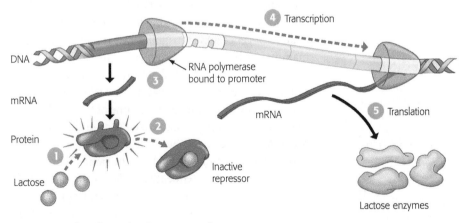

Operon turned on (lactose inactivates repressor)

199

Gene Regulation in Eukaryotic Cells

Eukaryotes, especially multicellular ones, have more sophisticated mechanisms than bacteria for regulating the expression of their genes. This is not surprising because a prokaryote, being a single cell, does not require the elaborate regulation of gene expression that leads to cell specialization in multicellular eukaryotic organisms. A bacterium does not have neurons that need to be different from blood cells, for example.

The pathway from gene to protein in eukaryotic cells is a long one, providing a number of points where the process can be turned on or off, speeded up or slowed down. Picture the series of pipes that carry water from your local reservoir to a faucet in your home. At various points, valves control the flow of water. We use this analogy in Figure 11.3 to illustrate the flow of genetic information from a eukaryotic chromosome—a reservoir of genetic information—to an active protein that has been made in the cell's cytoplasm. The multiple mechanisms that control gene expression are analogous to the control valves in your water pipes. In the figure, each control knob indicates a gene expression "valve." All these knobs represent possible control points, although only one or a few control points are likely to be important for a typical protein.

Using a reduced version of Figure 11.3 as a guide, we will explore several ways that eukaryotes can control gene expression, starting within the nucleus.

The Regulation of DNA Packing

Eukaryotic chromosomes may be in a more or less condensed state, with the DNA and accompanying proteins more or less tightly wrapped together (see Figure 8.4). DNA packing tends to prevent gene expression by preventing RNA polymerase and other transcription proteins from binding to the DNA.

Cells may use DNA packing for the long-term inactivation of genes. One intriguing case is seen in female mammals, where one X chromosome in each somatic cell is highly compacted and almost entirely inactive. This **X chromosome inactivation** first takes place early in embryonic development, when one of the two X chromosomes in each cell is inactivated at random. After one X chromosome is inactivated in each embryonic cell, all of that cell's descendants will have the same X chromosome turned off. Consequently, if a female has different versions of a gene on each of her X chromosomes, about half of her cells will express one version, while the other half will express the alternate version (Figure 11.4). ✅

✅ CHECKPOINT

Would a gene on the X chromosome be expressed more in human females (who have two copies of the X chromosome) than in human males (who have one copy)?

Answer: No, because in females one of the X chromosomes in each cell is inactivated.

▼ **Figure 11.3 The gene expression "pipeline" in a eukaryotic cell.** Each valve in the pipeline represents a stage at which the pathway from chromosome to functioning protein can be regulated, turned on or off, or speeded up or slowed down. Throughout this discussion we will use a miniature version of this figure to keep track of the stages as they are discussed.

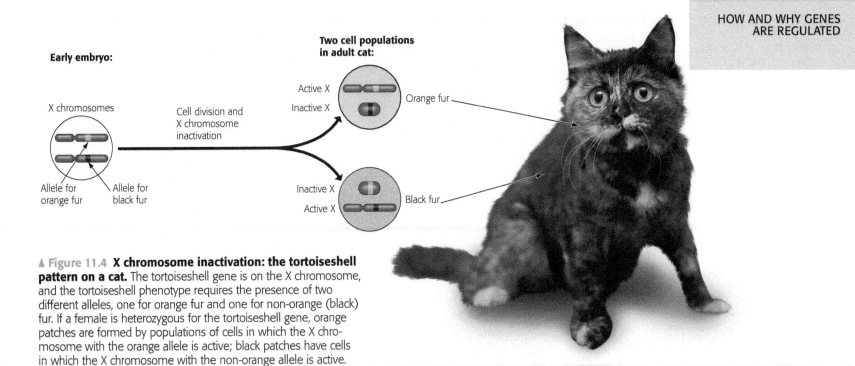

Early embryo:

X chromosomes

Allele for orange fur

Allele for black fur

Cell division and X chromosome inactivation

Two cell populations in adult cat:

Active X
Inactive X

Orange fur

Inactive X
Active X

Black fur

▲ Figure 11.4 **X chromosome inactivation: the tortoiseshell pattern on a cat.** The tortoiseshell gene is on the X chromosome, and the tortoiseshell phenotype requires the presence of two different alleles, one for orange fur and one for non-orange (black) fur. If a female is heterozygous for the tortoiseshell gene, orange patches are formed by populations of cells in which the X chromosome with the orange allele is active; black patches have cells in which the X chromosome with the non-orange allele is active.

The Initiation of Transcription

The initiation of transcription (whether transcription starts or not) is the most important stage for regulating gene expression. In both prokaryotes and eukaryotes, regulatory proteins bind to DNA and turn the transcription of genes on and off. Unlike prokaryotic genes, however, most eukaryotic genes are not grouped into operons. Instead, each eukaryotic gene usually has its own promoter and other control sequences.

As illustrated in Figure 11.5, transcriptional regulation in eukaryotes is complex, typically involving many proteins (collectively called **transcription factors**; shown in purple in the figure) acting in concert to bind to DNA sequences called **enhancers** (yellow) and to the promoter (green). The DNA-protein assembly promotes the binding of RNA polymerase (orange) to the promoter. Genes coding for related enzymes, such as those in a metabolic pathway, may share a specific kind of enhancer (or collection of enhancers), allowing these genes to be activated at the same time. Not shown in the figure are repressor proteins, which may bind to DNA sequences called **silencers**, inhibiting the start of transcription.

In fact, repressor proteins that turn genes off are less common in eukaryotes than **activators**, proteins that turn genes on by binding to DNA. Activators act by

making it easier for RNA polymerase to bind to the promoter. The use of activators is efficient because a typical animal or plant cell needs to turn on (transcribe) only a small percentage of its genes, those required for the cell's specialized structure and function. The "default" state for most genes in multicellular eukaryotes seems to be off, with the exception of "housekeeping" genes for routine activities such as the digestion of glucose. ☑

☑ **CHECKPOINT**

Of all the control points of DNA expression shown in Figure 11.3, which is under the tightest regulation?

Answer: the initiation of transcription

▼ Figure 11.5 **A model for turning on a eukaryotic gene.** A large assembly of transcription factors (proteins shown in purple) and several control sequences in the DNA are involved in initiating the transcription of a eukaryotic gene.

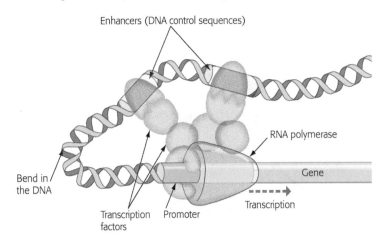

Enhancers (DNA control sequences)

RNA polymerase

Gene

Bend in the DNA

Transcription factors

Promoter

Transcription

RNA Processing and Breakdown

Within a eukaryotic cell, transcription occurs in the nucleus, where RNA transcripts are processed into mRNA before moving to the cytoplasm for translation by the ribosomes (see Figure 10.19). RNA processing includes the addition of a cap and a tail, as well as the removal of any introns—noncoding DNA segments that interrupt the genetic message—and the splicing together of the remaining exons.

Within a cell, exon splicing can occur in more than one way, generating different mRNA molecules from the same starting RNA molecule. Notice in **Figure 11.6**, for example, that one mRNA ends up with the green exon and the other with the brown exon. With this sort of **alternative RNA splicing**, an organism can produce more than one type of polypeptide from a single gene. A typical human gene contains about ten exons; nearly all genes are spliced in at least two different ways, and some are spliced hundreds of different ways.

After an mRNA is produced in its final form, its "lifetime" can be highly variable, from hours to weeks to months. Controlling the timing of mRNA breakdown provides another opportunity for regulation. But all mRNAs are eventually broken down and their parts recycled.

microRNAs

Recent research has established an important role for a variety of small single-stranded RNA molecules, called microRNAs (miRNAs), that can bind to complementary sequences on mRNA molecules in the cytoplasm. After binding, some miRNAs trigger breakdown of their target mRNA, whereas others block translation. It has been estimated that miRNAs may regulate the expression of one half of all human genes, a striking figure given that miRNAs were unknown 20 years ago. New techniques attempt to exploit miRNAs via a technique called RNA interference, the injection of small RNA molecules into a cell to turn off specific genes. By understanding the natural process of information flow through a cell, biologists may soon be able to artificially control gene expression in humans.

The Initiation of Translation

The process of translation—in which an mRNA is used to make a protein—offers additional opportunities for control by regulatory molecules. Red blood cells, for instance, have a protein that prevents the translation of hemoglobin mRNA unless the cell has a supply of heme, an iron-containing chemical group essential for hemoglobin function.

Protein Activation and Breakdown

The final opportunities for regulating gene expression occur after translation. For example, the hormone insulin is synthesized as one long, inactive polypeptide that must be chopped into pieces before it comes active **(Figure 11.7)**. Other proteins require chemical modification before they become active.

Another control mechanism operating after translation is the selective breakdown of proteins. Some proteins that trigger metabolic changes in cells are broken down within a few minutes or hours. This regulation allows a cell to adjust the kinds and amounts of its proteins in response to changes in its environment. ☑

▼ **Figure 11.6 Alternative RNA splicing: producing multiple mRNAs from the same gene.** Two different cells can use the same DNA gene to synthesize different mRNAs and proteins. In this example, one mRNA has ended up with exon 3 (brown) and the other with exon 4 (green). These mRNAs, which are just two of many possible outcomes, can then be translated into different proteins.

▼ **Figure 11.7 The formation of an active insulin molecule.** Only in its final form, with a central region removed, does insulin act as a hormone.

Initial polypeptide (inactive)   Insulin (active hormone)

Information Flow | Cell Signaling

The control of gene expression is a good example of one of biology's important themes: information flow. Through regulation, a cell can alter its activities in response to signals from the environment. So far, we have considered gene regulation only within a single cell. In a multicellular organism, the process can cross cell boundaries, allowing information to be communicated between and among cells. For example, a cell can produce and secrete chemicals, such as hormones, that affect gene regulation in another cell. Consider an analogy from your own experience: In grade school, did you ever station a classmate near the door to signal the teacher's return? Information from outside the room (the teacher's approach) was used to alter behavior within the classroom (stop messing around!). In a similar way, cells use protein "lookouts" to convey information into the cell, resulting in changes to cellular functions.

A signal molecule can act by binding to a receptor protein and initiating a **signal transduction pathway**, a series of molecular changes that converts a signal received outside a cell to a specific response inside the target cell. Figure 11.8 shows an example of cell-to-cell signaling in which the target cell's response is the transcription (turning on) of a gene. ❶ First, the signaling cell secretes the signal molecule (🝒). ❷ This molecule binds to a specific receptor protein (🝒) embedded in the target cell's plasma membrane. ❸ The binding activates a signal transduction pathway consisting of a series of relay proteins (green) within the target cell. Each relay molecule activates the next. ❹ The last relay molecule in the series activates a transcription factor (🝒) that ❺ triggers the transcription of a specific gene. ❻ Translation of the mRNA produces a protein that can then perform the function originally called for by the signal. ☑

✓ **CHECKPOINT**

How can a signal molecule from one cell alter gene expression in a target cell without entering the target cell?

Answer: by binding to a receptor protein in the membrane of the target cell and triggering a signal transduction pathway that activates transcription factors

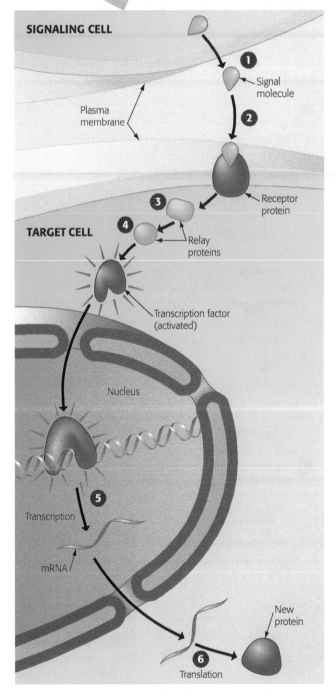

▲ Figure 11.8 **A cell-signaling pathway that turns on a gene.** The coordination of cellular activities in a multicellular organism depends on cell-to-cell signaling that helps regulate genes.

Labels in figure: SIGNALING CELL; Signal molecule; Plasma membrane; Receptor protein; TARGET CELL; Relay proteins; Transcription factor (activated); Nucleus; Transcription; mRNA; Translation; New protein

Homeotic Genes

Cell-to-cell signaling and the control of gene expression are particularly important during early embryonic development, when a single-celled zygote develops into a multicellular organism. Master control genes called **homeotic genes** regulate groups of other genes that determine what body parts will develop in which locations. For example, one set of homeotic genes in fruit flies instructs cells in the midbody to form legs. Elsewhere, these homeotic genes remain turned off, while others are turned on. Mutations in homeotic genes can produce bizarre effects. For example, fruit flies with mutations in homeotic genes may have extra sets of legs growing from their head (Figure 11.9).

► Figure 11.9 **The effect of homeotic genes.** The strange mutant fruit fly shown at the bottom results from a mutation in a homeotic (master control) gene.

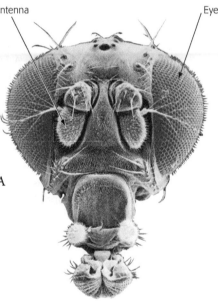

Antenna   Eye

Normal head due to presence of normal homeotic gene

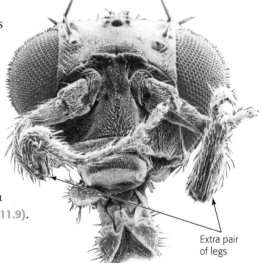

Extra pair of legs

Head with extra legs growing due to presence of mutant homeotic gene

203

☑ **CHECKPOINT**

How can a mutation
in just one homeotic
gene drastically affect
an organism's physical
appearance?

Answer: Because homeotic genes control many other genes, a single change can affect the expression of many of the proteins that control appearance.

One of the most significant biological discoveries in recent years uncovered the fact that similar homeotic genes help direct embryonic development in nearly every eukaryotic organism examined so far, including yeasts, plants, earthworms, frogs, chickens, mice, and humans. These similarities suggest that these homeotic genes arose very early in the history of life and that the genes have remained remarkably unchanged over eons of animal evolution. ☑

Someday a DNA chip might report on the activities of all your genes.

which genes were being transcribed in the starting cells. Researchers can thus learn which genes are active in different tissues, at different times, or in tissues from individuals in different states of health. Such information may contribute to a better understanding of diseases and suggest new therapies. For example, comparing patterns of gene expression in breast cancer tumors with noncancerous breast tissue has resulted in more effective treatment protocols.

DNA Microarrays: Visualizing Gene Expression

Scientists who study gene regulation often want to determine which genes are switched on or off in a particular cell. A **DNA microarray** is a slide with thousands of different kinds of single-stranded DNA fragments attached in a tightly spaced array (grid). Each DNA fragment is obtained from a particular gene; a single microarray thus carries DNA from thousands of genes, perhaps even all the genes of an organism.

Figure 11.10 outlines how microarrays are used. ❶ A researcher collects all of the mRNA transcribed in a particular type of cell at a given moment. This collection of mRNA is mixed with reverse transcriptase, a viral enzyme that ❷ produces DNA that is complementary to each mRNA sequence. This **complementary DNA (cDNA)** is synthesized using nucleotides that have been modified to fluoresce (glow). The fluorescent cDNA collection thus represents all of the genes being actively transcribed in the cell. ❸ A small amount of the fluorescently labeled cDNA mixture is added to the DNA fragments of the microarray. If a molecule in the cDNA mixture is complementary to a DNA fragment at a particular location on the grid, the cDNA molecule binds to it, becoming fixed there. ❹ After unbound cDNA is rinsed away, the remaining cDNA glows in the microarray. The pattern of glowing spots enables the researcher to determine

❶ mRNA isolated

Reverse transcriptase combined with fluorescent DNA nucleotides

❷ cDNA made from mRNA — Fluorescent cDNA

❸ cDNA mixture added to spots

DNA microarray (each spot contains DNA from a particular gene)

❹ Unbound cDNA rinsed away

Nonfluorescent spot

Fluorescent spot

Fluorescent cDNA

DNA of an expressed gene

DNA of an unexpressed gene

DNA microarray, actual size (6,400 genes)

▲ Figure 11.10 **Visualizing gene expression using a DNA microarray.**

Cloning Plants and Animals

Now that we have examined how gene expression is regulated, we will devote the rest of this chapter to discussing how gene regulation affects two important processes: cloning and cancer.

The Genetic Potential of Cells

One of the most important take-home lessons from this chapter is that all body cells contain a complete complement of genes, even if they are not expressing all of them. If you've ever grown a plant from a small cutting, you've seen evidence of this yourself: A single differentiated plant cell can undergo cell division and give rise to a complete adult plant. On a larger scale, the technique described in **Figure 11.11** can be used to produce hundreds or thousands of genetically identical organisms—clones—from the cells of a single plant.

Plant cloning is now used extensively in agriculture. For some plants, such as orchids, cloning is the only commercially practical means of reproducing plants. In other cases, cloning has been used to reproduce a plant with specific desirable traits, such as high fruit yield or resistance to disease. Seedless plants (such as seedless grapes, watermelons, and oranges) cannot reproduce sexually, leaving cloning as the sole means of mass-producing these common foods.

Is this sort of cloning possible in animals? A good indication that some animal cells can also tap into their full genetic potential is **regeneration**, the regrowth of lost body parts. When a salamander loses a tail, for example, certain cells in the tail stump reverse their differentiated state, divide, and then differentiate again to give rise to a new tail. Many other animals, especially among the invertebrates (sea stars and sponges, for example), can regenerate lost parts, and isolated pieces of a few relatively simple animals can dedifferentiate and then develop into an entirely new organism (see Figure 8.1).

▶ Figure 11.11 **Test-tube cloning of an orchid.** Tissue removed from the stem of an orchid plant and placed in growth medium may begin dividing and eventually grow into an adult plant. The new plant is a genetic duplicate of the parent plant. This process proves that mature plant cells can reverse their differentiation and develop into all the specialized cells of an adult plant.

| Cells removed from orchid plant | Cells in growth medium | Single cell / Cell division in culture | Young plant | Adult plant |

Reproductive Cloning of Animals

Animal cloning is achieved through a procedure called **nuclear transplantation** (Figure 11.12). First performed in the 1950s on frog embryos and in the 1990s on adult mammals, nuclear transplantation involves replacing the nucleus of an egg cell or a zygote with a nucleus removed from an adult body cell. If properly stimulated, the recipient cell may then begin to divide. Repeated cell divisions form a hollow ball of about 100 cells. At this point, the cells may be used for different purposes, as indicated by the two branches in Figure 11.12.

If the animal to be cloned is a mammal, further development requires implanting the early embryo into the uterus of a surrogate mother (Figure 11.12, upper branch). The resulting animal will be a "clone" (genetic copy) of the donor. This type of cloning is called **reproductive cloning** because it results in the birth of a new animal.

In 1996, researchers used reproductive cloning to produce the first mammal cloned from an adult cell, a sheep named Dolly. The researchers fused specially treated sheep cells with eggs from which they had removed the nuclei. After several days of growth, the resulting embryos were implanted in the uteruses of surrogate mothers. One of the embryos developed into Dolly—and, as expected, Dolly resembled the nucleus donor, not the egg donor or the surrogate mother.

Cloning may help save the giant panda from extinction.

Practical Applications of Reproductive Cloning

Since the first success in 1996, researchers have cloned many species of mammals, including mice, horses, dogs, mules, cows, pigs, rabbits, ferrets, camels, goats, and cats (Figure 11.13a). Why would anyone want to do this? In agriculture, farm animals with specific sets of desirable traits might be cloned to produce identical herds. In research, genetically identical animals can provide perfect "control animals" for experiments. The pharmaceutical industry is experimenting with cloning animals for potential medical use (Figure 11.13b). For example, researchers have produced pig clones that lack a gene for a protein that can cause immune system rejection in humans. Organs from such pigs may one day be used in human patients who require life-saving transplants.

Perhaps the most intriguing use of reproductive cloning is to restock populations of endangered animals. Among the rare animals that have been cloned are a wild mouflon (a small European sheep), a gaur (an Asian ox), and gray wolves (Figure 11.13c), and many others are being attempted. In 2003, a banteng (a Javanese cow whose numbers have dwindled to just a few in the wild) was cloned using frozen cells from a zoo-raised banteng that had died 23 years prior. Scientists obtained banteng skin tissue from "The Frozen Zoo," a facility in San Diego, California, where samples from rare or endangered animals are stored for conservation. The scientists transplanted nuclei from the frozen cells

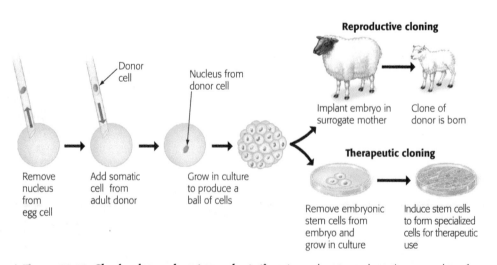

▲ Figure 11.12 **Cloning by nuclear transplantation.** In nuclear transplantation, a nucleus from an adult body cell is injected into a nucleus-free egg cell. The resulting embryo may then be used to produce a new organism (reproductive cloning, shown in the upper branch) or to provide stem cells (therapeutic cloning, lower branch).

into nucleus-free eggs from dairy cows. The resulting embryos were implanted into surrogate cows, leading to the birth of a healthy baby banteng. This success shows that it is possible to produce a baby even when a female of the donor species is unavailable. Scientists may someday be able to use similar cross-species methods to clone an animal from a recently extinct species.

The use of cloning to repopulate endangered species holds tremendous promise. However, cloning may also create new problems. Conservationists argue that cloning may detract from efforts to preserve natural habitats. They correctly point out that cloning does not increase genetic diversity and is therefore not as beneficial to endangered species as natural reproduction. In addition, an increasing body of evidence suggests that cloned animals are less healthy than animals produced via fertilization: Many cloned animals exhibit defects such as susceptibility to obesity, pneumonia, liver failure, and premature death. Dolly the cloned sheep, for example, was euthanized in 2003 after suffering complications from a lung disease usually seen only in much older sheep. She was 6 years old, while her breed has a life expectancy of 12 years. Some evidence suggests that chromosomal changes in the cloned animals are the cause, but the effects of cloning on animal health are still being investigated.

Human Cloning

The cloning of various mammals has heightened speculation that humans could be cloned. Critics point out the many practical and ethical objections to human cloning. Practically, cloning of mammals is extremely difficult and inefficient. Only a small percentage of cloned embryos (usually less than 10%) develop normally, and they appear less healthy than naturally born kin. Ethically, the discussion about whether or not people should be cloned—and if so, under what circumstances—is far from settled. Meanwhile, the research and the debate continue. ☑

☑ **CHECKPOINT**

Imagine that mouse coat color is always passed down from parent to offspring. Suppose a nucleus from an adult body cell of a black mouse is injected into an egg removed from a white mouse, and then the embryo is implanted into a brown mouse. What would be the color of the resulting cloned mice?

Answer: black, the color of the nucleus donor

▼ Figure 11.13 **Reproductive cloning of mammals.**

(a) The first clone. Dolly the sheep, shown in 1996 with her lone parent, was the first mammal cloned from an adult cell.

(b) Cloning for medical use. These piglets are clones of a pig that was genetically modified to lack a protein that causes transplant rejection in humans.

(c) Clones of endangered animals

Mouflon lamb with mother

Banteng

Gaur

207

Therapeutic Cloning and Stem Cells

The lower branch of Figure 11.12 shows the process of **therapeutic cloning**. The purpose of this procedure is not to produce a living organism but rather to produce embryonic stem cells.

Embryonic Stem Cells

In mammals, **embryonic stem cells (ES cells)** are obtained by removing cells from an early embryo and growing them in laboratory culture. Embryonic stem cells can divide indefinitely, and under the right conditions—such as the presence of certain growth-stimulating proteins—can (hypothetically) develop into a wide variety of different specialized cells (**Figure 11.14**). If scientists can discover the right conditions, they may be able to grow cells for the repair of injured or diseased organs. Some people speculate, for example, that ES cells may one day be used to replace cells damaged by spinal cord injuries or heart attacks. The use of embryonic stem cells in therapeutic cloning is controversial, however, because the removal of ES cells destroys the embryo.

Umbilical Cord Blood Banking

Another source of stem cells is blood collected from the umbilical cord and placenta at birth (**Figure 11.15**). Such stem cells appear to be partially differentiated. In 2005, doctors reported that an infusion of umbilical cord blood stem cells appeared to cure some babies of Krabbe disease, a fatal inherited disorder of the nervous system. Other people have received cord blood as a treatment for leukemia. To date, however, most attempts at umbilical cord blood therapy have not been successful. At present, the American Academy of Pediatrics recommends cord blood banking only for babies born into families with a known genetic risk.

Adult Stem Cells

Embryonic stem cells are not the only stem cells available to researchers. **Adult stem cells** can also generate replacements for some of the body's cells. Adult stem cells are further along the road to differentiation than ES cells and can therefore give rise to only a few related types of specialized cells. For example, stem cells in bone marrow generate different kinds of blood cells. Adult stem cells from donor bone marrow have long been used as a source of immune system cells in patients whose own immune systems have been destroyed by disease or cancer treatments.

Because no embryonic tissue is involved in their harvest, adult stem cells are less ethically problematic than ES cells. However, many researchers hypothesize that only the more versatile ES cells are likely to lead to groundbreaking advances in human health. Recent research has shown that some adult cells, such as human skin cells, may be reprogrammed to act like ES cells. In the near future, such cells may prove to be both therapeutically useful and ethically clear. ☑

☑ **CHECKPOINT**

How do the results of reproductive cloning and therapeutic cloning differ?

Answer: Reproductive cloning results in the production of a live individual; therapeutic cloning produces stem cells.

▼ Figure 11.14 **Differentiation of embryonic stem cells in culture.** Scientists hope to someday discover growth conditions that will stimulate cultured stem cells to differentiate into specialized cells.

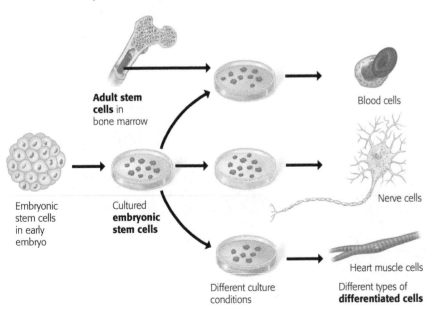

Adult stem cells in bone marrow

Embryonic stem cells in early embryo

Cultured **embryonic stem cells**

Different culture conditions

Blood cells

Nerve cells

Heart muscle cells

Different types of **differentiated cells**

▼ Figure 11.15 **Umbilical cord blood banking.** Just after birth, a doctor inserts a needle into the umbilical cord and extracts ¼ to ½ cup of blood. The umbilical cord blood (inset), rich in stem cells, is frozen and kept in a blood bank, where it is available if needed for medical treatment.

The Genetic Basis of Cancer

Cancer includes a variety of diseases in which cells escape from the control mechanisms that normally limit their growth and division (as introduced in Chapter 8). This escape involves changes in gene expression.

Genes That Cause Cancer

One of the earliest clues to the role of genes in cancer was the discovery in 1911 of a virus that causes cancer in chickens. Viruses that cause cancer can become permanent residents in host cells by inserting their nucleic acid into the DNA of host chromosomes. Over the last century, researchers have identified a number of viruses that harbor cancer-causing genes. One example is the human papillomavirus (HPV), which can be transmitted through sexual contact and is associated with several types of cancer, including cervical cancer.

Oncogenes and Tumor-Suppressor Genes

In 1976, American molecular biologists J. Michael Bishop, Harold Varmus, and their colleagues made a startling discovery. They found that a cancer-causing chicken virus contains a cancer-causing gene that is an altered version of a normal chicken gene. A gene that causes cancer is called an **oncogene** ("tumor gene"). Subsequent research has shown that the chromosomes of many animals, including humans, contain genes that can be converted to oncogenes. A normal gene with the potential to become an oncogene is called a **proto-oncogene**. (These terms can be confusing, so let's repeat them: A *proto-oncogene* is a normal, healthy gene that, if changed, can become a cancer-causing *oncogene*.) A cell can acquire an oncogene from a virus or from the mutation of one of its own proto-oncogenes.

How can a change in a gene cause cancer? Searching for the normal roles of proto-oncogenes in the cell, researchers found that many of these genes code for **growth factors**—proteins that stimulate cell division—or for other proteins that affect the cell cycle. When all these proteins are functioning normally, in the right amounts at the right times, they help keep the rate of cell division at an appropriate level. When they malfunction—if a growth factor becomes hyperactive, for example—cancer (uncontrolled cell growth) may result.

For a proto-oncogene to become an oncogene, a mutation must occur in the cell's DNA. **Figure 11.16** illustrates three kinds of changes in DNA that can produce active oncogenes. In all three cases, abnormal gene expression stimulates the cell to divide excessively.

Changes in genes whose products inhibit cell division are also involved in cancer. These genes are called **tumor-suppressor genes** because the proteins they encode normally help prevent uncontrolled cell growth (Figure 11.17). Any mutation that keeps a growth-inhibiting protein from being made or from functioning may contribute to the development of cancer. Researchers have identified many mutations in both tumor-suppressor and growth factor genes that are associated with cancer, as we'll discuss next.

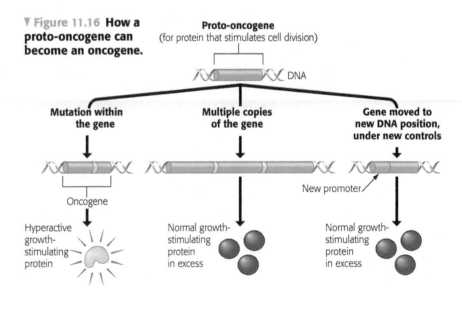

▼ Figure 11.16 **How a proto-oncogene can become an oncogene.**

Proto-oncogene
(for protein that stimulates cell division)

DNA

Mutation within the gene | Multiple copies of the gene | Gene moved to new DNA position, under new controls

Oncogene

New promoter

Hyperactive growth-stimulating protein | Normal growth-stimulating protein in excess | Normal growth-stimulating protein in excess

▼ Figure 11.17 **Tumor-suppressor genes.**

Tumor-suppressor gene

Mutated tumor-suppressor gene

Normal growth-inhibiting protein

Defective, nonfunctioning protein

Cell division under control

Cell division not under control

(a) **Normal cell growth.** A tumor-suppressor gene normally codes for a protein that inhibits cell growth and division. Such genes help prevent cancerous tumors from arising or spreading.

(b) **Uncontrolled cell growth (cancer).** When a mutation in a tumor-suppressor gene makes its protein defective, cells that are usually under the control of the normal protein may divide excessively, forming a tumor.

209

Cancer THE PROCESS OF SCIENCE

Are Childhood Tumors Different?

Medical researchers have made many **observations** of specific mutations that can lead to cancer. They therefore **question** whether different kinds of cancers are associated with specific mutations. A large research team led by the Johns Hopkins Kimmel Cancer Center in Baltimore formed the **hypothesis** that young patients with medulloblastoma (MB)—the most common pediatric brain cancer and the deadliest form of childhood cancer (Figure 11.18)—harbor unique mutations. They made the **prediction** that a genetic map of MB cells from childhood tumors would have cancer-associated mutations not found in adult brain cancer tissue.

The **experiment** involved sequencing all the genes in tumors removed from 22 pediatric MB patients and comparing them with normal tissue from these same patients. Their **results** showed that each tumor had an average of 11 mutations. Although this may seem like a lot, it is actually five to ten times fewer than the number of mutations associated with MB in adult patients. Young MB patients therefore seem to have fewer, but deadlier,

mutations. When they investigated the role that the mutated genes play, the research team found that some help control DNA packing, whereas others play a role in the development of organs. The researchers hope that this new knowledge about the genetic basis of MB may be used to develop new therapies for this often fatal disease.

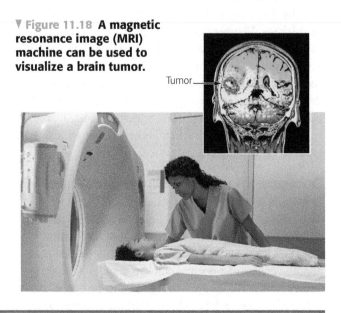

▼ Figure 11.18 **A magnetic resonance image (MRI) machine can be used to visualize a brain tumor.**

Tumor

The Progression of a Cancer

Nearly 150,000 Americans will be stricken by cancer of the colon (the main part of the large intestine) this year. One of the best-understood types of human cancer, colon cancer illustrates an important principle about how cancer develops: Although we still don't know exactly how a particular cell becomes a cancer cell, we do know that more than one mutation is needed to produce a full-fledged cancer cell. As in many cancers, the development of colon cancer is a gradual process.

As shown in Figure 11.19, ❶ colon cancer begins when an oncogene arises through mutation, causing unusually frequent division of normal-looking cells in the colon lining. ❷ Later, additional DNA mutations (such as the inactivation of a tumor-suppressor gene) cause the growth of a small benign tumor (called a polyp) in the colon wall. The cells of the polyp look normal, although they divide unusually frequently. If detected during a colonoscopy, suspicious polyps can usually be removed before they become a serious risk. ❸ Further mutations

▼ Figure 11.19 **Stepwise development of colon cancer.**

Colon wall

Colon wall

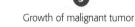

Cellular changes:	Increased cell division	Growth of benign tumor	Growth of malignant tumor
DNA changes:	Oncogene activated	Tumor-suppressor gene inactivated	Second tumor-suppressor gene inactivated

eventually lead to formation of a malignant tumor—a tumor that has the potential to metastasize (spread). It typically takes at least six DNA mutations (usually creating at least one active oncogene and disabling at least one tumor-suppressor gene) before a cell becomes fully cancerous.

The development of a malignant tumor is accompanied by a gradual accumulation of mutations that convert proto-oncogenes to oncogenes and knock out tumor-suppressor genes (Figure 11.20). The requirement for several DNA mutations—usually four or more—explains why cancers can take a long time to develop. This requirement may also help explain why the incidence of cancer increases with age; the longer we live, the more likely we are to accumulate mutations that cause cancer.

Inherited Cancer

The fact that multiple genetic changes are required to produce a cancer cell helps explain the observation that cancers can run in families. An individual inheriting an oncogene or a mutant version of a tumor-suppressor gene is one step closer to accumulating the necessary mutations for cancer to develop than is an individual without any such mutations. Geneticists are therefore devoting much effort to identifying inherited cancer mutations so that predisposition to certain cancers can be detected early in life.

About 15% of colorectal cancers, for example, involve inherited mutations. There is also evidence that inheritance plays a role in 5–10% of patients with breast cancer, a disease that strikes one out of every ten American women (Figure 11.21). Mutations in either or both of two genes—called *BRCA1* (pronounced "braca-1") and *BRCA2*—are found in at least half of inherited breast cancers. Both *BRCA1* and *BRCA2* are considered tumor-suppressor genes because the normal versions protect against breast cancer. A woman who inherits one mutant

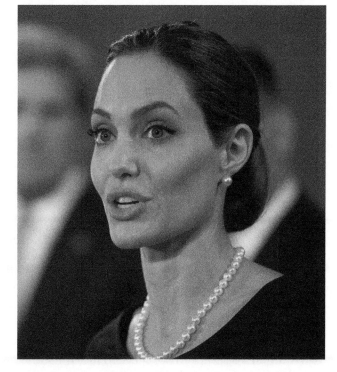

▲ Figure 11.21 **Breast cancer.** In 2013, at age 37, the actress Angelina Jolie underwent a preventive double mastectomy after learning she had a mutant *BRCA1* gene. Jolie's mother, grandmother, and aunt all died young from breast or ovarian cancer.

BRCA1 allele has a 60% probability of developing breast cancer before the age of 50, compared with only a 2% probability for an individual lacking the mutations. Tests using DNA sequencing can now detect these mutations. Unfortunately, these tests are of limited use because surgical removal of the breasts and/or ovaries is the only preventive option currently available to women who carry the mutant genes. ☑

☑ CHECKPOINT

How can a mutation in a tumor-suppressor gene contribute to the development of cancer?

Answer: A mutated tumor-suppressor gene may produce a defective protein that normally inhibits cell division and therefore normally suppresses tumors.

▼ Figure 11.20 **Accumulation of mutations in the development of a cancer cell.**
Mutations leading to cancer accumulate in a lineage of cells. In this figure, colors distinguish the normal cells from cells with one or more mutations, leading to increased cell division and cancer. Once a cancer-promoting mutation occurs (orange band on chromosome), it is passed to all the descendants of the cell carrying it.

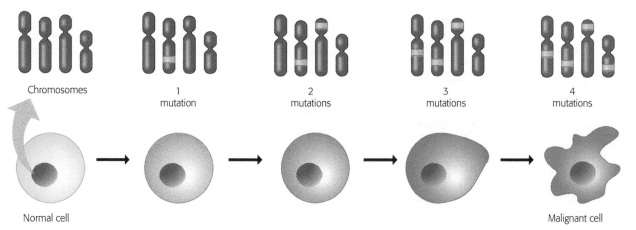

Chromosomes

1 mutation

2 mutations

3 mutations

4 mutations

Normal cell

Malignant cell

Cancer Risk and Prevention

Cancer is the second-leading cause of death (after heart disease) in most industrialized countries. Death rates due to certain forms of cancer have decreased in recent years, but the overall cancer death rate is still on the rise, currently increasing at about 1% per decade.

Although some cancers occur spontaneously, most cancers arise from mutations that are caused by **carcinogens**, cancer-causing agents found in the environment. Mutations often result from decades of exposure to carcinogens. One of the most potent carcinogens is ultraviolet (UV) radiation. Excessive exposure to UV radiation from the sun can cause skin cancer, including a deadly type called melanoma. You can decrease your risk by using sun protection (clothing, lotion, hats, etc.).

The one substance known to cause more cases and types of cancer than any other is tobacco. By a wide margin, more people die from lung cancer (nearly 160,000 Americans in 2014) than from any other form of cancer. Most tobacco-related cancers are due to smoking cigarettes, but smoking cigars, inhaling secondhand smoke, and smokeless tobacco also pose risks. As Table 11.1 indicates, tobacco use, sometimes in combination with alcohol consumption, causes several types of cancer. Exposure to some of the most lethal carcinogens is often a matter of individual choice: Tobacco use, the consumption of alcohol, and excessive time spent in the sun are all avoidable behaviors that affect cancer risk.

Some food choices significantly reduce a person's odds of developing cancer. For instance, eating 20–30 g of plant fiber daily (about the amount found in seven apples), while eating less animal fat may help prevent colon cancer. There is also evidence that certain substances in fruits and vegetables, including vitamins C and E and certain compounds related to vitamin A, may help protect against a variety of cancers. Cabbage and its relatives, such as broccoli and cauliflower, are thought to be especially rich in substances that help prevent cancer, although some of the specific substances have not yet been identified. Determining how diet influences cancer has become an important focus of nutrition research.

The battle against cancer is being waged on many fronts, and there is reason for optimism in the progress being made. It is especially encouraging that we can help reduce our risk of acquiring some of the most common forms of cancer by the choices we make in our daily lives. ☑

> Lifestyle choices you make can dramatically affect your risk of cancer.

☑ CHECKPOINT

Of all known behavioral factors, which one causes the most cancer cases and deaths?

Answer: *tobacco use*

Table 11.1	Cancer in the United States (Ranked by Number of Cases)		
Cancer	**Known or Likely Carcinogens or Factors**	**Estimated Cases (2014)**	**Estimated Deaths (2014)**
Breast	Estrogen; possibly dietary fat	235,000	40,400
Prostate	Testosterone; possibly dietary fat	233,000	29,500
Lung	Cigarette smoke	224,000	159,000
Colon and rectum	High dietary fat; low dietary fiber	136,800	50,310
Skin	Ultraviolet light	81,200	13,000
Lymphomas	Viruses (for some types)	80,000	20,100
Bladder	Cigarette smoke	74,700	15,600
Uterus	Estrogen	65,000	12,600
Kidney	Cigarette smoke	63,900	13,900
Leukemias	X-rays; benzene; viruses (for some types)	52,400	24,100
Pancreas	Cigarette smoke	46,400	39,600
Liver	Alcohol; hepatitis viruses	33,200	23,000
Brain and nerve	Trauma; X-rays	23,400	14,300
Stomach	Table salt; cigarette smoke	22,200	11,000
Ovary	Large number of ovulation cycles	22,000	14,300
Cervix	Viruses; cigarette smoke	12,400	4,000
All other types		259,940	101,010
Total		1,665,540	585,720

Data from: Cancer Facts and Figures 2014 (American Cancer Society Inc.).

Cancer EVOLUTION CONNECTION

The Evolution of Cancer in the Body

The theory of evolution describes natural selection acting on populations. Recently, medical researchers have been using an evolutionary perspective to gain insight into the development of tumors, such as the bone tumor shown in Figure 11.22. Evolution drives the growth of a tumor—which can be thought of as a population of cancer cells—and also affects how those cells respond to cancer treatments.

Recall that there are several assumptions behind Darwin's theory of natural selection (see Chapter 1). Let's consider how each one can be applied to cancer. First, all evolving populations have the potential to produce more offspring than can be supported by the environment. Cancer cells, with their uncontrolled growth, clearly demonstrate overproduction. Second, there must be variation among individuals of

the population. Studies of tumor cell DNA, like the one described in the Process of Science section, show genetic variability within tumors. Third, variations in the population must affect survival and reproductive success. Indeed, the accumulation of mutations in cancer cells renders them less susceptible to normal mechanisms of reproductive control. Mutations that enhance survival of malignant cancer cells are passed on to that cell's descendants. In short, a tumor evolves.

Viewing the progression of cancer through the lens of evolution helps explain why there is no easy "cure" for cancer but may also pave the way for novel therapies. For example, some researchers are attempting to "prime" tumors for treatment by increasing the reproductive success of only those cells that will be susceptible to a chemotherapy drug. Our understanding of cancer, like all other aspects of biology, benefits from an evolutionary perspective.

▼ Figure 11.22 **X-ray of shoulder and upper arm, revealing a large bone tumor.**

Chapter Review

SUMMARY OF KEY CONCEPTS

How and Why Genes Are Regulated

The various types of cells in a multicellular organism owe their distinctiveness to different combinations of genes being turned on and off via gene regulation in each cell type.

Gene Regulation in Bacteria

An operon is a cluster of genes with related functions together with their promoter and other DNA sequences that control their transcription. For example, the *lac* operon allows *E. coli* to produce enzymes for lactose use only when the sugar is present.

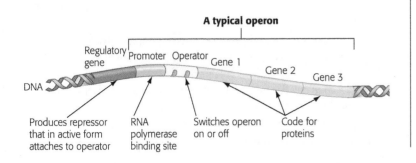

Gene Regulation in Eukaryotic Cells

In the nucleus of eukaryotic cells, there are several possible control points in the pathway of gene expression.

- DNA packing tends to block gene expression by preventing access of transcription proteins to the DNA. An extreme example is X chromosome inactivation in the cells of female mammals.

- The most important control point in both eukaryotes and prokaryotes is at gene transcription. Various regulatory proteins interact with DNA and with each other to turn the transcription of eukaryotic genes on or off.

- There are also opportunities for the control of eukaryotic gene expression after transcription, when introns are cut out of the RNA and a cap and tail are added to process RNA transcripts into mRNA.

- In the cytoplasm, presence of microRNAs may block the translation of an mRNA, and various proteins may regulate the start of translation.

- Finally, the cell may activate the finished protein in various ways (for instance, by cutting out portions or chemical modification). Eventually, the protein may be selectively broken down.

Information Flow: Cell Signaling

Cell-to-cell signaling is key to the development and function-ing of multicellular organisms. Signal transduction pathways convert molecular messages to cell responses, such as the transcription of particular genes.

Homeotic Genes

Evidence for the evolutionary importance of gene regulation is apparent in homeotic genes, master genes that regulate other genes that in turn control embryonic development.

DNA Microarrays: Visualizing Gene Expression

DNA microarrays can be used to determine which genes are turned on in a particular cell type.

Cloning Plants and Animals

The Genetic Potential of Cells

Most differentiated cells retain a complete set of genes, so an orchid plant, for example, can be made to grow from a single orchid cell. Under con-trolled conditions, animals can also be cloned.

Reproductive Cloning of Animals

Nuclear transplantation is a procedure whereby a donor cell nucleus is inserted into an egg from which the nucleus has been removed. First demonstrated in frogs in the 1950s, reproductive cloning was used in 1996 to clone a sheep from an adult cell and has since been used to create many other cloned animals.

Nucleus from donor cell — Early embryo resulting from nuclear transplantation — Embryo implanted in surrogate mother — Clone of nucleus donor

Therapeutic Cloning and Stem Cells

The purpose of therapeutic cloning is to produce embryonic stem cells for medical uses. Embryonic, umbilical cord, and adult stem cells all show promise for therapeutic uses.

Nucleus from donor cell — Early embryo resulting from nuclear transplantation — Embryonic stem cells in culture — Specialized cells

The Genetic Basis of Cancer

Genes That Cause Cancer

Cancer cells, which divide uncontrollably, can result from mutations in genes whose protein products regulate the cell cycle.

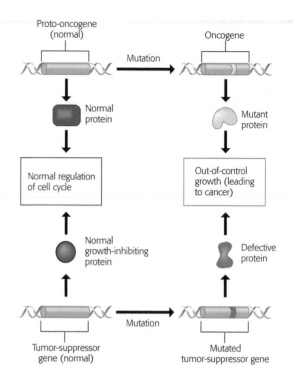

Proto-oncogene (normal) — Mutation → Oncogene
Normal protein — Mutant protein
Normal regulation of cell cycle — Out-of-control growth (leading to cancer)
Normal growth-inhibiting protein — Defective protein
Tumor-suppressor gene (normal) — Mutation → Mutated tumor-suppressor gene

Many proto-oncogenes and tumor-suppressor genes code for proteins active in signal transduction pathways regulating cell division. Mutations of these genes cause malfunction of the pathways. Cancer results from a series of genetic changes in a cell lineage. Researchers have identified many genes that, when mutated, promote the development of cancer.

Cancer Risk and Prevention

Reducing exposure to carcinogens (which induce cancer-causing mutations) and making other healthful lifestyle choices can help reduce cancer risk.

MasteringBiology®

For practice quizzes, BioFlix animations, MP3 tutorials, video tutors, and more study tools designed for this textbook, go to MasteringBiology®

SELF-QUIZ

1. Your bone cells, muscle cells, and skin cells look different because
   a. different kinds of genes are present in each kind of cell.
   b. they are present in different organs.
   c. different genes are active in each kind of cell.
   d. different mutations have occurred in each kind of cell.

2. A group of prokaryotic genes with related functions that are regulated as a single unit, along with the control sequences that perform this regulation, is called a(n) _____.

3. The regulation of gene expression must be more complex in multicellular eukaryotes than in prokaryotes because
   a. eukaryotic cells are much larger.
   b. in a multicellular eukaryote, different cells are specialized for different functions.
   c. prokaryotes are restricted to stable environments.
   d. eukaryotes have fewer genes, so each gene must do several jobs.

4. A eukaryotic gene was inserted into the DNA of a bacterium. The bacterium then transcribed this gene into mRNA and translated the mRNA into protein. The protein produced was useless and contained many more amino acids than the protein made by the eukaryotic cell. Why?
   a. The mRNA was not spliced as it is in eukaryotes.
   b. Eukaryotes and prokaryotes use different genetic codes.
   c. Repressor proteins interfered with transcription and translation.
   d. Ribosomes were not able to bind to tRNA.

5. How does dense packing of DNA in chromosomes prevent gene expression?

6. What evidence demonstrates that differentiated cells in a plant or animal retain their full genetic potential?

7. The most common procedure for cloning an animal is _____.

8. What is learned from a DNA microarray?

9. Which of the following is a substantial difference between embryonic stem cells and the stem cells found in adult tissues?
   a. In laboratory culture, only adult stem cells are immortal.
   b. In nature, only embryonic stem cells give rise to all the different types of cells in the organism.
   c. Only adult stem cells can be made to differentiate in the laboratory.
   d. Only embryonic stem cells are in every tissue of the adult body.

10. Name three potential sources of stem cells.

11. What is the difference between oncogenes and proto-oncogenes? How can one turn into the other? What function do proto-oncogenes serve?

12. A mutation in a single gene may cause a major change in the body of a fruit fly, such as an extra pair of legs or wings. Yet it takes many genes to produce a wing or leg. How can a change in just one gene cause such a big change in the body? What are such genes called?

Answers to these questions can be found in Appendix: Self-Quiz Answers.

THE PROCESS OF SCIENCE

13. Study the depiction of the *lac* operon in Figure 11.2. Normally, the genes are turned off when lactose is not present. Lactose activates the genes, which code for enzymes that enable the cell to use lactose. Mutations can alter the function of this operon. Predict how the following mutations would affect the function of the operon in the presence and absence of lactose:
   a. mutation of regulatory gene; repressor will not bind to lactose
   b. mutation of operator; repressor will not bind to operator
   c. mutation of regulatory gene; repressor will not bind to operator
   d. mutation of promoter; RNA polymerase will not attach to promoter

14. The human body has a far greater variety of proteins than genes, a fact that seems to highlight the importance of alternative RNA splicing, which allows several different mRNAs to be made from a single gene. Suppose you have samples of two types of adult cells from one person. Design an experiment using microarrays to determine whether or not the different gene expression is due to alternative RNA splicing.

15. Because a cat must have both orange and non-orange alleles to be tortoiseshell (see Figure 11.4), we would expect only female cats, which have two X chromosomes, to be tortoiseshell. Normal male cats (XY) can carry only one of the two alleles. Male tortoiseshell cats are rare and usually sterile. What might you guess their genotype to be?

16. Design a DNA microarray experiment that measures the difference in gene expression between normal colon cells and cells from a colon tumor.

17. **Interpreting Data** Review Table 11.1, which lists the number of diagnoses and the number of deaths for many types of cancer. We can estimate the deadliness of each type of cancer by dividing the number of deaths by the number of cases. (This is not accurate, however, because someone diagnosed during a particular year will not necessarily die during that same year, but it is a useful approximation.) If nearly everyone who received a diagnosis of one particular type of cancer dies, that ratio will be near 1 (or 100% deadly). If many more people receive diagnoses than die, the ratio will be near 0 (or near 0% deadly). Using this criteria, which two forms of cancer listed are the deadliest? The least deadly? What is the overall ratio for all types of cancer? What does this tell you about cancer survivability in general?

BIOLOGY AND SOCIETY

18. A chemical called dioxin is produced as a by-product of certain chemical manufacturing processes. Trace amounts of this substance were present in Agent Orange, a defoliant sprayed on vegetation during the Vietnam War. There has been a continuing controversy over its effects on soldiers exposed to Agent Orange during the war. Animal tests have suggested that dioxin can cause cancer, liver and thymus damage, immune system suppression, and birth defects; at high dosage it can be lethal. But such animal tests are inconclusive; a hamster is not affected by a dose that can kill a much larger guinea pig, for example. Researchers have discovered that dioxin enters a cell and binds to a protein that in turn attaches to the cell's DNA. How might this mechanism help explain the variety of dioxin's effects on different body systems and in different animals? How might you determine whether a particular individual became ill as a result of exposure to dioxin? Do you think this information is relevant in the lawsuits of soldiers suing over exposure to Agent Orange? Why or why not?

19. There are genetic tests available for several types of "inherited cancer." The results from these tests cannot usually predict that someone will get cancer within a particular amount of time. Rather, they indicate only that a person has an increased risk of developing cancer. For many of these cancers, lifestyle changes cannot decrease a person's risk. Therefore, some people consider the tests useless. If your close family had a history of cancer and a test were available, would you want to get screened? Why or why not? What would you do with this information? If a sibling decided to get screened, explain whether you would want to know the results.

DNA Technology

Why DNA Technology Matters

You have about the same number of genes as a microscopic worm, and only half as many as a rice plant.

Millions of individuals with diabetes live healthier lives thanks to insulin made by bacteria.

Someday, genetically modified potatoes could prevent tens of thousands of children from dying of cholera.

DNA Profiling BIOLOGY AND SOCIETY

Using DNA to Establish Guilt and Innocence

It was a horrific crime in the heart of the nation's capital: On February 24, 1981, a man broke into an apartment, just miles from the White House, and attacked a 27-year-old woman. After binding and raping her, the perpetrator stole traveler's checks and ran off. The victim had only glimpses of her attacker. Several weeks later, a police officer thought that 18-year-old Kirk Odom resembled a sketch of the perpetrator. A month later, the victim picked Odom out of a police lineup.

At trial, a Special Agent of the FBI testified that hair found in the victim's clothing, when viewed under a microscope, was "indistinguishable" from Odom's hair. Despite Odom having an alibi for his whereabouts on the night of the crime, after just a few hours of deliberation the jury convicted Odom of several charges, including rape while armed. He was sentenced to 20 to 66 years in prison. Odom served more than 20 years before being released on lifelong parole as a registered sex offender. However, in February 2011, prompted by recent discoveries that indicated that the FBI's microscopic hair analysis technique was flawed—and subsequent overturned convictions in other cases—a motion was filed to reopen the Odom case for DNA testing.

Modern forensic DNA analysis hinges on a simple fact: The cells of every person (except identical twins) contain unique DNA. DNA profiling is the analysis of DNA samples to determine whether they come from the same individual. In the Odom case, the government located sheets, clothing, and hair evidence from the 1981 crime scene. In the more recent analysis, the results were conclusive and irrefutable: The DNA left at the crime scene did *not* match Odom's. In fact, the DNA matched a different man, a convicted sex offender (who was never charged because the statute of limitations on the crime had expired). On July 13, 2012—Odom's 50th birthday—the court acknowledged that the original hair analysis data was erroneous and that Kirk Odom had "suffered a terrible injustice." After 30 years, Odom was officially declared innocent by the court.

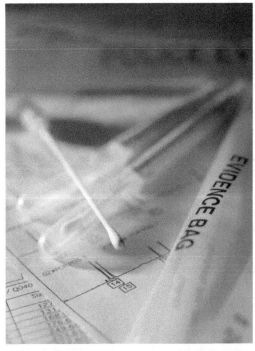

A DNA profile. Even minuscule bits of evidence can provide a DNA profile.

A steady stream of stories such as this one demonstrates that DNA technology can provide evidence of either guilt or innocence. Beyond the courtroom, DNA technology has led to some of the most remarkable scientific advances in recent years: Crop plants have been genetically modified to produce their own insecticides; human genes are being compared with those of other animals to help shed light on what makes us distinctly human; and significant advances have been made toward detecting and curing fatal genetic diseases. This chapter will describe these and other uses of DNA technology and explain how various DNA techniques are performed. We'll also examine some of the social, legal, and ethical issues that lie at the intersection of biology and society.

Genetic Engineering

You may think of **biotechnology**, the manipulation of organisms or their components to make useful products, as a modern phenomenon, but it actually dates back to the dawn of civilization. Consider such ancient practices as using yeast to make bread and beer and the selective breeding of livestock. But when people use the term *biotechnology* today, they are usually referring to DNA technology, modern laboratory techniques for studying and manipulating genetic material. Using the methods of DNA technology, scientists can modify specific genes and move them between organisms as different as bacteria, plants, and animals. Organisms that have acquired one or more genes by artificial means are called **genetically modified (GM) organisms**. If the newly acquired gene is from another organism, typically of another species, the recombinant organism is called a **transgenic organism**.

In the 1970s, the field of biotechnology exploded with the invention of methods for making recombinant DNA in the laboratory. Scientists can construct **recombinant DNA** by combining pieces of DNA from two different sources—often from different species—to form a single DNA molecule. Recombinant DNA technology is widely used in **genetic engineering**, the direct manipulation of genes for practical purposes. Scientists have genetically engineered bacteria to

mass-produce a variety of useful chemicals, from cancer drugs to pesticides. Scientists have also transferred genes from bacteria to plants and from one animal species to another (Figure 12.1). Such engineering can serve a variety of purposes, from basic research (What does this gene do?) to medical applications (Can we create animal models for this human disease?).

Recombinant DNA Techniques

Although genetic engineering can be performed on a variety of organisms, bacteria (*Escherichia coli*, in particular) are the workhorses of modern biotechnology. To manipulate genes in the laboratory, biologists often use bacterial **plasmids**, which are small, circular DNA molecules that duplicate separately from the larger bacterial chromosome (Figure 12.2). Because plasmids can carry virtually any gene and are passed from one generation of bacteria to the next, they are key tools for **gene cloning**, the production of multiple identical copies of a gene-carrying piece of DNA. Gene cloning methods are central to the production of useful products from genetically engineered organisms. ☑

▼ Figure 12.1 **Genetic engineers produced glowing fish by transferring a gene for a fluorescent protein originally obtained from jellies ("jellyfish").**

Plasmids

Bacterial chromosome

Remnant of bacterium

Colorized TEM 2,700x

▲ Figure 12.2 **Bacterial plasmids.** The micrograph shows a bacterial cell that has been ruptured, revealing one long chromosome and several smaller plasmids. The inset is an enlarged view of a single plasmid.

How to Clone a Gene

Consider a typical genetic engineering challenge: A genetic engineer at a pharmaceutical company identifies a gene of interest that codes for a valuable protein, such as a potential new drug. The biologist wants to manufacture the protein on a large scale. Figure 12.3 illustrates a way to accomplish this by using recombinant DNA techniques.

To start, the biologist isolates two kinds of DNA: bacterial plasmids that will serve as **vectors** (gene carriers, shown in blue in the figure) and DNA from another organism that includes the gene of interest (shown in yellow). This foreign DNA may be from any type of organism, even a human. ❶ The DNA from the two sources is joined together, resulting in recombinant DNA plasmids. ❷ The recombinant plasmids are then mixed with bacteria. Under the right conditions, the bacteria take up the recombinant plasmids. ❸ Each bacterium, carrying its recombinant plasmid, is allowed to reproduce via cell division to form a **clone**, a group of identical cells descended from a single original cell. As the bacteria multiply, the foreign gene carried by the recombinant plasmid is also copied. ❹ The transgenic bacteria with the gene of interest can then be grown in large tanks, producing the protein in marketable quantities. The end products of gene cloning may be copies of the gene itself, to be used in additional genetic engineering projects, or the protein product of the cloned gene, to be harvested and used. ✓

☑ **CHECKPOINT**

Why are plasmids valuable tools for the production of recombinant DNA?

Answer: Plasmids can carry virtually any foreign gene and are replicated by their bacterial host cells.

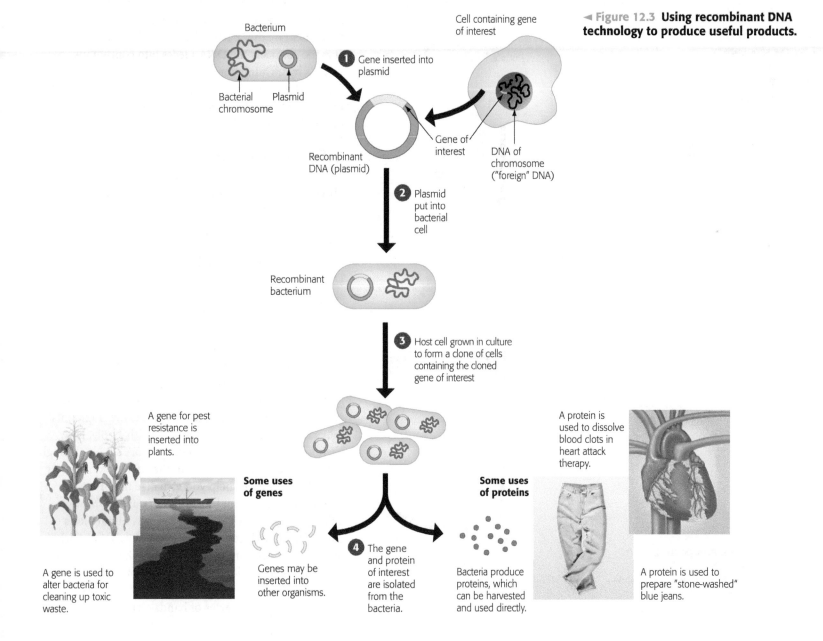

◄ Figure 12.3 **Using recombinant DNA technology to produce useful products.**

Bacterium

Bacterial chromosome   Plasmid

Cell containing gene of interest

❶ Gene inserted into plasmid

Recombinant DNA (plasmid)

Gene of interest

DNA of chromosome ("foreign" DNA)

❷ Plasmid put into bacterial cell

Recombinant bacterium

❸ Host cell grown in culture to form a clone of cells containing the cloned gene of interest

A gene for pest resistance is inserted into plants.

A protein is used to dissolve blood clots in heart attack therapy.

Some uses of genes

Some uses of proteins

A gene is used to alter bacteria for cleaning up toxic waste.

Genes may be inserted into other organisms.

❹ The gene and protein of interest are isolated from the bacteria.

Bacteria produce proteins, which can be harvested and used directly.

A protein is used to prepare "stone-washed" blue jeans.

219

Cutting and Pasting DNA with Restriction Enzymes

As shown in Figure 12.3, recombinant DNA is created by combining two ingredients: a bacterial plasmid and the gene of interest. To understand how these DNA molecules are spliced together, you need to learn how enzymes cut and paste DNA.

The cutting tools used for making recombinant DNA are bacterial enzymes called **restriction enzymes**. Biologists have identified hundreds of restriction enzymes, each recognizing a particular short DNA sequence, usually four to eight nucleotides long. For example, one restriction enzyme only recognizes the DNA sequence GAATTC, whereas another recognizes GGATCC. The DNA sequence recognized by a particular restriction enzyme is called a **restriction site**. After a restriction enzyme binds to its restriction site, it cuts the two strands of the DNA by breaking chemical bonds at

specific points within the sequence, like a pair of highly specific molecular scissors.

The top of Figure 12.4 shows a piece of DNA (blue) that contains one restriction site for a particular restriction enzyme. ❶ The restriction enzyme cuts the DNA strands between the bases A and G within the recognition sequence, producing pieces of DNA called **restriction fragments**. The staggered cuts yield two double-stranded DNA fragments with single-stranded ends, called "sticky ends." Sticky ends are the key to joining DNA restriction fragments originating from different sources. ❷ Next, a piece of DNA from another source (yellow) is added. Notice that the yellow DNA has single-stranded ends identical in base sequence to the sticky ends on the blue DNA because the same restriction enzyme was used to cut both types of DNA. ❸ The complementary ends on the blue and yellow fragments stick together by base pairing. ❹ The union between the blue and yellow fragments is then made permanent by the "pasting" enzyme **DNA ligase**. This enzyme connects the DNA pieces into continuous strands by forming bonds between adjacent nucleotides. The final outcome is a single molecule of recombinant DNA. The process just described explains what happens in step 1 of Figure 12.3. ☑

Gel Electrophoresis

To separate and visualize DNA fragments of different lengths, researchers carry out a technique called **gel electrophoresis**, a method for sorting macromolecules—usually proteins or nucleic acids—primarily by their electrical charge and size. Figure 12.5 shows how gel electrophoresis separates DNA fragments obtained from different sources. A sample with many copies of the DNA from each source is placed in a separate well (hole) at one end of a flat, rectangular gel. The gel is a thin slab of jellylike material that acts as a molecular sieve. A negatively charged electrode is then attached to the DNA-containing end of the gel and a positive electrode to the other end. Because the phosphate (PO_4^-) groups of nucleotides give DNA fragments a negative charge, the fragments move through the gel toward the positive pole. However, longer DNA fragments move more slowly through the thicket of polymer fibers in the gel than do shorter DNA fragments. To help you visualize the process, imagine a small animal scampering quickly through a thicket of jungle vines, while a large animal plods along the same distance much more slowly. Similarly, over time, shorter molecules move farther through a gel than longer molecules. Gel electrophoresis thus separates DNA fragments by length. When the current is turned off, a series of bands—visible as blue

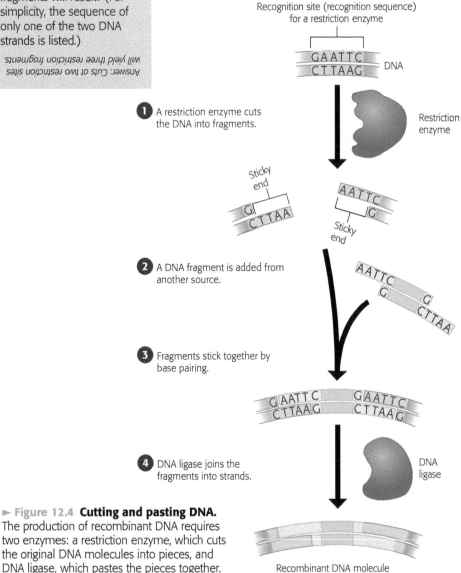

Recognition site (recognition sequence) for a restriction enzyme

GAATTC
CTTAAG   DNA

❶ A restriction enzyme cuts the DNA into fragments.

Restriction enzyme

Sticky end

G
CTTAA

AATTC
G

Sticky end

❷ A DNA fragment is added from another source.

AATTC
G   G
       CTTAA

❸ Fragments stick together by base pairing.

GAATTC   GAATTC
CTTAAG   CTTAAG

❹ DNA ligase joins the fragments into strands.

DNA ligase

Recombinant DNA molecule

▶ Figure 12.4 **Cutting and pasting DNA.** The production of recombinant DNA requires two enzymes: a restriction enzyme, which cuts the original DNA molecules into pieces, and DNA ligase, which pastes the pieces together.

▼ Figure 12.5 **Gel electrophoresis of DNA molecules.** The photo shows DNA fragments of various sizes visibly stained on the gel.

Mixture of DNA fragments of different sizes

Power source

Gel

Band of longest (slowest) fragments

Band of shortest (fastest) fragments

Completed gel

smudges in the photograph of the gel—is left in each column of the gel. Each band is a collection of DNA fragments of the same length. The bands can be made visible by staining, by exposure onto photographic film (if the DNA is radioactively labeled), or by measuring fluorescence (if the DNA is labeled with a fluorescent dye). ☑

Pharmaceutical Applications

By transferring the gene for a desired protein into a bacterium, yeast, or other kind of cell that is easy to grow in culture, scientists can produce large quantities of useful proteins that are present naturally only in small amounts. In this section, you'll learn about some applications of recombinant DNA technology.

Humulin is human insulin produced by genetically modified bacteria (**Figure 12.6**). In humans, insulin is a protein normally made by the

Millions of individuals with diabetes live healthier lives thanks to insulin made by bacteria.

▶ Figure 12.6 **Humulin, human insulin produced by genetically modified bacteria.**

pancreas. Insulin functions as a hormone and helps regulate the level of glucose in the blood. If the body fails to produce enough insulin, the result is type 1 diabetes. There is no cure, so people with this disease must inject themselves daily with doses of insulin for the rest of their lives.

Because human insulin is not readily available, diabetes was historically treated using insulin from cows and pigs. This treatment was problematic, however. Pig and cow insulins can cause allergic reactions in people because their chemical structures differ slightly from that of human insulin. In addition, by the 1970s, the supply of beef and pork pancreas available for insulin extraction could not keep up with the demand.

In 1978, scientists working at a biotechnology company chemically synthesized DNA fragments and linked them to form the two genes that code for the two polypeptides that make up human insulin (see Figure 11.7). They then inserted these artificial genes into *E. coli* host cells. Under proper growing conditions, the transgenic bacteria cranked out large quantities of the human protein. In 1982, Humulin hit the market as the world's first genetically engineered pharmaceutical product. Today, it is produced around the clock in gigantic fermentation vats filled with a liquid culture of bacteria. Each day, more than 4 million people with

☑ **CHECKPOINT**

You use a restriction enzyme to cut a long DNA molecule that has three copies of the enzyme's recognition sequence clustered near one end. When you separate the restriction fragments by gel electrophoresis, how do you expect the bands to appear?

Answer: three bands near the positive pole at the bottom of the gel (small fragments) and one band near the negative pole at the top of the gel (large fragment)

▲ Figure 12.7 **A factory that produces genetically engineered insulin.**

▲ Figure 12.8 **A genetically modified goat.**

diabetes use the insulin collected, purified, and packaged at such facilities (Figure 12.7).

Insulin is just one of many human proteins produced by genetically modified bacteria. Another example is human growth hormone (HGH). Abnormally low levels of this hormone during childhood and adolescence can cause dwarfism. Because growth hormones from other animals are not effective in people, HGH was an early target of genetic engineers. Before genetically engineered HGH became available in 1985, children with an HGH deficiency could only be treated with scarce and expensive supplies of HGH obtained from human cadavers. Another important pharmaceutical product produced by genetic engineering is tissue plasminogen activator (abbreviated as tPA), a natural human protein that helps dissolve blood clots. If administered shortly after a stroke, tPA reduces the risk of additional strokes and heart attacks.

Besides bacteria, yeast and mammalian cells can also be used to produce medically valuable human proteins. For example, genetically modified mammalian cells growing in laboratory cultures are currently used to produce a hormone called erythropoietin (EPO) that stimulates production of red blood cells. EPO is used to treat anemia; unfortunately, some athletes abuse the drug to seek the advantage of artificially high levels of oxygen-carrying red blood cells (a practice called "blood doping"). In recent decades, genetic engineers have even developed transgenic plant cells that can produce human drugs. Because they are easily grown in culture and are unlikely to be contaminated by human pathogens (such as viruses), some scientists believe that carrots may be the drug factories of the future!

Genetically modified whole animals are also used to produce drugs. Figure 12.8 shows a transgenic goat that carries a gene

> Someday, genetically modified potatoes could prevent tens of thousands of children from dying of cholera.

for an enzyme called lysozyme. This enzyme, found naturally in breast milk, has antibacterial properties. In another example, the gene for a human blood protein has been inserted into the genome of a goat so that the protein is secreted in the goat's milk. The protein is then purified from the milk. Because transgenic animals are difficult to produce, researchers may create a single transgenic animal and then breed or clone it. The resulting herd of transgenic animals could then serve as a grazing pharmaceutical factory—"pharm" animals.

DNA technology is also helping medical researchers develop vaccines. A vaccine is a harmless variant or derivative of a disease-causing microbe—such as a bacterium or virus—that is used to prevent an infectious disease. When a person is inoculated, the vaccine stimulates the immune system to develop lasting defenses against the microbe. For many viral diseases, the only way to prevent serious harm from the illness is to use vaccination to prevent the illness in the first place. For example, the vaccine against hepatitis B, a disabling and sometimes fatal liver disease, is produced by genetically engineered yeast cells that secrete a protein found on the microbe's outer surface.

Genetically Modified Organisms in Agriculture

Since ancient times, people have selectively bred agricultural crops to make them more useful (see Figure 1.13). Today, DNA technology is quickly replacing traditional breeding programs as scientists work to improve the productivity of agriculturally important plants and animals.

In the United States today, more than 80% of the corn crop, more than 90% of the soybean crop, and about 75% of the cotton crop are genetically modified. **Figure 12.9** shows corn that has been genetically engineered to resist attack by an insect called the European corn borer. Growing insect-resistant plants reduces the need for chemical insecticides. In another example, modified strawberry plants produce bacterial proteins that act as a natural antifreeze, protecting the delicate plants from the damages of cold weather. Potatoes and rice have been engineered to produce harmless proteins derived from the cholera bacterium; researchers hope that these modified foods will one day serve as an edible vaccine against cholera, a disease that kills thousands of children in developing nations every year. In India, the insertion of a natural but rare saltwater-resistance gene has enabled new varieties of rice to thrive in water three times as salty as seawater, allowing food to be grown in drought-stricken or flooded regions.

Scientists are also using genetic engineering to improve the nutritional value of crop plants **(Figure 12.10)**. One example is "golden rice 2," a transgenic variety of rice that carries genes from daffodils and corn. This rice could help prevent vitamin A deficiency and resulting blindness, especially in developing nations that depend on rice as a staple crop. Cassava, a starchy root crop that is a staple for nearly 1 billion people in developing nations, has similarly been modified to produce increased levels of iron and beta-carotene (which is converted to vitamin A in the body). However, controversy surrounds the use of GM foods, as we'll discuss at the end of the chapter.

Genetic engineers are targeting agricultural animals as well as plant crops. Although no transgenic animals are

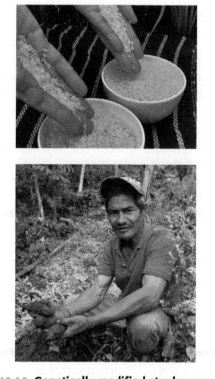

▲ Figure 12.10 **Genetically modified staple crops.** "Golden rice 2," the yellow grains shown here (top) alongside ordinary rice, has been genetically modified to produce high levels of beta-carotene, a molecule that the body converts to vitamin A. Transgenic cassava (bottom), a starchy root crop that serves as the main food source for nearly a billion people, has been modified to produce extra nutrients.

▼ Figure 12.9 **Genetically modified corn.** The corn plants in this field carry a bacterial gene that helps prevent infestation by the European corn borer (inset).

currently being sold as food, the Food and Drug Administration (FDA) has issued regulatory guidelines for their eventual introduction. Scientists might, for example, identify in one variety of cattle a gene that causes the development of larger muscles (which make up most of the meat we eat) and transfer it to other cattle or even to chickens. Researchers have genetically modified pigs to carry a roundworm gene whose protein converts less healthy fatty acids to omega-3 fatty acids. Meat from the modified pigs contains four to five times as much healthy omega-3 fat as regular pork. AquAdvantage is a trade name for Atlantic salmon that have been genetically modified to reach market size in half the normal time (18 months vs. 3 years). The FDA is currently reviewing AquAdvantage salmon; it may become the first GM animal approved for consumption in the United States. As of late 2014, the review continues. ☑

☑ **CHECKPOINT**

What is a genetically modified organism?

Answer: one that carries DNA introduced through artificial means

223

Human Gene Therapy

We've seen that bacteria, plants, and nonhuman animals can be genetically modified—so what about humans? **Human gene therapy** is intended to treat disease by introducing new genes into an afflicted person. In cases where a single defective gene causes a disorder, the mutant version of a gene may be replaced or supplemented with the normal allele. This could potentially correct a genetic disorder, perhaps permanently. In other cases, genes are inserted and expressed only long enough to treat a medical problem.

Figure 12.11 summarizes one approach to human gene therapy. The procedure closely resembles the gene cloning process shown in steps 1 through 3 of Figure 12.3, but in this instance human cells, rather than bacteria, are the targets. ❶ A gene from a normal individual is cloned, converted to an RNA version, and then inserted into the RNA genome of a harmless virus. ❷ Bone marrow cells are taken from the patient and infected with the recombinant virus. ❸ The virus inserts a DNA copy of its genome, including the normal human gene, into the DNA of the patient's cells. ❹ The engineered cells are then injected back into the patient. The normal gene is transcribed and translated within the patient's body, producing the desired protein. Ideally, the nonmutant version of the gene would be inserted into cells that multiply throughout a person's life. Bone marrow cells, which include the stem cells that give rise to all the types of blood cells, are prime candidates. If the procedure succeeds, the cells will multiply permanently and produce a steady supply of the missing protein, curing the patient.

The promise of gene therapy thus far exceeds actual results, but there have been some successes. In 2009, an international research team conducted a trial that focused on a form of progressive blindness linked to a defect in a gene responsible for producing light-detecting pigments in the eye. The researchers found that a single injection of a virus carrying the normal gene into one eye of affected children improved vision in that eye, sometimes enough to allow normal functioning, without significant side effects. The other eye was left untreated as a control.

From 2000 to 2011, gene therapy was used to cure 22 children with severe combined immunodeficiency (SCID), a fatal inherited disease caused by a defective gene that prevents development of the immune system, requiring patients to remain isolated within protective "bubbles." Unless treated with a bone marrow transplant, which is effective only 60% of the time, SCID patients quickly die from infections by microbes that most of us easily fend off. In these cases, researchers

❶ An RNA version is inserted into a virus

Normal human gene

Healthy person

RNA genome of virus

Inserted human RNA

❷ Bone marrow cells are infected

❸ Viral DNA inserts into the cell's chromosome

Human chromosome

Bone marrow cell from the patient

Bone of person with disease

Bone marrow

❹ The engineered cells are injected

▲ Figure 12.11 **One approach to human gene therapy.**

periodically removed immune system cells from the patients' blood, infected them with a virus engineered to carry the normal allele of the defective gene, then reinjected the blood into the patient. The treatment cured the patients of SCID, but there have been some serious side effects: Four of the treated patients developed leukemia, and one died after the inserted gene activated an oncogene (see Chapter 11), creating cancerous blood cells. Gene therapy remains promising, but there is very little evidence to date of safe and effective application. Active research continues, with new, tougher safety guidelines in place that are meant to minimize dangers. ☑

☑ CHECKPOINT

Why are bone marrow stem cells ideally suited as targets for gene therapy?

Answer: because bone marrow stem cells multiply throughout a person's life

DNA Profiling and Forensic Science

When a crime is committed, body fluids (such as blood or semen) or small pieces of tissue (such as skin beneath a victim's fingernails) may be left at the scene or on the victim or assailant. As discussed in the Biology and Society section at the start of the chapter, such evidence can be examined by **DNA profiling**, the analysis of DNA samples to determine whether they come from the same individual. Indeed, DNA profiling has rapidly transformed the field of **forensics**, the scientific analysis of evidence for crime scene investigations and other legal proceedings. To produce a DNA profile, scientists compare DNA sequences that vary from person to person.

Figure 12.12 presents an overview of a typical investigation using DNA profiling. ❶ First, DNA samples are isolated from the crime scene, suspects, victims, or other evidence. ❷ Next, selected sequences from each DNA sample are amplified (copied many times) to produce a large sample of DNA fragments. ❸ Finally, the amplified DNA fragments are compared. All together, these steps provide data about which samples are from the same individual and which samples are unique.

DNA Profiling Techniques

In this section, you'll learn about techniques for making a DNA profile.

The Polymerase Chain Reaction (PCR)

The **polymerase chain reaction** (**PCR**) is a technique by which a specific segment of DNA can be amplified: targeted and copied quickly and precisely. Through PCR, a scientist can obtain enough DNA from even minute amounts of blood or other tissue to allow a DNA profile to be constructed. In fact, a microscopic sample with as few as 20 cells can be sufficient for PCR amplification.

In principle, PCR is simple. A DNA sample is mixed with nucleotides, the DNA replication enzyme DNA polymerase, and a few other ingredients. The solution is then exposed to cycles of heating (to separate the DNA strands) and cooling (to allow double-stranded DNA to re-form). During these cycles, specific regions of each molecule of DNA are replicated, doubling the amount of that DNA (Figure 12.13). The result of this

▼ Figure 12.12 **Overview of DNA profiling.** In this example, DNA from suspect 1 does not match DNA found at the crime scene, but DNA from suspect 2 does match.

▼ Figure 12.13 **DNA amplification by PCR.** The polymerase chain reaction (PCR) is a method for making many copies of a specific segment of DNA. Each round of PCR, performed on a tabletop thermal cycler (shown at top), doubles the total quantity of DNA.

Crime scene   Suspect 1   Suspect 2

❶ DNA isolated

❷ DNA amplified

❸ DNA compared

Initial DNA segment

1   2   4   8

Number of DNA molecules

chain reaction is an exponentially growing population of identical DNA molecules. The key to automated PCR is an unusually heat-stable DNA polymerase, first isolated from prokaryotes living in hot springs (such as those shown in Figure 13.15B). Unlike most proteins, this enzyme can withstand the heat at the start of each cycle.

A DNA molecule within a starting sample is likely to be very long. But, most often, only a very small target region of that large DNA molecule needs to be amplified. The key to amplifying one particular segment of DNA and no others is the use of **primers**, short (usually 15–20 nucleotides long), chemically synthesized single-stranded DNA molecules. For each experiment, specific primers are chosen that are complementary to sequences found only at each end of the target sequence. The primers thus bind to sequences that flank the target sequence, marking the start and end points for the segment of DNA to be amplified. Beginning with a single DNA molecule and the appropriate primers, automated PCR can generate hundreds of billions of copies of the desired sequence in a few hours.

In addition to forensic applications, PCR can be used in the treatment and diagnosis of disease. For example, because the sequence of the genome of HIV (the virus that causes AIDS) is known, PCR can be used to amplify, and thus detect, HIV in blood or tissue samples. In fact, PCR is often the best way to detect this otherwise elusive virus. Medical scientists can now diagnose hundreds of human genetic disorders by using PCR with primers that target the genes associated with these disorders. The amplified DNA product is then studied to reveal the presence or absence of the disease-causing mutation. Among the genes for human diseases that have been identified are those for sickle-cell disease, hemophilia, cystic fibrosis, Huntington's disease, and Duchenne muscular dystrophy. Individuals afflicted with such diseases can often be identified before the onset of symptoms, even before birth, allowing for preventative medical care to begin. PCR can also be used to identify symptomless carriers of potentially harmful recessive alleles (see Figure 9.14). Parents may thus be informed of whether they have a risk of bearing a child with a rare disease that they do not themselves display. ☑

☑ **CHECKPOINT**

Why is only the slightest trace of DNA at a crime scene often sufficient for forensic analysis?

Answer: because PCR can be used to produce enough molecules for analysis

Short Tandem Repeat (STR) Analysis

How do you prove that two samples of DNA come from the same person? You could compare the entire genomes found in the two samples. But such an approach is impractical because the DNA of two humans of the same sex is 99.9% identical. Instead, forensic scientists typically compare about a dozen short segments of noncoding repetitive DNA that are known to vary between people. Have you ever seen a puzzle in a magazine that presents two nearly identical photos and asks you to find the few differences between them? In a similar way, scientists can focus on the few areas of difference in the human genome, ignoring the identical majority.

Repetitive DNA, which makes up much of the DNA that lies between genes in humans, consists of nucleotide sequences that are present in multiple copies in the genome. Some of this DNA consists of short sequences repeated many times tandemly (one after another); such a series of repeats in the genome is called a **short tandem repeat (STR)**. For example, one person might have the sequence AGAT repeated 12 times in a row at one place in the genome, the sequence GATA repeated 35 times at a second place, and so on; another person is likely to have the same sequences at the same places but with a different number of repeats. Like genes that cause physical traits, these stretches of repetitive DNA are more likely to be an exact match between relatives than between unrelated individuals.

STR analysis is a method of DNA profiling that compares the lengths of STR sequences at specific sites in the genome. The standard STR analysis procedure used by law enforcement compares the number of repeats of specific four-nucleotide DNA sequences at 13 sites scattered throughout the genome. Each repeat site, which typically contains from 3 to 50 four-nucleotide repeats in a row, varies widely from person to person. In fact, some STRs used in the standard procedure have up to 80 variations in the number of repeats. In the United States, the number of repeats at each site is entered into a database called CODIS (Combined DNA Index System) administered by the Federal Bureau of Investigation. Law enforcement agencies around the world can access CODIS to search for matches to DNA samples they have obtained from crime scenes or suspects.

Consider the two samples of DNA shown in Figure 12.14. Imagine that the top DNA segment was obtained at a crime scene and the bottom from a suspect's blood. The two segments have the same number of repeats at the first site: 7 repeats of the four-nucleotide DNA sequence AGAT (in orange). Notice, however, that they differ in the number of repeats at the second site: 8 repeats of GATA (in purple) in the crime scene DNA, compared with 12 repeats in the suspect's DNA. To create a DNA profile, a scientist uses PCR to specifically amplify the regions of DNA that include these STR sites. The resulting fragments are then compared.

STR site 1

STR site 2

Crime scene DNA

AGAT

GATA

Same number of
short tandem repeats

Different numbers of
short tandem repeats

Suspect's DNA

AGAT

GATA

◀ **Figure 12.14 Short tandem repeat (STR) sites.** Scattered throughout the genome, STR sites contain tandem repeats of four-nucleotide sequences. The number of repetitions at each site can vary from individual to individual. In this figure, both DNA samples have the same number of repeats (7) at the first STR site, but different numbers (8 versus 12) at the second.

Figure 12.15 shows the gel that would result from using gel electrophoresis to separate the DNA fragments from the example in Figure 12.14. (This figure simplifies the process; an actual STR analysis uses more sites than 2 and uses a different method to visualize the results.) The differences in the locations of the bands reflect the different lengths of the DNA fragments. This gel would provide evidence that the crime scene DNA did not come from the suspect.

As happened in the case discussed in the Biology and Society section, DNA profiling can provide evidence of either guilt or innocence. As of 2014, lawyers at the Innocence Project, a nonprofit legal organization located in New York City, have helped to exonerate more than 310 convicted criminals in 35 states, including 18 who were on death row. The average sentence served by those who were exonerated was 14 years. In nearly half of these cases, DNA profiling has also identified the true perpetrators. **Figure 12.16** presents some data from a real case in which STR analysis

proved a convicted man innocent and also helped identify the true perpetrator.

Just how reliable is a genetic profile? In forensic cases using STR analysis with the 13 standard markers, the probability of two people having identical DNA profiles is somewhere between one chance in 10 billion and one in several trillion. (The exact probability depends on the frequency of the individual's particular markers in the general population.) Thus, despite problems that can still arise from insufficient data, human error, or flawed evidence, genetic profiles are now accepted as compelling evidence by legal experts and scientists alike. ☑

☑ **CHECKPOINT**

What are STRs, and why are they useful for DNA profiling?

Answer: STRs (short tandem repeats) are nucleotide sequences repeated many times in a row within the human genome. STRs are valuable for DNA profiling because different people have different numbers of repeats at the various STR sites.

▼ **Figure 12.16 DNA profiling: proof of innocence and guilt.** In 1984, Earl Washington was convicted and sentenced to death for a 1982 rape and murder. In 2000, STR analysis showed conclusively that he was innocent. Because every person has two chromosomes, each STR site is represented by two numbers of repeats. The table shows the number of repeats for three STR markers in three samples: from semen found on the victim, from Washington, and from another man who was in prison after an unrelated conviction. These and other STR data (not shown) exonerated Washington and led the other man to plead guilty to the murder.

Amplified crime scene DNA

Amplified suspect's DNA

Longer fragments

Shorter fragments

▲ **Figure 12.15 Visualizing STR fragment patterns.** This figure shows the bands that would result from gel electrophoresis of the STR sites illustrated in Figure 12.14. Notice that one of the bands from the crime scene DNA does not match one of the bands from the suspect's DNA.

Source of sample	STR marker 1	STR marker 2	STR marker 3
Semen on victim	17,19	13,16	12,12
Earl Washington	16,18	14,15	11,12
Kenneth Tinsley	17,19	13,16	12,12

Investigating Murder, Paternity, and Ancient DNA

Since its introduction in 1986, DNA profiling has become a standard tool of forensics and has provided crucial evidence in many famous investigations. After the death of terrorist leader Osama bin Laden in 2011, U.S. Special Forces members obtained a sample of his DNA. Within hours, a military laboratory in Afghanistan compared the tissue against samples previously obtained from several of bin Laden's relatives, including his sister who had died of brain cancer in a Boston hospital in 2010. Although facial recognition and an eyewitness identification provided preliminary evidence, it was DNA that provided a conclusive match, officially ending the long hunt for the notorious terrorist.

DNA profiling can also be used to identify murder victims. The largest such effort in history took place after the World Trade Center attack on September 11, 2001. Forensic scientists in New York City worked for years to identify more than 20,000 samples of victims' remains. DNA profiles of tissue samples from the disaster site were matched to DNA profiles from tissue known to be from the victims or their relatives. More than half of the victims identified at the World Trade Center site were recognized solely by DNA evidence, providing closure to many grieving families. Since that time, the victims of other atrocities, such as mass killings during civil wars in Europe and Africa, have been identified using DNA profiling techniques. In 2010, for example, DNA analysis was used to identify the remains of war crime victims who had been buried in mass graves in Bosnia 15 years earlier. DNA profiling can also be used to identify victims of natural disasters. After a tsunami devastated southern Asian the day after Christmas 2004, DNA profiling was used to identify hundreds of victims, mostly foreign tourists.

Comparing the DNA of a mother, her child, and the purported father can settle a question of paternity. Sometimes paternity is of historical interest: DNA profiling proved that Thomas Jefferson or a close male relative fathered a child with an enslaved woman, Sally Hemings. In another historical case, researchers wished to investigate whether any descendants of Marie Antoinette (Figure 12.17), one-time queen of France, survived the French Revolution. DNA extracted from a preserved heart said to belong to her son was compared to DNA extracted from a lock of Marie's hair. A DNA match proved that her last known heir had, in fact, died in jail during the revolution. More recently, a former backup singer for the "Godfather of Soul" James Brown sued his estate after his death, claiming that her child was Brown's son. A DNA paternity test proved her claim, and 25% of Brown's estate was awarded to the mother and child.

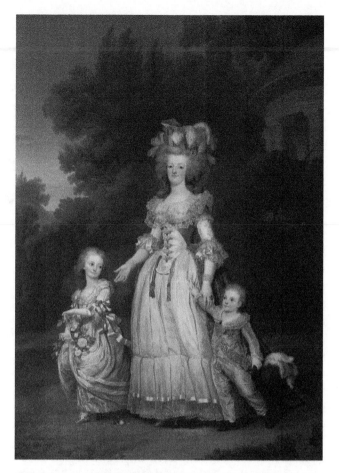

▲ Figure 12.17 **Marie Antoinette.** DNA profiling proved that Louis (depicted with his mother in this 1785 painting), the son of the Queen of France, did not survive the French Revolution.

DNA profiling can also help protect endangered species by conclusively proving the origin of contraband animal products. For example, analysis of seized elephant tusks can pinpoint the location of the poaching, allowing enforcement officials to increase surveillance and prosecute those responsible. In 2014, three tiger poachers in India were sentenced to five years in jail after DNA profiling matched the dead tigers' flesh to tissue under the poachers' fingernails.

Modern methods of DNA profiling are so specific and powerful that the DNA samples can be in a partially degraded state. Such advances are revolutionizing the study of ancient remains. For example, a 2014 study of DNA extracted from five mummified Egyptian heads (dating from 800 B.C. to 100 A.D.) was able to deduce the geographic origins of the individuals, as well as identify DNA from the pathogens that cause the diseases malaria and toxoplasmosis. Another study determined that DNA extracted from a 27,000-year-old Siberian mammoth was 98.6% identical to DNA from modern African elephants. Other studies involving a large collection of mammoth samples suggested that the last populations of the huge beasts migrated from North America to Siberia, where separate species interbred and, eventually, died out several thousand years ago.

Bioinformatics

In the past decade, new experimental techniques have generated enormous volumes of data related to DNA sequences. The need to make sense of an ever-increasing flood of information has spawned the field of **bioinformatics**, the application of computational methods to the storage and analysis of biological data. In this section, we'll explore some of the methods by which sequence data are accumulated, as well as many of the practical ways such knowledge can be put to use.

DNA Sequencing

Researchers can exploit the principle of complementary base pairing to determine the complete nucleotide sequence of a DNA molecule. This process is called **DNA sequencing**. In one standard procedure, the DNA is first cut into fragments, and then each fragment is sequenced (Figure 12.18). In the past decade, "next-generation sequencing" techniques have been developed that can simultaneously sequence thousands or hundreds of thousands of fragments, each of which can be 400–1,000 nucleotides long. This technology makes it possible to sequence nearly a million nucleotides per hour! This is an example of "high-throughput" DNA technology, which is currently the method of choice for studies where massive numbers of DNA samples—even representing an entire genome—are being sequenced. In "third-generation sequencing," a single, very long DNA molecule is sequenced on its own. Several groups of scientists have been working on the idea of moving a single strand of a DNA molecule through a very small pore in a membrane (a nanopore), detecting the bases one by one by their interruption of an electrical current.

▼ **Figure 12.18 A DNA sequencer.** This high-throughput DNA sequencing machine can process half a billion bases in a single 10-hour run.

The idea is that each type of base interrupts the current for a slightly different length of time. Such techniques, if perfected, may usher in a new era of faster, even more affordable sequencing.

Genomics

Improved DNA sequencing techniques have transformed the way in which we can explore fundamental biological questions about evolution and how life works. A major leap forward occurred in 1995 when a team of scientists announced that it had determined the nucleotide sequence of the entire genome of *Haemophilus influenzae*, a bacterium that can cause several human diseases, including pneumonia and meningitis. **Genomics**, the study of complete sets of genes (genomes), was born.

The first targets of genomics research were bacteria, which have relatively little DNA (as you can see in Table 12.1). But soon the attention of genomics researchers

Table 12.1	Some Important Sequenced Genomes*		
Organism	**Year Completed**	**Size of Genome (in base pairs)**	**Approximate Number of Genes**
Haemophilus influenzae (bacterium)	1995	1.8 million	1,700
Saccharomyces cerevisiae (yeast)	1996	12 million	6,300
Escherichia coli (bacterium)	1997	4.6 million	4,400
Caenorhabditis elegans (roundworm)	1998	100 million	20,100
Drosophila melanogaster (fruit fly)	2000	165 million	14,000
Arabidopsis thaliana (mustard plant)	2000	120 million	25,500
Oryza sativa (rice)	2002	430 million	42,000
Homo sapiens (human)	2003	3.0 billion	21,000
Rattus norvegicus (lab rat)	2004	2.8 billion	20,000
Pan troglodytes (chimpanzee)	2005	3.1 billion	20,000
Macaca mulatta (macaque)	2007	2.9 billion	22,000
Ornithorhynchus anatinus (duck-billed platypus)	2008	1.8 billion	18,500
Prunus persica (peach)	2013	227 million	27,900

*Some of the values listed are likely to be revised as genome analysis continues.

229

turned toward more complex organisms with much larger genomes. Baker's yeast (*Saccharomyces cerevisiae*) was the first eukaryote to have its full sequence determined, and the roundworm *Caenorhabditis elegans* was the first multicellular organism. Other sequenced animals include the fruit fly (*Drosophila melanogaster*) and lab rat (*Rattus norvegicus*), both model organisms for genetics research. Among the sequenced plants are *Arabidopsis thaliana*, a type of mustard plant used as a model organism, and rice (*Oryza sativa*), one of the world's most economically important crops.

As of 2014, the genomes of thousands of species have been published, and tens of thousands more are in progress. The majority of organisms sequenced to date are prokaryotes, including more than 4,000 bacterial species and nearly 200 archaea. Hundreds of eukaryotic genomes—including protists, fungi, plants, and animals both invertebrate and vertebrate—have also been completed. Genome sequences have been determined for cells from several cancers, for ancient humans, and for the many bacteria that live in the human intestine. ☑

Genome-Mapping Techniques

Genomes are most often sequenced using a technique called the **whole-genome shotgun method**. The first step is to chop the entire genome into fragments using restriction enzymes. Next, all the fragments are cloned and sequenced. Finally, computers running specialized mapping software reassemble the millions of overlapping short sequences into a single continuous sequence for every chromosome—an entire genome (Figure 12.19).

The DNA sequences determined by many research groups in the United States are deposited in GenBank, a database that is available to anyone via the Internet. You can browse it yourself at the National Center for Biotechnology Information: www.ncbi.nlm.nih.gov. GenBank includes the sequences of more than a hundred billion base pairs of DNA! The database is constantly updated, and the amount of data it contains doubles every 18 months.

Any sequence in the database can be retrieved and analyzed. For example, software can compare a collection of sequences from different species and diagram them as an evolutionary tree based on the sequence relationships. Bioinformatics has thereby revolutionized evolutionary biology by opening a vast new reservoir of data that can test evolutionary hypotheses. Next we'll discuss a particularly notable example of a sequenced animal genome—our own.

The Human Genome

The **Human Genome Project** was a massive scientific endeavor to determine the nucleotide sequence of all the DNA in the human genome and to identify the location and sequence of every gene. The project began in 1990 as

▼ Figure 12.19 **Genome sequencing.** In the photo at the bottom, a technician performs a step in the whole-genome shotgun method (depicted in the diagram).

Chromosome

Chop up with restriction enzyme

DNA fragments

Sequence fragments

AATC TTAATGTA TCGGAC GACGATTA

Align fragments

AATC GACGATTA
TCGGAC TTAATGTA

Reassemble full sequence

AATCGGACGATTAATGTA

an effort by government-funded researchers from six countries. Several years into the project, private companies joined the effort. At the completion of the project, more than 99% of the genome had been determined to 99.999% accuracy. (There remain a few hundred gaps of unknown sequence that require special methods to figure out.) This ambitious project has provided a wealth of data that may illuminate the genetic basis of what it means to be human.

The chromosomes in the human genome (22 autosomes plus the X and Y sex chromosomes) contain approximately 3 billion nucleotide pairs of DNA. If you imagine this sequence printed in letters (A, T, C, and G) the same size you see on this page, the sequence would fill a stack of books 18 stories high! However, the biggest surprise from the Human Genome Project is the relatively small number of human genes—currently estimated to be about 21,000—very close to the number found in a roundworm!

You have about the same number of genes as a microscopic worm, and only half as many as a rice plant.

The human genome was a major challenge to sequence because, like the genomes of most complex eukaryotes, only a small amount of our total DNA consists of genes that code for proteins, tRNAs, or rRNAs. Most complex eukaryotes have a huge amount of noncoding DNA—about 98% of human DNA is of this type. Some of this noncoding DNA is made up of gene control sequences such as promoters, enhancers, and microRNAs (see Chapter 11). Other noncoding regions include introns and repetitive DNA (some of which is used in DNA profiling). Some noncoding DNA is important to our health, with certain regions known to carry disease-causing mutations. But the function of most noncoding DNA remains unknown.

The human genome sequenced by government-funded scientists was actually a reference genome compiled from a group of individuals. As of today, the complete genomes of many individuals have been completed. Whereas sequencing the first human genome took 13 years and cost $100 million, we are rapidly approaching the day when an individual's genome can be sequenced in a matter of hours for less than $1,000.

Scientists have even begun to gather sequence data from our extinct relatives. In 2013, scientists sequenced the entire genome of a 130,000-year-old female Neanderthal (*Homo neanderthalensis*). Using DNA extracted from a toe bone found in a Siberian cave, the resulting genome was nearly as complete as that from a modern human. Analysis of the Neanderthal genome revealed evidence of interbreeding with *Homo sapiens*. A 2014 study provided evidence that many present-day humans of European and Asian descent (but not African descent) carry Neanderthal-derived genes that influence the production of keratin, a protein that is a key structural component of hair, nails, and skin. Modern humans appear to have inherited the gene from Neanderthals around 70,000 years ago and then passed it on to their descendants. Such studies provide valuable insight into our own evolutionary tree.

Bioinformatics can also provide insights into our evolutionary relationships with nonhuman animals. In 2005, researchers completed the genome sequence for our closest living relative on the evolutionary tree of life, the chimpanzee (*Pan troglodytes*). Comparisons with human DNA revealed that we share 96% of our genome. Genomic scientists are currently finding and studying the important differences, shedding scientific light on the age-old question of what makes us human.

The potential benefits of knowing many human genomes are enormous. Thus far, more than 2,000 disease-associated genes have been identified. A recent example involved Behcet's disease, a painful and life-threatening illness that involves swelling of blood vessels throughout the body. Researchers have long known that this disease is found most commonly among people living along the ancient trade route in Asia called the Silk Road (Figure 12.20). In 2013, researchers conducted a genome-wide search for genetic differences among Turkish people with and without the disease. They discovered four regions of the genome that are associated with the disease. The nearby genes are implicated in the immune system's ability to destroy invading microbes, to recognize infection sites, and to regulate autoimmune diseases. Interestingly, the function of the fourth gene has never been identified, but its close association with Behcet's disease may help researchers pinpoint its role. Next, we'll examine a much more common disease that may benefit from genomic analysis.

▼ Figure 12.20 **The Silk Road.** Behcet's disease is most commonly found along the Silk Road, part of which is shown in this map using modern place names.

Key

━━ = Silk Road

Can Genomics Cure Cancer?

Lung cancer, which kills more Americans every year than any other type of cancer, has long been the target of searches for effective chemotherapy drugs. One drug used to treat lung cancer, called gefitinib, targets the protein encoded by the *EGFR* gene. This protein is found on the surface of cells that line the lungs and is also found in lung cancer tumors.

Unfortunately, treatment with gefitinib is ineffective for many patients. While studying the effectiveness of gefitinib, researchers at the Dana-Farber Cancer Institute in Boston made the **observation** that a few patients responded quite well to the drug. This posed a **question:** Are genetic differences among lung cancer patients responsible for the differences in gefitinib's effectiveness? The researchers' **hypothesis** was that mutations in the *EGFR* gene were causing the different responses to gefitinib. The team made the **prediction** that DNA profiles focusing on the *EGFR* gene would reveal different DNA sequences in the tumors of responsive patients compared with the tumors of unresponsive patients. The researchers' **experiment** involved sequencing the *EGFR* gene in cells extracted from the tumors of five patients who responded to the drug and four who did not.

The **results** were quite striking: All five tumors from gefitinib-responsive patients had mutations in *EGFR*, whereas none of the other four tumors did (**Figure 12.21**). Although the small sample size means that additional tests are needed, these results suggest that doctors can use DNA profiling techniques to screen lung cancer patients

▲ Figure 12.21 **The *EGFR* protein: Fighting cancer with genomics.** Mutations (located at sites indicated by black arrows) in the *EGFR* protein can affect the ability of a cancer-fighting drug to destroy lung tumors. Here, the amino acid backbone of the protein is shown in green, with some important regions highlighted in orange, blue, and red.

for those who are most likely to benefit from treatment with this drug. In broader terms, this work suggests that fast and cheap sequencing may usher in an age of "personal genomics," where individual genetic differences among people will be put to routine medical use.

Applied Genomics

In 2001, a 63-year-old Florida man died from inhalation anthrax, a disease caused by breathing spores of the bacterium *Bacillus anthracis*. Because he was the first victim of this disease in the United States since 1976 (and coming so soon after the 9/11 terrorist attacks the month before), his death was immediately suspicious. By the end of the year, four more people had died from inhaling anthrax. Law enforcement officials realized that someone was sending anthrax spores through the mail (**Figure 12.22**). The United States was facing an unprecedented bioterrorist attack.

In the investigation that followed, one of the most helpful clues turned out to be the anthrax spores themselves. Investigators sequenced the genomes of the mailed anthrax spores. They quickly established that all of the mailed spores were genetically identical to a laboratory subtype stored in a single flask at the U.S. Army Medical Research Institute of Infectious Diseases in Fort Detrick, Maryland. Based in part on this evidence, the FBI named an army research scientist as a suspect in the case. Although never charged, that suspect committed suicide in 2008; the case officially remains unsolved.

The anthrax case is just one example of the investigative powers of genomics. Sequence data also provided strong evidence that a Florida dentist transmitted HIV to several patients and that a single natural strain of West Nile virus can infect both birds and people. A 2013 study used DNA sequencing to prove that cancerous skin cells that had spread to the brain had done so after fusing with red blood cells provided by a bone marrow donor. These results provided researchers with new insight into how cancer spreads throughout the body.

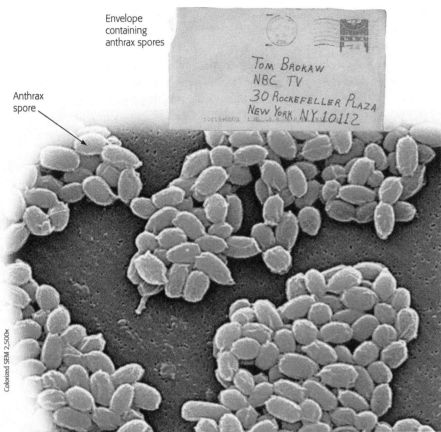

Envelope containing anthrax spores

Anthrax spore

Colorized SEM 2,500x

▲ Figure 12.22 **The 2001 anthrax attacks.** In 2001, envelopes containing anthrax spores caused five deaths.

contribute to our survival. The ability to sequence the DNA of mixed populations eliminates the need to culture each species separately in the lab, making it more efficient to study microbial species.

The successes in genomics have encouraged scientists to begin similar systematic studies of the full protein sets that genomes encode (proteomes), an approach called **proteomics** (Figure 12.23). The number of different proteins in humans far exceeds the number of different genes (about 100,000 proteins versus about 21,000 genes). And because proteins, not genes, actually carry out the activities of the cell, scientists must study when and where proteins are produced and how they interact to understand the functioning of cells and organisms.

Genomics and proteomics enable biologists to approach the study of life from an increasingly global perspective. Biologists are now compiling catalogs of genes and proteins—that is, listings of all the "parts" that contribute to the operation of cells, tissues, and organisms. As such catalogs become complete, researchers are

 Interconnections within Systems Systems Biology

The computational power provided by the tools of bioinformatics allows the study of whole sets of genes and their interactions, as well as the comparison of genomes from different species. Genomics is a rich source of new insights into fundamental questions about genome organization, regulation of gene expression, embryonic development, and evolution.

Technological advances have also led to metagenomics, the study of DNA from an environmental sample. When obtained directly from the environment, a sample will likely contain genomes from many species. After the whole sample is sequenced, computer software sorts out the partial sequences from different species and assembles them into the individual specific genomes. So far, this approach has been applied to microbial communities found in environments as diverse as the Sargasso Sea and the human intestine. A 2012 study cataloged the astounding diversity of the human "microbiome"—the many species of bacteria that coexist within and upon our bodies and that

▲ Figure 12.23 **Proteomics.** Each peak on this three-dimensional graph represents one protein separated by gel electrophoresis. The height of the peak correlates with the amount of that protein. By identifying every protein in a sample, researchers can gain a fuller understanding of the complete biological system.

shifting their attention from the individual parts to how these parts work together in biological systems. This approach, called systems biology, aims to model the dynamic behavior of whole biological systems based on the study of the interactions among the system's parts. Because of the vast amounts of data generated in these types of studies, advances in computer technology and bioinformatics have been crucial in making systems biology possible.

Such analyses may have many practical applications. For example, proteins associated with specific diseases may be used to aid diagnosis (by developing tests that search for a particular combination of proteins) and treatment (by designing drugs that interact with the proteins involved). As high-throughput techniques become more rapid and less expensive, they are increasingly being applied to the problem of cancer. The Cancer Genome Atlas project is a simultaneous investigation by multiple research teams of a large group of interacting genes and gene products. This project aims to determine how changes in biological systems lead to cancer. A three-year pilot project set out to find all the common mutations in three types of cancer—lung, ovarian, and brain—by comparing gene sequences and patterns of gene expression in cancer cells with those in normal cells. The results confirmed the role of several genes suspected to be linked to cancer and identified a few previously unknown ones, suggesting possible new targets for therapies. The research approach proved so fruitful for these three types of cancer that the project has been extended to ten other types of cancer, chosen because they are common and often lethal in humans.

Systems biology is a very efficient way to study emergent properties, novel properties that arise at each successive level of biological complexity as a result of the arrangement of building blocks at the underlying level. The more we can learn about the arrangement and interactions of the components of genetic systems, the deeper will be our understanding of whole organisms. ☑

☑ **CHECKPOINT**

What is the difference between genomics and proteomics?

Answer: Genomics concerns the complete set of an organism's genes, whereas proteomics concerns the complete set of an organism's proteins.

Safety and Ethical Issues

As soon as scientists realized the power of DNA technology, they began to worry about potential dangers. Early concerns focused on the possibility of creating hazardous new disease-causing organisms. What might happen, for instance, if cancer-causing genes were transferred into infectious bacteria or viruses? To address such concerns, scientists developed a set of guidelines that have become formal government regulations in the United States and some other countries.

One safety measure in place is a set of strict laboratory procedures to protect researchers from infection by engineered microbes and to prevent microbes from accidentally leaving the laboratory (Figure 12.24). In addition, strains of microbes to be used in recombinant DNA experiments are genetically crippled to ensure that they cannot survive outside the laboratory. As a further precaution, certain obviously dangerous experiments have been banned.

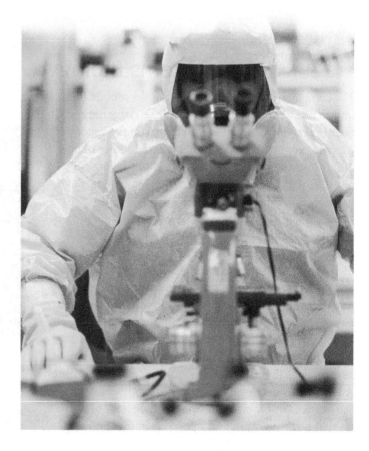

▶ Figure 12.24 **Maximum-security laboratory.** A scientist in a high-containment laboratory wears a biohazard suit, used for working with dangerous microorganisms.

The Controversy over Genetically Modified Foods

Today, most public concern about possible hazards centers on genetically modified (GM) foods. GM strains account for a significant percentage of several staple crops in the United States, Argentina, and Brazil; together these countries account for more than 80% of the world's supply of GM crops. Controversy about the safety of these foods is an important political issue (Figure 12.25). For example, the European Union has suspended the introduction into the market of new GM crops and considered banning the import of all GM foodstuffs. In the United States and other countries where the GM revolution has proceeded relatively unnoticed (until recently), mandatory labeling of GM foods is now being debated.

Advocates of a cautious approach are concerned that crops carrying genes from other species might harm the environment or be hazardous to human health (by, for example, introducing new allergens, molecules that can cause allergic reactions, into foods). A major worry is that transgenic plants might pass their new genes to close relatives in nearby wild areas. We know that lawn and crop grasses, for example, commonly exchange genes with wild relatives via pollen transfer. If domestic plants carrying genes for resistance to herbicides, diseases, or insect pests pollinated wild plants, the offspring might become "superweeds" that would be very difficult to control. However, researchers may be able to prevent the escape of such plant genes in various ways—for example, by engineering plants so that they cannot breed. Concern has also been raised that the widespread use of GM seeds may reduce natural genetic diversity, leaving crops susceptible to catastrophic die-offs in the event of a sudden change to the environment or introduction of a new pest. Although the U.S. National Academy of Sciences released a study finding no scientific evidence that transgenic crops pose any special health or environmental risks, the authors of the study also recommended more stringent long-term monitoring to watch for unanticipated environmental impacts.

Negotiators from 130 countries (including the United States) agreed on a Biosafety Protocol that requires exporters to identify GM organisms present in bulk food

▼ Figure 12.25 **Opposition to genetically modified organisms (GMOs).** Protesters in Oregon voice their displeasure against GMOs.

shipments and allows importing countries to decide whether the shipments pose environmental or health risks. The United States declined to sign the agreement, but it went into effect anyway because the majority of countries were in favor of it. Since then, European countries have, on occasion, refused crops from the United States and other countries for fear that they contain GM crops, leading to trade disputes.

Governments and regulatory agencies throughout the world are grappling with how to facilitate the use of biotechnology in agriculture, industry, and medicine while ensuring that new products and procedures are safe. In the United States, all genetic engineering projects are evaluated for potential risks by a number of regulatory agencies, including the Food and Drug Administration, the Environmental Protection Agency, the National Institutes of Health, and the Department of Agriculture. ☑

☑ **CHECKPOINT**

What is the main concern about adding genes for herbicide resistance to crop plants?

Answer: the possibility that the genes could escape, via cross-pollination, to wild plants that are closely related to the crop species

Ethical Questions Raised by Human DNA Technologies

Human DNA technology raises legal and ethical questions—few of which have clear answers. Consider, for example, how the treatment of dwarfism with injections of human growth hormone (HGH) produced by genetically engineered cells might be extended beyond its current use. Should parents of short but hormonally normal children be able to seek HGH treatment to make their kids taller? If not, who decides which children are "tall enough" to be excluded from treatment? In addition to technical challenges, human gene therapy also provokes ethical questions. Some critics believe that tampering with human genes in any way is immoral or unethical. Other observers see no fundamental difference between the transplantation of genes into somatic cells and the transplantation of organs.

Genetic engineering of gametes (sperm or ova) and zygotes has been accomplished in lab animals. It has not been attempted in humans because such a procedure raises very difficult ethical questions. Should we try to eliminate genetic defects in our children and their descendants? Should we interfere with evolution in this way? From a long-term perspective, the elimination of unwanted versions of genes from the gene pool could backfire. Genetic variety is a necessary ingredient for the adaptation of a species as environmental conditions change with time. Genes that are damaging under some conditions may be advantageous under others (one example is the sickle-cell allele—see the Evolution Connection in Chapter 17). Are we willing to risk making genetic changes that could be detrimental to our species in the future?

Similarly, advances in genetic profiling raise privacy issues (Figure 12.26). If we were to create a DNA profile of every person at birth, then theoretically we could match nearly every violent crime to a perpetrator because it is virtually impossible for someone to commit a violent crime without leaving behind DNA evidence. But are we, as a society, prepared to sacrifice our genetic privacy, even for such worthwhile goals? In 2014, the U.S. Supreme Court, by a 5–4 vote, upheld the practice of collecting DNA samples from suspects at the time of their arrest (before they had been convicted). Ruling that obtaining DNA is "like fingerprinting and photographing, a legitimate police booking procedure that is reasonable under the Fourth Amendment," the Supreme Court decision will likely usher in an era of expanded use of DNA profiling in many aspects of police work.

As more information becomes available about our personal genetic makeup, some people question whether greater access to this information is always beneficial. For example, mail-in kits (Figure 12.27) have become available that can tell healthy people their relative risk of developing various diseases (such as Parkinson's and Crohn's) later in life. Some argue that such information helps families to prepare. Others worry that the tests prey on our fears without offering any real benefit because certain diseases, such as Parkinson's, are not currently preventable or treatable. Other tests, however, such as for breast cancer risk, may help a person make changes that can prevent disease. How can we identify truly useful tests?

There is also a danger that information about disease-associated genes

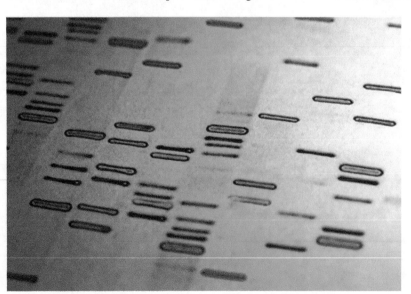

◄ Figure 12.26 **Access to genetic information raises privacy concerns.**

could be abused. One issue is the possibility of discrimination and stigmatization. In response, the U.S. Congress passed the Genetic Information Nondiscrimination Act of 2008. Title I of the act prohibits insurance companies from requesting or requiring genetic information during an application for health insurance. Title II provides similar protections in employment.

A much broader ethical question is how do we really feel about wielding one of nature's powers—the evolution of new organisms? Some might ask if we have any right to alter an organism's genes—or to create new organisms. DNA technologies raise many complex issues that have no easy answers. It is up to you, as a participating citizen, to make informed choices. ☑

► Figure 12.27 **Personalized genetic testing.** This kit can be used to send saliva for genetic analysis. The results can indicate a person's risk of developing certain diseases.

☑ CHECKPOINT

Why does genetically modifying a human gamete raise different ethical questions than genetically modifying a human somatic (body) cell?

Answer: A genetically modified somatic cell will affect only the patient. Modifying a gamete will affect an unborn individual as well as all of his or her descendants.

DNA Profiling EVOLUTION CONNECTION

The Y Chromosome as a Window on History

The human Y chromosome passes essentially intact from father to son. Therefore, by comparing Y DNA, researchers can learn about the ancestry of human males. DNA profiling can thus provide data about recent human evolution.

Geneticists have discovered that about 8% of males currently living in central Asia have Y chromosomes of striking genetic similarity. Further analysis traced their common genetic heritage to a single man living about 1,000 years ago. In combination with historical records, the data led to the speculation that the Mongolian ruler Genghis Khan (Figure 12.28) may have been responsible for the spread of the chromosome to nearly 16 million men living today. A similar study of Irish men suggested that nearly 10% of them were descendants of Niall of the Nine Hostages, a warlord who lived during the 1400s. Another study of Y DNA seemed to confirm the claim by the Lemba people of southern Africa that they are descended from ancient Jews (Figure 12.29). Sequences of Y DNA distinctive of the Jewish priestly caste called Kohanim are found at high frequencies among the Lemba.

Comparison of Y chromosome DNA profiles is part of a larger effort to learn more about the human genome. Other research efforts are extending genomic studies to many more species. These studies will advance our understanding of all aspects of biology, including health and ecology, as well as evolution. In fact, comparisons of the completed genome sequences of bacteria, archaea, and eukaryotes first supported the theory that these are the three fundamental domains of life—a topic we discuss further in the next unit, "Evolution and Diversity."

▲ Figure 12.28 **Genghis Khan.**

► Figure 12.29 **Lemba people of southern Africa.**

Chapter Review

SUMMARY OF KEY CONCEPTS

Genetic Engineering

DNA technology, the manipulation of genetic material, is a relatively new branch of biotechnology, the use of organisms to make helpful products. DNA technology often involves the use of recombinant DNA, the combination of nucleotide sequences from two different sources.

Recombinant DNA Techniques

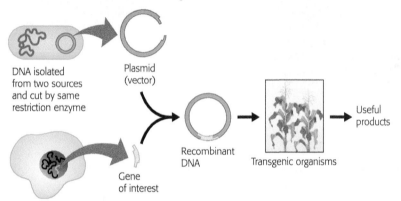

DNA isolated from two sources and cut by same restriction enzyme

Plasmid (vector)

Gene of interest

Recombinant DNA

Transgenic organisms

Useful products

Pharmaceutical Applications

By transferring a human gene into a bacterium or other easy-to-grow cell, scientists can mass-produce valuable human proteins to be used as drugs or vaccines.

Genetically Modified Organisms in Agriculture

Recombinant DNA techniques have been used to create genetically modified organisms, organisms that carry artificially introduced genes. Nonhuman cells have been engineered to produce human proteins, genetically modified food crops, and transgenic farm animals. A transgenic organism is one that carries artificially introduced genes, typically from a different species.

Human Gene Therapy

A virus can be modified to include a normal human gene. If this virus is injected into the bone marrow of a person suffering from a genetic disease, the normal human gene may be transcribed and translated, producing a normal human protein that may cure the genetic disease. This technique has been used in gene therapy trials involving a number of inherited diseases. There have been both successes and failures to date, and research continues.

DNA Profiling and Forensic Science

Forensics, the scientific analysis of legal evidence, has been revolutionized by DNA technology. DNA profiling is used to determine whether two DNA samples come from the same individual.

DNA Profiling Techniques

Short tandem repeat (STR) analysis compares DNA fragments using the polymerase chain reaction (PCR) and gel electrophoresis.

Crime scene   Suspect 1   Suspect 2

DNA

Polymerase chain reaction (PCR) amplifies STR sites

Longer DNA fragments

Shorter DNA fragments

Gel

DNA fragments compared by gel electrophoresis
(Bands of shorter fragments move faster toward the positive pole.)

Investigating Murder, Paternity, and Ancient DNA

DNA profiling can be used to establish innocence or guilt of a criminal suspect, identify victims, determine paternity, and contribute to basic research.

Bioinformatics

DNA Sequencing

Automated machines can now sequence many thousands of DNA nucleotides per hour.

Genomics

Advances in DNA sequencing have ushered in the era of genomics, the study of complete genome sets.

Genome-Mapping Techniques

The whole-genome shotgun method involves sequencing DNA fragments from an entire genome and then assembling the sequences.

The Human Genome

The nucleotide sequence of the human genome is providing a wealth of useful data. The 24 different chromosomes of the human genome contain about 3 billion nucleotide pairs and 21,000 genes. The majority of the genome consists of noncoding DNA.

Applied Genomics

Comparing genomes can aid criminal investigations and basic biological research.

Interconnections within Systems: Systems Biology

Success in genomics has given rise to proteomics, the systematic study of the full set of proteins found in organisms. Genomics and proteomics both contribute to systems biology, the study of how many parts work together within complex biological systems.

Safety and Ethical Issues

The Controversy over Genetically Modified Foods

The debate about genetically modified crops centers on whether they might harm humans or damage the environment by transferring genes through cross-pollination with other species.

Ethical Questions Raised by Human DNA Technologies

As members of society we must become educated about DNA technologies so that we can intelligently address the ethical questions raised by their use.

MasteringBiology®

For practice quizzes, BioFlix animations, MP3 tutorials, video tutors, and more study tools designed for this textbook, go to MasteringBiology®

SELF-QUIZ

1. Suppose you wish to create a large batch of the protein lactase using recombinant DNA. Place the following steps in the order you would have to perform them.
   a. Find the clone with the gene for lactase.
   b. Insert the plasmids into bacteria and grow the bacteria into clones.
   c. Isolate the gene for lactase.
   d. Create recombinant plasmids, including one that carries the gene for lactase.

2. A carrier that moves DNA from one cell to another, such as a plasmid, is called a _____.

3. In making recombinant DNA, what is the benefit of using a restriction enzyme that cuts DNA in a staggered fashion?

4. A paleontologist has recovered a bit of organic material from the 400-year-old preserved skin of an extinct dodo. She would like to compare DNA from the sample with DNA from living birds. The most useful method for initially increasing the amount of dodo DNA available for testing is _____.

5. Why do DNA fragments containing STR sites from different people tend to migrate to different locations during gel electrophoresis?

6. What feature of a DNA fragment causes it to move through a gel during electrophoresis?
   a. the electrical charges of its phosphate groups
   b. its nucleotide sequence
   c. the hydrogen bonds between its base pairs
   d. its double helix shape

7. After a gel electrophoresis procedure is run, the pattern of bars in the gel shows
   a. the order of bases in a particular gene.
   b. the presence of various-sized fragments of DNA.
   c. the order of genes along particular chromosomes.
   d. the exact location of a specific gene in the genome.

8. Name the steps of the whole-genome shotgun method.

9. Put the following steps of human gene therapy in the correct order.
   a. Virus is injected into patient.
   b. Human gene is inserted into a virus.
   c. Normal human gene is isolated and cloned.
   d. Normal human gene is transcribed and translated in the patient.

Answers to these questions can be found in Appendix: Self-Quiz Answers.

THE PROCESS OF SCIENCE

10. Some scientists once joked that when the DNA sequence of the human genome was complete, "we can all go home" because there would be nothing left for genetic researchers to discover. Why haven't they all "gone home"?

11. Interpreting Data When comparing genomes from different species, biologists often calculate the genome density, the number of genes per number of nucleotides in the genome. Refer to Table 12.1. You can calculate the gene density of each species by dividing the number of genes by the size of the genome (usually expressed in Mb, which is mega base pairs, or 1 million base pairs). Using a spreadsheet, calculate the gene density for every species in the table. (Don't forget that 1 billion = 1,000 million; for example, humans have 3,000 Mb.) How does the gene density of bacteria compare to humans? Humans and roundworms have nearly the same number of genes, but how do the gene densities of these two species compare? Can you identify any general correlation between gene density and the size or complexity of an organism?

12. Listed below are 4 of the 13 genome sites used to create a standard DNA profile. Each site consists of a number of short tandem repeats: sets of 4 nucleotides repeated in a row within the genome. For each site, the number of repeats found at that site for this individual are listed:

Chromosome number	Genetic site	# of repeats
3	D3S1358	4
5	D5S818	10
7	D7S820	5
8	D8S1179	22

Imagine you perform a PCR procedure to create a DNA profile for this individual. Which of the following four gels correctly represents the DNA profile of this person?

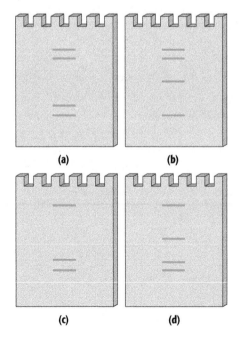

(a)   (b)

(c)   (d)

BIOLOGY AND SOCIETY

13. In the not-too-distant future, gene therapy may be used to treat many inherited disorders. What do you think are the most serious ethical issues to face before human gene therapy is used on a large scale? Explain.

14. Today, it is fairly easy to make transgenic plants and animals. What are some safety and ethical issues raised by this use of recombinant DNA technology? What are some dangers of introducing genetically engineered organisms into the environment? What are some reasons for and against leaving such decisions to scientists? Who should make these decisions?

15. In October 2002, the government of the African nation of Zambia announced that it was refusing to distribute 15,000 tons of corn donated by the United States, enough corn to feed 2.5 million Zambians for three weeks. The government rejected the corn because it was likely to contain genetically modified kernels. The government made the decision after its scientific advisers concluded that the studies of the health risks posed by GM crops "are inconclusive." Do you agree with Zambia's decision to turn away the corn? Why or why not? In your answer, consider that at the time, Zambia was facing food shortages, and 35,000 Zambians were expected to starve to death over the next six months. How do the risks posed by GM crops compare to the risk of starvation?

16. From 1977 to 2000, 12 convicts were executed in Illinois. During that same period, 13 death row inmates were exonerated based on DNA evidence. In 2000, the governor of Illinois declared a moratorium on all executions in his state because the death penalty system was "fraught with errors." Do you support the Illinois governor's decision? What rights should death penalty inmates have with regard to DNA testing of old evidence? Who should pay for this additional testing?

Unit 3
Evolution and Diversity

13 **How Populations Evolve**

Chapter Thread: **Evolution Past, Present, and Future**

14 **How Biological Diversity Evolves**

Chapter Thread: **Mass Extinctions**

15 **The Evolution of Microbial Life**

Chapter Thread: **Human Microbiota**

16 **The Evolution of Plants and Fungi**

Chapter Thread: **Plant-Fungus Interactions**

17 **The Evolution of Animals**

Chapter Thread: **Human Evolution**

13 How Populations Evolve

Thanks to natural selection, populations of more than 500 insect species are invulnerable to the most widely used pesticides.

▲ If it weren't for artificial selection, you'd be eating tomatoes the size of blueberries.

In some species, males engage in nonlethal combat in the hope of mating with females. ▶

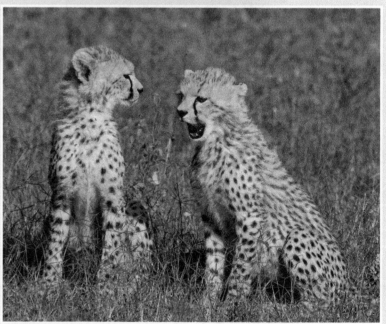

▲ Populations of endangered species may be doomed by their lack of genetic diversity.

242

Evolution Past, Present, and Future BIOLOGY AND SOCIETY

Evolution Today

Life on Earth is gloriously diverse. More than 1.3 million species have been identified, and scientists estimate that several million more await discovery. How did Earth come to be populated by this abundance of diversity? The answer is evolution. In studying evolution, we reach hundreds of millions of years into the past to trace the history of life up until the present time. It isn't all about stones and bones, though. Evolution is happening right now, somewhere near you.

Consider the biological diversity in your surroundings. The organisms that are our closest neighbors are those that are best adapted to a human-dominated environment—the birds that feed on seeds and insects in suburban yards or city parks; the plants that thrive in vacant lots or sidewalk cracks; the insects and other pests that feast on our discarded food, our crops, and even our blood. Then there's the vast variety of microscopic life teeming everywhere, including both beneficial and disease-causing species that have adapted to the human body. All of these organisms are products of evolution, and they continue to evolve generation by generation in the present day. As you will learn in this chapter, the environment plays a powerful role in evolution. Human activities—agriculture, mining, logging, development, the burning of fossil fuels, and the use of medicine, to name just a few—may alter the environments of organisms in ways that result in rapid, observable evolution. Evolutionary changes can also be studied in settings affected by natural environmental changes. Within a hundred thousand years, a blink of the eye in geologic time, lakes may appear or disappear; and newly minted volcanic islands can be clothed in plants and animals over a span of decades, centuries, or millennia, depending on the nearness of land.

An understanding of evolution informs all of biology, from exploring life's molecules to analyzing ecosystems. And applications of evolutionary biology are transforming medicine, agriculture, biotechnology, and conservation biology. In this chapter, you'll learn how the process of evolution works and read about verifiable, measurable examples of evolution that affect our world.

White-tailed deer. Suburban landscapes often include patches of forest that provide food and shelter for deer, such as this one nibbling on garden plants.

The Diversity of Life

For all of human history, people have named, described, and classified the inhabitants of the natural world. As trade and exploration connected all regions of the planet, these tasks became increasingly complex. For example, a scholar who sought to describe all the types of plants known to the Greeks in 300 B.C. had about 500 species to distinguish. Today, scientists recognize roughly 400,000 plant species.

By the 1700s, it was clear that a unified system of naming and classifying was needed. Agreement eventually coalesced around a scheme introduced by Carolus Linnaeus, a Swedish scientist. His system, which is still in use today, is the basis for **taxonomy**, the branch of biology concerned with identifying, naming, and classifying species. The Linnaean system includes a method of naming species and a hierarchical classification of species into broader groups of organisms.

Naming and Classifying the Diversity of Life

In the Linnaean system, each species is given a two-part Latinized name, or **binomial**. The first part of a binomial is the **genus** (plural, *genera*), a group of closely related species. For example, the genus of large cats is *Panthera*. The second part of a binomial is used to distinguish species within a genus. The two parts must be used together to name a species. Thus, the scientific name for the leopard is *Panthera pardus*. Notice that the first letter of the genus is capitalized and that the whole binomial is italicized. For instance, a newly discovered spider in the genus *Aptostichus* was named *Aptostichus stephencolberti*, after the television personality.

The Linnaean binomial solved the problem of the ambiguity of common names. Referring to an animal as a squirrel or a plant as a daisy is not specific—there are many species of squirrels and daisies. In addition, people in different regions may use the same common name for different species. For example, the flowers called bluebells in Scotland, England, Texas, and the eastern United States are actually four unrelated species.

Linnaeus also introduced a system for grouping species into a hierarchy of categories. The first step of this classification is built into the binomial. For example, the genus *Panthera* contains three other species: the lion (*Panthera leo*), the tiger (*Panthera tigris*), and the jaguar (*Panthera onca*). Beyond the grouping of species within genera, taxonomy extends to progressively broader categories of classification. It places similar genera in the same **family**, puts families into **orders**, orders into **classes**, classes into **phyla** (singular, *phylum*), phyla into **kingdoms**, and kingdoms into **domains**. Figure 13.1 places the leopard in this taxonomic scheme of groups within groups. The resulting classification of a particular organism is somewhat like a postal address identifying a person in a particular apartment, in a building with many apartments, on a street with many apartment buildings, in a city with many streets, and so on.

Grouping organisms into broader categories is a way to structure our understanding of the world. However, the criteria used to define more inclusive groups such as families, orders, and classes are ultimately arbitrary. After you learn about the processes by which the diversity of life evolved, we will introduce a classification system based on an understanding of evolutionary relationships (see Chapter 14). ☑

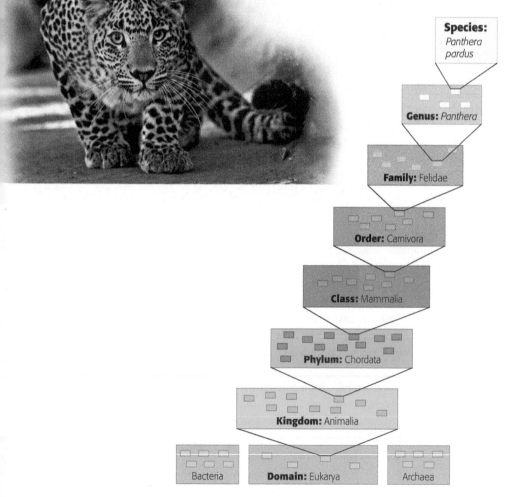

◄ **Figure 13.1 Hierarchical classification.** Taxonomy classifies species—the least inclusive groups—into increasingly broad categories. *Panthera pardus* is one of four species (indicated here with yellow boxes) in the genus *Panthera*; *Panthera* is a genus (orange box) in the family Felidae, and so on.

Species: *Panthera pardus*

Genus: *Panthera*

Family: Felidae

Order: Carnivora

Class: Mammalia

Phylum: Chordata

Kingdom: Animalia

Bacteria   **Domain:** Eukarya   Archaea

Explaining the Diversity of Life

While early naturalists and philosophers sought to describe and organize the diversity of life, they also sought to explain its origin. The explanation accepted by present-day biologists is the evolutionary theory proposed by Charles Darwin in his best-known book, *On the Origin of Species by Means of Natural Selection*, published in 1859. Before we introduce Darwin's theory, however, let's take a brief look at the scientific and cultural context that made the theory of evolution such a radical idea in Darwin's time.

The Idea of Fixed Species

The Greek philosopher Aristotle, whose ideas had an enormous impact on Western culture, generally held the view that species are fixed, permanent forms that do not change over time. Judeo-Christian culture reinforced this idea with a literal interpretation of the biblical book of Genesis, which tells the story of each form of life being individually created in its present-day form. In the 1600s, religious scholars used biblical accounts to estimate the age of Earth at 6,000 years. Thus, the idea that all living species came into being relatively recently and are unchanging in form dominated the intellectual climate of the Western world for centuries.

At the same time, however, naturalists were also grappling with the interpretation of **fossils**—imprints or remains of organisms that lived in the past. Although fossils were thought to be the remains of living creatures, many were puzzling. For example, if "snakestones"

(Figure 13.2a) were the coiled bodies of snakes, then why were none ever found with an intact head? Could some fossils represent species that had become extinct? Stunning discoveries in the early 1800s, including fossilized skeletons of a gigantic sea creature dubbed an ichthyosaur, or fish-lizard (Figure 13.2b), convinced many naturalists that extinctions had indeed occurred.

Lamarck and Evolutionary Adaptations

Fossils told of other changes in the history of life, too. Naturalists compared fossil forms with living species and noted patterns of similarities and differences. In the early 1800s, French naturalist Jean-Baptiste de Lamarck suggested that the best explanation for these observations is that life evolves. Lamarck explained evolution as the refinement of traits that equip organisms to perform successfully in their environments. He proposed that by using or not using its body parts, an individual may develop certain traits that it passes on to its offspring. For example, some birds have powerful beaks that enable them to crack tough seeds. Lamarck suggested that these strong beaks are the cumulative result of ancestors exercising their beaks during feeding and passing that acquired beak power on to offspring. However, simple observations provide evidence against the inheritance of acquired traits: A carpenter who builds up strength and stamina through a lifetime of pounding nails with a heavy hammer will not pass enhanced biceps on to children. Although Lamarck's idea of how species evolve was mistaken, his proposal that species evolve as a result of interactions between organisms and their environments helped set the stage for Darwin. ✓

> ✓ **CHECKPOINT**
>
> How do fossils contradict the idea of fixed species?
>
> *Answer: They don't match any living creature.*

▼ Figure 13.2 **Fossils that perplexed naturalists in the 1800s.**

(a) "Snakestone." This fossil is actually a mollusc called an ammonite, an extinct relative of the present-day nautilus (see Figure 17.13). Ammonites of this type ranged in size from about several inches to more than 7 feet in diameter.

(b) Icthyosaur skull and paddle-like forelimb. These marine reptiles—some more than 50 feet long—ruled the oceans for 155 million years before becoming extinct about 90 million years ago. The enormous eye is thought to be an adaptation to the dim light of the deep sea.

Charles Darwin and *The Origin of Species*

Although Charles Darwin was born more than 200 years ago—on the very same day as Abraham Lincoln—his work had such an extraordinary impact that many scientists mark his birthday with a celebration of his contributions to biology. How did Darwin become a rock star of science?

As a boy, Darwin was fascinated with nature. He loved collecting insects and fossils, as well as reading books about nature. His father, an eminent physician, could see no future for his son as a naturalist and sent him to medical school. But young Darwin, finding medicine boring and surgery before the days of anesthesia horrifying, quit medical school. His father then enrolled him at Cambridge University with the intention that he should become a clergyman. After college, however, Darwin returned to his childhood interests rather than following the career path mapped out by his father. At the age of 22, he began a sea voyage on the HMS *Beagle* that helped frame his theory of evolution.

Darwin's Journey

The *Beagle* was a survey ship. Although it stopped at many locations around the world, its main task was charting poorly known stretches of the South American coast (Figure 13.3). Darwin, a skilled naturalist, spent most of his time on shore doing what he enjoyed most—exploring the natural world. He collected thousands of specimens of fossils and living plants and animals. He also kept detailed journals of his observations. For a naturalist from a small, temperate country, seeing the glorious diversity of unfamiliar life-forms on other continents was a revelation. He carefully noted the characteristics of plants and animals that made them well suited to such diverse environments as the jungles of Brazil, the grasslands of Argentina, the towering peaks of the Andes, and the desolate and frigid lands at the southern tip of South America.

Observations

Many of Darwin's observations indicated that geographic proximity is a better predictor of relationships among organisms than similarity of environment. For example, the plants and animals living in temperate regions of South America more closely resembled species living in tropical regions of that continent than

▼ Figure 13.3 **The voyage of the *Beagle*.**

species living in similarly temperate regions of Europe. And the South American fossils Darwin found, though clearly examples of species different from living ones, were distinctly South American in their resemblance to the contemporary plants and animals of that continent. For instance, he collected fossilized armor plates resembling those of living armadillo species. Paleontologists later reconstructed the creature to which the armor belonged—which turned out to be an extinct armadillo the size of a Volkswagen Beetle.

Darwin was particularly intrigued by the geographic distribution of organisms on the Galápagos Islands. The Galápagos are relatively young volcanic islands about 900 kilometers (540 miles) off the Pacific coast of South America. Most of the animals that inhabit these remote islands are found nowhere else in the world, but they resemble South American species.

Darwin noticed that Galápagos marine iguanas—with a flattened tail that aids in swimming—are similar to, but distinct from, land-dwelling iguanas on the islands and on the South American mainland. Furthermore, each island had its own distinct variety of giant tortoise (Figure 13.4), the strikingly unique inhabitants for which the islands were named (*galápago* means "tortoise" in Spanish).

New Insights

While on his voyage, Darwin was strongly influenced by the newly published *Principles of Geology* by Scottish geologist Charles Lyell. The book presented the case for an ancient Earth sculpted over millions of years by gradual geological processes that continue today. Darwin witnessed the power of natural forces to change Earth's surface firsthand when he experienced an earthquake that raised part of the coastline of Chile almost a meter.

By the time Darwin returned to Great Britain five years after the *Beagle* first set sail, he had begun to seriously doubt that Earth and all its living organisms had been specially created only a few thousand years earlier. As he reflected on his observations, analyzed his specimen collections, and discussed his work with colleagues, he concluded that the evidence was better explained by the hypothesis that present-day species are the descendants of ancient ancestors that they still resemble in some ways. Over time, differences gradually accumulated by a process that Darwin called "descent with modification," his phrase to describe evolution. Unlike others who had explored the idea that organisms had changed over time, however, Darwin also proposed a scientific mechanism for *how* life evolves, a process he called natural selection. In **natural selection**, individuals with certain inherited traits are more likely to survive and reproduce than are individuals with other traits. He hypothesized that as the descendants of a remote ancestor spread into various habitats over millions and millions of years, natural selection resulted in diverse modifications, or **evolutionary adaptations**, that fit them to specific ways of life in their environment.

▼ Figure 13.4 **Two varieties of Galápagos tortoise.**

(a) The thick, domed shell and short neck and legs are characteristic of tortoises found on wetter islands that have more abundant, dense vegetation.

(b) Saddleback shells have an arch at the front, which allows the long neck to emerge. This, along with longer legs, enables the tortoise to stretch higher to reach the scarce vegetation on dry islands.

Evolution Darwin's Theory

Darwin spent the next two decades compiling and writing about evidence for evolution. He realized that his ideas would cause an uproar, however, and he delayed publishing. Meanwhile, Darwin learned that Alfred Russel Wallace, a British naturalist doing fieldwork in Indonesia, had conceived a hypothesis almost identical to Darwin's. Not wanting to have his life's work eclipsed by Wallace's, Darwin finally published *The Origin of Species*, a book that supported his hypothesis with immaculate logic and hundreds of pages of evidence drawn from observations and experiments in biology, geology, and paleontology. The hypothesis of evolution set forth in *The Origin of Species* has since generated predictions that have been tested and verified by more than 150 years of research. Consequently, scientists regard Darwin's concept of evolution by means of natural selection as a **theory**—a widely accepted explanatory idea that is broader in scope than a hypothesis, generates new hypotheses, and is supported by a large body of evidence.

In the next several pages, we examine lines of evidence for Darwin's theory of **evolution**, the idea that living species are descendants of ancestral species that were different from present-day ones. Then we will return to natural selection as the mechanism for evolutionary change. With our current understanding of how this mechanism works, we extend Darwin's definition of evolution to include genetic changes in a population from generation to generation. ✓

Evidence of Evolution

Evolution leaves observable signs. Such clues to the past are essential to any historical science. Historians of human civilization can study written records from earlier times. But they can also piece together the evolution of societies by recognizing vestiges of the past in modern cultures. Even if we did not know from written documents that Spaniards colonized the Americas, we would deduce this from the Hispanic stamp on Latin American culture. Similarly, biological evolution has left evidence in fossils, as well as in today's organisms.

Evidence from Fossils

Fossils—imprints or remains of organisms that lived in the past—document differences between past and present organisms and show that many species have become extinct. The soft parts of a dead organism usually decay rapidly, but the hard parts of an animal that are rich in minerals, such as the bones and teeth of vertebrates and the shells of clams and snails, may remain as fossils. Figure 13.5 (facing page) illustrates some of the ways that organisms can fossilize.

Not all fossils are the actual remnants of organisms. Some, such as the ammonite in Figure 13.2a, are casts. A cast forms when a dead organism that was buried in sediment decomposes and leaves an empty "mold" that is later filled by minerals dissolved in water. The minerals harden within the mold, making a replica of the organism. You may have seen crime scene investigators on TV shows use fast-acting plaster in the same way to make casts of footprints or tire tracks. Fossils may also be imprints, such as footprints or burrows, that remain after the organism decays. **Paleontologists** (scientists who study fossils) also eagerly examine coprolites—fossilized feces—for clues about the diets and digestive systems of extinct animals.

In rare instances, an entire organism, including its soft parts, is encased in a medium that prevents decomposition. Examples include insects trapped in amber (fossilized tree resin) and mammoths, bison, and even prehistoric humans frozen in ice or preserved in bogs.

Many fossils are found in fine-grained sedimentary rocks formed from the sand or mud that settles to the bottom of seas, lakes, swamps, and other aquatic habitats, covering dead organisms. Over millions of years, new layers of sediment are deposited atop older ones and compress them into layers of rock called strata (singular, *stratum*). Thus, the fossils in a particular stratum provide a glimpse of some of the organisms that lived in the area at the time the layer formed. Because younger strata are on top of older layers, the relative ages of fossils can be determined by the layer in which they are found. (Radiometric dating—see Figure 2.17—can be used to determine the approximate ages of fossils.) As a result, the sequence in which fossils appear within layers of sedimentary rocks is a historical record of life on

Earth. The **fossil record** is this ordered sequence of fossils as they appear in the rock layers, marking the passage of geologic time (see Figure 14.12).

Of course, as Darwin acknowledged, the fossil record is incomplete. Many of Earth's organisms did not live in areas that favor fossilization. Many fossils that did form were in rocks later distorted or destroyed by geologic processes. Furthermore, not all fossils that have been preserved are accessible to paleontologists. Even with its limitations, however, the fossil record is remarkably detailed. And although the incompleteness of the fossil record may seem frustrating (wouldn't it be nice to have all our questions answered!), it makes paleontology an unexpectedly thrilling occupation. Like a mystery series in which new clues are uncovered in each episode, the thousands of fossils newly discovered each year give paleontologists new opportunities to test hypotheses about how the diversity of life evolved. In the next section, you'll learn how fossils are revealing answers to a very old puzzle. ☑

☑ **CHECKPOINT**

Why are older fossils generally in deeper rock layers than younger fossils?

Answer: Sedimentation places younger rock layers on top of older ones.

▼ Figure 13.5 **A fossil gallery.**

Sedimentary fossils are formed when minerals seep into and replace organic matter. This petrified (stone) tree in Arizona's Petrified Forest National Park is about 190 million years old.

This 45-million-year-old insect is embedded in amber (hardened resin from a tree).

Sedimentary rocks are the richest hunting grounds for paleontologists, scientists who study fossils. This researcher is excavating a fossilized dinosaur skeleton from sandstone in Dinosaur National Monument, located in Utah and Colorado.

A dinosaur left these footprints 120 million years ago in what is now northern Spain. Biologists often study footprints to learn how extinct animals moved.

These tusks belong to a whole 23,000-year-old mammoth, which scientists discovered in Siberian ice in 1999.

Did Whales Evolve from Land-Dwelling Mammals?

In *The Origin of Species*, Darwin predicted the existence of fossils of transitional forms linking very different groups of organisms. The first such fossil was discovered shortly after Darwin's book was published—the 150-million-year-old *Archaeopteryx*, a fossil that displayed a combination of reptilian and birdlike features. Thousands of fossil discoveries have since shed light on the evolutionary origin of birds from a lineage of dinosaurs, as well as the origins of many other groups of plants and animals, including the transition of fish to amphibian and the evolution of mammals from a reptilian ancestor.

The origin of whales is one of the most intriguing evolutionary transitions. Whales are cetaceans, a group that also includes dolphins and porpoises. As you probably know, cetaceans are mammals that are thoroughly adapted to their aquatic environment. For example, their ears are internal and highly specialized for underwater hearing. They have forelimbs in the form of flippers but lack hind limbs. Overall, cetaceans are so very different from other mammals that scientists have long puzzled over their origins. In the 1960s, **observations** of fossil teeth led paleontologists to form the **hypothesis** that whales were the descendants of primitive hoofed, wolflike carnivores. They made the **prediction** that transitional fossils would show reduced hind limb and pelvic bones as whales evolved from these terrestrial, four-limbed

ancestors. Rather than a controlled **experiment**, paleontologists tested their hypothesis by making detailed measurements and other observations of fossils accumulated over 20 years of extraordinary discoveries in Pakistan and Egypt. The **results** supported their hypothesis. **Figure 13.6** illustrates the diminishing size of the hind limb and pelvic bones in a few of the specimens studied. As you will learn shortly, however, a different kind of evidence later called this conclusion into question.

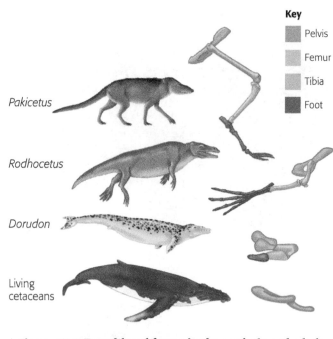

Key
- Pelvis
- Femur
- Tibia
- Foot

Pakicetus

Rodhocetus

Dorudon

Living cetaceans

▲ Figure 13.6 **Transitional forms in the evolution of whales.**

Evidence from Homologies

A second type of evidence for evolution comes from analyzing similarities among different organisms. Evolution is a process of descent with modification—characteristics present in an ancestral organism are altered over time by natural selection as its descendants face different environmental conditions. In other words, evolution is a remodeling process. As a result, related species can have characteristics that have an underlying similarity yet function differently. Similarity resulting from common ancestry is known as **homology**.

Darwin cited the anatomical similarities among vertebrate forelimbs as evidence of common ancestry. As **Figure 13.7** shows, the same skeletal elements make up the forelimbs of humans, cats, whales, and bats. The functions of these forelimbs differ. A whale's flipper does

not do the same job as a bat's wing, so if these structures had been uniquely engineered, then we would expect that their basic designs would be very different. The logical explanation instead is that the arms, forelegs, flippers, and wings of these different mammals are variations on an anatomical structure of an ancestral organism that over millions of years has become adapted to different functions. Biologists call such anatomical similarities in different organisms homologous structures—features that often have different functions but are structurally similar because of common ancestry.

As a result of advances in **molecular biology**, the study of the molecular basis of genes and gene expression, present-day scientists have a much deeper understanding of homologies than Darwin did. Just as your genetic background is recorded in the DNA you inherit from your parents, the evolutionary history of each

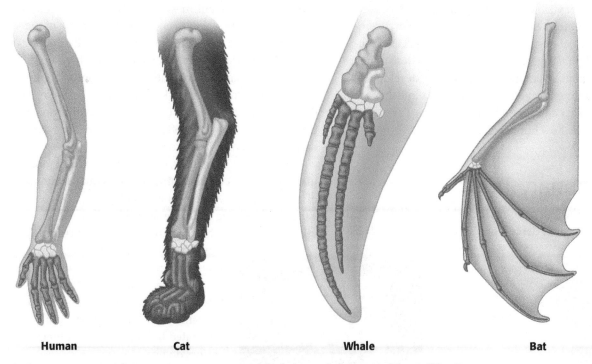

| Human | Cat | Whale | Bat |

▲ **Figure 13.7 Homologous structures: anatomical signs of descent with modification.** The forelimbs of all mammals are constructed from the same skeletal elements. (Homologous bones in each of these four mammals are colored the same.) The hypothesis that all mammals descended from a common ancestor predicts that their forelimbs, though diversely adapted, would be variations on a common anatomical theme.

species is documented in the DNA inherited from its ancestral species. If two species have homologous genes with sequences that match closely, biologists conclude that these sequences must have been inherited from a relatively recent common ancestor. Conversely, the greater the number of sequence differences between species, the more distant is their last common ancestor. Molecular comparisons between diverse organisms have allowed biologists to develop and test hypotheses about the evolutionary divergence of major branches on the tree of life.

Darwin's boldest hypothesis was that all life-forms are related. Molecular biology provides strong evidence for this claim: All forms of life use the same genetic language of DNA and RNA, and the genetic code—how RNA triplets are translated into amino acids—is essentially universal (see Figure 10.10). Thus, it is likely that all species descended from common ancestors that used this code. Because of these molecular homologies, bacteria engineered with human genes can produce human proteins such as insulin and human growth hormone. But molecular homologies go beyond a shared genetic code. For example, organisms as dissimilar as humans and bacteria share homologous genes inherited from a very distant common ancestor.

Geneticists have also uncovered hidden molecular homologies. Organisms may retain genes that have lost their function through mutations, even though homologous genes in related species are fully functional. Many

of these inactive genes have been identified in humans. For example, one such gene encodes an enzyme known as GLO that is used in making vitamin C. Almost all mammals have a metabolic pathway to make this essential vitamin from glucose. Although humans and other primates have functional genes for the first three steps in the pathway, the inactive GLO gene prevents us from making vitamin C—we must get sufficient amounts in our diet to maintain health.

Some of the most interesting homologies are "left-over" structures that are of marginal or perhaps no importance to the organism. These **vestigial structures** are remnants of features that served important functions in the organism's ancestors. For example, the small pelvis and hind-leg bones of ancient whales are vestiges (traces) of their walking ancestors. The eye remnants that are buried under scales in blind species of cave fishes—a vestige of their sighted ancestors—are another example. Humans have vestigial structures, too. When we're cold or agitated, we often get goose bumps caused by small muscles under the skin that make the body hair stand on end. The same response is more visible (and more functional) in a bird that fluffs up its feathery insulation (see Figure 18.9) or a cat that bristles when threatened.

An understanding of homology can also explain observations about embryonic development that are otherwise puzzling. For example, comparing early stages of development in different animal species reveals

► Figure 13.8 **Evolutionary signs from comparative embryology.** At the early stage of development shown here, the kinship of vertebrates is unmistakable. Notice, for example, the pharyngeal pouches and tails in both the chicken embryo and the human embryo.

similarities not visible in adult organisms (Figure 13.8). At some point in their development, all vertebrate embryos have a tail posterior to the anus, as well as structures called pharyngeal (throat) pouches. These pouches are homologous structures that ultimately develop to have very different functions, such as gills in fishes and parts of the ears and throat in humans.

Next we see how homologies help us trace evolutionary descent. ☑

Evolutionary Trees

Darwin was the first to visualize the history of life as a tree in which patterns of descent branch off from a common

Pharyngeal pouches

Post-anal tail

Chicken embryo

Human embryo

trunk—the first organism—to the tips of millions of twigs representing the species living today. At each fork of the evolutionary tree is an ancestor common to all evolutionary branches extending from that fork. Closely related species share many traits because their lineage of common descent traces to a recent fork of the tree of life. Biologists illustrate these patterns of descent with an **evolutionary tree**, although today they often turn the trees sideways so they can be read from left to right.

Homologous structures, both anatomical and molecular, can be used to determine the branching sequence of an evolutionary tree. Some homologous characters, such as the genetic code, are shared by all species because they date to the deep ancestral past. In contrast, traits that evolved more recently are shared by smaller groups of organisms. For example, all tetrapods (from the Greek *tetra*, four, and *pod*, foot) have the same basic limb bone structure illustrated in Figure 13.7, but their ancestors do not.

Figure 13.9 is an evolutionary tree of tetrapods (amphibians, mammals, and reptiles, including birds) and their closest living relatives, the lungfishes. In this diagram, each branch point represents the common ancestor of all species that

▼ Figure 13.9 **An evolutionary tree of tetrapods (four-limbed animals).**

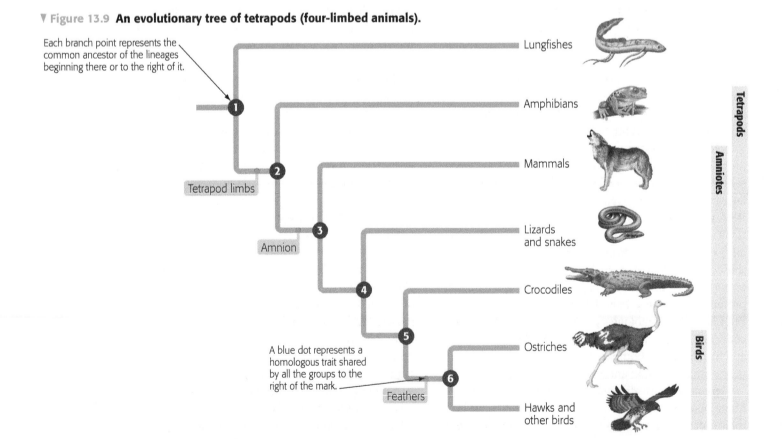

Each branch point represents the common ancestor of the lineages beginning there or to the right of it.

Lungfishes

Amphibians

Mammals

1

Tetrapod limbs

2

Amnion

3

Lizards and snakes

4

Crocodiles

5

A blue dot represents a homologous trait shared by all the groups to the right of the mark.

Feathers

6

Ostriches

Hawks and other birds

Tetrapods

Amniotes

Birds

descended from it. For example, lungfishes and all tetrapods descended from ancestor **1**. Three homologies are shown by the blue dots on the tree—tetrapod limbs, the amnion (a protective embryonic membrane), and feathers. Tetrapod limbs were present in common ancestor **2** and hence are found in its descendants (the tetrapods). The amnion was present in ancestor **3** and thus is shared only by mammals and reptiles, which are known as amniotes. Feathers were present only in **6** ancestor and hence are found only in birds.

Evolutionary trees are hypotheses reflecting our current understanding of patterns of evolutionary descent. Some trees, such as the one in Figure 13.9, are based on a convincing combination of fossil, anatomical, and molecular data. Others are more speculative because sufficient data are not yet available. ☑

Whale Evolution Revisited

Now let's resume the story of whale evolution. As we discussed, beginning in the 1970s, paleontologists unearthed a remarkable series of transitional fossils that supported the hypothesis that whales evolved from hoofed, wolflike carnivores. However, molecular biologists using DNA analysis to infer relationships among living animals found a close relationship between whales and hippopotamuses, which are members of a group of mostly herbivorous, cloven-hoofed mammals that includes pigs, deer, and camels **(Figure 13.10)**. Consequently, they proposed an alternative hypothesis of whale evolution: that whales and hippos are both descendants of a cloven-hoofed ancestor.

Paleontologists were taken aback by the contradictory results. Nevertheless, openness to new evidence is a hallmark of science, and the paleontologists had an idea

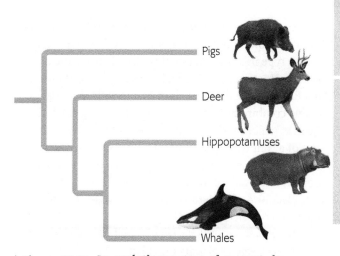

Pigs

Deer

Hippopotamuses

Whales

▲ Figure 13.10 **An evolutionary tree of present-day whales and herbivorous cloven-hoofed mammals.** Data from: M. Nikaido et al., Phylogenetic relationships among Cetartiodactyls based on insertions of short and long interspersed elements: hippopotamuses are the closest extant relatives of whales. *Proceedings of the National Academy of Sciences USA* 96: 10261–10266 (1999).

☑ CHECKPOINT
In Figure 13.9, which number represents the most recent common ancestor of humans and canaries?

Answer: The most recent ancestor of humans (mammals) and canaries (birds) is **3***.*

for resolving the issue. Cloven-hoofed mammals have a unique ankle bone. Like most fossilized skeletons, the specimens of early cetaceans that had been found were incomplete—none included an ankle bone. If the ancestor of whales was a wolflike carnivore, then the shape of its ankle bone would be similar to most present-day mammals. Two fossils discovered in 2001 provided the answer. Both *Pakicetus* and *Rodhocetus* (see Figure 13.6) had the distinctive ankle bone of a cloven-hoofed mammal, a result that supported the hypothesis based on the DNA analysis. Thus, as is often the case in science, scientists are becoming more certain about the evolutionary origin of whales as mounting evidence from different lines of inquiry converge.

Natural Selection as the Mechanism for Evolution

Now that you have learned about the lines of evidence supporting Darwin's theory of descent with modification, let's look at Darwin's explanation of *how* life evolves. Because he hypothesized that species formed gradually over long periods of time, Darwin knew that he would not be able to study the evolution of new species by direct observation. But he did have a way to gain insight into the process of incremental change: the practices used by plant and animal breeders.

All domesticated plants and animals are the products of selective breeding from wild ancestors. For example,

the baseball-sized tomatoes grown today are very different from their Peruvian ancestors, which were not much larger than blueberries. Having conceived the notion that **artificial selection**—the selective breeding of domesticated plants and animals to promote the occurrence of desirable traits in the offspring—was the key to understanding evolutionary change, Darwin bred pigeons to gain firsthand experience. He acquired further insight through conversations with farmers about livestock breeding. He learned that artificial selection

If it weren't for artificial selection, you'd be eating tomatoes the size of blueberries.

253

has two essential components: variation and heritability. Variation among individuals, for example, differences in coat type in a litter of puppies, size of corn ears, or milk production by individual cows in a herd, allows the breeder to select the animals or plants with the most desirable combination of characters as breeding stock for the next generation. Heritability refers to the transmission of a trait from parent to offspring. Despite their lack of knowledge of the underlying genetics, breeders had long understood the importance of heritability in artificial selection—if a character is not heritable, it cannot be improved by selective breeding.

Unlike most naturalists, who looked for consistency of traits as a way to classify organisms, Darwin was a careful observer of variations between individuals. He knew that individuals in natural populations have small but measurable differences, for example, variations in color and markings (Figure 13.11). But what forces in nature determined which individuals became the breeding stock for the next generation?

Darwin found inspiration in an essay written by economist Thomas Malthus, who contended that much of human suffering—disease, famine, and war—was the consequence of human populations increasing faster than food supplies and other resources. Darwin applied Malthus's idea to populations of plants and animals, reasoning that the resources of any given environment are limited. The production of more individuals than the environment can support leads to a struggle for existence, with only some offspring surviving in each generation (Figure 13.12). Of the many eggs laid, young born, and seeds spread, only a tiny fraction complete development and leave offspring themselves. The rest are eaten, starved, diseased, unmated, or unable to reproduce for other reasons. The essence of natural selection

▼ Figure 13.11 **Color variation within a population of Asian lady beetles.**

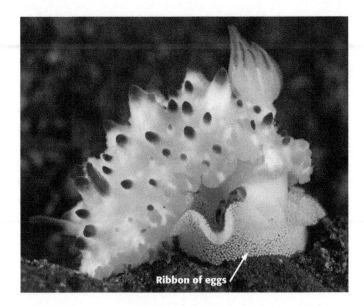

Ribbon of eggs

▲ Figure 13.12 **Overproduction of offspring.** This sea slug, a mollusc related to snails (see Figure 17.13), is laying thousands of eggs embedded in the yellow ribbon around its body. Only a tiny fraction of the eggs will actually give rise to offspring that survive and reproduce.

is this unequal reproduction. In the process of natural selection, individuals whose traits better enable them to obtain food, escape predators, or tolerate physical conditions will survive and reproduce more successfully, passing these adaptive traits to their offspring.

Darwin reasoned that if artificial selection can bring about significant change in a relatively short period of time, then natural selection could modify species considerably over hundreds or thousands of generations. Over vast spans of time, many traits that adapt a population to its environment will accumulate. If the environment changes, however, or if individuals move to a new environment, natural selection will select for adaptations to these new conditions, sometimes producing changes that result in the origin of a completely new species.

Next, let's look at an example of how natural selection operates.

Natural Selection in Action

Look at any natural environment and you will see the products of natural selection—adaptations that suit organisms to their environment. But can we see natural selection in action? Yes, indeed! Biologists have documented evolutionary change in thousands of scientific studies.

An unsettling example of natural selection in action is the evolution of pesticide resistance in hundreds of insect species. Pesticides control insects and prevent them from eating crops or transmitting diseases. But whenever a new type of pesticide is used to control pests, the outcome

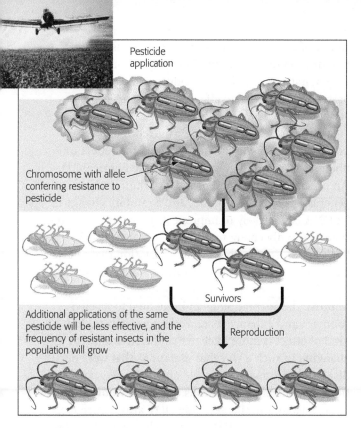

Pesticide
application

Chromosome with allele
conferring resistance to
pesticide

Survivors

Additional applications of the same
pesticide will be less effective, and the
frequency of resistant insects in the
population will grow

Reproduction

▲ Figure 13.13 **Evolution of pesticide resistance in
insect populations.** By spraying crops with poisons to kill
insect pests, people have unwittingly favored the reproductive
success of insects with inherent resistance to the poisons.

is similar (Figure 13.13): A relatively small amount of
poison initially kills most of the insects, but subsequent
applications are less and less effective. The few survivors
of the first pesticide wave are individuals that are
genetically resistant, carrying an allele (alternative form
of a gene) that somehow enables them to survive the
chemical attack. So the poison kills most members of the
population, leaving the resistant survivors to reproduce
and pass the alleles for pesticide resistance to their

offspring. Thus, the proportion of pesticide-resistant
individuals increases in each generation.

Key Points about Natural Selection

Before we move on, let's summarize how natural selection works in bringing about evolutionary change.

Natural selection affects individual organisms—in
Figure 13.13, each insect either survived the pesticide
or was killed by it. However, individuals do not evolve.
Rather, it is the population—the group of organisms—
that evolves over time as adaptive traits become more
common in the group and other traits change or
disappear. Thus, evolution refers to generation-to-
generation changes in populations.

Natural selection can amplify or diminish
only heritable traits. Although an organism
may, during its lifetime, acquire characters
that help it survive, such acquired characters
cannot be passed on to offspring.

Natural selection is more an editing process
than a creative mechanism. A pesticide does not create new alleles that allow insects to survive. Rather,
the presence of the pesticide leads to natural selection
for insects in the population that already have those
alleles.

Natural selection is not goal-directed; it does not
lead to perfectly adapted organisms. Whereas artificial
selection is a deliberate attempt by humans to produce
individuals with specific traits, natural selection is the
result of environmental factors that vary from place to
place and over time. A trait that is favorable in one situation may be useless—or even detrimental—in different
circumstances. And, as you will see, some adaptations
are compromises. ☑

Thanks to natural selection,
populations of more than
500 insect species are
invulnerable to the most
widely used pesticides.

The Evolution of Populations

In *The Origin of Species*, Darwin provided evidence that
life on Earth has evolved over time, and he proposed that
natural selection, in favoring some heritable traits over
others, was the primary mechanism for that change. But
how do the variations that are the raw material for natural
selection arise in a population? And how are these variations passed along from parents to offspring? Darwin
did not know that Gregor Mendel (see Figure 9.1) had
already answered these questions. Although both men
lived and worked at around the same time, Mendel's work

was largely ignored by the scientific community. Its redis-
covery in 1900 set the stage for understanding the genetic
differences on which evolution is based.

Sources of Genetic Variation

You have no trouble recognizing friends in a crowd.
Each person has a unique genome, reflected in individual phenotypic variations such as appearance and other
traits. Indeed, individual variation occurs in all species,

as illustrated by the garter snakes in Figure 13.14. In addition to obvious physical differences, such as the snakes' colors and patterns, most populations have a great deal of phenotypic variation that can be observed only at the molecular level, such as an enzyme that detoxifies a pesticide. Of course, not all variation in a population is heritable. Phenotype—the expressed traits of an organism—results from a combination of the genotype, which is inherited, and many environmental influences. For instance, if you have dental work to straighten and whiten your teeth, you will not pass your environmentally produced smile to your offspring. Only the genetic component of variation is relevant to natural selection. Many of the characters that vary in a population result from the combined effect of several genes. Other features, such as Mendel's purple and white pea flowers or human blood types, are determined by a single gene locus, with different alleles producing distinct phenotypes. But where do these alleles come from?

Mutation

New alleles originate by mutation, a change in the nucleotide sequence of DNA. Thus, mutation is the ultimate

▼ Figure 13.14 **Variation in a garter snake population.** These four garter snakes, which belong to the same species, were all captured in one Oregon field. The behavior of each physical type is correlated with its coloration. When approached, spotted snakes, which blend in with their background, generally freeze. In contrast, snakes with stripes, which make it difficult to judge the speed of motion, usually flee rapidly when approached.

source of the genetic variation that serves as raw material for evolution. In multicellular organisms, however, only mutations in cells that produce gametes can be passed to offspring and affect a population's genetic variability.

A change as small as a single nucleotide in a protein-coding gene can have a significant effect on phenotype, as in sickle-cell disease (see Figure 9.21). An organism is a refined product of thousands of generations of past selection, and a random change in its DNA is not likely to improve its genome any more than randomly changing some words on a page is likely to improve a story. In fact, mutation that affects a protein's function will probably be harmful. On rare occasions, however, a mutated allele may actually improve the adaptation of an individual to its environment and enhance its reproductive success. This kind of effect is more likely when the environment is changing in such a way that mutations that were once disadvantageous are favorable under the new conditions. For instance, mutations that endow houseflies with resistance to the pesticide DDT also reduce their growth rate. Before DDT was introduced, such mutations were a handicap to the flies that had them. But once DDT was part of the environment, the mutant alleles were advantageous, and natural selection increased their frequency in fly populations.

Chromosomal mutations that delete, disrupt, or rearrange many gene loci at once are almost certain to be harmful. But duplication of a gene or small pieces of DNA through errors in meiosis can provide an important source of genetic variation. If a repeated segment of DNA can persist over the generations, mutations may accumulate in the duplicate copies without affecting the function of the original gene, eventually leading to new genes with novel functions. This process may have played a major role in evolution. For example, the remote ancestors of mammals carried a single gene for detecting odors that has since been duplicated repeatedly. As a result, mice have about 1,300 different genes that encode smell receptors. It is likely that such dramatic increases helped early mammals by enabling them to distinguish among many different smells. And repeated duplications of genes that control development are linked to the origin of vertebrate animals from an invertebrate ancestor.

In prokaryotes, mutations can quickly generate genetic variation in a population. Because bacteria multiply so rapidly, a beneficial mutation can increase in frequency in a matter of hours or days. And because bacteria are haploid, with a single allele for each gene, a new allele can have an effect immediately. Mutation rates in animals and plants average about 1 in every 100,000 genes per generation. For these organisms, low mutation rates, long time spans between generations, and diploid genomes prevent most mutations from significantly affecting genetic variation from one generation to the next.

Sexual Reproduction

In organisms that reproduce sexually, most of the genetic variation in a population results from the unique combination of alleles that each individual inherits. (Of course, the origin of those allele variations is past mutations.)

Fresh assortments of existing alleles arise every generation from three random components of sexual reproduction: independent orientation of homologous chromosomes at metaphase I of meiosis (see Figure 8.16), crossing over (see Figure 8.18), and random fertilization. During meiosis, pairs of homologous chromosomes, one set inherited from each parent, trade some of their genes by crossing over. These homologous chromosomes separate into gametes independently of other chromosome pairs. Thus, gametes from any individual vary extensively in their genetic makeup. Finally, each zygote made by a mating pair has a unique assortment of alleles resulting from the random union of sperm and egg.

Populations as the Units of Evolution

One common misconception about evolution is that individual organisms evolve during their lifetimes. It is true that natural selection acts on individuals: Each individual's combination of traits affects its survival and reproductive success. But the evolutionary impact of natural selection is only apparent in the changes in a population of organisms over time.

A **population** is a group of individuals of the same species that live in the same area and interbreed. We can measure evolution as a change in the prevalence of certain heritable traits in a population over a span of generations. The increasing proportion of resistant insects in areas sprayed with pesticide is one example. Natural selection favored insects with alleles for pesticide resistance. As a result, these insects left more offspring than nonresistant individuals, changing the genetic makeup of the next generation's population.

Different populations of the same species may be geographically isolated from each other to such an extent that an exchange of genetic material never or only rarely occurs. Such isolation is common in populations confined to different lakes (Figure 13.15) or islands. For example, each population of Galápagos tortoise is restricted to its own island. Not all populations have such sharp boundaries, however; members of a population typically breed with one another and are therefore more closely related to each other than they are to members of a different population.

In studying evolution at the population level, biologists focus on the **gene pool**, which consists of all copies of every type of allele at every locus in all members of the population. For many loci, there are two or more alleles in the gene pool. For example, in a housefly population, there may be two alleles relating to DDT breakdown, one that codes for an enzyme that breaks down DDT and one for a version of the enzyme that does not. In populations living in fields sprayed with DDT, the allele for the enzyme conferring resistance will

▼ Figure 13.15 **Isolated lakes in Denali National Park and Preserve, Alaska.**

increase in frequency and the other allele will decrease in frequency. When the relative frequencies of alleles in a population change like this over a number of generations, evolution is taking place.

Next, we'll explore how to test whether evolution is occurring in a population. ☑

Analyzing Gene Pools

Imagine a wildflower population with two varieties of blooms that are different colors (Figure 13.16). An allele for red flowers, which we will symbolize by R, is dominant to an allele for white flowers, symbolized by r. These are the only two alleles for flower color in the gene pool of this hypothetical plant population. Now, let's say that 80%, or 0.8, of all flower-color loci in the gene pool have the R allele. We'll use the letter p to represent the relative frequency of the R allele in the population. Thus, $p = 0.8$. Because there are only two alleles in this example, the r allele must be present at the other 20% (0.2) of the gene pool's flower-color loci. (This accounts for 100% of the flower-color loci in the gene pool, or a relative frequency of 1.) Let's use the letter q for the frequency of the r allele in the population. For the wildflower population, $q = 0.2$. And since there are only two alleles for flower color, we can express their frequencies as follows:

Notice that if we know the frequency of either allele in the gene pool, we can subtract it from 1 to calculate the frequency of the other allele.

From the frequencies of alleles, we can also calculate the frequencies of different genotypes in the population if the gene pool is completely stable (not evolving). In the wildflower population, what is the probability of producing an RR individual by "drawing" two R alleles from the pool of gametes? (Here we apply the rule of multiplication that you learned in Chapter 9; review Figure 9.11.) The probability of drawing an R sperm multiplied by the probability of drawing an R egg is $p \times p = p^2$, or $0.8 \times 0.8 = 0.64$. In other words, 64% of the plants in the population will have the RR genotype. Applying the same math, we also know the frequency of rr individuals in the population: $q^2 = 0.2 \times 0.2 = 0.04$. Thus, 4% of the plants are rr, giving them white flowers. Calculating the frequency of heterozygous individuals, Rr, is trickier. That's because the heterozygous genotype can form in two ways, depending on whether the sperm or egg supplies the dominant allele. So the frequency of the Rr genotype is $2pq$, which is $2 \times 0.8 \times 0.2 = 0.32$. In our imaginary wildflower population, 32% of the plants are Rr, with red flowers. Figure 13.17 reviews these calculations graphically.

Now we can write a general formula for calculating the frequencies of genotypes in a gene pool from the frequencies of alleles, and vice versa:

▼ Figure 13.17 **A mathematical swim in the gene pool.** Each of the four boxes in the Punnett square corresponds to a probable "draw" of alleles from the gene pool.

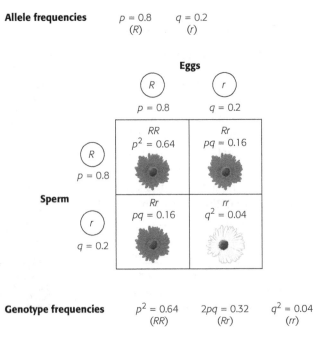

▼ Figure 13.16 **A population of wildflowers with two varieties of color.**

Notice that the frequencies of all genotypes in the gene pool must add up to 1. This formula is called the Hardy-Weinberg equation, named for the two scientists who derived it.

Population Genetics and Health Science

Public health scientists use the Hardy-Weinberg equation to calculate the percentage of a human population that carries the allele for certain inherited diseases. Consider phenylketonuria (PKU), which is an inherited inability to break down the amino acid phenylalanine. If untreated, the disorder has serious effects on brain development. PKU occurs in about 1 out of 10,000 babies born in the United States. Newborn babies are now routinely tested for PKU, and symptoms can be prevented if individuals living with the disease follow a strict diet that limits phenylalanine. In addition to occurring naturally, phenylalanine is found in the widely used artificial sweetener aspartame (Figure 13.18).

PKU is caused by a recessive allele (that is, one that must be present in two copies to produce the phenotype). Thus, we can represent the frequency of individuals in the U.S. population born with PKU with the q^2 term in the Hardy-Weinberg formula. For one PKU occurrence per 10,000 births, $q^2 = 0.0001$. Therefore, q, the frequency of the recessive allele in the population,

equals the square root of 0.0001, or 0.01. And p, the frequency of the dominant allele, equals $1 - q$, or 0.99.

Now let's calculate the frequency of carriers, who are heterozygous individuals who carry the PKU allele in a single copy and may pass it on to offspring. Carriers are represented in the formula by $2pq$: $2 \times 0.99 \times 0.01$, or 0.0198. Thus, the Hardy-Weinberg formula tells us that about 2% of the U.S. population are carriers for the PKU allele. Estimating the frequency of a harmful allele is essential for any public health program dealing with genetic diseases.

Microevolution as Change in a Gene Pool

As stated earlier, evolution can be measured as changes in the genetic composition of a population over time. It helps, as a basis of comparison, to know what to expect if a population is not evolving. A nonevolving population is in genetic equilibrium, which is also known as **Hardy-Weinberg equilibrium**. The population's gene pool remains constant. From generation to generation, the frequencies of alleles (p and q) and genotypes (p^2, $2pq$, and q^2) are unchanged. Sexual shuffling of genes cannot by itself change a large gene pool. Because a generation-to-generation change in allele frequencies of a population is evolution viewed on the smallest scale, it is sometimes referred to as **microevolution**. ✓

▼ Figure 13.18
A warning to individuals with PKU.

INGREDIENTS: SORBITOL, MAGNESIUM STEARATE, ARTIFICIAL FLAVOR, **ASPARTAME† (SWEETENER),** ARTIFICIAL COLOR (YELLOW 5 LAKE, BLUE 1 LAKE), ZINC GLUCONATE.
†PHENYLKETONURICS: CONTAINS PHENYLALANINE

☑ **CHECKPOINT**
1. Which term in the Hardy-Weinberg formula ($p^2 + 2pq + q^2 = 1$) corresponds to the frequency of individuals with *no* alleles for the recessive disease PKU?
2. Define microevolution.

Answers: 1. p^2 2. Microevolution is a change in a population's frequencies of alleles.

Mechanisms That Alter Allele Frequencies in a Population

Now that we've defined microevolution as changes in a population's genetic makeup from generation to generation, we come to an obvious question: What mechanisms can change a gene pool? Natural selection is the most important, because it is the only process that promotes adaptation. We'll examine natural selection in more detail shortly. But first, we look at two other mechanisms of evolutionary change: genetic drift, which is due to chance, and gene flow, the exchange of alleles between neighboring populations.

Genetic Drift

Flip a coin 1,000 times, and a result of 700 heads and 300 tails would make you very suspicious about that coin.

But flip a coin 10 times, and an outcome of 7 heads and 3 tails would seem within reason. With a smaller sample, there is a greater chance of deviation from an idealized result—in this case, an equal number of heads and tails.

Let's apply this coin toss logic to a population's gene pool. If a new generation draws its alleles at random from the previous generation, then the larger the population (the sample size), the better the new generation will represent the gene pool of the previous generation. Thus, one requirement for a gene pool to maintain the status quo is a large population size. The gene pool of a small population may not be accurately represented in the next generation because of sampling error. The changed gene pool is analogous to the erratic outcome from a small sample of coin tosses.

Figure 13.19 applies this concept of sampling error to a small population of wildflowers. Chance causes the frequencies of the alleles for red (R) and white (r) flowers to change over the generations. And that fits our definition of microevolution. This evolutionary mechanism, a change in the gene pool of a population due to chance, is called **genetic drift**. But what would cause a population to shrink down to a size where there is genetic drift? Two ways this can occur are the bottleneck effect and the founder effect, both of which we explore next.

The Bottleneck Effect

Disasters such as earthquakes, floods, and fires may kill large numbers of individuals, producing a small surviving population that is unlikely to have the same genetic makeup as the original population. Again, the gene pool of the surviving population is a small sample of the genetic diversity originally present. By chance, certain alleles may be overrepresented among the survivors. Other alleles may be underrepresented. And some alleles may be eliminated. Chance may continue to change the gene pool for many generations until the population is again large enough for sampling errors to be insignificant.

The analogy illustrated in Figure 13.20 shows why genetic drift due to a drastic reduction in population size is called the **bottleneck effect**.

▼ Figure 13.20 **The bottleneck effect.** The colored marbles in this analogy represent three alleles in an imaginary population. Shaking just a few of the marbles through the bottleneck is like an environmental disaster that drastically reduces the size of a population. Compared with the predisaster population, purple marbles are overrepresented in the new population, green marbles are underrepresented, and orange marbles are absent—all by chance. Similarly, a population that passes through a "bottleneck" event emerges with reduced variability.

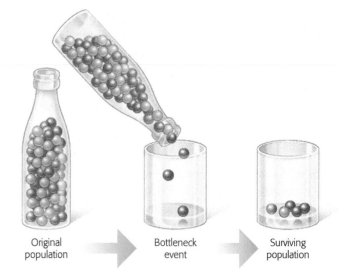

Original population → Bottleneck event → Surviving population

▼ Figure 13.19 **Genetic drift.** This hypothetical wildflower population consists of only ten plants. Due to random change over the generations, genetic drift can eliminate some alleles, as is the case for the r allele in generation 3 of this imaginary population.

Generation 1
p (frequency of R) = 0.7
q (frequency of r) = 0.3

Only 5 of 10 plants leave offspring

Generation 2
p = 0.5
q = 0.5

Only 2 of 10 plants leave offspring

Generation 3
p = 1.0
q = 0.0

Passing through a "bottleneck"—a severe reduction in population size—decreases the overall genetic variability in a population because at least some alleles are likely to be lost from the gene pool. We can see this concept at work in the potential loss of individual variation, and hence adaptability, in drastically reduced populations of endangered species.

One such endangered species is the cheetah (Figure 13.21). The fastest of all running animals, cheetahs are magnificent cats that were once widespread in Africa and Asia. Like many African mammals, the number of cheetahs fell dramatically during the last ice age (around 10,000 years ago). At that time, the species suffered a severe bottleneck, possibly as a result of disease, human hunting, and periodic droughts. The South African cheetah population may have suffered a second bottleneck during the 1800s, when farmers hunted the animals to near extinction. Today, only a few small populations of cheetahs exist in the wild. Genetic variability in these populations is very low. In addition, the cheetahs remaining in Africa are being crowded into nature preserves and parks as human demands on the land increase. Along with crowding comes an increased potential for the spread of disease. With so little variability, the cheetah has a reduced capacity to adapt to such environmental challenges. Although captive breeding programs can boost cheetah population sizes, the species' pre-bottleneck genetic diversity can never be restored. ☑

The Founder Effect

When a few individuals colonize an isolated island, lake, or other new habitat, the genetic makeup of the colony is only a sample of the gene pool in the larger population. The smaller the colony (in other words, the smaller the sample size), the less likely it is to be representative of all the genetic diversity present in the population from which the colonists emigrated. If the colony succeeds, genetic drift will continue to change the frequency of alleles randomly until the population is large enough for genetic drift to be minimal. The type of genetic drift resulting from the establishment of a small, new population whose gene pool differs from that of the parent population is called the **founder effect**.

Numerous examples of the founder effect have been identified in geographically or socially isolated human populations. In such situations, disease-causing alleles that are rare in the larger population may become common in a small colony. For example, Amish and Mennonite communities in North America were founded by small numbers of European immigrants in the 1700s, and individuals within the community have since intermarried, remaining genetically separate from the larger population (Figure 13.22). Dozens of genetic diseases that are extremely rare elsewhere are relatively common in these communities. On the other hand, the high frequency of genetic diseases in populations has enabled genetic researchers to identify the mutation responsible for certain genetic disorders. In some cases, a disorder is treatable if detected early.

Populations of endangered species may be doomed by their lack of genetic diversity.

▲ Figure 13.22 **The founder effect.** Small, isolated populations often have high frequencies of alleles that are rare in large populations.

☑ CHECKPOINT

Would you expect modern cheetahs to have more genetic variation or less than cheetahs did 1,000 years ago?

Answer: less, because the bottleneck effed reduces genetic variability

▼ Figure 13.21 **Implications of the bottleneck effect in conservation biology.** Some endangered species, such as the cheetah, have low genetic variability. As a result, they are less adaptable to environmental changes, such as new diseases, than are species with a greater resource of genetic variation.

▲ Figure 13.23 **Gene
flow.** The pollen of some
plants can be carried by the
wind for hundreds of miles,
allowing gene flow to occur
between distant populations.

Gene Flow

Another source of evolutionary change is **gene flow**,
which is genetic exchange with another population. A
population may gain or lose alleles when fertile individuals move into or out of the population or when gametes
(such as plant pollen) are transferred between populations (Figure 13.23). For example, consider our hypothetical wildflower population in Figure 13.16. Suppose
a neighboring population consists entirely of white-
flowered individuals. A wind storm may blow pollen
to our wildflowers from the neighboring population,
resulting in a higher frequency of the white-flower allele
in the next generation—a microevolutionary change.

Gene flow tends to reduce differences between
populations. If it is extensive enough, gene flow can
eventually join neighboring populations into a single
population with a common gene pool. As people began
to move about the world more freely, gene flow became
an important agent of microevolutionary change in
populations that were previously isolated. ☑

Natural Selection: A Closer Look

Genetic drift, gene flow, and even mutation can cause
microevolution. But only by rare chance would these
events result in improving a population's fit to its environment. In natural selection, on the other hand, only
the events that produce genetic variation (mutation and
sexual reproduction) are random. The process of natural selection, in which individuals better adapted to the
environment are more likely to survive and reproduce,
is *not* random. Consequently, only natural selection
consistently leads to adaptive evolution—evolution
that results in a better fit between organisms and their
environment.

The adaptations of organisms include many striking examples. Consider the blue-footed booby
(Figure 13.24), one of the most memorable creatures
that Darwin encountered on the Galápagos Islands. The
bird's body and bill are streamlined like a torpedo, mini-
mizing friction as it dives from heights up to 24 m (over
75 feet) into the shallow water below. To pull out of this
high-speed dive once it hits the water, the booby uses its
large tail as a brake. Those remarkable blue feet are an
essential requirement for the male's reproductive success. Female boobies prefer males with the brightest blue
feet. Thus, the male's courtship display is a dance that
features frequent flashes of his colorful assets.

Such adaptations are the result of natural selection.
By consistently favoring some alleles over others, natural

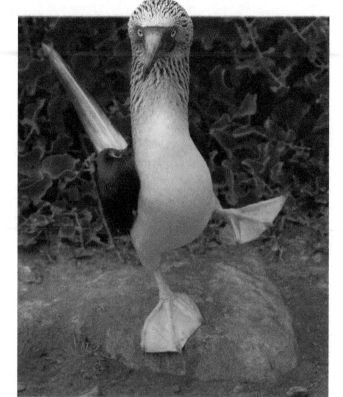

▲ Figure 13.24 **A blue-footed booby.** Although the booby's
large, webbed feet are highly advantageous in the water, they
are clumsy for walking on land.

selection improves the match between organisms and
their environment. However, the environment may
change over time. As a result, what constitutes a "good
match" between an organism and its environment is a
moving target, making adaptive evolution a continuous,
dynamic process.

Evolutionary Fitness

The commonly used phrase "survival of the fittest" is
misleading if we take it to mean head-to-head competition between individuals. Reproductive success, the key
to evolutionary success, is generally more subtle and
passive. In a varying population of moths, certain individuals may produce more offspring than others because
their wing colors hide them from predators better. Plants
in a wildflower population may differ in reproductive
success because some attract more pollinators, owing
to slight variations in flower color, shape, or fragrance.
In a given environment, such traits can lead to greater
relative fitness, the contribution an individual makes to
the gene pool of the next generation *relative to* the contributions of other individuals. The fittest individuals in
the context of evolution are those that produce the largest number of viable, fertile offspring and thus pass on
the most genes to the next generation. ☑

Three General Outcomes of Natural Selection

Imagine a population of mice with individuals ranging in fur color from very light to very dark gray. If we graph the number of mice in each color category, we get a bell-shaped curve like the one shown at the top of Figure 13.25. If natural selection favors certain fur-color phenotypes over others, the population of mice will change over the generations. Three general outcomes are possible, depending on which phenotypes are favored. These three modes of natural selection are called directional selection, disruptive selection, and stabilizing selection.

Directional selection shifts the overall makeup of a population by selecting in favor of one extreme phenotype—the darkest mice, for example (Figure 13.25a). Directional selection is most common when the local environment changes or when organisms migrate to a new environment. An actual example is the shift of insect populations toward a greater frequency of pesticide-resistant individuals.

Disruptive selection can lead to a balance between two or more contrasting phenotypes in a population (Figure 13.25b). A patchy environment, which favors different phenotypes in different patches, is one situation associated with disruptive selection. The variations seen in the snake population in Figure 13.14 result from disruptive selection.

Stabilizing selection favors intermediate phenotypes (Figure 13.25c). Such selection typically occurs in relatively stable environments, where conditions tend to reduce physical variation. This evolutionary conservatism works by selecting against the more extreme phenotypes. For example, stabilizing selection keeps the majority of human birth weights between 3 and 4 kg (approximately 6.5 to 9 pounds). For babies much lighter or heavier than this, infant mortality is greater.

Of the three selection modes, stabilizing selection occurs in most situations, resisting change in well-adapted populations. Evolutionary spurts occur when a population is stressed by a change in the environment or by migration to a new place. When challenged with a new set of environmental problems, a population either adapts through natural selection or dies off in that locale. The fossil record tells us that the population's extinction is the most common result. Those populations that do survive crises may change

enough to be designated new species. (You'll learn more about this in Chapter 14.) ☑

Sexual Selection

Darwin was the first to explore the implications of **sexual selection**, a form of natural selection in which individuals with certain traits are more likely than other individuals to obtain mates. The males and females of an animal species obviously have different reproductive organs. But they may also have secondary sexual traits, noticeable differences not directly associated with reproduction or survival. This distinction in appearance, called **sexual dimorphism**, is often manifested in a size difference. Among male vertebrates, sexual dimorphism may also be evident in adornment, such as manes on

☑ **CHECKPOINT**

The thickness of fur in a bear population increases over several generations as the climate in the region becomes colder. This is an example of which type of selection: directional, disruptive, or stabilizing?

Answer: *directional*

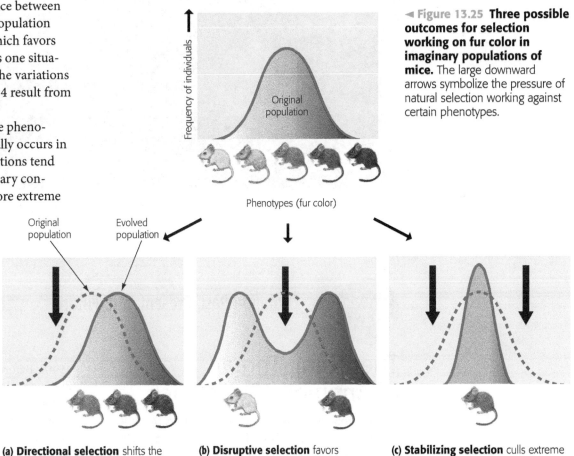

◄ **Figure 13.25 Three possible outcomes for selection working on fur color in imaginary populations of mice.** The large downward arrows symbolize the pressure of natural selection working against certain phenotypes.

(a) Directional selection shifts the overall makeup of the population by favoring variants at one extreme. In this case, the trend is toward darker color, perhaps because the landscape has been shaded by the growth of trees, making darker mice less noticeable to predators.

(b) Disruptive selection favors variants at opposite extremes over intermediate individuals. Here, the relative frequencies of very light and very dark mice have increased. Perhaps the mice have colonized a patchy habitat where a background of light soil is studded with dark rocks.

(c) Stabilizing selection culls extreme variants from the population, in this case eliminating individuals that are unusually light or dark. The trend is toward reduced phenotypic variation and increased frequency of an intermediate phenotype.

lions, antlers on deer, or colorful plumage on peacocks and other birds (Figure 13.26a).

In some species, secondary sex structures may be used to compete with members of the same sex (usually males) for mates. Contests may involve physical combat, but are more often ritualized displays (Figure 13.26b). Such selection is common in species in which the winner acquires a harem of mates—an obvious boost to that male's evolutionary fitness.

> In some species, males engage in nonlethal combat in the hope of mating with females.

In a more common type of sexual selection, individuals of one sex (usually females) are choosy in selecting their mates. Males with the largest or most colorful adornments are often the most attractive to females. The extraordinary feathers of a peacock's tail are an example of this sort of "choose me!" statement. Every time a female chooses a mate based on a certain appearance or behavior, she perpetuates the alleles that caused her to make that choice and allows a male with that particular phenotype to perpetuate his alleles.

What is the advantage to females of being choosy? One hypothesis is that females prefer male traits that are correlated with "good" alleles. In several bird species, research has shown that traits preferred by females, such as bright beaks or long tails, are related to overall male health.

▼ Figure 13.26 **Sexual dimorphism.**

(a) **Sexual dimorphism in a finch species.** Among vertebrates, including this pair of green-winged Pytilia (native to Africa), males (right) are usually the showier sex.

(b) **Competing for mates.** Male Spanish ibex engage in nonlethal combat for the right to mate with females.

Evolution Past, Present, and Future EVOLUTION CONNECTION

The Rising Threat of Antibiotic Resistance

As you probably know, antibiotics are drugs that kill infectious microorganisms. But antibiotics are a relatively recent development in medicine. Before antibiotics, people often died from diseases such as whooping cough, and a minor wound—a razor nick or a scratch from a rose thorn—could result in a fatal infection. A revolution in human health followed the introduction of penicillin, the first widely used antibiotic, in the 1940s. Before long, more antibiotics were developed, and many diseases that had once been fatal could easily be cured. But even amid the enthusiasm for the new wonder drugs, signs of trouble began to appear. Doctors reported cases of bacterial infections that did not respond to antibiotics. By 1952, a researcher had identified the reason: Some bacteria had genetic traits that enabled them to resist the killing power of the drugs. In the same way that pesticides select for resistant insects, antibiotics select for resistant bacteria. A gene that codes for an enzyme that breaks down an antibiotic or a mutation that alters the site where an antibiotic binds can make a bacterium and its offspring resistant to that antibiotic. Again we see both the random and nonrandom aspects of natural selection—the random genetic mutations in bacteria and the nonrandom selective effects as the environment favors the antibiotic-resistant phenotype.

Ironically, our enthusiasm for the curative powers of antibiotics has encouraged the evolution of antibiotic-resistant bacteria. Livestock producers add antibiotics to animal feed, a practice that may select for bacteria resistant to standard antibiotics. Doctors may overprescribe antibiotics—for example, to patients with viral infections, which do not respond to antibiotic treatment. You may also be part of the problem. If you stop taking a prescribed antibiotic as soon as you feel better, instead of taking the full course of medication your doctor has prescribed, you are allowing mutant bacteria that may be killed more slowly by the drug to survive and multiply. Subsequent mutations in such bacteria may lead to full-blown antibiotic resistance.

Natural selection for antibiotic resistance is particularly strong in hospitals, where antibiotic use is extensive. A formidable "superbug" known as MRSA (methicillin-resistant *Staphylococcus aureus*) can cause "flesh-eating disease" and potentially fatal systemic (whole-body) infections. Alarmingly, a growing number of incidents of MRSA infection now begin in community settings, such as athletic facilities, schools, and military barracks (Figure 13.27).

MRSA is not the only antibiotic-resistant microorganism. According to a report issued by the Centers for Disease Control (CDC), 17 bacterial infections are no longer treatable with standard antibiotics; most of these are considered urgent or serious threats to public health. The most recent "superbug" to emerge is a strain of the bacteria that cause gonorrhea, a sexually transmitted disease. Public health officials fear that as this strain spreads, gonorrhea will become an incurable disease.

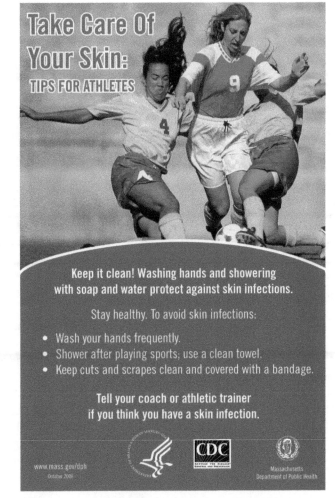

▲ Figure 13.27 **Cautioning athletes about MRSA.**

Drug resistance has also evolved in disease-causing viruses (for example, HIV and influenza) and parasites (for example, the organism that causes malaria).

Medical and pharmaceutical researchers are racing to develop new antibiotics and other drugs. However, experience suggests that our battle against the evolution of drug-resistant bacteria will continue for the foreseeable future.

Chapter Review

SUMMARY OF KEY CONCEPTS
The Diversity of Life

Naming and Classifying the Diversity of Life
In the Linnaean system of classification, each species is assigned a two-part name. The first part is the genus, and the second part is unique for each species within the genus. In the taxonomic hierarchy, domain > kingdom > phylum > class > order > family > genus > species.

Explaining the Diversity of Life
Present-day biologists accept Darwin's theory of evolution by means of natural selection as the best explanation for the diversity of life. However, when Darwin published his theory in 1859, it was a radical departure from the prevailing views.

Charles Darwin and *The Origin of Species*

Darwin's Journey

During his around-the-world voyage on the *Beagle*, Darwin observed adaptations of organisms that inhabited diverse environments. In particular, Darwin was struck by the geographic distribution of organisms on the Galápagos Islands, off the South American coast. When Darwin considered his observations in light of new evidence for a very old Earth that changed slowly, he arrived at ideas that were at odds with the long-held notion of a young Earth populated by unchanging species.

Evolution: Darwin's Theory

In his book *On the Origin of Species by Means of Natural Selection*, Darwin made two proposals: (1) Existing species descended from ancestral species, and (2) natural selection is the mechanism of evolution.

Evidence of Evolution

Evidence from Fossils

The fossil record shows that organisms have appeared in a historical sequence, and many fossils link ancestral species with those living today. For example, the evolution of whales from ancestral land-dwelling animals is documented by fossils of transitional forms.

Evidence from Homologies

Structural and molecular homologies reveal evolutionary relationships. Closely related species often have similar stages in their embryonic development. All species share a common genetic code, suggesting that all forms of life are related through branching evolution from the earliest organisms.

Evolutionary Trees

An evolutionary tree represents a succession of related species, with the most recent at the tips of the branches. Each branch point represents a common ancestor of all species that radiate from it.

Natural Selection as the Mechanism for Evolution

Darwin proposed natural selection as the mechanism that produces adaptive evolutionary change. In a population that varies, individuals best suited for a particular environment are more likely to survive and reproduce than those that are less suited to that environment.

Natural Selection in Action

Natural selection has been observed in many scientific studies, including in the evolution of pesticide-resistant insects.

Key Points about Natural Selection

Individuals do not evolve. Only heritable traits, not those acquired during an individual's lifetime, can be amplified or diminished by natural selection. Natural selection only works on existing variation—new variation does not arise in response to an environmental change. Natural selection does not produce perfect organisms.

The Evolution of Populations

Sources of Genetic Variation

Mutation and sexual reproduction produce genetic variation. Mutation is the ultimate source of genetic variation. Individual mutations have little short-term effect on a large gene pool, but in the long term, mutation is the source of genetic variation.

Populations as the Units of Evolution

A population, members of the same species living in the same time and place, is the smallest biological unit that can evolve.

Analyzing Gene Pools

A gene pool consists of all the alleles in all the individuals making up a population. The Hardy-Weinberg formula can be used to calculate the frequencies of genotypes in a gene pool from the frequencies of alleles, and vice versa:

Allele frequencies	$p + q = 1$
Genotype frequencies	$p^2 + 2pq + q^2 = 1$

Dominant homozygotes   Heterozygotes   Recessive homozygotes

Population Genetics and Health Science

The Hardy-Weinberg formula can be used to estimate the frequency of a harmful allele, which is useful information for public health programs dealing with genetic diseases.

Microevolution as Change in a Gene Pool

Microevolution is generation-to-generation change in allele frequencies in a population.

Mechanisms That Alter Allele Frequencies in a Population

Genetic Drift

Genetic drift is a change in the gene pool of a small population due to chance. A bottleneck event (a drastic reduction in population size) and the founder effect (occurring in a new population started by a few individuals) are two situations leading to genetic drift.

Gene Flow

A population may gain or lose alleles by gene flow, which is genetic exchange with another population.

Natural Selection: A Closer Look

Of all causes of evolution, only natural selection promotes evolutionary adaptations. Relative fitness is the contribution an individual makes to the gene pool of the next generation relative to the contributions of other individuals. The outcome of natural selection may be directional, disruptive, or stabilizing. Secondary sexual traits (such as sex-specific plumage or behaviors) can promote sexual selection, a type of natural selection in which mating preferences are determined by inherited traits.

Directional selection   Disruptive selection   Stabilizing selection

MasteringBiology®

For practice quizzes, BioFlix animations, MP3 tutorials, video tutors, and more study tools designed for this textbook, go to MasteringBiology®

SELF-QUIZ

1. Place these levels of classification in order from least inclusive to most inclusive: class, domain, family, genus, kingdom, order, phylum, species.

2. Which of the following is a true statement about Charles Darwin?
   a. He was the first to discover that living things can change, or evolve.
   b. He based his theory on the inheritance of acquired traits.
   c. He proposed natural selection as the mechanism of evolution.
   d. He was the first to realize that Earth is more than 6,000 years old.

3. How did the insights of Lyell and other geologists influence Darwin's thinking about evolution?

4. In a population with two alleles for a particular genetic locus, B and b, the allele frequency of B is 0.7. If this population is in Hardy-Weinberg equilibrium, what is the frequency of heterozygotes? What is the frequency of homozygous dominants? What is the frequency of homozygous recessives?

5. Define fitness from an evolutionary perspective.

6. Which of the following processes is the ultimate source of the genetic variation that serves as raw material for evolution?
   a. sexual reproduction   c. genetic drift
   b. mutation   d. natural selection

7. As a mechanism of evolution, natural selection can be most closely equated with
   a. random mating.   c. unequal reproductive success.
   b. genetic drift.   d. gene flow.

8. Compare and contrast how the bottleneck effect and the founder effect can lead to genetic drift.

9. In a particular bird species, individuals with average-sized wings survive severe storms more successfully than other birds in the same population with longer or shorter wings. Of the three general outcomes of natural selection (directional, disruptive, or stabilizing), this example illustrates _____.

10. Which of the following statements is (are) true about a population in Hardy-Weinberg equilibrium? (More than one may be true.)
    a. The population is quite small.
    b. The population is not evolving.
    c. Gene flow between the population and surrounding populations does not occur.
    d. Natural selection is not occurring.

Answers to these questions can be found in Appendix: Self-Quiz Answers.

THE PROCESS OF SCIENCE

11. **Interpreting Data** A population of snails has recently become established in a new region. The snails are preyed on by birds that break the snails open on rocks, eat the soft bodies, and leave the shells. The snails occur in both striped and unstriped forms. In one area, researchers counted both live snails and broken shells. Their data are summarized here:

	Striped Shells	Unstriped Shells
Number of live snails	264	296
Number of broken snail shells	486	377
Total	750	673

Based on these data, which snail form is subject to more predation by birds? Predict how the frequencies of striped and unstriped individuals might change over time.

12. Imagine that the presence or absence of stripes on the snails from the previous question is determined by a single gene locus, with the dominant allele (*S*) producing striped snails and the recessive allele (*s*) producing unstriped snails. Combining the data from both the living snails and broken shells, calculate the following: the frequency of the dominant allele, the frequency of the recessive allele, and the number of heterozygotes in the observed groups.

BIOLOGY AND SOCIETY

13. To what extent are people in a technological society exempt from natural selection? Explain your answer.

14. What plants and animals have you seen near your home or school? What evolutionary adaptations suit them to their environment?

14 How Biological Diversity Evolves

If you drove off the rim of the Grand Canyon, you would pass by 40 rock layers and several hundred million years of geologic history before hitting the ground.

Alleles from two wild grasses could be used to make a better ear of corn.

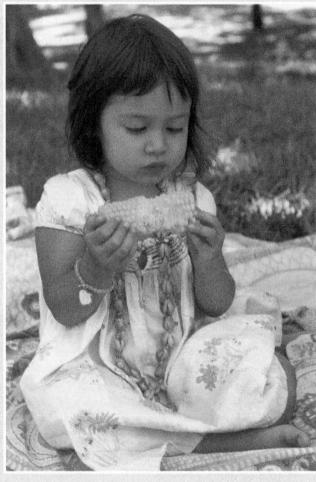

Piecing together evolutionary histories shows who's related to whom.

268

Mass Extinctions BIOLOGY AND SOCIETY

The Sixth Mass Extinction

The fossil record reveals that the evolutionary history of life on Earth has been episodic, with long, relatively stable periods punctuated by brief, cataclysmic ones. During these upheavals, new species formed and others died out in great numbers.

Extinctions are inevitable in a changing world, but the fossil record reveals a few instances of great change, times when the majority of life on Earth—between 50% and 90% of living species—suddenly died out, vanishing forever. Scientists have documented five such mass extinctions during the last 540 million years. Today, human activities are modifying the global environment to such an extent that many species are disappearing at an alarming rate. In the past 400 years— a very short time on a geologic scale—more than 1,000 species are known to have become extinct. Scientists estimate that this is 100 to 1,000 times the extinction rate seen in most of the fossil record.

Are we in the midst of a sixth mass extinction? In an extensive analysis published in *Nature* in 2011, researchers compared data from the fossil record of the "big five" mass extinctions with data from the modern era. The good news is that the current loss of biodiversity does not yet qualify as a mass extinction. The bad news is that we're teetering on the brink. The loss of species that are now at critical risk of extinction—like the sea otter pictured here—would push our planet into a period of mass extinction. When the researchers include species that are endangered or threatened (lower

An endangered species. Oil spills, entanglement in commercial fishing nets, and disease are among the causes of declining sea otter populations.

categories of risk) in their calculations, the picture becomes very grim indeed. In contrast to the ancient mass extinctions, which unfolded over hundreds of thousands of years, a human-driven sixth mass extinction could be completed in just a few centuries. And, as with prior mass extinctions, life on Earth may take millions of years to recover.

But the fossil record also shows a creative side to the destruction. Mass extinctions can pave the way for the evolution of many diverse species from a common ancestor, such as the diversification of mammals after the extinction of dinosaurs. Accordingly, we'll begin this chapter by discussing the birth of new species and then examine how biologists trace the evolution of biological diversity. We'll also take a closer look at how scientists classify living organisms.

The Origin of Species

Natural selection, a microevolutionary mechanism, explains the striking ways in which organisms are suited to their environment. But what accounts for the tremendous diversity of life, the millions of species that have existed during Earth's history? This question intrigued Darwin, who referred to it in his diary as "that mystery of mysteries—the first appearance of new beings on this Earth."

When, as a young man, Darwin visited the Galápagos Islands (see Figure 13.3), he realized that he was visiting a place of origins. Though the volcanic islands were geologically young, they were already home to many plants and animals known nowhere else in the world. Among these unique inhabitants were marine iguanas (Figure 14.1), Galápagos tortoises (see Figure 13.4), and numerous species of small birds called finches, which you will learn more about in this chapter (see Figure 14.11). Surely, Darwin thought, not all of these species could have been among the original colonists. Some of them must have evolved later on, the myriad descendants of the original colonists, modified by natural selection from those original ancestors.

In the century and a half since the publication of Darwin's *On the Origin of Species by Means of Natural Selection*, new discoveries and technological advances—especially in molecular biology—have given scientists a wealth of new information about the evolution of life on Earth. For example, researchers have explained the genetic patterns underlying the homology of vertebrate limbs (see Figure 13.7). Hundreds of thousands more fossil discoveries have been cataloged, including many of the transitional (intermediate) forms predicted by Darwin. In a fascinating convergence of old and new techniques, researchers have even been able to investigate the genetic material of certain fossils, including our ancient relatives, the Neanderthals (see Figure 14.23). New dating methods have confirmed that Earth is billions of years old, much older than even the most radical geologists of Darwin's time proposed. As you'll learn in this chapter, these dating methods have also enabled researchers to determine the ages of fossils and rocks, providing valuable insight into evolutionary relationships between groups of organisms. In addition, our enhanced understanding of geologic processes, such as the changing positions of continents, explains some of the geographic distributions of organisms and fossils that puzzled Darwin and his contemporaries.

In this chapter, you'll learn how evolution has woven the rich tapestry of life, beginning with **speciation**, the process in which one species splits into two or more species. Other topics include the origin of evolutionary novelty, such as the wings and feathers of birds and the large brains of humans, and the impact of mass extinctions, which clear the way for new adaptive explosions, such as the diversification of mammals following the disappearance of most of the dinosaurs.

▼ Figure 14.1 **A marine iguana (right), an example of the unique species inhabiting the Galápagos.** Darwin noticed that Galápagos marine iguanas—with a flattened tail that aids in swimming—are similar to, but distinct from, land-dwelling iguanas on the islands and on the South American mainland (left).

What Is a Species?

Species is a Latin word meaning "kind" or "appearance." Indeed, as children we learn to distinguish between the kinds of plants and animals—between dogs and cats, for example, or between roses and dandelions—from differences in their appearance. Although the basic idea of species as distinct life-forms seems intuitive, devising a more formal definition is not so easy.

One way of defining a species (and the main definition used in this book) is the **biological species concept**. It defines a **species** as a group of populations whose members have the potential to interbreed with one another in nature and produce fertile offspring (offspring that can reproduce) (Figure 14.2). Geography and culture may conspire to keep a Manhattan businesswoman and a Mongolian dairyman apart. But if the two did meet and mate, they could have viable babies who develop into fertile adults because all humans belong to the same species. In contrast, humans and chimpanzees, despite having a shared evolutionary history, are distinct species because they can't successfully interbreed.

We cannot apply the biological species concept to all situations. For example, basing the definition of species on reproductive compatibility excludes organisms that only reproduce asexually (producing offspring from a single parent), such as most prokaryotes. And because fossils are obviously not currently reproducing sexually, they cannot be evaluated by the biological species concept. In response to such challenges, biologists have developed other ways to define species. For example, most of the species named so far have been classified based on measurable physical traits such as number and type of teeth or flower structures. Another approach defines a species as the smallest group of individuals sharing a common ancestor and forming one branch on the tree of life. Yet another approach proposes defining a species solely on the basis of molecular data, a sort of bar code that identifies each species.

Each species concept is useful, depending on the situation and the questions being asked. The biological species concept, however, is particularly useful when focusing on how species originate, that is, when we ask: What prevents a member of one group from successfully interbreeding with a member of another group? You'll learn about the variety of answers to that question next. ☑

☑ CHECKPOINT

According to the biological species concept, what defines a species?

Answer: the ability of its members to interbreed with one another and produce fertile offspring in a natural setting

▼ Figure 14.2 **The biological species concept is based on reproductive compatibility rather than physical similarity.**

Similarity between different species. The eastern meadowlark (left) and the western meadowlark (right) are very similar in appearance, but they are separate species and do not interbreed.

Diversity within one species. Humans, as diverse in appearance as we are, belong to a single species (*Homo sapiens*) and can interbreed.

Reproductive Barriers between Species

Clearly, a fly will not mate with a frog or a fern. But what prevents closely related species from interbreeding? What, for example, maintains the species boundary between the eastern meadowlark and the western meadowlark (shown in Figure 14.2)? Their geographic ranges overlap in the Great Plains region, and they are so similar that only expert birders can tell them apart. And yet, these two bird species do not interbreed.

A **reproductive barrier** is anything that prevents individuals of closely related species from interbreeding. Let's examine the different kinds of reproductive barriers that isolate the gene pools of species (Figure 14.3). We can classify reproductive barriers as either prezygotic or postzygotic, depending on whether they block interbreeding before or after the formation of zygotes (fertilized eggs).

Prezygotic barriers prevent mating or fertilization between species (Figure 14.4). The barrier may be time-based (temporal isolation). For example, western spotted skunks breed in the fall, but the eastern species breeds in late winter. Temporal isolation keeps the species from mating even where they coexist on the Great Plains. In other cases, species live in the same region but not in the same habitats (habitat isolation). For example, one species of North American garter snake lives mainly in water, while a closely related species lives on land. Traits that enable individuals to recognize potential mates, such as a particular odor, coloration, or courtship ritual, can also function as reproductive barriers (behavioral isolation). In many bird species, for example,

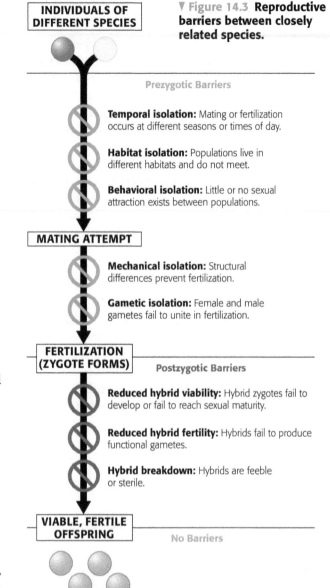

▼ Figure 14.3 **Reproductive barriers between closely related species.**

INDIVIDUALS OF DIFFERENT SPECIES

Prezygotic Barriers

Temporal isolation: Mating or fertilization occurs at different seasons or times of day.

Habitat isolation: Populations live in different habitats and do not meet.

Behavioral isolation: Little or no sexual attraction exists between populations.

MATING ATTEMPT

Mechanical isolation: Structural differences prevent fertilization.

Gametic isolation: Female and male gametes fail to unite in fertilization.

FERTILIZATION (ZYGOTE FORMS)

Postzygotic Barriers

Reduced hybrid viability: Hybrid zygotes fail to develop or fail to reach sexual maturity.

Reduced hybrid fertility: Hybrids fail to produce functional gametes.

Hybrid breakdown: Hybrids are feeble or sterile.

VIABLE, FERTILE OFFSPRING

No Barriers

► Figure 14.4 **Prezygotic barriers.** Prezygotic barriers prevent mating or fertilization.

PREZYGOTIC BARRIERS

Temporal Isolation

These two closely related species of skunks mate at different times of the year.

Habitat Isolation

These two closely related species of garter snakes do not mate because one lives in the water while the other lives on land.

courtship behavior is so elaborate that individuals are unlikely to mistake a bird of a different species as one of their kind. In still other cases, the egg-producing and sperm-producing structures of different species are anatomically incompatible (mechanical isolation). For example, the two closely related species of snails in Figure 14.4 cannot join their male and female sex organs because their shells spiral in opposite directions. In still other cases, gametes (eggs and sperm) of different species are incompatible, preventing fertilization (gametic isolation). Gametic isolation is very important when fertilization is external. Male and female sea urchins of many species release eggs and sperm into the sea, but fertilization occurs only if species-specific molecules on the surface of egg and sperm attach to each other.

Postzygotic barriers operate if interspecies mating actually occurs and results in hybrid zygotes (Figure 14.5). (In this context, "hybrid" means that the egg comes from one species and the sperm from another species.) In some cases, hybrid offspring die before reaching reproductive maturity (reduced hybrid viability). For example, although certain closely related salamander species will hybridize, the offspring fail to develop normally because of genetic incompatibilities between the two species. In other cases of hybridization, offspring may become vigorous adults, but are infertile (reduced hybrid fertility). A mule, for example, is the hybrid offspring of a female horse and a male donkey. Mules are sterile—they cannot successfully breed with each other. Thus, horses and donkeys remain distinct species. In other cases, the first-generation hybrids are viable and fertile, but when these hybrids mate with one another or with either parent species, the offspring are feeble or sterile (hybrid breakdown). For example,

different species of cotton plants can produce fertile hybrids, but the offspring of the hybrids do not survive.

In summary, reproductive barriers form the boundaries around closely related species. In most cases, it is not a single reproductive barrier but some combination of two or more that keeps species isolated. Next, we examine situations that make reproductive isolation and speciation possible. ☑

Answer: because it prevents mating and therefore the formation of a zygote

▼ Figure 14.5 **Postzygotic barriers.** Postzygotic barriers prevent development of fertile adults.

POSTZYGOTIC BARRIERS		
Reduced Hybrid Viability	**Reduced Hybrid Fertility**	**Hybrid Breakdown**

Some species of salamander can hybridize, but their offspring do not develop fully or, like this one, are frail and will not survive long enough to reproduce.

Horse

Donkey

The hybrid offspring of a horse and a donkey is a mule, which is sterile.

Mule

The rice hybrids at the left and right are fertile, but plants of the next generation (middle) are small and sterile.

Behavioral Isolation	**Mechanical Isolation**	**Gametic Isolation**

Galápagos blue-footed boobies mate only after a specific ritual of high stepping that advertises a mate's bright blue feet.

Because these snails' shells spiral in opposite directions, their genital openings (indicated by arrows) cannot be aligned and mating cannot occur.

Gametes of these red and purple urchins are unable to fuse because proteins on the surface of the eggs and sperm cannot bind to one another.

Evolution Mechanisms of Speciation

A key event in the origin of many species occurs when a population is somehow cut off from other populations of the parent species. With its gene pool isolated, the splinter population can follow its own evolutionary course. Changes in its allele frequencies caused by genetic drift and natural selection will not be diluted by alleles entering from other populations (gene flow). Such reproductive isolation can result from two general scenarios: allopatric ("different country") speciation and sympatric ("same country") speciation. In **allopatric speciation**, the initial block to gene flow is a geographic barrier that physically isolates the splinter population. In contrast, **sympatric speciation** is the origin of a new species without geographic isolation. The splinter population becomes reproductively isolated even though it is in the midst of the parent population.

Allopatric Speciation

Given the vast span of geologic time, we can imagine many scenarios that could fragment a population into two or more isolated populations. A mountain range may emerge and gradually split a population of organisms that can inhabit only lowlands. A land bridge, such as the Isthmus of Panama, may form and separate the marine life on either side. A large lake may subside and form several smaller lakes, with their populations now isolated. Glaciation could force small populations into ice-free areas that would remain isolated for millennia until the glaciers receded.

How formidable must a geographic barrier be to keep allopatric populations apart? The answer depends partly on the ability of the organisms to move about. Birds, mountain lions, and coyotes can cross mountain ranges, rivers, and canyons. Such barriers also do not hinder the windblown pollen of pine trees or the spread of seeds carried by animals capable of crossing the barrier. In contrast, small rodents may find a deep canyon or a wide river an impassable barrier (Figure 14.6).

Speciation is more common for a small, isolated population because it is more likely than a large population to have its gene pool changed substantially by both genetic drift and natural selection. But for each small, isolated population that becomes a new species, many more simply perish in their new environment. Life on the frontier is harsh, and most pioneer populations become extinct.

Even if a small, isolated population survives, it does not necessarily evolve into a new species. The population may adapt to its local environment and begin to look very different from the ancestral population, but that doesn't necessarily make it a new species. Speciation occurs with the evolution of reproductive barriers between the isolated population and its parent

▼ Figure 14.6 **Allopatric speciation of antelope squirrels on opposite rims of the Grand Canyon.** Harris's antelope squirrel (*Ammospermophilus harrisii*) is found on the south rim of the Grand Canyon. Just a few miles away on the north rim is the closely related white-tailed antelope squirrel (*Ammospermophilus leucurus*). Birds and other organisms that can disperse easily across the canyon have not diverged into different species on opposite rims.

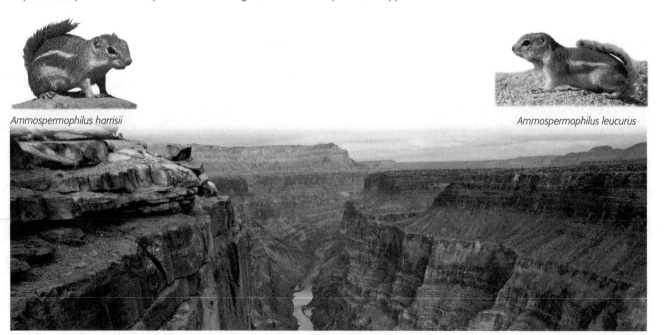

Ammospermophilus harrisii

Ammospermophilus leucurus

▶ **Figure 14.7 Possible outcomes after geographic isolation of populations.** In this diagram, the orange and green arrows track populations over time. The mountain symbolizes a period of geographic isolation during which time genetic changes may occur in both populations. After a period of time, the populations are no longer separated by a geographic barrier (right side of diagram) and come back into contact. If the populations can interbreed freely (top diagram), speciation has not occurred. If the populations cannot interbreed (bottom), then speciation has occurred.

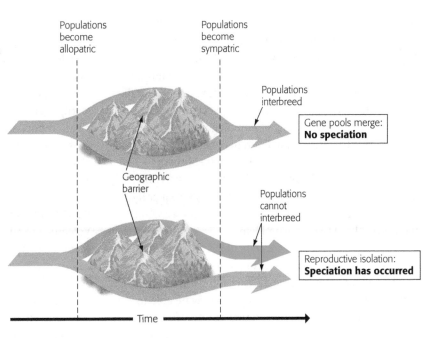

Populations become allopatric

Populations become sympatric

Populations interbreed

Gene pools merge: **No speciation**

Geographic barrier

Populations cannot interbreed

Reproductive isolation: **Speciation has occurred**

Time

population. In other words, if speciation occurs during geographic separation, the new species cannot breed with its ancestral population even if the two populations should come back into contact at some later time **(Figure 14.7).** ☑

Sympatric Speciation

Speciation doesn't necessarily require vast spans of time, nor is geographic isolation a prerequisite. A species may originate from an accident during cell division that results in an extra set of chromosomes, a condition called **polyploidy**. Examples of polyploid speciation have been found in some animal species, especially fish and amphibians **(Figure 14.8)**. However, it is most common in

plants—an estimated 80% of present-day plant species are descended from ancestors that arose by polyploid speciation **(Figure 14.9)**.

Two distinct forms of polyploid speciation have been observed. In one form, polyploidy arises from a single parent species. For example, a failure of cell division might double the chromosome number from the original diploid number ($2n$) to tetraploid ($4n$). Because the polyploid individual cannot produce fertile hybrids with its parent species, immediate reproductive isolation results.

A second form of polyploid speciation can occur when two different species interbreed and produce hybrid offspring. Most instances of polyploid speciation in plants resulted from such hybridizations. How did these

▼ **Figure 14.8 Gray tree frog.** This amphibian is thought to have originated by polyploid speciation.

▼ **Figure 14.9 Chinese hibiscus.** Many ornamental varieties of this species have been produced through polyploidy, which may make the flowers larger or increase the number of petals.

☑ **CHECKPOINT**

What mechanism accounts
for most observed instances
of sympatric speciation? Why
might this be the case?

*Answer: Accidents of cell division
that result in polyploidy. Polyploidy
produces "instant" reproductive
isolation.*

interspecies hybrids overcome the postzygotic barrier of sterility (see Figure 14.5)? A mule is sterile because its parents' chromosomes don't match. A horse has 64 chromosomes (32 pairs); a donkey has 62 chromosomes (31 pairs). Therefore, a mule has 63 chromosomes. Recall that gametes are produced by meiosis, a cell division process that involves pairing of homologous chromosomes (see Figure 8.14). Structural differences between the chromosomes of horses and donkeys prevent them from pairing correctly, and the odd number leaves one chromosome without a potential partner. Consequently, mules don't produce viable gametes. Now, let's see why plants don't have the same problem.

In **Figure 14.10**, species A hybridizes with species B. Like a mule, the resulting hybrid plant has an odd number of chromosomes, and its chromosomes are not homologous. However, the hybrid may be able to reproduce asexually, as many plants can do. If so, there may eventually be an error in cell division that results in polyploidy and thus reproductive isolation from the parent. Biologists have identified several plant species that originated via polyploidy within the past 150 years.

Many of the plant species we grow for food are polyploids, including oats, potatoes, bananas, strawberries, peanuts, apples, sugarcane, and wheat. The wheat used for bread is a hybrid of three different parent species and has six sets of chromosomes, two sets from each parent. Plant geneticists use chemicals to induce errors in cell division and generate new polyploids in the laboratory. By harnessing this evolutionary process, they can produce new hybrid species with desirable qualities.

Biologists have also identified cases in which subpopulations appear to be in the process of sympatric speciation. In some cases, subgroups of a population become adapted for exploiting food sources in different habitats,

such as the shallow versus deep habitats of a lake. In another example, a type of sexual selection in which female fish choose mates based on color has contributed to rapid reproductive isolation. Because of its direct effect on reproductive success, sexual selection can interrupt gene flow within a population and may therefore be an important factor in sympatric speciation. But the most frequently observed mechanism of sympatric speciation involves large-scale genetic changes that occur in a single generation. ☑

Island Showcases of Speciation

Volcanic islands, such as the Galápagos and Hawaiian island chains, are initially devoid of life. Over time, colonists arrive via ocean currents or winds. Some of these organisms gain a foothold and establish new populations. In their new environment, these populations may diverge significantly from their distant parent populations. In addition, islands that have physically diverse habitats and that are far enough apart to permit populations to evolve in isolation but close enough to allow occasional dispersals to occur are often the sites of multiple speciation events.

The Galápagos Islands, which were formed by underwater volcanoes from 5 million to 1 million years ago, are one of the world's great showcases of speciation. They are home to numerous plants, snails, reptiles, and birds that are found nowhere else on Earth. For example, the islands have 14 species of closely related finches, which are often called Darwin's finches because he collected them during his around-the-world voyage (see Figure 13.3). These birds share many finch-like traits, but they differ in their feeding habits and their beaks, which are specialized for what they eat. Their various foods include insects, large or small seeds, cactus fruits, and even eggs of other species. The woodpecker finch uses cactus spines or twigs as tools to pry insects from trees. The "vampire" finch supplements its diet of seeds and insects by pecking wounds on the backs of seabirds and drinking their blood. **Figure 14.11** (facing page) shows some of these birds, with their distinctive beaks adapted for their specific diets. The finches differ in their habitats as well as their beaks—some live in trees and others spend most of their time on the ground.

How might Darwin's finch species have evolved from a small population of ancestral birds that colonized one of the islands? Completely isolated on the island, the founder population may have changed significantly as natural selection adapted it to the new environment, and thus it became a new species. Later, a few individuals of this new species may have migrated to a neighboring island, where, under different conditions, this new founder population was changed enough through

▼ **Figure 14.10 Sympatric speciation in a plant.** The gametes from two different species result in a sterile hybrid, which may undergo asexual reproduction. Such a hybrid may eventually form a new species by polyploidy.

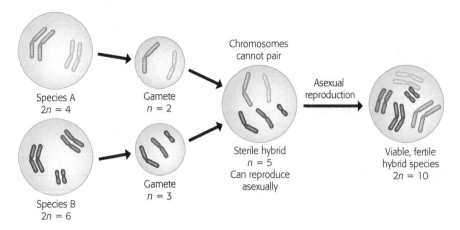

Species A
2n = 4

Gamete
n = 2

Species B
2n = 6

Gamete
n = 3

Chromosomes
cannot pair

Sterile hybrid
n = 5
Can reproduce
asexually

Asexual
reproduction

Viable, fertile
hybrid species
2n = 10

Cactus-seed-eater (cactus finch)

Tool-using insect-eater (woodpecker finch)

Blood, seed, and insect-eater (vampire finch)

▲ Figure 14.11 **Galápagos finches with beaks adapted for specific diets.**

process of speciation is often extremely slow. So you may be surprised to learn that we *can* see speciation occurring. Consider that life has been evolving over hundreds of millions of years and will continue to evolve. The species living today represent a snapshot, a brief instant in this vast span of time. The environment continues to change—sometimes rapidly due to human impact—and natural selection continues to act on affected populations. It is reasonable to assume that some of these populations are changing in ways that could eventually lead to speciation. Studying populations as they diverge gives biologists a window on the process of speciation.

Researchers have documented at least two dozen cases in which populations are currently diverging as they use different food resources or breed in different habitats. Numerous cases involve insects exploiting different food plants. In one well-studied example, a subpopulation of a fly that feeds on hawthorn fruits found a new resource when American colonists planted apple trees. Although the two fly populations are still regarded as subspecies, researchers have identified mechanisms that severely restrict gene flow between them. In other cases, biologists have identified animal populations that are diverging as a result of differences in male courtship behavior.

Although biologists are continually making observations and devising experiments to study evolution in progress, much of the evidence for evolution comes from the fossil record. So what does the fossil record say about the time frame for speciation—the length of time between when a new species forms and when its populations diverge enough to produce another new species? In one survey of 84 groups of plants and animals, the time for speciation ranged from 4,000 to 40 million years. Such long time frames tell us that it has taken vast spans of time for life on Earth to evolve.

natural selection to become yet another new species. Some of these birds may then have recolonized the first island and coexisted there with the original ancestral species if reproductive barriers kept the species distinct. Multiple rounds of colonization and speciation on the many separate islands of the Galápagos probably followed. Today, each of the Galápagos Islands has several species of finches, with as many as ten on some islands. Reproductive isolation due to species-specific songs helps keep the species separate.

Observing Speciation in Progress

In contrast to microevolutionary change, which may be apparent in a population within a few generations, the

As you've seen, speciation may begin with small differences. However, as speciation occurs again and again, these differences accumulate and may eventually lead to new groups that differ greatly from their ancestors, as in the origin of whales from four-legged land animals (see Figure 13.6). The cumulative effects of multiple speciations, as well as extinctions, have shaped the dramatic changes documented in the fossil record. We begin to examine such changes next.

Earth History and Macroevolution

Having examined how new species arise, we are ready to turn our attention to macroevolution. **Macroevolution** is evolutionary change above the species level, for example, the origin of a new group of organisms through a series of speciation events. Macroevolution also includes the impact of mass extinctions on the diversity of life and its subsequent recovery. An understanding of macroevolution begins with a look at the span of geologic time over which life's diversity has evolved.

The Fossil Record

Fossils are evidence of organisms that lived in the past (see Figure 13.5). The strata (layers) of sedimentary rocks provide a record of life on Earth—each rock layer contains a local sample of the organisms that existed at the time the sediment was deposited. Thus, the fossil record, the sequence in which fossils appear in rock strata, is an archive of macroevolution. For example, scan the wall of the Grand Canyon from rim to floor and you look back through hundreds of millions of years (Figure 14.12). Younger strata formed atop older ones; correspondingly, younger fossils are found in layers closer to the surface, whereas the deepest strata contain the oldest fossils. However, this only gives us the ages of fossils relative to each other. Like peeling off layers of wallpaper in an old house, we can infer the order in which the layers were applied but not the year that each layer was added.

If you drove off the rim of the Grand Canyon, you would pass by 40 rock layers and several hundred million years of geologic history before hitting the ground.

By studying many sites, geologists have established a **geologic time scale** that divides Earth's history into a sequence of geologic periods. The time line presented in Table 14.1 is separated into four broad divisions: the Precambrian (a general term for the time before about 540 million years ago), followed by the Paleozoic, Mesozoic, and Cenozoic eras. Each of these divisions represents a distinct age in the history of Earth and its life. The boundaries between eras are marked by mass extinctions, when many forms of life disappeared from the fossil record and were replaced by species that diversified from the survivors.

The most common method geologists use to learn the ages of rocks and the fossils they contain is **radiometric dating**, a method based on the decay of radioactive isotopes (see Figure 2.17). For example, a living organism contains both the common isotope carbon-12 and the radioactive isotope carbon-14 in the same ratio as that present in the atmosphere. Once an organism dies, it stops accumulating carbon, and the stable carbon-12 in its tissues does not change. Carbon-14, however, spontaneously decays to another element. Carbon-14 has a half-life of 5,730 years, so half the carbon-14 in a specimen decays in about 5,730 years, half the remaining carbon-14 decays in the next 5,730 years, and so on. Scientists measure the ratio of carbon-14 to carbon-12 in a fossil to calculate its age.

Carbon-14 is useful for dating relatively young fossils—up to about 75,000 years old. There are isotopes with longer half-lives, such as uranium-235 (half-life 71.3 million years) and potassium-40 (half-life 1.3 billion years). However, organisms don't incorporate those elements into their bodies. Therefore, scientists use indirect methods to date older fossils. One commonly used method is to date layers of volcanic rock or ash above and below the sedimentary layer in which fossils are found. By inference, the age of the fossils is between those two dates. Potassium-argon dating is often used for volcanic rock, for example. Isotopes of uranium are useful for other types of ancient rock.

▼ Figure 14.12 **Strata of sedimentary rock at the Grand Canyon.** The Colorado River has cut through more than a mile of rock, exposing sedimentary strata that are like huge pages from the book of life. Each stratum entombs fossils that represent some of the organisms from that period of Earth's history.

Table 14.1 | **The Geologic Time Scale**

Geologic Time	Period	Epoch	Age (millions of years ago)	Some Important Events in the History of Life
Cenozoic era	Quaternary	Recent		Historical time
			0.01	
		Pleistocene		Ice ages; humans appear
			1.8	
	Tertiary	Pliocene		Origin of genus *Homo*
			5	
		Miocene		Continued speciation of mammals and angiosperms
			23	
		Oligocene		Origins of many primate groups, including apes
			34	
		Eocene		Angiosperm dominance increases; origins of most living mammalian orders
			56	
		Paleocene		Major speciation of mammals, birds, and pollinating insects
			65	
Mesozoic era	Cretaceous			Flowering plants (angiosperms) appear; many groups of organisms, including most dinosaur lineages, become extinct at end of period (Cretaceous extinctions)
			145	
	Jurassic			Gymnosperms continue as dominant plants; dinosaurs become dominant
			200	
	Triassic			Cone-bearing plants (gymnosperms) dominate landscape; speciation of dinosaurs, early mammals, and birds
			251	
Paleozoic era	Permian			Extinction of many marine and terrestrial organisms (Permian extinctions); speciation of reptiles; origins of mammal-like reptiles and most living orders of insects
			299	
	Carboniferous			Extensive forests of vascular plants; first seed plants; origin of reptiles; amphibians become dominant
			359	
	Devonian			Diversification of bony fishes; first amphibians and insects
			416	
	Silurian			Early vascular plants dominate land
			444	
	Ordovician			Marine algae are abundant; colonization of land by diverse fungi, plants, and animals
			488	
	Cambrian			Origin of most living animal phyla (Cambrian explosion)
			542	
Precambrian			600	Diverse algae and soft-bodied invertebrate animals appear
			635	Oldest animal fossils
			2,100	Oldest eukaryotic fossils
			2,700	Oxygen begins accumulating in atmosphere
			3,500	Oldest fossils known (prokaryotes)
			4,600	Approximate time of origin of Earth

Relative Time Span

Cenozoic

Mesozoic

Paleozoic

Pre-cambrian

Plate Tectonics and Biogeography

If photographs of Earth were taken from space every 10,000 years and then spliced together, it would make a remarkable movie. The seemingly "rock solid" continents we live on drift about Earth's surface. According to the theory of **plate tectonics**, the continents and seafloors form a thin outer layer of solid rock, called the crust, which covers a mass of hot, viscous material called the mantle. The crust is not one continuous expanse, however. It is divided into giant, irregularly shaped plates that float atop the mantle (Figure 14.13). In a process called continental drift, movements in the mantle cause the plates to move. The boundaries of some plates are hotspots of geologic activity. In some cases, we feel an immediate, violent symptom of this activity, as when an earthquake signals that two plates are scraping past or colliding with each other (Figure 14.14). Although most movement is extremely slow, not much faster than the speed at which fingernails grow, continents have wandered thousands of miles over the long course of earth's history.

By reshaping the physical features of the planet and altering the environments in which organisms live, continental drift has had a tremendous impact on the evolution of life's diversity. Two chapters in the continuing saga of continental drift had an especially strong influence on life. About 250 million years ago, near the end of the Paleozoic era, plate movements brought all the previously separated landmasses together into a supercontinent called Pangaea, which means "all land" (Figure 14.15, facing page). Imagine some of the possible effects on life. Species that had been evolving in isolation came together and competed. As the landmasses joined, the total amount of shoreline was reduced. There is also evidence that the ocean basins increased in depth, lowering sea level and draining the shallow coastal seas. Then, as now, most

▲ Figure 14.14 **A tsunami caused by an earthquake off the coast of Japan in March 2011.** Japan sits atop four different plates. Frequent earthquakes occur as the plates move and bump against each other.

marine species inhabited shallow waters, and the formation of Pangaea destroyed a considerable amount of that habitat. It was probably a long, traumatic period for terrestrial life as well. The continental interior, which was drier and had a more erratic climate than the coastal regions, increased in area substantially when the land came together. Changing ocean currents also undoubtedly affected land life as well as sea life. Thus, the formation of Pangaea had a tremendous environmental impact that reshaped biological diversity by causing extinctions and providing new opportunities for diversification of the survivors.

The second dramatic chapter in the history of continental drift began during the mid-Mesozoic era. Pangaea started to break up, causing geographic isolation of colossal proportions. As the landmasses drifted apart, each continent became a separate evolutionary arena as its climates changed and its organisms diverged.

The history of continental mergers and separations explains many patterns of **biogeography**, the study of the past and present distribution of organisms. For example, almost all the animals and plants that live on Madagascar, a large island located off the southern coast of Africa, are unique—they diversified from ancestral populations after Madagascar was isolated from Africa and India. The more than 50 species of lemurs that currently inhabit Madagascar, for instance, evolved from a common ancestor over the past 40 million years.

▼ Figure 14.13 **Earth's tectonic plates.** The red dots indicate zones where violent geologic activity, such as earthquakes and volcanic eruptions, take place. Arrows indicate direction of continental drift.

Key

• Zones of violent tectonic activity

↑ Direction of movement

Continental drift also separated Australia from other landmasses. Australia and its neighboring islands are home to more than 200 species of marsupials, most of which are found nowhere else in the world (Figure 14.16). Marsupials are mammals such as kangaroos, koalas, and wombats whose young complete their embryonic development in a pouch outside the mother's body. The rest of the world is dominated by eutherian (placental) mammals, whose young complete their development in the mother's uterus. Looking at a current map of the world, you might hypothesize that marsupials evolved only on the island continent of Australia. But marsupials are not unique to Australia. More than a hundred species live in Central and South America. North America is also home to a few, including the Virginia opossum. The distribution of marsupials only makes sense in the context of continental drift—marsupials must have originated when the continents were joined. Fossil evidence suggests that marsupials originated in what is now Asia and later dispersed to the tip of South America while it was still connected to Antarctica. They made their way to Australia before continental drift separated Antarctica from Australia, setting "afloat" a great raft of marsupials. The few early eutherians that lived in Australia became extinct, whereas on other continents, most marsupials became extinct. Isolated on Australia, marsupials evolved and diversified, filling ecological roles analogous to those filled by eutherians on other continents. ☑

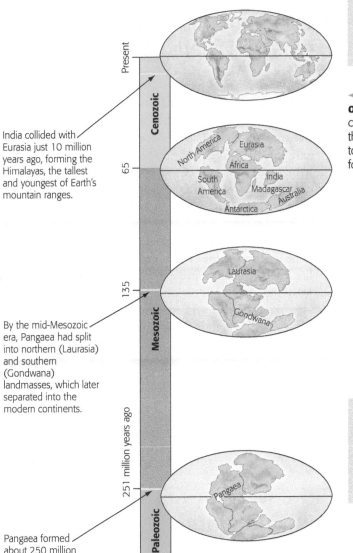

India collided with Eurasia just 10 million years ago, forming the Himalayas, the tallest and youngest of Earth's mountain ranges.

By the mid-Mesozoic era, Pangaea had split into northern (Laurasia) and southern (Gondwana) landmasses, which later separated into the modern continents.

Pangaea formed about 250 million years ago.

▲ Figure 14.15 **The history of plate tectonics.** The continents continue to drift, though not at a rate that's likely to cause any motion sickness for their passengers.

☑ CHECKPOINT

How many continents did Earth have at the time of Pangaea?

Answer: one

▼ Figure 14.16 **Australian marsupials.** The continent of Australia is home to many unique plants and animals, including diverse marsupials, mammals that have ecological roles filled by eutherians on other continents.

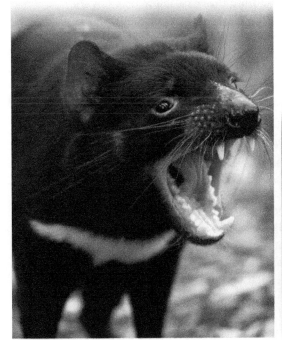

Tasmanian devil, a carnivore

Sugar glider, an omnivore

Koala, an herbivore

Mass Extinctions and Explosive Diversifications of Life

As discussed in the Biology and Society section at the beginning of the chapter, the fossil record reveals that five mass extinctions have occurred over the last 540 million years. In each of these events, 50% or more of Earth's species died out. Of all the mass extinctions, those marking the ends of the Permian and Cretaceous periods have been the most intensively studied.

The Permian mass extinction, at about the time the merging continents formed Pangaea, claimed about 96% of marine species and took a tremendous toll on terrestrial life as well. Equally notable is the mass extinction at the end of the Cretaceous period. For 150 million years prior, dinosaurs dominated Earth's land and air, whereas mammals were few and small, resembling today's rodents. Then, about 65 million years ago, most of the dinosaurs became extinct, leaving behind only the descendants of one lineage, the birds. Remarkably, the massive die-off (which also included half of all other species) occurred in less than 10 million years—a brief period in geologic time.

But there is a flip side to the destruction. Each massive dip in species diversity has been followed by explosive diversification of certain survivors. Extinctions seem to have provided the surviving organisms with new environmental opportunities. For example, mammals existed for at least 75 million years before undergoing an explosive increase in diversity just after the Cretaceous period. Their rise to prominence was undoubtedly associated with the void left by the extinction of the dinosaurs. The world would be a very different place today if many dinosaur lineages had escaped the Cretaceous extinctions or if none of the mammals had survived.

Mass Extinctions THE PROCESS OF SCIENCE

Did a Meteor Kill the Dinosaurs?

For decades, scientists have been debating the cause of the rapid dinosaur die-off that occurred 65 million years ago. Many **observations** provide clues. The fossil record shows that the climate had cooled and that shallow seas were receding from continental lowlands. It also shows that many plant species died out. Perhaps the most telling evidence was discovered by physicist Luis Alvarez and his geologist son Walter Alvarez, both of the University of California, Berkeley. In 1980, they found that rock deposited around 65 million years ago contains a thin layer of clay rich in iridium, an element very rare on Earth but common in meteors and other extraterrestrial material that occasionally falls to Earth. This discovery led the Alvarez team to ask the following **question**: Is the iridium layer the result of fallout from a huge cloud of dust that billowed into the atmosphere when a large meteor or asteroid hit Earth?

The father and son formed the **hypothesis** that the mass extinction 65 million years ago was caused by the impact of an extraterrestrial object. This hypothesis makes a clear **prediction**: A huge impact crater of the right age should be found somewhere on Earth's surface. (This is a good example of using verifiable observations rather than a direct **experiment** to test a hypothesis; see Chapter 1.) In 1981, two petroleum geologists found the **results** predicted by the Alvarezes' hypothesis: the Chicxulub crater, located near Mexico's Yucatán Peninsula in the Caribbean Sea **(Figure 14.17)**. This impact site, about 180 km wide (about 112 miles) and dating from the predicted time, was created when a meteor or asteroid about 10 km in diameter (about 6 miles, more than the length of 100 football fields) slammed into Earth, releasing thousands of times more energy than is stored in the world's combined stockpile of nuclear weapons. Such a cloud could have blocked sunlight and disturbed climate severely for months, perhaps killing off many plant species and, later, the animals that depended on those plants for food.

Debate continues about whether this impact alone caused the dinosaurs to die out or whether other factors—such as continental movements or volcanic activity—also contributed. Most scientists agree, however, that the collision that created the Chicxulub crater could indeed have been a major factor in global climatic change and mass extinctions.

▼ Figure 14.17 **Trauma for planet Earth and its Cretaceous life.**

Chicxulub crater

An artist's representation of the impact of an asteroid or comet.

The impact's immediate effect was most likely a cloud of hot vapor and debris that could have killed many of the plants and animals in North America within hours.

The 65-million-year-old Chicxulub impact crater is located in the Caribbean Sea near the Yucatán Peninsula of Mexico. The horseshoe shape of the crater and the pattern of debris in sedimentary rocks indicate that an asteroid or comet struck at a low angle from the southeast.

Mechanisms of Macroevolution

The fossil record can tell us what the great events in the history of life have been and when they occurred. Continental drift and mass extinctions followed by the diversification of survivors provide a big-picture view of how those changes came about. But now scientists are increasingly able to explain the basic biological mechanisms that underlie the macroevolutionary changes seen in the fossil record.

Large Effects from Small Genetic Changes

Scientists working at the interface of evolutionary biology and developmental biology—the research field abbreviated **evo-devo**—are studying how slight genetic changes can become magnified into major structural differences between species. Homeotic genes, the master control genes, program development by controlling the rate, timing, and spatial pattern of changes in an organism's form as it develops from a zygote into an adult. These genes determine such basic developmental events as where a pair of wings or legs will appear on a fruit fly (see Figure 11.9). A subtle change in the developmental program can have profound effects. Accordingly, changes in the number, nucleotide sequence, and regulation of homeotic genes have led to the huge diversity in body forms.

Changes in rate of developmental events explains changes in the homologous limb bones of vertebrates (see Figure 13.7). Increased growth rates produced the extra-long "finger" bones in bat wings. Slower growth rates of leg and pelvic bones led to the eventual loss of hind limbs in whales (see Figure 13.6). On the other hand, the loss of limbs in the evolution of snakes from a four-limbed lizard-like ancestor resulted from different spatial patterns of expression of homeotic genes.

Striking evolutionary transformations may also result from a change in the timing of developmental events. Figure 14.18 is a photograph of an axolotl, a salamander that illustrates a phenomenon called **paedomorphosis**, the retention in the adult of body structures that were juvenile features in an ancestral species. The axolotl grows to full size and reproduces without losing its external gills, a juvenile feature in most species of salamanders.

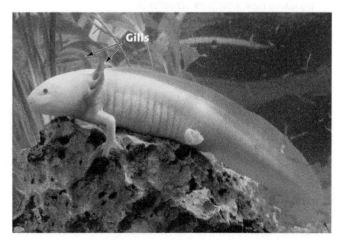

Gills

◄ Figure 14.18
Paedomorphosis. The axolotl, a salamander, becomes an adult (shown here) and reproduces while retaining certain tadpole characteristics, including gills.

Paedomorphosis has also been important in human evolution. Humans and chimpanzees are even more alike in body form as fetuses than they are as adults. In the fetuses of both species, the skulls are rounded and the jaws are small, making the face rather flat (Figure 14.19). As development proceeds, accelerated growth in the jaw produces the elongated skull, sloping forehead, and massive jaws of an adult chimpanzee. In the human lineage, genetic changes that slowed the growth of the jaw relative to other parts of the skull produced an adult whose head proportions still resembled that of a child—and that of a baby chimpanzee. Our large skull and complex brain are among our most distinctive features. The human brain is proportionately larger than the chimpanzee brain because growth of the organ is switched off much later in human development. Compared with the brain of a chimpanzee, our brain continues to grow for several more years, which can be interpreted as the prolonging of a juvenile process.

Next, we see how the process of evolution can produce new, complex structures.

Chimpanzee infant   Chimpanzee adult

Chimpanzee fetus   Chimpanzee adult

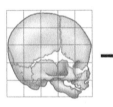

Human fetus   Human adult (paedomorphic features)

▲ **Figure 14.19 Comparison of human and chimpanzee skull development.** Starting with fetal skulls that are very similar (left), the differential growth rates of the bones making up the skulls produce adult heads with very different proportions. The grid lines will help you relate the fetal skulls to the adult skulls.

The Evolution of Biological Novelty

The two squirrels in Figure 14.6 are different species, but they are very similar animals that live very much the same way. How do we account for the dramatic differences between dissimilar groups—squirrels and birds, for example? Let's see how the Darwinian theory of gradual change can explain the evolution of intricate structures such as eyes or of new kinds of structures (novel structures) such as feathers.

Adaptation of Old Structures for New Functions

The feathered flight of birds is a perfect marriage of structure and function. Consider the evolution of feathers, which are clearly essential to avian aeronautics. In a flight feather, separate filaments called barbs emerge from a central shaft that runs from base to tip. Each barb is linked to the next by tiny hooks that act much like the teeth of a zipper, forming a tightly connected sheet of barbs that is strong but flexible. In flight, the shapes and arrangements of various feathers produce lift, smooth airflow, and help with steering and balance. How did such a beautifully intricate structure evolve? Reptilian features apparent in fossils of *Archaeopteryx*, one of the earliest birds, offered clues in Darwin's time (Figure 14.20), but the definitive answer came in 1996. Birds were not the first feathered animals on Earth—dinosaurs were.

The first feathered dinosaur to be discovered, a 130-million-year-old fossil found in northeastern China, was named *Sinosauropteryx* ("Chinese lizard-wing"). About the size of a turkey, it had short arms and ran on its hind legs, using its long tail for balance. Its

▼ **Figure 14.20 An extinct bird.** Called *Archaeopteryx* ("ancient wing"), this animal lived near tropical lagoons in central Europe about 150 million years ago. Despite its feathers, *Archaeopteryx* has many features in common with reptiles. *Archaeopteryx* is not considered an ancestor of today's birds. Instead, it probably represents an extinct side branch of the bird lineage.

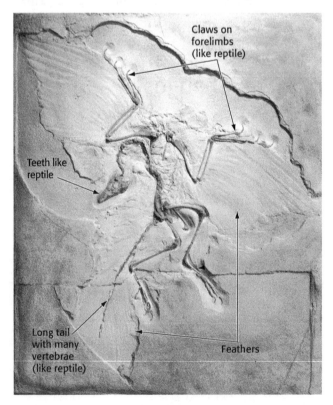

Claws on forelimbs (like reptile)

Teeth like reptile

Long tail with many vertebrae (like reptile)

Feathers

unimpressive plumage consisted of a downy covering of hairlike feathers. Since the discovery of *Sinosauropteryx*, thousands of fossils of feathered dinosaurs have been found and classified into more than 30 different species. Although none was unequivocally capable of flying, many of these species had elaborate feathers that would be the envy of any modern bird. But the feathers seen in these fossils could not have been used for flight, nor would their reptilian anatomy have been suited to flying. So if feathers evolved before flight, what was their function? Their first utility may have been for insulation. It is possible that longer, winglike forelimbs and feathers, which increased the surface area of these forelimbs, were co-opted for flight after functioning in some other capacity, such as mating displays, thermoregulation, or camouflage (all functions that feathers still serve today). The first flights may have been only short glides to the ground or from branch to branch in tree-dwelling species. Once flight itself became an advantage, natural selection would have gradually remodeled feathers and wings to fit their additional function.

Structures such as feathers that evolve in one context but become co-opted for another function are called exaptations. However, exaptation does not mean that a structure evolves in anticipation of future use. Natural selection cannot predict the future; it can only improve an existing structure in the context of its current use. ☑

From Simple to Complex Structures in Gradual Stages

Most complex structures have evolved in small steps from simpler versions having the same basic function—a process of refinement rather than the sudden appearance of complexity. Consider the amazing camera-like eyes of vertebrates and squids. Although these complex eyes evolved independently, the origin of both can be traced from a simple ancestral patch of photoreceptor cells through a series of incremental modifications that benefited their owners at each stage. Indeed, there appears to have been a single evolutionary origin of light-sensitive cells, and all animals with eyes—vertebrates and invertebrates alike—share the same master genes that regulate eye development.

Figure 14.21 illustrates the range of complexity in the structure of eyes among present-day molluscs, a large and diverse phylum of animals. Simple patches of pigmented cells enable limpets, single-shelled molluscs that cling to seaside rocks, to distinguish light from dark. When a shadow falls on them, they hold on more tightly—a behavioral adaptation that reduces the risk of being eaten. Other molluscs have eyecups that have no lenses or other means of focusing images but can indicate light direction. In those molluscs that do have complex eyes, the organs probably evolved in small steps of adaptation. You can see examples of such small steps in Figure 14.21.

☑ CHECKPOINT

Explain why the concept of exaptation does not imply that a structure evolves in anticipation of some future environmental change.

Answer: Although an exaptation has new or additional functions in a new environment, it existed earlier because it worked as an adaptation to the old environment.

▼ Figure 14.21 **A range of eye complexity among molluscs.** The complex eye of the squid evolved in small steps. Even the simplest eye was useful to its owner.

Patch of pigmented cells	Eyecup	Simple pinhole eye	Eye with primitive lens	Complex camera lens-type eye
Pigmented cells (photoreceptors); Nerve fibers	Pigmented cells; Eyecup; Nerve fibers	Fluid-filled cavity; Optic nerve; Layer of pigmented cells (retina)	Transparent protective tissue (cornea); Lens; Retina; Optic nerve	Cornea; Lens; Retina; Optic nerve
Limpet	Abalone	Nautilus	Marine snail	Squid

Classifying the Diversity of Life

The Linnaean system of taxonomy (see Figure 13.1) is quite a useful method of organizing life's diversity into groups. Ever since Darwin, however, biologists have had a goal beyond simple organization: to have classification reflect evolutionary relationships. In other words, how an organism is named and classified should reflect its place within the evolutionary tree of life. **Systematics**, which includes taxonomy, is a discipline of biology that focuses on classifying organisms and determining their evolutionary relationships.

Classification and Phylogeny

Biologists use **phylogenetic trees** to depict hypotheses about the evolutionary history, or phylogeny, of species. These branching diagrams reflect the hierarchical classification of groups nested within more in-clusive groups. The tree in Figure 14.22 shows the classification of some carnivores and their probable evolutionary relationships. Note that each branch point represents the divergence of two lineages from a common ancestor. (You may recall Figure 13.9, which is a phylogenetic tree of tetrapods.)

Alleles from two wild grasses could be used to make a better ear of corn.

Understanding phylogeny can have practical applications. For example, maize (corn) is an important food crop worldwide; it also pro-vides us with snack favorites such as pop-corn, tortilla chips, and corn dog batter. Thousands of years of artificial selection (selective breeding) transformed a scrawny grass with small ears of rock-hard kernels into the maize we know today. In the process, much of the plant's original genetic variation was stripped away. By constructing a phylogeny of maize, researchers have identified two species of wild grasses that may be maize's closest living relatives. The genomes of these plants may harbor alleles that offer disease resistance or other useful traits that could be transferred into culti-vated maize by crossbreeding or genetic engineering—insurance against future disease outbreaks or other environmental changes that might threaten corn crops.

Identifying Homologous Characters

Homologous structures in different species may vary in form and function but exhibit fundamen-tal similarities because they evolved from the same structure in a common ancestor. Among the verte-brates, for instance, the whale forelimb is adapted for steering in the water, whereas the bat wing is adapted for flight. Nonetheless, there are many basic similari-ties in the bones supporting these two structures (see Figure 13.7). Thus, homologous structures are one of the best sources of information for phylogenetic rela-tionships. The greater the number of homologous struc-tures between two species, the more closely the species are related.

There are pitfalls in the search for homology: Not all likeness is inherited from a common ancestor. Species from different evolutionary branches may have certain structures that are superficially similar if natural selec-tion has shaped analogous adaptations. This is called **convergent evolution**. Similarity due to convergence is called **analogy**, not homology. For example, the wings of insects and those of birds are analogous flight equip-ment: They evolved independently and are built from entirely different structures.

▼ Figure 14.22 **The relationship of classification and phylogeny for some members of the order Carnivora.** The hierarchical classification is reflected in the finer and finer branching of the phylogenetic tree. Each branch point in the tree represents an ancestor common to species to the right of that branch point.

▲ Figure 14.23 **Artist's reconstruction of Neanderthal.** DNA extracted from Neanderthals, extinct members of the human family, has allowed scientists to study their evolutionary relationship with modern humans.

Comparing the embryonic development of two species can often reveal homology that is not apparent in the mature structures (for example, see Figure 13.8). There is another clue to distinguishing homology from analogy: The more complex two similar structures are, the less likely it is they evolved independently. For example, compare the skulls of a human and a chimpanzee (see Figure 14.19). Although each is a fusion of many bones, they match almost perfectly, bone for bone. It is highly improbable that such complex structures matching in so many details could have separate origins. Most likely, the genes required to build these skulls were inherited from a common ancestor.

If homology reflects common ancestry, then comparing the DNA sequences of organisms gets to the heart of their evolutionary relationships. The more recently two species have branched from a common ancestor, the more similar their DNA sequences should be. Scientists have sequenced well over 150 billion bases of DNA from thousands of species. This enormous database has fueled a boom in the study of phylogeny and clarified many evolutionary relationships. In addition, some fossils are preserved in such a way that DNA fragments can be extracted for comparison with living organisms (Figure 14.23). ☑

Inferring Phylogeny from Homologous Characters

Once homologous characters—characters that reflect an evolutionary relationship—have been identified

Piecing together evolutionary histories shows who's related to whom.

for a group of organisms, how are these characters used to construct phylogenies? The most widely used approach is called cladistics. In **cladistics**, organisms are grouped by common ancestry. A **clade** (from the Greek word for "branch") consists of an ancestral species and all its evolutionary descendants—a distinct branch in the tree of life. Thus, identifying clades makes it possible to construct classification schemes that reflect the branching pattern of evolution.

Cladistics is based on the Darwinian concept of "descent with modification from a common ancestor"— species have some characters in common with their ancestors, but they also differ from them. To identify clades, scientists compare an ingroup with an outgroup (Figure 14.24). The ingroup (for example, the three mammals in Figure 14.24) is the group of species that is actually being analyzed. The outgroup (in Figure 14.24, the iguana, representing reptiles) is a species or group of species known to have diverged before the lineage that contains the groups being studied. By comparing members of the ingroup with each other and with the outgroup, we can determine what characters distinguish the ingroup from the outgroup.

All the mammals in the ingroup have hair and mammary glands. These characters were present in the ancestral mammal, but not in the outgroup. Next, gestation, the carrying of offspring in the uterus within the female parent, is absent from the duck-billed platypus (which lays eggs with a shell). From this absence we might infer that the duck-billed platypus represents an early branch point in the mammalian clade. Proceeding in this manner, we can construct a phylogenetic tree. Each branch represents the divergence of two groups from a

☑ CHECKPOINT

Our forearms and a bat's wings are derived from the same ancestral prototype; thus, they are _____. In contrast, the wings of a bat and the wings of a bee are derived from totally unrelated structures; thus, they are _____.

Answer: homologous; analogous

▼ Figure 14.24 **A simplified example of cladistics.**

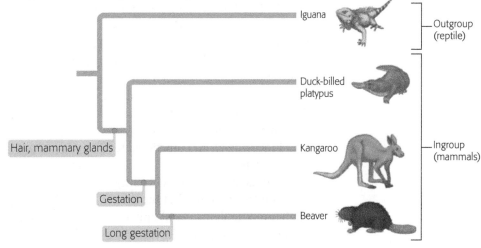

Iguana — Outgroup (reptile)

Duck-billed platypus

Kangaroo — Ingroup (mammals)

Beaver

Hair, mammary glands

Gestation

Long gestation

common ancestor, with the emergence of a lineage possessing one or more new features. The sequence of branching represents the order in which they evolved and when groups last shared a common ancestor. In other words, cladistics focuses on the changes that define the branch points in evolution.

The cladistics approach to phylogeny clarifies evolutionary relationships that were not always apparent in other taxonomic classifications. For instance, biologists traditionally placed birds and reptiles in separate classes of vertebrates (class Aves and class Reptilia, respectively). This classification, however, is inconsistent with cladistics. An inventory of homologies indicates that birds and crocodiles make up one clade, and lizards and snakes form another. If we go back as far as the ancestor that crocodiles share with lizards and snakes to make up a clade, then the class Reptilia must also include birds. The tree in **Figure 14.25** is thus more consistent with cladistics than with traditional classifications. ☑

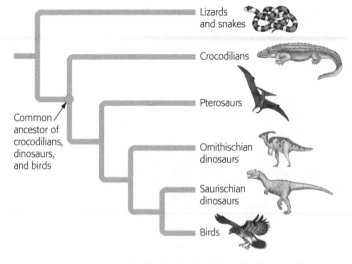

▲ Figure 14.25 **How cladistics is shaking phylogenetic trees.** Strict application of cladistics sometimes produces phylogenetic trees that conflict with classical taxonomy.

Classification: A Work in Progress

Phylogenetic trees are hypotheses about evolutionary history. Like all hypotheses, they are revised (or in some cases rejected) based on new evidence. Molecular systematics and cladistics are combining to remodel phylogenetic trees and challenge traditional classifications.

Linnaeus divided all known forms of life between the plant and animal kingdoms, and the two-kingdom system prevailed in biology for over 200 years. In the mid-1900s, the two-kingdom system was replaced by a five-kingdom system that placed all prokaryotes in one kingdom and divided the eukaryotes among four other kingdoms.

In the late 20th century, molecular studies and cladistics led to the development of a **three-domain system** (Figure 14.26). This current scheme recognizes three basic groups: two domains of prokaryotes—Bacteria and Archaea—and one domain of eukaryotes, called Eukarya. The domains Bacteria and Archaea differ in a number of important structural, biochemical, and functional features (see Chapter 15).

The domain Eukarya is currently divided into kingdoms, but the exact number of kingdoms is still under debate. Biologists generally agree on the kingdoms Plantae, Fungi, and Animalia. These kingdoms consist of multicellular eukaryotes that differ in structure, development, and modes of nutrition. Plants make their own food by photosynthesis. Fungi live by decomposing the remains of other

► Figure 14.26 **The three-domain classification system.** Molecular and cellular evidence supports the phylogenetic hypothesis that two lineages of prokaryotes, the domains Bacteria and Archaea, diverged very early in the history of life. Molecular evidence also suggests that domain Archaea is more closely related to domain Eukarya than to domain Bacteria.

organisms and absorbing small organic molecules. Most animals live by ingesting food and digesting it within their bodies.

The remaining eukaryotes, the protists, include all those eukaryotes that do not fit the definition of plant, fungus, or animal—effectively, a taxonomic grab bag. Most protists are unicellular (amoebas, for example). But the protists also include certain large, multicellular organisms that are believed to be direct descendants of unicellular protists. For example, many biologists classify the seaweeds as protists because they are more closely related to some single-celled algae than they are to true plants.

It is important to understand that classifying Earth's diverse species is a work in progress as we learn more about organisms and their evolution. Charles Darwin envisioned the goals of modern systematics when he wrote in *The Origin of Species*, "Our classifications will come to be, as far as they can be so made, genealogies." ☑

☑ **CHECKPOINT**

What lines of evidence caused biologists to develop the three-domain system of classification?

Answer: molecular studies and cladistics

 Mass Extinctions EVOLUTION CONNECTION

Rise of the Mammals

In this chapter, you've read about mass extinctions and their effects on the evolution of life on Earth. In the fossil record, each mass extinction was followed by a period of evolutionary change. Many new species arose as survivors became adapted to occupy new habitats or fill community roles vacated by extinctions.

For example, fossil evidence indicates that the number of mammal species increased dramatically after the extinction of most of the dinosaurs around 65 million years ago (Figure 14.27). Although mammals originated 180 million years ago, fossils older than 65 million years indicate that they were mostly small and not very diverse. Early mammals may have been eaten or outcompeted by the larger and more diverse dinosaurs. With the disappearance of most of the dinosaurs, mammals expanded greatly in both diversity and size, filling the ecological roles once occupied by dinosaurs. Had it not been for the dinosaur extinction, mammals may never have expanded their territories and become the predominant land animals. Therefore, we humans may owe our existence to the demise of older species. Through the process of evolution by natural selection, this pattern of death and renewal is repeated throughout the history of life on Earth.

▼ Figure 14.27 **The increase in mammalian species after the extinction of dinosaurs.** Although mammals originated more than 150 million years ago, they did not begin to widely diverge until after the demise of the dinosaurs.

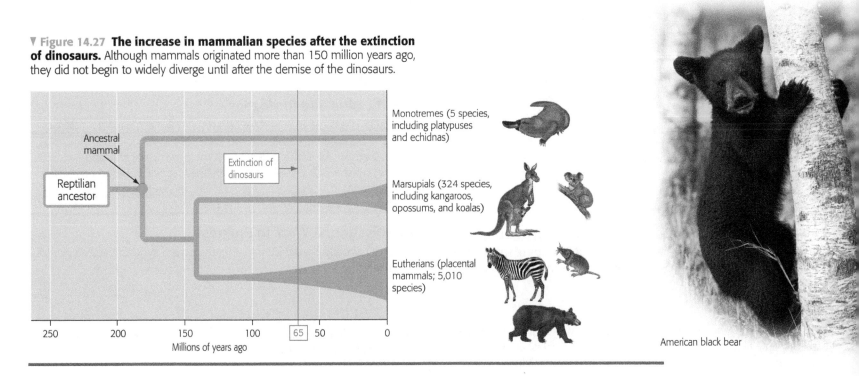

American black bear

Chapter Review

SUMMARY OF KEY CONCEPTS

The Origin of Species

What Is a Species?

The diversity of life evolved through speciation, the process in which one species splits into two or more species. According to the biological species concept, a species is a group of populations whose members have the potential to interbreed in nature to produce fertile offspring. The biological species concept is just one of several possible ways to define species.

Reproductive Barriers between Species

Gametes — Prezygotic barriers — Zygote — Postzygotic barriers — Viable, fertile offspring

Prezygotic barriers
- Temporal isolation
- Habitat isolation
- Behavioral isolation
- Mechanical isolation
- Gametic isolation

Postzygotic barriers
- Reduced hybrid viability
- Reduced hybrid fertility
- Hybrid breakdown

Evolution: Mechanisms of Speciation

When the gene pool of a population is severed from other gene pools of the parent species, the splinter population can follow its own evolutionary course.

Parent population

Allopatric speciation
(occurs after geographic isolation)

Sympatric speciation
(occurs without geographic isolation)

Hybridization leading to polyploids is a common mechanism of sympatric speciation in plants.

Earth History and Macroevolution

Macroevolution refers to evolutionary change above the species level, for example, the origin of evolutionary novelty and new groups of species and the impact of mass extinctions on the diversity of life and its subsequent recovery.

The Fossil Record

Geologists have established a geologic time scale with four broad divisions: Precambrian, Paleozoic, Mesozoic, and Cenozoic. The most common method for determining the ages of fossils is radiometric dating.

Plate Tectonics and Biogeography

Earth's crust is divided into large, irregularly shaped plates that float atop the viscous mantle. About 250 million years ago, plate movements brought all the landmasses together into the supercontinent Pangaea, causing extinctions and providing new opportunities for the survivors to diversify. About 180 million years ago, Pangaea began to break up, causing geographic isolation. Continental drift accounts for patterns of biogeography, such as the diversity of unique marsupials in Australia.

Mass Extinctions and Explosive Diversifications of Life

The fossil record reveals long, relatively stable periods punctuated by mass extinctions followed in turn by explosive diversification of certain survivors. For example, during the Cretaceous extinctions, about 65 million years ago, the world lost an enormous number of species, including most of the dinosaurs. Mammals greatly increased in diversity after the Cretaceous period.

Mechanisms of Macroevolution

Large Effects from Small Genetic Changes

A subtle change in the genes that control a species' development can have profound effects. In paedomorphosis, for example, the adult retains body features that were strictly juvenile in ancestral species.

The Evolution of Biological Novelty

An exaptation is a structure that evolves in one context and gradually becomes adapted for other functions. Most complex structures have evolved incrementally from simpler versions having the same function.

Classifying the Diversity of Life

Systematics, which includes taxonomy, focuses on classifying organisms and determining their evolutionary relationships.

Classification and Phylogeny

The goal of classification is to reflect phylogeny, the evolutionary history of species. Classification is based on the fossil record, homologous structures, and comparisons of DNA sequences. Homology (similarity based on shared ancestry) must be distinguished from analogy (similarity based on convergent evolution). Cladistics uses shared characters to group related organisms into clades—distinctive branches in the tree of life.

Classification: A Work in Progress

Biologists currently classify life into a three-domain system: Bacteria, Archaea, and Eukarya.

MasteringBiology®

For practice quizzes, BioFlix animations, MP3 tutorials, video tutors, and more study tools designed for this textbook, go to MasteringBiology®

SELF-QUIZ

1. Distinguish between microevolution, speciation, and macroevolution.

2. Bird guides once listed the myrtle warbler and Audubon's warbler as distinct species that lived side by side in parts of their ranges. However, recent books describe them as the eastern and western forms of a single species, the yellow-rumped warbler. Apparently, the two kinds of warblers
   a. live in the same areas.
   b. successfully interbreed.
   c. are almost identical in appearance.
   d. are merging to form a single species.

3. Identify each of the following reproductive barriers as prezygotic or postzygotic.
   a. One lilac species lives on acidic soil, another on basic soil.
   b. Mallard and pintail ducks mate at different times of the year.
   c. Two species of leopard frogs have different mating calls.
   d. Hybrid offspring of two species of jimsonweed always die before reproducing.
   e. Pollen of one kind of pine tree cannot fertilize another kind.

4. Why is a small, isolated population more likely to undergo speciation than a large one?

5. Many species of plants and animals adapted to desert conditions probably did not arise there. Their success in living in deserts could be due to _____, structures that originally had one use but became adapted for different functions.

6. Mass extinctions
   a. cut the number of species to the few survivors left today.
   b. resulted mainly from the separation of the continents.
   c. occurred regularly, about every million years.
   d. were followed by diversification of the survivors.

7. The animals and plants of India are almost completely different from the species in nearby Southeast Asia. Why might this be true?
   a. They have become separated by convergent evolution.
   b. The climates of the two regions are completely different.
   c. India is in the process of separating from the rest of Asia.
   d. India was a separate continent until relatively recently.

8. A paleontologist estimates that when a particular rock formed, it contained 12 mg of the radioactive isotope potassium-40. The rock now contains 3 mg of potassium-40. The half-life of potassium-40 is 1.3 billion years. From this information, you can conclude that the rock is approximately _____ billion years old.

9. Why are biologists careful to distinguish similarities due to homology from similarities due to analogy when constructing phylogenetic trees?

10. In the three-domain system, which two domains contain prokaryotic organisms?

Answers to these questions can be found in Appendix: Self-Quiz Answers.

THE PROCESS OF SCIENCE

11. Imagine you are conducting fieldwork and discover two groups of mice living on opposite sides of a river. Assuming that you will not disturb the mice, design a study to determine whether these two groups belong to the same species. If you could capture some of the mice and bring them to the lab, how might that affect your experimental design?

12. **Interpreting Data** The carbon-14/carbon-12 ratio of a fossilized skull is about 6.25% that of the skull of a present-day animal. Using the graph below, what is the approximate age of the fossil?

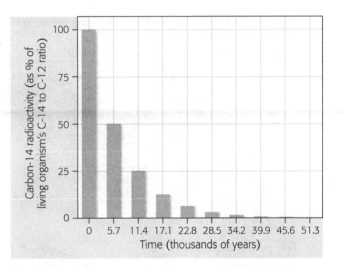

BIOLOGY AND SOCIETY

13. Most biologists are alarmed at the current rate of species extinction. What are some reasons for their concern? Considering that life has endured numerous mass extinctions and has always bounced back, how would this sixth mass extinction be different? What might be some consequences for the surviving species?

14. The red wolf (*Canis rufus*) was once widespread in the southeastern United States but was declared to be extinct in the wild. Biologists bred captive red wolf individuals and reintroduced them into areas of eastern North Carolina, where they are federally protected as endangered species. The current wild population is estimated to be about 100 individuals. However, a new threat to red wolves has arisen: hybridization with coyotes (*Canis latrans*), which have become more numerous in the areas inhabited by red wolves. Although red wolves and coyotes differ in morphology and DNA, they are capable of interbreeding and producing fertile offspring. Social behavior is the main reproductive barrier between the species and is more easily overcome when same-species mates are rare. For this reason, some people think that the endangered status of the red wolf should be withdrawn and resources should not be spent to protect what is not a "pure" species. Do you agree? Why or why not?

15 The Evolution of Microbial Life

Why Microorganisms Matter

If your family took a vacation in which you traveled 1 mile for every million years in the history of life, you'd still be asking, "Are we there yet?" after driving from Miami to Seattle.

According to a recent study, infection by the parasite *Toxoplasma* makes mice lose their fear of cats.

Seaweeds aren't just used for wrapping sushi—they're in your ice cream, too.

You have microorganisms to thank for the clean water you drink every day.

Human Microbiota BIOLOGY AND SOCIETY

Our Invisible Inhabitants

You probably know that your body contains trillions of individual cells, but did you know that they aren't all "you"? In fact, microorganisms residing in and on your body outnumber your own cells by 10 to 1. That means 100 trillion bacteria, archaea, and protists call your body home. Your skin, mouth, and nasal passages and your digestive and urogenital tracts are prime real estate for these microorganisms. Although each individual is so tiny that it would have to be magnified hundreds of times for you to see it, the weight of your microbial residents totals two to five pounds.

Colorized scanning electron micrograph of bacteria on a human tongue (14,500×).

We acquire our microbial communities during the first two years of life, and they remain fairly stable thereafter. However, modern life is taking a toll on that stability. We alter the balance of these communities by taking antibiotics, purifying our water, sterilizing our food, attempting to germproof our surroundings, and scrubbing our skin and teeth. Scientists hypothesize that disrupting our microbial communities may increase our susceptibility to infectious diseases, predispose us to certain cancers, and contribute to conditions such as asthma and other allergies, irritable bowel syndrome, Crohn's disease, and autism. Researchers are even investigating whether having the wrong microbial community could make us fat. In addition, scientists are studying how our microbial communities have evolved over the course of human history. As you'll discover in the Evolution Connection section at the end of this chapter, for example, dietary changes invited decay-causing bacteria to make themselves at home on our teeth.

Throughout this chapter, you will learn about the benefits and drawbacks of human-microbe interactions. You will also sample a bit of the remarkable diversity of prokaryotes and protists. This chapter is the first of three that explore the magnificent diversity of life. And so it is fitting that we begin with the prokaryotes, Earth's first life-form, and the protists, the bridge between unicellular eukaryotes and multicellular plants, fungi, and animals.

Major Episodes in the History of Life

To put our survey of diversity into perspective, let's look at a brief overview of major events in the history of life on Earth. Our planet's history began 4.6 billion years ago, a time span that is difficult to grasp. To visualize this immense scale, imagine taking a road trip across North America in which each mile traveled is the equivalent of passing through 1 million years. Our journey will take us from Kamloops, British Columbia, in Canada, to the finish line of the Boston Marathon in Boston, Massachusetts, on a route that covers 4,600 miles (Figure 15.1).

Setting out from Kamloops, we head southwest to Seattle, Washington, and then south toward San Francisco,

California. By the time we reach the California border, nearly 750 million years have passed, and the first rocks have formed on Earth's cooling surface.

Our arrival at the Golden Gate Bridge coincides with the appearance of the first cells in the fossil record. After 1,100 million years, life on Earth has begun! Those earliest organisms were all **prokaryotes**, having cells that lack true nuclei. You'll learn more about the origin of these first cells in the next section.

Conditions on the young Earth were very different from conditions today. One difference that was critical to the origin and

► Figure 15.1 **Some major episodes in the history of life.** On this 4,600-mile metaphorical road trip, each mile equals 1 million years in Earth's history.

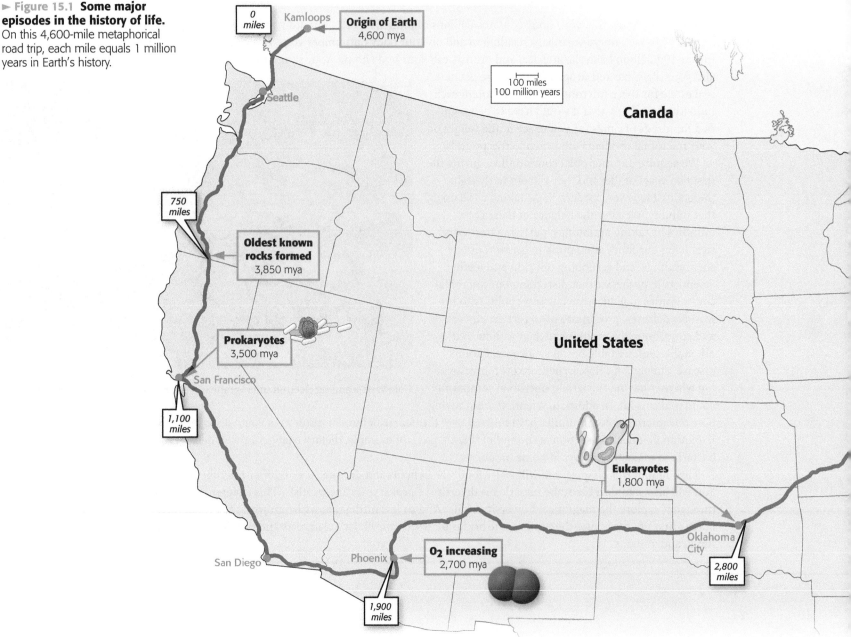

evolution of life was the lack of atmospheric O_2. As we continue driving south on our metaphoric journey, diverse metabolic pathways are evolving among the prokaryotes. However, we won't reach our next milestone for another 800 million years. By that time we have passed through San Diego and turned east across the desert. At Phoenix, Arizona, Earth is 2,700 million years old, and atmospheric O_2 has begun to increase as a result of photosynthesis by autotrophic prokaryotes.

Nine hundred million years later, just past Oklahoma City, we find the first fossils of eukaryotic organisms. **Eukaryotes** are composed of one or more cells that contain nuclei and many other membrane-bound organelles absent in prokaryotic cells. Eukaryotic cells evolved from ancestral host cells that engulfed smaller prokaryotes. The mitochondria of our cells and those of every other eukaryote are descendants of those prokaryotes, as are the chloroplasts of plants and algae.

Prokaryotes had been on Earth for 1.7 billion years before eukaryotes evolved. The appearance of these more complex cells, however, launched a period of tremendous diversification of eukaryotic forms. These new organisms were the protists. Protists are mostly microscopic and unicellular, and as you will learn in this chapter, they are represented today by a great diversity of species.

The next great event in the evolution of life was multicellularity. The oldest fossils that are clearly multicellular are 1.2 billion years old, or about midway between St. Louis, Missouri, and Terre Haute, Indiana, on our road trip. The organisms that left these fossils were tiny and not at all complex.

It isn't until 600 million years later (roughly 600 million years ago) that large, diverse, multicellular organisms appeared in the fossil record. At this point, we have traveled 4,000 miles—4 billion years—and now find ourselves in Erie, near the western edge of Pennsylvania (coincidentally, where one of the authors was born). Less than 15% of our journey remains, and we still have not encountered much diversity. But that's about to change. A great diversification of animals, the so-called Cambrian explosion, marked the beginning of the Paleozoic era, about 542 million years ago (see Table 14.1). By the end of that period, all the major animal body plans, as well as all the major groups, had evolved. The colonization of land by plants, fungi, and insects also occurred during the Paleozoic. This evolutionary transition began about 500 million years ago, a time that, in our road trip, corresponds to reaching Buffalo, New York.

By the time we get to Albany, New York, we're in the middle of the Mesozoic era, sometimes called the age of dinosaurs. At the end of the Mesozoic, 65 million years ago, we find ourselves about halfway across the state of Massachusetts. As we draw closer to Boston, more and more familiar organisms begin to dominate the landscape—flowering plants, birds, and mammals, including primates.

Modern humans, *Homo sapiens*, appeared roughly 195,000 years ago. At that point, we are less than two blocks shy of the finish line of our journey from the origin of Earth to the present day. Thus, spans of time that seem lengthy in the context of our own lives are brief moments in the history of life on Earth.

Mid-Mesozoic
180 mya

Colonization of land
500 mya

Homo sapiens
0.195 mya

Boston

4,600 miles

Albany

Buffalo

Erie

4,000 miles

Large, complex multicellular organisms
600 mya

Oldest multicellular fossils
1,200 mya

Terre Haute

St Louis

3,400 miles

If your family took a vacation in which you traveled 1 mile for every million years in the history of life, you'd still be asking, "Are we there yet?" after driving from Miami to Seattle.

295

The Origin of Life

Looking at the abundant diversity of life around us, it is difficult to imagine that Earth was not always like this. But early in its 4.6-billion-year history, our planet had no oceans, no lakes, very little oxygen, and no life at all. It was bombarded by debris left over from the formation of the solar system—gigantic chunks of rock and ice whose impact with Earth generated heat so fierce that it vaporized all available water. Indeed, for the first several hundred million years of its existence, conditions on the young Earth were so harsh that it's doubtful life could have originated; if it did, it could not have survived.

Although conditions had become considerably calmer, the Earth of 4 billion years ago was still in violent turmoil. Water vapor had condensed into oceans on the planet's cooling surface, but volcanic eruptions belched gases such as carbon dioxide, methane, and ammonia and other nitrogen compounds into its atmosphere (**Figure 15.2**). Although lack of atmospheric O_2 would be deadly to most of Earth's present-day inhabitants, this environment made the origin of life possible— O_2 is a corrosive agent that tends to disrupt chemical bonds and would have prevented the formation of complex molecules.

Life is an emergent property that arises from the specific arrangement and interactions of its molecular parts (see Figure 1.20). To learn how life originated from nonliving substances, biologists draw on research from the fields of chemistry, geology, and physics. In the next sections, we'll look at the attributes that must have arisen during the origin of life. Scientists agree on these properties, but which of several plausible scenarios led to them is still the subject of vigorous debate. ☑

A Four-Stage Hypothesis for the Origin of Life

According to one hypothesis for the origin of life, the first organisms were products of chemical evolution in four stages: (1) the synthesis of small organic molecules, such as amino acids and nucleotide monomers; (2) the joining of these small molecules into macromolecules, including proteins and nucleic acids; (3) the packaging of all these molecules into pre-cells, droplets with membranes that maintained an internal chemistry different from the surroundings; and (4) the origin of self-replicating molecules that eventually made inheritance possible. Although we'll never know for sure how life on Earth began, this hypothesis leads to predictions that can be tested in the laboratory. Let's look at some of the observations and experimental evidence for each of these four stages.

Stage 1: Synthesis of Organic Compounds

The chemicals mentioned above that formed Earth's early atmosphere, such as water (H_2O), methane (CH_4), and ammonia (NH_3), are all small, inorganic molecules. In contrast, the structures and functions of life depend on more complex organic molecules, such as sugars, fatty acids, amino acids, and nucleotides, which are composed of the same elements. Could these complex molecules have arisen from the ingredients available?

This stage was the first to be extensively studied in the laboratory. In 1953, Stanley Miller, a graduate student of Nobel laureate Harold Urey, performed a now-classic experiment. He devised an apparatus to simulate conditions thought to prevail on early Earth (**Figure 15.3**, facing page). A flask of warmed water simulated the primordial sea. An "atmosphere"—in the form of gases added to a reaction chamber—contained hydrogen gas, methane, ammonia, and water vapor. To mimic the prevalent lightning of the early Earth, electrical sparks were discharged into the chamber. A condenser cooled the atmosphere, causing water and any dissolved compounds to "rain" into the miniature "sea."

The results of the Miller-Urey experiments were front-page news. After the apparatus had run for a

☑ **CHECKPOINT**

One reason why the spontaneous generation of life on Earth could not occur today is the abundance of _____ in our modern atmosphere.

Answer: oxygen (O_2)

▼ Figure 15.2 **An artist's rendition of conditions on early Earth.**

▲ **Figure 15.3 Apparatus used to simulate early-Earth chemistry in Urey and Miller's experiments.**

Labels in figure:
- Sparks simulating lightning
- Water vapor
- "Atmosphere"
- CH_4
- NH_3
- H_2
- Electrode
- Condenser
- Cold water
- H_2O
- "Sea"
- Sample for chemical analysis

of amino acids, some in large amounts. Recent studies have shown that this meteorite also contains other key organic molecules, including lipids, simple sugars, and nitrogenous bases such as uracil.

Stage 2: Abiotic Synthesis of Polymers

Once small organic molecules were present on Earth, how were they linked together to form polymers such as proteins and nucleic acids without the help of enzymes and other cellular equipment? Researchers have brought about such polymerization in the laboratory by dripping solutions of organic monomers onto hot sand, clay, or rock. The heat vaporizes the water in the solutions and concentrates the monomers on the underlying material. Some of the monomers then spontaneously bond together to form polymers. On the early Earth, raindrops or waves may have splashed dilute solutions of organic monomers onto fresh lava or other hot rocks and then washed polypeptides and other polymers back into the sea. There they could accumulate in great quantities (since no life existed to consume them). ☑

Stage 3: Formation of Pre-Cells

The cell membrane forms a boundary that separates a living cell and its functions from the external environment. A key step in the origin of life would have been the isolation of a collection of organic molecules within a membrane. We'll call these molecular aggregates pre-cells—not really cells, but molecular packages with some of the properties of life. Within a confined space, certain combinations of molecules could be concentrated and interact more efficiently.

Researchers have demonstrated that pre-cells could have formed spontaneously from fatty acids (see Figure 3.11). The presence of a specific type of clay thought to be common on early Earth greatly speeds up the rate of spontaneous pre-cell formation. Unlike the plasma membranes of today's cells, these rudimentary membranes were quite porous, allowing organic monomers such as RNA nucleotides and amino acids to cross freely. However, polymers that formed inside the pre-cells were too large to exit. In addition to physically corralling molecules into a fluid-filled space, these pre-cells may have had certain properties of life. They may have had the ability to use chemical energy and grow. Most intriguingly, pre-cells made in laboratory experiments can divide to produce new pre-cells—a simple form of reproduction.

Stage 4: Origin of Self-Replicating Molecules

Life is defined partly by the process of inheritance, which is based on self-replicating molecules. Today's cells store their genetic information as DNA. They

☑ **CHECKPOINT**

What is the name of the chemical reaction whereby monomers are linked together into polymers? (*Hint*: Review Figure 3.4.)

Answer: dehydration reaction

week, an abundance of organic molecules essential for life, including amino acids, the monomers of proteins, had collected in the "sea." Many laboratories have since repeated Miller's experiment using various atmospheric mixtures and have also produced organic compounds. In 2008, one of Miller's former graduate students discovered some samples from an experiment that Miller had designed with a different atmosphere, one that would mimic volcanic conditions. Reanalyzing these samples using modern equipment, he identified additional organic compounds that had been synthesized. Indeed, 22 amino acids had been produced under Miller's simulated volcanic conditions, compared with the 11 produced with the atmosphere in his original 1953 experiment.

Scientists are also testing other hypotheses for the origin of organic molecules on Earth. Some researchers are exploring the hypothesis that life may have begun in submerged volcanoes or deep-sea hydrothermal vents, gaps in Earth's crust where hot water and minerals gush into deep oceans. These environments, among the most extreme environments in which life exists today, could have provided the initial chemical resources for life.

Another intriguing hypothesis proposes that meteorites were the source of Earth's first organic molecules. Fragments of a 4.5-billion-year-old meteorite that fell to Earth in Australia in 1969 contain more than 80 types transcribe the information into RNA and then translate RNA messages into specific enzymes and other proteins (see Figure 10.9). This mechanism of information flow probably emerged gradually through a series of small changes to much simpler processes.

What were the first genes like? One hypothesis is that they were short strands of RNA that replicated without the assistance of proteins. In laboratory experiments, short RNA molecules can assemble spontaneously from nucleotide monomers in the absence of enzymes (Figure 15.4). The result is a population of RNA molecules, each with a random sequence of monomers. Some of the molecules self-replicate, but their success at this reproduction varies. What happens can be described as molecular evolution: The RNA varieties that replicate fastest increase their frequency in the population.

In addition to the experimental evidence, there is another reason the idea of RNA genes in the primordial world is plausible. Cells actually have RNAs that can act as enzymes; they are called ribozymes. Perhaps early ribozymes catalyzed their own replication. That would help with the "chicken and egg" paradox of which came first, enzymes or genes. Maybe the "chicken and egg" came together in the same RNA molecules. The molecular biology of today may have been preceded by an ancient "RNA world."

The pre-cells described above could assemble spontaneously, reproduce, and grow. These abilities, however, would only result in endless copies of the original pre-cell. So how did cells acquire the ability to evolve? We consider this question next. ☑

From Chemical Evolution to Darwinian Evolution

Recall how present-day organisms evolve by natural selection. Genetic variation arises by mutations, errors that change the nucleotide sequence of the DNA. Some variations increase an organism's chance of reproductive success and are thus perpetuated in subsequent generations. In the same way, natural selection would have begun to shape the properties of pre-cells that contained self-replicating RNA. Those that contained genetic information that helped them grow and reproduce more efficiently than others would have increased in number, passing their abilities on to later generations. Mutations would have resulted in additional variation on which natural selection could work, and the most successful of these pre-cells would have continued to evolve. Of course, the gap between such pre-cells and even the simplest of modern cells is enormous. But with millions of years of incremental changes through natural selection, these molecular cooperatives could have become more and more cell-like. At some point during this time, pre-cells passed a fuzzy border to become true cells. The stage was then set for the evolution of diverse life-forms, changes that we see documented in the fossil record.

☑ **CHECKPOINT**

What are ribozymes? Why are they a logical step in the formation of life?

Answer: A ribozyme is an RNA molecule that functions as an enzyme. Ribozymes can perform some of the functions of both DNA and protein.

▼ Figure 15.4 **Self-replication of RNA "genes."**

RNA monomers

Formation of short RNA polymers: simple "genes"

Assembly of a complementary RNA chain (pairing rules are G with C and A with U)

Complementary chain serves as template for making a copy of original "gene"

Original "gene"

Complementary RNA chain

Prokaryotes

The history of prokary-
otic life is a success
story spanning billions
of years. Prokaryotes
lived and evolved all alone
on Earth for about 2 billion
years. They have continued to adapt
and flourish on a changing Earth and
in turn have helped to modify the planet. In this section,
you will learn about prokaryotic structure and function,
diversity, relationships, and ecological significance.

They're Everywhere!

Today, prokaryotes are found wherever there is life,
including in and on the bodies of multicellular organisms. The collective biological mass (biomass) of
prokaryotes is at least ten times that of all eukaryotes.
Prokaryotes also thrive in habitats too cold, too hot,
too salty, too acidic, or too alkaline for any eukaryote
(Figure 15.5). Scientists are just beginning to investigate the extensive prokaryotic diversity in the oceans.
Biologists have even discovered prokaryotes living on
the walls of a gold mine 3.3 km (2 miles) below Earth's
surface.

Though individual prokaryotes are small organisms
(Figure 15.6), they are giants in their collective impact
on Earth and its life. We hear most about the relatively
few species that cause illness. Bacterial infections are
responsible for about half of all human diseases, including tuberculosis, cholera, many sexually transmitted
infections, and certain types of food poisoning. However, prokaryotic life is much more than just a rogues'
gallery. The Biology and Society section introduced our
microbiota, the community of microorganisms that
live in and on our bodies. Each of us harbors several
hundred different species and genetic strains of prokaryotes, including a few whose positive effects are well
studied. For example, some of our intestinal inhabitants
supply essential vitamins and enable us to extract nutrition from food molecules that we can't otherwise digest.
Many of the bacteria that live on our skin perform
helpful housekeeping functions such as decomposing
dead skin cells. Prokaryotes also guard the body against
disease-causing intruders.

It would be hard to overstate the importance of prokaryotes to the health of the environment. Prokaryotes
living in the soil and at the bottom of lakes, rivers, and
oceans help to decompose dead organisms and other

◄ Figure 15.5 **A window to
early life?** An instrument on a
research submarine samples the
water around a hydrothermal
vent more than 1.5 km (about
a mile) below the ocean's
surface. Prokaryotes that live
near the vent use the emitted
gases as an energy source.
This environment, which is
very dark, hot, and under high
pressure, is among the most
extreme in which life is known
to exist.

► Figure 15.6 **Bacteria
on the point of a pin.**
The orange rods are
individual bacteria, each
about 5 μm long, on the
point of a pin. Besides
highlighting their tiny
size, this micrograph will
help you understand
why a pin prick can
cause infection.

Colorized SEM 605×

waste materials, returning vital chemical elements such
as nitrogen to the environment. If prokaryotes were to
disappear, the chemical cycles that sustain life would
come to a halt, and all forms of eukaryotic life would
also be doomed. In contrast, prokaryotic life would undoubtedly persist in the absence of eukaryotes, as it once
did for 2 billion years.

Structure/Function

Prokaryotes

Prokaryotes have a cellular organization fundamentally different from that of eukaryotes. Whereas eukaryotic cells have a membrane-enclosed nucleus and numerous other membrane-enclosed organelles, prokaryotic cells lack these structural features (see Figures 4.2 and 4.3). And nearly all species of prokaryotes have cell walls exterior to their plasma membranes. Despite the simplicity of the cell structures, though, prokaryotes display a remarkable range of diversity. In this section, you'll learn about aspects of their form, reproduction, and nutrition that help these organisms survive in their environments.

Prokaryotic Forms

Determining cell shape by microscopic examination is an important step in identifying a prokaryote. The micrographs in Figure 15.7 show the three most common shapes. Spherical prokaryotic cells are called **cocci** (singular, *coccus*). Rod-shaped prokaryotes are called **bacilli** (singular, *bacillus*). Spiral-shaped prokaryotes include spirochetes, different species of which cause syphilis and Lyme disease.

Although all prokaryotes are unicellular, the cells of some species usually exist as groups of two or more cells. For example, cocci that occur in clusters are called staphylococci. Other cocci, including the bacterium that causes strep throat, occur in chains; they are called streptococci. Some prokaryotes grow branching chains of cells (Figure 15.8a). And some species even exhibit a simple division of labor among specialized types of cells (Figure 15.8b). Among unicellular species, moreover, there are some giants that actually dwarf most eukaryotic cells (Figure 15.8c).

▼ Figure 15.8 **A diversity of prokaryotic shapes and sizes.**

(a) Actinomycete. An actinomycete is a mass of branching chains of rod-shaped cells. These bacteria are common in soil, where they secrete antibiotics that inhibit the growth of other bacteria. Various antibiotic drugs, such as streptomycin, are obtained from actinomycetes.

Colonized SEM 4,800×

LM 400×

(b) Cyanobacteria. These photosynthetic cyanobacteria exhibit division of labor. The box highlights a cell that converts atmospheric nitrogen to ammonia, which can then be incorporated into amino acids and other organic compounds.

LM 18×

(c) Giant bacterium. The larger white blob in this photo is the marine bacterium *Thiomargarita namibiensis*. This prokaryotic cell is more than 0.5 mm in diameter, about the size of the fruit fly's head below it.

▼ Figure 15.7 **Three common shapes of prokaryotic cells.**

SHAPES OF PROKARYOTIC CELLS		
Spherical (cocci)	**Rod-shaped (bacilli)**	**Spiral**

Colonized SEM 10,000×   Colonized SEM 10,000×   Colonized TEM 30,000×

About half of all prokaryotic species are mobile. Many of those that travel have one or more flagella that propel the cells away from unfavorable places or toward more favorable places, such as nutrient-rich locales.

In many natural environments, prokaryotes attach to surfaces in a highly organized colony called a **biofilm**. A biofilm may consist of one or several species of prokaryotes, and it may include protists and fungi as well. As a biofilm becomes larger and more complex, it develops into a "city" of microbes. Communicating by chemical signals, members of the community engage in division of labor, including defense against invaders, among other activities.

Biofilms can form on almost any type of surface, such as rocks, organic material (including living tissue), metal, and plastic. A biofilm known as dental plaque (Figure 15.9) can cause tooth decay, a topic you'll learn more about in the Evolution Connection section at the end of this chapter. Biofilms are common among bacteria that cause disease in humans. For instance, ear infections and urinary tract infections are often the result of biofilm-forming bacteria. Biofilms of harmful bacteria can also form on implanted medical devices such as catheters, replacement joints, and pacemakers. The structure of biofilms makes these infections especially difficult to defeat. Antibiotics may not be able to penetrate beyond the outer layer of cells, leaving much of the community intact.

Prokaryotic Reproduction

Many prokaryotes can reproduce at a phenomenal rate if conditions are favorable. The cells copy their DNA almost continuously and divide again and again by the

▼ Figure 15.9 **Dental plaque, a biofilm that forms on teeth.**

Colorized SEM 6,000x

▼ Figure 15.10 **Household sponge contaminated with bacteria (red, green, yellow, and blue objects in this colorized micrograph).**

Colorized SEM 8,400x

process of **binary fission**. Dividing by binary fission, a single cell becomes 2 cells, which then become 4, 8, 16, and so on. Some species can produce a new generation in only 20 minutes under optimal conditions. If reproduction continued unchecked at this rate, a single prokaryote could give rise to a colony outweighing Earth in only three days! Also, each time DNA is replicated prior to binary fission, spontaneous mutations occur. As a result, rapid reproduction generates a great deal of genetic variation in a prokaryotic population. If the environment changes, an individual that possesses a beneficial gene can quickly take advantage of the new conditions. For example, exposure to antibiotics may select for antibiotic resistance in a bacterial population (see the Evolution Connection section at the end of Chapter 13).

Fortunately, few prokaryotic populations can sustain exponential growth for long. Environments are usually limiting in resources such as food and space. Prokaryotes also produce metabolic waste products that may eventually pollute the colony's environment. Still, you can understand why kitchen sponges may harbor large numbers of bacteria (Figure 15.10) and why food can spoil so rapidly. Refrigeration retards food spoilage not because the cold kills bacteria, but because most microorganisms reproduce very slowly at such low temperatures.

Some prokaryotes can survive during very harsh conditions by forming specialized cells called endospores. An **endospore** is a thick-coated, protective cell produced within the prokaryotic cell when the prokaryote is exposed to unfavorable conditions. The endospore can survive all sorts of trauma and extreme temperatures—not even boiling water kills most of these resistant cells. And when the environment becomes more hospitable, the endospore can absorb water and resume growth. To ensure that all cells, including endospores, are killed when laboratory equipment is sterilized, microbiologists use an appliance called an autoclave, a pressure cooker that applies high-pressure steam at a temperature of 121°C (250°F). The food-canning industry uses similar methods to kill endospores of dangerous bacteria such as *Clostridium botulinum*, the cause of the potentially fatal disease botulism. ☑

Prokaryotic Nutrition

You are probably familiar with the methods by which multicellular organisms obtain energy and carbon, the two main resources needed for synthesizing organic compounds. Plants use carbon dioxide and the sun's energy in the process of photosynthesis; animals and fungi obtain both carbon and energy from organic matter. These modes of nutrition are both common among prokaryotes as well **(Figure 15.11)**. But the metabolic capabilities of prokaryotes are far more diverse than those of eukaryotes. Some species harvest energy from inorganic substances such as ammonia (NH_3) and hydrogen sulfide (H_2S). Soil bacteria that obtain energy

from inorganic nitrogen compounds are essential to the chemical cycle that makes nitrogen available to plants (see Figure 20.34). Because they don't depend on sunlight for energy, these prokaryotes can thrive in conditions that seem totally inhospitable to life—even between layers of rocks buried hundreds of feet below Earth's surface! Near hydrothermal vents, where scalding water and hot gases surge into the sea more than a mile below the surface, bacteria that use sulfur compounds as a source of energy support diverse animal communities.

The metabolic talents of prokaryotes make them excellent symbiotic partners with animals, plants, and fungi. **Symbiosis** ("living together") is a close association between organisms of two or more species. In some cases of symbiosis, both organisms benefit from the partnership. For example, many of the animals that inhabit hydrothermal vent communities, including the giant tube worm shown in **Figure 15.12**, harbor sulfur bacteria within their bodies. The animals absorb sulfur compounds from the water. The bacteria use the compounds as an energy source to convert CO_2 from seawater into organic molecules that, in turn, provide food for their hosts. Similarly, photosynthesis by cyanobacteria

▼ Figure 15.12 **Giant tube worm.** These animals, which can grow up to 2 m (over 6 ft) long, depend on symbiotic prokaryotes to supply them with food.

▼ Figure 15.11 **Two methods of obtaining energy and carbon.**

(a) *Oscillatoria.* This is a species of cyanobacteria, a type of prokaryote that undergoes photosynthesis.

LM 65×

(b) *Salmonella.* These bacteria, which cause a type of food poisoning, obtain energy and carbon from organic matter—in this case, living human cells.

Colorized SEM 21,000×

▲ Figure 15.13 *Azolla* (water fern, inset) floating in rice paddy. These small plants grow rapidly and cover the water's surface, which helps exclude weeds. Decomposition of the short-lived plants releases nitrogen that fertilizes the rice.

provides food for a fungal partner in the symbiosis that forms some lichens (see the Evolution Connection section at the end of Chapter 16).

In addition to photosynthesis, many cyanobacteria are also capable of nitrogen fixation, the process of converting atmospheric nitrogen (N_2) into a form usable by plants. Symbiosis with cyanobacteria gives plants such as the water fern *Azolla* an advantage in nitrogen-poor environments. This tiny, floating plant has been used to boost rice production for more than a thousand years (Figure 15.13). Other nitrogen-fixing bacteria live symbiotically in root nodules of plants in the legume family, a large group that includes many economically important species such as beans, soybeans, peas, and peanuts.

The Ecological Impact of Prokaryotes

As a result of their nutritional diversity, prokaryotes perform a variety of ecological services that are essential to our well-being. Let's turn our attention now to the vital role that prokaryotes play in sustaining the biosphere.

Prokaryotes and Chemical Recycling

Not too long ago, the atoms making up the organic molecules in your body were part of inorganic compounds found in soil, air, and water, as they will be again one day. Life depends on the recycling of chemical elements between the biological and physical components of ecosystems. Prokaryotes play essential roles in these chemical cycles. For example, nearly all the nitrogen that plants use to make proteins and nucleic acids comes from prokaryotic metabolism in the soil. In turn, animals get their nitrogen compounds from plants.

Another vital function of prokaryotes, mentioned earlier in the chapter, is the breakdown of organic wastes and dead organisms. Prokaryotes decompose organic matter and, in the process, return elements to the environment in inorganic forms that can be used by other organisms. If it were not for such decomposers, carbon, nitrogen, and other elements essential to life would become locked in the organic molecules of corpses and waste products. (You'll learn more about the role that prokaryotes play in chemical cycling in Chapter 20.)

Putting Prokaryotes to Work

People have put the metabolically diverse prokaryotes to work in cleaning up the environment. **Bioremediation** is the use of organisms to remove pollutants from water, air, or soil. One example of bioremediation is the use of prokaryotic decomposers to treat our sewage. Raw sewage is first passed through a series of screens and shredders, and solid matter settles out from the liquid waste. This solid matter, called sludge, is then gradually added to a culture of anaerobic prokaryotes, including both bacteria and archaea. The microbes decompose the organic matter in the sludge, converting it to material that can be used as landfill or fertilizer. The liquid wastes may then be passed through a trickling filter system consisting of a long horizontal bar that slowly rotates, spraying liquid wastes onto a bed of rocks (Figure 15.14). Aerobic prokaryotes and fungi growing on the rocks remove much of the organic matter from the liquid. The outflow from the rock bed is then sterilized and released back into the environment.

> You have microorganisms to thank for the clean water you drink every day.

▼ Figure 15.14 **Putting microbes to work in sewage treatment facilities.** This is a diagram of a trickling filter system, which uses bacteria, archaea, and fungi to treat liquid wastes after sludge is removed.

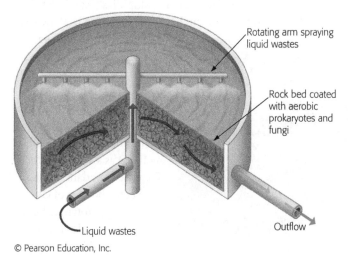

Rotating arm spraying liquid wastes

Rock bed coated with aerobic prokaryotes and fungi

Liquid wastes

Outflow

© Pearson Education, Inc.

Bioremediation has also become an important tool for cleaning up toxic chemicals released into the soil and water by industrial processes. Naturally occurring prokaryotes capable of degrading pollutants such as oil, solvents, and pesticides are often present in contaminated soil, but environmental workers may use methods of speeding up their activity. In Figure 15.15, an airplane is spraying chemical dispersants on oil from the disastrous 2010 Deepwater Horizon spill in the Gulf of Mexico. Like detergents that help clean greasy dishes, these chemicals break oil into smaller droplets that offer more surface area for microbial attack. Prokaryotes are also helping to decontaminate old mining sites where the soil and water are laced with heavy metals and other poisons. We are just beginning to explore the great potential that prokaryotes offer for bioremediation. In the future, genetically engineered microbes may be put to

▲ Figure 15.15 **Spraying chemical dispersants on an oil spill in the Gulf of Mexico.**

work cleaning up the wide variety of toxic waste products that continue to accumulate in our landscapes and landfills. ☑

The Two Main Branches of Prokaryotic Evolution: Bacteria and Archaea

By comparing diverse prokaryotes at the molecular level, biologists have identified two major branches of prokaryotic evolution: **bacteria** and **archaea**. Thus, life is organized into three domains—**Bacteria**, **Archaea**, and **Eukarya** (review Figure 14.26). Although bacteria and archaea have prokaryotic cell organization in common, they differ in many structural and physiological characteristics. In this section, we'll focus on the special characteristics of archaea before turning our attention to bacteria.

Archaea are abundant in many habitats, including places where few other organisms can survive. One group of archaea, the extreme thermophiles ("heat lovers"), live in very hot water (Figure 15.16); some archaea even populate the deep-ocean vents that gush near-boiling water, such as the one shown in Figure 15.5. Another group is the extreme halophiles ("salt lovers"), archaea that thrive in such environments as Utah's Great Salt Lake, the Dead Sea, and seawater-evaporating ponds used to produce salt.

A third group of archaea are methanogens, which live in anaerobic (oxygen-free) environments and give off methane as a waste product. They are abundant in the mud at the bottom of lakes and swamps. You may have seen methane, also called marsh gas, bubbling up from

a swamp. Methanogens flourish in the anaerobic conditions of solid waste landfills, where the large amount of methane they produce is a significant contributor to global warming (see Figure 18.43). Many municipalities collect this methane and use it as a source of energy (Figure 15.17).

Great numbers of methanogens also inhabit the digestive tracts of animals. In humans, intestinal gas is largely the result of their metabolism. More important, methanogens aid digestion in cattle, deer, and other animals that depend heavily on cellulose for their nutrition. Normally, bloating does not occur in these animals because they regularly expel large volumes of gas produced by the methanogens. (And that may be more than you wanted to know about these gas-producing microbes!)

Archaea are also abundant in more moderate conditions, especially the oceans, where they can be found at all depths. They are a substantial fraction of the prokaryotes in waters 150 m (nearly 500 ft) below the surface and half of the prokaryotes that live below 1,500 m (0.9 mi). Archaea are thus one of the most abundant cell types in Earth's largest habitat.

Bacteria That Cause Disease

Although most bacteria are harmless or even beneficial to us, a tiny minority of species cause a disproportionate amount of misery. Bacteria and other organisms that cause disease are called **pathogens**. We're healthy most of the time because our body's defenses check the growth of pathogen populations. Occasionally, the balance shifts in favor of a pathogen, and we become ill. Even some of

▼ Figure 15.16 **Heat-loving archaea.** In this photo, you can see yellow and orange colonies of heat-loving prokaryotes growing in the Abyss Pool, West Thumb Geyser, in Yellowstone Park, Wyoming.

▲ Figure 15.17 **Pipes for collecting gas generated by methanogenic archaea from a landfill.**

◄ Figure 15.18 **Bacteria that cause meningitis.** *Neisseria meningitidis*, an endotoxin-producing pathogen.

the bacteria that are normal residents of the human body can make us sick when our defenses have been weakened by poor nutrition or a viral infection.

Most pathogenic bacteria cause disease by producing a poison—either an exotoxin or an endotoxin. **Exotoxins** are proteins that bacterial cells secrete into their environment. For example, *Staphylococcus aureus* (abbreviated *S. aureus*) produces several exotoxins. Although *S. aureus* is commonly found on the skin and in the nasal passages, if it enters the body through a wound, it can cause serious disease. One of its exotoxins causes layers of skin to slough off ("flesh-eating disease"); another can produce a potentially deadly disease called toxic shock syndrome, which has been associated with improper use of tampons. *S. aureus* exotoxins are also a leading cause of food poisoning. If food contaminated with *S. aureus* is not refrigerated, the bacteria reproduce and release exotoxins so potent that ingesting a millionth of a gram causes vomiting and diarrhea. Once the food has been contaminated, even boiling it will not destroy the exotoxins.

Endotoxins are chemical components of the outer membrane of certain bacteria. All endotoxins induce the same general symptoms: fever, aches, and sometimes a dangerous drop in blood pressure (septic shock). Septic shock triggered by an endotoxin of the pathogen that causes bacterial meningitis (Figure 15.18) can kill a healthy person in a matter of days, or even hours. Because the bacteria are easily transmitted among people living in close contact, many colleges require students to be vaccinated against this disease. Other examples of endotoxin-producing bacteria include the species of *Salmonella* that cause food poisoning and typhoid fever.

Sanitation is generally the most effective way to prevent bacterial disease. The installation of water treatment and sewage systems continues to be a public health priority throughout the world. Antibiotics have been discovered that can cure most bacterial diseases.

However, resistance to widely used antibiotics has evolved in many of these pathogens.

In addition to sanitation and antibiotics, a third defense against bacterial disease is education. A case in point is Lyme disease, which is caused by a spirochete bacterium carried by ticks (Figure 15.19). Disease-carrying ticks live on deer and field mice but also bite humans. Lyme disease usually starts as a red rash shaped like a bull's-eye around a tick bite. Antibiotics can cure the disease if administered within a month of exposure. If untreated, Lyme disease can cause debilitating arthritis, heart disease, and nervous system disorders. Because there is no vaccine, the best defense against Lyme disease is public education about avoiding tick bites and the importance of seeking treatment if a rash develops.

▼ Figure 15.19 **Lyme disease, a bacterial disease transmitted by ticks.** The bacterium that causes Lyme disease (shown in micrograph at right) is carried from deer to humans by ticks.

"Bull's-eye" rash

Tick that carries the Lyme disease bacterium

Spirochete that causes Lyme disease

The potential of some pathogens to cause serious harm has led to their use as biological weapons. One of the greatest threats is from endospores of the bacterium that causes anthrax. When anthrax endospores enter the lungs, they germinate, and the bacteria multiply, producing an exotoxin that eventually accumulates to lethal levels in the blood. Although the bacteria can be killed by certain antibiotics, the antibiotics don't eliminate the toxin already in the body. As a result, inhalation anthrax has a very high death rate. In an incident in 2001, five people died when anthrax spores were mailed to members of the news media and the U.S. Senate.

Another bacterium considered to have dangerous potential as a weapon is *Clostridium botulinum*. Unlike other biological agents, the weapon form of *C. botulinum* is the exotoxin it produces, botulinum, rather than the living microbes. Botulinum, the deadliest poison on Earth, blocks transmission of the nerve signals that cause muscle contraction, resulting in paralysis of the muscles required for breathing. Thirty grams of botulinum, a bit more than an ounce, could kill every person in the United States. On the other hand, the minute amount of botulinum in Botox is used for cosmetic purposes. When the toxin is injected under the skin, it relaxes the facial muscles that cause wrinkles. ☑

Human Microbiota THE PROCESS OF SCIENCE

Are Intestinal Microbiota to Blame for Obesity?

As you learned in the Biology and Society section, our bodies are home to trillions of bacteria that cause no harm or are even beneficial to our health. In the past decade, researchers have made enormous strides in characterizing our microbiota and have begun to investigate the specific effects of these residents on our physiological processes. Because our intestinal microbes are known to be involved in some aspects of food processing, researchers speculate that they might be involved in obesity. Let's examine how a team of scientists investigated the impact of microbiota on body composition—the amount of fat versus lean body mass.

Using **observations** from previous studies, the scientists asked the following **question**: Can microbiota from an obese person affect the body composition of another person? Although this is the question that we ultimately want answered, researchers routinely test hypotheses in animal models before using human subjects. Mice that have been raised in germ-free conditions have no microbiota, making them ideal subjects for this type of experiment. Therefore, the scientists formed the **hypothesis** that intestinal microbiota of an obese person would increase the amount of body fat in mice. Their **prediction** was that if the hypothesis was correct, then lean, germ-free mice that received transplants of microbes from the intestines of obese individuals would show a greater increase of body fat than would germ-free mice that received transplants of microbes from the intestines of lean individuals.

The researchers recruited four pairs of female twins for the **experiment**. In each pair, one twin was obese and the other was lean. Microbiota from the feces of each individual were transplanted into separate groups of germ-free mice (Figure 15.20). The **results**, shown in Figure 15.21, supported the hypothesis. Mice that received microbiota from an obese donor became more obese; mice that received microbiota from a lean donor remained lean.

Is a microbe-based cure for obesity just around the corner? It's not likely. The experiment described here—and many similar experiments—represent an early stage of scientific investigation. A great deal more research is needed to determine whether our microbial residents are responsible for obesity. If that proves to be the case, the next challenge will be figuring out how to safely manipulate the complex ecosystem within our bodies.

▼ Figure 15.20 **Experiment to investigate the effect of microbiota on body composition.**

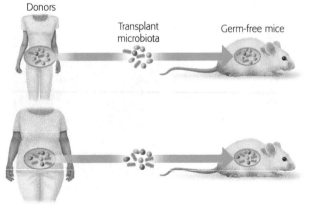

Donors

Transplant microbiota

Germ-free mice

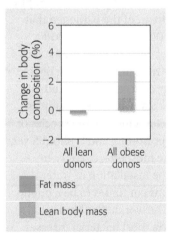

◄ Figure 15.21 **Results of microbiota transplantation experiment.** The graph shows the change in body composition (lean vs. fat mass) of mice that received microbiota from a lean donor (left) or an obese donor (right).

Data from: V. K. Ridaura et al., Gut microbiota from twins discordant for obesity modulate metabolism in mice. *Science* 341 (2013). DOI: 10.1126/science.1241214.

Protists

The fossil record indicates that the first eukaryotes evolved from prokaryotes around 2 billion years ago. **Endosymbiosis**, a relationship in which one organism lives inside the cell or cells of a host organism, played a key role in the evolution of eukaryotic cells. Extensive evidence supports the theory that mitochondria and chloroplasts originated as prokaryotes that established residence inside larger host cells. Hosts and endosymbionts became interdependent and eventually became single organisms with inseparable parts. These primal eukaryotes were not only the predecessors of the great variety of modern protists; they were also ancestral to all other eukaryotes—plants, fungi, and animals.

The term protists is not a taxonomic category. At one time, protists were classified in a fourth eukaryotic kingdom (kingdom Protista). However, recent genetic and structural studies shattered the notion of protists as a unified group—some protists are more closely related to fungi, plants, or animals than they are to each other. Hypotheses about protist phylogeny (and thus, classification) are changing rapidly as new information causes scientists to revise their ideas. Although there is general agreement about some relationships, others are hotly disputed. Thus, **protist** is a bit of a catch-all category that includes all eukaryotes that are not fungi, animals, or plants. Most, but not all, protists are unicellular. Because their cells are eukaryotic, even the simplest protists are much more complex than any prokaryote.

One mark of protist diversity is the variety of ways they obtain their nutrition. Some protists are autotrophs, producing their food by photosynthesis. Photosynthetic protists belong to an informal category called **algae** (singular, *alga*), which also includes cyanobacteria. Protistan algae may be unicellular, colonial, or multicellular, such as the one shown in Figure 15.22a. Other protists are heterotrophs, acquiring their food from other organisms. Some heterotrophic protists eat bacteria or other protists; some are fungus-like and obtain organic molecules by absorption. Still others are parasitic. A **parasite** derives its nutrition from a living host, which is harmed by the interaction. For example, the parasitic trypanosomes shown among human red blood cells in Figure 15.22b cause sleeping sickness, a debilitating disease common in parts of Africa. Yet other protists are mixotrophs, capable of both photosynthesis and heterotrophy. *Euglena* (Figure 15.22c), a common inhabitant of pond water, can change its mode of nutrition, depending on availability of light and nutrients.

Protist habitats are also diverse. Most protists are aquatic, living in oceans, lakes, and ponds, but they are found almost anywhere there is moisture, including terrestrial habitats such as damp soil and leaf litter. Others are symbionts that reside in the bodies of various host organisms.

Because the classification of protists remains a work in progress, our brief survey of protists is not organized to correspond with any hypothesis about phylogeny. Instead, we'll look at four informal categories of protists: protozoans, slime molds, unicellular and colonial algae, and seaweeds.

▼ Figure 15.22 **Protist modes of nutrition.**

(a) An autotroph: *Caulerpa*, a multicellular alga

(b) A heterotroph: parasitic trypanosome (arrow)

Colorized SEM 5,440×

(c) A mixotroph: *Euglena*

LM 700×

Protozoans

Protists that live primarily by ingesting food are called **protozoans** (Figure 15.23). Protozoans thrive in all types of aquatic environments. Most species eat bacteria or other protozoans, but some can absorb nutrients dissolved in the water. Protozoans that live as parasites in animals, though in the minority, cause some of the world's most harmful diseases.

Flagellates are protozoans that move by means of one or more flagella. Most species are free-living (nonparasitic). However, this group also includes some nasty parasites that make people sick. An example is *Giardia*, a common waterborne parasite that causes severe diarrhea. People most often pick up *Giardia* by drinking water contaminated with feces containing the parasite. For example, a swimmer in a lake or river might accidentally ingest water, or a hiker might drink contaminated water from a seemingly pristine stream. (Boiling the water first will kill *Giardia*.) Another flagellate is *Trichomonas*, a common sexually transmitted parasite. The parasite travels through the reproductive tract by moving its flagella and undulating part of its membrane. In women, these protozoans feed on white blood cells and bacteria living on the cells lining the vagina. *Trichomonas* also infects the cells lining the male reproductive tract, but limited availability of food results in very small population sizes. Consequently, males typically have no symptoms of infection.

Other flagellates live symbiotically in a relationship that benefits both partners. Termites are notoriously destructive to wooden structures, but they lack enzymes to digest the tough, complex cellulose molecules that make up wood. Flagellates that reside in the termite's digestive tract break down the cellulose into simpler molecules, sharing the bounty with their hosts.

Amoebas are characterized by great flexibility in their body shape and the absence of permanent organelles for locomotion. Most species move and feed by means of **pseudopodia** (singular, *pseudopodium*), temporary extensions of the cell. Amoebas can assume virtually any shape as they creep over rocks, sticks, or mud at the bottom of a pond or ocean. One species of parasitic amoeba causes amoebic dysentery, a disease that is responsible for an estimated 100,000 deaths worldwide every year. Other protozoans with pseudopodia include the **forams,** which have shells. Although they are single-celled, the largest forams grow to a diameter of several centimeters. Ninety percent of forams that have been identified are fossils. The fossilized shells, which are a component of sedimentary rock such as limestone, are excellent markers for relating the ages of rocks in different parts of the world.

Apicomplexans are all parasitic, and some cause serious human diseases. They are named for a structure at their apex (tip) that is specialized for penetrating host cells and tissues. This group of protozoans includes *Plasmodium*, the parasite that causes malaria. Another apicomplexan is *Toxoplasma*, which requires a feline host to complete its complex life cycle. Cats that eat wild birds or rodents may be infected and shed the parasite in their feces. People can become infected by handling cat litter of outdoor cats, but they don't become sick because the immune system keeps the parasite in check. However, a woman who is newly infected with *Toxoplasma* during pregnancy can pass the parasite to her unborn child, who may suffer damage to the nervous system as a result.

Ciliates are protozoans named for their hairlike structures called cilia, which provide movement of the protist and sweep food into the protist's "mouth." Nearly all ciliates are free-living (nonparasitic) and include both heterotrophs and mixotrophs. If you have had the opportunity to explore protist diversity in a droplet of pond water, you may have seen the common freshwater ciliate *Paramecium*. ☑

> According to a recent study, infection by the parasite *Toxoplasma* makes mice lose their fear of cats.

☑ **CHECKPOINT**

According to a recent study, mice infected with *Toxoplasma* lose their fear of cats. How would altering the behavior of mice in this way be a beneficial adaptation for the *Toxoplasma* parasite?

Answer: Fearless mice are more likely to be caught and eaten by a cat, thus transmitting the parasite to a host in which it can complete its life cycle (that is, successfully reproduce).

▼ Figure 15.23 **A diversity of protozoans.**

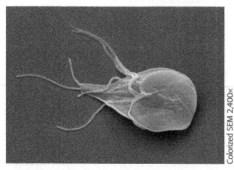

A flagellate: *Giardia*. This flagellated protozoan parasite can colonize and reproduce within the human intestine, causing disease.

Colorized SEM 2,400×

Another flagellate: *Trichomonas*. This common sexually transmitted parasite causes an estimated 5 million new infections each year.

Colorized SEM 3,200×

An amoeba. This amoeba is beginning to wrap pseudopodia around an algal cell in preparation for engulfing it.

Colorized TEM 2,300×

Slime Molds

Slime molds are multicellular protists related to amoebas. Although slime molds were once classified as fungi, DNA analysis showed that they arose from different evolutionary lineages. Like many fungi, slime molds feed on dead plant material. Two distinct types of slime molds have been identified.

In plasmodial slime molds, the feeding body is an amoeboid mass called a plasmodium (Figure 15.24) that extends pseudopodia among the leaf litter and other decaying material on a forest floor. A plasmodium can measure several centimeters across, with its network of fine filaments taking in bacteria and bits of dead organic matter amoeboid-style. Large as it is, though, the plasmodium is actually a single cell with many nuclei. Its mass of cytoplasm is not divided by plasma membranes. When the plasmodium runs out of food,

or its environment dries up, the slime mold grows reproductive structures. Stalked bodies that arise from the plasmodium bear tough-coated spores that can survive harsh conditions. If you look closely at a decaying log or the mulch in landscaped areas, you may notice these spore-bearing structures. Like the endospores of anthrax bacteria, slime mold spores can absorb water and grow once favorable conditions return.

In cellular slime molds, the feeding stage consists of solitary amoeboid cells that function independently of each other rather than a plasmodium (Figure 15.25). But when food is in short supply, the amoeboid cells swarm together to form a slug-like colony that moves and functions as a single unit. After a brief period of mobility, the colony extends a stalk and develops into a multicellular reproductive structure.

▲ Figure 15.24 **A plasmodial slime mold.** The weblike form of the slime mold's feeding stage (yellow structure) is an adaptation that enlarges the organism's surface area, increasing its contact with food, water, and oxygen.

Amoeboid cells

Slug-like colony

Reproductive structure

▲ Figure 15.25 **Life stages of a cellular slime mold.**

A foram. A foram cell secretes a shell made of organic material hardened with calcium carbonate. The pseudopodia, seen here as thin rays, extend through small pores in the shell.

Apical complex

Red blood cell

An apicomplexan. *Plasmodium*, which causes malaria, enters red blood cells of its human host. The parasite feeds on the host cell from within, eventually destroying it.

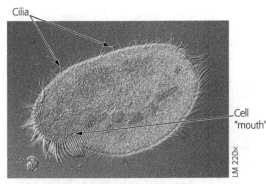

Cilia

Cell "mouth"

A ciliate. The ciliate *Paramecium* uses its cilia to move through pond water. Cilia lining the oral groove keep a current of water containing food moving toward the cell "mouth."

Unicellular and Colonial Algae

Algae are protists and cyanobacteria whose photosynthesis supports food chains in freshwater and marine ecosystems. Researchers are currently trying to harness their ability to convert light energy to chemical energy for another purpose—to produce biofuels. We'll look at four groups of protistan algae. Three of these groups—dinoflagellates, diatoms, and green algae—are unicellular, and one group is colonial.

Many unicellular algae are components of **phytoplankton**, the photosynthetic organisms, mostly microscopic, that drift near the surfaces of ponds, lakes, and oceans. Dinoflagellates are abundant in the vast aquatic pastures of phytoplankton. Each **dinoflagellate** species has a characteristic shape reinforced by external plates made of cellulose (Figure 15.26a). The beating of two flagella in perpendicular grooves produces a spinning movement. Dinoflagellate blooms—population explosions—sometimes cause warm coastal waters to turn pinkish orange, a phenomenon known as a red tide. Toxins produced by some red-tide dinoflagellates have caused massive fish kills and are poisonous to humans as well. One group of dinoflagellates resides within the cells of reef-building corals. Without these algal partners, corals could not build and sustain the massive reefs that provide the food, living space, and shelter that support the splendid diversity of the reef community.

Diatoms have glassy cell walls containing silica, the mineral used to make glass (Figure 15.26b). The cell wall consists of two halves that fit together like the bottom and lid of a shoe box. Diatoms store their food reserves in the form of an oil that provides buoyancy, keeping diatoms floating as plankton near the sunlit surface. The organic remains of diatoms that lived hundreds of millions of years ago are thought to be the main component of oil deposits. But why wait millions of years? Researchers are currently working on methods of growing diatoms and processing the oil into biodiesel.

Green algae are named for their grass-green chloroplasts. Unicellular green algae flourish in most freshwater lakes and ponds, as well as many home pools and aquariums. The green algal group also includes colonial forms, such as *Volvox*, shown in Figure 15.26c. Each *Volvox* colony is a hollow ball of flagellated cells (the small green dots in the photo) that are very similar to certain unicellular green algae. The balls within the balls in Figure 15.25c are daughter colonies that will be released when the parent colonies rupture. Of all photosynthetic protists, green algae are the most closely related to plants.

Seaweeds

Defined as large, multicellular marine algae, **seaweeds** grow on rocky shores and just offshore. Their cell walls have slimy and rubbery substances that cushion their bodies against the agitation of the waves. Some seaweeds are as large and complex as many plants. And although the word *seaweed* implies a plantlike appearance, the similarities between these algae and plants are a consequence of convergent evolution. In fact, the closest relatives of seaweeds are certain unicellular algae, which is why many biologists include seaweeds with the protists. Seaweeds are classified into three different groups (Figure 15.27), based partly on the types of pigments present in their chloroplasts: green algae, red algae, and brown algae (some of which are known as kelp).

Many coastal people, particularly in Asia, harvest seaweeds for food. For example, in Japan and Korea, some seaweed species, including brown algae called kombu, are ingredients in soups. Other seaweeds, such as red algae called nori, are used to wrap sushi. Marine algae are rich

▼ Figure 15.26 **Unicellular and colonial algae.**

Colorized SEM 667×

(a) **Dinoflagellate:** Note the wall of protective plates

Colorized SEM 165×

(b) **Diatom:** Note the glassy walls

LM 195×

(c) **Volvox:** A colonial green alga

▼ Figure 15.27 **The three major groups of seaweeds.**

Green algae. This sea lettuce is an edible species that inhabits the intertidal zone, where the land meets the ocean.

Red algae. These seaweeds are most abundant in the warm coastal waters of the tropics.

Brown algae. This group includes the largest seaweeds, known as kelp, which grow as marine "forests."

in iodine and other essential minerals, but much of their organic material consists of unusual polysaccharides that humans cannot digest. They are eaten mostly for their rich tastes and unusual textures. The gel-forming substances in the cell walls of seaweeds are widely used as thickeners for such processed foods as puddings, ice cream, and salad dressing. The seaweed extract called agar provides the gel-forming base for the media microbiologists use to culture bacteria in petri dishes. ☑

Seaweeds aren't just used for wrapping sushi—they're in your ice cream, too.

Human Microbiota EVOLUTION CONNECTION

The Sweet Life of *Streptococcus mutans*

Did you ever wonder why candy causes cavities? A biofilm-forming species of bacteria called *Streptococcus mutans* is the culprit. *S. mutans* thrives in the anaerobic environment found in the tiny crevices in tooth enamel. Using sucrose (table sugar) to make a sticky polysaccharide, the bacteria glue themselves in place and build up thick deposits of plaque. Unless you make an effort to remove it, the plaque becomes mineralized, turning into a crusty tartar that must be scraped off your teeth by a dental hygienist (Figure 15.28). Within this fortress, *S. mutans* ferments sugars to obtain energy, releasing lactic acid as a by-product. The acid attacks tooth enamel and eventually eats through it. Other bacteria then use the entrance and infect the soft tissue in the interior of the tooth.

Early humans were hunter-gatherers, living on food foraged in the wild. In a major cultural shift, this lifestyle was replaced by agriculture, which provided a diet rich in carbohydrates from grain. A later dietary shift brought processed flour and sugar to the table. Each change in diet altered the environment inhabited by our oral microbiota. Studies of prehistoric human remains have correlated dental disease with these changes in diet.

Recent research links *S. mutans* directly to these increases in tooth decay. In one study, researchers analyzed DNA from tartar on the teeth of prehistoric humans who lived in Europe from 7,500 to 400 years ago. The tartar of hunter-gatherers included many species of bacteria but few known to cause tooth decay. *S. mutans* first appeared as one member of a diverse bacterial community after the agricultural diet had been established. Diversity of the oral microbiota dropped dramatically about 400 years ago, around the time sugar was introduced into the diet, and *S. mutans* became the overwhelmingly dominant species. Thus, we can infer that natural selection in the high-sugar environment favored *S. mutans*.

What adaptations gave *S. mutans* an advantage over other species? Another research team investigated genetic changes that allowed *S. mutans* to thrive in a high-sugar environment. Their results turned up more than a dozen genes that improved the ability of *S. mutans* to metabolize sugars and survive increased acidity. They also discovered chemical weapons produced by *S. mutans* that kill harmless bacteria—their competitors for space in the limited terrain of the human oral cavity.

It appears that *S. mutans* took full advantage of an evolutionary opportunity afforded by the human sweet tooth. Having adapted to new environmental conditions and ousted its competitors, it is now firmly entrenched as the dominant member of the mouth's microbial community.

▲ Figure 15.28 **Checking the effects of *Streptococcus mutans*.**

Chapter Review

SUMMARY OF KEY CONCEPTS

Major Episodes in the History of Life

Major Episode	Millions of Years Ago
Plants and fungi colonize land	500
Fossils of large, diverse multicellular organisms	600
Oldest fossils of multicellular organisms	1,200
Oldest eukaryotic fossils	1,800
Beginning of atmospheric accumulation of O_2	2,700
Oldest prokaryotic fossils	3,500
Origin of Earth	4,600

The Origin of Life

A Four-Stage Hypothesis for the Origin of Life

One scenario suggests that the first organisms were products of chemical evolution in four stages:

Inorganic compounds → Organic monomers → Polymer → Membrane-enclosed compartment → Complementary chain

Abiotic synthesis of organic monomers → **Abiotic synthesis of polymers** → **Formation of pre-cells** → **Self-replicating molecules**

From Chemical Evolution to Darwinian Evolution

Over millions of years, natural selection favored the most efficient pre-cells, which evolved into the first prokaryotic cells.

Prokaryotes

They're Everywhere!

Prokaryotes are found wherever there is life and greatly outnumber eukaryotes. Prokaryotes thrive in habitats where eukaryotes cannot live. A few prokaryotic species cause serious disease, but most are either benign or beneficial to other forms of life.

Structure/Function: Prokaryotes

Prokaryotic cells lack nuclei and other membrane-enclosed organelles. Most have cell walls. Prokaryotes exhibit three common shapes.

Spherical   **Rod-shaped**   **Spiral**

About half of all prokaryotic species are mobile, most of these using flagella to move. Some prokaryotes can survive extended periods of harsh conditions by forming endospores. Many prokaryotes can reproduce by binary fission at high rates if conditions are favorable, but growth is usually restricted by limited resources.

Prokaryotes include species that obtain energy from the sun (like plants) and from organic material (like animals and fungi). Some species derive energy from inorganic substances such as ammonia (NH_3) or hydrogen sulfide (H_2S). Some prokaryotes live in symbiotic associations with animals, plants, or fungi.

The Ecological Impact of Prokaryotes

Prokaryotes help recycle chemical elements between the biological and physical components of ecosystems. People use prokaryotes to remove pollutants from water, air, and soil in the process called bioremediation.

The Two Main Branches of Prokaryotic Evolution: Bacteria and Archaea

The prokaryotic lineage includes domains Bacteria and Archaea. Many archaea are "extremophiles" capable of surviving under conditions (such as high heat or salt concentrations) that would kill other forms of life; other archaea are found in more moderate environments. Some bacteria cause disease, mostly by producing exotoxins or endotoxins. Sanitation, antibiotics, and education are the best defenses against bacterial disease.

Protists

Protists are unicellular eukaryotes and their closest multicellular relatives.

Protozoans

Protozoans, including flagellates, amoebas, apicomplexans, and ciliates, primarily live in aquatic environments and ingest their food.

Slime Molds

Slime molds (including plasmodial slime molds and cellular slime molds) resemble fungi in appearance and lifestyle as decomposers but are not at all closely related.

Unicellular and Colonial Algae

Unicellular algae, including dinoflagellates, diatoms, and unicellular green algae, are photosynthetic protists that support food chains in freshwater and marine ecosystems.

Seaweeds

Seaweeds—which include green, red, and brown algae—are large, multicellular marine algae that grow on and near rocky shores.

MasteringBiology®

For practice quizzes, BioFlix animations, MP3 tutorials, video tutors, and more study tools designed for this textbook, go to MasteringBiology®

SELF-QUIZ

1. Place these events in the history of life on Earth in the order that they occurred.
   a. accumulation of O_2 in Earth's atmosphere
   b. colonization of land by plants and fungi
   c. diversification of animals (Cambrian explosion)
   d. origin of eukaryotes
   e. origin of humans
   f. origin of multicellular organisms
   g. origin of prokaryotes

2. Place the following steps in the origin of life in the order that they are hypothesized to have occurred.
   a. integration of abiotically produced molecules into membrane-enclosed pre-cells
   b. origin of the first molecules capable of self-replication
   c. abiotic joining of organic monomers into polymers
   d. abiotic synthesis of organic monomers
   e. natural selection among pre-cells

3. DNA replication relies on the enzyme DNA polymerase. Why does this suggest that the earliest genes were made from RNA?

4. Contrast exotoxins with endotoxins.

5. Some species of cyanobacteria form symbiotic relationships with other organisms. What benefit might a protist or fungus receive from a cyanobacterial symbiont? What benefit might a plant receive from a cyanobacterial symbiont?

6. The bacteria that cause tetanus can be killed only by prolonged heating at temperatures considerably above boiling. What does this suggest about tetanus bacteria?

7. How is the process used in sewage treatment similar to the decomposition of leaf litter in a forest?

8. What do all protists have in common?

9. Which of the following protists is *not* a human pathogen?
   a. *Toxoplasma*
   b. *Trichomonas*
   c. *Paramecium*
   d. *Giardia*

10. Which algal group is most closely related to plants?
    a. diatoms
    b. green algae
    c. dinoflagellates
    d. seaweeds

Answers to these questions can be found in Appendix: Self-Quiz Answers.

THE PROCESS OF SCIENCE

11. Imagine you are on a team designing a moon base that will be self-contained and self-sustaining. Once supplied with building materials, equipment, and organisms from Earth, the base will be expected to function indefinitely. One of the members of your team has suggested that everything sent to the base be chemically treated or irradiated so that no bacteria of any kind are present. Do you think this is a good idea? Predict some of the consequences of eliminating all bacteria from an environment.

12. **Interpreting Data** Because bacteria divide by binary fission, the population size doubles every generation. Suppose the generation time for bacteria that cause food poisoning (for example, *Staphylococcus aureus* or *Salmonella*) is 30 minutes at room temperature. The number of cells in a population can be calculated using this formula.

Initial number of cells $\times 2^{(\text{Number of generations})}$ = Population size

For example, if a dish of potato salad is contaminated with 10 bacteria, the bacterial population after 1 hour (2 generations) is $10 \times 2^2 = 40$. Fill in the table below to show how the bacterial population increases when a dish of potato salad is left on the kitchen counter after dinner instead of being refrigerated overnight.

Time (Hours)	Number of Generations	Number of Bacteria
0	0	10
1	2	40
2	4	
3	6	
4	8	
5	10	
6	12	
8	16	
10	20	
12	24	

Why does the rate of increase change over time? Describe how a graph of the data would look.

BIOLOGY AND SOCIETY

13. State or local public health departments regularly inspect restaurants to ensure that safe food-handling procedures are used. In most states, detailed reports are available online. Locate such a report for a restaurant in your area. Mark the items on the checklist that cover hygiene and food handling, and explain how each item prevents potential contamination by pathogenic prokaryotes. Use the same checklist to inspect your own kitchen and evaluate whether corrective measures are needed.

14. Probiotics, foods and supplements that contain living microorganisms, are thought to cure problems of the digestive tract by restoring the natural balance of its microbial community. Sales of these products total billions of dollars a year. Explore the topic of probiotics and evaluate the scientific evidence for their beneficial effects. A good starting point is the website of the U.S. Food and Drug Administration, the agency that regulates advertising claims of health benefits of dietary supplements (www.fda.gov/Food/DietarySupplements/default.htm).

16 The Evolution of Plants and Fungi

Why Plants and Fungi Matter

If you were to hug one of the largest giant sequoia trees, you would need more than a dozen friends to help you reach around its circumference.

If you've ever had mushroom pizza, you've snacked on the fungi's reproductive structure.

Fungi may not always be pretty, but if you find the right one, it could pay your way through college.

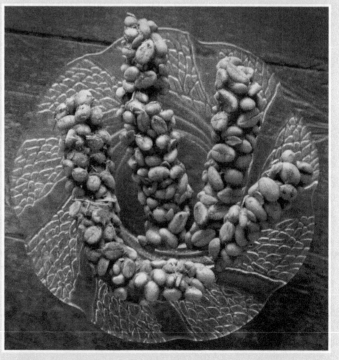

The most expensive coffee in the world has passed through the digestive tract of a catlike animal called a civet.

Plant-Fungus Interactions BIOLOGY AND SOCIETY

The Diamond of the Kitchen

To the untrained eye, a truffle (the fungus, not the chocolate) is an unappealing lump that you probably wouldn't eat on a dare. But despite their unappetizing appearance, truffles are treasured by gourmets as "diamonds of the kitchen." They command prices up to hundreds of dollars per ounce for the best specimens. A 3.3-pound white truffle—an unusually large individual of the rarest variety—brought a record $330,000 at auction. What's the attraction? Rather than their taste, truffles are prized for their powerful scent, which has been described as earthy or moldy. A little truffle goes a long way. Chefs only need to add a few shavings from a truffle to infuse a dish with its delectable essence.

Truffles are the subterranean reproductive bodies of certain fungi. Their job is to produce spores, single cells that are capable of growing into a new fungus, just as a seed can grow into a new plant. It is generally advantageous for seeds or spores to start their lives in a new place, away from the ground inhabited by their parents. And that's where the potent truffle smell comes in. Attracted by the heady aroma, certain animals excavate and eat the fungi and later deposit the hardy spores in their feces. Human noses are not sensitive enough to locate the buried treasures, so truffle hunters use pigs or trained dogs to sniff out their quarry.

Thinly sliced black truffles top a pasta dish. Black truffles, which can be cultivated, are much less expensive than the white variety, which are found only in a small region of Italy.

Besides being culinary gems, truffles represent the essential role of fungi as the hidden power behind the throne of the plant kingdom. The roots of most plants are surrounded—in some cases even permeated—by a finely woven web of fungal filaments. Truffles, for example, have such a relationship with certain species of trees, which is why skilled truffle hunters look for their treasures beneath oak and hazelnut trees. This association is an example of symbiosis, an interaction in which one species lives in or on another species. The ultrathin fungal filaments reach into pockets between the soil grains that are too small for roots to enter, absorbing water and inorganic nutrients and passing them to the plant. The plant returns the favor by supplying the fungus with sugars and other organic molecules. This relationship between fungus and root is evident in some of the oldest plant fossils, suggesting that the mutually beneficial symbiosis was crucial to the colonization of land.

Colonizing Land

What exactly is a plant? A **plant** is a multicellular eukaryote that carries out photosynthesis and has a set of adaptations for living on land. Photosynthesis distinguishes plants from the animal and fungal kingdoms, which are also made up of eukaryotic, multicellular organisms. Large algae, including seaweeds, are also eukaryotic, multicellular, and photosynthetic. However, they lack terrestrial adaptations and thus are classified as protists rather than plants (see Figure 15.27). It is true that some, such as water lilies, have returned to the water, but they evolved from terrestrial ancestors (just as several species of aquatic mammals, such as whales, evolved from terrestrial mammals).

Terrestrial Adaptations of Plants

Why does life on land require a special set of adaptations? Consider how algae fare after being washed up on the

beach. Bodies that were upright in the buoyant water go limp on land and soon shrivel in the drying air. In addition, algae are not equipped to obtain the carbon dioxide needed for photosynthesis from the air. Clearly, living on land poses different problems than living in water. In this section, we discuss some of the terrestrial adaptations that distinguished plants from algae and allowed plants to colonize land. As you will see in later sections, it took more than 100 million years to complete the transition. The earliest land plants lacked some of the adaptations that made subsequent groups more successful in the terrestrial environment.

Adaptations of the Plant Body

For algae, carbon dioxide and minerals are available by diffusion from the surrounding water (Figure 16.1). Resources on land are found in two very different places: Carbon dioxide is mainly available in the air, whereas mineral nutrients and water are found mainly in the soil. Thus, the complex bodies of plants have organs specialized in different ways to function in these two environments. Subterranean organs called **roots** anchor the plant in soil and absorb minerals and water from the soil. Aboveground, **shoots** are organ systems that consist of photosynthetic leaves supported by stems.

Roots typically have many fine branches that thread among the grains of soil, providing a large surface area that maximizes contact with mineral-bearing water in the soil. In addition, as you learned in the Biology and Society section in the beginning of this chapter, most plants have symbiotic fungi associated with their roots. These root-fungus combinations, called **mycorrhizae** ("fungus roots"), enlarge the root's functional surface area (Figure 16.2). For their part, the fungi absorb water and essential minerals from the soil and provide these materials to the plant. The sugars produced by the plant nourish the fungi. Mycorrhizae are key adaptations that made it possible for plants to live on land.

Shoots also show structural adaptations to the terrestrial environment. Leaves are the main photosynthetic organs of most plants. Exchange of carbon dioxide (CO_2) and oxygen (O_2) between the atmosphere and the photosynthetic interior of a leaf occurs via **stomata** (singular, *stoma*), the microscopic pores found on a leaf's surface (see Figure 7.2). A waxy layer called the **cuticle** coats the leaves and other aerial parts of most plants, helping the plant body retain water (see Figure 18.8b).

To transport vital materials between roots and shoots, most plants have **vascular tissue**, a network

▼ Figure 16.1 **Structural adaptations of algae and plants.**

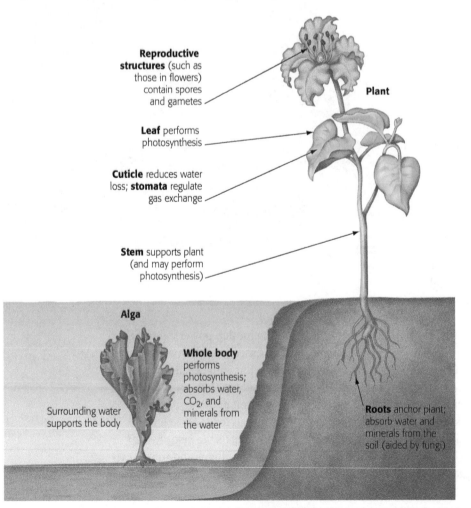

Reproductive structures (such as those in flowers) contain spores and gametes

Leaf performs photosynthesis

Cuticle reduces water loss; **stomata** regulate gas exchange

Stem supports plant (and may perform photosynthesis)

Plant

Alga

Whole body performs photosynthesis; absorbs water, CO_2, and minerals from the water

Surrounding water supports the body

Roots anchor plant; absorb water and minerals from the soil (aided by fungi)

▼ Figure 16.2 **Mycorrhizae: symbiotic associations of fungi and roots.** The finely branched filaments of the fungus (white in the photo) provide an extensive surface area for absorption of water and minerals from the soil.

Roots

Fungus

Root surrounded by fungus

▼ Figure 16.3 **Network of vascular tissue in a leaf.** The vascular tissue is visible as yellow veins on the underside of the leaf in the photograph.

Vascular tissue

Oak leaf

of tube-shaped cells that branch throughout the plant (Figure 16.3). There are two types of vascular tissue. One type is specialized for transporting water and minerals from roots to leaves, and the other distributes sugars from the leaves to the roots and other nonphotosynthetic parts of the plant.

Vascular tissue also solved the problem of structural support on land. The cell walls of many of the cells in vascular tissue are hardened by a chemical called **lignin**. The structural strength of lignified vascular tissue, otherwise known as wood, is amply demonstrated by its use as a building material.

Reproductive Adaptations

Adapting to land also required a new mode of reproduction. For algae, the surrounding water ensures that gametes (sperm and eggs) and developing offspring stay moist. The aquatic environment also provides a means of dispersing the gametes and offspring. Plants, however, must keep their gametes and developing offspring from drying out in the air. Plants produce their gametes in a structure that allows gametes to develop without dehydrating. In addition, the egg remains within tissues of the mother plant and is fertilized there. In plants, but not algae, the zygote (fertilized egg) develops into an embryo while still contained within the female parent, which protects the embryo and keeps it from dehydrating (Figure 16.4). Further adaptations in some plant groups allow sperm to travel via air and improve the survival of offspring during dispersal. ☑

▼ Figure 16.4 **The protected embryo of a plant.** Internal fertilization, with sperm and egg combining within a moist chamber on the female plant, is an adaptation for living on land. The female plant continues to nourish and protect the plant embryo, which develops from the zygote.

LM 55x

Embryo

Maternal tissue

The Origin of Plants from Green Algae

The algal ancestors of plants carpeted moist fringes of lakes or coastal salt marshes more than 500 million years ago. These shallow-water habitats were subject to occasional drying, and natural selection would have favored algae that could survive periodic droughts. Some species accumulated adaptations that enabled them to live permanently above the water line. A modern-day lineage of green algae, the **charophytes** (Figure 16.5), may resemble one of these early plant ancestors. Plants and present-day charophytes probably evolved from a common ancestor.

Adaptations making life on dry land possible had accumulated by about 470 million years ago, the age of the oldest known plant fossils. The evolutionary novelties of these first land plants opened the new frontier of a terrestrial habitat. Early plant life would have thrived in the new environment. Bright sunlight was abundant on land, the atmosphere had a wealth of carbon dioxide, and at first there were relatively few pathogens and plant-eating animals. The stage was set for an explosive diversification of plant life.

▼ Figure 16.5 **Two species of charophytes, the closest algal relatives of plants.**

LM 265x

Plant Diversity

As we survey the diversity of modern plants, remember that the evolutionary past is the key to the present. The history of the plant kingdom is a story of adaptation to diverse terrestrial habitats.

Bacteria
Archaea
Protists
Eukarya **Plants**
Fungi
Animals

Highlights of Plant Evolution

▼ Figure 16.6 **Highlights of plant evolution.** This phylogenetic tree highlights the evolution of structures that allowed plants to move onto land; these structures still exist in modern plants. As we survey the diversity of plants, miniature versions of this tree will help you place each plant group in its evolutionary context.

The fossil record chronicles four major periods of plant evolution, which are also evident in the diversity of modern plants (Figure 16.6). Each stage is marked by the evolution of structures that opened new opportunities on land.

❶ After plants originated from an algal ancestor approximately 470 million years ago, early diversification gave rise to nonvascular plants, including mosses, liverworts, and hornworts. These plants, called **bryophytes**, lack true roots and leaves. Bryophytes also lack lignin, the wall-hardening material that enables other plants to stand tall. Without lignified cell walls, bryophytes have weak upright support. The most familiar bryophytes are **mosses**. A mat of moss actually consists of many plants growing in a tight pack, holding one another up. Structures that protect the gametes and embryos are a terrestrial adaptation that originated in bryophytes.

❷ The second period of plant evolution, begun about 425 million years ago, was the diversification of

Ancestral green algae

❶ Origin of first terrestrial adaptations (about 470 mya)

❷ Origin of vascular tissue (about 425 mya)

❸ Origin of seeds (about 360 mya)

❹ Origin of flowers (about 140 mya)

Charophytes (a group of green algae)

Bryophytes

Ferns and other seedless vascular plants

Gymnosperms

Angiosperms

Nonvascular plants (bryophytes)

Seedless vascular plants

Seed plants

Land plants

Vascular plants

600   500   400   300   200   100   0
Millions of years ago (mya)

plants with vascular tissue. The presence of conducting tissues hardened with lignin allowed vascular plants to grow much taller, rising above the ground to achieve significant height. The earliest vascular plants lacked seeds. Today, this seedless condition is retained by **ferns** and a few other groups of vascular plants.

3 The third major period of plant evolution began with the origin of the seed about 360 million years ago. Seeds advanced the colonization of land by further protecting plant embryos from drying and other hazards. A **seed** consists of an embryo packaged along with a store of food within a protective covering. The seeds of early seed plants were not enclosed in any specialized chambers. These plants gave rise to the **gymnosperms** ("naked seeds"). Today, the most widespread and diverse

gymnosperms are the **conifers**, consisting mainly of cone-bearing trees, such as pines.

4 The fourth major episode in the evolutionary history of plants was the emergence of flowering plants, or **angiosperms** ("contained seeds"), at least 140 million years ago. The **flower** is a complex reproductive structure that bears seeds within protective chambers called ovaries. This contrasts with the naked seeds of gymnosperms. The great majority of living plants—some 250,000 species—are angiosperms, including all our fruit and vegetable crops, grains and other grasses, and most trees.

With these highlights as our framework, we are now ready to survey the four major groups of modern plants: bryophytes, ferns, gymnosperms, and angiosperms **(Figure 16.7).** ☑

☑ **CHECKPOINT**

Name the four major groups of plants. Name an example of each.

Answer: bryophytes (mosses), seedless vascular plants (ferns), gymnosperms (conifers), angiosperms (plants that produce fruits and vegetables)

▼ Figure 16.7 **The major groups of plants.**

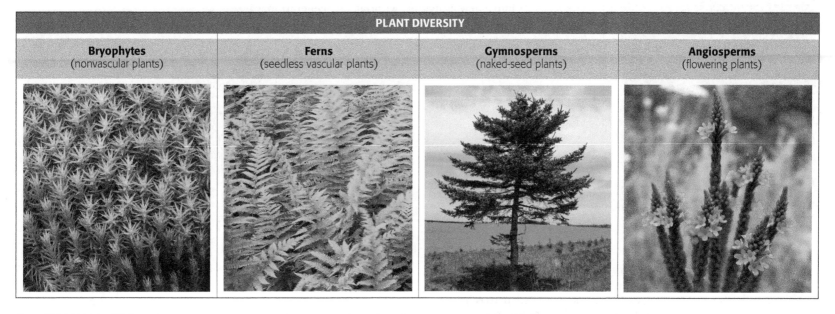

PLANT DIVERSITY			
Bryophytes (nonvascular plants)	**Ferns** (seedless vascular plants)	**Gymnosperms** (naked-seed plants)	**Angiosperms** (flowering plants)

Bryophytes

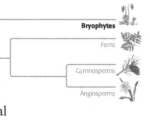

Mosses, which are bryophytes, may sprawl as low mats over acres of land **(Figure 16.8)**. Mosses display two of the key terrestrial adaptations that made the move onto land possible: (1) a waxy cuticle that helps prevent dehydration and (2) the retention of developing embryos within the female plant. However, mosses are not totally liberated from their ancestral aquatic habitat. Mosses need water to reproduce because their sperm need to swim to reach eggs located within the female plant. (A film of rainwater or dew is enough moisture for the sperm to travel.) In addition, because most mosses have no vascular

▼ Figure 16.8 **A peat moss bog in Scotland.** Mosses are bryophytes, which are nonvascular plants. Sphagnum mosses, collectively called peat moss, carpet at least 3% of Earth's land surface. They are most commonly found in high northern latitudes. The ability of peat moss to absorb and retain water makes it an excellent addition to garden soil.

319

tissue to carry water from soil to aerial parts of the plant, they need to live in damp places.

If you examine a mat of moss closely, you can see two distinct forms of the plant. The green, spongelike plant that is the more obvious is called the **gametophyte**. Careful examination will reveal the other form of the moss, called a **sporophyte**, growing out of a gametophyte as a stalk with a capsule at its tip (Figure 16.9). The cells of the gametophyte are haploid—they have one set of chromosomes (see Figure 8.12). In contrast, the sporophyte is made up of diploid cells (with two chromosome sets). These two different stages of the plant life cycle are named for the types of reproductive cells they produce. Gametophytes produce gametes (sperm and eggs), while sporophytes produce spores. A **spore** is a haploid cell that can develop into a new individual without

fusing with another cell (two gametes must fuse to form a zygote). Spores usually have tough coats that enable them to survive in harsh environments. Seedless plants, including mosses and ferns, disperse their offspring as spores rather than as multicellular seeds.

The gametophyte and sporophyte are alternating generations that take turns producing each other. Gametophytes produce gametes that unite to form zygotes, which develop into new sporophytes. And sporophytes produce spores that give rise to new gametophytes. This type of life cycle, called **alternation of generations**, occurs only in plants and multicellular green algae (Figure 16.10). Among plants, mosses and other bryophytes are unique in having the gametophyte as the larger, more obvious plant. As we continue our survey of plants, we'll see an increasing dominance of the sporophyte as the more highly developed generation. ✓

▼ Figure 16.9 **The two forms of a moss.** The feathery plant we generally know as a moss is the gametophyte. The stalk with the capsule at its tip is the sporophyte.

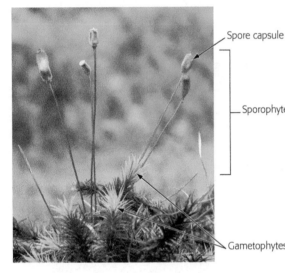

Spore capsule

Sporophytes

Gametophytes

▶ Figure 16.10 **Alternation of generations.** Plants have life cycles very different from ours. Each of us is a diploid individual; the only haploid stages in the human life cycle, as for nearly all animals, are sperm and eggs. By contrast, plants have alternating generations: Diploid (2n) individuals (sporophytes) and haploid (n) individuals (gametophytes) generate each other in the life cycle.

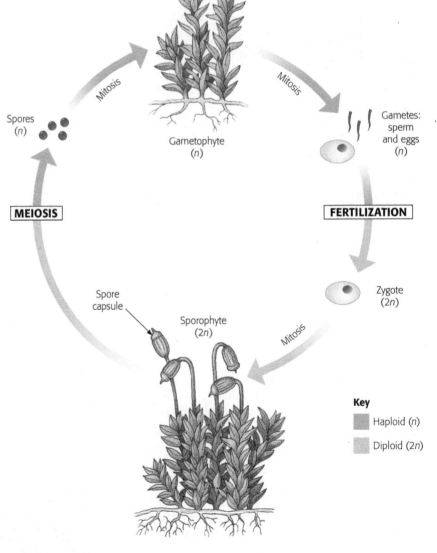

Spores
(n)

Mitosis

Gametophyte
(n)

Mitosis

Gametes: sperm and eggs
(n)

MEIOSIS

FERTILIZATION

Spore capsule

Sporophyte
(2n)

Mitosis

Zygote
(2n)

Key

Haploid (n)

Diploid (2n)

✓ **CHECKPOINT**

Bryophytes, like all plants, have a life cycle that involves an alternation of generations. What are the two generations called? Which generation dominates in bryophytes?

Answer: *gametophyte, sporophyte; gametophyte*

Ferns

The evolution of vascular tissue allowed ferns to colonize a greater variety of habitats than mosses. Ferns are by far the most diverse seedless vascular plants, with more than 12,000 known species. However, the sperm of ferns, like those of mosses, have flagella and must swim through a film of water to fertilize eggs. Most ferns inhabit the tropics, although many species are found in temperate forests, such as many woodlands in the United States (Figure 16.11).

During the Carboniferous period, from about 360 to 300 million years ago, ancient ferns were part of a much greater diversity of seedless plants that formed vast, swampy tropical forests over much of what is now Eurasia and North America (Figure 16.12). As the plants died, they fell into stagnant wetlands and did not decay completely. Their remains formed thick organic deposits. Later, seawater flooded the swamps, marine sediments covered the organic deposits, and pressure and heat gradually converted them to coal. Coal is black sedimentary rock made up of fossilized plant material. Like coal, oil and natural gas also formed from the remains of long-dead organisms; thus, all three are known as **fossil fuels**. Since the Industrial Revolution, coal has been a crucial source of energy for people. However, burning these fossil fuels releases CO_2 and other gases that contribute to global climate change (see Figure 18.46). ☑

▼ Figure 16.11 **Ferns (seedless vascular plants).** The ferns in the foreground are growing on the forest floor in Redwood National Park, California. The fern generation familiar to us is the sporophyte generation. You would have to crawl on the forest floor and explore with careful hands and sharp eyes to find fern gametophytes (upper right), tiny plants growing on or just below the soil surface.

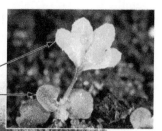

New sporophyte

Gametophyte

Cluster of spore capsules

"Fiddlehead" (young leaf ready to unfurl)

◀ Figure 16.12 **A "coal forest" of the Carboniferous period.** This painting, based on fossil evidence, reconstructs one of the great seedless forests. Most of the large trees belong to ancient groups of seedless vascular plants that are represented by just a few present-day species. The plants near the base of the trees are ferns.

☑ CHECKPOINT

Why are ferns able to grow taller than mosses?

Answer: Vascular tissue hardened with lignin allows ferns to stand taller and transport nutrients farther.

Gymnosperms

"Coal forests" dominated the North American and Eurasian landscapes until near the end of the Carboniferous period. At that time, the global climate turned drier and colder, and the vast swamps began to disappear. This climatic change provided an opportunity for seed plants, which can complete their life cycles on dry land and withstand long, harsh winters. Of the earliest seed plants, the most successful were the gymnosperms, and several kinds grew along with the seedless plants in the Carboniferous swamps. Their descendants include the conifers, or cone-bearing plants.

If you were to hug one of the largest giant sequoia trees, you would need more than a dozen friends to reach around its circumference.

Conifers

Perhaps you have had the fun of hiking or skiing through a forest of conifers, the most common gymnosperms. Pines, firs, spruces, junipers, cedars, and redwoods are all conifers. A broad band of coniferous forests covers much of northern Eurasia and North America and extends southward in mountainous regions (Figure 16.13). Today, about 190 million acres of coniferous forests in the United States are designated national forests.

Conifers are among the tallest, largest, and oldest organisms on Earth. Coastal redwoods, native to the northern California coast, are the world's tallest trees—up to 110 m, the height of a 33-story building. Giant sequoias, relatives of redwoods that grow in the Sierra Nevada mountains of California, are massive. One, known as the General Sherman tree, is about 84 m (275 feet) high and outweighs the combined weight of a dozen space shuttles. Bristlecone pines, another species of California conifer, are among the oldest organisms alive. A specimen discovered in 2012 is more than 5,000 years old; it was a seedling when people invented writing.

Nearly all conifers are evergreens, meaning they retain leaves throughout the year. Even during winter, they perform a limited amount of photosynthesis on sunny days. And when spring comes, conifers already have fully developed leaves that can take advantage of the sunnier days. The needle-shaped leaves of pines and firs are also adapted to survive dry seasons. A thick cuticle covers the leaf, and the stomata are located in pits, further reducing water loss.

Coniferous forests are highly productive; you probably use products harvested from them every day. For example, conifers provide much of our lumber for building and wood pulp for paper production. What we call wood is actually an accumulation of vascular tissue with lignin, which gives the tree structural support.

Evolution   Terrestrial Adaptations of Seed Plants

Compared with ferns, most gymnosperms have three additional adaptations that make survival in diverse terrestrial habitats possible: (1) further reduction of the gametophyte, (2) pollen, and (3) seeds.

The first adaptation is an even greater development of the diploid sporophyte compared with the haploid gametophyte generation (Figure 16.14). A pine tree or

▼ Figure 16.13 **A coniferous forest in Tetlin National Wildlife Refuge, Alaska.** Coniferous forests are widespread in northern North America and Eurasia; conifers also grow in the Southern Hemisphere, though they are less numerous there.

► Figure 16.14 **Three variations on alternation of generations in plants.**

Key
Haploid (*n*)
Diploid (2*n*)

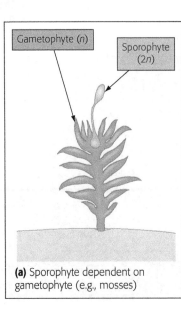

(a) Sporophyte dependent on gametophyte (e.g., mosses)

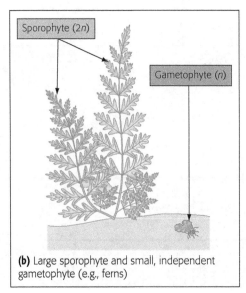

(b) Large sporophyte and small, independent gametophyte (e.g., ferns)

(c) Reduced gametophyte dependent on sporophyte (seed plants) other conifer is a sporophyte with tiny gametophytes living in its cones (Figure 16.15). In contrast to what is seen in bryophytes and ferns, gymnosperm gametophytes are totally dependent on and protected by the tissues of the parent sporophyte.

A second adaptation of seed plants to dry land came with the evolution of pollen. A **pollen grain** is actually the much-reduced male gametophyte; it houses cells that will develop into sperm. In the case of conifers, **pollination**, the delivery of pollen from the male parts of a plant to the female parts of a plant, occurs via wind. This mechanism for sperm transfer contrasts with the swimming sperm of mosses and ferns. In seed plants, the use of tough, airborne pollen that carries sperm to egg is a terrestrial adaptation that led to even greater success and diversity of plants on land.

The third important terrestrial adaptation of seed plants is the seed itself. A seed consists of a plant embryo packaged along with a food supply within a protective coat. Seeds develop from **ovules**, structures that contain the female gametophytes (Figure 16.16). In conifers, the ovules are located on the scales of

▼ Figure 16.15 **A pine tree, the sporophyte, bearing two types of cones containing gametophytes.** Each scale of the female cone is actually a modified leaf that bears a structure called an ovule containing a female gametophyte. Male cones release clouds of millions of pollen grains, the male gametophytes. Some of these pollen grains land on female cones on trees of the same species. The sperm can fertilize eggs in the ovules of the female cones. The ovules eventually develop into seeds.

Scale

Ovule-producing cones; the scales contain female gametophytes

Pollen-producing cones; they produce male gametophytes

Ponderosa pine

female cones. Once released from the parent plant, the seed can remain dormant for days, months, or even years. Under favorable conditions, the seed can then **germinate**, or sprout: Its embryo emerges through the seed coat as a seedling. Some seeds drop close to their parents, while others are carried far by the wind or animals. ☑

▼ Figure 16.16 **From ovule to seed.**

Female cone, cross section

Cross section of scale

Key

Haploid (*n*)

Diploid (*2n*)

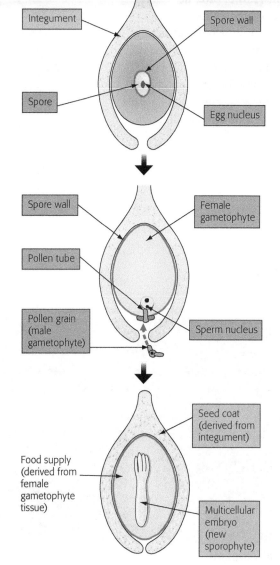

Integument

Spore wall

Spore

Egg nucleus

(a) Ovule. The sporophyte produces spores within a tissue surrounded by a protective integument, which may be multilayered. The spore develops into a female gametophyte, which produces an egg nucleus.

Spore wall

Female gametophyte

Pollen tube

Pollen grain (male gametophyte)

Sperm nucleus

(b) Fertilized ovule. After pollination, the pollen grain grows a tiny tube that enters the ovule, where it releases a sperm nucleus that fertilizes the egg.

Seed coat (derived from integument)

Food supply (derived from female gametophyte tissue)

Multicellular embryo (new sporophyte)

(c) Seed. Fertilization triggers the transformation of ovule to seed. The fertilized egg (zygote) develops into a multicellular embryo; the rest of the gametophyte forms a tissue that stockpiles food; and the integument of the ovule hardens to become the seed coat.

Angiosperms

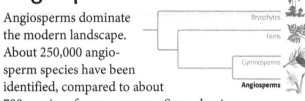

Angiosperms dominate the modern landscape. About 250,000 angiosperm species have been identified, compared to about 700 species of gymnosperms. Several unique adaptations account for the success of angiosperms. For example, refinements in vascular tissue make water transport even more efficient in angiosperms than in gymnosperms. Of all terrestrial adaptations, however, it is the flower that accounts for the unparalleled success of the angiosperms.

Flowers, Fruits, and the Angiosperm Life Cycle

No organism makes a showier display of its sex life than the angiosperm. From roses to dandelions, flowers are the site of procreation. This showiness helps to attract go-betweens—insects and other animals—that transfer pollen from one flower to another of the same species. Angiosperms that rely on wind pollination, including grasses and many trees, have much smaller, less flamboyant flowers. In those species, the plant's reproductive energy is allocated to making massive amounts of pollen for release into the wind.

A flower is a short stem bearing modified leaves that are attached in concentric circles at its base (Figure 16.17). The outer layer consists of the **sepals**, which are usually green. They enclose the flower before it opens (think of the green "wrapping" on a rosebud). When the sepals are peeled away, the next layer is the **petals**, which are often colorful—these are the showy structures that attract pollinators. Plucking off the petals reveals the **stamens**, the male reproductive structures. Pollen grains develop in the **anther**, a sac at the top of each stamen. At the center of the flower is the **carpel**, the female reproductive structure. It includes the **ovary**, a protective chamber containing one or more ovules, in which eggs develop. The sticky tip of the carpel, called the **stigma**, traps pollen. As you can see in Figure 16.18, the basic structure of a flower can exist in many beautiful variations.

◀ Figure 16.17 **Structure of a flower.**

▼ Figure 16.18 **A diversity of flowers.**

Prickly pear cactus

Bleeding heart

California poppy

Summer snapdragon

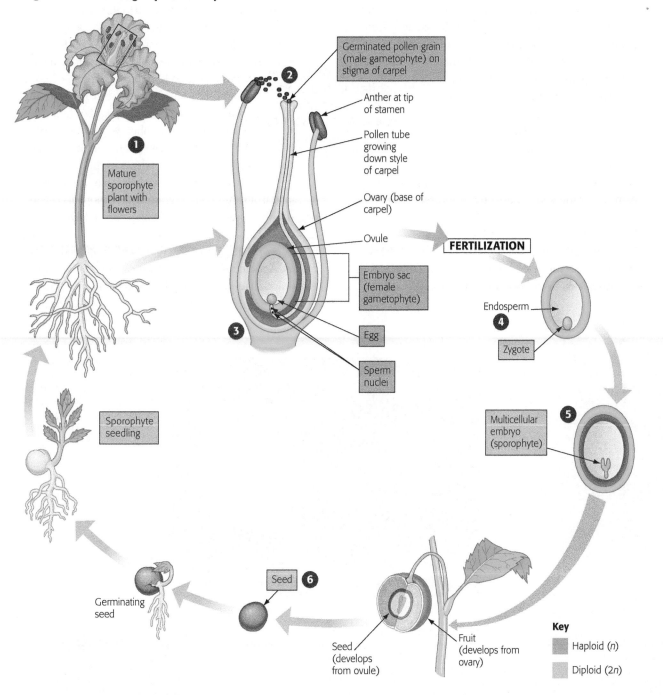

▼ Figure 16.19 **The angiosperm life cycle.**

In angiosperms, as in gymnosperms, the sporophyte generation is dominant and produces the gametophyte generation within its body. **Figure 16.19** highlights key stages in the angiosperm life cycle. ❶ The flower is part of the sporophyte plant. As in gymnosperms, the pollen grain is the male gametophyte of angiosperms. The female gametophyte is located within an ovule, which in turn resides within a chamber of the ovary. ❷ After a pollen grain lands on the stigma, a pollen tube grows down to the ovule and ❸ releases a sperm nucleus that fertilizes an egg within the embryo sac. ❹ This produces a zygote, which ❺ develops into an embryo. The tissue surrounding the embryo develops into nutrient-rich **endosperm**, which will provide a food supply for the growing plant. ❻ The whole ovule develops into a seed, which can germinate and develop into a new sporophyte to begin the cycle anew. The seed's enclosure within an ovary is what distinguishes angiosperms (from the Greek *angion*, container, and *sperm*, seed) from gymnosperms (from the Greek *gymnos*, naked), which have a naked seed.

▼ Figure 16.20 **Fruits and
seed dispersal.** Different
types of fruits are adapted
for different methods of
dispersal.

A **fruit** is the ripened ovary of a flower. Thus, fruits are produced only by angiosperms. As seeds are developing from ovules, the ovary wall thickens, forming the fruit that encloses the seeds. A pea pod is an example of a fruit with seeds (mature ovules, the peas) encased in the ripened ovary (the pod). Fruits protect and help disperse seeds. As Figure 16.20 demonstrates, many angiosperms depend on animals to disperse seeds, often passing them through the digestive tract. Conversely, most land animals, including humans, rely on angiosperms as a food source, directly or indirectly. ☑

The most expensive coffee in the world has passed through the digestive tract of a catlike animal called a civet.

Angiosperms and Agriculture

Whereas gymnosperms supply most of our lumber and paper, angiosperms supply nearly all of our food—as well as the food eaten by domesticated animals, such as cows and chickens. More than 90% of the plant kingdom is made up of angiosperms, including cereal grains such as wheat and corn, citrus and other fruit trees, coffee and tea, and cotton. Many types of garden produce—tomatoes, squash, strawberries, and oranges, to name just a few—are the edible fruits of plants we have domesticated. Fine hardwoods from flowering plants such as oak, cherry, and walnut trees supplement the lumber we get from conifers. We also grow angiosperms for fiber, medications, perfumes, and decoration.

Early humans probably collected wild seeds and fruits. Agriculture gradually developed as people began sowing seeds and cultivating plants to have a more dependable food source. And as they domesticated certain plants, people began to select those with improved yield and quality. Agriculture can thus be seen as yet another facet of the evolutionary relationship between plants and animals.

Animal transportation.
Some fruits are adapted to hitch free rides on animals. The cockleburs attached to the fur of this dog may be carried miles before opening and releasing seeds.

Animal ingestion. Many angiosperms produce fleshy, edible fruits that are attractive to animals as food. The animal digests the fleshy part of the fruit, but most of the tough seeds pass unharmed through the digestive tract. The seeds are later deposited, along with a fertilizer supply, some distance from where the fruit was eaten. The Asian palm civet shown here is eating coffee berries. The civet's digestive enzymes reportedly give the seeds (coffee beans) an exquisite flavor. Coffee beans "processed" in this way, known as kopi luwak, cost up to $500 per pound.

Wind dispersal. Some angiosperms depend on wind for seed dispersal. Here, milkweed pods open to release masses of seeds (brown) carried by silken parachutes (part of the seed coat).

Plant Diversity as a Nonrenewable Resource

The ever-increasing human population, with its demand for space and natural resources, is extinguishing plant species at an unprecedented rate. The problem is especially critical for forest ecosystems, which are home to as many as 80% of the world's plant and animal species. Deforestation has been an ongoing human activity for centuries. Worldwide, less than 25% of the original forests remain; the figure in the contiguous United States is around 10%. Typically, forests are cut down to harvest timber or to clear land for housing or large-scale agriculture (Figure 16.21). Much of the forest that remains is tropical, and it is disappearing at an estimated 150,000 km^2 per year (about 58,000 mi^2), which is roughly equal to the area of Illinois. Government policies in Brazil have produced a marked slowdown in Amazonian deforestation. Nevertheless, the global rate of tropical deforestation has increased by 2,101 km^2 (more than 800 mi^2) per year over the past decade.

Why does the loss of tropical forests matter? In addition to forests being centers of biodiversity, millions of people worldwide depend on these forests for their livelihood. There are other practical reasons to be concerned about the loss of plant diversity represented in tropical forests. More than 120 prescription drugs are made from substances derived from plants (Table 16.1). Pharmaceutical companies were led to most of these species by local peoples who use the plants in preparing their traditional medicines. Today, researchers are seeking to combine their scientific skills with the stores of local knowledge in partnerships that will develop new drugs and also benefit the local economies.

Scientists are working to slow the loss of plant diversity, in part by researching sustainable ways for people to benefit from forests. The goal of such efforts is to encourage management practices that use forests as resources without damaging them. The solutions we propose must be economically realistic; people who live where there are tropical rain forests must be able to make a living. But if the only goal is profit for the short term, then the destruction will continue until the forests are gone. We need to appreciate the rain forests and other ecosystems as living treasures that can regenerate only slowly. Only then will we learn to work with them in ways that preserve their biological diversity for the future.

Throughout our survey of plants in this chapter, we have seen how entangled the botanical world is with other terrestrial life. We switch our attention now to that other group of organisms that moved onto land with plants: the kingdom Fungi. ✓

✓ CHECKPOINT

In what way are forests renewable resources? In what way are they not?

Answer: Forests are renewable in the sense that new trees can grow where old growth has been removed by logging. Habitats that are permanently destroyed cannot be replaced, however, so forests must be harvested in a sustainable manner.

▼ Figure 16.21 **Cultivated land bordering a tropical forest in Uganda.**
Bwindi Impenetrable National Park (on the right) is renowned for its biodiversity, which includes half the world's remaining mountain gorillas.

Table 16.1	A Sampling of Medicines Derived from Plants		
Compound	**Source**		**Example of Use**
Atropine	Belladonna plant		Pupil dilator in eye exams
Digitalin	Foxglove		Heart medication
Menthol	Wild mint		Ingredient in cough medicines, decongestants
Morphine	Opium poppy		Pain reliever
Quinine	Quinine tree		Malaria preventive
Paclitaxel (Taxol)	Pacific yew		Ovarian cancer drug
Tubocurarine	Curare tree		Muscle relaxant during surgery
Vinblastine	Periwinkle		Leukemia drug

Source: Adapted from Randy Moore et al., Botany, 2nd ed. Dubuque, IA: Brown, 1998, Table 2.2, p. 37.

Fungi

The word *fungus* often evokes unpleasant images. Fungi rot timbers, spoil food, and afflict people with athlete's foot and worse.

However, ecosystems would collapse without fungi to decompose dead organisms, fallen leaves, feces, and other organic materials. Fungi recycle vital chemical elements back to the environment in forms that other organisms can assimilate. And you have already learned that nearly all plants have mycorrhizae, fungus-root associations that help plants absorb minerals and water from the soil. In addition to these ecological roles, fungi have been used by people in various ways for centuries. We eat fungi (mushrooms and extremely expensive truffles, for instance), culture fungi to produce antibiotics and other drugs, add them to dough to make bread rise, culture them in milk to produce a variety of cheeses, and use them to ferment beer and wine.

Fungi may not always be pretty, but if you find the right one, it could pay your way through college.

Fungi are eukaryotes, and most are multicellular, but many have body structures and modes of reproduction unlike those of any other organism (Figure 16.22). Molecular studies indicate that fungi and animals arose from a common ancestor around 1.5 billion years ago. The oldest undisputed fossils of fungi, however, are only about 460 million years old, perhaps because the ancestors of terrestrial fungi were microscopic and fossilized poorly. Despite appearances, a mushroom is more closely related to you than it is to any plant!

Biologists who study fungi have described more than 100,000 species, but there may be as many as 1.5 million. Classifying fungi is an ongoing area of research. (One widely accepted phylogenetic tree divides the kingdom Fungi into five groups.) You are probably familiar with several kinds of fungi, including mushrooms, mold, and yeast. In this section, we'll discuss the characteristics common to all fungi and then survey their wide-ranging ecological impact. ☑

☑ **CHECKPOINT**

Name three ways that we benefit from fungi in our environment.

Answer: Fungi help recycle nutrients by decomposing dead organisms; mycorrhizae help plants absorb water and nutrients; some fungi serve us as food.

▼ Figure 16.22 **A gallery of diverse fungi.**

Bracket fungi. These are the reproductive structures of a fungus that absorbs nutrients as it decomposes a fallen tree on a forest floor. The green "leafy" material is lichens, which are described in the Evolution Connection section in this chapter.

A "fairy ring." Some mushroom-producing fungi poke up "fairy rings," which can appear on a lawn overnight. A ring develops at the edge of the main body of the fungus, which consists of an underground mass of tiny filaments (hyphae) within the ring. As the underground fungal mass grows outward from its center, the diameter of the fairy ring produced at its expanding perimeter increases annually.

Colonized SEM 2,800x

Mold. Molds grow rapidly on their food sources, which are often our food sources as well. The mold on this orange reproduces asexually by producing chains of microscopic spores (inset) that are dispersed via air currents.

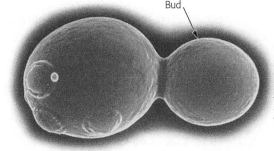

Colonized SEM 6,400x

Bud

Budding yeast. Yeasts are unicellular fungi. This yeast cell is reproducing asexually by a process called budding.

Corn smut. This parasitic fungus plagues corn growers. To gourmets, however, it is a delicacy known as *huitlacoche*.

Structure/Function Characteristics of Fungi

We'll begin our look at the structure and function of fungi with an overview of how fungi obtain nutrients.

Fungal Nutrition

Fungi are heterotrophs that acquire their nutrients by **absorption**. In this mode of nutrition, small organic molecules are absorbed from the surrounding medium. A fungus digests food outside its body by secreting powerful digestive enzymes into the food. The enzymes decompose complex molecules to simpler compounds that the fungus can absorb. Fungi absorb nutrients from such nonliving organic material as fallen logs, animal corpses, and the wastes of live organisms.

Fungal Structure

The bodies of most fungi are constructed of threadlike filaments called **hyphae** (singular, *hypha*). Fungal hyphae are minute threads of cytoplasm surrounded by a plasma membrane and cell wall. The cell walls of fungi differ from the cellulose walls of plants. Fungal cell walls are usually built mainly of chitin, a strong but flexible polysaccharide that is also found in the external skeletons of insects. Most fungi have multicellular hyphae, which consist of chains of cells separated by cross-walls with pores. In many fungi, cell-to-cell channels allow ribosomes, mitochondria, and even nuclei to flow between cells.

Fungal hyphae branch repeatedly, forming an interwoven network called a **mycelium** (plural, *mycelia*), the feeding structure of the fungus (Figure 16.23). Fungal mycelia usually escape our notice because they are often subterranean, but they can be huge. In fact, scientists have discovered that the mycelium of one humongous fungus in Oregon is 5.5 km—that's 3.4 miles!—in diameter and spreads through 2,200 acres of forest. This fungus is at least 2,600 years old and weighs hundreds of tons, qualifying it as one of Earth's oldest and largest organisms.

A mycelium maximizes contact with its food source by mingling with the organic matter it is decomposing and absorbing. A bucketful of rich organic soil may contain as much as a kilometer of hyphae. A fungal mycelium grows rapidly, adding hyphae as it branches within its food. The great majority of fungi are nonmotile; they cannot run, swim, or fly in search of food. But the mycelium makes up for the lack of mobility by swiftly extending the tips of its hyphae into new territory. ☑

Fungal Reproduction

The mushroom in Figure 16.23 is actually made up of tightly packed hyphae. Mushrooms arise from an underground mycelium. While the mycelium obtains food from organic material via absorption, the function of the mushroom is reproduction. Unlike a truffle, which relies on animals to disperse its spores, a mushroom pops up above ground to disperse its spores on air currents.

Fungi typically reproduce by releasing haploid spores that are produced either sexually or asexually. The output of spores is mind-boggling. For example, puffballs, which are the reproductive structures of certain fungi, can spew clouds containing trillions of spores. Easily carried by wind or water, spores germinate to produce mycelia if they land in a moist place where there is food. Spores thus function in dispersal and account for the wide geographic distribution of many species of fungi. The airborne spores of fungi have been found more than 160 km (100 miles) above Earth. Closer to home, try leaving a slice of bread out for a week and you will observe the furry mycelia that grow from the invisible spores raining down from the surrounding air.

If you've ever had mushroom pizza, you've snacked on the fungi's reproductive structure.

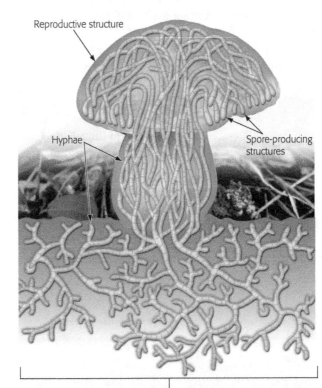

Reproductive structure

Hyphae

Spore-producing structures

Mycelium

◄ Figure 16.23 **The fungal mycelium.** A mushroom consists of tightly packed hyphae that extend upward from a much more massive mycelium of hyphae growing underground. The photo at the bottom shows a mycelium made up of the cottony threads that decompose organic litter.

☑ CHECKPOINT

Describe how the structure of a fungal mycelium reflects its function.

Answer: The extensive network of hyphae puts a large surface area in contact with the food source.

The Ecological Impact of Fungi

Fungi have been major players in terrestrial communities ever since plants and fungi together moved onto land. Let's examine a few examples of how fungi continue to have an enormous ecological impact, including numerous interactions with people.

Fungi as Decomposers

Fungi and bacteria are the principal decomposers that keep ecosystems stocked with the inorganic nutrients essential for plant growth. Without decomposers, carbon, nitrogen, and other elements would accumulate in nonliving organic matter. Plants and the animals they feed would starve because elements taken from the soil would not be returned.

Fungi are well adapted as decomposers of organic refuse. Their invasive hyphae enter the tissues and cells of dead organisms and digest polymers, including the cellulose of plant cell walls. A succession of fungi, in concert with bacteria and, in some environments, invertebrate animals, is responsible for the complete breakdown of organic litter. The air is so loaded with fungal spores that as soon as a leaf falls or an insect dies, it is covered with spores and soon after infiltrated by fungal hyphae.

We may applaud fungi that decompose forest litter or dung, but it's a different story when molds attack our food or our shower curtains. A significant amount of the world's fruit harvest is lost each year to fungal attack. And a wood-digesting fungus does not distinguish between a fallen oak limb and the oak planks of a boat. During the Revolutionary War, the British lost more ships to fungal rot than to enemy attack. What's more, soldiers stationed in the tropics during World War II watched as their tents, clothing, and boots were destroyed by molds.

Parasitic Fungi

Parasitism is a relationship in which two species live in contact and one organism benefits while the other is harmed. Parasitic fungi absorb nutrients from the cells or body fluids of living hosts. Of the 100,000 known species of fungi, about 30% make their living as parasites.

About 500 species of fungi are known to be parasitic in humans and other animals. A baffling disease known as coccidioidomycosis, or valley fever, causes devastating illness in some people; others suffer only mild flu-like symptoms. People contract the disease when they inhale the spores of a fungus that lives in the soil of the southwestern United States. In recent years, researchers have noticed an uptick in reported cases of valley fever, perhaps due to changes in climate patterns or development of once-rural areas inhabited by the fungus. Less serious fungal diseases include vaginal yeast infections and ringworm, so named because it appears as circular red areas on the skin. The ringworm fungus can infect almost any skin surface, where it produces intense itching and sometimes blisters. One species attacks the feet, causing athlete's foot. Another species is responsible for the misery known as jock itch.

The great majority of fungal parasites infect plants. American chestnut and American elm trees, once common in forests, fields, and city streets, were devastated by fungal epidemics in the 20th century (Figure 16.24a). Fungi are also serious agricultural pests, and some of the fungi that attack food crops are toxic to humans. The seed heads of many kinds of grain and grasses, including rye, wheat, and oats, are sometimes infected with fungal growths called ergots (Figure 16.24b). Consumption of flour made from ergot-infested grain can cause hallucinations, temporary insanity, and death. In fact, lysergic acid, the raw material from which the hallucinogenic drug LSD is made, has been isolated from ergots. This fact may help explain a centuries-old mystery, as we'll see next.

(a) An American elm tree killed by Dutch elm disease fungus

(b) Ergots on rye

Ergots

◄ Figure 16.24 **Parasitic fungi that cause plant disease.**
(a) The parasitic fungus that causes Dutch elm disease evolved with European species of elm trees, and it is relatively harmless to them. But it has been deadly to American elms since it was accidentally introduced in 1926. (b) Ergots, parasitic fungi, are the dark structures on these rye seed heads.

Plant-Fungus Interactions THE PROCESS OF SCIENCE

Did a Fungus Lead to the Salem Witch Hunt?

In January 1692, eight young girls in the town of Salem, Massachusetts, began to act bizarrely. The girls suffered from incomprehensible speech, odd skin sensations, convulsions, and hallucinations. The worried community blamed the girls' symptoms on witchcraft and began to accuse one another. By the time the hysteria ended that autumn, more than 150 villagers had been accused of witchcraft, and 20 of them had been hanged as a result. Finding the cause behind the "Salem witch hunt" has long intrigued historians.

In 1976, a University of California psychology graduate student offered a new explanation. She began with the **observation** that the symptoms reported by the girls were consistent with ergot poisoning (Figure 16.25). This led her to **question** whether an ergot outbreak could have been behind the witch hunt. The researcher tested her **hypothesis** by examining the historical records, making the **prediction** that facts consistent with ergot poisoning would be uncovered.

Her **results** were suggestive, though not conclusive. Agricultural records confirm that rye—the principal host for ergot—grew abundantly around Salem at that time and that the growing season of 1691 had been particularly warm and wet, conditions under which ergot thrives. This suggests that the rye crop consumed during the winter of 1691–1692 could easily have been contaminated. The summer of 1692, when the accusations began to die down, was dry, consistent with an ergot die-off. Most important, the reported symptoms appear consistent with those of ergot poisoning. These clues suggest (but do not prove) that the girls, and perhaps others in Salem, were in the grips of ergot-induced illness. Some historians dispute this idea, and other hypotheses have been proposed. Conclusive evidence may never be found, but this story reinforces the unifying thread of this chapter—the importance of the interaction of plants and fungi—and illustrates how the scientific method can be applied in a wide variety of academic disciplines.

▼ Figure 16.25 **Ergot and the Salem witch hunt.** Ergot poisoning may have been the catalyst for the Salem witch hunt of 1692.

Commercial Uses of Fungi

It would not be fair to fungi to end our discussion with an account of diseases. In addition to their positive global impact as decomposers, fungi also have a number of practical uses for people.

Most of us have eaten mushrooms, although we may not have realized that we were ingesting the reproductive extensions of subterranean fungi. Your grocery store probably stocks Portobello, shiitake, and oyster mushrooms along with common button mushrooms. If you like to cook with mushrooms, you can buy a mushroom "garden"—mycelium embedded in a rich food source—that makes it easy to grow your own. Some enthusiasts gather edible fungi from fields and forests (Figure 16.26), but only experts should dare to eat wild fungi. Some poisonous species resemble edible ones, and there are no simple rules to help the novice distinguish one from the other.

Other fungi are used in food production. The distinctive flavors of certain kinds of cheeses, including Roquefort and blue cheese, come from the fungi used to ripen them. And people have used yeasts (unicellular fungi) for thousands of years to produce alcoholic beverages and cause bread to rise (see Figure 6.15).

▼ Figure 16.26 **Fungi eaten by people.**

Chicken of the woods. This fleshy shelf fungus is said to taste like chicken.

Chanterelle mushrooms. Gourmet mushrooms are highly prized by chefs for their earthy flavors and interesting textures.

Giant puffball. These humongous fungi can grow to more than 2 feet in diameter. They are only edible when immature, before the spores form. Beware: Deadly fungi often resemble small puffballs.

Fungi are medically valuable as well. Some fungi produce antibiotics that are used to treat bacterial diseases. In fact, the first antibiotic discovered was penicillin, made by the common mold *Penicillium* (Figure 16.27). Researchers are also investigating fungal products that show potential as anticancer drugs.

As sources of medicines and food, as decomposers, and as partners with plants in mycorrhizae, fungi play vital roles in life on Earth. ☑

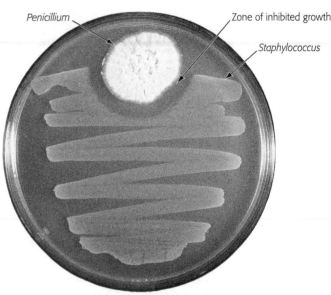

Penicillium   Zone of inhibited growth

Staphylococcus

▶ Figure 16.27 **Fungal production of an antibiotic.** Penicillin is made by the common mold *Penicillium*. In this petri dish, the clear area between the mold and the growing *Staphylococcus* bacteria is where the antibiotic produced by the *Penicillium* inhibits the growth of the bacteria.

Plant-Fungus Interactions EVOLUTION CONNECTION

A Mutually Beneficial Symbiosis

Discussing fungi in the same chapter as plants may seem to indicate that these two kingdoms are close relatives, but as we've discussed, fungi are more closely related to animals than to plants. However, the success of plants on land and the great diversity of fungi are interconnected; neither could have populated the land without the other.

Evolution is not just about the origin and adaptation of individual species. Relationships between species are also an evolutionary product. For example, prokaryotes and protists partner with a variety of organisms in mutually beneficial symbioses (see Figures 15.12 and 15.13). Bacteria living in the roots of certain plants provide nitrogen compounds to their host and receive food in exchange. We even have our own symbiotic bacteria that help keep our skin healthy and produce certain vitamins in our intestines. Particularly relevant to this chapter is the symbiotic association of fungi and plant roots—mycorrhizae—that made life's move onto land possible.

Lichens, symbiotic associations of unicellular algae or photosynthetic bacteria held in a mass of fungal hyphae, are striking examples of how intimate these relationships can be. At a distance, it is easy to mistake lichens for mosses or other simple plants growing on rocks, rotting logs, or trees (Figure 16.28). The partners are so closely entwined that they appear to be a single organism. The fungus receives food from its photosynthetic partner. The fungal mycelium, in turn, provides a suitable habitat for the algae, helping the algae absorb and retain water and minerals. The merger is so complete that lichens are actually named as species, as though they were individual organisms.

After protists and plants, fungi is the third group of eukaryotes that we have surveyed so far. Strong evidence suggests that they evolved from protist ancestors that also gave rise to the fourth and most diverse group of eukaryotes: the animals, the topic of the next chapter.

▼ Figure 16.28 **Lichens: symbiotic associations of fungi and algae.** Lichens generally grow very slowly, sometimes less than a millimeter per year. Some lichens are thousands of years old, rivaling the oldest plants as Earth's elders. The close relationship between the fungal and algal partners is evident in the microscopic blowup of a lichen.

Algal cell

Fungal hyphae

Colorized SEM 1,000x

Chapter Review

SUMMARY OF KEY CONCEPTS

Colonizing Land

Terrestrial Adaptations of Plants

Plants are multicellular photosynthetic eukaryotes with adaptations for living on land.

Leaves are the main photosynthetic organs

Stomata regulate gas exchange between plant and atmosphere

Cuticle reduces water loss

Lignin hardens cell walls

Stem supports plant; may perform photosynthesis

Vascular tissues transport water, minerals, and sugars; provide support

Roots anchor plant; mycorrhizae (root-fungus associations) help absorb water and minerals from the soil

The Origin of Plants from Green Algae

Plants evolved from a group of multicellular green algae called charophytes.

Plant Diversity

Highlights of Plant Evolution

Four periods of plant evolution are marked by terrestrial adaptations in major plant groups.

| **Bryophytes** have structures that protect gametes and embryos. | **Ferns** have vascular tissue that conducts water and nutrients. | **Gymnosperms** have seeds that protect embryos from dessication. | **Angiosperms** have ovaries that protect ovules and disperse seeds. |

Bryophytes

 The most familiar bryophytes are mosses. Mosses display two key terrestrial adaptations: a waxy cuticle that prevents dehydration and the retention of developing embryos within the female plant's body. Mosses are most common in moist environments because their sperm must swim to the eggs and because they lack lignin in their cell walls and thus cannot stand tall. Bryophytes are unique among plants in having the gametophyte as the dominant generation in the life cycle.

Ferns

 Ferns are seedless plants that have vascular tissues but still use flagellated sperm to fertilize eggs. During the Carboniferous period, giant ferns were among the plants that decayed to thick deposits of organic matter, which were gradually converted to coal.

Gymnosperms

 A drier and colder global climate near the end of the Carboniferous period favored the evolution of the first seed plants. The most successful were the gymnosperms, represented by conifers. Needle-shaped leaves with thick cuticles and sunken stomata are adaptations to dry conditions. Conifers and most other gymnosperms have three additional terrestrial adaptations: (1) further reduction of the haploid gametophyte and greater development of the diploid sporophyte; (2) sperm-bearing pollen, which doesn't require water for transport; and (3) seeds, which consist of a plant embryo packaged along with a food supply inside a protective coat.

Angiosperms

 Angiosperms supply nearly all our food and much of our fiber for textiles. The evolution of the flower and more efficient water transport help account for the success of the angiosperms. The dominant stage is a sporophyte with gametophytes in its flowers. The female gametophyte is located within an ovule, which in turn resides within a chamber of the ovary. Fertilization of an egg in the female gametophyte produces a zygote, which develops into an embryo. The whole ovule develops into a seed. The seed's enclosure within an ovary is what distinguishes angiosperms from gymnosperms, which have naked seeds. A fruit is the ripened ovary of a flower. Fruits protect and help disperse seeds. Angiosperms are a major food source for animals, while animals aid plants in pollination and seed dispersal. Agriculture constitutes a unique kind of evolutionary relationship among plants, people, and other animals.

Plant Diversity as a Nonrenewable Resource

Deforestation to meet the demand of human activities for space and natural resources is causing the extinction of plant species at an unprecedented rate. The problem is especially critical for tropical forests.

Fungi

Characteristics of Fungi

Fungi are unicellular or multicellular eukaryotes; they are heterotrophs that digest their food externally and absorb the nutrients from the environment. They are more closely related to animals than to plants. A fungus usually consists of a mass of threadlike hyphae, forming a mycelium. The cell walls of fungi are mainly composed of chitin. Although most fungi are nonmotile, a mycelium can grow very quickly, extending the tips of its hyphae into new territory. Mushrooms are reproductive structures that extend from the underground mycelium. Fungi reproduce and disperse by releasing spores that are produced either sexually or asexually.

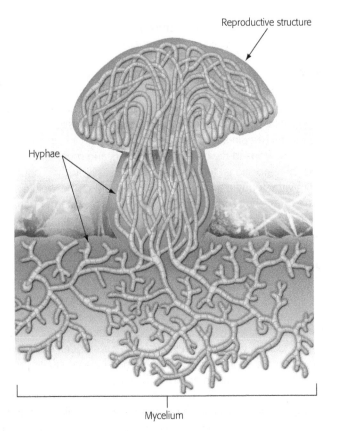

Reproductive structure

Hyphae

Mycelium

The Ecological Impact of Fungi

Fungi and bacteria are the principal decomposers of ecosystems. Many molds destroy fruit, wood, and human-made materials. About 500 species of fungi are known to be parasites of people and other animals. Fungi are also commercially important as food and in baking, beer and wine production, and the manufacture of antibiotics.

MasteringBiology®

For practice quizzes, BioFlix animations, MP3 tutorials, video tutors, and more study tools designed for this textbook, go to MasteringBiology®

1. Which of the following structures is common to all four major plant groups? vascular tissue, flowers, seeds, cuticle, pollen

2. Angiosperms are distinguished from all other plants because only angiosperms have reproductive structures called _____.

3. Complete the following analogies:
   a. Gametophyte is to haploid as _____ is to diploid.
   b. _____ are to conifers as flowers are to _____.
   c. Ovule is to seed as ovary is to _____.

4. Under a microscope, a piece of a mushroom would look most like
   a. jelly.
   b. a tangle of string.
   c. grains of sand.
   d. a sponge.

5. During the Carboniferous period, the dominant plants, which later formed the great coal beds, were mainly
   a. mosses and other bryophytes.
   b. ferns and other seedless vascular plants.
   c. charophytes and other green algae.
   d. conifers and other gymnosperms.

6. You discover a new species of plant. Under the microscope, you find that it produces flagellated sperm. A genetic analysis shows that its dominant generation has diploid cells. What kind of plant do you have?

7. How does the evergreen nature of pines and other conifers adapt the plants for living where the growing season is very short?

8. Which of the following terms includes all others in the list? angiosperm, fern, vascular plant, gymnosperm, seed plant

9. Plant diversity is greatest in
   a. tropical forests.
   b. the temperate forests of Europe.
   c. deserts.
   d. the oceans.

10. What is a fruit?

11. Lichens are symbionts of photosynthetic _____ with _____.

12. Contrast the heterotrophic nutrition of a fungus with your own heterotrophic nutrition.

Answers to these questions can be found in Appendix: Self-Quiz Answers.

13. In April 1986, an accident at a nuclear power plant in Chernobyl, Ukraine, scattered radioactive fallout for hundreds of miles. In assessing the biological effects of the radiation, researchers found mosses to be especially valuable as organisms for monitoring the damage. Radiation damages organisms by causing mutations. Explain why it is faster to observe the genetic effects of radiation on mosses than on other types of

plants. Imagine that you are conducting tests shortly after a nuclear accident. Using potted moss plants as your experimental organisms, design an experiment to test the hypothesis that the frequency of mutations decreases with the organism's distance from the source of radiation.

14. **Interpreting Data** Airborne pollen of wind-pollinated plants such as pines, oaks, weeds, and grasses causes seasonal allergy symptoms in many people. As global warming lengthens the growing season for plants, scientists predict longer periods of misery for allergy sufferers. However, global warming does not affect all regions equally (see Figure 18.44). The table below shows the length of the average season in nine locations for ragweed pollen, an allergen that affects millions of people. Calculate the change in length of the pollen season from 1995 to 2009 for each location and graph this information against latitude. Is there a latitudinal trend in the length of ragweed season? You may want to record the data on a map to help you visualize the geographic locations at which samples were taken.

Average Length of Ragweed Pollen Season in Nine Locations (averages obtained from at least 15 years of data)

Location	Latitude (°N)	Length of Pollen Season in 1995 (days)	Length of Pollen Season in 2009 (days)	Change in Length of Pollen Season (days)
Oklahoma City, OK	35.47	88	89	
Rogers, AR	36.33	64	69	
Papillion, WI	41.15	69	80	
Madison, WI	43.00	64	76	
La Crosse, WI	43.80	58	71	
Minneapolis, MN	45.00	62	78	
Fargo, ND	46.88	36	52	
Winnipeg, MB, Canada	50.07	57	82	
Saskatoon, SK, Canada	52.07	44	71	

Data from: L. Ziska et al., Recent warming by latitude associated with increased length of ragweed pollen season in central North America. *Proceedings of the National Academy of Sciences* 108: 4248–4251 (2011).

BIOLOGY AND SOCIETY

15. Why are tropical forests being destroyed so rapidly? What kinds of social, technological, and economic factors are responsible? Most forests in more industrialized Northern Hemisphere countries have already been cut. Do the more industrialized nations have a right to pressure the less industrialized nations in the Southern Hemisphere to slow or stop the destruction of their forests? Defend your answer. What kinds of benefits, incentives, or programs might slow the destruction of tropical forests?

16. As you learned in this chapter, many prescription drugs are derived from natural plant products. Numerous other plant substances, including caffeine and nicotine, have effects in the human body, as well. There is also a wide array of plant products, in the form of pills, powders, or teas, marketed as herbal medicines. Some people prefer taking these "natural" products to pharmaceuticals. Others use herbal supplements to boost energy, promote weight loss, strengthen the immune system, relieve stress, and more. The U.S. Federal Drug Administration, which approves pharmaceuticals, is also responsible for regulating herbal remedies. What does the label "FDA-approved" on an herbal remedy mean? How does that compare to FDA approval of a drug? The FDA website http://www.fda.gov/ForConsumers/default.htm is a good place to start your research. (Note that the FDA classifies herbal remedies as dietary supplements.)

The Evolution of Animals

Why Animal Diversity Matters

Evolutionary biologists have discovered the answer to the riddle "Which came first, the chicken or the egg?"

If you want to find nightcrawlers for fishing bait, look in a field of dairy cows.

According to recent DNA analysis, many of us have a bit of Neanderthal in our genes.

If all the arthropods on Earth were divided equally among the human population, we would each get about 140 million.

Human Evolution BIOLOGY AND SOCIETY

The Discovery of the Hobbit People

In 2003, Australian anthropologists digging on the Indonesian island of Flores stumbled upon bones of some highly unusual people, including the nearly complete skeleton of an adult female. Next to a modern woman, this fully grown individual would stand about waist-high. Features of her skull, such as the shape and thickness of the bones, were human-like, but its size was proportional to her tiny body, and her brain was the size of a chimpanzee's. Surprisingly, the bones were accompanied by tools for hunting and butchering animals, along with evidence of cooking fires. Most startling of all, the remains dated to roughly 18,000 years ago, a time when scientists had thought that *Homo sapiens* was the only surviving human species. Since the initial discovery, researchers have unearthed the bones of a dozen or so more of these miniature humans.

The discoverers attributed their astonishing find to a previously unknown species, which they named *Homo floresiensis* and nicknamed "hobbits." They speculated that a band of ancestral humans arrived on Flores millions of years ago from Africa and, within the isolated environment of the island, evolved into the diminutive *Homo floresiensis*. There is precedent for animal evolution of this type: Biologists have discovered island-bound dwarf populations of deer, elephants, and hippos. One hypothesis is that a lack of predators favors the evolution of smaller, more energy-efficient forms. Controversy erupted as

A skull from one of Indonesia's "hobbit people." Scientists are debating whether the skull is from an ancient human-like species.

soon as the research team announced their findings. Skeptical scientists suggested that the bones were from *Homo sapiens* with diseases that cause skeletal malformations. As you'll find out in the Process of Science section, the more scientists learn about the "hobbit" people, the more puzzling their findings become.

Homo sapiens and *Homo floresiensis* are just two of the 1.3 million species of animals that have been named and described by biologists. This amazing diversity arose through hundreds of millions of years of evolution as natural selection shaped animal adaptations to Earth's many environments. In this chapter, we'll look at the 9 most abundant and widespread of the roughly 35 phyla (major groups) in the kingdom Animalia. We'll give special attention to the major milestones in animal evolution and conclude by reconnecting with the fascinating subject of human evolution.

The Origins of Animal Diversity

Animal life began in Precambrian seas with the evolution of multicellular creatures that ate other organisms. We are among their descendants.

What Is an Animal?

Animals are eukaryotic, multicellular, heterotrophic organisms that obtain nutrients by eating. This mode of nutrition contrasts animals with plants and other organisms that construct organic molecules through photosynthesis. It also contrasts with fungi, which obtain nutrients by absorption after digesting the food outside their bodies (see Figure 16.23). Most animals digest food within their bodies after ingesting other organisms, dead or alive, whole or by the piece (Figure 17.1).

Animal cells lack the cell walls that provide strong support in the bodies of plants and fungi. And most animals have muscle cells for movement and nerve cells that control the muscles. The most complex animals can use their muscular and nervous systems for many functions other than eating. Some species even use massive networks of nerve cells called brains to think.

Most animals are diploid and reproduce sexually; eggs and sperm are the only haploid cells. The life cycle of a sea star (Figure 17.2) includes basic stages found in most animal life cycles. ❶ Male and female adult animals make haploid gametes by meiosis, and ❷ an egg and a sperm fuse, producing a zygote. ❸ The zygote divides by mitosis, forming ❹ an early embryonic stage called a **blastula**, which is usually a hollow ball of cells. ❺ In most animals, one side of the blastula folds inward, forming a stage called a **gastrula**. ❻ The gastrula develops into a saclike embryo with inner, outer, and middle cell layers and an opening at one end. After the gastrula stage, many animals develop directly into adults. Others, such as the sea star, develop into a **larva** ❼, an immature individual that looks different from the adult animal. (A tadpole, for another example, is a larval frog.) ❽ The larva undergoes a major change of body form, called **metamorphosis**, in becoming an adult capable of reproducing sexually. ☑

☑ CHECKPOINT

What mode of nutrition distinguishes animals from fungi, both of which are heterotrophs?

Answer: *ingestion (eating)*

▼ Figure 17.2 **The life cycle of a sea star as an example of animal development.**

MEIOSIS

Egg

Sperm

❷ FERTILIZATION

Zygote (fertilized egg)

MITOSIS

❸

Eight-cell stage

❹

Blastula (cross section)

❺

Early gastrula (cross section)

Outer cell layer

Future middle layer of cells

❻

Later gastrula (cross section)

Inner cell layer

Internal sac

Larva ❼

METAMORPHOSIS

Digestive tract

❽ Adult

Key
➡ Haploid (*n*)
➡ Diploid (2*n*)

▼ Figure 17.1 **Nutrition by ingestion, the animal way of life.** Few animals ingest a piece of food as large as the gazelle being eaten by this rock python. The snake will spend two weeks or more digesting its meal.

Early Animals and the Cambrian Explosion

Scientists hypothesize that animals evolved from a colonial flagellated protist (Figure 17.3). Although molecular data point to a much earlier origin, the oldest animal fossils that have been found are 550–575 million years old. Animal evolution must have already been under way for some time prior to that—the fossils reveal a variety of shapes, and sizes range from 1 cm to 1 m in length (Figure 17.4).

Animal diversification appears to have accelerated rapidly from 535 to 525 million years ago, during the Cambrian period. Because so many animal body plans and new phyla appear in the fossils from such an evolutionarily short time span, biologists call this episode the Cambrian explosion. The most celebrated source of Cambrian fossils is located in the mountains of British Columbia, Canada. The Burgess Shale, as it is known, provided a cornucopia of perfectly preserved animal fossils. In contrast to the Precambrian animals, many Cambrian animals had hard parts such as shells, and many are clearly related to existing animal groups. For example, scientists have classified more than a third of the species found in the Burgess Shale as arthropods, the group that includes present-day crabs, shrimps, and insects (Figure 17.5). Other fossils are more difficult to place. Some are downright weird, like the spiky creature near the center of the drawing, known as *Hallucigenia*, and *Opabinia*, the five-eyed predator grasping a worm with the long, flexible appendage that protrudes in front of its mouth.

What ignited the Cambrian explosion? Scientists have proposed several hypotheses, including increasingly complex predator-prey relationships and an increase in atmospheric oxygen. But whatever the cause of the rapid diversification, it is likely that the set of "master control" genes—the genetic framework for complex bodies—was already in place. Much of the diversity in body form among the animal phyla is associated with variations in where and when these genes are expressed within developing embryos.

In the last half billion years, animal evolution has to a large degree merely generated variations of the animal forms that originated in the Cambrian seas. Continuing research will help test hypotheses about the Cambrian explosion. But even as the explosion becomes less mysterious, it will seem no less wondrous. ✓

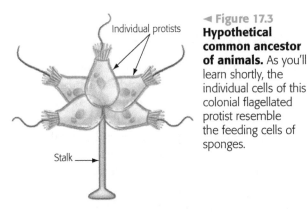

◄ Figure 17.3 **Hypothetical common ancestor of animals.** As you'll learn shortly, the individual cells of this colonial flagellated protist resemble the feeding cells of sponges.

Individual protists

Stalk

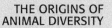 **CHECKPOINT**

Why is animal evolution during the early Cambrian referred to as an "explosion"?

Answer: because a great diversity of animals evolved in a relatively short time span

► Figure 17.4 **Fossils of Precambrian animals.** All of the oldest animal fossils are impressions of soft-bodied animals. Most of them do not appear to be related to any living group of animals.

Sea pen, possibly related to present-day colonial Cnidarians

Impression of upper surface of *Tribrachidium heraldicum*, which had a hemispheric shape and three-part symmetry unlike any living animal (up to 5 cm across)

▼ Figure 17.5 **A Cambrian seascape.** This drawing is based on fossils from the Burgess Shale. The flat-bodied animals are extinct arthropods called trilobites. A photo of a fossil trilobite is shown at the right.

Evolution — Animal Phylogeny

Historically, biologists have categorized animals by "body plan"—general features of body structure. Distinctions between body plans were used to construct phylogenetic trees showing the evolutionary relationships among animal groups. More recently, a wealth of genetic data has allowed evolutionary biologists to modify and refine groups. Figure 17.6 represents a revised set of hypotheses about the evolutionary relationships among nine major animal phyla based on both structural and genetic similarities.

▼ Figure 17.7 **Body symmetry.**

Radial symmetry. Parts radiate from the center, so any slice through the central axis divides into mirror images.

Bilateral symmetry. Only one slice can divide left and right sides into mirror-image halves.

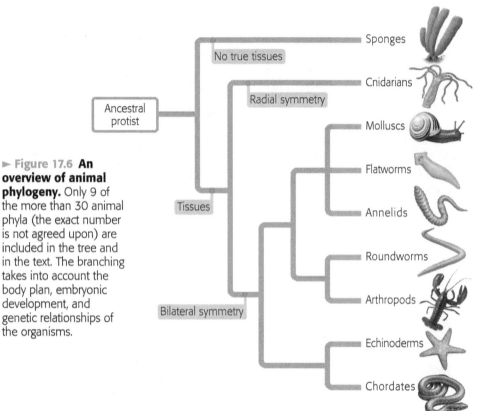

► Figure 17.6 **An overview of animal phylogeny.** Only 9 of the more than 30 animal phyla (the exact number is not agreed upon) are included in the tree and in the text. The branching takes into account the body plan, embryonic development, and genetic relationships of the organisms.

that first encounters food, danger, and other stimuli when traveling. In most bilateral animals, a nerve center in the form of a brain is at the head end, near a concentration of sense organs such as eyes. Thus, bilateral symmetry is an adaptation that aids movement, such as crawling, burrowing, or swimming. Indeed, many radial animals are stationary, whereas most bilateral animals are mobile.

Among bilateral animals, analysis of embryonic development sets the echinoderms and chordates apart from the evolutionary branch that includes molluscs, flatworms, annelids, roundworms, and arthropods. Molluscs, flatworms, and annelids have genetic similarities that are not shared by roundworms and arthropods.

The evolution of body cavities also helped lead to more complex animals. A **body cavity** (Figure 17.8, facing page) is a fluid-filled space separating the digestive tract from the outer body wall. The cavity enables the internal organs to grow and move independently of the outer body wall, and the fluid cushions them from injury. In soft-bodied animals such as earthworms, the fluid is under pressure and functions as a hydrostatic skeleton. Of the phyla shown in Figure 17.6, only sponges, cnidarians, and flatworms lack a body cavity.

With the overview of animal evolution in Figure 17.6 as our guide, we're ready to take a closer look at the nine most numerous animal phyla. ☑

☑ CHECKPOINT

1. In the phylogeny shown in Figure 17.6, chordates (the phylum that includes humans) are most closely related to which other animal phylum?
2. A round pizza displays _____ symmetry, whereas a slice of pizza displays _____ symmetry.

Answers: 1. echinoderms 2. radial; bilateral

A major branch point in animal evolution distinguishes sponges from all other animals based on structural complexity. Unlike more complex animals, sponges lack true tissues, groups of similar cells that perform a function (such as nervous tissue). A second major evolutionary split is based on body symmetry: radial versus bilateral (Figure 17.7). Like the flowerpot, the sea anemone has **radial symmetry**, identical all around a central axis. The shovel has **bilateral symmetry**, which means there's only one way to split it into two equal halves—right down the midline. A bilateral animal, such as the lobster in Figure 17.7, has a definite "head end"

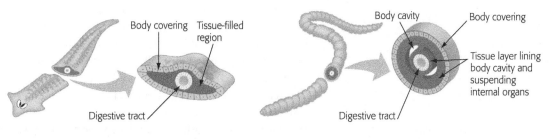

▼ Figure 17.8 **Body plans of bilateral animals.** The various organ systems of these animals develop from the three tissue layers that form in the embryo.

(a) **No body cavity:** for example, flatworm

(b) **Body cavity:** for example, earthworm

Major Invertebrate Phyla

Living on land as we do, our sense of animal diversity is biased in favor of vertebrates, animals with a backbone, such as amphibians, reptiles, and mammals. However, vertebrates make up less than 5% of all animal species. If we were to sample the animals in an aquatic habitat, such as a pond, tide pool, or coral reef, or if we were to consider the millions of insects that share our terrestrial world, we would find ourselves in the realm of **invertebrates**, animals without backbones. We give special attention to the vertebrates simply because we humans are among the backboned ones. However, by exploring the other 95% of the animal kingdom—the invertebrates—we'll discover an astonishing diversity of beautiful creatures that too often escape our notice.

is drawn through the pores into a central cavity and then flows out of the sponge through a larger opening (Figure 17.9). Flagella on specialized cells called choanocytes sweep water through the sponge's porous body. Tiny nets encircling the flagella trap bacteria and other food particles, which the choanocytes then engulf. Specialized cells called amoebocytes pick up food from the choanocytes, digest it, and carry the nutrients to other cells. Amoebocytes also manufacture the fibers that make up a sponge's skeleton. In some sponges, these fibers are sharp and spur-like, like the ones shown in Figure 17.9. Other sponges have softer, more flexible skeletons; these pliable, honeycombed skeletons are often used as natural sponges in the bath or to wash cars. ☑

☑ **CHECKPOINT**

In what fundamental way does the structure of a sponge differ from that of all other animals?

Answer: A sponge has no true tissues.

Sponges

Sponges (phylum Porifera) are stationary animals that appear so immobile that you might mistake them for plants. The simplest of all animals, sponges probably evolved very early from colonial protists. They have no nerves or muscles, but their individual cells can sense and react to changes in the environment. The cell layers of sponges are loose associations that are not considered true tissues. Sponges range in height from 1 cm (about half an inch) to 2 m (over 6 ft). Although some live in fresh water, the majority of the 5,500 or so species of sponges are marine.

Sponges are examples of suspension feeders, animals that collect food particles from water passed through some type of food-trapping equipment. The body of a sponge resembles a sac perforated with holes. Water

Sponges
Cnidarians
Molluscs
Flatworms
Annelids
Roundworms
Arthropods
Echinoderms
Chordates

▼ Figure 17.9 **Anatomy of a sponge.** To obtain enough food to grow by 3 ounces, a sponge must filter roughly 275 gallons of water through its body, enough to fill 3.5 typical-size bathtubs.

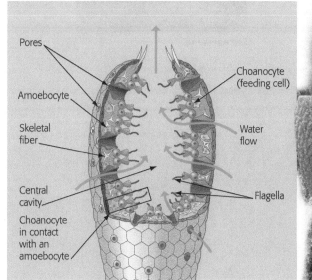

Pores
Amoebocyte
Skeletal fiber
Central cavity
Choanocyte in contact with an amoebocyte
Choanocyte (feeding cell)
Water flow
Flagella

Cnidarians

Cnidarians (phylum Cnidaria) are characterized by the presence of body tissues—as are all the remaining animals we will discuss—as well as by radial symmetry and tentacles with stinging cells. Cnidarians include sea anemones, hydras, corals, and jellies (sometimes called jellyfish, though they are not fish). Most of the 10,000 cnidarian species are marine.

Sponges
Cnidarians
Molluscs
Flatworms
Annelids
Roundworms
Arthropods
Echinoderms
Chordates

The basic body plan of a cnidarian is a sac with a central digestive compartment, the **gastrovascular cavity**. A single opening to this cavity functions as both mouth and anus. This basic body plan has two variations: the stationary **polyp** and the floating **medusa** (Figure 17.10). Polyps adhere to larger objects and extend their tentacles, waiting for prey. Examples of the polyp body plan are corals, sea anemones, and hydras. A medusa (plural, *medusae*) is a flattened, mouth-down version of the polyp. It moves freely by a combination of passive drifting and contractions of its bell-shaped body. The largest jellies are medusae with tentacles 60–70 m long (more than half the length of a football field) dangling from an umbrella-like body up to 2 m in diameter. There are some species of cnidarians that live only as polyps, others only as medusae, and still others that pass through both a medusa stage and a polyp stage in their life cycle.

Cnidarians are carnivores that use tentacles arranged in a ring around the mouth to capture prey and push the food into the gastrovascular cavity, where digestion begins. The undigested remains are eliminated through the mouth/anus. The tentacles are armed with batteries of cnidocytes ("stinging cells") that function in defense and in the capture of prey (Figure 17.11). The phylum Cnidaria is named for these stinging cells. ☑

☑ CHECKPOINT

In what fundamental way does the body plan of a cnidarian differ from that of other animals?

Answer: The body of a cnidarian is radially symmetric.

▼ **Figure 17.10 Polyp and medusa forms of cnidarians.** Note that cnidarians have two tissue layers, distinguished in the diagrams by blue and yellow. The gastrovascular cavity has only one opening, which functions as both mouth and anus.

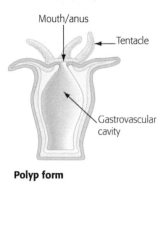

Mouth/anus
Tentacle
Gastrovascular cavity
Polyp form

Coral

Sea anemone

Hydra

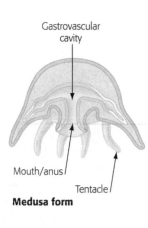

Gastrovascular cavity
Mouth/anus
Tentacle
Medusa form

Jelly

▼ **Figure 17.11 Cnidocyte action.** When a trigger on a tentacle is stimulated by touch, a fine thread shoots out from a capsule. Some cnidocyte threads entangle prey, while others puncture the prey and inject a poison.

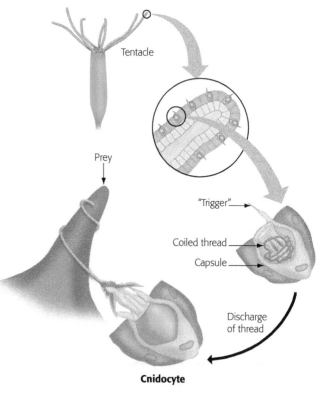

Tentacle
Prey
"Trigger"
Coiled thread
Capsule
Discharge of thread
Cnidocyte

Molluscs

Snails and slugs, oysters and clams, and octopuses and squids are all **molluscs** (phylum Mollusca). Molluscs are soft-bodied animals, but most are protected by a hard shell. Many molluscs feed by extending a file-like organ called a **radula** to scrape up food. For example, the radula of some aquatic snails slides back and forth like a backhoe, scraping and scooping algae off rocks. You can observe a radula in action by watching a snail graze on the glass wall of an aquarium. In cone snails, a group of predatory marine molluscs, the radula is modified to inject venom into prey. The sting of some cone snails is painful, or even fatal, to people.

There are 100,000 known species of molluscs, with most being marine animals. All molluscs have a similar body plan (Figure 17.12). The body has three main parts: a muscular foot, usually used for movement; a visceral mass containing most of the internal organs; and a fold of tissue called the mantle. The **mantle** drapes over the visceral mass and secretes the shell if one is present. The three major groups of molluscs are gastropods, bivalves, and cephalopods (Figure 17.13).

Most **gastropods**, including snails, are protected by a single spiraled shell into which the animal can retreat when threatened. Slugs and sea slugs lack shells. Many gastropods have a distinct head with eyes at the tips of tentacles (think of a garden snail). Marine, freshwater, and terrestrial gastropods make up about three-quarters of the living mollusc species.

The **bivalves**, including clams, oysters, mussels, and scallops, have shells divided into two halves hinged

together. None of the bivalves have a radula. There are both marine and freshwater species, with most being sedentary, using their muscular foot for digging and anchoring in sand or mud.

Cephalopods are all marine animals and generally differ from gastropods and sedentary bivalves in that their bodies are fast and agile. A few have large, heavy shells, but in most the shell is small and internal (as in squids) or missing (as in octopuses). Cephalopods have large brains and sophisticated sense organs, which contribute to their success as mobile predators. They use beak-like jaws and a radula to crush or rip prey apart. The mouth is at the base of the foot, which is drawn out into several long tentacles for catching and holding prey. The colossal squid, discovered in the ocean depths near Antarctica, is the largest living invertebrate. Scientists estimate that this massive cephalopod grows to an average length of 13 m—as long as a school bus. ☑

◄ Figure 17.12 **The general body plan of a mollusc.** Note the small body cavity (brown) and the complete digestive tract, with both mouth and anus (pink).

☑ **CHECKPOINT**

Classify these molluscs: A garden snail is an example of a _____; a clam is an example of a _____; a squid is an example of a _____.

Answer: gastropod; bivalve; cephalopod

▼ Figure 17.13 **Mollusc diversity.**

MAJOR GROUPS OF MOLLUSCS		
Gastropods	**Bivalves** (hinged shell)	**Cephalopods** (large brain and tentacles)

Snail (spiraled shell)

Sea slug (no shell)

Scallop. This scallop has many eyes (small round structures) peering out between the two halves of the hinged shell.

Octopus. Octopuses live on the seafloor, where they search for crabs and other food. They have no shell. The brain of an octopus is larger and more complex, proportionate to body size, than that of any other invertebrate.

Nautilus. The shell of the nautilus is a coiled series of chambers. The animal inhabits only the outermost chamber; the others contain gas and fluid that enable the nautilus to regulate its buoyancy.

Flatworms

Flatworms (phylum Platyhelminthes) are the simplest animals with bilateral symmetry. True to their name, these worms are ribbonlike and range from about 1 mm to about 20 m (about 65 ft) in length. Most flatworms have a gastrovascular cavity with a single opening. There are about 20,000 species of flatworms living in marine, freshwater, and damp terrestrial habitats (Figure 17.14).

The gastrovascular cavity of free-living flatworms called planarians is highly branched, providing an extensive surface area for the absorption of nutrients. When the animal feeds, a muscular tube projects through the mouth and sucks food in. Planarians live on the undersurfaces of rocks in freshwater ponds and streams.

Parasitic flatworms include blood flukes called schistosomes, which are a major health problem in the tropics. These worms have suckers that attach to the inside of the blood vessels near the human host's intestines. Infection by these flatworms causes a long-lasting disease called schistosomiasis, with such symptoms as severe abdominal pain, anemia, and dysentery. Although schistosomes are not found in the United States, more than 200 million people around the world are infected by these parasites each year.

Tapeworms parasitize many vertebrates, including people. Most tapeworms have a very long, ribbonlike body with repeated parts. There is no mouth and no gastrovascular cavity. The head of a tapeworm is equipped with suckers and hooks that lock the worm to the intestinal lining of the host. Bathed in partially digested food in the intestines of its host, the tapeworm simply absorbs nutrients across its body surface. Behind the head is a long ribbon of units that are little more than sacs of sex organs. At the back of the worm, mature units containing thousands of eggs break off and leave the host's body with the feces. People can become infected with tapeworms by eating undercooked beef, pork, or fish containing tapeworm larvae. The larvae are microscopic, but the adults can reach lengths of 2 m (6.5 ft) in the intestine. Such large tapeworms can cause intestinal blockage and rob enough nutrients from the host to cause nutritional deficiencies. Fortunately, an orally administered drug can kill the adult worms. ✓

▼ Figure 17.14 **Flatworm diversity.**

Annelids

Annelids (phylum Annelida) are worms that have **body segmentation**, which is the subdivision of the body along its length into a series of repeated parts called segments. In annelids, the segments look like a set of fused rings. There are about 16,500 annelid species, ranging in length from less than 1 mm to the giant Australian earthworm, which can grow up to 3 m (nearly 10 ft) long. Annelids live in damp soil, the sea, and most freshwater habitats. There are three main groups: earthworms, polychaetes, and leeches (Figure 17.15).

Annelids exhibit two characteristics shared by all other bilateral animals except flatworms. One is a **complete digestive tract**, which is a digestive tube with two openings: a mouth and an anus. A complete digestive tract can process food and absorb nutrients as a meal moves in one direction from one specialized digestive organ to the next. In people, for example, the mouth, stomach, and intestines act as digestive organs. A second characteristic is a body cavity (see Figure 17.8b).

Earthworms, like all annelids, are segmented both externally and internally (Figure 17.16). The body cavity is partitioned by walls (only two segment walls are fully shown here). Many of the internal structures, such as the nervous system (yellow in the figure) and organs that dispose of fluid wastes (green) are repeated in each segment. Segmental blood vessels include one main heart and five pairs of accessory hearts. The digestive tract, however, is not segmented; it passes through the segment walls from the mouth to the anus.

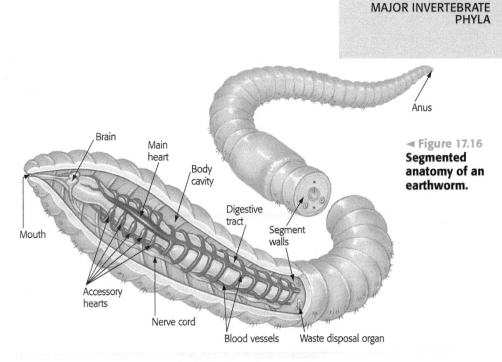

◄ **Figure 17.16**
Segmented anatomy of an earthworm.

Earthworms eat their way through the soil, extracting nutrients from organic matter as the soil passes through the digestive tract. Undigested material is eliminated as castings through the anus. Farmers and gardeners value earthworms because the animals aerate the soil and increase the amount of mineral nutrients available to plants. Because crops provide the earthworms' food, land use and farming practices have a huge effect on earthworm populations. In one study, for example, corn fields that were plowed yearly averaged 39,000 earthworms per acre, while populations in unplowed dairy pastures numbered at least 1,333,000 million per acre.

If you want to find nightcrawlers for fishing bait, look in a field of dairy cows.

▼ Figure 17.15 **Annelid diversity.**

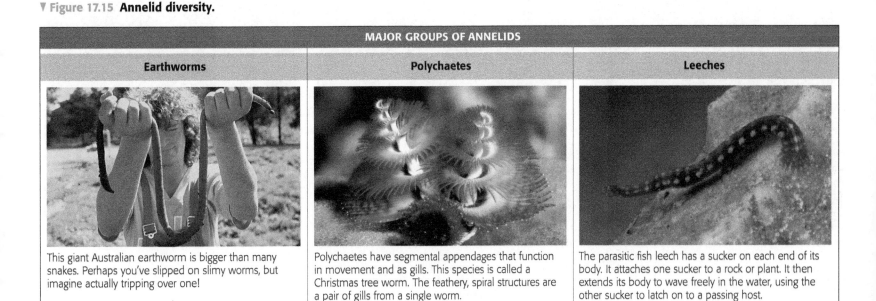

MAJOR GROUPS OF ANNELIDS		
Earthworms	**Polychaetes**	**Leeches**
This giant Australian earthworm is bigger than many snakes. Perhaps you've slipped on slimy worms, but imagine actually tripping over one!	Polychaetes have segmental appendages that function in movement and as gills. This species is called a Christmas tree worm. The feathery, spiral structures are a pair of gills from a single worm.	The parasitic fish leech has a sucker on each end of its body. It attaches one sucker to a rock or plant. It then extends its body to wave freely in the water, using the other sucker to latch on to a passing host.

In contrast to earthworms, most **polychaetes** are marine, mainly crawling on or burrowing in the seafloor. Segmental appendages with hard bristles help the worm wriggle about in search of small invertebrates to eat. The appendages also increase the animal's surface area for taking up oxygen and disposing of metabolic wastes, including carbon dioxide.

The third group of annelids, **leeches**, are notorious for the bloodsucking habits of some species. However, most species are free-living carnivores that eat small invertebrates such as snails and insects. A few terrestrial species inhabit moist vegetation in the tropics, but the majority of leeches live in fresh water. A European freshwater

Medicinal leech

species called *Hirudo medicinalis* is used for the treatment of circulatory complications. Most commonly, leeches are applied after reconstructive microsurgery in which limbs or digits are reattached. Because arteries (which transport blood into a reattached area) are easier to reconnect than veins (which transport blood out), blood can pool in the reattached area and stagnate, starving the healing tissue of oxygen. Medicinal leeches have razor-like jaws with hundreds of tiny teeth that cut through the skin. They secrete saliva containing an anesthetic and an anticoagulant into the wound. The anesthetic makes the bite virtually painless, and the anticoagulant prevents clotting as the leech drains excess blood from the wound. ☑

☑ **CHECKPOINT**

The body plan of an annelid displays _____, meaning that the body is divided into a series of repeated regions.

Answer: segmentation

Roundworms

Roundworms (also called **nematodes**, members of the phylum Nematoda) get their common name from their cylindrical body, which is usually tapered at both ends **(Figure 17.17)**. Roundworms are among the most numerous and widespread of all animals. About 25,000 species of roundworms are known, and perhaps ten times that number actually exist. Roundworms range in length from about 1 mm to 1 m. They

Sponges
Cnidarians
Molluscs
Flatworms
Annelids
Roundworms
Arthropods
Echinoderms
Chordates

are found in most aquatic habitats, in wet soil, and as parasites in the body fluids and tissues of plants and animals.

Free-living roundworms are important decomposers. They live virtually everywhere there is decaying organic matter, and their numbers are huge. Ninety thousand nematodes have been found in a single rotting apple. Recently, researchers even found nematodes living 2 miles underground, where they survive by grazing on microbes. Other species of nematodes thrive as parasites in plants and animals. Some are major agricultural pests that attack the roots of plants. At least 50 parasitic roundworm species infect people; they include pinworms, hookworms, and the parasite that causes trichinosis. ☑

☑ **CHECKPOINT**

Which phylum is most closely related to the roundworms? (*Hint*: Refer to the phylogenetic tree.)

Answer: arthropods

▼ **Figure 17.17 Roundworm diversity.**

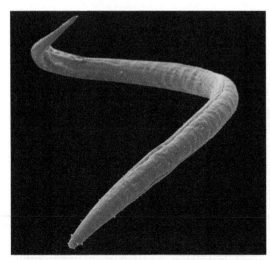

(a) A free-living roundworm. This species has the classic roundworm shape: cylindrical with tapered ends. The ridges indicate muscles that run the length of the body.

(b) Parasitic roundworms in pork. The potentially fatal disease trichinosis is caused by eating undercooked pork infected with *Trichinella* roundworms. The worms (shown here in pork tissue) burrow into a person's intestine and then invade muscle tissue.

(c) Head of hookworm. Hookworms sink their hooks into the wall of the host's small intestine and feed on blood. Although the worms are small (less than 1 cm), a severe infestation can cause serious anemia.

Arthropods

Arthropods (phylum Arthropoda) are named for their jointed appendages. Crustaceans (such as crabs and lobsters), arachnids (such as spiders and scorpions), and insects (such as grasshoppers and moths) are examples of arthropods (**Figure 17.18**). Zoologists estimate that the total arthropod population numbers about a billion billion (10^{18}) individuals. Researchers have identified more than a million arthropod species, mostly insects. In fact, two out of every three species of life that have been scientifically described are arthropods. And arthropods are represented in nearly all habitats of the biosphere. In species diversity, distribution, and sheer numbers, arthropods must be regarded as the most successful animal phylum.

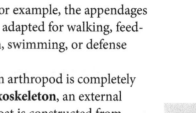

Sponges
Cnidarians
Molluscs
Flatworms
Annelids
Roundworms
Arthropods
Echinoderms
Chordates

◄ **Figure 17.18 Arthropod diversity.**

MAJOR GROUPS OF ARTHROPODS

Arachnids

Crustaceans

Millipedes and Centipedes

Insects

General Characteristics of Arthropods

Arthropods are segmented animals. In contrast with the repeating similar segments of annelids, however, arthropod segments and their appendages have become specialized for a great variety of functions. This evolutionary flexibility contributed to the great diversification of arthropods. Specialization of segments (or of fused groups of segments) provides for an efficient division of labor among body regions. For example, the appendages of different segments may be adapted for walking, feeding, sensory reception, swimming, or defense (**Figure 17.19**).

If all the arthropods on Earth were divided equally among the human population, we would each get about 140 million.

The body of an arthropod is completely covered by an **exoskeleton**, an external skeleton. This coat is constructed from layers of protein and a tough polysaccharide called chitin. The exoskeleton can be a thick, hard armor over some parts of the body (such as the head), yet be paper-thin and flexible in other locations (such as the joints). The exoskeleton protects the animal and provides points of attachment for the muscles that move the appendages. There are, of course, advantages to wearing hard parts on the outside. Our own skeleton is interior to most of our soft tissues, an arrangement that doesn't provide much protection from injury. But our skeleton does offer the advantage of being able to grow along with the rest of our body. In contrast, a growing arthropod must occasionally shed its old exoskeleton and secrete a larger one. This process, called molting, leaves the animal temporarily vulnerable to predators and other dangers. The next five pages explore the major groups of arthropods. ☑

☑ **CHECKPOINT**

Seafood lovers look forward to soft-shell crab season, when almost the entire animal can be eaten without cracking a hard shell to get at the meat. An individual crab is only a "soft-shell" for a matter of hours; harvesters therefore capture crabs and keep them in holding tanks until they are ready. What process makes soft-shell crabs possible?

Answer: Crabs have a thick exoskeleton that must be shed (molted) to allow the crab's body to grow. Soft-shell crabs have molted but have not yet secreted a new hard shell.

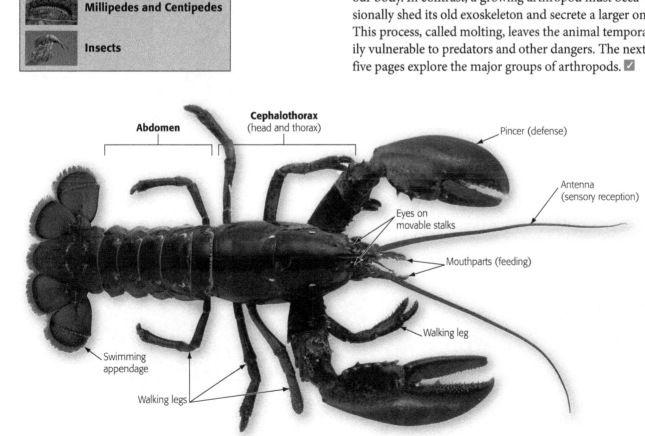

◄ **Figure 17.19 Anatomy of a lobster, a crustacean.** The whole body, including the appendages, is covered by an exoskeleton. The body is segmented, but this characteristic is obvious only in the abdomen.

Abdomen

Cephalothorax (head and thorax)

Pincer (defense)

Antenna (sensory reception)

Eyes on movable stalks

Mouthparts (feeding)

Walking leg

Swimming appendage

Walking legs

347

Arachnids

Arachnids include scorpions, spiders, ticks, and mites (Figure 17.20). Most arachnids live on land. Members of this arthropod group usually have four pairs of walking legs and a specialized pair of feeding appendages. In spiders, these feeding appendages are fang-like and equipped with poison glands. As a spider uses these appendages to immobilize and dismantle its prey, it spills digestive juices onto the torn tissues and sucks up its liquid meal.

▼ Figure 17.20 **Arachnid characteristics and diversity.**

Pair of feeding appendages

Leg (four pairs)

Pair of silk-spinning appendages

Scorpion. Scorpions have a pair of large pincers that function in defense and food capture. The tip of the tail bears a poisonous stinger. Scorpions sting people only when prodded or stepped on.

Dust mite. This microscopic house dust mite is a ubiquitous scavenger in our homes. Dust mites are harmless except to people who are allergic to the mites' feces.

Spider. Like most spiders, including the tarantula in the large photo above, this black widow spins a web of liquid silk, which solidifies as it comes out of specialized glands. A black widow's venom can kill small prey but is rarely fatal to humans.

Wood tick. Wood ticks and other species carry bacteria that cause Rocky Mountain spotted fever. Lyme disease is carried by several different species of ticks.

Crustaceans

Crustaceans, which are nearly all aquatic, include delectable species of crabs, lobsters, crayfish, and shrimps (Figure 17.21). Barnacles, which anchor themselves to rocks, boat hulls, and even whales, are also crustaceans. One group of crustaceans, the isopods, is represented on land by pill bugs. All of these animals exhibit the arthropod characteristic of multiple pairs of specialized appendages.

▼ Figure 17.21 **Crustacean characteristics and diversity.**

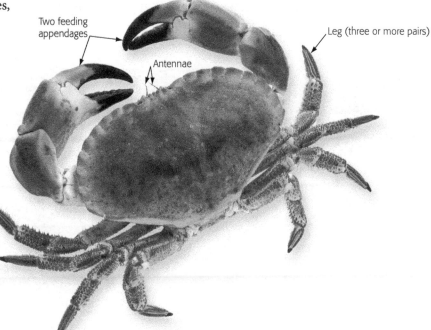

Two feeding appendages

Antennae

Leg (three or more pairs)

Crab. Ghost crabs are common along shorelines throughout the world. They scurry along the surf's edge and then quickly bury themselves in sand.

Shrimp. Naturally found in Pacific waters from Africa to Asia, giant prawns are widely cultivated as food.

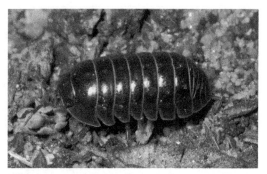

Pill bug. Commonly found in moist locations with decaying leaves, such as under logs, pill bugs get their name from their tendency to roll up into a tight ball when they sense danger.

Crayfish. The red swamp crayfish, cultivated worldwide for food, is native to the southeastern United States. When released outside its native range, it competes aggressively with other species, endangering the local ecosystem.

Barnacles. Barnacles are stationary crustaceans with exoskeletons hardened into shells by calcium carbonate (lime). The jointed appendages projecting from the shell capture small plankton.

Millipedes and Centipedes

Millipedes and **centipedes** are terrestrial arthropods that have similar segments over most of the body. Although they superficially resemble annelids, their jointed legs reveal they are arthropods (Figure 17.22).

Millipedes eat decaying plant matter. They have two pairs of short legs per body segment. Centipedes are carnivores, with a pair of poison claws used in defense and to paralyze prey, such as cockroaches and flies. Each of a centipede's body segments bears a single pair of legs.

► Figure 17.22 **Millipedes and centipedes.**

One pair of legs per segment

Two pairs of legs per segment

Millipede. Like most millipedes, this one has an elongated body with two pairs of legs per trunk segment.

Centipede. Centipedes can be found in dirt and leaf litter. Their venomous claws can harm cockroaches and spiders but not people.

Insect Anatomy

Like the grasshopper in Figure 17.23, most **insects** have a three-part body: head, thorax, and abdomen. The head usually bears a pair of sensory antennae and a pair of eyes. The mouthparts of insects are adapted for particular kinds of eating—for example, for biting and chewing plant material in grasshoppers, for lapping up fluids in houseflies, and for piercing skin and sucking blood in mosquitoes. Most adult insects have three pairs of legs and one or two pairs of wings, all extending from the thorax.

Flight is obviously one key to the great success of insects. An animal that can fly can escape many predators, more readily find food and mates, and disperse to new habitats much faster than an animal that must crawl on the ground. Because their wings are extensions of the exoskeleton and not true appendages, insects can fly without sacrificing legs. By contrast, the flying vertebrates—birds and bats—have one of their two pairs of legs modified for wings, which explains why these vertebrates are generally not very swift on the ground.

▼ Figure 17.23 **Anatomy of a grasshopper.**

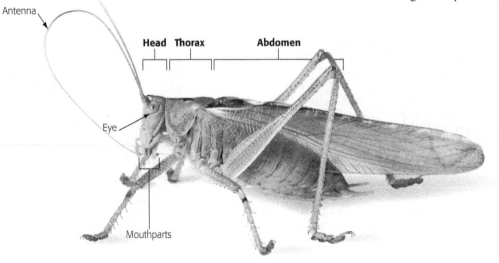

Antenna

Head Thorax Abdomen

Eye

Mouthparts

Insect Diversity

In species diversity, insects outnumber all other forms of life combined (Figure 17.24). They live in almost every terrestrial habitat and in fresh water, and flying insects fill the air. Insects are rare in the seas, where crustaceans are the dominant arthropods. The oldest insect fossils date back to about 400 million years ago. Later, the evolution of flight sparked an explosion in insect variety.

▼ Figure 17.24 **Insect diversity.**

Robber fly. This predatory insect injects prey with enzymes that liquefy the tissues, and then suck in the resulting fluid.

Rhinoceros beetle. Only males have a "horn," which is used for fighting other males and for digging.

Candy-striped leafhopper. Leafhoppers are tiny insects–about the width of the nail on your little finger–that can jump 40 times their body length.

Greater arid-land katydid. Often called the red-eyed devil, this scary-looking predator displays its wings and spiny legs when threatened.

Praying mantis. There are more then 2,000 species of praying mantises throughout the world.

Weevil. Light reflected from varying thicknesses of chitin produces the brilliant colors of this weevil.

Buckeye butterfly. The eyespots on the wings of this butterfly may startle predators.

Blue dasher dragonfly. The huge multifaceted eyes of dragonflies wrap around the head for nearly 360° vision. Each of the four wings works independently, giving dragonflies excellent maneuverability as they pursue prey.

351

Many insects undergo metamorphosis in their development. In the case of grasshoppers and some other insect groups, the young resemble adults but are smaller and have different body proportions. The animal goes through a series of molts, each time looking more like an adult, until it reaches full size. In other cases, insects have distinctive larval stages specialized for eating and growing that are known by such names as maggots (fly larvae), grubs (beetle larvae), or caterpillars (larvae of moths and butterflies). The larval stage looks entirely different from the adult stage, which is specialized for dispersal and reproduction. Metamorphosis from the larva to the adult occurs during a pupal stage (Figure 17.25).

Forensic entomologists (forensic scientists who study insects) use their knowledge of insect life cycles to help solve criminal cases. For example, blowfly maggots feed on decaying flesh. Female blowflies, which can smell a dead body from up to a mile away, typically arrive and lay their eggs in a fresh corpse within minutes. By knowing the length of each stage in the life cycle of a blowfly, an entomologist can determine how much time has passed since death occurred.

Animals so numerous, diverse, and widespread as insects are bound to affect the lives of all other terrestrial organisms, including people, in many ways. On the one hand, we depend on bees, flies, and other insects to pollinate our crops and orchards. On the other hand, insects are carriers of the microbes that cause many human diseases, such as malaria and West Nile disease. Insects also compete with people for food by eating our field crops. In an effort to minimize their losses, farmers in the United States spend billions of dollars each year on pesticides, spraying crops with massive doses of insecticide poisons. But try as they might, not even humans have significantly challenged the preeminence of insects and their arthropod kin. Rather, the evolution of pesticide resistance has caused humans to change their pest-control methods (see Figure 13.13). ☑

☑ **CHECKPOINT**

Which major arthropod group is mainly aquatic? Which is the most numerous?

Answer: *crustaceans; insects*

▼ Figure 17.25 **Metamorphosis of a monarch butterfly.**

The **larva (caterpillar)** spends its time eating and growing, molting as it grows.

After several molts, the larva becomes a **pupa** encased in a cocoon.

Within the pupa, the larval organs break down and adult organs develop from cells that were dormant in the larva.

Finally, the **adult** emerges from the cocoon.

The butterfly flies off and reproduces, nourished mainly by calories stored when it was a caterpillar.

Echinoderms

The **echinoderms** (phylum Echinodermata) are named for their spiny surfaces (*echin* is Greek for "spiny"). Among the echinoderms are sea stars, sea urchins, sea cucumbers, and sand dollars (Figure 17.26).

Echinoderms include about 7,000 species, all of them marine. Most move slowly, if at all. Echinoderms lack body segments, and most have radial symmetry as adults. Both the external and the internal parts of a sea star, for instance, radiate from the center like the spokes of a wheel. In contrast to the adult, the larval stage of echinoderms is bilaterally symmetrical. This supports other evidence that echinoderms are not closely related to other radial animals, such as cnidarians, that never show bilateral symmetry. Most echinoderms have an **endoskeleton** (interior skeleton) constructed from hard plates just beneath the skin. Bumps and spines of this endoskeleton account for the animal's rough or prickly surface. Unique to echinoderms is the **water vascular system**, a network of water-filled canals that circulate water throughout the echinoderm's body, facilitating gas exchange (the entry of O_2 and the removal of CO_2) and waste disposal. The water vascular system also branches into extensions called tube feet. A sea star or sea urchin pulls itself slowly over the seafloor using its suction-cup-like tube feet. Sea stars also use their tube feet to grip prey during feeding.

Looking at sea stars and other adult echinoderms, you may think they have little in common with humans and other vertebrates. But as shown by the phylogenetic tree at the left, echinoderms share an evolutionary branch with chordates, the phylum that includes vertebrates. Analysis of embryonic development can differentiate the echinoderms and chordates from the evolutionary branch that includes molluscs, flatworms, annelids, roundworms, and arthropods. With this context in mind, we're now ready to make the transition in our discussion from invertebrates to vertebrates. ☑

☑ CHECKPOINT

Contrast the skeleton of an echinoderm with that of an arthropod.

Answer: An echinoderm has an endoskeleton; an arthropod has an exoskeleton.

▼ Figure 17.26 **Echinoderm diversity.**

Sea star. When a sea star encounters an oyster or clam, it grips the mollusc's shell with its tube feet (see inset) and positions its mouth next to the narrow opening between the two halves of the prey's shell. The sea star then pushes its stomach out through its mouth and the crack in the mollusc's shell.

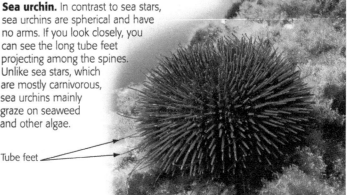

Sea urchin. In contrast to sea stars, sea urchins are spherical and have no arms. If you look closely, you can see the long tube feet projecting among the spines. Unlike sea stars, which are mostly carnivorous, sea urchins mainly graze on seaweed and other algae.

Tube feet

Sea cucumber. On casual inspection, this sea cucumber does not look much like other echinoderms. However, a closer look would reveal many echinoderm traits, including five rows of tube feet.

Sand dollar. Live sand dollars have a skin of short, movable spines covering a rigid skeleton. A set of five pores (arranged in a star pattern) allows seawater to be drawn into the sand dollar's body.

Vertebrate Evolution and Diversity

Most of us are curious about our family ancestry. Biologists are also interested in the larger question of tracing human ancestry within the animal kingdom. In this section, we trace the evolution of the vertebrates, the group that includes humans and their closest relatives. All vertebrates have endoskeletons, a characteristic shared with most echinoderms. However, vertebrate endoskeletons are unique in having a skull and a backbone, a series of bones called vertebrae (singular, *vertebra*), for which the group is named (Figure 17.27). Our first step in tracing the vertebrate lineage is to determine where vertebrates fit in the animal kingdom.

▼ Figure 17.27 **A vertebrate endoskeleton.** This snake skeleton, like those of all vertebrates, has a skull and a backbone consisting of vertebrae.

Skull
(protects brain)

Vertebra

Characteristics of Chordates

Sponges

Cnidarians

Molluscs

Flatworms

Annelids

Roundworms

Arthropods

Echinoderms

Chordates

The last phylum in our survey of the animal kingdom is the phylum Chordata. **Chordates** share four key features that appear in the embryo and sometimes in the adult (Figure 17.28). These four chordate characteristics are (1) a **dorsal, hollow nerve cord**, (2) a **notochord**, which is a flexible, longitudinal rod located between the digestive tract and the nerve cord, (3) **pharyngeal slits**, which are grooves in the pharynx, the region of the digestive tube just behind the mouth, and (4) a **post-anal tail**, which is a tail to the rear of the anus. Though these chordate characteristics are often difficult to recognize in the adult animal, they are always present in chordate embryos. For example, the notochord, for which our phylum is named, persists in adult humans only in the form of the cartilage disks that function as cushions between the vertebrae. Back injuries described as "ruptured disks" or "slipped disks" refer to these notochord remnants.

Body segmentation is another chordate characteristic. Chordate segmentation is apparent in the backbone of vertebrates (see Figure 17.27) and is also evident in the segmental muscles of all chordates (see the chevron-shaped—<<<<—muscles in the lancelet in Figure 17.29). Segmental musculature is not so obvious in adult humans unless one is motivated to sculpt "washboard abs."

Two groups of chordates, **tunicates** and **lancelets** (Figure 17.29), are invertebrates. All other chordates

▼ Figure 17.28 **Chordate characteristics.**

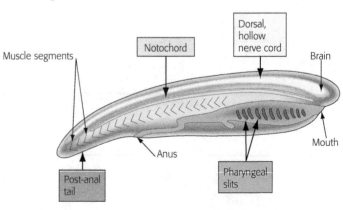

Muscle segments

Notochord

Dorsal, hollow nerve cord

Brain

Anus

Mouth

Post-anal tail

Pharyngeal slits

are **vertebrates**, which retain the basic chordate characteristics but have additional features that are unique—including, of course, the backbone. **Figure 17.30** is an overview of chordate and vertebrate evolution that will provide a context for our survey. ☑

▼ **Figure 17.29 Invertebrate chordates.**

Lancelet. This marine invertebrate owes its name to its bladelike shape. Only a few centimeters long, lancelets wiggle backward into the gravel, leaving their mouth exposed, and filter tiny food particles from the seawater.

Tunicates. The tunicate, or sea squirt, is a stationary animal that filters food from the water. These pastel sea squirts get their nickname from their coloration and the fact that they can quickly expel water to startle intruders.

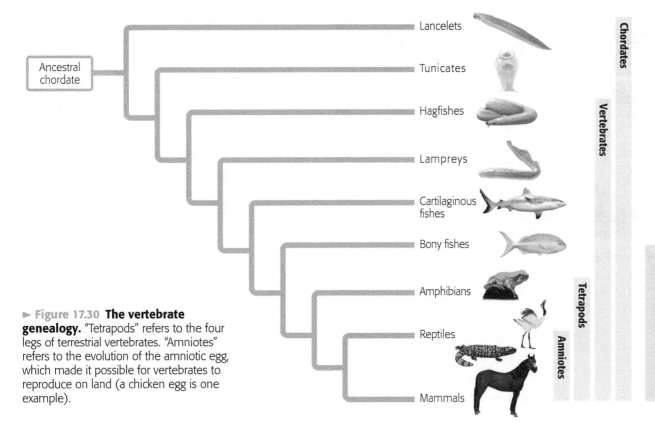

► **Figure 17.30 The vertebrate genealogy.** "Tetrapods" refers to the four legs of terrestrial vertebrates. "Amniotes" refers to the evolution of the amniotic egg, which made it possible for vertebrates to reproduce on land (a chicken egg is one example).

☑ **CHECKPOINT**

During our early embryonic development, what four features do we share with invertebrate chordates such as lancelets?

Answer: (1) dorsal, hollow nerve cord, (2) notochord, (3) pharyngeal slits, (4) post-anal tail

Fishes

The first vertebrates were
aquatic and probably evolved
during the early Cambrian period about 542 million years ago.
In contrast with most living vertebrates, they lacked jaws, hinged
bone structures that work the mouth.

Lancelets
Tunicates
Hagfishes
Lampreys
Cartilaginous fishes
Bony fishes
Amphibians
Reptiles
Mammals

   Two types of jawless fishes survive
today: hagfishes and lampreys. Present-
day hagfishes scavenge dead or dying animals on the
cold, dark seafloor (Figure 17.31a). When threatened,
a hagfish exudes an enormous amount of slime from
special glands on the sides of its body. Recently, some
hagfishes have become endangered because their skin
is used to make "eel-skin" belts, purses, and boots. Most
species of lampreys are parasites that use their jawless
mouths as suckers to attach to the sides of large fish
(Figure 17.31b). The rasping tongue then penetrates the
skin, allowing the lamprey to feed on its victim's blood
and tissues.

   We know from the fossil record that the first jawed
vertebrates were fishes that evolved about 440 million
years ago. They had two pairs of fins, making them agile
swimmers. Some early fishes were active predators up to
10 m (33 ft) in length that could chase prey and bite off
chunks of flesh. Even today, most fishes are carnivores.

   Cartilaginous fishes, such as sharks and rays, have
a flexible skeleton made of cartilage (Figure 17.31c).
Most sharks are adept predators because they are fast
swimmers with streamlined bodies, acute senses, and
powerful jaws. A shark does not have keen eyesight, but
its sense of smell is very sharp. In addition, special elec-
trosensors on the head can detect minute electrical fields
produced by muscle contractions in nearby animals.
Sharks also have a **lateral line system**, a row of sensory
organs running along each side of the body. Sensitive to
changes in water pressure, the lateral line system enables
a shark to detect minor vibrations caused by animals
swimming in its neighborhood. There are about 1,000
living species of cartilaginous fishes, nearly all of them
marine.

   The skeletons of **bony fishes** are reinforced by calcium (Figure 17.31d). Bony fishes have a lateral line
system, a keen sense of smell, and excellent eyesight.
On each side of the head, a protective flap called the
operculum (plural, *opercula*) covers a chamber housing
the gills, feathery external organs that extract oxygen
from water. Movement of the operculum allows the fish
to breathe without swimming. By contrast, sharks lack
opercula and must swim to pass water over their gills.
The need to move water over the gills is why a shark
must keep moving to stay alive. Also unlike sharks, bony
fishes have a **swim bladder**, a gas-filled sac that enables
the fish to control its buoyancy. Thus, many bony fishes
can conserve energy by remaining almost motionless, in
contrast to sharks, which sink if they stop swimming.

   Most bony fishes, including familiar species such as
tuna, trout, and goldfish, are **ray-finned fishes**. Their
fins are webs of skin supported by thin, flexible skeletal
rays, the feature for which the group was named. There
are approximately 27,000 species of ray-finned fishes,
the greatest number of species of any vertebrate group.

   A second evolutionary branch includes the **lobe-
finned fishes**. In contrast to the ray-finned fishes, their
fins are muscular and are supported by stout bones
that are homologous to amphibian limb bones. Early
lobe-fins lived in coastal wetlands and may have used
their fins to "walk" underwater. Today, three lineages of
lobe-fins survive. The coelacanth is a deep-sea dweller
once thought to be extinct. The lungfishes are represented by several Southern Hemisphere species that inhabit stagnant waters and gulp air into lungs connected
to the pharynx. The third lineage of lobe-fins adapted to
life on land and gave rise to amphibians, the first terrestrial vertebrates. ☑

☑ **CHECKPOINT**

A shark has a _____
skeleton, whereas a tuna
has a _____ skeleton.

Answer: cartilaginous; bony

▼ Figure 17.31 **Fish diversity.**

(a) Hagfish

(b) Lamprey (inset: mouth)

(c) Shark, a cartilaginous fish

Lateral line

Operculum

(d) Bony fish

Amphibians

In Greek, the word *amphibios* means "living a double life." Most **amphibians** exhibit a mixture of aquatic and terrestrial adaptations. Most species are tied to water because their eggs, lacking shells, dry out quickly in the air. A frog may spend much of its time on land, but it lays its eggs in water **(Figure 17.32a)**. An egg develops into a larva called a tadpole, a legless, aquatic algae-eater with gills, a lateral line system resembling that of fishes, and a long-finned tail. The tadpole undergoes a radical metamorphosis when changing into

Lancelets
Tunicates
Hagfishes
Lampreys
Cartilaginous fishes
Bony fishes
Amphibians
Reptiles
Mammals

a frog **(Figure 17.32b)**. When a young frog crawls onto shore and begins life as a terrestrial insect-eater, it has four legs, air-breathing lungs instead of gills, external eardrums, and no lateral line system. But even as adults, amphibians are most abundant in damp habitats, such as swamps and rain forests. This is partly because amphibians depend on their moist skin to supplement lung function in exchanging gases with the environment. Thus, even those frogs that are adapted to relatively dry habitats spend much of their time in humid burrows or under piles of moist leaves. The amphibians of today, including frogs and salamanders, account for about 12% of all living vertebrates, or about 6,000 species **(Figure 17.32c)**.

Amphibians were the first vertebrates to colonize land. They descended from fishes that had lungs and fins with muscles and skeletal supports strong enough to enable some movement, however clumsy, on land **(Figure 17.33)**. The fossil record chronicles the evolution of four-limbed amphibians from fishlike ancestors. Terrestrial vertebrates—amphibians, reptiles, and mammals—are collectively called **tetrapods**, which means "four feet." ✓

☑ CHECKPOINT

Amphibians were the first _____, four-footed terrestrial vertebrates.

Answer: tetrapods

▼ Figure 17.32 **Amphibian diversity.**

(a) Frog eggs

(b) Tadpole and adult tree frog (right)

Malayan horned frog

Texas barred tiger salamander

(c) Frogs and salamanders: the two major groups of amphibians

▼ Figure 17.33 **The origin of tetrapods.**

Lobe-finned fish. Fossils of some lobe-finned fishes have skeletal supports extending into their fins.

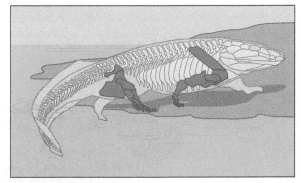

Early amphibian. Fossils of early amphibians have limb skeletons that probably functioned in helping them move on land.

Reptiles

Reptiles (including birds) and mammals are **amniotes**. The evolution of amniotes from an amphibian ancestor included many adaptations for living on land. The adaptation that gives the group its name is the **amniotic egg**, a fluid-filled egg with a waterproof shell that encloses the developing embryo (Figure 17.34).

The amniotic egg functions as a self-contained "pond" that enables amniotes to complete their life cycle on land.

The **reptiles** include snakes, lizards, turtles, crocodiles, alligators, and birds, along with a number of extinct groups, including most of the dinosaurs. The European grass snake in Figure 17.34 displays two reptilian adaptations to living on land: scaled waterproof skin, preventing dehydration in dry air, and amniotic eggs with shells, providing a watery, nutritious internal environment where the embryo can develop. These adaptations allowed reptiles to break their ancestral ties to aquatic habitats. Reptiles cannot breathe through their dry skin and so obtain most of their oxygen through their lungs.

Nonbird Reptiles

Nonbird reptiles are sometimes referred to as "cold-blooded" animals because they do not use their metabolism extensively to control body temperature. Reptiles do regulate body temperature, but largely through behavioral adaptations. For example, many lizards regulate their internal temperature by basking in the sun when the air is cool and seeking shade when the air is too warm. Because lizards and other nonbird reptiles absorb external heat rather than generating much of their own, they are said to be **ectotherms**, a term more accurate than "cold-blooded." By heating directly with solar energy rather than through the metabolic breakdown of food, a nonbird reptile can survive on less than 10% of the calories required by a mammal of equivalent size.

As successful as reptiles are today, they were far more widespread, numerous, and diverse during the Mesozoic era, which is sometimes known as the "age of reptiles." Reptiles diversified extensively during that era, producing a dynasty that lasted until about 65 million years ago. Dinosaurs, the most diverse reptile group, included the largest animals ever to inhabit land. Some were gentle giants that lumbered about while browsing vegetation. Others were voracious carnivores that chased their larger prey on two legs.

The age of reptiles began to fade about 70 million years ago. Around that time, the global climate became cooler and more variable. This was a period of mass extinctions that claimed all the dinosaurs by about 65 million years ago, except for one lineage (see Table 14.1). That lone surviving lineage is represented today by the reptilian group we know as birds. ☑

Evolutionary biologists have discovered the answer to the riddle "Which came first, the chicken or the egg?"

Lancelets
Tunicates
Hagfishes
Lampreys
Cartilaginous fishes
Bony fishes
Amphibians
Reptiles
Mammals

✅ **CHECKPOINT**

What is an amniotic egg?

Answer: a shelled egg surrounding fluid that contains an embryo

► Figure 17.34 **Reptile diversity.**

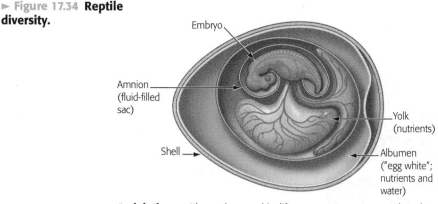

Embryo
Amnion (fluid-filled sac)
Shell
Yolk (nutrients)
Albumen ("egg white"; nutrients and water)

Aminiotic egg. The embryo and its life-support system are enclosed in a waterproof shell.

Snake. The shells of nonbird reptile eggs are leathery and flexible. This European grass snake is nonvenomous. When threatened, it may hiss and strike. If the bluff fails, it goes limp, pretending to be dead.

Lizard. The Gila monster, a desert-dweller of the Southwest, is the only venomous lizard native to the United States. Although large (up to 2 feet long), it moves too slowly to pose any danger to people.

Birds

You may have noticed that the reptilian egg resembles the more familiar chicken egg. Birds have scaly skin on their legs and feet; even feathers—their signature feature—are modified scales. Genetic and fossil evidence shows that **birds** are indeed reptiles, having evolved from a lineage of small, two-legged dinosaurs called theropods. Today, birds look quite different from reptiles because of their distinctive flight equipment—almost all of the 10,000 living bird species are airborne. The few flightless species, including the ostrich and the penguin, evolved from flying ancestors.

Almost every element of bird anatomy is adapted in some way that enhances flight. The bones have a honeycombed structure that makes them strong but light. (The wings of airplanes have the same basic construction.) For example, a huge seagoing species called the frigate bird has a wingspan of more than 2 m (6.6 ft), but its whole skeleton weighs only about 113 g (a mere 4 ounces, about as much as an iPhone). Another adaptation that reduces the weight of birds is the absence of some internal organs found in other vertebrates. Female birds, for instance, have only one ovary instead of a pair. Also, today's birds are toothless, an adaptation that trims the weight of the head, preventing uncontrolled nosedives. Birds do not chew food in the mouth but grind it in the gizzard, a muscular chamber of the digestive tract near the stomach.

Flying requires a great expenditure of energy and an active metabolism. Unlike other reptiles, birds are **endotherms**, meaning they use their own metabolic heat to maintain a warm, constant body temperature.

A bird's most obvious flight equipment is its wings. Bird wings are airfoils that illustrate the same principles of aerodynamics as the wings of an airplane **(Figure 17.35)**. A bird's flight motors are its powerful breast muscles, which are anchored to a keel-like breastbone. It is mainly these flight muscles that we call "white meat" on chicken and turkey breasts. Some birds, such as eagles and hawks, have wings adapted for soaring on air currents and flap their wings only occasionally. Other birds, including hummingbirds, excel at maneuvering but must flap continuously to stay aloft. Feathers are made of the same protein that forms the scales of reptiles. Feathers may have functioned first as insulation, helping birds retain body heat, or for courtship displays. Only later were they adapted as flight gear. ☑

> ☑ **CHECKPOINT**
> Birds differ from other reptiles in their main source of body heat, with birds being _____ and other reptiles being _____.
>
> *Answer: endotherms; ectotherms*

▶ Figure 17.35 **The aerodynamics of a bald eagle in flight.** Both birds and airplanes owe their "lift" to changes in air pressure caused by the shape of their wings.

Lower air pressure

Higher air pressure

Airfoil

Crocodile. Found throughout central and southern Africa, the Nile crocodile can grow up to 20 feet long and weigh nearly 2,000 pounds.

Birds. These red-crowned cranes, native to China, are performing an elaborate courtship dance.

Dinosaur. This *Herrerasaurus* skeleton is from a carnivorous theropod discovered in Argentina.

Mammals

There are two major lineages of amniotes: one that led to the reptiles and one that produced the mammals. The first **mammals** arose about 200 million years ago and were probably small, nocturnal insect-eaters. Mammals became much more diverse after the downfall of the dinosaurs. Most mammals are terrestrial. These include nearly 1,000 species of winged mammals, the bats. And the roughly 80 species of dolphins, porpoises, and whales are totally aquatic. The blue whale—an endangered mammal that grows to lengths of nearly 30 m (about as long as a basketball court)—is the largest animal that has ever lived. Mammals have two unique characteristics: mammary glands (which produce milk, a nutrient-rich substance to feed the young) and hair. The main function of hair is to insulate the body and help maintain a warm, constant internal temperature; like birds, mammals are endotherms.

The major groups of mammals are monotremes, marsupials, and eutherians (**Figure 17.36**). The duck-billed platypus and the echidna, or spiny anteater, are the only existing species of **monotremes**, egg-laying mammals. The platypus lives along rivers in eastern Australia and on the nearby island of Tasmania. The female usually lays two eggs and incubates them in a leaf nest. After hatching, the young nurse by licking up milk secreted by rudimentary mammary glands onto the mother's fur.

Most mammals are born rather than hatched. During pregnancy in marsupials and eutherians, the embryos are nurtured inside the mother by an organ called the **placenta**. Consisting of both embryonic and maternal tissues, the placenta joins the embryo to the mother within the uterus. The embryo receives oxygen and nutrients from maternal blood that flows close to the embryonic blood system in the placenta.

Marsupials, the so-called pouched mammals, include kangaroos, koalas, and opossums. These mammals have a brief pregnancy and give birth to embryonic offspring. After birth, the tiny offspring make their way to an external pouch on the mother's abdomen, where they attach to mammary glands. Nearly all marsupials live in Australia, New Zealand, and North and South America. Australian marsupials have diversified extensively, filling terrestrial habitats that on the other continents are occupied by eutherian mammals (see Figure 14.16).

Eutherians are also called **placental mammals** because their placentas provide a more intimate and longer-lasting association between the mother and her developing young than do marsupial placentas. Eutherians make up almost 95% of the 5,300 species of living mammals. Dogs, cats, cows, rodents, rabbits, bats, and whales are all examples of eutherian mammals. One of the eutherian groups is the primates, which include monkeys, apes, and humans. ☑

Lancelets
Tunicates
Hagfishes
Lampreys
Cartilaginous fishes
Bony fishes
Amphibians
Reptiles
Mammals

▼ Figure 17.36 **Mammalian diversity.**

MAJOR GROUPS OF MAMMALS		
Monotremes (hatched from eggs)	**Marsupials** (embryonic at birth)	**Eutherians** (fully developed at birth)
Monotremes, such as this duck-billed platypus, are the only mammals that lay eggs. Like other mammals, platypus mothers nourish their young with milk.	The young of marsupials are born very early in their development. The newborn kangaroo will finish its growth while nursing from a nipple in its mother's pouch.	In eutherians (placental mammals), young develop within the uterus of the mother. There they are nurtured by the flow of blood through the dense network of vessels in the placenta. This newborn foal is coated by remnants of the placenta.

The Human Ancestry

We have now traced animal phylogeny to the **primates**, the mammalian group that includes us—*Homo sapiens*—and our closest kin. To understand what that means, we must follow our ancestry back to the trees, where some of our most treasured traits originated.

The Evolution of Primates

Primate evolution provides a context for understanding human origins. The fossil record supports the hypothesis that primates evolved from insect-eating mammals during the late Cretaceous period, about 65 million years ago. Those early primates were small, arboreal (tree-dwelling) mammals. Thus, primates were first distinguished by characteristics that were shaped, through natural selection, by the demands of living in the trees. For example, primates have limber shoulder joints, which make it possible to swing from branch to branch. The agile hands of primates can hang on to branches and manipulate food. Nails have replaced claws in many primate species, and the fingertips are very sensitive. The eyes of primates are close together on the front of the face. The overlapping fields of vision of the two eyes enhance depth perception, an obvious advantage when swinging in trees. Excellent eye-hand coordination is also important for arboreal maneuvering. Parental care is essential for young animals in the trees. Mammals devote more energy to caring for their young than most other vertebrates, and primates are among the most attentive parents of all mammals. Most primates have single births and nurture their offspring for a long time. Although humans never lived in trees, we retain in modified form many traits that originated there.

Taxonomists divide the primates into three main groups (**Figure 17.37**). The first includes lemurs, lorises, and bush babies. These primates live in Madagascar, southern Asia, and Africa. Tarsiers, small nocturnal tree-dwellers found only in Southeast Asia, form the second group of primates. The third group of primates, **anthropoids**, includes monkeys and apes. All monkeys in the New World (the Americas) are arboreal and are distinguished by prehensile (grasping) tails that function as an extra appendage for swinging. If you see a monkey in a zoo swinging by its tail, you know it's from the New World. Although some Old World (African and Asian) monkeys are also arboreal, their tails are not prehensile. And many Old World monkeys, including baboons, macaques, and mandrills, are mainly ground-dwellers.

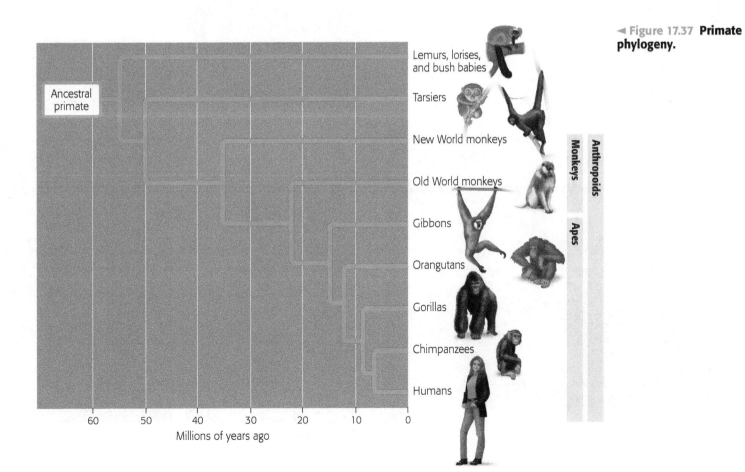

◄ Figure 17.37 **Primate phylogeny.**

Lemurs, lorises, and bush babies

Tarsiers

New World monkeys

Old World monkeys

Gibbons

Orangutans

Gorillas

Chimpanzees

Humans

Ancestral primate

60   50   40   30   20   10   0
Millions of years ago

Monkeys — Anthropoids

Apes

Anthropoids also have a fully opposable thumb; that is, they can touch the tips of all four fingers with their thumb.

Our closest anthropoid relatives are the nonhuman apes: gibbons, orangutans, gorillas, and chimpanzees. They live only in tropical regions of the Old World. Except for some gibbons, apes are larger than monkeys, with relatively long arms, short legs, and no tail.

Although all apes are capable of living in trees, only gibbons and orangutans are primarily arboreal. Gorillas and chimpanzees are highly social. Apes have larger brains proportionate to body size than monkeys, and their behavior is more adaptable. And, of course, the apes include humans. Figure 17.38 shows examples of primates.

▼ Figure 17.38 **Primate diversity.**

Red ruffed lemur

Tarsier

Black spider monkey
(New World monkey)

Gibbon (ape)

Orangutan (ape)

Patas monkey (Old World monkey)

Gorilla (ape)

Chimpanzee (ape)

Human

The Emergence of Humankind

Humanity is one very young twig on the tree of life. In the continuum of life spanning 3.5 billion years, the fossil record and molecular systematics indicate that humans and chimpanzees have shared a common African ancestry for all but the last 6–7 million years (see Figure 17.37). Put another way, if we compressed the history of life to a year, the human branch has existed for only 18 hours.

Some Common Misconceptions

Certain misconceptions about human evolution persist in the minds of many, long after these myths have been debunked by the fossil evidence. One of these myths is expressed in the question "If chimpanzees were our ancestors, then why do they still exist?" In fact, scientists do not think that humans evolved from chimpanzees. Rather, as illustrated in Figure 17.37, the lineages that led to present-day humans and chimpanzees diverged from a common ancestor several million years ago. Each branch then evolved separately. As an analogy, consider a large family reunion attended by the descendants of a man who was born in 1830. Although the attendees share this common ancestor who lived several generations ago, they may be only distantly related to each other, as sixth or seventh cousins. Similarly, chimpanzees are not our parent species, but more like our very distant phylogenetic cousins, related through a common ancestor that lived hundreds of thousands of generations in the past.

Another myth envisions human evolution as a ladder with a series of steps leading directly from an ancestral anthropoid to *Homo sapiens*. This is often illustrated as a parade of fossil **hominins** (members of the human family) becoming progressively more modern as they march across the page. In fact, as Figure 17.39 shows, there were times in hominin history when several human species coexisted. Scientists have identified about 20 species of fossil hominins, demonstrating that human phylogeny is more like a multibranched bush than a ladder, with our species being the tip of the only twig that still lives.

Although evidence from hundreds of thousands of hominin fossils debunks these and other myths about human evolution, many fascinating questions about our ancestry remain. The discovery of each new hominin fossil brings scientists a little closer to solving the puzzle of how we became human. In the following pages, you'll learn about some of the important clues that have been discovered so far.

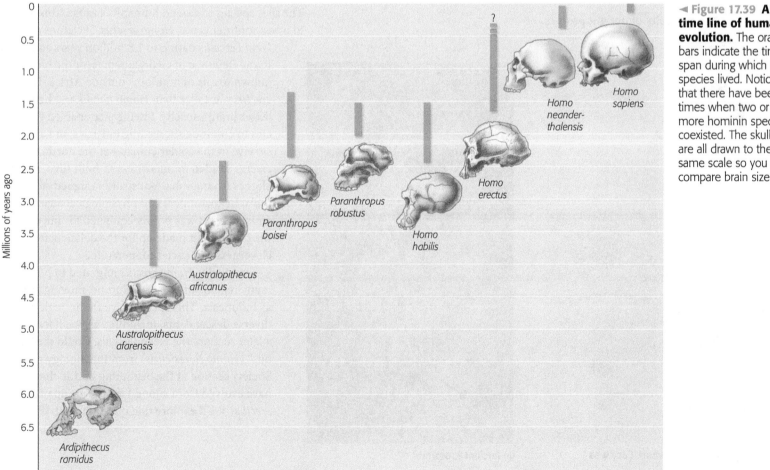

◄ Figure 17.39 **A time line of human evolution.** The orange bars indicate the time span during which each species lived. Notice that there have been times when two or more hominin species coexisted. The skulls are all drawn to the same scale so you can compare brain sizes.

Australopithecus and the Antiquity of Bipedalism

Present-day humans and chimpanzees clearly differ in two major physical features: Humans are bipedal (walk upright) and have much larger brains. When did these features emerge? In the early 1900s, scientists hypothesized that increased brain size was the initial change that separated hominins from other apes. That hypothesis was overturned when a team of researchers in Ethiopia (Figure 17.40a) unearthed a stunning 3.24-million-year-old female hominin that had a small brain and walked on two legs. Officially named *Australopithecus afarensis*, but nicknamed Lucy by her discoverers, the individual was only about 3 feet tall and with a head about the size of a softball. Corroborating evidence of early bipedalism was found soon after—the footprints of two upright-walking hominins preserved in a 3.6-million-year-old layer of volcanic ash (Figure 17.40b). Since these initial discoveries, many more *Australopithecus afarensis* fossils have been found, including most of the skeleton of a 3-year-old member of the species. Other species of *Australopithecus* have also been discovered. The first analysis of the most recent addition to the genus, *Australopithecus sediba*, was published in 2010.

▼ Figure 17.40 **The antiquity of upright posture.**

(a) Afar region of Ethiopia, where Lucy was discovered

(b) Ancient footprints

Scientists are now certain that bipedalism is a very old trait. Another lineage known as "robust" australopiths—including *Paranthropus boisei* and *Paranthropus robustus* in Figure 17.39—were also small-brained bipeds. So was *Ardipithecus ramidus*, the oldest hominin shown in Figure 17.39.

Homo habilis and the Evolution of Inventive Minds

Enlargement of the human brain is first evident in fossils from East Africa dating to about 2.4 million years ago. Thus, the fundamental human trait of an enlarged brain evolved a few million years after bipedalism.

Anthropologists have found skulls with brain capacities intermediate in size between those of the latest *Australopithecus* species and those of *Homo sapiens*. Simple handmade stone tools are sometimes found with the larger-brained fossils, which have been dubbed *Homo habilis* ("handy man"). After walking upright for about 2 million years, humans were finally beginning to use their manual dexterity and big brains to invent tools that enhanced their hunting, gathering, and scavenging on the African savanna.

Homo erectus and the Global Dispersal of Humanity

The first species to extend humanity's range from Africa to other continents was *Homo erectus*. Skeletons of *Homo erectus* dating to 1.8 million years ago found in the Republic of Georgia represent the oldest known fossils of hominins outside Africa. *Homo erectus* was taller than *Homo habilis* and had a larger brain capacity. Intelligence enabled this species to continue succeeding in Africa and also to survive in the colder climates of the north. *Homo erectus* resided in huts or caves, built fires, made clothes from animal skins, and designed stone tools. In anatomical and physiological adaptations, *Homo erectus* was poorly equipped for life outside the tropics, but made up for the deficiencies with cleverness and social cooperation.

Eventually, *Homo erectus* migrated to populate many regions of Asia and Europe, moving as far as Indonesia. This species gave rise to regionally diverse descendants, including, as you'll learn in a later section, the Neanderthals. Could the "hobbits" (*Homo floresiensis*) from the Biology and Society section at the beginning of this chapter have evolved from a long-isolated group of *Homo erectus*? We'll explore that question next. ☑

Human Evolution THE PROCESS OF SCIENCE

Who Were the Hobbit People?

How do scientists test hypotheses about events that occurred in the distant past? One approach involves using fossils, the historical record of life on Earth. If you have watched TV shows like *Bones*, in which forensic scientists use skeletal remains to solve crimes, you know that even a small piece of a skeleton can provide a wealth of information to an expert. Researchers have applied this method of hypothesis testing to the scientific debate over the "hobbit" people.

The first **observations** made by the researchers who discovered hominin fossils on the island of Flores revealed that the new fossils did not belong to any known species. This led researchers to ask the **question**, Where does this hominin fit in our evolutionary history? The scientists formed the **hypothesis** that the hobbits evolved from an isolated population of *Homo erectus*, the ancient hominin whose far-flung travels predated those of *Homo sapiens*. They made the **prediction** that key traits of the new species, such as its skull characteristics and body proportions, would resemble those of a miniature *Homo erectus* individual. Rather than a controlled **experiment**, the investigation consisted of making detailed measurements and other observations of the new fossils and comparing them with data from *Homo erectus* fossils. The initial **results** supported their hypothesis.

As you have learned, however, preliminary conclusions are often overturned by new evidence. In the past several years, further analyses have been carried out, and additional specimens have been examined. Many scientists now think that the evidence supports an alternative hypothesis: *Homo floresiensis* is most closely related to *Homo habilis*,

a smaller and more ancient species than *Homo erectus*. Other researchers continue to test the hypothesis that the hobbits are not a species at all but a *Homo sapiens* population with a disorder that caused bone malformations.

How can scientists determine which hypothesis is correct? By accumulating further evidence. While some researchers continue to excavate the site where *Homo floresiensis* was discovered (Figure 17.41), others are widening the search to additional locations. The most helpful information would come from finding a second skull or unearthing bones or teeth from which DNA could be extracted and analyzed. Meanwhile, the mystery of the hobbit people continues.

▼ Figure 17.41 **Searching for hobbits.** Researchers continue to excavate Liang Bua Cave, on the Indonesian island of Flores, where *Homo floresiensis* was discovered.

Homo neanderthalensis

Homo floresiensis is not the only mystery on our family tree. The first discovery of fossilized remains in the Neander Valley in Germany 150 years ago, *Homo neanderthalensis*—commonly called Neanderthals—stimulated the public's imagination. This intriguing species had a large brain and hunted big game with tools made from stone and wood. Neanderthals were living in Europe as far back as 350,000 years ago and spread to the Near East, central Asia, and southern Siberia. By 28,000 years ago, the species was extinct. Who were the Neanderthals?

Analysis of DNA extracted from Neanderthal fossils proved that humans are not the descendants of Neanderthals, as was once thought. Rather, humans and Neanderthals shared a common ancestor, and their lineages diverged about 400,000 years ago. You may

be surprised to learn that sequencing of Neanderthal genomes suggests that interbreeding between Neanderthals and some populations of *Homo sapiens* left a genetic legacy in our species. Roughly 2% of the genomes of most present-day humans came from Neanderthals. Africans are the exception—their DNA carries no detectable trace of Neanderthal ancestry. Scientists also learned that at least some Neanderthals had pale skin and red hair (see Figure 14.23). In the most recent analysis of a Neanderthal genome, published in 2014, researchers identified specific genes and gene regulation sequences (see Figure 11.3) that distinguish modern humans from Neanderthals. Clues such as these will help scientists understand the genetic differences that were important in the evolution of *Homo sapiens*.

According to recent DNA analysis, many of us have a bit of Neanderthal in our genes.

The Origin and Dispersal of *Homo sapiens*

Evidence from fossils and DNA studies is coming together to support a compelling hypothesis about how our own species, *Homo sapiens*, emerged and spread around the world. The oldest known fossils of *Homo sapiens* were discovered in Ethiopia and date from 160,000 to 195,000 years ago. These early humans lacked the heavy browridges of *Homo erectus* and *Homo neanderthalensis* and were more slender, suggesting that they belong to a distinct lineage. The Ethiopian fossils support molecular evidence about the origin of humans: DNA studies strongly suggest that all living humans can trace their ancestry back to a single African *Homo sapiens* lineage that began 160,000 to 200,000 years ago.

The oldest fossils of *Homo sapiens* outside Africa are from the Middle East and date back about 115,000 years.

Evidence suggests that our species emerged from Africa in one or more waves, spreading first into Asia and then to Europe, Southeast Asia, Australia, and finally to the New World (North and South America) (Figure 17.42). The date of the first arrival of humans in the New World is uncertain, although the generally accepted evidence suggests a minimum of 15,000 years ago.

Certain uniquely human traits have allowed for the development of human societies. The primate brain continues to grow after birth, and the period of growth is longer for a human than for any other primate. The extended period of human development also lengthens the time parents care for their offspring, which contributes to the child's ability to benefit from the experiences of earlier generations. This is the basis of human culture—social transmission of accumulated knowledge, customs, beliefs, and art over generations (Figure 17.43). The major means of this transmission is language, spoken and written. Humans have evolved culturally as well as biologically.

Nothing has had a greater impact on life on Earth than *Homo sapiens*. The global consequences of human evolution have been enormous. Cultural evolution made modern *Homo sapiens* a new force in the history of life—a species that could defy its physical limitations. We do not have to wait to adapt to an environment through natural selection; we simply change the environment to meet our needs.

We are the most numerous and widespread of all large animals, and wherever we go, we bring environmental change faster than many species can adapt. In the next unit, on ecology, we'll examine the interactions of humans—as well as other species—with the environment. ☑

▼ Figure 17.42 **The spread of *Homo sapiens* (dates given as years before present, BP)**

☑ CHECKPOINT

1. Humans first evolved on which continent?
2. When would a *Homo sapiens* individual have had an opportunity to meet a Neanderthal?

Answers: 1. Africa 2. between the time Homo sapiens reached the regions inhabited by Neanderthals (no sooner than 115,000 years ago) and the time when the Neanderthals died out (28,000 years ago)

◄ Figure 17.43 **Art history goes back a long way.** Beautiful ancient art, such as this 30,000-year-old painting from Lascaux Cave in France, is just one example of our cultural roots in early societies.

Human Evolution EVOLUTION CONNECTION

Are We Still Evolving?

Imagine that you could take a time machine 100,000 years into the past and bring back a *Homo sapiens* man. If you dressed him in jeans and a T-shirt and took him for a stroll around campus, chances are that no one would look twice. Did we stop evolving after becoming *Homo sapiens*? In some ways, yes. The human body has not changed much in the past 100,000 years. And by the time *Homo sapiens* began to travel out of Africa, all of the complex characteristics that define our humanity, including our big-brained intelligence and our capacity for language and symbolic thought, had already evolved.

But as humans wandered far from their site of origin and settled in diverse environments, populations encountered different selective forces. Some traits of people today reflect evolutionary responses of ancient ancestors to their physical and cultural environment. For example, the high frequency of sickle hemoglobin (see Figure 9.21) in certain populations is an adaptation that protects against the deadly disease malaria. In other malarial regions, a group of inherited blood disorders called thalassemia serve the same adaptive function.

Diet has had a significant effect on human evolution, too. For example, the ability to digest lactose as adults (see the Evolution Connection section of Chapter 3) evolved in populations that kept dairy herds. Reliance by early farmers on starchy crops such as rice or tubers also left a genetic trace: extra copies of the gene that encodes the starch-digesting enzyme amylase.

One of the most striking differences among people is skin color (Figure 17.44). The loss of skin pigmentation in humans who migrated north from Africa is thought to be an adaptation to low levels of ultraviolet (UV) radiation in northern latitudes. Dark pigment blocks the UV radiation necessary for synthesizing vitamin D—essential for proper bone development—in the skin. Recent research has turned up numerous other examples of adaptations that enabled us to colonize Earth's varied environments. For instance, Tibetans live at altitudes up to 14,000 feet (2.6 miles), where the air has 40% less oxygen than at sea level. Researchers have identified genes that have undergone evolutionary changes in response to this challenging environment (Figure 17.45). High-altitude adaptations have also been discovered in populations that inhabit the Andes Mountains in South America. Despite evolutionary tweaks such as these, however, we remain a single species.

▼ Figure 17.45 **Tibetans, a population adapted to living at high altitude.**

▼ Figure 17.44 **People with different adaptations to UV radiation.**

Chapter Review

■ SUMMARY OF KEY CONCEPTS
The Origins of Animal Diversity

What Is an Animal?
Animals are eukaryotic, multicellular, heterotrophic organisms that obtain nutrients by ingestion. Most animals reproduce sexually and develop from a zygote to a blastula and then to a gastrula. After the gastrula stage, some develop directly into adults, whereas others pass through a larval stage.

Early Animals and the Cambrian Explosion
Animals probably evolved from a colonial flagellated protist. Precambrian animals were soft-bodied. Animals with hard parts appeared during the Cambrian period. Between 535 and 525 million years ago, animal diversity increased rapidly.

Evolution: Animal Phylogeny
Major branches of animal evolution are defined by two key evolutionary differences: the presence or absence of tissues and radial versus bilateral body symmetry. A tissue-lined body cavity evolved in a number of later branches.

Radial symmetry   Bilateral symmetry

Major Invertebrate Phyla

This tree shows the eight major invertebrate phyla, as well as chordates, which include a few invertebrates.

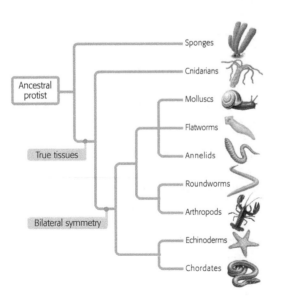

Sponges
Sponges (phylum Porifera) are stationary animals with porous bodies but no true tissues. Specialized cells draw water through pores in the sides of the body and trap food particles.

Cnidarians
Cnidarians (phylum Cnidaria) have radial symmetry, a gastrovascular cavity with a single opening, and tentacles with stinging cnidocytes. The body is either a stationary polyp or a floating medusa.

Molluscs
Molluscs (phylum Mollusca) are soft-bodied animals often protected by a hard shell. The body has three main parts: a muscular foot, a visceral mass, and a fold of tissue called the mantle.

MOLLUSCS		
Gastropods	Bivalves	Cephalopods

Flatworms
Flatworms (phylum Platyhelminthes) are the simplest bilateral animals. They may be free-living (such as planarians) or parasitic (such as tapeworms).

Annelids
Annelids (phylum Annelida) are segmented worms with complete digestive tracts. They may be free-living or parasitic.

Roundworms
Roundworms, also called nematodes (phylum Nematoda), are unsegmented and cylindrical with tapered ends. They may be free-living or parasitic.

Arthropods
Arthropods (phylum Arthropoda) are segmented animals with an exoskeleton and specialized, jointed appendages.

ARTHROPODS			
Arachnids	Crustaceans	Millipedes and Centipedes	Insects

Echinoderms
Echinoderms (phylum Echinodermata) are stationary or slow-moving marine animals that lack body segments and possess a unique water vascular system. Bilaterally symmetric larvae usually change to radially symmetric adults. Echinoderms have a bumpy endoskeleton.

Vertebrate Evolution and Diversity

Characteristics of Chordates

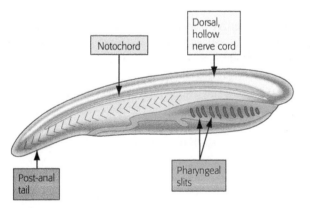

Tunicates and lancelets are invertebrate chordates. The vast majority of chordates are vertebrates, possessing a skull and backbone.

Fishes

Hagfishes and lampreys are jawless vertebrates. Cartilaginous fishes, such as sharks, are mostly predators with powerful jaws and a flexible skeleton made of cartilage. Bony fishes have a stiff skeleton reinforced by calcium. Bony fishes are further classified into ray-finned fishes and lobe-finned fishes (including lungfishes).

Amphibians

Amphibians are tetrapod vertebrates that usually deposit their eggs (lacking shells) in water. Aquatic larvae typically undergo a radical metamorphosis into the adult stage. Their moist skin requires that amphibians spend much of their adult life in humid environments.

Reptiles

Reptiles are amniotes, vertebrates that develop in a fluid-filled egg enclosed by a shell. Reptiles include terrestrial ectotherms with lungs and waterproof skin covered by scales. Scales and amniotic eggs enhanced reproduction on land. Birds are endothermic reptiles with wings, feathers, and other adaptations for flight.

Mammals

Mammals are endothermic vertebrates with mammary glands and hair. There are three major groups of mammals: Monotremes lay eggs; marsupials use a placenta but give birth to tiny embryonic offspring that usually complete development while attached to nipples inside the mother's pouch; and eutherians, or placental mammals, use their placenta in a longer-lasting association between the mother and her developing young.

MAMMALS		
Monotremes	**Marsupials**	**Eutherians**

The Human Ancestry

The Evolution of Primates

The first primates were small, arboreal mammals that evolved from insect-eating mammals about 65 million years ago. Anthropoids consist of New World monkeys (with prehensile tails), Old World monkeys (without prehensile tails), apes, and humans.

The Emergence of Humankind

Chimpanzees and humans evolved from a common ancestor about 6–7 million years ago. Species of the genus *Australopithecus*, which lived at least 4 million years ago, walked upright and had a small brain. Enlargement of the human brain in *Homo habilis* came later, about 2.4 million years ago. *Homo erectus* was the first species to extend humanity's range from its birthplace in Africa to other continents. *Homo erectus* gave rise to regionally diverse descendants, including the Neanderthals (*Homo neanderthalensis*). Current data indicate a relatively recent dispersal of modern Africans that gave rise to today's human diversity.

MasteringBiology®

For practice quizzes, BioFlix animations, MP3 tutorials, video tutors, and more study tools designed for this textbook, go to MasteringBiology®

SELF-QUIZ

1. Bilateral symmetry in the animal kingdom is best correlated with
   a. an ability to sense equally in all directions.
   b. the presence of a skeleton.
   c. motility and active predation and escape.
   d. development of a body cavity.
2. Identify which of the following categories includes all others in the list: arthropod, arachnid, insect, butterfly, crustacean, millipede.

3. The oldest group of tetrapods is the _____.

4. Reptiles are much more extensively adapted to life on land than amphibians because reptiles
   a. have a complete digestive tract.
   b. lay eggs that are enclosed in shells.
   c. are endothermic.
   d. go through a larval stage.

5. What is the name of the phylum to which humans belong? For what anatomical structure is the phylum named? Where in your body is a derivative of this anatomical structure found?

6. Fossils suggest that the first major trait distinguishing human primates from other primates was _____.

7. Which of the following types of animals is not included in the human ancestry? (*Hint*: See Figure 17.30.)
   a. a bird
   b. a bony fish
   c. an amphibian
   d. a primate

8. Put the following list of species in order, from the oldest to the most recent: *Homo erectus*, *Australopithecus* species, *Homo habilis*, *Homo sapiens*.

9. Match each of the following animals to its phylum:
   a. human   1. Echinodermata
   b. leech   2. Arthropoda
   c. sea star   3. Cnidaria
   d. lobster   4. Chordata
   e. sea anemone   5. Annelida

Answers to these questions can be found in Appendix: Self-Quiz Answers.

THE PROCESS OF SCIENCE

10. Imagine that you are a marine biologist. As part of your exploration, you dredge up an unknown animal from the seafloor. Describe some of the characteristics you should look at to determine the phylum to which the creature should be assigned.

11. Vegan and vegetarian diets are increasingly popular. While vegans consume no animals or animal products, many vegetarians are less strict. Talk to acquaintances who describe themselves as vegetarians, or who follow a meat-free diet, and determine which taxonomic groups they avoid eating (see Figures 17.6 and 17.30). Try to generalize about their diet. What do they consider "meat"? For example, do they avoid eating vertebrates but eat some invertebrates? Do they avoid only birds and mammals? What about fish? Do they eat dairy products or eggs?

12. What adaptations inherited from our primate ancestors enable humans to make and use tools?

13. Interpreting Data Average brain size, relative to body mass, gives a rough indication of the intelligence of a species. Graph the data below for hominins. Which species is most similar to *Homo floresiensis*? Does this information support the hypothesis that *Homo floresiensis* is a dwarf form of *Homo erectus* or an alternative explanation?

Hominin Species	Mean Brain Volume (cm³)	Mean Body Mass (kg)
Australopithecus afarensis	440	37
Homo erectus	940	58
Homo floresiensis	420	32
Homo habilis	610	34
Homo neanderthalensis	1480	65
Homo sapiens	1330	64
Paranthropus boisei	490	41

BIOLOGY AND SOCIETY

14. This chapter presents a scientific understanding of human origins. Science is one approach to understanding the natural world (as you learned in Chapter 1). Reread the Biology and Society section and underline words or phrases that reflect a scientific approach to the study of *Homo floresiensis*. You are probably also familiar with at least one way of understanding human origins that is outside the scope of science. How does that approach to understanding life differ from a scientific one? What might be the potential value of studying human evolution in a scientific context?

15. Coral reefs harbor a greater diversity of animals than any other environment in the sea. Australia's Great Barrier Reef has been protected as a marine reserve and is a mecca for scientists and nature enthusiasts. Elsewhere, such as in Indonesia and the Philippines, coral reefs are in danger. Many reefs have been depleted of fish, and runoff from the shore has covered coral with sediment. Nearly all the changes in the reefs can be traced back to human activities. What kinds of activities do you think might be contributing to the decline of the reefs? What are some reasons to be concerned about this decline? Do you think the situation is likely to improve or worsen in the future? Why? What might the local people do to halt the decline? Should the more industrialized countries help? Why or why not?

16. The human body has not changed much in the last 100,000 years, but human culture has changed a great deal. As a result of our culture, we change the environment at a rate far greater than the rate at which many species, including our own, can evolve. What evidence of rapid environmental change do you see around you? What aspects of human culture are responsible for these changes? Do you see any evidence of a decrease in the rate of human-caused environmental changes?

Appendix A Metric Conversion Table

Measurement	Unit and Abbreviation	Metric Equivalent	Approximate Metric-to-English Conversion Factor	Approximate English-to-Metric Conversion Factor
Length	1 kilometer (km)	= 1,000 (10^3) meters	1 km = 0.6 mile	1 mile = 1.6 km
	1 meter (m)	= 100 (10^2) centimeters	1 m = 1.1 yards	1 yard = 0.9 m
		= 1,000 millimeters	1 m = 3.3 feet	1 foot = 0.3 m
			1 m = 39.4 inches	
	1 centimeter (cm)	= 0.01 (10^{-2}) meter	1 cm = 0.4 inch	1 foot = 30.5 cm
				1 inch = 2.5 cm
	1 millimeter (mm)	= 0.001 (10^{-3}) meter	1 mm = 0.04 inch	
	1 micrometer (μm)	= 10^{-6} meter (10^{-3} mm)		
	1 nanometer (nm)	= 10^{-9} meter (10^{-3} μm)		
	1 angstrom (Å)	= 10^{-10} meter (10^{-4} μm)		
Area	1 hectare (ha)	= 10,000 square meters	1 ha = 2.5 acres	1 acre = 0.4 ha
	1 square meter (m^2)	= 10,000 square centimeters	1 m^2 = 1.2 square yards	1 square yard = 0.8 m^2
			1 m^2 = 10.8 square feet	1 square foot = 0.09 m^2
	1 square centimeter (cm^2)	= 100 square millimeters	1 cm^2 = 0.16 square inch	1 square inch = 6.5 cm^2
Mass	1 metric ton (t)	= 1,000 kilograms	1 t = 1.1 tons	1 ton = 0.91 t
	1 kilogram (kg)	= 1,000 grams	1 kg = 2.2 pounds	1 pound = 0.45 kg
	1 gram (g)	= 1,000 milligrams	1 g = 0.04 ounce	1 ounce = 28.35 g
			1 g = 15.4 grains	
	1 milligram (mg)	= 10^{-3} gram	1 mg = 0.02 grain	
	1 microgram (μg)	= 10^{-6} gram		
Volume (solids)	1 cubic meter (m^3)	= 1,000,000 cubic centimeters	1 m^3 = 1.3 cubic yards	1 cubic yard = 0.8 m^3
			1 m^3 = 35.3 cubic feet	1 cubic foot = 0.03 m^3
	1 cubic centimeter (cm^3 or cc)	= 10^{-6} cubic meter	1 cm^3 = 0.06 cubic inch	1 cubic inch = 16.4 cm^3
	1 cubic millimeter (mm^3)	= 10^{-9} cubic meter (10^{-3} cubic centimeter)		
Volume (liquids and gases)	1 kiloliter (kL or kl)	= 1,000 liters	1 kL = 264.2 gallons	1 gallon = 3.79 L
	1 liter (L)	= 1,000 milliliters	1 L = 0.26 gallon	1 quart = 0.95 L
			1 L = 1.06 quarts	
	1 milliliter (mL or ml)	= 10^{-3} liter	1 mL = 0.03 fluid ounce	1 quart = 946 mL
		= 1 cubic centimeter	1 mL = approx. ¼ teaspoon	1 pint = 473 mL
			1 mL = approx. 15–16 drops	1 fluid ounce = 29.6 mL
	1 microliter (μL or μl)	= 10^{-6} liter (10^{-3} milliliters)		1 teaspoon = approx. 5 mL
Time	1 second (s)	= $\frac{1}{60}$ minute		
	1 millisecond (ms)	= 10^{-3} second		
Temperature	Degrees Celsius (°C)		°F = $\frac{9}{5}$°C + 32	°C = $\frac{5}{9}$(°F − 32)

Appendix B The Periodic Table

Atomic number (number of protons)
Atomic mass (number of protons plus number of neutrons averaged over all isotopes)
Element symbol

6
C
12.01

Metals   Metalloids   Nonmetals

Representative elements

Groups: Elements in a vertical column have the same number of electrons in their valence (outer) shell and thus have similar chemical properties.

Periods: Each horizontal row contains elements with the same total number of electron shells. Across each period, elements are ordered by increasing atomic number.

Alkali metals   Alkaline earth metals   Halogens   Noble gases

Transition elements

Period number	Group 1A	Group 2A	3B	4B	5B	6B	7B	8B	8B	8B	1B	2B	Group 3A	Group 4A	Group 5A	Group 6A	Group 7A	Group 8A
	1	2	3	4	5	6	7	8	9	10	11	12	13	14	15	16	17	18
1	H 1.008																	He 4.003
2	Li 6.941	Be 9.012											B 10.81	C 12.01	N 14.01	O 16.00	F 19.00	Ne 20.18
3	Na 22.99	Mg 24.31											Al 26.98	Si 28.09	P 30.97	S 32.07	Cl 35.45	Ar 39.95
4	K 39.10	Ca 40.08	Sc 44.96	Ti 47.87	V 50.94	Cr 52.00	Mn 54.94	Fe 55.85	Co 58.93	Ni 58.69	Cu 63.55	Zn 65.41	Ga 69.72	Ge 72.64	As 74.92	Se 78.96	Br 79.90	Kr 83.80
5	Rb 85.47	Sr 87.62	Y 88.91	Zr 91.22	Nb 92.91	Mo 95.94	Tc (98)	Ru 101.1	Rh 102.9	Pd 106.4	Ag 107.9	Cd 112.4	In 114.8	Sn 118.7	Sb 121.8	Te 127.6	I 126.9	Xe 131.3
6	Cs 132.9	Ba 137.3	La 138.9	Hf 178.5	Ta 180.9	W 183.8	Re 186.2	Os 190.2	Ir 192.2	Pt 195.1	Au 197.0	Hg 200.6	Tl 204.4	Pb 207.2	Bi 209.0	Po (209)	At (210)	Rn (222)
7	Fr (223)	Ra (226)	Ac (227)	Rf (261)	Db (262)	Sg (266)	Bh (264)	Hs (269)	Mt (268)	Ds (271)	Rg (272)	Cn (285)	— (284)	— (289)	— (288)	— (293)	— (294?)	— (294)

Atomic numbers across periods 4–7, groups: Sc21, Ti22, V23, Cr24, Mn25, Fe26, Co27, Ni28, Cu29, Zn30; Y39, Zr40, Nb41, Mo42, Tc43, Ru44, Rh45, Pd46, Ag47, Cd48; La57*, Hf72, Ta73, W74, Re75, Os76, Ir77, Pt78, Au79, Hg80; Ac89†, Rf104, Db105, Sg106, Bh107, Hs108, Mt109, Ds110, Rg111, Cn112.

*Lanthanides

| 58 Ce 140.1 | 59 Pr 140.9 | 60 Nd 144.2 | 61 Pm (145) | 62 Sm 150.4 | 63 Eu 152.0 | 64 Gd 157.3 | 65 Tb 158.9 | 66 Dy 162.5 | 67 Ho 164.9 | 68 Er 167.3 | 69 Tm 168.9 | 70 Yb 173.0 | 71 Lu 175.0 |

†Actinides

| 90 Th 232.0 | 91 Pa 231.0 | 92 U 238.0 | 93 Np (237) | 94 Pu (244) | 95 Am (243) | 96 Cm (247) | 97 Bk (247) | 98 Cf (251) | 99 Es 252 | 100 Fm 257 | 101 Md 258 | 102 No 259 | 103 Lr 260 |

Name (Symbol)	Atomic Number	Name (Symbol)	Atomic Number	Name (Symbol)	Atomic Number	Name (Symbol)	Atomic Number	Name (Symbol)	Atomic Number
Actinium (Ac)	89	Copernicium (Cn)	112	Iridium (Ir)	77	Palladium (Pd)	46	Sodium (Na)	11
Aluminum (Al)	13	Copper (Cu)	29	Iron (Fe)	26	Phosphorus (P)	15	Strontium (Sr)	38
Americium (Am)	95	Curium (Cm)	96	Krypton (Kr)	36	Platinum (Pt)	78	Sulfur (S)	16
Antimony (Sb)	51	Darmstadtium (Ds)	110	Lanthanum (La)	57	Plutonium (Pu)	94	Tantalum (Ta)	73
Argon (Ar)	18	Dubnium (Db)	105	Lawrencium (Lr)	103	Polonium (Po)	84	Technetium (Tc)	43
Arsenic (As)	33	Dysprosium (Dy)	66	Lead (Pb)	82	Potassium (K)	19	Tellurium (Te)	52
Astatine (At)	85	Einsteinium (Es)	99	Lithium (Li)	3	Praseodymium (Pr)	59	Terbium (Tb)	65
Barium (Ba)	56	Erbium (Er)	68	Lutetium (Lu)	71	Promethium (Pm)	61	Thallium (Tl)	81
Berkelium (Bk)	97	Europium (Eu)	63	Magnesium (Mg)	12	Protactinium (Pa)	91	Thorium (Th)	90
Beryllium (Be)	4	Fermium (Fm)	100	Manganese (Mn)	25	Radium (Ra)	88	Thulium (Tm)	69
Bismuth (Bi)	83	Fluorine (F)	9	Meitnerium (Mt)	109	Radon (Rn)	86	Tin (Sn)	50
Bohrium (Bh)	107	Francium (Fr)	87	Mendelevium (Md)	101	Rhenium (Re)	75	Titanium (Ti)	22
Boron (B)	5	Gadolinium (Gd)	64	Mercury (Hg)	80	Rhodium (Rh)	45	Tungsten (W)	74
Bromine (Br)	35	Gallium (Ga)	31	Molybdenum (Mo)	42	Roentgenium (Rg)	111	Uranium (U)	92
Cadmium (Cd)	48	Germanium (Ge)	32	Neodymium (Nd)	60	Rubidium (Rb)	37	Vanadium (V)	23
Calcium (Ca)	20	Gold (Au)	79	Neon (Ne)	10	Ruthenium (Ru)	44	Xenon (Xe)	54
Californium (Cf)	98	Hafnium (Hf)	72	Neptunium (Np)	93	Rutherfordium (Rf)	104	Ytterbium (Yb)	70
Carbon (C)	6	Hassium (Hs)	108	Nickel (Ni)	28	Samarium (Sm)	62	Yttrium (Y)	39
Cerium (Ce)	58	Helium (He)	2	Niobium (Nb)	41	Scandium (Sc)	21	Zinc (Zn)	30
Cesium (Cs)	55	Holmium (Ho)	67	Nitrogen (N)	7	Seaborgium (Sg)	106	Zirconium (Zr)	40
Chlorine (Cl)	17	Hydrogen (H)	1	Nobelium (No)	102	Selenium (Se)	34		
Chromium (Cr)	24	Indium (In)	49	Osmium (Os)	76	Silicon (Si)	14		
Cobalt (Co)	27	Iodine (I)	53	Oxygen (O)	8	Silver (Ag)	47		

Appendix C Credits

PHOTO CREDITS

UNIT OPENERS: Unit 1 top left Vaclav Volrab/Shutterstock; **unit 1 left** Stone/Getty Images; **unit 2 top left** Nhpa/Age Fotostock; **unit 3 top left** Gay Bumgarner/Alamy; **unit 3 left** Eric Isselee/Shutterstock; **unit 4 top left** Jean-Paul Ferrero/Mary Evans Picture Library Ltd/Age Fotostock; **unit 4 left** Masyanya/Shutterstock; **unit 6 top right** John Coletti/Getty Images; **unit 6 left** Vilor/Shutterstock.

CHAPTER 1: Chapter opening photo right David Malan/Getty Images; **chapter opening photo bottom** Katherine Dickey; **chapter opening photo top** Eric J. Simon; **p. 3 right** Eric J. Simon; **1.1 left** M. I. Walker/Science Source; **1.1 center** SPL/Science Source; **1.1 right** Educational Images Ltd./Custom Medical Stock; **1.2 left** Michael Nichols/National Geographic/Getty Images; **1.2 right** Tim Ridley/Dorling Kindersley; **1.3** Adrian Sherratt/Alamy; **1.4a p. 6** xtock/Shutterstock; **1.4b p. 6** Lorne Chapman/Alamy; **1.4c p. 6** Trevor Kelly/Shutterstock; **1.4d p. 6** Eric J. Simon; **1.4e p. 7** Cathy Keife/Fotolia; **1.4f p. 7** Eric J. Simon; **1.4g p. 7** Redchanka/Shutterstock; **1.5** NASA/JPL California Institute of Technology; **1.6** Edwin Verin/Shutterstock; **1.7 top to bottom** Science Source; Neil Fletcher/Dorling Kindersley; Kristin Piljay/Lonely Planet Images/Getty Images; Stockbyte/Getty Images; Dr. D. P. Wilson/Science Source; **1.10 bottom** Michael Nolan/Robert Harding; **1.10 top left** Mike Hayward/Alamy; **1.10 top right** Public domain/Wikipedia; **1.11 top left** The Natural History Museum/Alamy; **1.13 left to right** Africa Studio/Shutterstock; Pablo Paul/Alamy; Foodcollection/Alamy; Barbro Bergfeldt/Shutterstock; Volff/Fotolia; Sarycheva Olesia/Shutterstock; **1.14 left to right** Eric Baccega/Nature Picture Library; Erik Lam/Shutterstock; **1.15** Martin Dohrn/Royal College of Surgeons/Science Source; **1.16** Susumu Nishinaga/Science Source; **1.18** Ian Hooton/Science Source; **1.19** Sergey Novikov/Shutterstock; **1.20 top to bottom** NASA Goddard Institute for Space Studies and Surface Temperature Analysis; Prasit Chansareekorn/Moment Collection/Getty Images; Dave G. Houser/Alamy; Biology Pics/Science Source.

CHAPTER 2: Chapter opening photo top Kevin Grant/Fotolia; **chapter opening photo bottom** PM Images/Ocean/Corbis; **chapter opening photo right** Ji Zhou/Shutterstock; **p. 23 right** Vaclav Volrab/Shutterstock **p. 24 top** Geoff Dann/Dorling Kindersley; **p. 24 bottom** Clive Streeter/Dorling Kindersley; **2.3 woman left** Ivan Polunin/Photoshot; **montage clockwise from bottom left** Jiri Hera/Fotolia; Anne Dowie/Pearson Education; Howard Shooter/Dorling Kindersley; Alessio Cola/Shutterstock; Ulkastudio/Shutterstock; **2.5** Raguet H/Age Fotostock; **2.9** William Allum/Shutterstock; **2.10 left** Stephen Alvarez/National Geographic/Getty Images; **2.10 right** Andrew Syred/Science Source; **2.11** Alasdair Thomson/Getty Images; **2.12** Ohn Leyba/The Denver Post/Getty Images; **2.13** Nexus 7/Shutterstock; **2.14** Kristin Piljay/Pearson Education; **p. 31 left** Doug Allan/Science Source; **2.15 top to bottom** Beth Van Trees/Shutterstock; Steve Gschmeissner/Science Source; VR Photos/Shutterstock; Terekhov igor/Shutterstock; Jsemeniuk/E+/Getty Images; **2.16** Luiz A. Rocha/Shutterstock.

CHAPTER 3: Chapter opening photo top left Nikola Bilic/Shutterstock; **chapter opening photo top right** Monkey Business/Fotolia; **chapter opening photo bottom right** Brian P. Hogan; **chapter opening photo bottom left** Eric J. Simon; **p. 37 right** Sean Justice/Cardinal/Corbis; **p. 37 top left** Sean Justice/Cardinal/Corbis; **3.3 left** James Marvin Phelps/Shutterstock; **3.3 right** Ilolab/Fotolia; **p. 39 center** Gavran333/Fotolia; **3.5** StudioSmart/Shutterstock; **3.8 bottom** Kristin Piljay/Pearson Education; **3.8 top** Stieberszabolcs/Fotolia; **3.9 top** Science Source; **3.9 center** Dr. Lloyd M. Beidler; **3.9 bottom** Biophoto Associates/Science Source; **3.10** Martyn F. Chillmaid/SPL/Science Source; **3.12 left box clockwise from left** Thomas M Perkins/Shutterstock; Hannamariah/Shutterstock; Valentin Mosichev/Shutterstock; Kellis/Fotolia; **3.12 right box clockwise from left** Kayros Studio/Fotolia; Multiart/Shutterstock; Maksim Shebeko/Fotolia; Subbotina Anna/Fotolia; Vladm/Shutterstock; **3.13 left** EcoPrint/Shutterstock; **3.13 right** Stockbyte/Getty Images; **3.14 top left** Brian Cassella/Rapport Press/Newscom; **3.14 top right** Matthew Cavanaugh/epa/Corbis Wire/Corbis; **3.14 bottom left** Gabriel Bouys/AFP/Getty Images; **3.14 bottom right** Shannon Stapleton/Reuters; **3.15 left to right** GlowImages/Alamy; Geoff Dann/Dorling Kindersley; Dave King/Dorling Kindersley; Tim Parmenter/Dorling Kindersley; Starsstudio/Fotolia; Steve Gschmeissner/Science Source; Kristin Piljay/Pearson Education; **3.19b** Ingram Publishing/Vetta/Getty Images; **3.20 top to bottom** Science Source/Science Source; Michael Patrick O'Neill/Alamy; Stefan Wackerhagen/imageBROKER/Newscom; **3.27** Ralph Morse/Contributor/Time Life Pictures/Getty Images.

CHAPTER 4: Chapter opening photo top left Asfloro/Fotolia; **chapter opening photo top right** Lily/Fotolia; **chapter opening photo bottom left** Jennifer Waters/Science Source; **chapter opening photo bottom right** Viktor Fischer/Alamy; **p. 55 right** SPL/Science Source; **p. 55 top left** SPL/Science Source; **p. 56 top left** Tmc_photos/Fotolia; **4.5** Science Source; **4.6 left** Biophoto Associates/Science Source; **4.6 right** Don W. Fawcett/Science Source; **4.9** MedImage/Science Source; **4.13 left** SPL/Science Source; **4.14 right** Daniel S. Friend; **4.15a** Michael Abbey/Science Source; **4.15b** Dr. Jeremy Burgess/Science Source; **4.17** Biology Pics/Science Source; **4.18** Daniel S. Friend; **4.19a** Dr. Torsten Wittmann/Science Source; **4.19b** Roland Birke/Photolibrary/Getty Images; **4.20a** Eye of Science/Science Source; **4.20b** Science Source; **4.20c** Charles Daghlian/Science Source.

CHAPTER 5: Chapter opening photo bottom left Jdwfoto/Fotolia; **chapter opening photo bottom right** William87/Fotolia; **chapter opening photo top left** Dmitrimaruta/Fotolia; **chapter opening photo top right** Eric J. Simon; **p. 75 right** Don W. Fawcett/Science Source; **p. 75 top left** Don W. Fawcett/Science Source; **5.1** Stephen Simpson/Photolibrary/Getty Images; **5.3a** George Doyle/Stockbyte/Getty Images; **5.3b** Monkey Business/Fotolia; **5.19** Peter B. Armstrong.

CHAPTER 6: Chapter opening photo right National Motor Museum/Motoring Picture Library/Alamy; **chapter opening photo top** Allison Herreid/Shutterstock; **chapter opening photo bottom** Nickola_che/Fotolia; **p. 91 right** Philippe Psaila/Science Source; **p. 91 top left** Philippe Psaila/Science Source; **6.1** Eric J. Simon; **6.2 left to right** Dudarev Mikhail/Shutterstock; Eric Isselée/Shutterstock; **6.3** Dmitrimaruta/Fotolia; **6.12** Alex Staroseltsev/Shutterstock; **6.13** Maridav/Shutterstock; **6.16** Kristin Piljay/Alamy.

CHAPTER 7: Chapter opening photo top right NASA; **chapter opening photo top left** Sunny studio/Shutterstock; **chapter opening photo bottom** Mangostock/Shutterstock; **p. 107 right** Martin Bond/Science Source; **p. 107 top left** Martin Bond/Science Source; **7.1 left to right** Neil Fletcher/Dorling Kindersley; Jeff Rotman/Nature Picture Library; Susan M. Barns, Ph.D; **7.2 top center** John Fielding/Dorling Kindersley; **7.2 top right** John Durham/Science Source; **7.2 center left** Biophoto Associates/Science Source; **7.6** Joyce/Fotolia; **7.7** JulietPhotography/Fotolia; **7.8b** Photos by LQ/Alamy; **7.14** Pascal Goetgheluck/Science Source.

CHAPTER 8: Chapter opening photo top left Franco Banfi/Science Source; **chapter opening photo bottom left** Brian Jackson/Fotolia; **chapter opening photo bottom right** Zephyr/Science Source; **chapter opening photo top right** Andrew Syred/Science Source; **p. 121 right** Nhpa/Age Fotostock; **p. 121 top left** Nhpa/Age Fotostock; **8.1 p. 122 left to right** Dr. Torsten Wittmann/Science Source; Dr. Yorgos Nikas/Science Source; **8.1 p. 123 left to right** Biophoto Associates/Science Source; Image Quest Marine; John Beedle/Getty Images; **8.2 top to bottom** Eric Isselee/Shutterstock; Christian Musat/Shutterstock; Michaeljung/Fotolia; Eric Isselee/Shutterstock; Milton H. Gallardo; **8.3** Ed Reschke/Getty Images; **8.4** Biophoto Associates/Science Source; **8.7** Conly L. Rieder, Ph.D; **8.8a** Don W. Fawcett/Science Source; **8.8b** Kent Wood/Science Source; **8.10** Sarahwolfephotography/Getty Images; **8.11** CNRI/Science Source; **8.12** Iofoto/Shutterstock; **8.14** Ed Reschke/Getty Images; **8.17** David M. Phillips/Science Source; **8.19** Dr. David Mark Welch; **8.22 bottom** CNRI/Science Source; **8.22 top** Lauren Shear/Science Source; **8.23** Nhpa/Superstock.

CHAPTER 9: Chapter opening photo top left Dora Zett/Shutterstock; **chapter opening photo bottom** ICHIRO/Getty Images; **chapter opening photo top right** Classic Image/Alamy; **p. 145 right** Eric J. Simon; **p. 145 top left** Eric J. Simon; **9.1** Science Source; **9.4** Patrick Lynch/Alamy; **9.5** James King-Holmes/Science Source; **9.8** Martin Shields/Science Source; **9.9 left to right** Tracy Morgan/Dorling Kindersley; Tracy Morgan/Dorling Kindersley; Eric Isselee/Shutterstock; Victoria Rak/Shutterstock; **9.10 left to right** Tracy Morgan/Dorling Kindersley; Eric Isselee/Shutterstock; **9.12 top left to right** James Woodson/Getty Images; Ostill/Shutterstock; Oleksii Sergieiev/Fotolia; **9.12 bottom left to right** Blend Images - KidStock/Getty Images; Image Source/Getty Images; Blend Images/Shutterstock; **9.13 left to right** Jupiterimages/Stockbyte/Getty Images; Diego Cervo/Fotolia; **Table 9.1 top to bottom** David Terrazas Morales/Corbis; Editorial Image, LLC/Alamy; Eye of Science/Science Source; Science Source; **9.16 left to right** Cynoclub/Fotolia; CallallooAlexis/Fotolia; **p. 156 center left** Eric J. Simon; **p. 157 bottom** Astier/BSIP SA/Alamy; **9.20** Mauro Fermariello/Science

Source; **9.21** Oliver Meckes & Nicole Ottawa/Science Source; **9.23** Eric J. Simon; **p. 161 center** Szabolcs Szekeres/Fotolia; **9.25 top left to right** In Green/Shutterstock; Rido/Shutterstock; **9.25 bottom left to right** Dave King/Dorling Kindersley; Jo Foord/Dorling Kindersley; **9.25 right** Andrew Syred/Science Source; **9.28** Archive Pics/Alamy; **9.29 left to right** Jerry Young/Dorling Kindersley; Gelpi/Fotolia; Dave King/Dorling Kindersley; Dave King/Dorling Kindersley; Tracy Morgan/Dorling Kindersley; Dave King/Dorling Kindersley; Jerry Young/Dorling Kindersley; Dave King/Dorling Kindersley; Dave King/Dorling Kindersley; Shutterstock; Tracy Morgan/Dorling Kindersley.

CHAPTER 10: Chapter opening photo bottom right Mopic/Alamy; **chapter opening photo top right** Oregon Health Sciences University, ho/AP Images; **chapter opening photo top left** Science Source; **chapter opening photo bottom left** Marcobarone/Fotolia; **p. 171 right** Stringer Russia/Kazbek Basaev/Reuters; **p. 171 top left** Stringer Russia/Kazbek Basaev/Reuters; **10.3 left to right** Barrington Brown/Science Source; Library of Congress; **10.11** Jay Cheng/Reuters; **10.22** Michael Follan - Mgfotouk.com/Getty Images; **10.23** Mixa/Alamy; **10.24** Oliver Meckes/Science Source; **10.25** Russell Kightley/Science Source; **10.26** N. Thomas/Science Source; **10.28** Hazel Appleton, Health Protection Agency Centre for Infections/Science Source; **10.29** Jeff Zelevansky JAZ/Reuters; **10.31** NIBSC/Science Photo Library/Science Source; **10.32** Will & Deni McIntyre/Science Source.

CHAPTER 11: Chapter opening photo top left Alila Medical Media/Shutterstock; **chapter opening photo right** Keren Su/Corbis; **chapter opening photo bottom left** Chubykin Arkady/Shutterstock; **p. 197 right** David McCarthy/Science Source; **p. 197 top left** David McCarthy/Science Source; **11.1 left to right** Steve Gschmeissner/Science Source; Steve Gschmeissner/Science Photo Library/Alamy; Ed Reschke/Getty Images; **11.4** Iuliia Lodia/Fotolia; **11.9 top to bottom** F. Rudolf Turner; F. Rudolf Turner; **11.10** American Association for the Advancement of Science; **11.11** Videowokart/Shutterstock; **p. 205 top center** Joseph T. Collins/Science Source; **11.13a** Courtesy of the Roslin Institute, Edinburgh; **11.13b** University of Missouri; **11.13c left to right** Pasqualino Loi; Robert Lanza; Robert Lanza/F. Rudolf Turner; **11.15** Mauro Fermariello/Science Source; **11.15 bottom right inset** Craig Hammell/Cord Blood Registry; **11.18 bottom** ERproductions Ltd/Blend Images/Alamy; **11.18 top** Simon Fraser/Royal Victoria Infirmary, Newcastle upon Tyne/Science Source; **11.19** Geo Martinez/Shutterstock; **11.21** Alastair Grant/AP Images; **11.22** CNRI/Science Source.

CHAPTER 12: Chapter opening photo top right Alexander Raths/Shutterstock; **chapter opening photo bottom** Stocksnapper/Shutterstock; **chapter opening photo top left** Gerd Guenther/Science Source; **p. 217 right** Tek Image/Science Source; **p. 217 top left** Tek Image/Science Source; **12.1** AP Images; **12.2** Huntington Potter/University of South Florida College of Medicine; **12.2 inset** Prof. S. Cohen/Science Source; **12.5** Andrew Brookes/National Physical Laboratory/Science Source; **12.6** Eric Carr/Alamy; **12.7** Volker Steger/

Science Source; **12.8** Inga Spence/Alamy; **12.9** Christopher Gable and Sally Gable/Dorling Kindersley; **12.9 inset** U.S. Department of Agriculture (USDA); **12.10 top to bottom** International Rice Research Institute; Fotosearch RM/Age Fotostock; **12.13** Applied Biosystems, Inc; **12.16** Steve Helber/AP Images; **12.17** Fine Art Images/Heritage Image Partnership Ltd/Alamy; **12.18** Volker Steger/Science Source; **12.19 bottom** David Parker/Science Photo Library/Science Source; **12.19 top** Edyta Pawlowska/Shutterstock; **12.22** Scott Camazine/Science Source; **12.23** James King-Holmes/Science Source; **12.24** 68/Ben Edwards/Ocean/Corbis; **12.25** Alex Milan Tracy/NurPhoto/Sipa U/Newscom; **12.26** Isak55/Shutterstock; **12.27** Image Point Fr/Shutterstock; **12.28** Public domain; **12.29** Daily Mail/Rex/Alamy.

CHAPTER 13: Chapter opening photo top left victoriaKh/Shutterstock; **chapter opening photo top center** BW Folsom/Shutterstock; **chapter opening photo top right** Parameswaran Pillai Karunakaran/FLPA; **chapter opening photo bottom right** John Bryant/Getty Images; **chapter opening photo center left** W. Perry Conway/Ramble/Corbis; **chapter opening photo bottom left** G. Newman Lowrance/AP Images; **p. 243 right** Gay Bumgarner/Alamy; **p. 243 top left** Gay Bumgarner/Alamy; **13.1** Aditya Singh/Moment/Getty Images; **13.2 left to right** Chris Pole/Shutterstock; Sabena Jane Blackbird/Alamy; **13.3 left** Science Source; **13.3 right** Classic Image/Alamy; **13.4a** Celso Diniz/Shutterstock; **13.4b** Tim Laman/National Geographic/Getty Images; **13.5 top left** Francois Gohier/Science Source; **13.5 center** Francois Gohier/Science Source; **13.5 top right** Science Source; **13.5 bottom left** Pixtal/SuperStock; **13.5 bottom right** Vostok Sarl/Mammuthus; **13.8 left to right** Dr. Keith Wheeler/Science Source; Lennart Nilsson/Tidningarnas Telelgrambyra AB Nilsson/TT Nyhetsbyrun; **13.10 top to bottom** Eric Isselee/Shutterstock; Tom Reichner/Shutterstock; Eric Isselee/Shutterstock; Christian Musat/Shutterstock; **13.11** Laura Jesse; **13.12** Zoonar/Poelzer/Age Fotostock; **13.13** Philip Wallick/Spirit/Corbis; **13.14** Edmund D. Brodie III; **13.15** Adam Jones/The Image Bank/Getty Images; **13.16** Andy Levin/Science Source; **13.18** Pearson Education; **13.21** Steve Bloom Images/Alamy; **13.22** Planetpix/Alamy; **13.23** Heather Angel/Natural Visions/Alamy; **13.24** Mariko Yuki/Shutterstock; **13.26a** Reinhard/ARCO/Nature Picture Library; **13.26b** John Cancalosi/Age Fotostock; **13.27** Centers for Disease Control and Prevention

CHAPTER 14: Chapter opening photo top left Keneva Photography/Shutterstock; **chapter opening photo right** Peter Augustin/Photodisc/Getty Images; **chapter opening photo bottom left** Oberhaeuser/Caro/Alamy; **chapter opening photo bottom right** GL Archive/Alamy; **p. 269 right** Kevin Schafer/Lithium/Age Fotostock; **p. 269 top left** Kevin Schafer/Lithium/Age Fotostock; **14.1 left to right** Cathleen A Clapper/Shutterstock; Peter Scoones/Nature Picture Library; **14.2 Clockwise from far left** Rolf Nussbaumer Photography/Alamy; David Kjaer/Nature Picture Library; Jupiterimages/Stockbyte/Getty images; Photos.com; Phil Date/Shutterstock; Robert Kneschke/Shutterstock; Comstock/Stockbyte/Getty Images; Comstock Photos/Fotosearch; **14.4 p. 272 left to right** USDA/

APHIS Animal and Plant Health Inspection Service; Brian Kentosh; McDonald/Photoshot Holdings Ltd.; Michelsohn Moses; **14.4 p. 273 left to right** J & C Sohns/Tier und Naturfotografie/Age Fotostock; Asami Takahiro; Danita Delimont/Gallo Images/Age Fotostock; **14.5 left** Brown Charles W; **14.5 center top to bottom** Dogist/Shutterstock; Alistair Duncan/Dorling Kindersley; Dorling Kindersley/Dorling Kindersley; **14.5 right** Okuno Kazutoshi; **14.6** Morey Milbradt/Getty Images; **14.6 top left inset** John Shaw/Photoshot; **14.6 top right inset** Clement Vezin/Fotolia; **14.8** Michelle Gilders/Alamy; **14.9** Loraart8/Shutterstock; **14.11 top to bottom** Interfoto/Alamy; Mary Plage/Oxford Scientific/Getty Images; Jim Clare/Nature Picture Library; **14.12** Robert Glusic/Corbis; **14.14** Kyodo/Xinhua/Photoshot/Newscom; **14.16 left to right** Jurgen & Christine Sohns/FLPA; Eugene Sergeev/Shutterstock; Kamonrat/Shutterstock; **14.17 right** Mark Pilkington/Geological Survey of Canada/SPL/Science Source; **14.18** Juniors Bildarchiv GmbH/Alamy; **14.19** Jean Kern; **14.20** Chris Hellier/Science Source; **14.21 left to right** Image Quest Marine; Christophe Courteau/Science Source; Reinhard Dirscherl/Alamy; Image Quest Marine; Image Quest Marine; **p. 286 top right** FloridaStock/Shutterstock.com; **14.23** National Geographic Image Collection/Alamy; **14.27** Arco Images GmbH/Alamy.

CHAPTER 15: Chapter opening photo bottom right vlabo/Shutterstock; **chapter opening photo bottom left** Harry Vorsteher/Cultura Creative (RF)/Alamy; **chapter opening photo bottom center** Odilon Dimier/PhotoAlto sas/Alamy; **p. 293 right** Steve Gschmeissner/Science Source; **p. 293 top left** Steve Gschmeissner/Science Source; **15.2** Mark Garlick/Science Photo Library/Corbis; **15.5** George Luther; **15.6 left to right** Jupiter Images; Dr. Tony Brain and David Parker/Science Photo Library/Science Source; **15.7 left to right** Scimat/Science Source; Niaid/CDC/Science Source; CNRI/SPL/Science Source; **15.8a** David M. Phillips/Science Source; **15.8b** Susan M. Barns; **15.8c** Heide Schulz/Max-Planck Institut für Marine Mikrobiologie; **15.9** Science Photo Library - Steve Gschmeissner/Brand X Pictures/Getty Images; **15.10** Eye of Science/Science Source; **15.11a** Sinclair Stammers/Science Source; **15.11b** Dr. Gary Gaugler/Science Source; **15.12** Image Quest Marine; **15.13 inset** Arco Images/Huetter, C./Alamy; **15.13** Nigel Cattlin/Alamy; **15.15** SIPA USA/SIPA/Newscom; **15.16** Eric J. Simon; **15.17 left** Jim West/Alamy; **15.18 right** SPL/Science Source; **15.19 left to right** Centers for Disease Control and Prevention (CDC); Scott Camazine/Science Source; Dariusz Majgier/Shutterstock; David M. Phillips/Science Source; **15.22a** Carol Buchanan/F1online/Age Fotostock; **15.22b** Oliver Meckes/Science Source; **15.22c** blickwinkel/Alamy; **15.23 p. 308 left to right** Eye of Science/Science Source; David M. Phillips/The Population Council/Science Source; Biophoto Associates/Science Source; **15.23 p. 309 left to right** Claude Carre/Science Source; Dr. Masamichi Aikawa; Michael Abbey/Science Source; **15.24** The Hidden Forest, www.hiddenforest.co.nz; **15.25 right top to bottom** Courtesy of Matt Springer, Stanford University; Courtesy of Robert Kay, MRC Cambridge; Courtesy of Robert Kay, MRC Cambridge; **15.26a** Eye of Science/Science Source;

ILLUSTRATION AND TEXT CREDITS

Appendix D Self-Quiz Answers

CHAPTER 1

1. b (some living organisms are single-celled)
2. atom, molecule, cell, tissue, organ, organism, population, ecosystem, biosphere; the cell
3. Photosynthesis cycles nutrients by converting the carbon in carbon dioxide to sugar, which is then consumed by other organisms. Additionally, the oxygen in water is released as oxygen gas. Photosynthesis contributes to energy flow by converting sunlight to chemical energy, which is then also consumed by other organisms, and by producing heat.
4. a4, b1, c3, d2
5. On average, those individuals with heritable traits best suited to the local environment produce the greatest number of offspring that survive and reproduce. This increases the frequency of those traits in the population over time. The result is the accumulation of evolutionary adaptations.
6. d
7. c
8. evolution
9. a3, b2, c1, d4

CHAPTER 2

1. electrons; neutrons
2. protons
3. Nitrogen-14 has an atomic number of 7 and a mass number of 14. The radioactive isotope, nitrogen-16, has an atomic number of 7 and a mass number of 16.
4. Organisms incorporate radioactive isotopes of an element into their molecules just as they do nonradioactive isotopes, and researchers can detect the presence of the radioactive isotopes.
5. Each carbon atom has only three covalent bonds instead of the required four.
6. The positively charged hydrogen regions would repel each other.
7. d
8. a
9. The positive and negative poles cause adjacent water molecules to become attracted to each other, forming hydrogen bonds. The properties of water such as

cohesion, temperature regulation, and water's ability to act as a solvent all arise from this atomic "stickiness."
10. Because a nonpolar molecule cannot form hydrogen bonds, it would not have the properties that allow water to act as the basis of life, such as the ability to dissolve substances and water's cohesive properties.
11. The cola is an aqueous solution, with water as the solvent, sugar as the main solute, and the CO_2 making the solution acidic.

CHAPTER 3

1. Isomers have different structures, or shapes, and the shape of a molecule usually helps determine the way it functions in the body.
2. dehydration reactions; water
3. hydrolysis
4. b
5. $C_6H_{12}O_6 + C_6H_{12}O_6 \rightarrow C_{12}H_{22}O_{11} + H_2O$
6. fatty acid; glycerol; triglyceride
7. b
8. c
9. If the change does not affect the shape of the protein in any way, then that change would not affect the function of the protein.
10. Hydrophobic amino acids are most likely to be found within the interior of a protein, far from the watery environment.
11. a
12. starch (or glycogen or cellulose); nucleic acid
13. Both DNA and RNA are polynucleotides; both have the same phosphate group along the backbone; and both use A, C, and G bases. But DNA uses T while RNA uses U as a base; the sugar differs between them; and DNA is usually double-stranded, while RNA is usually single-stranded.
14. Structurally, a gene is a long stretch of DNA. Functionally, a gene contains the information needed to produce a protein.

CHAPTER 4

1. b
2. A membrane is fluid because its components are not locked into

place. A membrane is mosaic because it contains a variety of suspended proteins.
3. endomembrane system
4. smooth ER; rough ER
5. rough ER, Golgi apparatus, plasma membrane
6. Both organelles use membranes to organize enzymes and both provide energy to the cell. But chloroplasts capture energy from sunlight during photosynthesis, whereas mitochondria release energy from glucose during cellular respiration. Chloroplasts are only in photosynthetic plants and protists, whereas mitochondria are in almost all eukaryotic cells.
7. a3, b1, c5, d2, e4
8. nucleus, nuclear pores, ribosomes, rough ER, Golgi apparatus
9. Both are appendages that aid in movement and that extend from the surface of a cell. Cells with flagella typically have one long flagellum that propels the cell in a whiplike motion; cilia are usually shorter, are more numerous, and beat in a coordinated fashion.

CHAPTER 5

1. You convert the chemical energy from food to the kinetic energy of your upward climb. At the top of the stairs, some of the energy has been stored as potential energy because of your higher elevation. The rest has been converted to heat.
2. Energy; entropy
3. 10,000 g (or 10 kg); remember that 1 Calorie on a food label equals 1,000 calories of heat energy.
4. The three phosphate groups store chemical energy, a form of potential energy. The release of a phosphate group makes some of this potential energy available to cells to perform work.
5. Hydrolases are enzymes that participate in hydrolysis reactions, breaking down large molecules into the smaller molecules that make them up. Enzymes often have names that end in -ase, so a hydrolase is an enzyme that performs hydrolysis reactions.
6. An inhibitor's binding to another site on the enzyme can cause the

enzyme's active site to change shape.
7. b
8. *Hypertonic* and *hypotonic* are relative terms. A solution that is hypertonic to tap water could be hypotonic to seawater. When using these terms, you must provide a comparison, as in "The solution is hypertonic to the cell's cytoplasm."
9. Passive transport moves atoms or molecules along their concentration gradient (from higher to lower concentration), and active transport moves them against their concentration gradient.
10. b

CHAPTER 6

1. d
2. Plants produce organic molecules by photosynthesis. Consumers must acquire organic material by consuming it rather than making it.
3. In breathing, your lungs exchange CO_2 and O_2 between your body and the atmosphere. In cellular respiration, your cells consume the O_2 in extracting energy from food and release CO_2 as a waste product.
4. the electron transport chain
5. O_2
6. The majority of the energy provided by cellular respiration is generated during the electron transport chain. Shutting down that pathway will deprive cells of energy very quickly.
7. b
8. Glycolysis
9. b
10. Because fermentation supplies only 2 ATP per glucose molecule compared with about 32 from cellular respiration, the yeast will have to consume 16 times as much glucose to produce the same amount of ATP.

CHAPTER 7

1. thylakoids; stroma
2. Because NADPH and ATP are produced by the light reactions on the stroma side, they are more readily available for the Calvin cycle, which consumes the NADPH and ATP and occurs in the stroma.
3. inputs: a, d, e; outputs: b, c

4. "Photo" refers to the light required for photosynthesis to proceed, and "synthesis" refers to the fact that it makes sugar. Putting it together, the word "photosynthesis" means "to make using light."

5. Green light is reflected by chlorophyll, not absorbed, and therefore cannot drive photosynthesis.

6. H_2O

7. c

8. The reactions of the Calvin cycle require the outputs of the light reactions (ATP and NADPH).

9. c

CHAPTER 8

1. c

2. They have identical genes (DNA).

3. They are in the form of very long, thin strands.

4. b

5. prophase and telophase

6. a. 1, 1; b. 1, 2; c. 2, 4; d. $2n$, n; e. individually, by homologous pair; f. identical, unique; g. repair, growth, asexual reproduction; gamete formation

7. 39

8. Prophase II or metaphase II; it cannot be during meiosis I because then you would see an even number of chromosomes; it cannot be during a later stage of meiosis II because then you would see the sister chromatids separated.

9. benign; malignant

10. 16 ($2n = 8$, so $n = 4$ and $2^n = 2^4 = 16$)

11. Nondisjunction would create just as many gametes with an extra copy of chromosome 3 or 16, but extra copies of chromosome 3 or 16 are probably fatal.

CHAPTER 9

1. genotype; phenotype

2. Statement **a.** is the law of independent assortment; statement **b.** is the law of segregation.

3. c

4. c

5. d

6. d

7. d

8. Rudy must be X^DY^0. Carla must be X^DX^d (because she had a son with the disease). There is a ¼ chance

that their second child will be a male with the disease.

9. Height appears to result from polygenic inheritance, like human skin color. See Figure 9.22.

10. The brown allele appears to be dominant, the white allele recessive. The brown parent appears to be homozygous dominant, BB, and the white mouse is homozygous recessive, bb. The F_1 mice are all heterozygous, Bb. If two of the F_1 mice are mated, ¾ of the F_2 mice will be brown.

11. The best way to find out whether a brown F_2 mouse is homozygous dominant or heterozygous is to do a testcross: Mate the brown mouse with a white mouse. If the brown mouse is homozygous, all the offspring will be brown. If the brown mouse is heterozygous, you would expect half the offspring to be brown and half to be white.

12. Freckles are dominant, so Tim and Jan must both be heterozygous. There is a ¾ chance that they will produce a child with freckles and a ¼ chance that they will produce a child without freckles. The probability that the next two children will have freckles is $\frac{3}{4} \times \frac{3}{4} = \frac{9}{16}$.

13. According to the odds, half their children will be heterozygous and have elevated cholesterol levels. There is a ¼ chance that their next child will be homozygous, hh, and have an extremely high cholesterol level, like Katerina.

14. Because it is the father's sperm (that could carry either an X or a Y chromosome) that determines the sex of the offspring, not the mother's egg (which always carries an X).

15. The mother is a heterozygous carrier, and the father is normal. See the brown boxed area at the bottom of Figure 9.28 for a pedigree. One-quarter of their children will be boys suffering from hemophilia; ¼ will be female carriers.

16. For a woman to be colorblind, she must inherit X chromosomes bearing the colorblindness allele from both parents. Her father has only one X chromosome, which

he passes on to all his daughters, so he must be colorblind. A male only needs to inherit the colorblindness allele from a carrier mother; both his parents are usually phenotypically normal.

17. The genotype of the black short-haired parent rabbit is $BBSS$. The genotype of the brown long-haired parent is $bbss$. The F_1 rabbits will all be black and short-haired, $BbSs$. The F_2 rabbits will be black short-haired, black long-haired, brown short-haired, and brown long-haired, in a proportion of 9:3:3:1.

CHAPTER 10

1. polynucleotides; nucleotides

2. sugar (deoxyribose), phosphate, nitrogenous base

3. b

4. Each daughter DNA molecule will have half the radioactivity of the parent molecule, because one polynucleotide from the original parental DNA molecule winds up in each daughter DNA molecule.

5. CAU; GUA; histidine (His)

6. A gene is the polynucleotide sequence with information for making one polypeptide. Each codon—a triplet of bases in DNA or RNA—codes for one amino acid. Transcription occurs when RNA polymerase produces mRNA using one strand of DNA as a template. A ribosome is the site of translation, or polypeptide synthesis, and tRNA molecules serve as interpreters of the genetic code. Each tRNA molecule has an amino acid attached at one end and a three-base anticodon at the other end. Beginning at the start codon, mRNA moves relative to the ribosome a codon at a time. A tRNA with a complementary anticodon pairs with each codon, adding its amino acid to the polypeptide chain. The amino acids are linked by peptide bonds. Translation stops at a stop codon, and the finished polypeptide is released. The polypeptide folds to form a functional protein, sometimes in combination with other polypeptides.

7. a3, b3, c1, d2, e2 and 3

8. d

9. d

10. The genetic material of these viruses is RNA, which is replicated inside the infected cell by special enzymes encoded by the virus. The viral genome (or its complement) serves as mRNA for the synthesis of viral proteins.

11. reverse transcriptase; The process of reverse transcription occurs only in infections by RNA-containing retroviruses like HIV. Cells do not require reverse transcriptase (their RNA molecules do not undergo reverse transcription), so reverse transcriptase can be knocked out without harming the human host.

CHAPTER 11

1. c

2. operon

3. b

4. a

5. DNA polymerase and other proteins required for transcription do not have access to tightly packed DNA.

6. the ability of these cells to produce entire organisms through cloning

7. nuclear transplantation

8. which genes are active in a particular sample of cells

9. b

10. embryonic tissue (ES cells), umbilical cord blood, and bone marrow (adult stem cells)

11. Proto-oncogenes are normal genes involved in the control of the cell cycle. Mutation or viruses can cause them to be converted to oncogenes, or cancer-causing genes. Proto-oncogenes are necessary for normal control of cell division.

12. Master control genes, called homeotic genes, regulate many other genes during development.

CHAPTER 12

1. c, d, b, a

2. vector

3. Such an enzyme creates DNA fragments with "sticky ends," single-stranded regions whose unpaired bases can hydrogen-bond to the complementary sticky ends of other fragments created by the same enzyme.

4. PCR

5. Different people tend to have different numbers of repeats at each STR site. DNA fragments prepared from the STR sites of different people will thus have different lengths, causing them to migrate to different locations on a gel.

6. a

7. b

8. Chop the genome into fragments using restriction enzymes, clone and sequence each fragment, and reassemble the short sequences into a continuous sequence for every chromosome.

9. c, b, a, d

CHAPTER 13

1. species, genus, family, order, class, phylum, kingdom, domain

2. c

3. Lyell and other geologists presented evidence for the gradual change of geologic features over millions of years. Darwin applied this idea to suggest that species evolve through the slow accumulation of small changes over long periods of time.

4. *Bb*: 0.42; *BB*: 0.49; *bb*: 0.09

5. The fitness of an individual (or of a particular genotype) is measured by the relative number of alleles that it contributes to the gene pool of the next generation compared with the contribution of others. Thus the number of fertile offspring produced determines an individual's fitness.

6. b

7. c

8. Both effects result in populations small enough for significant sampling error in the gene pool for the first few generations. A bottleneck event reduces the size of an existing population in a given location. The founder effect occurs when a new, small population colonizes a new territory.

9. stabilizing selection

10. b, c, d

CHAPTER 14

1. Microevolution is a change in the gene pool of a population, often associated with adaptation. Speciation is an evolutionary process in which one species splits into two or more

species. Macroevolution is evolutionary change above the species level, for example, the origin of evolutionary novelty and new taxonomic groups and the impact of mass extinctions on the diversity of life and its subsequent recovery. Macroevolution is marked by major changes in the history of life, and these changes are often noticeable enough to be evident in the fossil record.

2. b

3. prezygotic: a, b, c, e; postzygotic: d

4. because a small gene pool is more likely to be changed substantially by genetic drift and natural selection

5. exaptations

6. d

7. d

8. 2.6

9. Homologies reflected a shared evolutionary history, while analogies do not. Analogies result from convergent evolution.

10. Archaea and Bacteria

CHAPTER 15

1. g, a, d, f, c, b, e

2. d, c, a, b, e

3. DNA polymerase is a protein, which must be transcribed from a gene. But a DNA gene requires DNA polymerase to be replicated. This creates a paradox about which came first—DNA or protein. But RNA can act as both an information storage molecule and an enzyme, suggesting that dual-role RNA may have preceded both DNA and proteins.

4. Exotoxins are poisons secreted by pathogenic bacteria; endotoxins are components of the outer membrane of pathogenic bacteria.

5. food (products of photosynthesis); usable form of nitrogen

6. They can form endospores.

7. Prokaryotes in soil or water decompose the organic matter in leaves and other plant and animal remains, returning the elements to the environment in inorganic form. Prokaryotes in a sewage treatment facility decompose the organic matter in sewage, converting it to an inorganic form.

8. They are eukaryotes that are not plants, animals, or fungi.

9. c

10. b

CHAPTER 16

1. cuticle

2. flowers

3. a. sporophyte b. cones; angiosperms c. fruit

4. b

5. b

6. a fern

7. Because the plants do not lose their leaves during autumn and winter, the leaves are already fully developed for photosynthesis when the short growing season begins in spring.

8. vascular plant

9. a

10. a ripened ovary of a flower that protects and aids in the dispersal of seeds contained in the fruit

11. algae or cyanobacteria; fungi

12. A fungus digests its food externally by secreting digestive juices into the food and then absorbing the small nutrients that result from digestion. In contrast, humans and most other animals ingest relatively large pieces of food and digest the food within their bodies.

CHAPTER 17

1. c

2. arthropod

3. amphibians

4. b

5. chordata; notochord; cartilage disks between your vertebrae

6. bipedalism

7. a

8. *Australopithecus* species, *Homo habilis, Homo erectus, Homo sapiens*

9. a4, b5, c1, d2, e3

CHAPTER 18

1. organismal ecology, population ecology, community ecology, ecosystem ecology

2. light, water temperature, chemicals added

3. physiological; behavioral

4. d

5. a. desert; b. grassland; c. tropical rain forest; d. temperate broadleaf forest; e. coniferous forest; f. tundra

6. chaparral

7. permafrost, very cold winters, and high winds

8. agriculture

9. Carbon dioxide and other gases in the atmosphere absorb heat energy radiating from Earth and reflect it back toward Earth. This is called the greenhouse effect. As the carbon dioxide concentration in the atmosphere increases, more heat is retained, causing global warming.

10. c

11. populations of organisms that have high genetic variability and short life spans

CHAPTER 19

1. the number of people and the land area in which they live

2. III; I

3. a. The *x*-axis is time; the *y*-axis is the number of individuals; the red curve represents exponential growth; the blue curve represents logistic growth.

b. carrying capacity

c. In exponential growth, the size of the population increases more and more rapidly. In logistic growth, the population grows fastest when it is about one-half the carrying capacity.

d. exponential growth curve, though the worldwide growth rate is slowing

4. d

5. opportunistic

6. c

7. c

CHAPTER 20

1. habitat destruction

2. d

3. c

4. a2, b5, c5, d3 or d4, e1

5. because the pesticides become concentrated in their prey

6. succession

7. Only 10% of the energy trapped by photosynthesis is turned into biomass by the plant, and only 10% of that energy is turned into the meat of a grazing animal. Therefore, grain-fed beef provides only about 1% of the energy captured by photosynthesis.

8. Many nutrients come from the soil, but carbon comes from the air.

9. landscape

10. a

Glossary

A

abiotic factor (ā'bī-ot'-ik)
A nonliving component of an ecosystem, such as air, water, light, minerals, or temperature.

abiotic reservoir
The part of an ecosystem where a chemical, such as carbon or nitrogen, accumulates or is stockpiled outside of living organisms.

ABO blood groups
Genetically determined classes of human blood that are based on the presence or absence of carbohydrates A and B on the surface of red blood cells. The ABO blood group phenotypes, also called blood types, are A, B, AB, and O.

absorption
The uptake of small nutrient molecules by an organism's own body. In animals, absorption is the third main stage of food processing, following digestion; in fungi, it is acquisition of nutrients from the surrounding medium.

acclimation (ak'-li-mā'-shun)
Physiological adjustment that occurs gradually, though still reversibly, in response to an environmental change.

acid
A substance that increases the hydrogen ion (H⁺) concentration in a solution.

activation energy
The amount of energy that reactants must absorb before a chemical reaction will start. An enzyme lowers the activation energy of a chemical reaction, allowing it to proceed faster.

activator
A protein that switches on a gene or group of genes by binding to DNA.

active site
The part of an enzyme molecule where a substrate molecule attaches—typically, a pocket or groove on the enzyme's surface.

active transport
The movement of a substance across a biological membrane against its concentration gradient, aided by specific transport proteins and requiring the input of energy (often as ATP).

adenine (A) (ad'-uh-nēn)
A double-ring nitrogenous base found in DNA and RNA.

ADP Adenosine diphosphate
(a-den'-ō-sēn dī-fos'-fāt)
A molecule composed of adenosine and two phosphate groups. The molecule ATP is made by combining a molecule of ADP with a third phosphate in an energy-consuming reaction.

adult stem cell
A cell present in adult tissues that generates replacements for nondividing differentiated cells.

aerobic (ār-ō'-bik)
Containing or requiring molecular oxygen (O₂).

age structure
The relative number of individuals of each age in a population.

AIDS
Acquired immunodeficiency syndrome; the late stages of HIV infection, characterized by a reduced number of T cells; usually results in death caused by infections that would be defeated by a properly functioning immune system.

alga (al'-guh)
(plural, **algae**) An informal term that describes a great variety of photosynthetic protists, including unicellular, colonial, and multicellular forms. Prokaryotes that are photosynthetic autotrophs are also regarded as algae.

allele (uh-lē'-ul)
An alternative version of a gene.

allopatric speciation
The formation of a new species in populations that are geographically isolated from one another. *See also* sympatric speciation.

alternation of generations
A life cycle in which there is both a multicellular diploid form, the sporophyte, and a multicellular haploid form, the gametophyte; a characteristic of plants and multicellular green algae.

alternative RNA splicing
A type of regulation at the RNA-processing level in which different mRNA molecules are produced from the same primary transcript, depending on which RNA segments are treated as exons and which as introns.

amino acid (uh-mēn'-ō)
An organic molecule containing a carboxyl group, an amino group, a hydrogen atom, and a variable side chain (also called a radical group or R group); serves as the monomer of proteins.

amniote
Member of a clade of tetrapods that has an amniotic egg containing specialized membranes that protect the embryo. Amniotes include mammals and reptiles (including birds).

amniotic egg (am'-nē-ot'-ik)
A shelled egg in which an embryo develops within a fluid-filled amniotic sac and is nourished by yolk. Produced by reptiles (including birds) and egg-laying mammals, it enables them to complete their life cycles on dry land.

amoeba (uh-mē'-buh)
A general term for a protozoan (animal-like protist) characterized by great structural flexibility and the presence of pseudopodia.

amphibian
Member of a class of vertebrate animals that includes frogs and salamanders.

anaerobic (an'-ār-ō'-bik)
Lacking or not requiring molecular oxygen (O₂).

analogy
The similarity between two species that is due to convergent evolution rather than to descent from a common ancestor with the same trait.

anaphase
The third stage of mitosis, beginning when sister chromatids separate from each other and ending when a complete set of daughter chromosomes has arrived at each of the two poles of the cell.

angiosperm (an'-jē-ō-sperm)
A flowering plant, which forms seeds inside a protective chamber called an ovary.

animal
A eukaryotic, multicellular, heterotrophic organism that obtains nutrients by ingestion.

annelid (an'-uh-lid)
A segmented worm. Annelids include earthworms, polychaetes, and leeches.

anther
A sac in which pollen grains develop, located at the tip of a flower's stamen.

anthropoid (an'-thruh-poyd)
Member of a primate group made up of the apes (gibbons, orangutans, gorillas, chimpanzees, and bonobos), monkeys, and humans.

anticodon (an'-tī-kō'-don)
On a tRNA molecule, a specific sequence of three nucleotides that is complementary to a codon triplet on mRNA.

aphotic zone (ā-fō'-tik)
The region of an aquatic ecosystem beneath the photic zone, where light levels are too low for photosynthesis to take place.

apicomplexan (ap'-ē-kom-pleks'-un)
A type of parasitic protozoan (animal-like protist). Some apicomplexans cause serious human disease.

aqueous solution (ā'-kwē-us)
A solution in which water is the solvent.

arachnid
Member of a major arthropod group that includes spiders, scorpions, ticks, and mites.

Archaea (ar-kē'-uh)
One of two prokaryotic domains of life, the other being Bacteria.

archaean (ar-kē'-uhn)
(plural, **archaea**) An organism that is a member of the domain Archaea.

arthropod (ar'-thruh-pod)
Member of the most diverse phylum in the animal kingdom; includes the horseshoe crab, arachnids (for example, spiders, ticks, scorpions, and mites), crustaceans (for example, crayfish, lobsters, crabs, and barnacles), millipedes, centipedes, and insects. Arthropods are characterized by a chitinous exoskeleton, molting, jointed appendages, and a body formed of distinct groups of segments.

artificial selection
The selective breeding of domesticated plants and animals to promote the occurrence of desirable traits in the offspring.

asexual reproduction
The creation of genetically identical offspring by a single parent, without the participation of gametes (sperm and egg).

atom
The smallest unit of matter that retains the properties of an element.

atomic mass
The total mass of an atom.

atomic number
The number of protons in each atom of a particular element. Elements are ordered by atomic number in the periodic table of the elements.

ATP Adenosine triphosphate (a-den'-ō-sēn trī-fos'-fāt)
A molecule composed of adenosine and three phosphate groups; the main energy source for cells. A molecule of ATP can be broken down to a molecule of ADP (adenosine diphosphate) and a free phosphate; this reaction releases energy that can be used for cellular work.

ATP synthase
A protein cluster, found in a cellular membrane (including the inner membrane of mitochondria, the thylakoid membrane of chloroplasts, and the plasma membrane of prokaryotes), that uses the energy of a hydrogen ion concentration gradient to make ATP from ADP. An ATP synthase provides a port through which hydrogen ions (H^+) diffuse.

autosome
A chromosome not directly involved in determining the sex of an organism; in mammals, for example, any chromosome other than X or Y.

autotroph (ot'-ō-trōf)
An organism that makes its own food from inorganic ingredients, thereby sustaining itself without eating other organisms or their molecules. Plants, algae, and photosynthetic bacteria are autotrophs.

B

bacillus (buh-sil'-us)
(plural, **bacilli**) A rod-shaped prokaryotic cell.

Bacteria
One of two prokaryotic domains of life, the other being Archaea.

bacteriophage (bak-tēr'-ē-ō-fāj)
A virus that infects bacteria; also called a phage.

bacterium
(plural, **bacteria**) An organism that is a member of the domain Bacteria.

base
A substance that decreases the hydrogen ion (H^+) concentration in a solution.

benign tumor
An abnormal mass of cells that remains at its original site in the body.

benthic realm
A seafloor or the bottom of a freshwater lake, pond, river, or stream. The benthic realm is occupied by communities of organisms known as benthos.

bilateral symmetry
An arrangement of body parts such that an organism can be divided equally by a single cut passing longitudinally through it. A bilaterally symmetric organism has mirror-image right and left sides.

binary fission
A means of asexual reproduction in which a parent organism, often a single cell, divides into two individuals of about equal size.

binomial
A two-part Latinized name of a species; for example, *Homo sapiens*.

biocapacity
Earth's capacity to produce the resources such as food, water, and fuel consumed by humans and to absorb human-generated waste.

biodiversity
The variety of living things; includes genetic diversity, species diversity, and ecosystem diversity.

biodiversity hot spot
A small geographic area that contains a large number of threatened or endangered species and an exceptional concentration of endemic species (those found nowhere else).

biofilm
A surface-coating cooperative colony of prokaryotes.

biogeochemical cycle
Any of the various chemical circuits occurring in an ecosystem, involving both biotic and abiotic components of the ecosystem.

biogeography
The study of the past and present distribution of organisms.

bioinformatics
A scientific field of study that uses mathematics to develop methods for organizing and analyzing large sets of biological data.

biological control
The intentional release of a natural enemy to attack a pest population.

biological magnification
The accumulation of persistent chemicals in the living tissues of consumers in food chains.

biological species concept
The definition of a species as a population or group of populations whose members have the potential in nature to interbreed and produce fertile offspring.

biology
The scientific study of life.

biomass
The amount, or mass, of living organic material in an ecosystem.

biome (bī'-ōm)
A major terrestrial or aquatic life zone, characterized by vegetation type in terrestrial biomes and the physical environment in aquatic biomes.

biophilia
The human desire to affiliate with other life in its many forms.

bioremediation
The use of living organisms to detoxify and restore polluted and degraded ecosystems.

biosphere
The global ecosystem; the entire portion of Earth inhabited by life; all of life and where it lives.

biotechnology
The manipulation of living organisms to perform useful tasks.

biotic factor (bī-ot'-ik)
A living component of a biological community; any organism that is part of an individual's environment.

bird
Member of a group of reptiles with feathers and adaptations for flight.

bivalve
Member of a group of molluscs that includes clams, mussels, scallops, and oysters.

blastula (blas'-tyū-luh)
An embryonic stage that marks the end of cleavage during animal development; a hollow ball of cells in many species.

body cavity
A fluid-filled space separating the digestive tract from the outer body wall.

body segmentation
Subdivision of an animal's body into a series of repeated parts called segments.

bony fish
A fish that has a stiff skeleton reinforced by calcium salts.

bottleneck effect
Genetic drift resulting from a drastic reduction in population size. Typically, the surviving population is no longer genetically representative of the parent population.

bryophyte (brī'-uh-fīt)
A type of plant that lacks xylem and phloem; a nonvascular plant. Bryophytes include mosses and their close relatives.

buffer
A chemical substance that resists changes in pH by accepting hydrogen ions from or donating hydrogen ions to solutions.

C

calorie
The amount of energy that raises the temperature of 1 g of water by 1°C. Commonly reported as Calories, which are kilocalories (1,000 calories).

Calvin cycle
The second of two stages of photosynthesis; a cyclic series of chemical reactions that occur in the stroma of a chloroplast, using the carbon in CO_2 and the ATP and NADPH produced by the light reactions to make the energy-rich sugar molecule G3P, which is later used to produce glucose.

cancer
A malignant growth or tumor caused by abnormal and uncontrolled cell division.

cap
Extra nucleotides added to the beginning of an RNA transcript in the nucleus of a eukaryotic cell.

carbohydrate (kar'-bō-hī'-drāt)
A biological molecule consisting of a simple sugar (a monosaccharide), two monosaccharides joined into a double sugar (a disaccharide), or a chain of monosaccharides (a polysaccharide).

carbon fixation
The initial incorporation of carbon from CO_2 into organic compounds by autotrophic organisms such as photosynthetic plants, algae, or bacteria.

carbon footprint
The amount of greenhouse gas emitted as a result of the actions of a person, nation, or other entity.

carcinogen (kar-sin'-uh-jin)
A cancer-causing agent, either high-energy radiation (such as X-rays or UV light) or a chemical.

carnivore
An animal that mainly eats other animals. *See also* herbivore; omnivore.

carpel (kar'-pul)
The egg-producing part of a flower, consisting of a stalk with an ovary at the base and a stigma, which traps pollen, at the tip.

carrier
An individual who is heterozygous for a recessively inherited disorder and who therefore does not show symptoms of that disorder.

carrying capacity
The maximum population size that a particular environment can sustain.

cartilaginous fish (kar-ti-laj'-uh-nus)
A fish that has a flexible skeleton made of cartilage.

cell cycle
An ordered sequence of events (including interphase and the mitotic phase) that extends from the time a eukaryotic cell is first formed from a dividing parent cell until its own division into two cells.

cell cycle control system
A cyclically operating set of proteins that triggers and coordinates events in the eukaryotic cell cycle.

cell division
The reproduction of a cell.

cell plate
A membranous disk that forms across the midline of a dividing plant cell. During cytokinesis, the cell plate grows outward, accumulating more cell wall material and eventually fusing into a new cell wall.

cell theory
The theory that all living things are composed of cells and that all cells come from earlier cells.

cellular respiration
The aerobic harvesting of energy from food molecules; the energy-releasing chemical breakdown of food molecules, such as glucose, and the storage of potential energy in a form that cells can use to perform work; involves glycolysis, the citric acid cycle, the electron transport chain, and chemiosmosis.

cellulose (sel'-yū-lōs)
A large polysaccharide composed of many glucose monomers linked into cable-like fibrils that provide structural support in plant cell walls. Because cellulose cannot be digested by animals, it acts as fiber, or roughage, in the diet.

centipede
A carnivorous terrestrial arthropod that has one pair of long legs for each of its numerous body segments, with the front pair modified as poisonous claws.

central vacuole (vak'-yū-ōl)
A membrane-enclosed sac occupying most of the interior of a mature plant cell, having diverse roles in reproduction, growth, and development.

centromere (sen'-trō-mer)
The region of a chromosome where two sister chromatids are joined and where spindle microtubules attach during mitosis and meiosis. The centromere divides at the onset of anaphase during mitosis and anaphase II of meiosis.

cephalopod
Member of a group of molluscs that includes squids and octopuses.

chaparral (shap-uh-ral')
A terrestrial biome limited to coastal regions where cold ocean currents circulate offshore, creating mild, rainy winters and long, hot, dry summers; also known as the Mediterranean biome. Chaparral vegetation is adapted to fire.

character
A heritable feature that varies among individuals within a population, such as flower color in pea plants or eye color in humans.

charophyte (kar'-uh-fīt')
A member of the green algal group that shares features with land plants. Charophytes are considered the closest relatives of land plants; modern charophytes and modern plants likely evolved from a common ancestor.

chemical bond
An attraction between two atoms resulting from a sharing of outer-shell electrons or the presence of opposite charges on the atoms.

chemical cycling
The use and reuse of chemical elements such as carbon within an ecosystem.

chemical energy
Energy stored in the chemical bonds of molecules; a form of potential energy.

chemical reaction
A process leading to chemical changes in matter, involving the making and/or breaking of chemical bonds. A chemical reaction involves rearranging atoms, but no atoms are created or destroyed.

chemotherapy (kē'-mō-ther'-uh-pē)
Treatment for cancer in which drugs are administered to disrupt cell division of the cancer cells.

chlorophyll (klor'-ō-fil)
A light-absorbing pigment in chloroplasts that plays a central role in converting solar energy to chemical energy.

chlorophyll _a_ (klor'-ō-fil ā)
A green pigment in chloroplasts that participates directly in the light reactions.

chloroplast (klō'-rō-plast)
An organelle found in plants and photosynthetic protists. Enclosed by two membranes, a chloroplast absorbs sunlight and uses it to power the synthesis of organic food molecules (sugars).

chordate (kōr'-dāt)
An animal that at some point during its development has a dorsal, hollow nerve cord, a notochord, pharyngeal slits, and a post-anal tail. Chordates include lancelets, tunicates, and vertebrates.

chromatin (krō'-muh-tin)
The combination of DNA and proteins that constitutes chromosomes; often used to refer to the diffuse, very extended form taken by the chromosomes when a eukaryotic cell is not dividing.

chromosome (krō'-muh-sōm)
A gene-carrying structure found in the nucleus of a eukaryotic cell and most visible when compacted during mitosis and meiosis; also, the main gene-carrying structure of a prokaryotic cell. Each chromosome consists of one very long threadlike DNA molecule and associated proteins. *See also* chromatin.

chromosome theory of inheritance
A basic principle in biology stating that genes are located on chromosomes and that the behavior of chromosomes during meiosis accounts for inheritance patterns.

ciliate (sil'-ē-it)
A type of protozoan (animal-like protist) that moves and feeds by means of cilia.

cilium (sil'-ē-um)
(plural, **cilia**) A short appendage that propels some protists through the water and moves fluids across the surface of many tissue cells in animals.

citric acid cycle
The metabolic cycle that is fueled by acetyl CoA formed after glycolysis in cellular respiration. Chemical reactions in the cycle complete the metabolic breakdown of glucose molecules to carbon dioxide. The cycle occurs in the matrix of mitochondria and supplies most of the NADH molecules that carry energy to the electron transport chains. Also referred to as the Krebs cycle.

clade
An ancestral species and all its descendants—a distinctive branch in the tree of life.

cladistics (kluh-dis'-tiks)
The study of evolutionary history; specifically, an approach to systematics in which organisms are grouped by common ancestry.

class
In classification, the taxonomic category above order.

cleavage
The process of cytokinesis in animal cells, characterized by pinching of the plasma membrane.

clone
As a verb, to produce genetically identical copies of a cell, organism, or DNA molecule. As a noun, the collection of cells, organisms, or molecules resulting from cloning; also (colloquially), a single organism that is genetically identical to another because it arose from the cloning of a somatic cell.

cnidarian (*nī-dār'-ē-an*)
An animal characterized by cnidocytes, radial symmetry, a gastrovascular cavity, and a polyp or medusa body form. Cnidarians include hydras, jellies, sea anemones, and corals.

coccus (*kok'-us*)
(plural, **cocci**) A spherical prokaryotic cell.

codominant
Expressing two different alleles of a gene in a heterozygote.

codon (*kō'-don*)
A three-nucleotide sequence in mRNA that specifies a particular amino acid or polypeptide termination signal; the basic unit of the genetic code.

cohesion (*kō-hē'-zhun*)
The attraction between molecules of the same kind.

community
All the organisms inhabiting and potentially interacting in a particular area; an assemblage of populations of different species.

community ecology
The study of how interactions between species affect community structure and organization.

competitive exclusion principle
The concept that populations of two species cannot coexist in a community if their niches are nearly identical. Using resources more efficiently and having a reproductive advantage, one of the populations will eventually outcompete and eliminate the other.

complementary DNA (cDNA)
A DNA molecule made in vitro using mRNA as a template and the enzyme reverse transcriptase. A cDNA

molecule therefore corresponds to a gene but lacks the introns present in the DNA of the genome.

complete digestive tract
A digestive tube with two openings, a mouth and an anus.

compound
A substance containing two or more elements in a fixed ratio; for example, table salt (NaCl) consists of one atom of the element sodium (Na) for every atom of chlorine (Cl).

concentration gradient
An increase or decrease in the density of a chemical substance within a given region. Cells often maintain concentration gradients of hydrogen ions across their membranes. When a gradient exists, the ions or other chemical substances involved tend to move from where they are more concentrated to where they are less concentrated.

conifer (*kon'-uh-fer*)
A gymnosperm, or naked-seed plant, most of which produce cones.

coniferous forest (*kō-nif'-rus*)
A terrestrial biome characterized by conifers, cone-bearing evergreen trees.

conservation biology
A goal-oriented science that seeks to understand and counter the loss of biodiversity.

conservation of energy
The principle that energy can be neither created nor destroyed.

consumer
An organism that obtains its food by eating plants or by eating animals that have eaten plants.

convergent evolution
The evolution of similar features in different evolutionary lineages, which can result from living in very similar environments.

coral reef
Tropical marine biome characterized by hard skeletal structures secreted primarily by the resident cnidarians.

covalent bond (*kō-vā'-lent*)
An attraction between atoms that share one or more pairs of electrons.

cross
The cross-fertilization of two different varieties of an organism or of two different species; also called hybridization.

crossing over
The exchange of segments between chromatids of homologous chromosomes during prophase I of meiosis.

crustacean
Member of a major arthropod group that includes lobsters, crayfish, crabs, shrimps, and barnacles.

cryptic coloration
Adaptive coloration that makes an organism difficult to spot against its background.

cuticle (*kyū'-tuh-kul*)
(1) In animals, a tough, nonliving outer layer of the skin. (2) In plants, a waxy coating on the surface of stems and leaves that helps retain water.

cystic fibrosis (CF)
A human genetic disorder caused by a recessive allele and characterized by an excessive secretion of mucus and consequent vulnerability to infection; fatal if untreated.

cytokinesis (*sī'-tō-kuh-nē'-sis*)
The division of the cytoplasm to form two separate daughter cells. Cytokinesis usually occurs during telophase of mitosis, and the two processes (mitosis and cytokinesis) make up the mitotic (M) phase of the cell cycle.

cytoplasm (*sī'-tō-plaz'-um*)
Everything within a eukaryotic cell inside the plasma membrane and outside the nucleus; consists of a semifluid medium (cytosol) and organelles; can also refer to the interior of a prokaryotic cell.

cytosine (C) (*sī'-tuh-sēn*)
A single-ring nitrogenous base found in DNA and RNA.

cytoskeleton
A meshwork of fine fibers in the cytoplasm of a eukaryotic cell; includes microfilaments, intermediate filaments, and microtubules.

cytosol (*sī'-tuh-sol*)
The fluid part of the cytoplasm, in which organelles are suspended.

D

data
Recorded verifiable observations.

decomposer
An organism that absorbs nutrients from nonliving organic material,

such as dead organisms, fallen plant material, and the wastes of living organisms, and converts them to inorganic forms.

dehydration reaction (*dē-hī-drā'-shun*)
A chemical process in which a polymer forms when monomers are linked by the removal of water molecules. One molecule of water is removed for each pair of monomers linked. The atoms in the water molecule are provided by the two monomers involved in the reaction. A dehydration reaction is essentially the reverse of a hydrolysis reaction.

density-dependent factor
A limiting factor whose effects intensify with increasing population density.

density-independent factor
A limiting factor whose occurrence and effects are not related to population density.

desert
A terrestrial biome characterized by low and unpredictable rainfall (less than 30 cm per year).

detritivore (*di-trī'-tuh-vor*)
An organism that consumes dead organic matter (detritus).

detritus (*di-trī'-tus*)
Dead organic matter.

diatom (*dī'-uh-tom*)
A unicellular photosynthetic alga with a unique glassy cell wall containing silica.

diffusion
The spontaneous movement of particles of any kind down a concentration gradient, that is, movement of particles from where they are more concentrated to where they are less concentrated.

dihybrid cross (*dī'-hī'-brid*)
A mating of individuals differing at two genetic loci.

dinoflagellate (*dī'-nō-flaj'-uh-let*)
A unicellular photosynthetic alga with two flagella situated in perpendicular grooves in cellulose plates covering the cell.

diploid (*dip'-loid*)
Containing two sets of chromosomes (pairs of homologous chromosomes) in each cell, one set inherited from each parent; referring to a 2*n* cell.

directional selection
Natural selection that acts in favor of the individuals at one end of a phenotypic range.

disaccharide (*dī-sak'-uh-rīd*)
A sugar molecule consisting of two monosaccharides (simple sugars) linked by a dehydration reaction.

discovery science
The process of scientific inquiry that focuses on using observations to describe nature. *See also* hypothesis, science.

disruptive selection
Natural selection that favors extreme over intermediate phenotypes.

disturbance
In an ecological sense, a force that damages a biological community, at least temporarily, by destroying organisms and altering the availability of resources needed by organisms in the community. Disturbances such as fires and storms play a pivotal role in structuring many biological communities.

DNA Deoxyribonucleic acid
(*dē-ok'-sē-rī'-bō-nū-klā'-ik*)
The genetic material that organisms inherit from their parents; a double-stranded helical macromolecule consisting of nucleotide monomers with deoxyribose sugar, a phosphate group, and the nitrogenous bases adenine (A), cytosine (C), guanine (G), and thymine (T). *See also* gene.

DNA ligase (*lī'-gās*)
An enzyme, essential for DNA replication, that creates new chemical bonds between adjacent DNA nucleotides; used in genetic engineering to paste a specific piece of DNA containing a gene of interest into a bacterial plasmid or other vector.

DNA microarray
A glass slide containing thousands of different kinds of single-stranded DNA fragments arranged in an array (grid). Tiny amounts of DNA fragments, representing different genes, are attached to the glass slide. These fragments are tested for hybridization with various samples of cDNA molecules, thereby measuring the expression of thousands of genes at one time.

DNA polymerase (*puh-lim'-er-ās*)
An enzyme that assembles DNA nucleotides into polynucleotides using a preexisting strand of DNA as a template.

DNA profiling
A procedure that analyzes an individual's unique collection of genetic markers using PCR and gel electrophoresis. DNA profiling can be used to determine whether two samples of genetic material came from the same individual.

DNA sequencing
Determining the complete nucleotide sequence of a gene or DNA segment.

domain
A taxonomic category above the kingdom level. The three domains of life are Archaea, Bacteria, and Eukarya.

dominant allele
In a heterozygote, the allele that determines the phenotype with respect to a particular gene; the dominant version of a gene is usually represented with a capital italic letter (e.g., *F*).

dorsal, hollow nerve cord
One of the four hallmarks of chordates; the chordate brain and spinal cord.

double helix
The form assumed by DNA in living cells, referring to its two adjacent polynucleotide strands wound into a spiral shape.

Down syndrome
A human genetic disorder resulting from a condition called trisomy 21, the presence of an extra chromosome 21; characterized by heart and respiratory defects and varying degrees of developmental disability.

E

earthworm
A type of annelid, or segmented worm, that extracts nutrients from soil.

echinoderm (*ih-kī'-nuh-derm*)
Member of a group of slow-moving or stationary marine animals characterized by a rough or spiny skin, a water vascular system, typically an endoskeleton, and radial symmetry in adults. Echinoderms include sea stars, sea urchins, and sand dollars.

ecological footprint
An estimate of the amount of land required to provide the resources, such as food, water, fuel, and housing, that an individual or a nation consumes and to absorb the waste it generates.

ecological niche
The sum of a species' use of the biotic and abiotic resources in its environment.

ecological succession
The process of biological community change resulting from disturbance; transition in the species composition of a biological community, often following a flood, fire, or volcanic eruption. *See also* primary succession; secondary succession.

ecology
The scientific study of the interactions between organisms and their environments.

ecosystem (*ē'-kō-sis-tem*)
All the organisms in a given area, along with the nonliving (abiotic) factors with which they interact; a biological community and its physical environment.

ecosystem ecology
The study of energy flow and the cycling of chemicals among the various biotic and abiotic factors in an ecosystem.

ecosystem service
Function performed by an ecosystem that directly or indirectly benefits people.

ectotherm (*ek'-tō-therm*)
An animal that warms itself mainly by absorbing heat from its surroundings.

electromagnetic spectrum
The full range of radiation, from the very short wavelengths of gamma rays to the very long wavelengths of radio signals.

electron
A subatomic particle with a single unit of negative electrical charge. One or more electrons move around the nucleus of an atom.

electron transport
A reaction in which one or more electrons are transferred to carrier molecules. A series of such reactions, called an electron transport chain, can release the energy stored in high-energy molecules such as glucose. *See also* electron transport chain.

electron transport chain
A series of electron carrier molecules that shuttle electrons during the final stage of cellular respiration, ultimately using the energy of the electrons to make ATP; located in the inner membrane of mitochondria, the thylakoid membrane of chloroplasts, and the plasma membrane of prokaryotes.

element
A substance that cannot be broken down into other substances by chemical means. Scientists recognize 92 chemical elements that occur naturally and several more that have been created in the laboratory.

embryonic stem cell (ES cell)
Any of the cells in the early animal embryo that differentiate during development to give rise to all the kinds of specialized cells in the body.

emerging virus
A virus that has appeared suddenly or has recently come to the attention of medical scientists.

endangered species
As defined in the U.S. Endangered Species Act, a species that is in danger of extinction throughout all or a significant portion of its range.

endemic species
A species whose distribution is limited to a specific geographic area.

endocytosis (*en'-dō-sī-tō'-sis*)
The movement of materials from the external environment into the cytoplasm of a cell via vesicles or vacuoles.

endomembrane system
A network of organelles that partitions the cytoplasm of eukaryotic cells into functional compartments. Some of the organelles are structurally connected to each other, whereas others are structurally separate but functionally connected by the traffic of vesicles among them.

endoplasmic reticulum (ER)
(*reh-tik'-yuh-lum*)
An extensive membranous network in a eukaryotic cell, continuous with the outer nuclear membrane and composed of ribosome-studded

(rough) and ribosome-free (smooth) regions. See also rough ER; smooth ER.

endoskeleton
A hard interior skeleton located within the soft tissues of an animal; found in all vertebrates and a few invertebrates (such as echinoderms).

endosperm
In flowering plants, a nutrient-rich mass formed by the union of a sperm cell with the diploid central cell of the embryo sac during double fertilization; provides nourishment to the developing embryo in the seed.

endospore
A thick-coated, protective cell produced within a prokaryotic cell exposed to harsh conditions.

endosymbiosis
A relationship in which one organism lives inside the cell or cells of a host organism.

endotherm
An animal that derives most of its body heat from its own metabolism.

endotoxin
A poisonous component of the outer membrane of certain bacteria.

energy
The capacity to cause change, or to move matter in a direction it would not move if left alone.

energy flow
The passage of energy through the components of an ecosystem.

enhancer
A eukaryotic DNA sequence that helps stimulate the transcription of a gene at some distance from it. An enhancer functions by means of a transcription factor called an activator, which binds to it and then to the rest of the transcription apparatus.

entropy (en'-truh-pē)
A measure of disorder, or randomness. One form of disorder is heat, which is random molecular motion.

enzyme (en'-zīm)
A protein that serves as a biological catalyst, changing the rate of a chemical reaction without itself being changed in the process.

enzyme inhibitor
A chemical that interferes with an enzyme's activity by changing the enzyme's shape, either by plugging up the active site or by binding to another site on the enzyme.

epigenetic inheritance
Inheritance of traits transmitted by mechanisms not directly involving the nucleotide sequence of a genome; frequently involves chemical modification of DNA bases and/or histone proteins.

equilibrial life history (ē-kwi-lib'-rē-ul)
The pattern of reaching sexual maturity slowly and producing few offspring but caring for the young; often seen in long-lived, large-bodied species.

estuary (es'-chuh-wār-ē)
The area where a freshwater stream or river merges with seawater.

Eukarya (yū-kār'-yuh)
The domain of eukaryotes, organisms made up of eukaryotic cells; includes all of the protists, plants, fungi, and animals.

eukaryote (yū-kār'-ē-ōt)
An organism characterized by eukaryotic cells. See also eukaryotic cell.

eukaryotic cell (yū-kār'-ē-ot'-ik)
A type of cell that has a membrane-enclosed nucleus and other membrane-enclosed organelles. All organisms except bacteria and archaea (including protists, plants, fungi, and animals) are composed of eukaryotic cells.

eutherian (yū-thēr'-ē-un)
See placental mammal.

evaporative cooling
A property of water whereby a body becomes cooler as water evaporates from it.

evo-devo
Evolutionary developmental biology, which studies the evolution of developmental processes in multicellular organisms.

evolution
Descent with modification; genetic change in a population or species over generations; the heritable changes that have produced Earth's diversity of organisms.

evolutionary adaptation
Modification resulting from natural selection that suits organisms to their environment.

evolutionary tree
A branching diagram that reflects a hypothesis about evolutionary relationships between groups of organisms.

exocytosis (ek'-sō-sī-tō'-sis)
The movement of materials out of the cytoplasm of a cell via membranous vesicles or vacuoles.

exon (ek'-son)
In eukaryotes, a coding portion of a gene. See also intron.

exoskeleton
A hard, external skeleton that protects an animal and provides points of attachment for muscles.

exotoxin
A poisonous protein secreted by certain bacteria.

exponential population growth
A model that describes the expansion of a population in an ideal, unlimited environment.

extracellular matrix
The meshwork that surrounds animal cells, consisting of a web of protein and polysaccharide fibers embedded in a liquid, jelly, or solid.

F

F_1 generation
The offspring of two parental (P generation) individuals. F_1 stands for first filial.

F_2 generation
The offspring of the F_1 generation. F_2 stands for second filial.

facilitated diffusion
The passage of a substance across a biological membrane down its concentration gradient aided by specific transport proteins.

family
In classification, the taxonomic category above genus.

fat
A large lipid molecule made from an alcohol called glycerol and three fatty acids; a triglyceride. Most fats function as energy-storage molecules.

fermentation
The anaerobic harvest of energy from food by some cells. Different pathways of fermentation can produce different end products, including ethanol and lactic acid.

fern
Any of a group of seedless vascular plants.

fertilization
The union of a haploid sperm cell with a haploid egg cell, producing a zygote.

flagellate (flaj'-uh-lit)
A protozoan (animal-like protist) that moves by means of one or more flagella.

flagellum (fluh-jel'-um)
(plural, **flagella**) A long appendage that propels protists through the water and moves fluids across the surface of many tissue cells in animals. A cell may have one or more flagella.

flatworm
A bilateral animal with a thin, flat body form, a gastrovascular cavity with a single opening, and no body cavity. Flatworms include planarians, flukes, and tapeworms.

flower
In an angiosperm, a short stem with four sets of modified leaves, bearing structures that function in sexual reproduction.

fluid mosaic
A description of membrane structure, depicting a cellular membrane as a mosaic of diverse protein molecules suspended in a fluid bilayer of phospholipid molecules.

food chain
The sequence of food transfers between the trophic levels of a community, beginning with the producers.

food web
A network of interconnecting food chains.

foram
A marine protozoan (animal-like protist) that secretes a shell and extends pseudopodia through pores in its shell.

forensics
The scientific analysis of evidence for crime scene investigations and other legal proceedings.

fossil
A preserved imprint or remains of an organism that lived in the past.

fossil fuel
An energy deposit formed from the fossilized remains of long-dead plants and animals.

fossil record
The ordered sequence of fossils as they appear in rock layers, marking the passing of geologic time.

founder effect

The genetic drift resulting from the establishment of a new, small population whose gene pool represents only a sample of the genetic variation present in the parent population.

fruit

A ripened, thickened ovary of a flower, which protects dormant seeds and aids in their dispersal.

functional group

A group of atoms that form the chemically reactive part of an organic molecule. A particular functional group usually behaves similarly in different chemical reactions.

fungus

(plural, **fungi**) A heterotrophic eukaryote that digests its food externally and absorbs the resulting small nutrient molecules. Most fungi consist of a netlike mass of filaments called hyphae. Molds, mushrooms, and yeasts are examples of fungi.

G

gamete (*gam'-ēt*)

A sex cell; a haploid egg or sperm. The union of two gametes of opposite sex (fertilization) produces a zygote.

gametophyte (*guh-mē'-tō-fīt*)

The multicellular haploid form in the life cycle of organisms undergoing alternation of generations; results from a union of spores and mitotically produces haploid gametes that unite and grow into the sporophyte generation.

gastropod

Member of the largest group of molluscs, including snails and slugs.

gastrovascular cavity

A digestive compartment with a single opening that serves as both the entrance for food and the exit for undigested wastes; may also function in circulation, body support, and gas exchange. Jellies and hydras are examples of animals with a gastrovascular cavity.

gastrula (*gas'-trū-luh*)

The embryonic stage resulting from gastrulation in animal development. Most animals have a gastrula made up of three layers of cells: ectoderm, endoderm, and mesoderm.

gel electrophoresis

(*jel e-lek'-trō-fōr-ē'-sis*) A technique for sorting macromolecules. A mixture of molecules is placed on a gel between a positively charged electrode and a negatively charged one; negatively charged molecules migrate toward the positive electrode. The molecules separate in the gel according to their rates of migration.

gene

A unit of inheritance in DNA (or RNA, in some viruses) consisting of a specific nucleotide sequence that programs the amino acid sequence of a polypeptide. Most of the genes of a eukaryote are located in its chromosomal DNA; a few are carried by the DNA of mitochondria and chloroplasts.

gene cloning

The production of multiple copies of a gene.

gene expression

The process whereby genetic information flows from genes to proteins; the flow of genetic information from the genotype to the phenotype: DNA → RNA → protein.

gene flow

The gain or loss of alleles from a population by the movement of individuals or gametes into or out of the population.

gene pool

All the alleles for all the genes in a population at any one time.

gene regulation

The turning on and off of specific genes within a living organism.

genetic code

The set of rules giving the correspondence between nucleotide triplets (codons) in mRNA and amino acids in protein.

genetic drift

A change in the gene pool of a population due to chance.

genetic engineering

The direct manipulation of genes for practical purposes.

genetically modified (GM) organism

An organism that has acquired one or more genes by artificial means. If the gene is from another organism, typically of another species, the recombinant organism is also known as a transgenic organism.

genetics

The scientific study of heredity (inheritance).

genome

The genetic material of an organism or virus; the complete complement of an organism's or virus's genes along with its noncoding nucleic acid sequences.

genomics

The study of whole sets of genes and their interactions.

genotype (*jē'-nō-tīp*)

The genetic makeup of an organism.

genus (*jē'-nus*)

(plural, **genera**) In classification, the taxonomic category above species; the first part of a species' binomial; for example, *Homo*.

geologic time scale

A time scale established by geologists that reflects a consistent sequence of geologic periods, grouped into four divisions: Precambrian, Paleozoic, Mesozoic, and Cenozoic.

germinate

To initiate growth, as in a plant seed or a plant or fungal spore.

glycogen (*glī'-kō-jen*)

A complex, extensively branched polysaccharide made up of many glucose monomers; serves as a temporary energy-storage molecule in liver and muscle cells.

glycolysis (*glī-kol'-uh-sis*)

The multistep chemical breakdown of a molecule of glucose into two molecules of pyruvic acid; the first stage of cellular respiration in all organisms; occurs in the cytoplasmic fluid.

Golgi apparatus (*gol'-jē*)

An organelle in eukaryotic cells consisting of stacks of membranous sacs that modify, store, and ship products of the endoplasmic reticulum.

granum (*gran'-um*)

(plural, **grana**) A stack of hollow disks formed of thylakoid membrane in a chloroplast. Grana are the sites where light energy is trapped by chlorophyll and converted to chemical energy during the light reactions of photosynthesis.

green alga

One of a group of photosynthetic protists that includes unicellular,

colonial, and multicellular species. Green algae are the photosynthetic protists most closely related to plants.

greenhouse effect

The warming of the atmosphere caused by CO_2, CH_4, and other gases that absorb heat radiation and slow its escape from Earth's surface.

greenhouse gas

Any of the gases in the atmosphere that absorb heat radiation, including CO_2, methane, water vapor, and synthetic chlorofluorocarbons.

growth factor

A protein secreted by certain body cells that stimulates other cells to divide.

guanine (G) (*gwa'-nēn*)

A double-ring nitrogenous base found in DNA and RNA.

gymnosperm (*jim'-nō-sperm*)

A naked-seed plant. Its seed is said to be naked because it is not enclosed in an ovary.

H

habitat

A place where an organism lives; a specific environment in which an organism lives.

haploid

Containing a single set of chromosomes; referring to an *n* cell.

Hardy-Weinberg equilibrium

The condition describing a nonevolving population (one that is in genetic equilibrium).

heat

The amount of kinetic energy contained in the movement of the atoms and molecules in a body of matter. Heat is energy in its most random form.

herbivore

An animal that eats mainly plants, algae, or phytoplankton. *See also* carnivore; omnivore.

herbivory

The consumption of plant parts or algae by an animal.

heredity

The transmission of traits from one generation to the next.

heterotroph (*het'-er-ō-trōf*)

An organism that cannot make its own organic food molecules from inorganic ingredients and must obtain them by consuming other organisms or their organic products; a consumer (such as an animal) or a decomposer (such as a fungus) in a food chain.

heterozygous (het'-er-ō-zī'-gus)
Having two different alleles for a given gene.

histone (his'-tōn)
A small protein molecule associated with DNA and important in DNA packing in the eukaryotic chromosome.

HIV
Human immunodeficiency virus; the retrovirus that attacks the human immune system and causes AIDS.

homeotic gene (hō'-mē-ot'-ik)
A master control gene that determines the identity of a body structure of a developing organism, presumably by controlling the developmental fate of groups of cells. (In plants, such genes are called organ identity genes.)

hominin (hah'-mi-nin)
Any anthropoid on the human branch of the evolutionary tree, more closely related to humans than to chimpanzees.

homologous chromosomes
(hō-mol'-uh-gus)
The two chromosomes that make up a matched pair in a diploid cell. Homologous chromosomes are of the same length, centromere position, and staining pattern and possess genes for the same characteristics at corresponding loci. One homologous chromosome is inherited from the organism's father, the other from the mother.

homology (hō-mol'-uh-jē)
Similarity in characteristics resulting from a shared ancestry.

homozygous (hō'-mō-zī'-gus)
Having two identical alleles for a given gene.

host
An organism that is exploited by a parasite or pathogen.

human gene therapy
A recombinant DNA procedure intended to treat disease by altering an afflicted person's genes.

Human Genome Project
An international collaborative effort that sequenced the DNA of the entire human genome.

hybrid
The offspring of parents of two different species or of two different varieties of one species; the offspring of two parents that differ in one or more inherited traits; an individual that is heterozygous for one or more pairs of genes.

hydrogen bond
A type of weak chemical bond formed when a partially positive hydrogen atom from one polar molecule is attracted to the partially negative atom in another molecule (or in another part of the same molecule).

hydrogenation
The artificial process of converting unsaturated fats to saturated fats by adding hydrogen.

hydrolysis (hī-drol'-uh-sis)
A chemical process in which macromolecules are broken down by the chemical addition of water molecules to the bonds linking their monomers; an essential part of digestion. A hydrolysis reaction is essentially the opposite of a dehydration reaction.

hydrophilic (hī'-drō-fil'-ik)
"Water-loving"; pertaining to polar, or charged, molecules (or parts of molecules), which are soluble in water.

hydrophobic (hī'-drō-fō'-bik)
"Water-fearing"; pertaining to nonpolar molecules (or parts of molecules), which do not dissolve in water.

hypertonic
In comparing two solutions, referring to the one with the greater concentration of solutes.

hypha (hī'-fuh)
(plural, **hyphae**) One of many filaments making up the body of a fungus.

hypothesis (hī-poth'-uh-sis)
(plural, **hypotheses**) A tentative explanation that a scientist proposes for a specific phenomenon that has been observed.

hypotonic
In comparing two solutions, referring to the one with the lower concentration of solutes.

I

incomplete dominance
A type of inheritance in which the phenotype of a heterozygote (*Aa*) is intermediate between the phenotypes of the two types of homozygotes (*AA* and *aa*).

induced fit
The interaction between a substrate molecule and the active site of an enzyme, which changes shape slightly to embrace the substrate and catalyze the reaction.

insect
An arthropod that usually has three body segments (head, thorax, and abdomen), three pairs of legs, and one or two pairs of wings.

interphase
The phase in the eukaryotic cell cycle when the cell is not actually dividing. During interphase, cellular metabolic activity is high, chromosomes and organelles are duplicated, and cell size may increase. Interphase accounts for 90% of the cell cycle. *See also* mitosis.

interspecific competition
Competition between populations of two or more species that require similar limited resources.

interspecific interaction
Any interaction between members of different species.

intertidal zone (in'-ter-tīd'-ul)
A shallow zone where the waters of an estuary or ocean meet land.

intraspecific competition
Competition between individuals of the same species for the same limited resources.

intron (in'-tron)
In eukaryotes, a nonexpressed (noncoding) portion of a gene that is excised from the RNA transcript. *See also* exon.

invasive species
A non-native species that has spread far beyond the original point of introduction and causes environmental or economic damage

by colonizing and dominating suitable habitats.

invertebrate
An animal that does not have a backbone.

ion (ī'-on)
An atom or molecule that has gained or lost one or more electrons, thus acquiring an electrical charge.

ionic bond (ī-on'-ik)
An attraction between two ions with opposite electrical charges. The electrical attraction of the opposite charges holds the ions together.

isomer (ī'-sō-mer)
One of two or more molecules with the same molecular formula but different structures and thus different properties.

isotonic (ī-sō-ton'-ik)
Having the same solute concentration as another solution.

isotope (ī'-sō-tōp)
A variant form of an atom. Different isotopes of an element have the same number of protons and electrons but different numbers of neutrons.

K

karyotype (kār'-ē-ō-tīp)
A display of micrographs of the meta-phase chromosomes of a cell, arranged by size and centromere position.

keystone species
A species whose impact on its community is much larger than its biomass or abundance indicates.

kinetic energy (kuh-net'-ik)
Energy of motion. Moving matter performs work by transferring its motion to other matter, such as leg muscles pushing bicycle pedals.

kingdom
In classification, the broad taxonomic category above phylum.

L

lancelet
One of a group of bladelike invertebrate chordates.

landscape
A regional assemblage of interacting ecosystems.

landscape ecology
The application of ecological principles to the study of land-use patterns; the scientific study of the biodiversity of interacting ecosystems.

larva
An immature individual that looks different from the adult animal.

lateral line system
A row of sensory organs along each side of a fish's body. Sensitive to changes in water pressure, it enables a fish to detect minor vibrations in the water.

law of independent assortment
A general rule of inheritance, first proposed by Gregor Mendel, that states that when gametes form during meiosis, each pair of alleles for a particular character segregates (separates) independently of each other pair.

law of segregation
A general rule of inheritance, first proposed by Gregor Mendel, that states that the two alleles in a pair segregate (separate) into different gametes during meiosis.

leech
A type of annelid, or segmented worm, that typically lives in fresh water.

lichen (lī'-ken)
A symbiotic association between a fungus and an alga or between a fungus and a cyanobacterium.

life
Defined by the set of common characteristics that distinguish living organisms from nonliving matter, including such properties and processes as order, regulation, growth and development, energy use, response to the environment, reproduction, and the capacity to evolve over time.

life cycle
The entire sequence of stages in the life of an organism, from the adults of one generation to the adults of the next.

life history
The traits that affect an organism's schedule of reproduction and survival.

life table
A listing of survivals and deaths in a population in a particular time period and predictions of how long, on average, an individual of a given age will live.

light reactions
The first of two stages in photosynthesis; the steps in which solar energy is absorbed and converted to chemical energy in the form of ATP and NADPH. The light reactions power the sugar-producing Calvin cycle but produce no sugar themselves.

lignin (lig'-nin)
A chemical that hardens the cell walls of plants. Lignin makes up most of what we call wood.

limiting factor
An environmental factor that restricts the number of individuals that can occupy a particular habitat, thus holding population growth in check.

linked genes
Genes located close enough together on a chromosome that they are usually inherited together.

lipid
An organic compound consisting mainly of carbon and hydrogen atoms linked by nonpolar covalent bonds and therefore mostly hydrophobic and insoluble in water. Lipids include fats, waxes, phospholipids, and steroids.

lobe-finned fish
A bony fish with strong, muscular fins supported by bones. *See also* ray-finned fish.

locus
(plural, **loci**) The particular site where a gene is found on a chromosome. Homologous chromosomes have corresponding gene loci.

logistic population growth
A model that describes population growth that decreases as population size approaches carrying capacity.

lysogenic cycle (lī-sō-jen'-ik)
A bacteriophage reproductive cycle in which the viral genome is incorporated into the bacterial host chromosome as a prophage. New phages are not produced, and the host cell is not killed or lysed unless the viral genome leaves the host chromosome.

lysosome (lī'-sō-sōm)
A digestive organelle in eukaryotic cells; contains enzymes that digest the cell's food and wastes.

lytic cycle (lit'-ik)
A viral reproductive cycle resulting in the release of new viruses by lysis (breaking open) of the host cell.

M

macroevolution
Evolutionary change above the species level. Examples of macroevolutionary change include the origin of a new group of organisms through a series of speciation events and the impact of mass extinctions on the diversity of life and its subsequent recovery.

macromolecule
A giant molecule formed by joining smaller molecules. Examples of macromolecules include proteins, polysaccharides, and nucleic acids.

malignant tumor
An abnormal tissue mass that spreads into neighboring tissue and to other parts of the body; a cancerous tumor.

mammal
Member of a class of endothermic amniotes that possesses mammary glands and hair.

mantle
In molluscs, the outgrowth of the body surface that drapes over the animal. The mantle produces the shell and forms the mantle cavity.

marsupial (mar-sū'-pē-ul)
A pouched mammal, such as a kangaroo, opossum, or koala. Marsupials give birth to embryonic offspring that complete development while housed in a pouch and attached to nipples on the mother's abdomen.

mass
A measure of the amount of matter in an object.

mass number
The sum of the number of protons and neutrons in an atom's nucleus.

matter
Anything that occupies space and has mass.

medusa (med-ū'-suh)
(plural, **medusae**) One of two types of cnidarian body forms; a floating, umbrella-like body form; also called a jelly.

meiosis (mī-ō'-sis)
In a sexually reproducing organism, the process of cell division that produces haploid gametes from diploid cells within the reproductive organs.

messenger RNA (mRNA)
The type of ribonucleic acid that encodes genetic information from DNA and conveys it to ribosomes, where the information is translated into amino acid sequences.

metabolism (muh-tab'-uh-liz-um)
The total of all the chemical reactions in an organism.

metamorphosis (met'-uh-mōr'-fuh-sis)
The transformation of a larva into an adult.

metaphase (met'-eh-fāz)
The second stage of mitosis. During metaphase, the centromeres of all the cell's duplicated chromosomes are lined up along the center line of the cell.

metastasis (muh-tas'-tuh-sis)
The spread of cancer cells beyond their original site.

microbiota
The community of microorganisms that live in and on the body of an animal.

microevolution
A change in a population's gene pool over a succession of generations.

microtubule
The thickest of the three main kinds of fibers making up the cytoskeleton of a eukaryotic cell; a straight, hollow tube made of globular proteins called tubulins. Microtubules form the basis of the structure and movement of cilia and flagella.

millipede
A terrestrial arthropod that has two pairs of short legs for each of its numerous body segments and that eats decaying plant matter.

mitochondrion (mī'-tō-kon'-drē-on)
(plural, **mitochondria**) An organelle in eukaryotic cells where cellular respiration occurs. Enclosed by two concentric membranes, it is where most of the cell's ATP is made.

mitosis (mī-tō'-sis)
The division of a single nucleus into two genetically identical daughter nuclei. Mitosis and cytokinesis make

up the mitotic (M) phase of the cell cycle.

mitotic (M) phase

The phase of the cell cycle when mitosis divides the nucleus and distributes its chromosomes to the daughter nuclei and cytokinesis divides the cytoplasm, producing two daughter cells.

mitotic spindle

A spindle-shaped structure formed of microtubules and associated proteins that is involved in the movement of chromosomes during mitosis and meiosis. (A spindle is shaped roughly like a football.)

molecular biology

The study of the molecular basis of heredity.

molecule

A group of two or more atoms held together by covalent bonds.

mollusc (*mol'-lusk*)

A soft-bodied animal characterized by a muscular foot, mantle, mantle cavity, and radula. Molluscs include gastropods (snails and slugs), bivalves (clams, oysters, and scallops), and cephalopods (squids and octopuses).

monohybrid cross

A mating of individuals differing at one genetic locus.

monomer (*mon'-uh-mer*)

A chemical subunit that serves as a building block of a polymer.

monosaccharide

(*mon'-uh-sak'-uh-rīd*)

The smallest kind of sugar molecule; a single-unit sugar; also known as a simple sugar.

monotreme (*mon'-uh-trēm*)

An egg-laying mammal, such as the duck-billed platypus.

moss

Any of a group of seedless nonvascular plants.

movement corridor

A series of small clumps or a narrow strip of quality habitat (usable by organisms) that connects otherwise isolated patches of quality habitat.

mutagen (*myū'-tuh-jen*)

A chemical or physical agent that inter-acts with DNA and causes a mutation.

mutation

A change in the nucleotide sequence of DNA; a major source of genetic diversity.

mutualism

An interspecific interaction in which both partners benefit.

mycelium (*mī-sē'-lē-um*)

(plural, **mycelia**) The densely branched network of hyphae in a fungus.

mycorrhiza (*mī'-kō-rī'-zuh*)

(plural, **mycorrhizae**) A mutually beneficial symbiotic association of a plant root and fungus.

N

NADH

An electron carrier (a molecule that carries electrons) involved in cellular respiration and photosynthesis. NADH carries electrons from glucose and other fuel molecules and deposits them at the top of an electron transport chain. NADH is generated during glycolysis and the citric acid cycle.

NADPH

An electron carrier (a molecule that carries electrons) involved in photosynthesis. Light drives electrons from chlorophyll to NADP$^+$, forming NADPH, which provides the high-energy electrons for the reduction of carbon dioxide to sugar in the Calvin cycle.

natural selection

A process in which organisms with certain inherited characteristics are more likely to survive and reproduce than are organisms with other characteristics; unequal reproductive success.

nematode (*nēm'-uh-tōd*)

See roundworm.

neutron

An electrically neutral particle (a particle having no electrical charge), found in the nucleus of an atom.

nitrogen fixation

The conversion of atmospheric nitrogen (N_2) to ammonia (NH_3). NH_3 then picks up another H$^+$ to become NH_4^+ (ammonium), which plants can absorb and use.

nondisjunction

An accident of meiosis or mitosis in which a pair of homologous chromosomes or a pair of sister chromatids fails to separate at anaphase.

notochord (*nō'-tuh-kord*)

A flexible, cartilage-like, longitudinal rod located between the digestive tract and nerve cord in chordate animals, present only in embryos in many species.

nuclear envelope

A double membrane, perforated with pores, that encloses the nucleus and separates it from the rest of the eukaryotic cell.

nuclear transplantation

A technique in which the nucleus of one cell is placed into another cell that already has a nucleus or in which the nucleus has been previously destroyed. The cell is then stimulated to grow, producing an embryo that is a genetic copy of the nucleus donor.

nucleic acid (*nū-klā'-ik*)

A polymer consisting of many nucleotide monomers; serves as a blueprint for proteins and, through the actions of proteins, for all cellular structures and activities. The two types of nucleic acids are DNA and RNA.

nucleoid

A non–membrane-enclosed region in a prokaryotic cell where the DNA is concentrated.

nucleolus (*nū-klē'-ō-lus*)

A structure within the nucleus of a eukaryotic cell where ribosomal RNA is made and assembled with proteins to make ribosomal subunits; consists of parts of the chromatin DNA, RNA transcribed from the DNA, and proteins imported from the cytoplasm.

nucleosome (*nū'-klē-ō-sōm*)

The bead-like unit of DNA packing in a eukaryotic cell; consists of DNA wound around a protein core made up of eight histone molecules.

nucleotide (*nū'-klē-ō-tīd*)

An organic monomer consisting of a five-carbon sugar covalently bonded to a nitrogenous base and a phosphate group. Nucleotides are the building blocks of nucleic acids, including DNA and RNA.

nucleus

(plural, **nuclei**) (1) An atom's central core, containing protons and neutrons. (2) The genetic control center of a eukaryotic cell.

O

omnivore

An animal that eats both plants and animals. *See also* carnivore; herbivore.

oncogene (*on'-kō-jēn*)

A cancer-causing gene; usually contributes to malignancy by abnormally enhancing the amount or activity of a growth factor made by the cell.

operator

In prokaryotic DNA, a sequence of nucleotides near the start of an operon to which an active repressor can attach. The binding of repressor prevents RNA polymerase from attaching to the promoter and transcribing the genes of the operon.

operculum (*ō-per'-kyū-lum*)

(plural, **opercula**) A protective flap on each side of a bony fish's head that covers a chamber housing the gills.

operon (*op'-er-on*)

A unit of genetic regulation common in prokaryotes; a cluster of genes with related functions, along with the promoter and operator that control their transcription.

opportunistic life history

The pattern of reproducing when young and producing many offspring that receive little or no parental care; often seen in short-lived, small-bodied species.

order

In classification, the taxonomic category above family.

organelle (*ōr-guh-nel'*)

A membrane-enclosed structure with a specialized function within a eukaryotic cell.

organic compound

A chemical compound containing the element carbon.

organism

An individual living thing, such as a bacterium, fungus, protist, plant, or animal.

organismal ecology

The study of the evolutionary adaptations that enable individual organisms to meet the challenges posed by their abiotic environments.

osmoregulation

The control of the gain or loss of water and dissolved solutes in an organism.

osmosis (oz-mō´-sis)
The diffusion of water across a selectively permeable membrane.

ovary
(1) In animals, the female gonad, which produces egg cells and reproductive hormones. (2) In flowering plants, the base of a carpel in which the egg-containing ovules develop.

ovule (ō´-vyūl)
In a seed plant, a reproductive structure that contains the female gametophyte and the developing egg. An ovule develops into a seed.

P

P generation
The parent individuals from which offspring are derived in studies of inheritance. P stands for parental.

paedomorphosis (pē´-duh-mōr´-fuh-sis)
The retention in the adult of features that were juvenile in ancestral species.

paleontologist
A scientist who studies fossils.

parasite
An organism that lives in or on another organism (the host) from which it obtains nourishment; an organism that benefits at the expense of another organism, which is harmed in the process.

passive transport
The diffusion of a substance across a biological membrane without any input of energy.

pathogen
A disease-causing virus or organism.

pedigree
A family tree representing the occurrence of heritable traits in parents and offspring across a number of generations.

pelagic realm (puh-laj´-ik)
The open-water region of an ocean.

peptide bond
The covalent linkage between two amino acid units in a polypeptide, formed by a dehydration reaction between two amino acids.

periodic table of the elements
A table listing all of the chemical elements (both natural and human-made) ordered by atomic number (the number of protons in the nucleus of a single atom of that element).

permafrost
Continuously frozen subsoil found in the arctic tundra.

petal
A modified leaf of a flowering plant. Petals are the often colorful parts of a flower that advertise it to insects and other pollinators.

pH scale
A measure of the relative acidity of a solution, ranging in value from 0 (most acidic) to 14 (most basic).

phage (fāj)
See bacteriophage.

phagocytosis (fag´-ō-sī-tō´-sis)
Cellular "eating"; a type of endocytosis whereby a cell engulfs large molecules, other cells, or particles into its cytoplasm.

pharyngeal slit (fuh-rin´-jē-ul)
A gill structure in the pharynx, found in chordate embryos and some adult chordates.

phenotype (fē´-nō-tīp)
The expressed traits of an organism.

phospholipid (fos´-fō-lip´-id)
A molecule that is a part of the inner bilayer of biological membranes, having a hydrophilic head and a hydrophobic tail.

phospholipid bilayer
A double layer of phospholipid molecules (each molecule consisting of a phosphate group bonded to two fatty acids) that is the primary component of all cellular membranes.

photic zone (fō´-tik)
Shallow water near the shore or the upper layer of water away from the shore; region of an aquatic ecosystem where sufficient light is available for photosynthesis.

photon (fō´-ton)
A fixed quantity of light energy. The shorter the wavelength of light, the greater the energy of a photon.

photosynthesis (fō´-tō-sin´-thuh-sis)
The process by which plants, algae, and some bacteria transform light energy to chemical energy stored in the bonds of sugars. This process requires an input of carbon dioxide (CO_2) and water (H_2O) and produces oxygen gas (O_2) as a waste product.

photosystem
A light-harvesting unit of a chloroplast's thylakoid membrane; consists of several hundred molecules, a reaction-center chlorophyll, and a primary electron acceptor.

phylogenetic tree (fī´-lō-juh-net´-ik)
A branching diagram that represents a hypothesis about evolutionary relationships between organisms.

phylum (fī´-lum)
(plural, **phyla**) In classification, the taxonomic category above class. Members of a phylum all have a similar general body plan.

phytoplankton
Photosynthetic organisms, mostly microscopic, that drift near the surfaces of ponds, lakes, and oceans.

placenta (pluh-sen´-tuh)
In most mammals, the organ that provides nutrients and oxygen to the embryo and helps dispose of its metabolic wastes. The placenta is formed from embryonic tissue and the mother's endometrial blood vessels.

placental mammal (pluh-sen´-tul)
Mammal whose young complete their embryonic development in the uterus, nourished via the mother's blood vessels in the placenta; also called a eutherian.

plant
A multicellular eukaryote that c arries out photosynthesis and has a set of structural and reproductive terrestrial adaptations, including a multicellular, dependent embryo.

plasma membrane
The thin double layer of lipids and proteins that sets a cell off from its surroundings and acts as a selective barrier to the passage of ions and molecules into and out of the cell; consists of a phospholipid bilayer in which proteins are embedded.

plasmid
A small ring of self-replicating DNA separate from the larger chromosome(s). Plasmids are most frequently derived from bacteria.

plate tectonics (tek-tahn´-iks)
The theory that the continents are part of great plates of Earth's crust that float on the hot, underlying portion of the mantle. Movements in the mantle cause the continents to move slowly over time.

pleiotropy (plī´-uh-trō-pē)
The control of more than one phenotypic character by a single gene.

polar ice
A terrestrial biome that includes regions of extremely cold temperature and low precipitation located at high latitudes north of the arctic tundra and in Antarctica.

polar molecule
A molecule containing an uneven distribution of charge due to the presence of polar covalent bonds (bonds having opposite charges on opposite ends). A polar molecule will have a slightly positive pole (end) and a slightly negative pole.

pollen grain
In a seed plant, the male gametophyte that develops within the anther of a stamen. It houses cells that will develop into sperm.

pollination
In seed plants, the delivery, by wind or animals, of pollen from the male (pollen-producing) parts of a plant to the stigma of a carpel on the female part of a plant.

polychaete (pahl´-ē-kēt)
A type of annelid, or segmented worm, that typically lives on the seafloor.

polygenic inheritance (pol´-ē-jen´-ik)
The additive effect of two or more genes on a single phenotypic character.

polymer (pol´-uh-mer)
A large molecule consisting of many identical or similar molecular units, called monomers, covalently joined together in a chain.

polymerase chain reaction (PCR) (puh-lim´-uh-rās)
A technique used to obtain many copies of a DNA molecule or many copies of part of a DNA molecule. A small amount of DNA mixed with the enzyme DNA polymerase, DNA nucleotides, and a few other ingredients replicates repeatedly in a test tube.

polynucleotide (pol´-ē-nū´-klē-ō-tīd)
A polymer made up of many nucleotides covalently bonded together.

polyp (pol´-ip)
One of two types of cnidarian body forms; a stationary (sedentary), columnar, hydra-like body.

polypeptide
A chain of amino acids linked by peptide bonds.

polyploidy
Having more than two complete sets of chromosomes as a result of an accident of cell division.

polysaccharide (*pol'-ē-sak'-uh-rīd*)
A carbohydrate polymer consisting of many monosaccharides (simple sugars) linked by covalent bonds.

population
A group of interacting individuals belonging to one species and living in the same geographic area at the same time.

population density
The number of individuals of a species per unit area or volume of the habitat.

population ecology
The study of how members of a population interact with their environment, focusing on factors that influence population density and growth.

population momentum
In a population in which fertility (the number of live births over a woman's lifetime) averages two children (replacement rate), the continuation of population growth as girls reach their reproductive years.

post-anal tail
A tail posterior to the anus, found in chordate embryos and most adult chordates.

postzygotic barrier (*pōst'-zī-got'-ik*)
A reproductive barrier that operates if interspecies mating occurs and forms hybrid zygotes.

potential energy
Stored energy; the energy that an object has due to its location and/or arrangement. Water behind a dam and chemical bonds both possess potential energy.

predation
An interaction between species in which one species, the predator, kills and eats the other, the prey.

prezygotic barrier (*prē'-zī-got'-ik*)
A reproductive barrier that impedes mating between species or hinders fertilization of eggs if members of different species attempt to mate.

primary consumer
An organism that eats only autotrophs; an herbivore.

primary production
The amount of solar energy converted to the chemical energy stored in organic compounds by autotrophs in an ecosystem during a given time period.

primary succession
A type of ecological succession in which a biological community begins in an area without soil. *See also* secondary succession.

primate
Member of the mammalian group that includes lorises, bush babies, lemurs, tarsiers, monkeys, apes, and humans.

primer
A short stretch of nucleic acid bound by complementary base pairing to a DNA sequence and elongated with DNA nucleotides. During PCR, primers flank the desired sequence to be copied.

prion (*prī'-on*)
An infectious form of protein that may multiply by converting related proteins to more prions. Prions cause several related diseases in different animals, including scrapie in sheep, mad cow disease, and Creutzfeldt-Jakob disease in humans.

producer
An organism that makes organic food molecules from carbon dioxide, water, and other inorganic raw materials: a plant, alga, or autotrophic bacterium; the trophic level that supports all others in a food chain or food web.

product
An ending material in a chemical reaction.

prokaryote (*prō-kār'-ē-ōt*)
An organism characterized by prokaryotic cells. *See also* prokaryotic cell.

prokaryotic cell (*prō-kār'-ē-ot'-ik*)
A type of cell lacking a nucleus and other membrane-bound organelles. Prokaryotic cells are found only among organisms of the domains Bacteria and Archaea.

promoter
A specific nucleotide sequence in DNA, located at the start of a gene, that is the binding site for RNA polymerase and the place where transcription begins.

prophage (*prō'-fāj*)
Phage DNA that has inserted into the DNA of a prokaryotic chromosome.

prophase
The first stage of mitosis. During prophase, duplicated chromosomes condense to form structures visible with a light microscope, and the mitotic spindle forms and begins moving the chromosomes toward the center of the cell.

protein
A biological polymer constructed from hundreds to thousands of amino acid monomers. Proteins perform many functions within living cells, including providing structure, transport, and acting as enzymes.

proteomics
The systematic study of the full protein sets (proteomes) encoded by genomes.

protist (*prō'-tist*)
Any eukaryote that is not a plant, animal, or fungus.

proton
A subatomic particle with a single unit of positive electrical charge, found in the nucleus of an atom.

proto-oncogene (*prō'-tō-on'-kō-jēn*)
A normal gene that can be converted to a cancer-causing gene.

protozoan (*prō'-tō-zō'-un*)
A protist that lives primarily by ingesting food; a heterotrophic, animal-like protist.

provirus
Viral DNA that inserts into a host genome.

pseudopodium (*sū'-dō-pō'-dē-um*)
(plural, **pseudopodia**) A temporary extension of an amoeboid cell. Pseudopodia function in moving cells and engulfing food.

Punnett square
A diagram used in the study of inheritance to show the results of random fertilization.

pyramid of production
A diagram depicting the cumulative loss of energy with each transfer in a food chain.

Q

quaternary consumer (*kwot'-er-nār-ē*)
An organism that eats tertiary consumers.

R

radial symmetry
An arrangement of the body parts of an organism like pieces of a pie around an imaginary central axis. Any slice passing longitudinally through a radially symmetric organism's central axis divides the organism into mirror-image halves.

radiation therapy
Treatment for cancer in which parts of the body that have cancerous tumors are exposed to high-energy radiation to disrupt cell division of the cancer cells.

radioactive isotope
An isotope whose nucleus decays spontaneously, giving off particles and energy.

radiometric dating
A method for determining the age of fossils and rocks from the ratio of a radioactive isotope to the nonradioactive isotope(s) of the same element in the sample.

radula (*rad'-yū-luh*)
A file-like organ found in many molluscs, typically used to scrape up or shred food.

ray-finned fish
A bony fish in which fins are webs of skin supported by thin, flexible skeletal rays. All but one living species of bony fishes are ray-fins. *See also* lobe-finned fish.

reactant
A starting material in a chemical reaction.

recessive allele
In heterozygotes, the allele that has no noticeable effect on the phenotype; the recessive version of a gene is usually represented with a lowercase italic letter (e.g., *f*).

recombinant DNA
A DNA molecule carrying genes derived from two or more sources, often from different species.

regeneration

The regrowth of body parts from pieces of an organism.

relative abundance

The proportional representation of a species in a biological community; one component of species diversity.

relative fitness

The contribution an individual makes to the gene pool of the next generation relative to the contribution of other individuals in the population.

repetitive DNA

Nucleotide sequences that are present in many copies in the DNA of a genome. The repeated sequences may be long or short and may be located next to each other or dispersed in the DNA.

repressor

A protein that blocks the transcription of a gene or operon.

reproductive barrier

Anything that prevents individuals of closely related species from interbreeding, even when populations of the two species live together.

reproductive cloning

Using a body cell from a multicellular organism to make one or more genetically identical individuals.

reptile

Member of the clade of amniotes that includes snakes, lizards, turtles, crocodiles, alligators, birds, and a number of extinct groups (including most of the dinosaurs).

restoration ecology

A field of ecology that develops methods of returning degraded ecosystems to their natural state.

restriction enzyme

A bacterial enzyme that cuts up foreign DNA at one very specific nucleotide sequence. Restriction enzymes are used in DNA technology to cut DNA molecules in reproducible ways.

restriction fragment

A molecule of DNA produced from a longer DNA molecule cut up by a restriction enzyme.

restriction site

A specific sequence on a DNA strand that is recognized and cut by a restriction enzyme.

retrovirus

An RNA virus that reproduces by means of a DNA molecule. It reverse-transcribes its RNA into DNA, inserts the DNA into a cellular chromosome, and then transcribes more copies of the RNA from the viral DNA. HIV and a number of cancer-causing viruses are retroviruses.

reverse transcriptase (tran-skrip'-tās)

An enzyme that catalyzes the synthesis of DNA on an RNA template.

ribosomal RNA (rRNA) (rī'-buh-sōm'-ul)

The type of ribonucleic acid that, together with proteins, makes up ribosomes.

ribosome (rī'-buh-sōm)

A cellular structure consisting of RNA and protein organized into two subunits and functioning as the site of protein synthesis in the cytoplasm. The ribosomal subunits are constructed in the nucleolus and then transported to the cytoplasm where they act.

RNA Ribonucleic acid (rī'-bō-nū-klā'-ik)

A type of nucleic acid consisting of nucleotide monomers, with a ribose sugar, a phosphate group, and the nitrogenous bases adenine (A), cytosine (C), guanine (G), and uracil (U); usually single-stranded; functions in protein synthesis and as the genome of some viruses.

RNA polymerase (puh-lim'-uh-rās)

An enzyme that links together the growing chain of RNA nucleotides during transcription, using a DNA strand as a template.

RNA splicing

The removal of introns and joining of exons in eukaryotic RNA, forming an mRNA molecule with a continuous coding sequence; occurs before mRNA leaves the nucleus.

root

The underground organ of a plant. Roots anchor the plant in the soil, absorb and transport minerals and water, and store food.

rough ER (rough endoplasmic reticulum) (reh-tik'-yuh-lum)

A network of interconnected membranous sacs in a eukaryotic cell's cytoplasm. Rough ER membranes are studded with ribosomes that make membrane proteins and secretory proteins. The rough ER constructs membrane from phospholipids and proteins.

roundworm

An animal characterized by a cylindrical, wormlike body form and a complete digestive tract; also called a nematode.

rule of multiplication

A rule stating that the probability of a compound event is the product of the separate probabilities of the independent events.

S

saturated

Pertaining to fats and fatty acids whose hydrocarbon chains contain the maximum number of hydrogens and therefore have no double covalent bonds. Because of their straight, flat shape, saturated fats and fatty acids tend to be solid at room temperature.

savanna

A terrestrial biome dominated by grasses and scattered trees. The temperature is warm year-round. Frequent fires and seasonal drought are significant abiotic factors.

scavenger

An animal that feeds on the carcasses of dead animals.

science

Any method of learning about the natural world that follows the scientific method. See also discovery science; hypothesis.

scientific method

Scientific investigation involving the observation of phenomena, the formulation of a hypothesis concerning the phenomena, experimentation to demonstrate the truth or falseness of the hypothesis, and results that validate or modify the hypothesis.

seaweed

A large, multicellular marine alga.

secondary consumer

An organism that eats primary consumers.

secondary succession

A type of ecological succession that occurs where a disturbance has destroyed an existing biological community but left the soil intact. See also primary succession.

seed

A plant embryo packaged with a food supply within a protective covering.

sepal (sē'-pul)

A modified leaf of a flowering plant. A whorl of sepals encloses and protects the flower bud before it opens.

sex chromosome

A chromosome that determines whether an individual is male or female; in mammals, for example, the X or Y chromosome.

sex-linked gene

A gene located on a sex chromosome.

sexual dimorphism

Distinction in appearance based on secondary sexual characteristics, noticeable differences not directly associated with reproduction or survival.

sexual reproduction

The creation of genetically distinct offspring by the fusion of two haploid sex cells (gametes: sperm and egg), forming a diploid zygote.

sexual selection

A form of natural selection in which individuals with certain characteristics are more likely than other individuals to obtain mates.

shoot

The aerial organ of a plant, consisting of stem and leaves. Leaves are the main photosynthetic structures of most plants.

short tandem repeat (STR)

DNA consisting of tandem (in a row) repeats of a short sequence of nucleotides.

signal transduction pathway

A series of molecular changes that converts a signal received on a target cell's surface to a specific response inside the cell.

silencer

A eukaryotic DNA sequence that inhibits the start of gene transcription; may act analogously to an enhancer, binding a repressor.

sister chromatid (krō'-muh-tid)

One of the two identical parts of a duplicated chromosome. While joined, two sister chromatids make up one chromosome; chromatids are eventually separated during mitosis or meiosis II.

slime mold
A multicellular protist related to amoebas.

smooth ER (smooth endoplasmic reticulum) (reh-tik'-yuh-lum)
A network of interconnected membranous tubules in a eukaryotic cell's cytoplasm. Smooth ER lacks ribosomes. Enzymes embedded in the smooth ER membrane function in the synthesis of certain kinds of molecules, such as lipids.

solute (sol'-yūt)
A substance that is dissolved in a liquid (which is called the solvent) to form a solution.

solution
A liquid consisting of a homogeneous mixture of two or more substances: a dissolving agent, the solvent, and a substance that is dissolved, the solute.

solvent
The dissolving agent in a solution. Water is the most versatile known solvent.

somatic cell (sō-mat'-ik)
Any cell in a multicellular organism except a sperm or egg cell or a cell that develops into a sperm or egg; a body cell.

speciation (spē'-sē-ā'-shun)
An evolutionary process in which one species splits into two or more species.

species
A group of populations whose members possess similar anatomical characteristics and have the ability to interbreed. *See also* biological species concept.

species diversity
The variety of species that make up a biological community; the number and relative abundance of species in a biological community.

species richness
The total number of different species in a community; one component of species diversity.

sponge
An aquatic stationary animal characterized by a highly porous body, choanocytes (specialized cells used for suspension feeding), and no true tissues.

spore
(1) In plants and algae, a haploid cell that can develop into a multicellular haploid individual, the gametophyte, without fusing with another cell. (2) In fungi, a haploid cell that germinates to produce a mycelium.

sporophyte (spōr'-uh-fīt)
The multicellular diploid form in the life cycle of organisms undergoing alternation of generations; results from a union of gametes and meiotically produces haploid spores that grow into the gametophyte generation.

stabilizing selection
Natural selection that favors intermediate variants by acting against extreme phenotypes.

stamen (stā'-men)
A pollen-producing part of a flower, consisting of a stalk (filament) and an anther.

starch
A storage polysaccharide found in the roots of plants and certain other cells; a polymer of glucose.

start codon (kō'-don)
On mRNA, the specific three-nucleotide sequence (AUG) to which an initiator tRNA molecule binds, starting translation of genetic information.

steroid (stir'-oyd)
A type of lipid with a carbon skeleton in the form of four fused rings: three 6-sided rings and one 5-sided ring. Examples are cholesterol, testosterone, and estrogen.

stigma (stig'-muh)
(plural, **stigmata**) The sticky tip of a flower's carpel that traps pollen.

stoma (stō'-muh)
(plural, **stomata**) A pore surrounded by guard cells in the epidermis of a leaf. When stomata are open, CO_2 enters the leaf, and water and O_2 exit. A plant conserves water when its stomata are closed.

stop codon (kō'-don)
In mRNA, one of three triplets (UAG, UAA, UGA) that signal gene translation to stop.

STR analysis
A method of DNA profiling that compares the lengths of STR sequences at specific sites in the genome.

stroma (strō'-muh)
A thick fluid enclosed by the inner membrane of a chloroplast. Sugars are made in the stroma by the enzymes of the Calvin cycle.

substrate
(1) A specific substance (reactant) on which an enzyme acts. Each enzyme recognizes only the specific substrate of the reaction it catalyzes. (2) A surface in or on which an organism lives.

sugar-phosphate backbone
The alternating chain of sugar and phosphate to which DNA and RNA nitrogenous bases are attached.

survivorship curve
A plot of the number of individuals that are still alive at each age in the maximum life span; one way to represent the age-specific death rate.

sustainability
The goal of developing, managing, and conserving Earth's resources in ways that meet the needs of people today without compromising the ability of future generations to meet their needs.

sustainable development
Development that meets the needs of people today without limiting the ability of future generations to meet their needs.

swim bladder
A gas-filled internal sac that helps bony fishes maintain buoyancy.

symbiosis (sim'-bē-ō'-sis)
An interaction between organisms of different species in which one species, the symbiont, lives in or on another species, the host.

sympatric speciation
The formation of a new species in populations that live in the same geographic area. *See also* allopatric speciation.

systematics
A discipline of biology that focuses on classifying organisms and determining their evolutionary relationships.

T

taiga (tī'-guh)
The northern coniferous forest, characterized by long, snowy winters and short, wet summers. Taiga extends across North America and Eurasia, to the southern border of the arctic tundra; it is also found just below alpine tundra on mountainsides in temperate zones.

tail
Extra nucleotides added at the end of an RNA transcript in the nucleus of a eukaryotic cell.

taxonomy
The branch of biology concerned with identifying, naming, and classifying species.

telophase
The fourth and final stage of mitosis, during which daughter nuclei form at the two poles of a cell. Telophase usually occurs together with cytokinesis.

temperate broadleaf forest
A terrestrial biome located throughout midlatitude regions where there is sufficient moisture to support the growth of large, broadleaf deciduous trees.

temperate grassland
A terrestrial biome located in the temperate zone and characterized by low rainfall and nonwoody vegetation. Tree growth is hindered by occasional fires and periodic severe drought.

temperate rain forest
A coniferous forest of coastal North America (from Alaska to Oregon) supported by warm, moist air from the Pacific Ocean.

temperate zones
Latitudes between the tropics and the Arctic Circle in the north and the Antarctic Circle in the south; regions with milder climates than the tropics or polar regions.

terminator
A special sequence of nucleotides in DNA that marks the end of a gene. It signals RNA polymerase to release the newly made RNA molecule, which then departs from the gene.

tertiary consumer (ter'-shē-ār-ē)
An organism that eats secondary consumers.

testcross
The mating between an individual of unknown genotype for a particular character and an individual that is

homozygous recessive for that same character.

tetrapod
A vertebrate with four limbs. Tetrapods include mammals, amphibians, and reptiles (including birds).

theory
A widely accepted explanatory idea that is broader in scope than a hypothesis, generates new hypotheses, and is supported by a large body of evidence.

therapeutic cloning
The cloning of human cells by nuclear transplantation for therapeutic purposes, such as the replacement of body cells that have been irreversibly damaged by disease or injury. *See also* nuclear transplantation; reproductive cloning.

threatened species
As defined in the U.S. Endangered Species Act, a species that is likely to become endangered in the foreseeable future throughout all or a significant portion of its range.

three-domain system
A system of taxonomic classification based on three basic groups: Bacteria, Archaea, and Eukarya.

thylakoid (*thī'-luh-koyd*)
One of a number of disk-shaped membranous sacs inside a chloroplast. Thylakoid membranes contain chlorophyll and the enzymes of the light reactions of photosynthesis. A stack of thylakoids is called a granum.

thymine (T) (*thī'-mēn*)
A single-ring nitrogenous base found in DNA.

trace element
An element that is essential for the survival of an organism but is needed in only minute quantities. Examples of trace elements needed by people include iron and zinc.

trait
A variant of a character found within a population, such as purple flowers in pea plants or blue eyes in people.

trans fats
An unsaturated fatty acid produced by the partial hydrogenation of vegetable oils and present in hardened vegetable oils, most margarines, many commercial baked foods, and many fried foods.

transcription
The synthesis of RNA on a DNA template.

transcription factor
In the eukaryotic cell, a protein that functions in initiating or regulating transcription. Transcription factors bind to DNA or to other proteins that bind to DNA.

transfer RNA (tRNA)
A type of ribonucleic acid that functions as an interpreter in translation. Each tRNA molecule has a specific anticodon, picks up a specific amino acid, and conveys the amino acid to the appropriate codon on mRNA.

transgenic organism
An organism that contains genes from another organism, typically of another species.

translation
The synthesis of a polypeptide using the genetic information encoded in an mRNA molecule. There is a change of "language" from nucleotides to amino acids. *See also* genetic code.

transport vesicle
A tiny membranous sphere in a cell's cytoplasm carrying molecules produced by the cell. The vesicle buds from the endoplasmic reticulum or Golgi apparatus and eventually fuses with another organelle or the plasma membrane, releasing its contents.

triglyceride (*trī-glis'-uh-rīd*)
A dietary fat that consists of a molecule of glycerol linked to three molecules of fatty acids.

trisomy 21
See Down syndrome.

trophic structure (*trō'-fik*)
The feeding relationships among the various species in a community.

tropical forest
A terrestrial biome characterized by warm temperatures year-round.

tropics
The region between the Tropic of Cancer and the Tropic of Capricorn; latitudes between 23.5° north and south.

tumor
An abnormal mass of cells that forms within otherwise normal tissue.

tumor-suppressor gene
A gene whose product inhibits cell division, thereby preventing uncontrolled cell growth.

tundra
A terrestrial biome characterized by bitterly cold temperatures. Plant life is limited to dwarf woody shrubs, grasses, mosses, and lichens. Arctic tundra has permanently frozen subsoil (permafrost); alpine tundra, found at high elevations, lacks permafrost.

tunicate
One of a group of stationary invertebrate chordates.

U

unsaturated
Pertaining to fats and fatty acids whose hydrocarbon chains lack the maximum number of hydrogen atoms and therefore have one or more double covalent bonds. Because of their bent shape, unsaturated fats and fatty acids tend to stay liquid at room temperature.

uracil (U) (*yū'-ruh-sil*)
A single-ring nitrogenous base found in RNA.

V

vacuole (*vak'-ū-ōl*)
A membrane-enclosed sac, part of the endomembrane system of a eukaryotic cell, having diverse functions.

vascular tissue
Plant tissue consisting of cells joined into tubes that transport water and nutrients throughout the plant body. Xylem and phloem make up vascular tissue.

vector
A piece of DNA, usually a plasmid or a viral genome, that is used to move genes from one cell to another.

vertebrate (*ver'-tuh-brāt*)
A chordate animal with a backbone. Vertebrates include lampreys, cartilaginous fishes, bony fishes,

amphibians, reptiles (including birds), and mammals.

vesicle
A membranous sac in the cytoplasm of a eukaryotic cell.

vestigial structure (*ve-sti'-gē-al*)
A structure of marginal, if any, importance to an organism. Vestigial structures are historical remnants of structures that had important functions in ancestors.

virus
A microscopic particle capable of infecting cells of living organisms and inserting its genetic material. Viruses have a very simple structure and are generally not considered to be alive because they do not display all of the characteristics associated with life.

W

warning coloration
The bright color pattern, often yellow, red, or orange in combination with black, of animals that have effective chemical defenses.

water vascular system
In echinoderms, a radially arranged system of water-filled canals that branch into extensions called tube feet. The system provides movement and circulates water, facilitating gas exchange and waste disposal.

wavelength
The distance between crests of adjacent waves, such as those of the electromagnetic spectrum including light.

wetland
An ecosystem intermediate between an aquatic ecosystem and a terrestrial ecosystem. Wetland soil is saturated with water permanently or periodically.

whole-genome shotgun method
A method for determining the DNA sequence of an entire genome by cutting it into small fragments, sequencing each fragment, and then placing the fragments in the proper order.

wild-type trait
The trait most commonly found in nature.

X

X chromosome inactivation
In female mammals, the inactivation of one X chromosome in each somatic cell. Once X inactivation occurs in a given cell (during embryonic development), all descendants of that cell will have the same copy of the X chromosome inactivated.

Z

zooplankton
In aquatic environments, free-floating animals, including many microscopic ones.

zygote (*zī'-gōt*)
The fertilized egg, which is diploid, that results from the union of haploid gametes (sperm and egg) during fertilization.

Index

Giant panda, cloning and, 196, 206
Giant sequoias, 314, 322
Giant tube worms, 302f, 376f
Giardia, 308, 308f
Gibbons, 362f
Gila monsters, 358f
GLO (enzyme), 251
Global biogeochemical cycles, 440
Global climate change, 394–95
    accumulation of greenhouse gases
        and, 394–95
    as agent of evolution by natural selection, 399
    atmospheric concentration of carbon dioxide,
        394–95
    carbon cycle, carbon dioxide, and, 394–95
    cheatgrass and, 413f
    effects of, on ecosystems, 394–95
    effects of, on freshwater biomes, 380
    effects of, on global water cycle, 391
    effects of, on polar bears and penguins,
        373, 399
    effects of, on species distribution, 396
    effects of, on terrestrial biomes, 394–95
    fossil fuels and, 394–95
    global human ecological footprint and, 420–21
    greenhouse effect and, 373
    human carbon footprints and, **398**
    krill habitat and, 390
    ocean acidification and, 394–95
    photosynthesis and, 394–95
    rate of, reducing, 106, 110
    sea ice decline, 390
    water resources and, 393
Global ecological footprints, 420–21
Global warming. *See* Global climate change
Global water cycle, 391f
Glucose
    in cellular respiration, 93, 94–95, 100
    in chemical cycling between photosynthesis
        and cellular respiration, 92–93
    conversion of to cellular energy, 40
    in fermentation, 96, 101
    in glycolysis, 96–97
    linear and ring structure of, 40
    as monosaccharide, 40
    in muscle cells, 91
    ring structure of, 40f
Glyceraldehyde 3–phosphate (G3P), 115
Glycogen, 36, **42**

Glycolysis, **95,** 96f
    in cellular respiration, 96, 100
    in fermentation, 101
    nanotechnology and, 75
    oxygen and, 103
GM (genetically modified) foods, 223. *See also*
        Genetically modified (GM) organisms
Goiter, iodine deficiencies and, 25
Golden rice, 2, 223
Golgi, Camillo, 65
Golgi apparatus, 64, **65,** 65f,
    lysosomes and, 66
    vacuoles and, 67
Goodall, Jane, 5, 5f
Gorillas, 362f
Grana, 68, **109**
Grand Canyon, 274f, 278, 278f
Grasshoppers, 350f
Graves' disease, 23
Gray tree frogs, 275f
"Great Pacific Garbage Patch," 383
Greater arid-land katydid, 351f
Green algae, **310,** 317, 320
Green energy. *See* Biofuels
Greenhouse effect. *See* Greenhouse gases
Greenhouse gases, 394–96
Growth factors, **209**
Guanine (G) , 49, 173
Gulf of Mexico
    dead zone in, 443, 443f
    oil spill in, 428f
Gymnosperms, **319**

H

H1N1 influenza virus, 171
Habitat isolation, 272, 272f
Habitats
    declining biodiversity in destruction of, 427
    in ecology, **375**
    of the red-cockaded woodpecker, 412f
Hagfishes, 356f
Halophiles, extreme, 304
Haploid cells, **131**
Hardy-Weinberg
    equation, 259
    equilibrium, 258
Health, human. *See* Diseases and disorders, human

Heat, **77**
    energy conversions and generation of, 16
    greenhouse effect and, 394–95
    solar energy and uneven, in zones
        of Earth, 376
HeLa cells, 129
Helicobacter pylori, 55f, 57f
Helium (He), 25
Hemoglobin, 48
Hemophilia, 144, 164, 164f
Herbivores, **432**
Herbivory, **431**
Heredity, **146**–57. *See also* Genetics
Heritable traits, 11
Herrerasaurus, 359f
Heterotrophs, **92,** 307f
Heterozygotes, 158
HGH. *See* Human growth hormone
High-fructose corn syrup (HFCS), 41
Hill, A. V., 102, 102f
Hirudo medicinalis, 346
Histones, **124**
History of life on Earth, 292, 294–95, 294f
HIV (human immunodeficiency virus),
        190–91, 190f
    nucleic acid in an infected cell, 191f
    as retrovirus causing AIDS, 190
    as RNA virus, 190
Hobbit people. *See Homo floresienes*
Homeotic genes, **203**
    in gene regulation, 203–4
    in macroevolution by developmental
        processes, 283
Hominins. *See* Human Evolution
Homo erectus, 364
Homo floresiensis (Hobbit people), 337
Homo habilis, 364
Homologies, **250**
    as evidence of evolution, 250–52
    molecular, 251
Homologous characters, 286–87
Homologous chromosomes, **130**
    alleles and, 149f
    independent assortment of, 135–36
    during meiosis, 257
    Gregor Mendel's law of segregation and, 149
    in sexual reproduction, 130–31
Homologous structures, 251f
Homo sapiens. See also Human evolution; Humans